PennyPress ®

MW00737523

PUZZLER'S GIANT BOOK OF CROSSWORDS 79 ™

Penny Press is the publisher of a fine family of puzzle magazines and books renowned for their editorial excellence.

This delightful collection has been carefully selected by the editors of Penny Press for your special enjoyment and entertainment.

Puzzler's Giant Book of Crosswords, No. 79, August 2021. Published four times a year by Penny Publications, LLC, 6 Prowitt Street, Norwalk, CT 06855-1220. On the web at PennyDellPuzzles.com. Copyright © 2021 by Penny Publications, LLC. Penny Press is a trademark registered in the U.S. Patent Office. All rights reserved. No material from this publication may be reproduced or used without the written permission of the publisher.
ISBN-13: 978-1-59238-238-5   Printed by The P.A. Hutchison Co., Mayfield, PA, U.S.A. 7/7/21

PENNY PRESS PUZZLE PUBLICATIONS

✦ PUZZLE MAGAZINES ✦

All-Star Word Seeks
Approved Variety Puzzles
Classic Variety Puzzles
   Plus Crosswords
Easy & Fun Variety Puzzles
Easy Crossword Express
Family Variety Puzzles & Games
Famous Fill-In Puzzles
Fast & Easy Crosswords
Favorite Easy Crosswords
Favorite Fill-In
Favorite Variety Puzzles
Fill-In Puzzles
Garfield's Word Seeks
Good Time Crosswords
Good Time Easy Crosswords
Good Time Variety Puzzles

Large-Print Word Seek Puzzles
Master's Variety Puzzles
Merit Variety Puzzles & Games
Original Logic Problems
Penny's Finest Favorite Word Seeks
Penny's Finest Good Time Word Seeks
Penny's Finest Super Word Seeks
Quick & Easy Crosswords
Spotlight Celebrity Word Seek
Spotlight Movie & TV Word Seek
Spotlight Remember When Word Seek
Tournament Variety Puzzles
Variety Puzzles and Games
Variety Puzzles and Games
   Special Issue
Word Seek Puzzles
World's Finest Variety Puzzles

✦ SPECIAL SELECTED COLLECTIONS ✦

Alphabet Soup
Anagram Magic
   Square
Brick by Brick
Codewords
Cross Pairs Word Seeks
Crostics
Crypto-Families
Cryptograms
Diagramless
Double Trouble
England's Best
   Logic Puzzles

Flower Power
Frameworks
Large-Print
   Crosswords
Large-Print
   Cryptograms
Large-Print
   Missing Vowels
Letterboxes
Match-Up
Missing List Word
   Seeks
Missing Vowels

Number Fill-In
Number Seek
Patchwords
Places, Please
Quotefalls
Simon Says
Stretch Letters
Syllacrostics
What's Left?
Word Games
   Puzzles
Zigzag

✦ PUZZLER'S GIANT BOOKS ✦

Crosswords   Sudoku   Word Games   Word Seeks

ACROSS

1. Former Islamic title
6. Makes lace
10. Private high school
14. ____-Hartley Act
18. Unaccompanied
19. Republic of Ireland
20. "____ Man"
21. Arab prince
22. Actress Massey
23. Rage
25. Wading bird
26. Ethereal
27. Vacation spots
29. Emergency wards
32. ". . . not ____ for tribute"
33. Johnny ____
35. Paternally kin
36. Superior
40. Lean
42. Saltpeter
43. "A Visit from St. Nicholas" author
44. Of a musical key
47. TV spots
49. Natives: suffix
50. Lost interest
51. Map line
53. Failing grades
55. Trite
56. Temperance leader Nation
57. Town in 88 Across
58. Witty remarks
59. Chat
62. Canadian province: abbr.
63. Fractions
66. Kind of dancer
67. Chide
70. Long-haired cats
71. Teacakes
73. Hoople's expletive
74. Never in bondage
75. Cereal grain
76. Male turkey
77. Tuber
79. Compos mentis
80. Mental grasp
84. Annoy
86. Present
87. Checked typesetting
88. Neighbor of Sudan
90. Females
92. Three: prefix
94. Good-bys
95. Dance
96. Church images
97. Nahuatl
99. ____ Tagh
100. ____-La Guardia Act
102. Sailor
103. Mythical monster
107. Wambaugh work, with "The"
110. Drive back
112. Worry
115. Japanese measure
116. More pleasant
118. Ranked
119. Rose's lover
120. At any time
121. ____ Alto
122. Eared seal
123. Queen of Jordan
124. Spreads hay
125. Goddess of discord
126. Intrinsically

DOWN

1. Capital of Egypt
2. Edgar ____ Poe
3. At liberty
4. Twain work, with "The"
5. Dread
6. Mosaic pieces
7. River island
8. Run
9. ____ Junipero
10. Ranking archbishop
11. Discounts
12. Earthquake hub
13. Strike an attitude
14. Recipe measure
15. Soul: Fr.
16. Evergreen
17. Attempt
24. Douglas work
28. Refrain syllable
30. Squadrons
31. Grapevine news
34. River bottom
37. Many-sided solid
38. Prior to, poetically
39. Cerise
41. Grievance
44. Twitch
45. Explorer Johnson
46. And not
48. Moon goddess
50. Bunk
52. French city
54. Counterfeit
55. Romaine
57. To one side
58. Middle, at law
60. Years of life
61. Cattle genus
64. Bellowing
65. January stone
66. Mercer sentiment, "You've ____ the positive"
67. Lay odds
68. Conceit
69. Unbridled
71. Whiskey cocktail
72. Writer Truman ____
74. Opponent
77. Altered
78. Eggs
81. Astern
82. New Zealand parrot
83. Magazine execs
85. Locomotive driver
86. Painter Matisse
87. Spanish explorers
88. Actress Hagen
89. Vapor
90. Scrubbed
91. "The Little Shop of ____"
93. Squealer
96. Stimulus
98. Three: Ital.
101. Sandpiper
104. Sacrifice table
105. Customers
106. Change the color
108. Hone
109. Dueling status symbol
111. Brace
112. Tin
113. Australian native
114. ____ Grande
117. Hebrew judge

PUZZLE 2

• GREAT MOVIES •

ACROSS

1. Con game
5. Snub
10. Gaelic
14. Jordan's capital
19. ____ Alto
20. French book
21. Air
22. Owing service
23. Sour
24. Tatum ____
25. Space
26. False: pref.
27. 1975 Sada Thompson vehicle
30. Davis and Midler
31. Logic
32. Arabian
33. Respect
35. Social
37. Dated
39. Beg, of old
43. Lemmon-Matthau hit
50. Donkey
51. Competition
52. Crone
53. Italian poet
54. Sweetsop
56. Magazine sections, for short
57. Greek resistance: abbr.
59. Chekhov
60. ____-mutuel
61. Cancel
62. "Indiana Jones and the Temple ____"
64. Opaque gem
66. Offspring
67. ____ Lind
68. Sailboat part
70. Small-intestine section
72. Equipment
74. Bakery output
77. Inlet
79. Turkish weights
81. Stellar
85. ____ from the blue
86. Motels
88. "____ of robins"
90. Trig function
91. French roasts
92. Support
93. 7, in Tijuana
94. Put on
95. Fictional friar
96. Full of: suff.
97. Shirley MacLaine flick
101. "Young ____"
103. "Rose ____ rose . . ."
104. Affirmative vote
105. Truly
107. Show feeling
112. Brooks
116. Praying ____
119. Janet Leigh film
122. Potato state
123. "Venus de ____"
124. Gold unit
125. Ancient shout
126. Squelched
127. ____ breve
128. Vote in
129. Auberjonois
130. Gaits
131. Secretary
132. Balance: Fr.
133. Prophet

DOWN

1. Disagreements
2. Hiding place
3. UFO passenger
4. California city
5. Pigeonhole
6. Dressed to the ____
7. Unconcealed
8. Harangue
9. Membranes
10. Writer Hunter
11. Go over again
12. Mortimer ____
13. Greek letter
14. Trumpeter Herb ____
15. Henry Fonda film
16. Run into
17. Chills and fever
18. Beatty and Sparks
28. Lack
29. Revered person
30. Onion holders
34. Sissy Spacek film
36. "The ____ Family"
38. Ballet step
40. Colonial administrator
41. Oak nut
42. Crotchety
43. Cliff Huxtable's son
44. 50%
45. Mild oath
46. Pantry article
47. Having awareness of
48. Idealists
49. Punitive
50. Of flight
55. Commonwealth of Australia state
56. Indian princes
58. Marilyn Monroe picture
63. Malt kilns
65. Summer sign
69. Commendation
71. Tsar's decree
73. Diner
74. Magna ____
75. Concerning
76. Movie directed by Jack Lemmon
78. Malayan peak
80. Percolate
82. Needle
83. Soon
84. Let borrow
87. Backdrops
89. Depot: abbr.
96. Public injunctions: abbr.
98. Mata ____
99. Actress Garr
100. Norman and family
102. Negative atoms
103. Pastoral poems
106. Zola
108. Glacial ridge
109. "____ of Two Cities"
110. Goddess of agriculture
111. Parcel
113. Riverbank
114. Sierra ____
115. Smirk
116. Haze
117. Hebrew month
118. Western alliance: abbr.
120. Flood
121. Diminutive suffix
123. Rabid

ACROSS
1. Timid
5. "Elephant Boy"
9. Salinger miss
13. Ignite
18. Height: prefix
19. Heavens: prefix
21. Con game
22. Veranda
23. Thomas Wolfe hero
24. Fable ender
25. Corrida beast
26. "Rudy" star
27. Start of a four-line verse
31. Detail
32. Clayey soil
33. Biochemical compound
34. Presley's "It's ____ Never"
36. English diarist
38. Navigational abbrs.
39. Switch word
42. Ames native
43. Arias
44. Snick or ____
45. Inland sea
46. Second line of the verse
51. Fortuneteller's words
52. ____ time (quickly)
53. ____ coming (deserved the comeuppance)
54. Perfume
55. Place
56. Darlings' dog
57. Quotes
58. Park supervisor
59. Gainsay
60. Indy 500 participant
61. Wedding-band material
62. House addition
65. Recurring taps
66. Seaweed
67. Avril's follower
70. Fresh air, informally
71. Jabber
72. Orchestra member
73. Pound
74. Third line of the verse
78. Greek god of love
79. For fear that
80. Thaw
81. Photocopying-machine need
82. Celtic Neptune
83. Paving stone
84. Complicate
86. Motorist's stopover
87. Abode
88. Air
89. Red and Dead
90. Last line of the verse
99. Stud
100. Surrealist
101. Dogma
102. Undo
103. Straighten
104. Ancient town near Salerno
105. Minneapolis's neighbor
106. Woe!
107. Grinder
108. Actor Bruce
109. List concluder, for short
110. Father, in Paris

DOWN
1. Wise men
2. Duke of Edom
3. Sicilian spewer
4. Gull
5. South Carolina fort
6. "____ with a View"
7. Insult
8. Sloth
9. Ethyl acetate et al.
10. Look mean
11. Chagall
12. Salary
13. Political line-ups
14. Turkish title
15. One not for
16. Weather forecast
17. Comedian Alan
20. Actress Dukakis
28. Jackets or collars
29. Vocal turndown
30. Made spherical
34. Lasso end
35. Young hooter
36. Indian city
37. Nevada town
38. Nin
39. Rubber sealant
40. Test answer
41. Flout
42. "Your ____ the only peacemaker" ("As You Like It")
43. Mayor Bono
44. Jewish feast
45. Correct
47. Climbing plant
48. Coagulate
49. Wins at chess
50. Milan's La ____
56. Mideast desert
57. Plants of 56 Down
58. His name is Mudd
59. Hamlet's countrymen
60. Laughing
61. Delight in one's self
62. Comic George
63. Blue
64. Copter mechanism
65. Secret meeting
66. "____ for Adano"
67. WWI battle site
68. Photographer Adams
69. Stravinsky
71. Was part of a masquerade
72. Terminer's partner
73. Footwear leather loop
75. Resin
76. Issue
77. Porticos
83. Less steely
84. Ape
85. Beak
86. Kind of health
87. Jungle laugher
88. Coe, for one
89. Tuscan city
90. Mine vehicle
91. Hawaiian port
92. Satanic
93. Roy's wife
94. Grant
95. Use needles and yarn
96. Festive season
97. Prevaricator
98. First word in the motto of Massachusetts

PUZZLE 4

• FIRST AND LAST •

ACROSS
1. Bellow
5. "Peg Woffington" author
10. Canadian flyers
15. Central European
19. German river
20. Senior
21. Speckled or red tree
22. Guadalcanal village
23. Not too distant astronaut?
25. Clemens's purpose?
27. Tune
28. Colosseum et al.
29. Report
30. Strange
31. St. Peter's birds
33. Messenger
34. Desirous
35. Hartman of "Dan August"
36. Reconcile
38. Spotted cavy
40. Tennis player's bug?
44. Affluent goodnight girl?
49. "____ from the Bridge"
50. Adjutant
51. Urgency
52. Melville work
53. Ceremonial staff
54. Merriment
55. Liabilities
56. Finnish bath
57. BPOE member
58. Track star Sebastian ____
59. Sandwich type
60. Kind of hut
61. Prime minister to lose strength?
65. Coasted
68. Unfamiliar
69. Bride's phrase
70. "____ the season . . ."
73. Vary
74. Traveled over, in winter
75. Expunge
77. Bygone
78. Impression
79. Spreads
80. Math subj.
81. Specialist
82. Side-show painting?
84. Kentucky county taxi?
86. Parts
87. Trails
88. Metric measure
89. Angora material
93. Heap of wood
94. Lengthen
98. Swedish area
99. Lavin role
101. Present
103. Greek letter
104. Crazier chromosome?
106. Australian actor bit?
108. Eternally
109. '60s slogan
110. Oriental
111. Orbit point
112. "____ Mable"
113. Ecbatana natives
114. Dances
115. Turkey

DOWN
1. Conclusion
2. Fran's pal
3. Call off
4. Legal subject
5. Coffee order
6. New York island
7. Arabian gulf
8. Studies
9. Directional suffix
10. Sale location
11. Escape
12. Move slightly
13. Prophet
14. Stray
15. Cut
16. French river
17. Tired
18. Hatrack
24. Before this time, before
26. Near Eastern inn
29. Glass section
32. Adoree
33. Meddle
34. Discomfort
36. Pierre's girlfriend
37. Motion
38. Motorcycle part
39. Bag of tricks
40. Transpired
41. Shape
42. Carla Tortelli's ex
43. House of the Seven Gables site
44. Temple bigwig
45. Smolder
46. Ostriches' kin
47. Zilch
48. Relating to dawn
51. One of the Masters of the Universe
54. Induce
55. Dealt
56. Fodder tower
58. "Mask" star
59. Yells
60. Brood
61. Untainted
62. Chet and family
63. Evans's pseudonym
64. Okay on the radio
65. Ketch
66. "Betsy's Wedding" director
67. Roman way
70. Powder
71. Spanish island
72. Gore
74. Scoria
75. Carnegie
76. Wings
77. Check receiver
79. ____ and terminer
80. Thrash
81. Rabbit home
83. Skip over
84. Attention
85. Doctor and Tom
87. Parisian schools
89. Trimmed the grass
90. Popeye's girl
91. Healthier
92. Previn
93. ____-nez (glasses)
94. Fiber plant
95. Rhetorical device
96. Singled out
97. Place to stay
99. "Let Us Now Praise Famous Men" writer
100. Pencil component
101. Ascension
102. Irish Rose lover
105. Record letters, for short
106. Long fish
107. Exclamation

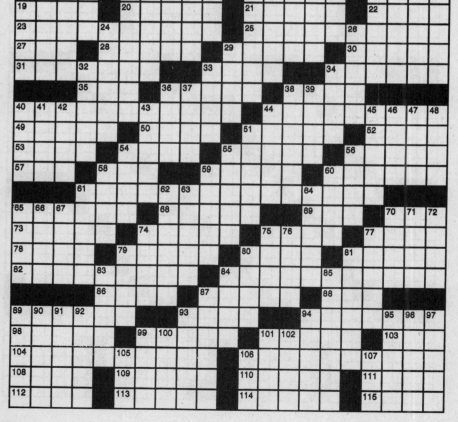

ACROSS

1. Kind of joint
5. Comedian Johnson
9. Close gem setting
13. Resolute
17. Wife of Zeus
18. Fate
19. All the same, to Fifi
20. Fancy
21. Ellipse
22. Former Atlanta arena
23. Place to think?
24. Furnished
25. Maine
28. Famous cow
29. Star metal
30. Auction
31. One: pref.
32. Egyptian Christians
35. Rugged peak
37. Come a _____ (fall)
41. Part of the orchestra
42. Play the provinces
43. City on the Loire
45. Labor org.
46. Pothole filler
47. Southern forest
49. Cookie
50. Audience pleasers
52. Seaweed
53. Itty-bitty
54. Secondhand
55. Oscar nominee in "Exodus"
57. Parc bench
58. Stowe child
60. "Walk on the _____ Side"
61. Too-curious lady of myth
64. Samoan port
65. Hand grenades
68. Tuck's partner
69. Outlaw
70. Penchants
71. Arena sound
72. Art _____
73. Scissored sheep
75. Glove for Gary Carter
76. Passport stamps
77. Chew the fat
78. Consider
80. Intention
81. Saunter
84. Western evergreen
90. Edmonton's prov.
91. Drake's "Golden _____"
92. Conceal
93. Diving waterfowl
94. Comedy
95. Mine, to Mimi
96. Singing son of Woody
97. Harrow's rival
98. Holiday herb
99. Filly's mom
100. ". . . _____ we forget"
101. Without

DOWN

1. Karate blow
2. Son of Leah
3. Meshed's land
4. Gear for Chagall
5. Embellish
6. Cicero's city
7. Accent
8. Envoy
9. Rose part
10. Chalcedony
11. Weathercock
12. Wapiti
13. Stimulus
14. Caesar's fatal date
15. Italian painter
16. Win for Kasparov
26. Poet's contraction
27. Catching game
28. Baseball's Slaughter
31. "Battle Cry" author
32. Sheep shelter
33. Scottish resort
34. Prickly rodent
35. Tricks
36. Have regrets
37. Musical ending
38. Wreath decor
39. Enthusiasm
40. Stringy
42. _____ the knot
43. Tree trunk
44. Corporate symbol
47. Quarry
48. "A Fish Called _____"
49. Make ecstatic
51. Peak in Thessaly
53. Sunbathes
55. Dinner candy
56. _____ du Vent
57. 1934 heavyweight champ
58. Dinner checks
59. Colorful fish
60. Zephyr
61. _____ du jour
62. Wealthy, to Juanita
63. Mil. addresses
65. Sneak a look
66. "This is the forest _____"
67. Kitty
70. Heehaw
72. Shirley Temple film
74. Sailor's assent
75. "Little Women" woman
76. Compete
78. Benefactor
79. Comic Murphy
80. Apportion
81. Travel charts
82. Earthen pot
83. _____ party
84. Bean type
85. French father
86. Olive and canola
87. Whit
88. Meridian hour
89. River of Austria
91. Amateur actor

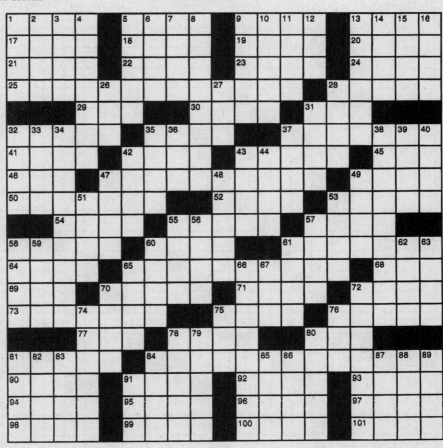

PUZZLE 6

• END PLAY •

ACROSS

1. Be merciful to
6. Blemish
10. Carry on
14. Under
19. French path
20. Slice off
21. Butterine
22. Duck
23. 5 ANDs
27. Sault ____ Marie
28. Hits lightly
29. Merit
30. Newest
31. Dock
33. Teen's problem
34. Horsehair
35. Snakes
38. Powder ingredient
40. Routine food
42. Southeastern electric inits.
45. 5 ONDs
50. Housetops
51. Is situated
52. Singing brothers
53. Dolly's greeting
54. ____ uncertain terms
55. Glen
56. Skidded
57. Scatter refuse
58. Horned animal
59. Numero ____
60. Seasoning
61. Refinement
62. 4 INDs
66. Legislative bodies
69. Soil
70. Wheel part
71. Title
75. Teases
76. Island dance
77. TV's Calucci
78. "Dies ____"
79. Palm
80. Brownish purple
81. Aching
82. Balmy
83. 6 ENDs
87. Dutch commune
88. Once, once
89. Race units
90. Hermits
91. Biblical word for cattle
93. Persia, today
95. Attenuated
96. In the direction of
99. IV
100. Deadlocks
102. Male child
105. 6 UNDs
110. Actress Sophia ____
111. Trim
112. Crude metals
113. Actress Faye
114. New Hampshire city
115. Confederate
116. Spherical roof
117. Piano part

DOWN

1. Adages
2. Cabal
3. Century plant
4. Primary color
5. Snaky fish
6. Trident
7. Tent city
8. Rainbows
9. ____ Speedwagon
10. Ancient Italian
11. 1928 presidential candidate
12. Night light
13. "High ____"
14. Playwright Brendan ____
15. Creme de la creme
16. Clare Boothe ____
17. Poems
18. Garment-seam finish
24. Word before up or down
25. Capital of Hejaz
26. Gladden
31. Act
32. Incenses
33. Charity
34. Army cafeteria
35. Harsh-smelling
36. "Lorna ____"
37. Buzz
38. Suit man
39. Aweather's opposite
41. Like summertime tea
42. Lists
43. Glens
44. Italian love
46. Boards
47. Graceful dance
48. Great Wall site
49. Deciding
55. Sand hills
56. Native Israeli
57. Suspension
60. Grins
61. Spigot
63. Petal oil
64. Instructive
65. Rosebush features
66. Long look
67. Auriculate
68. Nine, to Pedro
72. Turk's decree
73. Healthier
74. Percolates
76. Embraces
77. Fly the ____
80. "Le ____ Goriot"
81. Grocery check-out process
82. Pig or wrought
84. Imparts
85. Mild, as a cigar
86. Fiber thread
91. Actress Valentine
92. Peace goddess
94. Corroded
95. Rent
96. Chat
97. Reed instrument
98. Deteriorated
99. Stoke
100. Picador's target
101. List component
102. Port ____, Egypt
103. Killer whale
104. Christmas
106. Stop ____ dime
107. Tennis-star Laver
108. Draw off
109. Speed-boat champion Bardahl

ACROSS

1. Capacitance unit
6. Food listing
10. Laugh
14. Auditor: abbr.
17. Nimble
18. King of comedy
19. Popeye's lady
21. Ladies of Spain: abbr.
22. Kill-joy
24. Closely contested
26. Society-page word
27. "Bus Stop" playwright
28. French notions
30. Electronic devices
31. Wicked things
32. Hollywood's Laura ___
33. Some entertainments
34. Kind of checkers
37. Lubricants
38. Halley's, for one
39. Adore
40. Pod item
41. Jai follower
42. Polaris, e.g.
46. Author Cleveland ___
47. Still care
51. Giant great
52. Poi beginning
53. Several
54. Part of QED
55. Rudimentary seed
57. Tarzan portrayer
58. Bedrock beast?
59. Singer Jacques ___
60. Summary
61. Shelley verse play
64. Notwithstanding
67. Actor Peter ___
69. Formicary dwellers
71. Propellers
72. Garfunkel
75. Stair part
76. Yen
77. Sea bird
78. Unique item
79. Three, in Turin
80. Useless thing
84. Insect
85. Hockey family
87. Some dada paintings
88. Kin: abbr.
89. Scorches
90. Land parcels
92. Father
93. Religious singers
94. Compensation
96. On
97. Storms
98. Salt, e.g.
99. Kind of acid
100. Hebrew month
101. Ovine comment
104. Equal
106. Jogs the memory
109. Scant
110. Bird sound
111. Ash, for one
112. Faithful
113. Fast plane: abbr.
114. Miscalculates
115. Prophet
116. Fresh

DOWN

1. Bambi, once
2. Author of "The Morning Watch"
3. Ceremony
4. Priestly garb
5. Execution
6. Twist
7. Actress Sommer et al.
8. Laird's refusal
9. Less neat
10. Those who sharpen on whetstone
11. E.T., e.g.
12. Torso features
13. Ms. Gardner
14. Not refined
15. Steps
16. Questions
20. Indigenous
21. Ales
23. Flavoring seed
25. Dingy nightclub
29. Procrastinator
31. January, in Juarez
33. Crowd noise
34. Box
35. Pertaining to blood
36. Remote place
37. Nashville tourist attraction, for short
38. Coagulate
41. Heart's "Nothing ___"
43. Too close to call
44. Hun leader
45. Rds.
47. Split rattan
48. Presently
49. Spaces
50. Solar deity
53. Rodents
56. British beet
58. Mason's Street
59. Numbers game
60. Opening
62. Agrarian's implement
63. Fusses
65. Picador's focus
66. Dangle
67. Aware
68. Region: abbr.
70. Stress
73. German composer Max ___
74. Lock
76. Refs
77. European river
78. Consecrates, formerly
81. Elizabeth ___ Browning
82. Nobel Prize chemist
83. LAX and Metro
84. Quartz and feldspar
86. Briny
89. Epics
91. Bounders
92. Is frugal
93. Freeloader
94. Reserves
95. Wakeful
96. Omani VIP
97. Rajah's lady
98. Shortens a skirt
99. State
101. Turkish officials
102. Pity!
103. Backer
105. Ram's mate
107. Indignation
108. Feathery scarf

PUZZLE 8

ACROSS

1. Ten-percenter
6. Summary
11. Tortes et al.
16. Pugilist
17. Moslem decree
18. Playing marble
19. Montana city
20. Disaster
22. Wordsworth work
23. Murray and West
25. Pith
26. Zip
27. Game fish
29. Electrical unit
30. Autos
31. Shopping place
32. Sea cow
34. Chats
36. Element
37. Make beloved
41. Ash Wednesday's season
42. Nerd
43. Cuban province
44. Pie ___ mode: 2 wds.
45. Goad
46. A famous Piper
47. Soft metal
48. Couches
50. Feral
51. Rummy coup
52. Goes stealthily
53. Highland girl
54. Injures
55. Implore
57. Ninny
58. Bath et al.
61. Basket contents
62. Loose
65. Grain unit
66. Malay craft
67. Depend
68. Conglomerate inits.
69. Offer
72. Ms. Shore
74. Plus
75. French legislature
76. Ms. Astaire
77. Villainous looks
78. Nicholas and Alexander
79. Alpine song

DOWN

1. Monastery head
2. Kind of cheese
3. Wipe out
4. Seine, e.g.
5. Quakes
6. Does kitchen work
7. Pitchers' stats
8. Feline
9. Insistent
10. Spanish coin, once
11. Two-wheeled vehicle
12. Give it ___ (try): 2 wds.
13. Greek letter
14. Early anesthetic
15. Oozes
21. In shreds
24. Picnic crasher
28. Gasp
29. Disfigure
30. Yield
32. ___ of honor
33. Geraint's wife
34. Grade
35. She of Troy
36. Arguments for
38. Amused
39. Leaning
40. Tears
42. Bureaus
43. Lubricates
45. Short dog, for short
46. Nonsense!
49. Labels
50. WWII women
51. Slipper
53. Envoys
54. ___ of obligation: 2 wds.
56. Self-centered one
57. Dolores ___ Rio
58. Flower part
59. Break down grammatically
60. Got up
62. Hires
63. Like old bread
64. A Barrymore
66. Does greenhouse work
67. Pride sound
70. Each
71. Actress Claire
73. Altar phrase: 2 wds.

PUZZLE 9

ACROSS

1. Difficult
5. River of Paraguay
8. Ratify
12. Pitcher
13. Plunder
14. River in Ireland
15. Buttercup family
18. Serious play
19. Barber's call
20. Japanese coin
21. Grown-up scrod
23. Down provider
27. Cup for liquid
29. Greasy
30. Search around
33. Botch
35. Surface measurement
36. Facing a glacier
38. Moment
40. Opposite of WSW
41. Swiss mountain
44. Acute
46. Wireless
48. Consequences
52. Finished
53. Dernier ____
54. Genealogy chart
55. Is victorious
56. Author Deighton
57. Dispatch

DOWN

1. Droves
2. Cognizant
3. French author
4. Percussion instrument
5. Curve
6. Hammers
7. Adept
8. Divisions
9. Previous to, poetically
10. Literary collection
11. Shelter
16. Mother-of-pearl
17. Edged tool
22. Ins' counterparts
24. Burrow
25. Kay-em connector
26. Seeded bread
27. Thin biscuits
28. Deep black
30. Corpulent
31. Misstep
32. Supporter of David
34. Employers
37. Duration
39. Byron's eternity
41. Idolize
42. Flax fabric
43. Sat for a portrait
45. Biblical book: abbr.
47. River islands
48. Tier
49. King of Midian
50. Hoosegow
51. Commit a moral wrong

PUZZLE 10

ACROSS

1. Trudge
5. New Haven trees
9. Long for
10. Ferocious cats
12. Trickster's forte
14. Aye
15. Sister's daughter
16. ____, right in the kisser
18. Vittles
20. Animal doc
21. Only
22. State policeman
24. Braved
25. Sustained
26. Small dog
27. Leather belt
30. Dexterity
34. Historical times
35. Bambi's mom
36. Hint
37. Spider's trap
38. Carried chair
40. In the manner of: 2 wds.
41. Conjurer's word
44. Singer Ross
45. Fencing rapiers
46. He, she, and it
47. Legal document

DOWN

1. Quickly
2. Delay
3. Oast
4. Secondary
5. Choose by vote
6. Citrus fruit
7. Extinct bird
8. Critic
9. Distinct
11. Saw wood
13. "The ____ Hunter"
14. Hitherto
17. Unite
19. Divans
21. Sorcery
23. Vim
24. Payable
26. Implored
27. Stitch
28. Trample
29. Peter Cottontail
30. Soft drink
31. Looked fiercely
32. Hawaiian dances
33. Darjeeling, for one
35. Rot
38. Lucid
39. Back of the neck
42. Rally cry
43. Buzzer

PUZZLE 11

ACROSS

1. Pace
5. Historic time
8. Spoken
12. Singer Guthrie
13. Cold-cut marts
15. One million: pref.
16. Year with February 29
17. Wear away
18. Orangutans
19. Take food
20. Applaud
21. Stop
23. Iron alloy
25. Darn
27. "Born in the ___"
28. Pear-shaped instrument
30. Opposite of WNW
32. Faucet
35. Renter
38. Give temporary use
39. Building addition
40. Comfort
41. Escape
43. Locale
44. Double curve
45. Cut
46. Ascended
48. French holy woman: abbr.
49. Citrus refresher
50. Integument
51. Butt
53. Beaver's construction
55. Aquatic mammal
59. Valet's kin
62. Flavorful leaf
64. "The Greatest"
65. ___ were (seemingly)
66. Delicious or Granny Smith
68. Landed
69. French dream
70. Heaped
71. Love excessively
72. ___-do-well
73. Palmer's need
74. "The Defiant ___"

DOWN

1. Store transactions
2. Pick up the bill
3. Make happy
4. "___ Goes the Weasel"
5. Marry on the run
6. Free
7. On the briny
8. Sharif and Bradley
9. Certain pistols
10. "Rock of ___"
11. Endure
13. Dolores ___ Rio
14. Rub out
20. Hint
22. Lamented
24. Otherwise
26. Unwanted plant
29. Tendency
31. Skulk
33. To the sheltered side
34. Design
35. Pinky and Peggy
36. Orient
37. Firm
38. Track circuit
42. Competed
43. "___ She Sweet"
45. Ditto
47. Melee
50. Grin
52. Change
54. Enough
56. Eagle's claw
57. Cream of the crop
58. Certain religious practices
59. Farm building
60. One who benefits from another's lawsuit
61. Entranced
63. Sparks or Beatty
67. Simple Simon's desire
68. Commotion

PUZZLE 12

Start and Finish

Form 5-letter words which start and finish with the same letter. ___O A S ___ for example becomes TOAST when a T is placed at the beginning and end of that set of letters. Use a different letter for each set.

1. ___ N O C ___
2. ___ L U M ___
3. ___ E M P ___
4. ___ O Z E ___
5. ___ E C U ___

6. ___ Y N I ___
7. ___ I B E ___
8. ___ U T D ___
9. ___ A G L ___
10. ___ I T C ___

ACROSS

1. Dance
5. Campus group: abbr.
9. S'il vous ____
14. Biblical weed
15. Lead in "To Sir with Love"
16. Sonata's finish
17. Rainbow goddess
18. Seaweed product
19. Canadian island
20. Strive to beat a deadline: 3 wds.
23. Gratuity
24. Inhabitant: suff.
25. In the vanguard: 4 wds.
34. Baby's food
35. Winged
36. Shapes, as muscles
37. Handle
39. Ventriloquist Bergen
42. Jeff's partner
43. Haley opus
45. Sir Guinness
47. Female ruff
48. Idle period: 4 wds.
52. Hair mass
53. First-down yardage
54. Almost too late: 5 wds.
63. Removed the center from
64. ____ and dear
65. "Gentlemen Prefer Blondes" author
66. Type of glasses or house
67. Sea eagle
68. Sonny Shroyer role
69. Penniless
70. Feat
71. Assess

DOWN

1. Mix
2. Scarlett's mansion
3. Sevareid or Clapton
4. Spanish coin
5. Place for a sitter?
6. Anatomical fold
7. Asian range
8. Retire for the night: 2 wds.
9. Object
10. Boor
11. Opposed
12. Bibliography entry
13. Raced
21. Verdi work
22. ____ Anne de Beaupre
25. Asunder
26. Red River city
27. Surrey's ____ and Ewell
28. Passing fancy
29. Heart or liver
30. Selleck or Brokaw
31. Bury
32. Distributed
33. ____ Park, Colorado
38. Chowed down
40. "Cakes and ____"
41. Refinished
44. At an indefinite future time
46. Kitchen big cheese?
49. ____ sequitur
50. Expressed a thought
51. Elk feature
54. Religious object
55. No way
56. Type of surgeon
57. Livestock
58. Beak-base covering
59. Noted citizen
60. Hebrides island
61. Theoretical
62. ____ est percipi

Categories

For each of the categories listed, can you think of a word or phrase beginning with each letter on the left? Count 1 point for each correct answer. A score of 15 is good, and 21 is excellent.

	BIRDS	CLOTHING	DOGS	ISLANDS	SCIENTISTS
D					
E					
C					
O					
R					

PUZZLE 15

ACROSS

1. Confront
5. Shawl
9. Habit
13. Atop
17. Songster Logan
18. Hoop or dance beginner
19. Camelot lady
20. Verne captain
21. Hideaway
22. Letters before thetas
23. Deer
24. "Kukla, ___ and Ollie"
25. Intrepid
28. "The Thin ___": 2 wds.
30. Conger
31. Jason's sweetheart
33. 52, to Cato
34. Persevere
38. "Picnic" playwright
40. No-see-ums
44. "Waiting for Lefty" playwright
45. Oriental
48. Fanfare
49. Recreation room
50. Crown
52. Comedian Aykroyd
53. Partake
54. Social climber
56. Warble
58. Craftsman
60. Harvest goddess
62. Furlough
65. American fleet: abbr.
66. Starry
70. Epics
72. Clothing
76. Director of "Sahara"
77. The cruelest month: abbr.
80. Acronym for a beam
82. Barnyard sound
83. Operatic highlights
84. Here!
86. Boot-shaped country
88. Browned bread
89. Drink to excess
90. Asks
92. Gunn from "Treasure Island"
94. Primp
97. Above, to Keats
98. Dispute
102. Never-say-die
107. Constellation bear
108. Witticisms
110. Author Murdoch
111. Entryway
112. Ripens
113. Inter ___
114. Use as proof
115. John-Boy's sister
116. Biblical affirmatives
117. Calm
118. Makes lace
119. Rational

DOWN

1. Plopped
2. **Kirghiz mountain** range
3. Muse of history
4. Serious
5. Man's greatest inventions?
6. Actress Lee
7. Frighten
8. Glue
9. Blushed
10. Lennon's wife
11. Layer
12. A Ford
13. Staunch
14. Persian fairy
15. Muscat's land
16. Not a soul
26. Burglary
27. Revise for print
29. Condensations
32. Taj Mahal city
34. Schools of whales
35. Anthony or Barbara
36. Gambling city
37. Rip
39. Sicilian resort
41. Alack
42. Movie plantation
43. British weapon
46. Seed cover
47. Auction
51. "___ Wonderful World": 2 wds.
55. Audacious: 3 wds.
57. ___ Cruces
59. Stratagem
61. Building compound
63. Canyon
64. Portrayer of TV's Redigo
66. Star in Aquarius
67. Barcelona bull
68. Silkworm
69. Engrossed
71. Italian wine district
73. One of a Latin trio
74. Function
75. Lads
78. Support
79. Retaliation
81. Rosie's fastener
85. Witnessed
87. Harangues
91. Sounds
93. Katmandu's land
95. Decree
96. Oriental wheel
98. Wharf
99. Exhort
100. On the ocean
101. Humdinger
103. Pitcher's glove
104. Adriatic wind
105. Cut of meat
106. Ocean flier
109. Zip

ACROSS
1. Beat it!
6. Robin Cook novel
10. 21-gun event
16. Addison's partner
17. Avow
18. Stretching out the neck
20. "The Messiah" composer
21. Undiluted
22. Love affair
23. Table scraps
24. Cattle marking
26. Inhale quickly
27. "Hiroshima, ___ Amour"
28. Boulevard: abbr.
29. Declared
30. Blockhead
31. ___ cheap
32. Succinct
34. Turbine, for one
37. Sea vessel
38. Tropical trees
40. Whetstone
41. "The Divine ___"
42. Primarily
44. Smoke
45. Small mammal
46. Resting
47. Shop
49. Haul
50. Droop
53. Linus's sister
54. Interchange
56. Farm structure
57. French season
58. Shine
59. Confidence
60. Supplication
61. Stringed instrument
62. Fish catcher
63. Table protector
65. Apropos
68. Discrimination
69. French river
70. Of a region
71. Dream-bringer?
73. Poetry
76. Irishman
77. Arid
78. In addition
80. Indian weight
81. Leaf of 38 Across
82. Chopped
83. Investigate
85. Vega, e.g.
86. Not natural: hyph.
88. Duo
89. Turned into
91. Gaunt
92. Stewpot
93. Cheered up
94. Fiends
95. Rind
96. Napery material

DOWN
1. Go hungry
2. Table decoration
3. Buttons and Skelton
4. Rarebit ingredient
5. Word before toast and after peach
6. Neighbor of the United States
7. Hot spot
8. Anthropologist Margaret
9. Skill
10. Abrade
11. Wakened
12. Lantern
13. Actress Merkel
14. Malaysian quarry: 2 wds.
15. Sang again, e.g.
16. Young pig
19. Upper class
25. Edges
26. "___ with the Wind"
29. Merchandise
30. Break bread
31. Coin
33. Dog in "Annie"
35. Butter maker
36. Settler's place
37. Lounge around
39. Enigma
41. French author of "Gigi"
42. Adam was the first
43. Be adjacent
44. Froth
45. Disarray
48. Ensnare
49. Serve tea
50. Nevada's nickname: 2 wds.
51. Toward shelter
52. Billy or nanny
55. Chandelier ornament
56. Thorn
58. Cotillion
61. Passion
62. Zinfandel or Merlot
64. Sunder
65. Washington city
66. Emerald Isle
67. Hodgepodge
68. Farm building
69. Haughty one
71. Where Ed Norton worked
72. Without principles
74. Tars
75. Blundered
77. Automobile type
79. Revolutionary
82. Nimbus
83. Colorless
84. Irritate
85. Glance through
87. Taciturn
88. Soda
90. Samuel's mentor

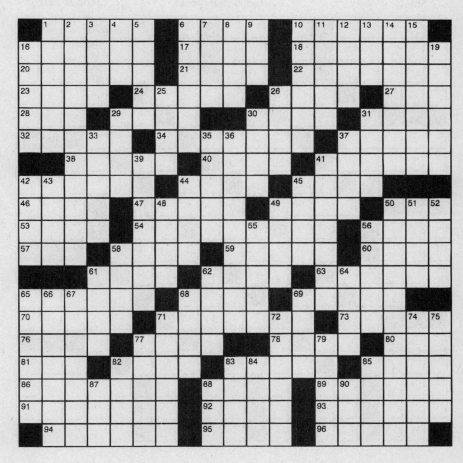

PUZZLE 17

ACROSS

1. Snowbank
6. House cleaner, in London
10. Nor'easter
14. God of the underworld
17. Copland ballet
18. Old Norse poem
19. Black, poetically
20. Ethan Allen's brother
21. Apparent
22. Geraint's wife
23. Period following Mardi Gras
24. Unused
25. 100 centavos
26. Make a choice
27. Apartment
29. Pointless
31. Acquiesce
33. Jack's relative
34. Panic-striken
35. Easily managed
38. Percolate
39. Reckon
40. Distant
41. Showy flower, for short
42. Skier's line
43. Lace shade
47. Computer pick list
48. County event
49. Argument
50. Wight and Ely
51. Rapier
53. Patched
55. Mischievous Olympian
56. Craze
59. Mortar trough
60. Sugarcane liquor
61. Type of graph
62. Sycophant's word
63. Mountain birthplace of Zeus
64. Football team
66. Ethical
68. "____ Doll"
70. Small bite
71. Rake
72. Midwestern state
76. Mine car
77. Huckleberry's friend
78. Unmannerly person
79. Live coal
80. Indonesian boat
82. "Wind in the Willows" character, with Mr.
83. Dodges
84. Overpower
87. Sort
88. Biblical hunter
89. Praise
90. Succotash ingredient
91. In favor of
92. River to the Moselle
96. Type of store: abbr.
97. Shout of contempt
99. Midday
101. Terra ____
102. Semicircle
103. Highlands language
104. Novelist Grey
105. Edible bulb
106. Pigpen
107. Charlie Brown's word
108. Greek god
109. Animal

DOWN

1. Pendant
2. Gad about
3. Roman calendar days
4. Savage
5. Small portion
6. Crinkled fabric
7. Linda or Leigh
8. Black cuckoo
9. Diminished
10. Icy
11. Succor a scofflaw
12. Cartography term: abbr.
13. Tempt
14. Tunisian money
15. Goddess of peace
16. Cut
26. Poet's output
28. Fabric pile
30. Designates
32. Santa's helper
33. Burn
34. Suture
35. Foal's mother
36. Spanish rah
37. Lifer
38. Came in feetfirst
39. Deluge
41. Fragrant flower
42. High craggy hill
44. Potter's material
45. Anatomical network
46. Exercises
48. Deceive
49. Hit suddenly
50. Comic strip's light bulb
52. At what time
53. Demand for payment
54. Paddy's land
56. Clenched hand
57. Hebrew month
58. Computer fodder
60. Ribbed fabric
65. Vitality
66. State of mind
67. Chauffeur-driven car
69. Urge forward
71. Course
73. Accessory for Yum-Yum
74. Tie the knot
75. ____ gratia artis
77. Write quickly
78. Rich mass of ore
79. Entertainer Tanguay
81. Preferably
82. Lyricist Rice
83. Kyushu island volcano
84. French impressionist
85. Put forth
86. Ornamental
87. Flying toys
88. Birds of prey
90. Without direction
91. Corn bread
93. Operatic highlight
94. Hebrew prophet
95. Carry on
98. ____ pro nobis
100. Bireme's need
101. Watch pocket

ACROSS

1. Genie's abode
5. Tried for office again
10. Freshet
15. Patriot Nathan
19. Inter ____
20. Sidestep
21. Zodiac's ram
22. Lackaday!
23. Intuitive perception
25. Best airline cabin
27. All the people
28. Relinquish
29. Mount
30. Determined
31. ____ diem
32. Tranquillity
34. At a distance
35. Bobbsey girl
36. Hair style
37. Cache
39. Divan
42. Less moist
45. Afternoon custom
46. Portico
50. Excitedly
51. Ragtime dance
55. News anchor
57. Literal
58. Sugar: suff.
59. ____ beaver
61. Letter embellishment
62. Ever, to a poet
63. Arab chieftains
65. Tree trunk
66. Iron alloy
67. ____ heaven
69. Be unfaithful to
71. Thespian
72. Promissory notes: abbr.
75. Cutlass
76. Barnyard wallower
79. Rill
80. Loft
82. Soak flax
83. Cornbread
84. More uncanny
86. Oliver's desire
88. Religious gp.
89. Liang
90. Globe
93. Volumetric flow unit
95. Smell
96. "Purple People ____"
98. Torrid
99. Turkish unit of weight
101. Man with the figures: abbr.
104. Ignoble
105. Chinese pagoda
106. Not pro-fessionally done
111. Fly or coat
113. Turkeys, in Madrid
115. Notifies
116. Octagonal
118. Variety shop
120. Sailing
121. Amphitheater
122. Oak's seed
123. Weapon: Fr.
124. Time in office
125. Piece of lingerie
126. Decompose
127. Defeat

DOWN

1. Type of surgery
2. Still kicking
3. Blends
4. Endorsement
5. Echo
6. Happening
7. Madras queen
8. Public attention-getters
9. Born: Fr.
10. Journalist Morley
11. Puritanical
12. Most breezy
13. Having a will
14. Id ____
15. Nimbus
16. Pertaining to wings
17. Riata
18. German city
24. Tree frog genus
26. Star of "Moonstruck"
28. Boy Scout unit
31. Pucker
33. Glide
36. Spelling contest
38. Homage
39. Satisfy
40. Fairy-tale villain
41. Gettysburg Address starter
43. Pitcher's bag's contents
44. Idleness
47. Trio
48. ____-de-boeuf
49. Sandy's line
52. Flap
53. Self-conceit
54. Stones
56. Up and about
58. Hebrew dry measure
60. Honoraria
63. Call forth
64. Pellets
66. Printer's direction
68. Star: Fr.
70. Rotund
71. Tract
73. Shoshonean Indian
74. Incite to attack
77. Formerly
78. Feeble
79. Risk
81. After-sledding drink
83. Shaped like an Egyptian tomb
85. Agenda
87. Kernel
91. Breathe
92. Coated with crumbs
94. Guests
97. Spur on
98. Possesses
100. "Ol' Man River" composer
101. Defraud
102. Aplomb
103. Boring tool
105. Time before tomorrow
106. Destruction
107. Musical drama
108. Houston player
109. Considers
110. Medieval workers
112. Fake
114. Market
117. Posed
118. Craze
119. Hamill's milieu

PUZZLE 19

· STADIUM OR DISH ·

ACROSS

1. Incline
5. Niagara River island
9. Extol
13. Paul Bunyan's ox
17. Inspiration
18. Type of worm
19. Caen's river
20. War god
21. Life, for some
24. Spanish lad
25. Instrument of old
26. Export
27. Artist's color
29. Helps
31. Plunge
32. Isinglass
33. Struck
34. To-do
35. Citadel
38. Base
39. Cattail
41. Contends
42. Uncooked
44. Woody's son
46. United States region
   in the 1930s
49. Troglodyte's home
50. Saturday and Sunday
52. Sari-wearer
53. French painter
54. Statistics
55. Rides the waves
56. Tennis champ
57. Hillside
59. Puccini's forte
60. Choirboys
63. Sitarist Shankar
64. Pasadena stadium
66. Old Greek coin
67. Orangutan
68. Separate
70. Ladies
72. Comedian Olsen
73. Archbishop
75. Nimble
77. Handled roughly
79. Trim
80. Caliber
81. Shopping places
82. Yacht basin
85. Festive
86. James ___ Carter, Jr.
87. Race-track shape
88. Mammoth Cave's
   neighbor
94. Fast-food order
95. Emblem of Wales
96. Aquatic bird
97. Thrown glove
98. Foul-up
99. Marine birds
100. No problem
101. Wanes

DOWN

1. Adam's loss
2. Flurry
3. Sea gull
4. Shipping platform
5. Talents
6. Fairy-tale starter
7. Alas, in Ulm
8. Dissertation
9. Actor Greene
10. Parched
11. One, to Fifi
12. Abhor
13. Potted dwarf tree
14. Door to ore
15. Twining plant stem
16. Organic compound
22. External
23. Guns while idling
28. Takes steps
29. Love, in Livorno
30. Flabbergasted
31. Fizzlers
32. Sugar source
33. Cabbage salad
34. Vendetta
35. Radio's major of "The
   Amateur Hour"
36. Miami stadium, once
37. Main church area
40. Best or Millay
41. Chat, for short
43. Rainy
45. Giraffe's kin
47. Most faithful
48. Wilkes- ___ ,
   Pennsylvania
49. Freight
51. Summer, in Sevres
53. Back-to-work time:
   abbr.
55. Germ cell
56. Pelican's feature
57. Lady of Spain: abbr.
58. Northern Swede
59. Proclaim
60. Influence
61. Acting parts
62. Travois
65. Grimm villain
68. Young or Ladd
69. Allegory
71. Tenpin feat
74. Conclusion
75. Arias
76. Cavort
78. Maintain
80. Refuses
81. Borgnine film
82. Quips
83. Stratford's river
84. Hindu melody
85. Actress Verdon
86. Selves
89. "___ the land . . ."
90. Part of India
91. Arrest
92. Soviet agency: abbr.
93. Referendum vote

ACROSS

1. Stylish
5. Gator's kin
9. Eight: prefix
13. Soft drink
17. Western weed
18. Leander's love
19. Stuff
20. The same, to Cato: abbr.
21. Soon
22. Conception
23. Animal shelter
24. Street
25. Writing implements
27. Clever accomplishment
29. Speeders
31. Ancient
32. Burn
33. European bunting
34. Chatter
37. Cook
38. Consented
42. Kiln
43. Dressed
44. Unconscious periods
46. Anger
47. Recline
48. Pen
49. Group of witches
50. Imprison
51. Outlining
53. Carp
54. Shade
55. Had a meal
56. Removed the center of
57. Vehicle
58. Impertinent
61. Hints
62. Actress Bergen
66. Patriot Nathan ____
67. Record
68. Dray
69. Milk-producer
70. Spanish gold
71. Actor Eastwood
72. Remedy
73. Yield
74. Medium
76. Ringlet
77. Legal actions
78. Pig's utterance
79. Taxis
80. Narrow bed
81. Brandy
84. Muslim judge
85. Musical performance
89. Eager
90. New Year's noisemaker
92. Fragment
94. Cilium
95. Only
96. Paradise
97. Overdue
98. Bacchanal's cry
99. Nobleman
100. Wet
101. Black-____ Susan
102. Network

DOWN

1. Applaud
2. Sharpen
3. Religious statue
4. Fabricate
5. Youngster
6. Skelton and Buttons
7. Mine deposit
8. Tutored
9. Happen
10. Trim
11. Do needlework
12. U.S. citizen
13. Come full ____
14. Woodwind
15. Fibber
16. Totals
26. Sort
28. Dolt
30. Rainbows
32. Fellow
33. Desert animal
34. Filly's counterpart
35. Den
36. Confused
37. Blockage
39. Use a phone
40. Hence
41. Ruminant mammal
43. Pine nut
44. Bays
45. Roman poet
48. Urban place
49. Proofreader's mark
50. Wood measure
52. Baked dessert
53. Woo
54. Tilt
56. Family group
57. Concern
58. Hew
59. Sculls
60. Surfeit
61. Young bird
62. Astronomer Sagan
63. Frozen desserts
64. Cipher
65. Female sheep
67. Settled decisively
68. Mongrels
71. Mexican mint plant
72. Small chamber
73. Baseball position
75. Eel
76. Heel
77. Against
79. Shrewd
80. Made do
81. Pitch a tent
82. Molding
83. Stab
84. Work gang
85. Summon
86. Roof edge
87. Tumult
88. Woody plant
91. Pindar poem
93. Fodder

PUZZLE 21

ACROSS
1. Trudge
5. Injure
9. Huck's vessel
13. ___ David
17. Impertinent
18. Butter substitute
19. Ohio Indian
20. Potpourri
21. Unrefined minerals
22. Esteemed
24. Spar
25. Abhor
27. ___ Cruces
28. Inventories
29. Star player
30. Nob or Sam
32. Tale
34. Bind again
37. Animal hair
38. Burdened
40. Legendary bird
43. Above
44. Roadside eatery
46. Thaw
47. Australian bird
48. "A Few Good ___"
49. Classify
50. Occurrence
52. Russian ruler
53. Able was I ___ . . .
54. Minuscule
55. Baker's need
56. Word following up or down
58. Large extinct bird
60. Relies
63. Plus
64. Design
67. Fat
68. Fasten
70. Psyche part
73. Rail
74. Prepare, as fish
76. Beep
77. Currently
78. Liable
79. Proofreader's word
80. Blotch
82. Israeli city
83. Written documents: abbr.
84. Sharpens
86. Hooter
87. Skedaddles
88. Engrossed
89. Central or Menlo
91. Decay
92. Vapor
95. Feel unwell
96. Atones
100. Assists
101. "Two ___ of Verona"
105. Seldom
106. Goad
107. Medicinal plant
108. Road division
109. Emerald Isle
110. Dregs
111. Forbids
112. Store
113. Bureaucracy section: abbr.

DOWN
1. Wand for cattle
2. Bewitch
3. Poetic works
4. Lose hope
5. Steed
6. On the sheltered side
7. Legal thing
8. Thick mass of hair
9. Conjure up again
10. Martial ___
11. Old-fashioned expletive
12. Koppel or Bessell
13. Funny guy
14. Woe is me!
15. Haze
16. Utensils
23. Addition
26. Freeze
28. Fabric fuzz
30. Pursue
31. Rage
32. Heavenly garden
33. Skins
34. City on the Tiber
35. Eternally
36. Urban housing
37. Discharged
39. Improve
40. Domicile
41. General Bradley
42. Mongrels
44. Female rabbit
45. Paul and his kin
49. Hit hard
51. Sell
52. Light brown
55. October's gem
57. Military vehicle
59. Morsel for Dobbin
61. Make joyous
62. Ruin
64. Stuff
65. Talks candidly
66. Prevent legally
69. Hostel
71. Skirt panel
72. Is indebted
75. Copper coin
76. Peddle
79. Bogus
81. Peak
82. Metamorphosed
85. Acts against with malice
87. Dandy
88. Tears down, in London
90. "___ for one . . ."
91. Renovate
92. Author Bellow
93. Grow weary
94. "The Razor's ___"
95. Momentarily
96. Gambling town
97. Nostril
98. Pilgrimage
99. Transmitted
101. Gossip
102. Guido's note
103. Chicago trains
104. Welcome or place pad

MOVIES AND TELEVISION

ACROSS

1. "My Gal ____" (1942 film)
4. "Animal ____" (1954 film)
8. "The ____ Horizons" (1955 film)
11. John ____ of "Good Times"
13. "____ Predators" (1987 film)
15. Robertson or Evans
16. "Queen of the ____" (1962 film)
17. "The Name Above the ____" (Frank Capra autobiography)
18. Thicke or Arkin
19. Martin or Jones
20. "Mr. ____" (1946 film)
21. "Easter ____" (1948 film)
23. "Ready, Willing and ____" (1937 film)
25. "White ____ and Tails" (1946 film)
26. "Soap" family name
28. "____ Children" (1940 film)
34. "____ Fiddle" (1939 film)
36. 1981 Bacall film, with "The"
37. Meadow
38. ____ about (approximately): 2 wds.
39. Clarinetist Shaw
41. TV's ____ Maxwell
42. Garry Moore show singer Denise ____
43. Payment
44. Ed Norton's workplace
46. Tennessee ____: 2 wds.
50. Brownie part
51. "Flying Down to ____" (1933 film)
52. "____ Camera" (1955 film): 3 wds.
54. "My ____ Flicka" (1943 film)
57. Explosive
58. Old salts
62. Merit
63. TV actress Graff
65. Actress McClurg
66. Blackthorn fruit
67. Priscilla and Rosemary
68. Pro ____
69. Japanese coin

70. Collate
71. "My ____ Godfrey" (1936 film)

DOWN

1. "Blood and ____" (1941 film)
2. Gaston's gal
3. "____ Montes" (1955 film)
4. "____ Attraction" (1987 film)
5. Faye and Cooper
6. Ceremony
7. Brooks or Torme
8. New Deal pooch
9. "When I was ____ . . .": 2 wds.
10. French director Clair
12. "The ____ Was Indiscreet" (1947 film)
14. "____ Daughter" (1949 film)
15. "Ten Who ____" (1960 film)
22. "____ Mail" (1932 film)
24. Cross or Gazzara
26. Lanza's voice
27. "The ____ People" (1981 film)
29. "It's Love I'm ____" (1937 film)
30. Skater Babilonia
31. Steve or Woody

32. "The Best ____ of Our Lives" (1946 film)
33. "____ at Sea" (1940 film)
34. "____ Survivor" (1970 film)
35. Spring bloom
40. Old car
41. "____ Girl" (1942 film)
45. "A Nightmare on ____ Street" (1984 film)
47. Dunne or Cara
48. One, to Dietrich
49. "My ____ with Andre" (1982 film)
53. "____ of Love" (1985 film): 2 wds.
54. Actor Parker
55. Abnormal lung sound
56. "The ____ Petticoat" (1956 film)
57. ____'clock scholar: 2 wds.
59. Rich or West
60. Hayworth
61. Penn
64. "The ____ Vegas Story" (1952 film)

PUZZLE 23

• BLOW BY BLOW •

ACROSS

1. Bend out of shape
5. Engendered
10. Cutter, for one
14. African lily
15. Straighten
16. Impulse
17. Comic Laurel
18. Special talent
19. Cheer the team
20. Cornucopia
23. Theater award
24. Virginia willow
27. Massenet opera
29. Megaphone
33. Sheriff's group
34. Pitchfork part
35. ____ homo
36. Termite
37. Endure a situation
40. Munch
41. Palm, e.g.
43. Jason's ship
44. Makes (one's way)
46. Seaman's dance
48. Ouida's real appellation
49. ____'acte
50. TV's Tennille
51. Swindled
58. Hindu teacher
61. Takes on
62. Ceremony
63. Without warranty
64. Song for eight
65. Kind of cheese
66. Prey
67. Two on the aisle
68. How Lindy flew

DOWN

1. Scrub down
2. Choir member
3. Bellow
4. Banners
5. Bay of the Arctic
6. Wed on the run
7. Jeune fille
8. ____-bellum
9. Young miss
10. ____ hatchet
11. Spanish galleon's cargo
12. Past
13. Asian holiday
21. Orchestra instruments
22. Sesame plant
25. Geological epoch
26. Penny ____
27. James or Marilyn
28. Aft
29. Spree
30. Open
31. Waikiki garland
32. Trawlers' tools
33. Trail
34. Diamond cover: abbr.
38. ____ Babilonia
39. Guitar sound
42. Rave
45. Refugees
47. Old hand
48. Perches
50. Bird sound
52. Greek letters
53. Resort near Cannes
54. Spanish miss: abbr.
55. Isle near Venice
56. Kin to etc.
57. DJ's disk
58. Joke
59. Made in the ____
60. Grand Canyon area

PUZZLE 24   Crypto-Limerick

To read this humorous verse, you must first decode it as you would a regular cryptogram.

```
AXDQD   ZSMD   YCF   C   FPKKV   ZKU   TCPU

YXZ   ZSKV   CAD   NQCJD   TCQTCKCUD.

     CA   ZSD   XLSUQDU   CSU   ADS

        FXD   FCPU   AZ   AXD   TDS,

''XZY   SPMDKV   JQDFDQEDU   P   XCED   FACVDU!''
```

PUZZLE 25

ACROSS
1. Individuality
5. Play on words
8. Beseech
12. Egg-shaped
13. Exist
14. Comfort
15. Concluding
17. Request
18. Passing craze
19. Show up
21. Part of an arrow
24. Remain
25. Very small
26. Slender
27. Knock
30. Actor Carney
31. Courageous
32. Frost, as a cake
33. Stinging insect
34. Uncommon
35. Alaskan city
36. Candy _____
37. Thirst quencher
38. Athletic events
41. Took a chair
42. Adore
43. Fictitious
48. Space
49. Pride
50. Clamp
51. Beauty-shop offer
52. Tier
53. Mild oath

DOWN
1. Turf
2. Actress Arden
3. Young boy
4. Downy
5. Reimbursed
6. Vase
7. Pessimistic
8. Vigorous
9. Rattling sound
10. On the ocean
11. Time period
16. Feline
20. Window glass
21. Pierce
22. Employ
23. Feed the kitty
24. Portion
26. The Manhattan _____
27. Uprising
28. Top
29. Equal
31. Unruly child
35. Original inhabitant
36. Dairy product
37. 1943 fem. army-member
38. Hit
39. Skin opening
40. Above
41. White precipitation
44. In the past
45. Dried fruit
46. Neighbor of Can.
47. Was ahead

PUZZLE 26

ACROSS
1. Pack
5. Distant
8. Pig's home
11. Verdi opera
12. Ripen
13. Noose
15. Narrow opening
16. Compress
18. Calm
20. Chalkboard's need
21. Stick
22. Existed
23. Use an explosive
26. Penalty for misconduct
30. Atmosphere
31. Turf
32. "We _____ the World"
33. Lure
36. Go very fast
38. First woman
39. Mimic
40. Complete agreement
43. Bull's-eye
47. Good-bye
49. Rescue
50. Leave out
51. Narrow inlet
52. Unwrap
53. Twisty curve
54. Affirmative
55. Dolt

DOWN
1. Talk back
2. Roof covering
3. Aroma
4. Tasteless liquids
5. Stood up to
6. Gone by
7. Restored
8. Accommodate
9. Time periods
10. Sniffer
14. _____ capita
17. Small drink of liquor
19. "Death Be _____ Proud"
23. Sheep sound
24. Afire
25. Mr. Linkletter
26. Speck
27. "Norma _____"
28. Anger
29. Actor Danson
31. Vista
34. Adjusts, as a clock
35. Declare openly
36. Health resort
37. Human being
39. Book of maps
40. Unusual sky sighting
41. Title
42. Part of the eye
44. Yawn
45. Always
46. Take care of
48. Fabrication

PUZZLE 27

Codeword is a special crossword puzzle in which conventional clues are omitted. Instead, answer words in the diagram are represented by numbers. Each number represents a different letter of the alphabet, and all of the letters of the alphabet are used. When you are sure of a letter, put it in the code key chart for easy reference. Two letters have been given to start you off.

1	14
2	15
3	16
4	17
5	18
6	19
7	20
8	21
9	22
10	23
11	24
12	25 O
13	26 W

PUZZLE 28

CODEWORD

1	14
2	15
3	16
4	17
5	18
6	19
7 I	20
8	21 N
9	22
10	23
11	24
12	25
13	26

ACROSS

1. Gabs
6. Schedule
11. Like raw carrots
16. Restrict
17. Kitchen tool
18. Go to bed
20. Fragrance
21. Fairy-tale opener
24. Veneration
26. Part of a den wall, perhaps
27. Oath
28. Locale
29. Matured
30. Ascots
31. Destiny
32. Snout
34. Brooches
35. Elector
36. Center
39. French painter
41. Fondle
42. Mountain ridge
43. Shiny fabric
44. Formerly, of old
45. Son of Leah
46. Theater curtain
47. Slink
50. Writer Bagnold
51. Serenity
53. Part of Q.E.D.
55. Luxurious
57. Grew weary
58. Carry on the back
59. Metal thread
60. Bishop's cap
61. Make broader
62. Bravery awards
65. Street urchin
66. Dromedaries
67. Shun
68. Painful
69. Weight allowance
70. Monthly payment
71. Indonesian island
72. Farm unit
74. Green pear
78. Writer Levin
79. Songstress Reddy
80. Sicilian peak
82. Simultaneously
85. Actress Moreno et al.
86. Flew high
87. Storms
88. Motionless
89. Indian peasants
90. Athletic game
91. Monsters

DOWN

1. Actress Bow
2. Employer
3. Get ____ on
4. "____ for no man"
5. Headliner
6. Square of foam rubber
7. Spear
8. Curved across
9. Summer shirt
10. Outbreak
11. Hags
12. Actor Auberjonois et al.
13. Slanting type: abbr.
14. Hold a session
15. York, e.g.
19. Overacts
22. Enamel
23. Water pitchers
25. Facilitate
31. Temporarily
33. Bullfight cheer: Sp.
34. Evening TV period
35. Extensive
36. Masculine
37. Goddess of peace
38. Imp
39. Gem weight
40. Of the ear
41. Wept
43. Vista
44. "____ Gantry"
46. Masts
47. Ambulance horn
48. Wear away
49. Badgerlike animal
52. Small monkey
54. Hamilton bills
56. Cover with gold
60. Seamen
61. Conflict
62. Diva Callas
63. Turns inside out
64. Contributor
65. Jewish folklore character
66. French city
68. Luncheon entrees
69. Most reliable
71. Assail
72. Friend: Sp.
73. Potential leader
75. Aquatic mammal
76. Trap
77. Hurls
79. Man of the hour
81. Quartet less one
83. Dried grass
84. Spigot

PUZZLE 29

• BEAT THE CLOCK •

PUZZLE 30

ACROSS

1. "____ the Titanic!"
6. Warty creature
10. Football play
14. Building addition
15. Grimm's monster
16. Smallest of the litter
17. Actress Debra
18. Actor Tim
19. Singer Adams
20. Hi-fi
22. Cotton gin inventor
23. "West ____ Story"
24. Pinch
26. Distribute
28. Frying pans
33. Long, long ____
34. Shoe strings
35. Nutty cake
37. Not near
40. Currier and ____
41. Riotous fight
42. North Sea feeder
43. Flower plot
44. Wait on
45. ____-footed
46. For each
47. Guess
49. Put back
53. Unit of corn
54. Bread spread
55. Bad actor
57. Cockroach, to some
62. There ought to be ____
63. Culture medium
65. Mathematical matrix, for one
66. Playing cubes
67. Pianist Peter
68. ____ Janeiro
69. Plant
70. Playing card
71. Allots

DOWN

1. Chats
2. Medical school subject: abbr.
3. Playwright William
4. Crystal-ball gazer
5. Stretches out
6. Rocky pinnacle
7. Curved molding
8. Seed pods
9. Consecrate
10. Pronto
11. Examine
12. Nastily derogatory
13. Cowpoke's charge
21. Lubricant
25. ____ Cottontail
27. Grow old
28. Suave
29. Critic's superior rating
30. Frosted
31. ____ Plaines
32. Figure out
36. Della or Pee Wee
37. ____ market
38. Aid a criminal
39. Network
41. Storekeeper
42. Graceful tree
44. Red, White, or Black
45. Rifle
46. Removed snow by machine
48. Check
49. Highways
50. Miss ____ Ewing ("Dallas" character)
51. Calm
52. Avid
56. Female horse
58. Pennsylvania port
59. Jog
60. Burden
61. "The ____ of Texas"
64. Cowboy Rogers

PUZZLE 31   ANAGRAM QUOTES

Unscramble each set of letters below the dashes to complete the humorous quotations.

1. _____ : _____ who catches _____ by _____, by _____, and _____ by _____.

   HSMNFRAEI   EOSMENO   IHFS   CTEPAIEN   KLUC   MMETIEOSS   LTAE

2. A _____ _____ is like a _____ who _____ _____.

   ODGO KOCO   SSOEECRSR   SPNEEIDSS   EPHAINSSP

ACROSS

1. Wild guess
5. Neighbor of Miss.
8. Short swim
11. Jason's ship
12. Prohibit
13. Century plant
15. Duplicitious ones
18. Red-ink items
19. Musical pauses
20. Bandleader Brown
21. "___ Impossible"
22. Girlfriend, to Jacques
25. Liston opponent
26. Costa
29. Look twice
33. Rowan or Rather
34. AAA suggestion
35. Bassoon, e.g.
36. Gambling cube
37. Fruity dessert
39. Cosmetics queen Lauder
42. Alter
45. Some baseball games
48. Australian bird
49. Hair preparation
50. Period following Mardi Gras
51. Erhard's prog.
52. Vapor
53. Foil's kin

DOWN

1. Dispirited
2. Walked on
3. Malarial fever
4. Fumbled, as a baseball
5. Helps in wrongdoing
6. Young men
7. Metric land measure
8. Evans and Roberts
9. French land masses
10. Sweet wine
14. Windy road curve
16. Taradiddle
17. Bandleader Shaw
21. Under the weather
22. Put two and two together
23. Extinct bird
24. Author Fleming
25. Humorist Burrows
26. Actress Charlotte ___
27. Mamie's husband
28. Fourposter
30. Bay window
31. Shoshonean Indian
32. Foot-operated lever
36. First public appearance
37. Removes the rind
38. "___ Believer"
39. Netherlands commune
40. Several
41. Day before Wed.
42. Mother of Zeus
43. Maintain
44. Shore soarer
46. Omelet ingredient
47. Fr. holy woman

ACROSS

1. Couple
5. Needlefish
8. "Moonstruck" actress
12. Indian tourist site
13. Primate
14. Topnotch
15. Whitman work
18. Appear
19. Nostradamus, e.g.
20. Not as much
23. Banal
26. Offers for viewing
30. Site for a labyrinth
31. Escape
32. Equipment for a rodeo
34. Mineral springs
35. Actress Foster of "Punky Brewster"
36. Church officials
38. Morsel
41. Pole
42. Certain transaction
44. Connections
47. E.B. White work
52. O.K. Corral good guy
53. Prefix for recent
54. Henri's head
55. Bridge expert Culbertson and others
56. Hampshire's home
57. Adj.

DOWN

1. Crony
2. Distinctive periods
3. "Dies ___"
4. Untwists
5. Auto fuel
6. Mil. address
7. Umps' cousins
8. Concerned person
9. Most ancient
10. Naval off.
11. Legal thing
16. Mideast bigwig
17. Obtain
21. Sassy person
22. Headliners
24. Recording ribbon
25. Precambrian and Paleozoic
26. Land map
27. Hindu deity
28. Representative
29. Tread
33. Winged
37. Awn
39. Field covers, for short
40. Wright wing
43. Endless times
45. Meadow mowers
46. Prepares for dining, as a table
47. Third letter
48. Computer in "2001"
49. Laotian holiday
50. Miniature
51. Stake

PUZZLE 34

Two clues for each number and two puzzle diagrams—which answer goes where? That's your dilemma. Answer the clues and then decide in which crossword pattern the answer fits. The first two words have been entered for you.

ACROSS

1. Male cat
   Actor Hutton
4. Wet dirt
   Paving liquid
7. Swiftly
   Make amends
9. At a distance
   Pub brews
11. Military student
    Pastimes
12. Man's servant
    Sum
14. Bullring cheer
    Time period
15. That woman
    Flightless bird
17. Wrath
    Adam's mate
18. Needle hole
    Curved letter
20. Speechified
    Deletes
22. Not now
    Singer Rogers
24. Next to
    Make a choice
27. Devour
    Rug
30. Actress Lupino
    Actress Gardner
31. Doctrine
    Globe
33. Ribbon loop
    Tear
35. Estate
    Metal fastener
37. Sheeplike
    Gladden
39. Further
    Theater box
40. Positioned
    More sagacious
41. Scepter
    Actor Beatty
42. Fruit drink
    Grant's foe

DOWN

1. Domesticates
   At this time
2. Individual
   Rink material
3. Dole
   Disarray
4. Pub
   Ripen
5. Chicken _____ king
   Alien vessel: abbr.
6. Appointments
   Kindled again
7. King topper
   Gone by
8. Ashen
   Vetch
10. Rant
    Withered
13. Bandleader Brown
    Actor Knight
16. Sharpens
    Gauge
19. Glide on snow
    Inventor Whitney
21. Upper limb
    Affirmative vote
23. Blue-penciled
    Worshiped
24. Faint
    Stripe
25. Wicked
    Dutch cheese
26. Church law
    Delight in
28. Get up
    Lessen
29. Carry
    Prong
32. Cereal dish
    Plateau
34. _____ diem
    Marry
36. Self
    Crude metal
38. Compete
    Box top

Movies and Television

ACROSS

1. "Take Her, She's ___"
   (1963 movie)
5. Actor Andrews
9. Cleo's downfall
12. Italian actress Valli ("The
    Third Man")
14. Thicke of "Growing Pains"
15. Choir voice
16. Graves or Falk
17. Give temporarily
18. Ooze
19. Actor Clark
20. State, to Bardot
21. TV's Johnson
22. "The Love ___" (1951
    movie)
24. "___ Street" (1974 movie)
26. "___ Eagles" (1986 Redford
    movie)
29. "___ in My Heart" (1933
    Stanwyck movie)
31. "Never ___ at a WAC"
    (1952 movie)
32. Stimson of "Little Miss
    Marker" (1980)
34. Cara of "Fame"
39. TV's "___ World"
41. "The ___ Was Indiscreet"
    (1947 movie)
43. Singer-actress Della
44. Prop for Julia Child
46. "The ___ the Merrier"
    (1943 movie)
47. Frog genus
49. Actress Canova
51. Donahue of "Father Knows
    Best"
55. "A Fine ___" (1986 Danson
    movie)
57. Actress Anderson
58. Small tastes
60. Lambs' mothers
64. "September ___"
65. Give out
66. " . . . ruler of the Queen's
    ___"
68. In mid-Atlantic
69. Dry
70. 1962 Welles movie, with
    "The"
71. Actor Beatty

72. Bernadette et al.: abbr.
73. "Desire Under the ___"
    (1958 movie)

DOWN

1. Atlas page
2. "___ Three Lives": 2 wds.
3. Silent-screen actress Naldi
4. "East of ___" (1954)
5. Evans and Robertson
6. "___ to Three Wives":
   2 wds.
7. 1934 Anna Sten film
8. "The Old Man ___ Sea":
   2 wds.
9. "Red ___" (1977 TV movie)
10. "___ Fair" (1945 movie)
11. "The Outcasts of ___ Flat"
    (1952 movie)
13. 1953 Gig Young movie
15. Woe!
23. Other
25. Moran or Gray
26. Lois ___ of "Superman"
27. Reveler's cry
28. Obtains
30. Urn

31. "___ Games" (1983 movie)
33. Eisenberg of "Star Trek:
    Deep Space Nine"
35. "Nine Hours to ___" (1962)
36. "A Yank at ___" (1942)
37. Charles of "The Thin Man"
38. Before
40. "Hail the Conquering ___"
    (1944 movie)
42. "To the ___ of the Earth"
    (1948 movie)
45. Dracula, e.g.
48. James of "Gunsmoke"
50. "___ a Letter to My Love"
    (1981): 2 wds.
51. Violinist Mischa
52. "___ Shoes" (1980 movie)
53. "The Lady ___": 2 wds.
54. Actress Foch
56. ___ Kefauver
59. "___ My Love Again"
    (1937 movie): 2 wds.
61. Pottery
62. "So ___ My Love" (1948
    movie)
63. Cloth joining
67. Overhead railways

The answers to the clues can be found in a diagram, but they have been camouflaged. Their letters are in correct order, but sometimes they are separated by extra letters which have been inserted throughout the diagram. You must black out all the extra camouflage letters. The remaining letters will be used in words reading across and down. Solve Across and Down together to determine the correct letters where there is a choice. The number of answer words in a row or column is indicated by the number of clues.

	1	2	3	4	5	6	7	8	9	10	11	12	13	14	15
1	S	E	V	A	E	R	T	A	A	L	E	D	A	R	E
2	T	R	A	C	T	E	H	O	M	E	L	R	R	U	N
3	A	R	I	L	M	A	I	M	E	D	A	I	M	E	D
4	I	N	N	T	E	R	R	E	N	D	S	L	O	W	E
5	A	S	W	O	U	R	D	N	E	X	T	E	R	I	B
6	R	E	O	U	R	O	E	P	R	O	I	E	A	S	E
7	P	R	E	Y	E	S	A	L	T	N	E	R	V	E	S
8	O	W	I	N	G	I	V	E	I	T	E	M	I	R	E
9	O	V	A	T	E	N	E	A	R	S	L	E	D	E	S
10	L	E	T	R	E	S	T	D	E	F	T	T	R	E	E
11	S	C	H	A	M	H	O	G	G	L	E	H	A	T	E
12	A	P	E	P	T	I	N	A	R	E	N	A	N	A	P
13	L	E	N	T	H	E	E	L	O	D	D	S	G	A	S
14	A	N	S	W	E	R	R	E	A	D	S	P	E	L	I
15	T	U	T	O	R	S	S	A	D	Y	E	S	V	E	X

ACROSS

1. Disconnect • Story • Risk
2. Tiny amount • 4-base hit • Hosiery mishap
3. Feel unwell • Mutilated • Aspired
4. Hotel • Made a mistake • Scatter seed
5. Excalibur, e.g. • Mesh • Chest bone
6. Vintage car • Caviar • Expert • Comfort
7. Hunted animal • Seasoning • Audacity
8. Gothic arch • List entry • Anger
9. Egg-shaped • Adjacent • Winter toys
10. Allow • Relax • Skillful • Hardwood source
11. Iranian ruler • Gawk • Despise
12. Energy • Sn • Stadium • Snooze
13. Pre-Easter period • Shoe part • Gambler's concern • Fuel
14. Reply • File • Inventor Whitney
15. Craggy peak • Unhappy • Male or female

DOWN

1. Flight unit • Pond • Bed board
2. Sea eagle • Tennis stroke • Writing tool
3. Futile • Trouble • Greek capital
4. Satiate • Snare • Couple
5. Come into view • Anesthetic
6. Hindmost • Violinist's need • More bashful
7. Show position • Chalet feature • Duplicating-machine fluids
8. Portent • Supplicate • Festivity
9. Moslem prince • Wheel shoe • Highway
10. Went ahead • Prohibitions • Ran away
11. The Orient • Conger • Inclines
12. Less moist • Encountered • Lock parts
13. Knight's protection • Enthusiastic • Scope
14. French street • Sager • Greek letter • Pub order
15. Finale • Drone • Ooze • Half-dozen

This puzzle is like a regular crossword, but without black squares. All words in the same line overlap by one or two letters.

ACROSS

1. Mall units
6. Sailor
14. Ma or pa
15. Narration
16. Ambassador
17. Impenetrable to light
19. Ovum
20. Four quarts
21. Redford film, with "The"
23. Kind of sail
25. Alfonso's queen
27. Blackthorn
29. Lamprey hunters
32. Play a guitar
34. Skiff's propellers
36. Leda's lover, for one
37. Feeble-minded
38. De Valera's land
40. Public disturbance
41. Equipment
43. Remainder
46. Forever
48. Sanaa's country
50. Gave medicine to
52. Made a call
55. Spanish lady
56. Communion tables
57. Break suddenly
58. Cooking vessel
59. Make lace
61. Quantity of paper
62. Bland
63. Explorer Bartholomeu ___
64. Location
65. Border
66. Fencing blade
67. Salad greens
68. Performers
69. Emphasizes
70. Ar-Tee connector

DOWN

1. Backed
2. Spigot
3. Soapbox user
4. Ask for
5. Accustom
6. Baseball manuever
7. Certain gold coin
8. Seaweed
9. Daring deeds
10. Shoelace tip
11. Chest sound
12. Buckinghamshire's college
13. Title again
18. Bosom buddy
22. Recoil
24. "Tempest" spirit
25. Buffalo's lake
26. Michael Learned series
28. Cafe au ___
30. Hawaiian porches
31. New ___ (Maine native)
32. Do in
33. Shipworm
35. European deer
36. Pennant
39. Sicilian volcano
42. Folksinger Jenkins
44. Exciting feelings
45. Legislative bodies
47. Ohio city
48. Informal affirmative
49. Musician King Cole
50. Challenged
51. Raised platform
52. Leaks
53. Small land mass
54. Singer Frankie ___
55. Spanish two
58. Cushions
60. Kinski film
64. Family member, for short

PUZZLE 38

• **FOR THOSE WHO ARE ABLE** •

ACROSS

1. Soft fuel
5. Punctuation mark
10. Whitened
15. Destiny
19. ___ mater
20. Not whispered
21. Straighten
22. Nuclear bit
23. 3 ABLE additions
27. Semi-solid
28. Footwear
29. Pays up
30. Ore worker
31. Before
32. Misplace
33. Liquid measure
34. Dressed to the ___
35. Possessive pronoun
36. Hurok
37. Heat liquid
38. 3 ABLE additions
50. The best
51. College head
52. Swap
53. Songwriter ___ Novello
54. Delicate fabric
55. Cans
56. Dens
57. Dish
58. Even score
59. Covered feet
60. Chair maker
61. Freed
62. 2 ABLE additions
65. Mares
68. Arrives
69. Throw
70. "___ Boot"
73. Jagged
74. Soupy
75. Pope name
76. Cooped
77. Baseball name
78. More competent
79. Press
80. Chatter
81. 3 ABLE additions
85. Golf score
86. ___ Rogers
87. Serling
88. Command
91. Pertaining to bees
94. Chair
96. Noticed
99. Spin
100. Odor
101. Edison's park
102. Spanish aunt
103. 3 ABLE additions
107. Consider
108. Childlike
109. Fire cause
110. Matures
111. Ferber
112. Snake
113. Cubic meter
114. Assay

DOWN

1. Baseballer Satchel ___
2. Fudd
3. Sufficient
4. Roof material
5. Freight-train car
6. Mixtures
7. ___ Cristo
8. Rumple
9. Oklahoma town
10. Enamel
11. Winged
12. Ship
13. Finales
14. Hideaway
15. Dickens villain
16. Make up
17. Carries
18. Near East prince
24. Accommodate
25. Last ends
26. Zola
33. Bank deal
34. Brood of pheasants
35. Despise
36. Resorts
37. Percentages
38. Thaw
39. Jai ___
40. Agreeable
41. Peculiar speech
42. Beggar
43. Loses a lap
44. Airy spirit
45. Running talk
46. Steersman
47. Gabor namesakes
48. Musical sound
49. ___ Scott
55. The thing here
56. Alleys
57. Lily ___
59. Snicker ___
60. Judge's chamber
61. Not so much
62. Come out
63. Rent sign
64. Small hill
65. Boss
66. Heraldry bearing
67. Tree foundation
70. Unheeding
71. Against
72. Let it be
74. European coal area
75. Address a god
76. Urge
78. Headliner
79. Privy to
80. Charged particle
82. List the letters
83. Angry
84. Nut candy
88. Possessed
89. Split
90. Play
91. Harsh to the taste
92. Anger
93. Deduce
94. Feel
95. Witch's home
96. Theater section
97. Buenos ___
98. Middle section
99. Lateral section
100. Mining nail
101. Store
104. Actress Merkel
105. Ethiopian prince
106. Large tub

PUZZLE 39

• "THE DOCK OF THE BAY" •

ACROSS

1. Tropical fish
5. Recorded proceedings
9. Tattered
13. Footnote abbr.
17. Songwriter Porter
18. Eastern European
19. Turkish general
20. Carbonated beverage
21. Early man
22. Pudding starch
23. Arctic bay
25. New Jersey bay
27. Bistro
29. Succor
30. Author Talese
31. Like some lingerie
32. Ceremonial staff
34. Entertainer
37. Mediterranean juniper
38. Sounds of laughter
39. Cross
42. Sortie
43. Cincinnati's river
44. Biological fluids
45. Emit coherent light
46. Biblical craft
47. Matured
48. Dab
49. Protection
50. Trestles
52. Coral island
53. Inuit boat
54. Vicinity
55. Sound of derision
56. Beige
58. Liturgical cloth
61. Shellfish
63. Squirreled away
67. Barrier
68. Assuage
69. Designer Chapman
70. Epoch
71. Baltic port
72. Apiece
73. Singer Edith ____
74. Funds
75. Low cardinal number
76. Stained with writing fluid
77. Foremost place
78. Alpine song
79. Ordered
80. Flight prefix
81. Coat
82. Warning signal
85. Doctrines
86. Lake Huron bay
90. Maine bay
93. Southern vegetable
95. Solo
96. Division word
97. Motorcar
98. Illuminated sign
99. Shade
100. Uttered
101. Skier's tow
102. Sweeten the pot
103. Fencing implement

DOWN

1. Wound reminder
2. Musical division
3. Winglike
4. Inferior deity
5. Test
6. Faction
7. Type of sale
8. Alligator pear
9. Sticky confection
10. Fairy-tale figure
11. Greek letter
12. Snatch
13. Publish
14. Nobel-winning physicist
15. March date
16. Early Virginian
24. Old Peruvian
26. Pitch
28. "Mr. ____" (George Raft film)
31. Put down
32. Massachusetts harbor
33. Norwegian trio
34. OPEC member
35. Singer Vicki ____
36. "Kon-____"
37. Virginia/ Maryland bay
38. Recuperate
39. Biblical visitors
40. English rock group
41. Office item
43. Curved molding
44. Faint
45. Nocturnal mammal
47. Concur
48. Vermont ski town
49. Pertaining to the ear
51. City in Bangladesh
52. Intimidate
57. Style hair
58. Hair style
59. Chow or lo
60. Author of "Summer Brave"
62. Suggestive
64. Defunct
65. Gaelic
66. Arlene or Roald
69. Roman greeting
72. Finish
73. ____ non grata
74. Related by blood
76. Metrical division
77. Astronaut's vehicle
78. Personal pronoun
79. Litter
80. Mary or John Jacob
81. Scottish lord
82. Egyptian sacred bull
83. Russian river
84. Oppositionist
85. Speck
86. Horse's gait
87. Certain coffee grind
88. Countdown-ending number, in Berlin
89. Cadence
91. Met
92. Bear's young
94. Understanding

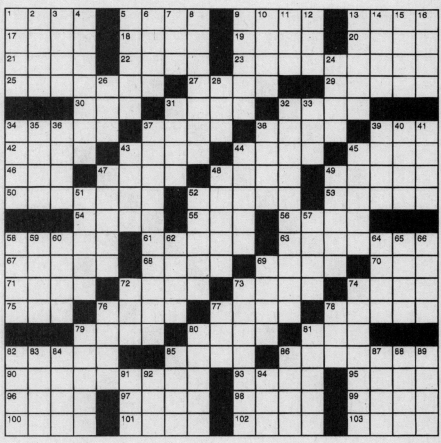

35

PUZZLE 40

ACROSS

1. Biological pouches
5. Current
9. Beatles movie
13. Verve
17. Actor Kincaid
18. Hawkeye State
19. Fragrance
20. Identical
21. Teamster's rig
22. Midday period
24. Fierce feline
25. Tasted
27. Leafy vegetable
28. Fear
30. Mimicked
31. Sly
32. Unearthly
33. Expropriate
35. Swimming contest
36. Write comments on
39. Producer
    Michael ___
40. Stadium part
41. Joy
42. Malleable metal
43. Singleton
44. Await action
45. Move smoothly
46. Entrepreneur Griffin
47. Stump
49. Marinates
50. Overly inquisitive
51. Actor Chaney
52. Slack
53. Outlaw Holliday
54. Confess
57. Wild creature
58. Connection
62. Cargo
63. Hang loosely
64. "Dream Along with
    Me" singer
65. "___ Folks"
    (Schulz cartoon)
66. Rod
67. House of Lords
    members
68. Completed
69. Spill the beans
70. North-of-the-border
    inhabitant
72. Fight site
73. Bout place
74. Symbolic archer
75. Several
76. Norse monarch
77. Residences
79. Ersatz
80. Enduring
83. Titled lady
84. Back talk
87. Hideaway
88. Explorer Tasman
89. Lode
90. Chips off the
    old block
91. Lab burner
92. Pickford or Astor
93. Grub
94. Arboretum dweller
95. Favorable votes

DOWN

1. Lip
2. Two-dimensional
   computation
3. Leader
4. Cropped
5. Used a rasp
6. Ear-splitting
7. Have title to
8. Zanier
9. With fervor
10. Peter Gunn's girl
11. Herbert ___ of the
    "Pink Panther" series
12. Fabrication
13. ___ de corps
14. Highly honored poets
15. Arsenal contents, for
    short
16. Nigh
23. Moratorium
26. Superman's foe
    Luthor
29. Piccadilly Circus
    statue
31. Unwanted plant
32. Markey and Bagnold
33. At the summit
34. Zilch
35. Flirtatious girl
36. Equivalent
37. Recap
38. Green-eyed
    monster?
40. "Harold ___"
41. Explosion
44. Deere's device
45. Honker
46. Needle
48. Trudge
49. Daytime TV fare
50. Taboo
52. Get wind
53. Thin coin
54. Fresh-water plant
55. Soil
56. Tardy individual
57. Sandwich requisite
58. Louisiana
    governor
59. Assuage
60. Composer Carlo
    Menotti
61. Exile isle
63. Crucial
64. Geometric figure
67. Duct
68. Least bright
69. Bill or Omar
71. In an uncivil
    manner
72. Turnpike
73. Mohammed ___
    Pasha
75. Eschews
76. Corpulent
77. Politician Clayton
    Powell
78. Gilda Radner's ___
    Wa Wa
79. ___ in the ocean
    (card game)
80. Skin problem
81. Singer Simone
82. Mardi ___
85. ___ culpa
86. Conjunction

36

ACROSS

1. Desert wear
5. TV's Zack Wheeler
9. Bernese mountains
13. Curing chemical
17. Clay pigment
18. Author Ephron
19. Usher
20. Mrs. Munster
21. 21
23. Evergreen
25. First ___ (rock group)
26. Letters before thetas
28. Formerly named
29. Berlin's "___ Bonds Today"
30. West African linguistic family
31. Rests against
35. ___ firma
38. Cipher
39. Complain
40. Literary inits.
41. Chinese port
42. Southern city
44. Danish fjord
45. Comedian Caesar
46. French father
47. Seine feeder
48. Biting
49. Pittsburgh teammate
51. Accustom
53. Slammer
54. War god
55. 747, e.g.
56. Fluff
57. Actor Foy
59. Insipid
60. Get
63. Singer Lesley ___
64. Theoretical
65. Sound of surf
66. Some army men, for short
67. Actress Meyers
68. Roving impulse
71. "Old ___" (Presley hit)
72. Antonym of convergence: abbr.
73. Speeds
74. Scottish island
75. Actress Palmer
76. Island near Greenland
78. Nicklaus's cry
79. Chinese temple
80. Hesitation sounds
81. Small monkey
82. Deceive
86. Bittersweet
90. Meeting place
92. Half of a quart
93. Actor Holliman
94. English river
95. Liberate
96. Gibb or Williams
97. Fermented beverage
98. French state
99. Trepidation

DOWN

1. French priest
2. Cheeky
3. Turkish regiment
4. Cult member
5. Like
6. Mortgage
7. Rainbow
8. Gets along
9. Very, in music
10. Pastures
11. Baby's food
12. Caveman's period
13. Stranger
14. Gerard or Young
15. Annex
16. Scandinavian rug
22. New Guinea money
24. Diplomat Silas ___
27. Yesterday
30. Handbag
31. Scalawag
32. Bur marigold
33. Actor Davis
34. Indigent
35. Russian news agency
36. Give out
37. Beverly Hills street
38. Singer Vikki ___
39. Watered silk
42. Existed
43. Type of song
46. Ballet exercise
48. Topnotch
50. Plimpton book
51. Cause to smile
52. Band-singer Wynn
53. Pakistani money
55. Moves slowly
56. Balto-Slav
57. Italian island group
58. Greek dialect
59. Studied
60. Artist Bonheur
61. Contends
62. See
64. Town's chief drag
65. Old Norse poem
68. Jetty
69. Uproar
70. Leather corselets
71. Close
75. Party
77. Baseball's Grove
78. Diamond
79. Nepal's neighbor
81. Prefix for trillion
82. Japanese hamlet
83. Seine feeder
84. Confused
85. Antelope's song companion
86. Resort of sorts
87. Malleable metal
88. Plus
89. Actress Dawn Chong
91. Ignited

PUZZLE 42

• GUYS AND DOLLS •

ACROSS

1. Cays
6. "I ___ Sheriff" (song)
13. Actress Jessica
18. Hope
19. Stays awhile
20. "Once Is Not ___"
22. Tulsa man, e.g.
23. Not distributed
24. Harsh
25. Trudge
26. Literary inits.
27. Jug handle
29. Son of Jacob (Douay Bible)
30. "Saratoga Trunk" author
34. ___ Perry awards
37. Legal thing
38. Satanic
39. Georg Simon ___
41. Ms. Maxwell
42. Conscription inits.
43. Dancer Castle
44. Apiary insect
45. Singapore ___
47. Corpulent
49. Sedaka and Simon
51. "___ Love with Amy"
54. Punitive
55. Ozzie's Mrs.
57. Sana's land
59. Newfoundland zone inits.
60. Mr. Borgnine
63. Song of 1925
66. Milkfish
67. Greek gods' mount
68. From soup to ___
69. French composer
70. Dugout VIP
71. Title for Ralph Richardson
72. Actors Jack and Frank
74. Affects
76. Motorist's gp.
77. Not considered
79. Alert in advance
81. Natives of 96 Across
83. ___ plenty
86. Kenton and Lee
87. Baseball's Reese
89. Assembled
91. Product of Bolivia
92. TV's "December ___"
93. Fitting
96. Capital of Latvia
97. Mr. Whitney
98. Author Lardner
99. French preposition
102. Two-time Nobelist
105. B. Truman followed her
108. Molding edge
109. Sea eagle
110. Bern's river
111. Turkish regiment
112. Fur pieces
115. Veteran
119. "___ Mame"
121. Staid
122. Actor Stamp
123. Makes spotless
124. Imp
125. Racetrack official
126. Cafe cup

DOWN

1. Tristan's love
2. Pitches woo
3. Actress Evans
4. Poetic palindrome
5. Indian unit of weight
6. Five o'clock shadow
7. Medieval guild
8. California fort
9. Three, in Rome
10. Spanish relative
11. Ms. Hayes
12. Landed properties
13. Bandleader Brown
14. Chemical suffix
15. Celestial flares
16. Edgar and others
17. Herons
18. Turkish money of account
21. ___ looking at you
26. Pulverize
28. Psychologist May
31. Flat stick
32. Level
33. Author Graves
34. Aviatrix Earhart
35. Beauty ___ the eye of the beholder
36. Walker and Kelly
40. ___ apparent
43. Philippine native
46. ___ whiz
47. Somewhat scarlet
48. Smallest of the Great Lakes
49. Egypt's Gamal Abdel and kin
50. Actor Peter
52. State of a Moslem chief
53. Former London prison
54. Old coin of India
55. Riled
56. "and never the ___ . . ."
58. African desert shrub
61. Genetic messenger: abbr.
62. Only, in Bonn
64. Mathematics subj.
65. Over there
72. "The Raven" maiden
73. Sofa
74. Ms. Flagg
75. Heavy hammer
78. Sketch: abbr.
80. Banshee sound
82. Ram's mate
84. Aural
85. Bach composition
87. Poet Matthew
88. One, in Berlin
90. Macaws
92. Of greater width
93. Accumulate
94. Separated
95. Electron tube
99. River deposits
100. Comedienne May
101. Porker pens
103. Koran's creed
104. Ria
106. Belgian marble
107. Windmill blades
113. Command for DDE
114. Japanese coin
116. Libyan measure
117. That girl
118. Emmet
119. Make like Olivier
120. Diminutive suffix

Note to Solvers: This Crossword does not have aids such as "2 wds." and "hyph."

ACROSS

1. Peepers
5. Music or food
9. Footless one
13. Fear or Hatteras
17. Song for Ferrante and Teicher
18. Caen's river
19. Famous Roman
20. Mars
21. ___ Place (Sundance's girlfriend)
22. Exult
25. Ambassador Black
27. Speck
28. Robust
29. Scratch
30. Saharan
31. Soft drink
33. Vexed
35. Roadwork barrier
36. In high spirits
40. Joust
41. Part of QED
42. Entices
43. Contend
44. Allhallows ___
45. Type of joint
46. Hot drink
47. 1492 ship
48. Remedy
50. Vicinity
51. Duck for down
52. Applaud
56. Conspiracy
59. Diana or Betsy
60. Least amount
64. Hebrew letter
65. Oodles
67. Walter ___ Mare
68. Mohammed Emin ___ Pasha
69. Grassland
70. Alan Ladd classic
71. Excellent
72. Star in Aquarius
73. Riant
75. Antiquated
76. Redolence
77. Spiel
78. Bobby and family
79. Thailand, formerly
80. Up and about
83. Vivacity: Ital.
84. Oriental
87. ___ stars (rejoice)
91. Peter, Paul and Mary
92. Legal wrong
93. Reverse
94. Negative replies
95. Therefore
96. Western Indians
97. "Harold ___"
98. Extinct bird
99. Actor O'Neal

DOWN

1. Poems
2. Comedienne Buzzi
3. Feel elation
4. Budding actress
5. ". . . owed by so many to ___"
6. Airport in Paris
7. Starter for sex or form
8. Charitable
9. Keen
10. "___ Don't Preach"
11. Sioux
12. Singer Ho
13. Laid-back
14. Rainbows
15. Bog fuel
16. View
23. Blood and guts
24. New York island
26. Chap
30. TV serial
31. Casein
32. Comply
33. Road: Lat.
34. ___-de-Gier
35. Crunchy
36. Son of Jacob
37. Zealous
38. Square root of 81
39. Lachrymose drop
41. Actress Martinelli
42. Silt
45. Unit of life
46. Ringlet
47. Unless: Lat.
49. U.S. neighbor's pilot's org.
50. Battery terminal
51. Actress Best
53. Borneo ape
54. Improve
55. African river
56. Summon
57. Epithet of Athena
58. Boyfriend
61. Celebrate
62. German lancer
63. Glove
65. Leg bone
66. Walking stick
67. Female rabbits
70. Neglect
71. Stuck in the mud
72. Strew
74. Shines
75. Seed cover
76. Bro's sib
78. Actor Bean
79. Final authority
80. Aleutian island
81. Injection
82. Biblical weed
83. "Adam ___"
84. Supplemented
85. Latvian capital
86. Midday
88. Umpire's decision
89. Opposite of SSW
90. Cote sound

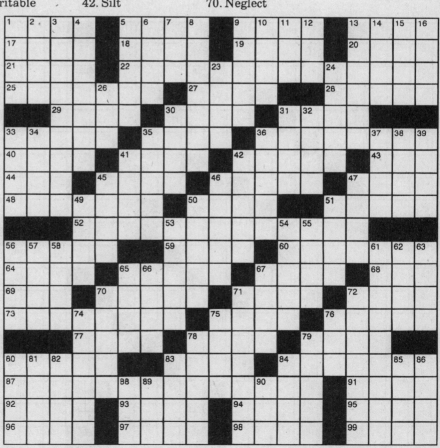

PUZZLE 44

• COMPLICATED MATTERS •

ACROSS

1. Hardwood
4. Shades of brown
8. Unwanted adipose tissue
12. Flat-topped buoy
15. Certain beans
17. Herschfield's agent
18. Foment
19. "Lonesome ___"
20. Mediocre
21. It holds water
22. Hairstyle
23. Once more
24. Competitor
26. Trail behind
28. Charge
30. Slippery
31. Upstanding
33. Slay
34. Inferior
36. Puzzler
38. Terminated
41. Redact
42. Leg part
43. Sign of assent
45. Dreary
46. Golf-ball position
47. Card term
48. Straightened
51. Container
52. Regardless of
54. Brownish purple
55. Squinchlike structure
57. Mischievous Greek god
58. More easily manuevered
59. Belonging to you and me
60. Room below ground
63. Ardent
64. Bicker
68. ___ pro nobis
69. Thallophytic plant
71. Bit of Little Miss Muffet's fare
72. Otic appendage
73. Lettuce type
75. "Name of the Rose" author
76. Clark's friend
77. Remus, to Romulus
78. Hit a high fly
80. Fail
83. June celebrant
84. Change
86. Finalize
87. Banshee cry
88. Chilling
91. ___ of iniquity
92. Outbursts
95. Weaken
96. "I Married ___"
98. Increase
100. Moolah
101. Part of B.A.
102. Part of QED
103. Leprechaun land
104. Gaelic
105. Ultimate degree
106. Solar plexus
107. A Scott
108. Asian coin

DOWN

1. Being, to Cato
2. Waterfowl
3. Enigmas
4. Lion's color
5. Egg on
6. Zilch
7. Get rid of
8. Thrifty
9. Sever
10. General's help
11. Fair-haired
12. Perplexity
13. Hellos, to Caesar
14. Amphibian
16. Most tender
19. Bold
25. Mum
27. Sandy's sound
29. Type of shoe
31. Gander, e.g.
32. Usurer
34. Actress Tuesday ___
35. ___ Cologne (cartoon skunk)
36. Cotton unit
37. Louis XVI, e.g.
39. O.K. Corral gunfighter
40. Force unit
42. Clique
44. Bypasses
47. Urgent
48. Italian city
49. Rubbed out
50. Celtic priest
53. Chum
54. Setting of stones
56. Ball
58. Oafs
60. Certain fowls
61. Composer Satie
62. Maze
64. Stop
65. Boggles
66. Deposited
67. Marine flier
70. 250, to Cassius
71. Sudden takeover
74. Steers
76. Lazed
77. Medical priority system
79. Presidential monogram
81. Calm
82. Lamb's ma
83. Impede
85. Restaurant selection
87. Gave spirits to
88. "___ Lake"
89. Deer
90. Time past
92. Radial
93. What ___ is new?
94. British gun
97. Pied Piper's follower
99. Publicize

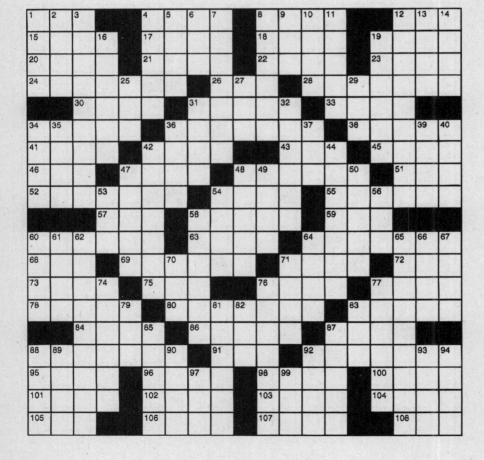

PUZZLE 45

• I'LL TAKE ROMANCE •

ACROSS

1. Exile island
5. Tiff
9. Church court
13. Eye inflammation
17. Mend socks
18. Apiece
19. Unwritten
20. Those people
21. Etching fluid
22. Quartet member
23. Thaw
24. Raise
25. Jason's wife
27. Jason's ship
29. Quality, in England
31. Home planet
34. Piano novelty
36. Lion's cry
37. Edge of civilization
40. Need
42. Rigid
45. Lout
46. Water nymph
48. Point
50. Songstress Adams
51. "Carmina Burana" composer
53. Bandleader Shaw
54. Yard-sale sign
56. Finis
57. Actress Garr et al.
59. Volunteer State: abbr.
60. Random tries
62. Extemporaneous remark
64. Pair
66. Near-sighted cartoon man
67. Bete ____
68. General Robert ____
70. "____ ed Euridice"
73. Floating menagerie
75. Dappled
77. Daggers
79. At a distance
80. Prophet
82. Undercover agent
83. Mr. Chips portrayer
84. "Born in the ____"
85. Church council
87. Hindu dress
89. Film daredevils
92. Self-satisfied
94. Shallow hollow
96. Nine: prefix
97. Bullfighter
100. Matured
102. Texas town
105. Writer Wister
106. Deities
108. Fruit fiber
111. Unbleached
112. Secular
113. Margarine
114. Brainstorm
115. At that time
116. Unit of force
117. Tilt
118. Contradict
119. Foam

DOWN

1. Dutch cheese
2. Doily fabric
3. 1935 film, with "The"
4. Of South American mountains
5. Vast expanse
6. Crony
7. Official proceedings
8. Rose prickle
9. Eliot work
10. Metallic dirt
11. Soft mineral
12. Communion table
13. Mark with furrows
14. 1966 film
15. Twelve months
16. "Jane ____"
26. Actor Carney
28. 50th anniversary
30. ____ Angeles
32. Songstress Turner
33. 1981 film
35. Deeds
37. Twelve inches
38. Scarce
39. Ceremony
41. 1953 film
43. Five-dollar bill
44. Nourished
47. "____ Misbehavin' "
49. Pocket bread
52. Cliche dog name
55. Pudding starch
58. Chemise
61. Adriatic wind
63. Blue flag
65. Hodgepodge
69. Sea eagles
71. Facility
72. Algerian port
73. Donkey
74. King: Sp.
76. Couple
78. Daze
81. Love story
86. Defective bomb
88. Motive
90. Opposite of SSW
91. Doctrines
93. "Taras Bulba" author
95. Lukewarm
97. Form
98. Out
99. Part in a play
101. Ranch vacationer
103. Angered
104. Basks
107. Goddess: Latin
109. Actor Cariou
110. Salary

41

PUZZLE 46

ACROSS
1. Neon, e.g.
4. ____ Vegas
7. Brittle
12. Fruit drink
13. Fore and ____
14. Bart Simpson's dad
15. Prune
16. Harbor
17. Vacant
18. Biblical queen
20. Epoch
21. Snakelike fish
22. Emulated Monet
26. Actress Irving
27. Paves
28. Singer Charles
29. Wheel part
30. "____ or Dare"
31. "Butterflies ____ Free"
32. Wrath
33. Quiet
34. Consumer lures: abbr.
35. Canned fish
37. Actress MacGraw
38. Bother
39. Emulates Sonja Henie
42. Daddies
45. Negative conjunction
46. Pension fund: abbr.
47. Happening
48. Flying saucer: abbr.
49. Car engine's need
50. Return the favor
51. Beige
52. Tennis court divider

DOWN
1. Strong wind
2. Uproars
3. Ninth month
4. Tag
5. Distant
6. Piggery
7. Adore
8. Old Italian
9. Brat
10. Place
11. Nose around
19. "____ Jude"
20. Globe
22. Take a break
23. Custom
24. Jug handles
25. Change color
26. Air
27. Elephant's snout
29. Not hers
30. Parched
34. Wing
36. Songstress Ross
37. Ohio city
39. Couch
40. Toledo's lake
41. Season
42. Each
43. Hail, to Caesar
44. Energy
45. Filbert, e.g.

ACROSS

1. Cover
4. Belly or garden
8. Aid and ____
12. Wrath
13. Encourage
14. Vanished
15. Fish propeller
16. Tramped
17. Motored
18. Personal property
20. Exploit
22. Stick
23. Deceives
27. Foreign
30. Quilter's gathering
31. Water tester
32. Soft drink
33. Dispose of
34. Skeleton part
35. Printing liquid
36. Breakfast cereal
37. Specified
38. Sahara, e.g.
40. Bear's burrow
41. Allow
42. Cash in
46. Enthusiastic
49. Excel
51. Exist
52. Recipe direction
53. Horrible
54. Preacher's subject
55. Antlered animal
56. Rational
57. Actor Cassidy ("The Addams Family")

DOWN

1. Existence
2. Garden bloomer
3. Parking-lot mishap
4. Shirt fastener
5. Did wrong
6. Conceit
7. Lost weight
8. Approve
9. Shout of disapproval
10. Cut short
11. Peg used by golfers
19. Length times width
21. "____ Loves You"
24. Powerful particle
25. Mood
26. Sow
27. Boric ____
28. Sole
29. Kinds
30. Chomped
33. Fazes
34. Dance orchestra
36. Lode yield
37. Sewing item
39. Senior citizen
40. Empty
43. "____ of Eden"
44. Part of HOMES
45. Patch
46. Include
47. Strive
48. Freezer cube
50. Ms. Peron

PUZZLE 48

ACROSS
1. Swabs
5. Actor Guinness
9. Negative
12. Region
13. Molten rock
14. Woolly one
15. Journal
17. By means of
18. Owns
19. Signs
21. Raise
24. Grow
26. Paddles
27. Philosophy
28. Imitate
29. More unusual
30. Lad
33. Intended
34. Get lighter
35. Plodded
38. Ties
39. Severe
40. Embrace
41. Hen product
42. Financial officer
48. Observe
49. Lounge
50. Gambling site
51. Road curve
52. Cheer
53. Swirl

DOWN
1. Operate
2. Prospector's find
3. Church bench
4. Soft belts
5. Sad cry
6. Circuit
7. "All About ___"
8. Yuletide singer
9. "___ on Sunday"
10. Being in debt
11. Make fun of
16. Tablet
20. Furious
21. Feather stole
22. Shoot the breeze
23. Sooner than, in poetry
24. Made a mistake
25. Lack
27. Arrived
29. Justly
30. Prohibit
31. Peculiar
32. Definitely!
33. Yellow pages, e.g.
34. Physique
35. The things here
36. Fads
37. Whims
38. Commuter vehicle
40. Corridor
43. Fish eggs
44. Building addition
45. Blushing
46. Finish
47. Actor Scheider

PUZZLE 49

ACROSS
1. Fearless
5. High-school formal
9. Car type
14. Sills's solo
15. Enthusiastic review
16. Felony
17. Talk noisily
18. Vase-shaped jug
19. Ethnic groups
20. Scornful smirks
22. Victoria's principal outlet
24. Double curve
25. Window part
27. Rip
29. Bunny's jump
32. Assemble
34. Priest's vestment
37. Samoan port
39. Cocktail
41. Nine-____ battery
43. Jeans inventor Strauss
44. Dollar bill
45. New York canal
46. Cupid
47. Winged spirit
49. Darn!
50. Map book
52. Dutch cheese
54. Allow
55. Give off
57. Diamonds or spades
59. Rocky hill
62. Bucket
64. Fastened
68. Overweight
70. Jewelry metal
72. "A ____ of Two Cities"
73. Forty-niner
74. Dueling weapon
75. Similar
76. Rock
77. Backside
78. Tidy

DOWN
1. Pubs
2. Algerian port
3. Queue
4. Social appointments
5. Ironed
6. Uncooked
7. Baker's need
8. Deserve
9. Yell
10. Time period
11. Gaming cubes
12. Singing brothers
13. Loch ____ monster
21. Butt into
23. Plumbing problem
26. Wading bird
28. Rhine or Amazon
29. Healthy
30. Musical drama
31. Swivel
33. Trace
35. Reef material
36. Cream of the crop
38. Wedding walkway
40. Requires
42. Trial
47. Largest continent
48. Wash
51. Unit of current
53. Ms. Farrow
56. Striped cat
58. Mythological god
59. Jones and Selleck
60. Newspaper notice, for short
61. Nevada city
63. Prance
65. Large pond
66. Lamb's pen name
67. Ding
69. Japanese coin
71. Pasture

PUZZLE 50

ACROSS

1. Thy ___ is brought down. (Isa. 14:11)
5. Shall say to his brother, ___. (Matt. 5:22)
9. And she took a ___. (2 Sam. 13:9)
12. Notion
13. And it became ___ in his hand. (Ex. 4:4)
14. ___ Grande
15. And ___ the book. (Dan. 12:4)
16. A fugitive and a ___ in the earth. (Gen. 4:14)
18. Let the proud be ___. (Ps. 119:78)
20. Topaz or opal
21. Who ___ tell him when it shall be? (Eccles. 8:7)
22. They knew that the island was called ___. (Acts 28:1)
25. Yet he restored the ___ unto his mother. (Judg. 17:4)
28. Owns
29. To him it is ___. (James 4:17)
30. They bring forth their young ___. (Job 39:3)
31. The ___ shall take him by the heel. (Job 18:9)
32. So that they ___ unto them. (Ex. 12:36)
33. And bring to pass his ___. (Isa. 28:21)
34. While Mordecai ___ in the king's gate. (Esth. 2:21)
35. They set the altar upon his ___. (Ezra 3:3)
36. ___ not him that wandereth. (Isa. 16:3)
38. Appointed with weapons of ___. (Judg. 18:11)
39. And all that handle the ___. (Ezek. 27:29)
40. Bind them upon thy ___. (Prov. 7:3)
44. Then Paul and ___ waxed bold. (Acts 13:46)
47. Shimei the son of ___. (1 Kings 4:18)
48. They set the ___ of God upon a new cart. (2 Sam. 6:3)
49. Tarry ___ to day also. (2 Sam. 11:12)
50. For his hand is ___ upon us. (1 Sam. 5:7)
51. Said unto him, ___, Lord. (Mark 7:28)
52. Then Asa was wroth with the ___. (2 Chron. 16:10)
53. They ___ unto it a lace of blue. (Ex. 39:31)

DOWN

1. Leaning Tower site
2. Lyric poems
3. Even unto the tower of ___ they sanctified it. (Neh. 3:1)
4. Because the ___ will be forsaken. (Isa. 32:14)
5. And black as a ___. (Song of Sol. 5:11)
6. And King ___ the Canaanite. (Num. 33:40)
7. Gear tooth
8. Maxims
9. To Abraham . . . were the ___ made. (Gal. 3:16)
10. And ___ with her suburbs. (Josh. 21:16)
11. Dwelt in the land of ___. (Gen. 4:16)
17. I will punish ___ in Babylon. (Jer. 51:44)

19. That utterance _____ be given unto me. (Eph. 6:19)
22. As if a _____ did flee from a lion. (Amos 5:19)
23. Fork prong
24. The _____ are a people not strong. (Prov. 30:25)
25. And Moses went up from the plains of _____. (Deut. 34:1)
26. Thou mayest not consume them at _____. (Deut. 7:22)
27. Two _____, to cover the two bowls. (1 Kings 7:41)
28. And the archers _____ him. (1 Chron. 10:3)
31. Respect . . . him that weareth the _____ clothing. (James 2:3)
32. Most spacious
34. Hagar the Egyptian, _____ hand maid. (Gen. 25:12)
35. Outlaw

37. The herd _____ violently down a steep place. (Luke 8:33)
38. For he was _____ than all men. (1 Kings 4:31)
40. Look how thy brethren _____. (1 Sam. 17:18)
41. Jesus cried with a loud voice, saying _____. (Mark 15:34)
42. It is a _____ thing that the king requireth. (Dan. 2:11)
43. Their feet are swift to _____ blood. (Rom. 3:15)
44. Like a green _____ tree. (Ps. 37:35)
45. But these _____ written. (John 20:31)
46. For the _____ that is in the land of Assyria. (Isa. 7:18)

PUZZLE 51

ACROSS

1. Just manages
5. Moderate
9. Cinderella's dance
13. Zoo attraction
17. Toro
18. Put on a pedestal
20. Toast topping
21. Woody's son
22. Wall Street totes
24. Prince Charles's horses
26. Pittsburgh export
27. Step
29. Spiffiest
30. Mover's vehicle
32. Liner
33. Moisten
34. Broke a rule, in cards
38. Author Jong
40. Hoists
44. "Arabian Nights" name
45. Harmless slitherer
49. Author Levin
50. Newton fruits
52. Credible
53. Expanded
54. Greek cross
55. Western resort
57. Place for a watch

60. Gels
63. Facial spasm
64. U or good
66. Unbroken
68. Wharf pest
69. Three Dog Night song
70. Sail holder
72. Curbs
74. Scour
76. Spectator's cry
78. Lennon's wife
79. Busybody
81. Actress Capshaw
82. Inventor Whitney
83. Director Fritz ____
85. Barren
87. Race refreshment
90. Melmac native
91. Pandora's find
94. List of items
96. Get out of sight
97. Turned on
98. Layer of enamel
102. Conceit
103. Desert formations
106. Greek marketplace
107. Tantrums

109. To say the ____
112. Sculling equipment
114. Egyptian king, for short
115. Mobile home
118. Eskimo shelter
119. Melting snow
123. Doris Day film, with "The"
125. Inappropriate
129. Writer Hunter
130. Biblical weed
131. Jeer
132. Char
133. Foxy
134. J, F, or K: abbr.
135. Sluggers' stats: abbr.
136. Word-processing goof

DOWN

1. Diminishes
2. Author Vonnegut
3. Author Wiesel
4. Jacket part
5. Unidentified male
6. Lupino of films
7. Part of L.A.
8. Put on clothes

9. Lout
10. Winner's take
11. Hotel magnate Helmsley
12. Runs lightly
13. South Carolina river
14. Ontario's sister lake
15. Pub orders
16. Missing
19. Swimmer Williams
23. Writer Fannie ____
24. Pillow trimming
25. Solemnly sworn vow
28. Ventilates
31. Close at hand
33. Roasts
34. Huck's craft
35. Lamb's pen name
36. Factory work forces
37. Sketched
39. Gas guzzler
41. Furious
42. Work out
43. Bechamel, e.g.
46. Frigate hands
47. Poet T. S. ____
48. Pitchers
51. Broth
56. Actor Flynn
58. Do in
59. Uses a stopwatch
61. Strategy
62. Certain piggy's house

65. Songstress Simone
67. Nick
71. Gin's go-with
73. Post office purchase
75. Orrin Hatch's state
76. Kingdom
77. Pitcher Reynolds
80. Location
84. Be a poor winner

86. Make a sweater
88. Verge
89. Old autos
92. Jet ____
93. Curly or Moe
95. Part of BTU
99. Type of exam
100. Radical
101. Confidence
104. City on the Hudson
105. Petticoat junction?

108. Finally!
110. Violin maker
111. Astronomer Carl ____
113. Submarine detector
115. Mimics
116. Launder
117. Trojan warrior
118. "____ Her on Monday"

120. Heed
121. Whack
122. Big sandwich
124. Uris character
126. Stand-in, for short
127. Prefix for cycle or corn
128. That thing's

PUZZLE 52

ACROSS

1. Certainly!
4. Closed
8. Laos's continent
12. Sail's support
16. Peel
17. Seize
18. Ringlet
19. Pain
20. One's old school
22. Valuables
24. Pekoe portion
25. Coral barrier
27. Kilt feature
28. Before, in verse
29. Small lake
30. Enemies
32. Expensive metal
35. Swiss ___ (beet variety)
37. Caution
38. Brief swim
41. "Much ___ About Nothing"
42. Christmas
43. Cut, as a cake
45. "It Had to Be ___"
46. Haze
47. Certain noblemen
49. Nights before holidays
50. Stitched
51. Romps
53. Modeled
55. Soft drinks
56. Cry of disgust
57. Mirror
58. Ruby, e.g.
59. Nab
62. Egypt's capital
63. ___ spring (spa)
67. Submit to
68. Marshal Dillon
69. Middays
71. ___-Wan Kenobi
72. Tavern beverage
73. Broadest
75. Craving
76. Filmmaker Spike ___
77. Half a score
78. Point-scoring serves
79. Consent
81. African grassland
82. Eating plan
83. Frosts
84. "Comin' Thro' the ___"
86. Petite
89. Rust-prone metal
90. Peaceful
94. Cattle and sheep, e.g.
97. Twin
100. Zone
101. Sunburn soother
102. Atmosphere
103. Clip
104. Hair wave
105. Fix
106. Jump
107. Actor Brynner

DOWN

1. Ivy League school
2. Columnist Bombeck
3. Ocean floor
4. Horse-drawn vehicle
5. Head topper
6. Hawaiian instrument, for short
7. Extreme fear
8. Played a part
9. Ride the waves
10. Outrage
11. Pie ___ mode
12. Heavy hammers
13. Land measure
14. Mets' former stadium
15. Exam
16. TV host Sajak
21. Deface
23. Pay out
26. Concludes
29. Gloom
30. Confronted
31. Unrefined metals
32. Fisherman's hook
33. Smell
34. Trademark
36. Belonging to that girl
37. "Husbands and ___"
38. Changed the color of
39. Hawkeye State
40. Word plays
42. Whinny
44. School assignment
48. Divides
50. Not all
52. "Peanuts" character
54. Canoe paddle

55. Common or sixth
57. Fence doors
58. Spicy cookie
59. Outer garment
60. Capable
61. High schooler
62. West Point student
63. Additional
64. Audition goal
65. Cain's brother
66. Bent the truth
68. "Of _____ and Men"
70. Belonging to us
73. Stands in line
74. Mexican dish
80. Friendly
81. Truth
82. "I _____ of Jeannie"
83. Annoyed
85. Still
86. Smack
87. Put on the payroll
88. Mind _____ matter
89. Sacred image
91. Off-white
92. Hammer's target
93. Shade tree
95. Scot's cap
96. Bullfight cheer
98. Expected
99. Gay Nineties, e.g.

PUZZLE 53

ACROSS
1. Object
5. Part of CD
9. Cut the grass
12. Burrowing rodent
13. Locale
14. Politician Beame
15. Arctic animal
17. Bumped into
18. Pump purchase
19. Approves
21. "Little ___"
24. Patriot Nathan ___
26. Smell
27. Hot pepper
30. Seine
31. Added liquor to
32. Nincompoop
34. Decreases in size
36. Melt together
37. Frosts
38. Took ore
39. Swap
42. Barnyard female
43. Possessed
44. Elected
50. Id's kin
51. Disparaging remark
52. Volcanic output
53. Word of assent
54. Brink
55. Raced

DOWN
1. Little demon
2. Also
3. House wing
4. Scanty
5. Bits
6. Infuriate
7. Sargasso or Adriatic
8. Sang
9. "I Remember ___"
10. Heed
11. Moistens
16. Bled, as a color
20. Barbie's friend
21. Was victorious
22. Pindar products
23. Wool-eater
24. Chops
25. Votes for
27. Walking stick
28. Part of speech
29. Relieve
31. Permit
33. Nourished
35. Eliminate
36. Certain exams
38. "A Few Good ___"
39. Those people
40. Frenzy
41. Fusses
42. Charter
45. Timeworn
46. Coffee cup
47. Knock
48. Night before
49. Pa

CAMOUFLAGE

The answers to the clues can be found in the diagram, but they have been camouflaged. Their letters are in the correct order, but sometimes they are separated by extra letters which have been inserted throughout the diagram. You must black out all the extra camouflage letters. The remaining letters will be used in words reading across and down. Solve Across and Down together to determine the correct letters where there is a choice. The number of answer words in a row or column is indicated by the number of clues.

	1	2	3	4	5	6	7	8	9	10	11	12	13
1	D	R	Y	P	R	S	A	L	I	M	N	N	E
2	L	S	C	R	E	E	O	G	C	H	T	A	N
3	S	T	B	A	L	T	W	A	O	F	J	R	T
4	G	R	A	T	Y	V	O	N	E	V	A	R	L
5	A	B	Q	C	O	T	H	I	T	U	T	O	R
6	W	A	I	T	Y	A	W	D	U	A	T	N	Y
7	P	W	R	I	T	C	L	O	S	E	T	V	C
8	E	P	O	C	M	H	C	A	K	N	O	W	S
9	M	I	T	E	Y	R	O	M	U	O	O	S	E
10	P	E	A	S	L	A	L	E	W	E	R	N	T
11	A	T	C	H	E	T	A	G	M	O	A	T	Y
12	T	H	E	U	N	I	L	D	R	S	I	A	O
13	Y	A	R	N	T	O	G	A	C	E	L	M	S

ACROSS
1. Nutty candy
2. Shrill cry • Light brown
3. Valiant
4. Hose fiber • Lend an ____
5. Behave • Teach privately
6. Be ready • Import tax
7. Decree • Intimate
8. Time period • Recognizes
9. Bishop's cap • Bullwinkle, e.g.
10. Legumes • Vigilant
11. Greek letter • Billy
12. North African country
13. Tall tale • Roman garb • Shade trees

DOWN
1. Old saying • Vacant
2. Kind of hat • Michelangelo work
3. Egypt's capital • Sailor
4. Rehearsal • Avoid
5. Depend • Camp shelter
6. Write on glass • Proportion
7. Mil. truancy • Fall behind
8. Come ashore • Greek letter
9. Hot diamonds • Ivory source
10. Shade • Rope loop
11. "The Rose ____" • Scold
12. Straits • Round cap
13. Foyer • Groups

PUZZLE 55

ACROSS
1. Hot coal
6. Charge per unit
10. Walk like an expectant father
14. Postman's walk
15. Eve's boy
16. Notes from Guido
17. Synthetic material
18. Pond denizens
20. Producer Lesser
21. Cream of the crop
23. New Delhi coin
24. Bequeathed
26. Stage signals
28. Iris part
29. Trotted
33. Goofed
35. Sale condition
36. Roman greeting
37. Actor Bert ____
38. Gives off
40. Rounded molding
41. ____ glance
42. Neighbor of Turkey
43. Duck-hunter's lair
44. Jr., e.g.
46. Adult wannabe
47. Old person: Ger.
48. Strut
51. Final letter
54. Helicopter part
56. Speller's exam
57. Teddy Roosevelt's party
59. Harden
61. Heraldic border
62. Lopez favorite
63. Firm
64. Periods of note
65. Out of kilter
66. Pits

DOWN
1. Serrate
2. Imbecile
3. Costner baseball film
4. Region for DDE
5. Subscribed again
6. Violent
7. Rest against
8. Network output
9. Right angle
10. Scan
11. Skewed
12. Actor Nicolas ____
13. To be, to Pliny
19. Stews
22. Land for grazing
25. ____ and out
27. Etats ____
29. Actor Michael ____
30. Jake La Motta's story
31. Tied score
32. Act
33. Verve
34. Pro ____
38. Part of QED
39. "____ for Daddy"
40. Skater Protopopov
42. Muslim's faith
43. Rude
45. Aerie dwellers
46. Noah's count
48. Porterhouse, for one
49. Strange
50. Marsh stalks
51. Hautboy
52. Catarrh
53. First lady of scat
55. Norse capital
58. Stop ____ dime
60. Now, in Edinburgh

ACROSS

1. Drove a formula car
6. Puppeteer Tony ____
10. Need for liniment
14. Where Greek met Greek
15. Excuse
16. Skidded
17. North Dakota city
18. Nab
20. Back gate
22. Sea eagle
23. Muslim title
24. Tower city
25. Windflowers
27. Fashionable
29. Squander
31. Greek queen of heaven
32. Little bit
33. Range
37. Land measure
38. After FDR
39. Cry of disgust
41. Sun. speech
42. Duck
44. Do wrong
45. Male party
46. Feeler
49. Jason's ship
50. Small anchors
53. Artistic style
55. Auricle
56. Some
57. Large-billed bird
60. Business board member
63. Top-drawer
64. Camp equipment
65. Prevalent
66. Firefighters' needs
67. Spoken
68. Feeds
69. About

DOWN

1. Inclined way
2. Exchange premium
3. Plotted
4. Amatory literature
5. Appointments
6. Bridge
7. Swiss peak
8. Atone
9. Room at the top
10. Residue
11. Spotless
12. Door pivot
13. Icelandic literary works
19. Catch, in a net
21. Oodles
25. Assist
26. Killer whale
27. Actor Everett
28. Superman, e.g.
30. Ship deserter
34. Blacklist, British-style
35. Wampum
36. Therefore
38. Hair dyes
39. Coffee server
40. Make the ____
43. Hiatus
44. Printers' letters
45. Presser
47. Term
48. Northern Ohio city
50. Contact
51. More uncommon
52. Scene of action
54. ____ and omega
57. Lincoln, e.g.: abbr.
58. Prayer ending
59. Snuggery
61. Ocean: abbr.
62. Newt

PUZZLE 57

ACROSS

1. Melodies
6. Thickening agent
10. Endure
14. Heavenly food
15. Wash
16. Nick and Nora's canine
17. Western desert plant
20. Understand
21. Break bread
22. Hamburger toppings
23. Crave
24. Chooses from the menu
25. Man with a monkey
29. Leaving
30. Dakota Indians
31. Jazz music
34. Hay place
35. Prepare eggs, in a way
37. Rhyme king
38. Newt
39. "___ Yellow Ribbon . . ."
40. American painter
41. Association
44. Source
46. Fluff
47. La Scala's city
48. Lilt
49. German river
52. Musical instrument
55. European blackbird
56. Of an historic age
57. Golfer's goal
58. Bone: pref.
59. Take-out phrase
60. Manner

DOWN

1. Old Testament prophet
2. Steak order
3. "Picnic" playwright
4. Literary collection
5. Doing a carpentry job
6. Straightener
7. Gawk
8. Forum greeting
9. Flute's kin
10. Having more frills
11. American fur merchant
12. Knocks out
13. Russian news agency
18. Metallic sound
19. South American range
23. Breathe hard
24. Humdinger
25. Rubberneck
26. House top
27. ___ of gab
28. ___ Jaya, New Guinea
31. Diva Lucrezia ___
32. Medley
33. Famous Quaker
35. French actress Simone
36. Warmth
37. Famous suffragist
39. Italian city
40. Tropical fruits
41. Psychic
42. Panay seaport
43. Bluish-white metal
44. Heaps
45. On one's toes
47. Short note, for short
48. Obstacle
49. Covered with yolk
50. Large shopping place
51. Snick's pal
53. Rio de ___
54. Pied Piper follower

All of the four-letter words in this crossword puzzle are listed separately and are in alphabetical order. Use the numbered clues as solving aids to help determine where each four-letter word goes in the diagram.

4 Letters
ALAN
ALOE
ANTE
AREA
ARNE
ARTE
BONE
BRAN
CARE
CENT
DINS
EELS
ELLA
EVIL
HEAD
IRAN
JABS
KATE
LANA
NEST
NOTE
OATS
OVAL
OVER
PANT
PASS
POET
RANT
RATE
RAVE
SAWS
SELL
SETS
SHAH
SNEE
SOON
TARA
TILE
TOSS
TRAY

ACROSS
14. Biblical weeds
18. Washer cycle
20. Valuable find
22. Wading birds
24. Singer Grant
26. Authorizes
31. Letter adjuncts: abbr.
34. Planters' plantings
35. Blue _____ special
36. Under the weather
38. Coagulates
40. Bitter vetch
41. Bed boards
42. Passe
43. Fast plane: abbr.
45. Sky chiefs
47. Storage place
48. Oak starters
51. Cosmetic-bag item
57. Raise one's spirits
61. More rational

DOWN
5. Plays a guitar
6. Like Bigfoot, perhaps
8. "_____ So Shy"
9. Yokohama's location
15. Service and agent
25. Dories and runabouts
26. Cigar remains
27. Sidelong glances
28. Minimal
29. Word for Simon's couple
30. Novelists' needs
31. Kind of bean
32. Frozen rain
33. Winter vehicles
35. Town maps
38. School groups
39. Erie Canal mule
45. Some Scottish musicians
46. Threes, in cards
47. Munches
58. Baby's seat

PUZZLE 59

ACROSS

1. Bewilder
5. Narrative
9. Smack
13. Flush
17. Washington bills
18. Muslim chief
19. Asian range
20. Repetition
21. Defeat
22. Shade of blue
23. Earthy deposit
24. Sacred bull
25. Wrote down
27. Ruff's mate
29. Sincere
31. Buff
32. Prefer
34. Face
35. Stretch
38. Island dance
39. Constituents
44. Dominion
45. Wealth
46. Shop-window sign
47. Chess piece
48. Keats work
49. Mr. Rogers
50. Exults
52. Cycle prefix
53. Shaft
55. Store employee
56. Opinion
58. English brew
59. Characteristic
60. Dog's greeting
61. Make proud
64. Long
65. Most immense
69. Free
70. Derrick
72. Fissure
73. Strive
74. Conception
76. Harness part
77. Accustomed
78. Greek letter
79. Plot
81. Illegal pitching move
82. Blunder
83. ____ passim
84. Flock
86. Cookie holder
87. Reduces
91. Be beholden to
92. Common
96. Popular shirts
97. Aria
99. True
101. Facts
102. Issue
103. Cupid
104. Treacherous
105. Complete
106. Skip
107. Assay
108. Refute
109. Repair

DOWN

1. Distribute
2. Shortly
3. Gusto
4. Substance
5. Roof of the World
6. Within
7. 100,000 rupees
8. Deep green
9. Engraved gem
10. Diminutive suffix
11. Sustenance
12. Fine thread
13. Farmer
14. Easy gait
15. Elevator name
16. Compass point
26. Groove
28. Zsa Zsa's sister
30. Daiquiri liquor
32. Brimming
33. Disclose
35. Stepped
36. Impertinent
37. Author Waugh
38. Place for an ace?
40. Divulge
41. Sentence need
42. Pitch
43. Taunt
45. Bestow
46. Fat component
49. Ruses
50. Showiness
51. Commence
54. Have a bite
55. Desire
57. Easter-basket item

59. Swarmed
60. Float
61. Skater Heiden
62. Adriatic
    resort
63. Arabian Sea
    gulf
64. Decade part
65. Join
66. Balanced
67. Position

68. Race
71. Stocky
72. Character
75. Baseball
    plays
77. Fluctuated
78. Ennui
80. Bowling
    target
81. Curtsy
82. Outlaw

85. Perch
86. Doughnut
    filler
87. Arise
88. Sphere prefix
89. Old Brazilian
    money
90. Cross
92. Advancement

93. Enthuse
94. Solar deity
95. Fat
98. ____
    Alamos
100. Genesis
    name

PUZZLE 60

ACROSS

1. Amnesia, e.g.
5. Bedouin
9. Octagonal sign
13. Humid
17. Aid in wrongdoing
18. Soft-drink
19. Bucket
20. Type of rug
21. Leonine greeting
22. Continuously
23. "____ was I ere I saw Elba"
24. Initiate a telephone call
25. Postpone
27. Diamond miscue
29. Roman shoes
31. Anymore
33. Finger count
34. Mouth
35. Sat on the throne
39. Orchestrated
41. "Charlotte's ____"
42. Low, despicable person
45. Mystery writer Gardner
46. Morning condensation
48. Carnival attractions
50. Irksome
51. Be unwell
52. ____ and vigor
54. Understand
55. Sad song
56. ____ we forget
58. Meeting record
60. Scorched
61. Race-track shape
63. 3 dots, 3 dashes, 3 dots
64. Aria
65. Not as fast
68. Giggles
70. ____ of tables
74. Plebe
75. Female G.I.
76. White or Yellow
77. American short-story writer
78. Finished
79. Reef animal
81. Pitcher spout
83. Vassal
84. No longer is
85. Opponent
86. Palindromic female name
88. Stream
90. Actor Dailey
91. Convened
93. Give him his ____
94. Leaves
98. Oyster's gem
100. No!
104. Actress Barbara
105. Miss Cinders
107. Thailand, once
109. White or Blue water
110. Poker starter
111. "High ____"
112. Sicilian mount
113. Actress Lanchester
114. Scottish maid
115. Long quiz
116. Leak
117. Judge

DOWN

1. Rendered hog fat
2. Hautboy
3. Close an envelope
4. Weird
5. Expert flier
6. Gambol
7. Wide-awake
8. Keg
9. Mast
10. Flap
11. Greases
12. Gratifies
13. Mr. Warbucks
14. Formal song
15. Ground grain
16. Boon companions
26. Hither and ____
28. Pip
30. Capture
32. Unite
35. Genuine
36. Cedar Point's waterfront
37. Contents of Pandora's box
38. Fiend
40. Absorbs food
41. Soggy
42. Maize
43. Prod
44. Marsh plant
47. Take first prize
49. ____ Plaines, Illinois
50. Seductive woman
53. Melodious
55. Collection-agency's term
57. Tall building
58. Blemish
59. Moppet
60. School transportation

62. Old soldier, for short
64. Peculiarity
65. Type of boat
66. Fluid rock
67. Poems
68. Paving liquid
69. Sniggler's quarry
71. Duel tool
72. Anon
73. Canopy
75. Misfortune
79. Satisfied
80. This prevents scurvy
82. Whale's group
83. Smoothed feathers
85. Not close
87. Rental agreements
89. Seek office
90. Hamlet et al.
92. Overused
94. FDR's New ____
95. ____ St. Vincent Millay
96. Household animals
97. ____ gin fizz
98. Labored breath
99. Garden path
101. Despicable
102. In some other way
103. Bore
106. ____ Angeles
108. Atlas illustration

PUZZLE 60

PUZZLE 61

ACROSS

1. Combine
5. Son of Venus
9. Fit to ___
13. Call or top
17. Range
18. Shake
19. Caspian Sea feeder
20. Perception
21. Dill
22. Mirthful
25. Of a planet
27. Leeds river
28. Splits
29. Panel
30. Weaver's reed
31. Char
33. Place for a party?
35. Worked in the garden
36. On cloud nine
40. Actress Martha ___
41. Platform
42. Make happy
43. Nigerian native
44. Enlarge
45. Hit
46. West Point cadet
47. Polish lancer
48. Most flushed
50. Motel offering
51. Employers
52. Cheerful
56. Vibrant
59. Mrs. Kennedy
60. Squirrel, e.g.
64. Ancient unit of weight
65. Alan Ladd film
67. Accompanied by
68. Son of Gad
69. Rainbow
70. Cast
71. Columnist Barrett
72. Illegal football move
73. Beautiful
75. "___ Not Dressing"
76. Sky ram
77. A Johnson
78. Mean
79. Snug as ___ in a rug
80. Ago
83. Cuban coin
84. Humiliated
87. Thrilled
91. Tamarisk
92. Cognate
93. Dispossess
94. Defense gp.
95. Forest creature
96. Cellar filler
97. Brooklyn cagers
98. Colorist
99. Xanadu

DOWN

1. Baby buggy
2. Mrs. Chaplin
3. Rapturous
4. Rabbit food
5. Quiet
6. Lament
7. Columbus coll.
8. Wines and dines
9. Actor Gene ___
10. Nest locale, often
11. Attention
12. Measure of length
13. Talk show host Geraldo
14. Scandinavian god
15. Furnish
16. Dawdles
23. Sped
24. Proclaim
26. Vex
30. Defame
31. Wound protector
32. Noble Italian family
33. ___ Rabbit
34. Superior, e.g.
35. West Indies republic
36. Fragrant resin
37. Roofing material
38. Bridge support
39. Fools
41. Dart
42. Emulate Romeo and Juliet
45. Hilo bird
46. ___ comitatus
47. "Back in the ___"
49. Opera star
50. French wine-growing region
51. Beehive State

53. Boat or train
54. German river
55. Whit
56. Indian nurse
57. Italian money, once
58. Andean Indian
61. Glad
62. Troy's canal
63. Slashes
65. Posted
66. Irwin of golf
67. Had on
70. Toast starter
71. Echo
72. Campaign
74. Like some lots
75. Social insect
76. Camel's-hair cloth
78. Eclipses
79. Loathe
80. Vichy and Bad Ems
81. Actress Chase
82. Young or Bush
83. Bygone
84. Entr'____
85. Gen. Robert ____
86. Laura or Bruce
88. Eternity
89. Directly
90. Denial

PUZZLE 61

PUZZLE 62

ACROSS

1. Trade
6. Former Senator Thurmond
11. Scallop or rum
14. Vietnamese dress
15. Religious statue
16. Opposite of WSW
17. Hawaiian memorial site
19. Tabasco two
20. Bowlers' milieu
21. Santiago's locale
23. Prom dances, e.g.
27. Ecological communities
28. Glacial epoch
29. Charlie or Martin
31. Take to court again
32. Performance record, for short
33. Bones
37. Primary
38. Hilo hello
39. Mary's follower
40. Author Sewell
41. Actress Merrill
42. Engraver's tool
43. Churchgoers
45. Civil
46. Duty
49. Scanner
50. ____ Lama
51. Western lake
53. Akkadian god of heaven
54. Oahu landmark
60. Like a jalapeno
61. Actress Barkin
62. Top
63. Barcelona gold
64. Greek theater structure
65. Union General George ____

DOWN

1. Soda stopper
2. Fish eggs
3. Minnesota city
4. "____ from the Madding Crowd"
5. Geoponics
6. Extends
7. Fatigue
8. Lee's men, for short
9. Amerind
10. "Peanuts" character
11. Obscure
12. Iguana's kin
13. Agreements
18. Healthy
22. Hawaiian capital
23. Terra ____
24. Indian, for one
25. Varnish ingredient
26. Hawaiian sizzling spot
27. Phi ____ Kappa
29. ____ Brook, New York
30. Music to a comic's ears
32. Gash
34. Eastern garments
35. Strike
36. "Lum and ____" (radio show)
38. Miner's access
42. Monotony
44. Stage whispers
45. Unskilled worker
46. Boise's land
47. Estate
48. Disney dog
49. Buzz
51. Whopper
52. Congregation's response
55. Category
56. Tinge
57. O'Hare guess, for short
58. Put two and two together
59. Anonymous John

ACROSS

1. Pillow cover
5. Bean curd
9. Axiom
14. Snare
15. Scientist Pavlov
16. Forty-____
17. Cupidinous
18. Beatty film
19. Obscure
20. Cliff dwellings locale
22. Tailless amphibians
23. Carpet fiber
24. Tropical vines
26. California spouter
28. French friends
32. Baste
35. Ninth mo.
36. Most sincere
38. They locate lost parcels
40. Hymn
41. African republic
42. Thick slice
43. Detective Archer
44. Sway
45. Guatemalan
47. ____ out (selection process)
49. Powders
54. Bay of Naples island
57. Part of the Rocky Mountains
59. Comedian Sherman
60. Oklahoma city
61. Hindu spouse
62. Fine china
63. Split
64. Bear or pass leader
65. John Jacob ____
66. Anxious
67. Bower

DOWN

1. Pundit
2. Skin eruption
3. Heeling
4. Emblem
5. Radial, e.g.
6. Imbricates
7. Follower of passing fancies
8. Oust
9. Hill or Bryant
10. Sauropod, e.g.
11. Singer Moffo
12. Turned right
13. Blunders
21. Bottle
25. American hero ____ Hale
27. Proclaim
29. Groats
30. Man or Wight
31. Ragout
32. Play lead
33. Marine bird
34. Stipend
37. Androids
39. The Centennial state
40. Rehearsal dinner sound
42. Blemished
46. Electrical unit
48. Greasy spoon
50. Chef's garment
51. Ship out
52. Staffs
53. Kilt or tutu
54. Hacienda
55. European mountains
56. Cabal
58. Gurge

PUZZLE 64

ACROSS

1. Unthreatened
5. Bouquet
10. First principles
14. Advanced degs.
18. Damage
19. Egyptian amulet
20. Castle trench
21. High nest
22. Epochs
23. Summer fete
25. Yearn
26. Buddhist festival
27. Invites
28. Lolls
29. Not as smart
30. Short socks
32. First pope
33. Lacking
34. Devotees
35. Dust specks
36. French range
39. Crimp
41. Irrigate
42. Average
43. Land unit
44. Tradition
45. Cry of woe
46. Closes
47. ___ of Wight
48. Clever
49. ___ point
51. Cursed
52. Loved too much
53. Symbol of Utah
55. Western
57. Proboscis: pref.
59. Dancer Paul ___
60. "Bonnie and ___"
61. Approve
64. Semester
65. Dragged
66. Emerging part
68. Lobbed
71. High society
73. Boot country
75. Old Tokyo
76. Double over
77. Declivity
78. Gene materials: abbr.
79. Change for a five
80. Miss Gardner
81. Mix, as a salad
82. U.S. poet
83. "___ Vanya"
84. Left behind
87. Badger's kin
88. Roguish
89. Makes beer
90. Stratum
91. In a nutshell
94. Knives
96. Malay island
97. Peas: Fr.
98. ___ deer
99. Preferred
100. Wimpy's preferences
102. Broadcasts
103. Balances
104. Asian river
105. Uncanny
106. "Pretty Woman" actor
107. Occident
108. Hialeah margin
109. Attire
110. "___ Death"

DOWN

1. Queen of ___
2. High priest
3. Ball-park treat
4. German spa
5. Boundaries
6. Orchestra section
7. Tierra del Fuego natives
8. Singer Davis
9. Sportsmen
10. Confounds
11. Auger
12. Felines
13. Messy place
14. Pulpit talk
15. Cookout
16. Clip joint
17. Visionary
21. Sharp
24. "___ Noster"
27. Nota ___
29. Pesos
31. Overdue
32. Dip accompaniments
33. Cookout
35. African land
36. Serve tea
37. ___ Stanley Gardner
38. Budgie food
39. Unsightly fat
40. Ran easily
41. July 4th fruits
42. Seafood fare
46. Stockholm native
47. Column order
49. Tootled
50. Eternally
51. Fashion
52. Jingle

54. Loathed
56. Winged
58. Do trucking
62. Fast-food fare
63. Swiss song
67. Emulate Brooke Shields
68. Long way off
69. Travel widely
70. Summer feasts
72. Forgotten
74. Asian weight
77. Mulligan and Irish
78. Dissuaded
79. In the past
82. Swamp
83. "Topaz" author
85. Passionate
86. Requirements
87. Roam
88. Crops up
90. Large beans
91. "___ Godunov"
92. "Mr. Moto" actor
93. Assents
94. Puffed
95. Not taped
96. Starchy root
97. "Le ___ Goriot"
100. Attila, e.g.
101. Eur. land
102. ___ Khan

PUZZLE 64

PUZZLE 65

ACROSS

1. Greatest amount
5. Ann or Cod
9. Punch
13. Side post of a doorway
17. Poet Khayyam
18. Unfold
19. Table spread
20. Mitch Miller's instrument
21. Building location
22. Cozy home
23. Color shade
24. Withered
25. Robs
27. Assay
29. Pioneer
31. Cravats
33. Bank on
35. Erie Canal mule of song
36. Displays
40. Let tears fall
42. First Pope
46. Actor Barker
47. Denude
49. Podium
51. Female knight
52. Component
54. Flounder's relative
55. Let
57. Keep your ___ on!
58. Go by car
60. Intentions
63. Supervises
65. Flight book
67. Actor Marvin
68. Explode
69. Tapers
73. Frets
76. Shy
80. Commotion
81. Compliment
83. Nobleman
85. Lawsuit
86. A person's record
88. Saxophone's need
90. Lucky number
92. Neptune's domain
93. Smudge
95. Tapering seam
97. Left
99. Spinning toy
101. Year with an extra day
103. ___ Beauty
104. Break glass
108. Between
110. Gathered a harvest
114. Money drawer
115. Boulevard
117. Verse maker
119. Give charity, with "out"
120. Actress Sedgwick
121. Not busy
122. Raison d'___
123. Anagram for eels
124. Favorites
125. Guide
126. Singe
127. ___ admiral

DOWN

1. Lichen
2. Skip
3. Satisfy
4. Picks up the check
5. Agrees
6. Orangutan
7. Annoying insect
8. Penetrate
9. ___ in bond
10. Actor Wallach
11. Camera eye
12. Lugs
13. Elbowed
14. Cain's brother
15. Supplemental
16. Lager
26. Perjury
28. Use a needle and thread
30. Metal added to a dancer's shoe
32. Razor hone
34. Twelve months
36. Potential prune
37. Nevada city
38. Doorway out
39. Window ledge
41. Mottled
43. Soft mineral
44. Expel
45. Cincinnati team
48. Rings
50. Cut a small piece
53. "Twice-___ Tales"
56. Jog
59. Bagel
61. Clear profit
62. Percolates
64. Homer's forte
66. Cogwheel
69. Surpasses
70. Rocker Ant
71. Won by a ___
72. Took to court

74. Unwanted plant
75. Break, as relations
77. Sail support
78. "____, "said the blind man: 2 wds.
79. ____ on your feet
82. Give out cards
84. Newspaper-man
87. Lets the cat out of the bag
89. Revered
91. Baptize
94. Bosh
96. ____-o'shanter
98. McGuffey opus
100. Unsafe situation
102. Water mains
104. Footfall
105. ____ nor hair
106. Descended to earth
107. Went by bus
109. Fawn over
111. North or South
112. Miss Maxwell
113. Doe
116. Neighbor of Georgia: abbr.
118. Dynasty

PUZZLE 66

Diagramless crosswords are solved by using the clues and their numbers to fill in the answer words and the arrangement of black squares. Insert the number of each clue with the first letter of its answer, across and down. Fill in a black square at the end of each word. Every black square must have a corresponding black square on the opposite side of the diagram to form a diagonally symmetrical pattern.

ACROSS
1. Hat
4. Evergreen
7. Tree fluid
10. Lemon drink
11. Exist
12. Duo
13. Show agreement
14. Knock
15. Auditory organ
16. Make a speech
18. Turn away
20. Slithery fish
21. Dramatist's device
22. Female relatives
24. Most terrible
26. Examination
30. Worthless stuff
31. Satire
32. Ventilate
33. Epoch
35. Source of metal
36. Highway: abbr.
37. Groove
38. Actor Knotts
39. Actor Danson
40. Observe
41. Asner and McMahon

DOWN
1. Hiawatha's craft
2. Worship
3. Operate by foot
4. Passenger
5. Author Levin
6. Meal
7. Horse
8. Cognizant
9. Ship landing
17. Former Russian rulers
19. Porthole view
21. Picnic spoiler
23. Theater employees
24. Inscribe
25. Paddled
27. Wear away
28. Food fish
29. Adolescents
30. Small pie
31. Destiny
34. Regret

Grid (first row): C A P

PUZZLE 67

ACROSS
1. Notebook
4. Press to a pulp
8. ____ de Janeiro
9. Peddler
11. Poems
13. Dove-colored horse
16. January 1 event in Pasadena
18. Walked through water
19. Enemy
20. Requirement
21. Finales
23. Did office work
26. First man
28. Eager
32. Isle: Fr.
33. Gem weight
35. Ringling Bros. event
39. Tusked animal
42. Comfort
43. Departs
44. Behold
45. Short, sharp blow
46. Attach

DOWN
1. Support
2. Verdi opus
3. Busy one
4. ____ culpa
5. Everyone
6. Sluggish
7. Macho guy: hyph.
9. Quick
10. Amusement park attraction
12. Secure
14. Wedding-announcement word
15. Unusual
17. "____ Be Cruel"
22. Resort
24. Decrees
25. Painter Salvador
27. Nothing more than
28. King topper
29. Lass
30. Russian city
31. Opens wide
34. Melt
36. Spanish house
37. Employed
38. Kernel
40. Ms. Gardner
41. Court divider

ACROSS

1. Midday
5. Skirt edges
9. Broadcast
11. December song
12. Dishes
14. Spin
15. Gel
16. Armed conflict
18. Small cabin
19. Turf
20. Lair
22. Chuck Yeager, e.g.
24. Each
25. Distress signal
27. Period
28. Blue
29. Tatter
31. Nut
33. Stripling
35. Moo
36. Salary
38. Church bench
40. Wooden stick
41. Ignited
43. Party concoction
45. Corral
46. Panama, e.g.
48. Label
50. Chum
51. Horse food
52. Cheer
54. Rodent
56. Up
58. Buccaneer
60. Number of seas
61. Lateral surfaces
62. Brooklyn growth
63. Beat

DOWN

1. Siestas
2. Greased
3. Speaks publicly
4. Tennis divider
5. Chapeau
6. Rubbed out
7. Engine
8. Winter toy
10. Morning moisture
11. Little bed
13. Pine ooze
14. Daily grind
17. Free
18. James Brolin TV show
21. Neither's partner
23. Cut off
24. Skillet
26. Green toss-up
28. Cut like a logger
30. Joke
32. Beat walker
34. Put off
36. Took the blue ribbon
37. Transgression
39. Humor
40. Experience again
42. Paving goo
44. Easter event
45. Peeler
46. Tin
47. Track distance
49. Pearly ____
50. Gone by
51. Layer
53. Towel word
55. Oral, e.g.
57. Observe
59. Eve's source

Starting box on page 562

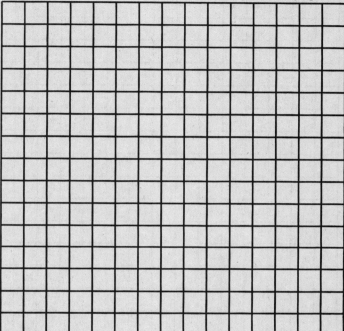

WORD MATH

PUZZLE 69

In these long-division problems letters are substituted for numbers. Determine the value of each letter. Then arrange the letters in order from 0 to 9, and they will spell a word or phrase.

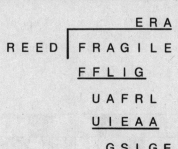

1

0	1	2	3	4	5	6	7	8	9

```
                O A K
       ┌─────────────────
S A C K │ C O N T A C T
         C D D C W
         ─────────
         R A D K C
         R T K D W
         ─────────
         A R O S T
         A T N C D
         ─────────
         W R K
```

2

0	1	2	3	4	5	6	7	8	9

```
                E R A
       ┌─────────────────
R E E D │ F R A G I L E
         F F L I G
         ─────────
         U A F R L
         U I E A A
         ─────────
         G S L G E
         G G L F D
         ─────────
         U L I U
```

3

0	1	2	3	4	5	6	7	8	9

```
                T W O
       ┌─────────────────
R O D S │ D R O W S Y
         U U R B
         ─────────
         N R W S
         W D S S
         ─────────
         O D B Y
         O S U B
         ─────────
         O W Y
```

PUZZLE 70

ACROSS

1. Potatolike tuber
4. Filch
7. Used to be
10. Saga
12. Make a mistake
13. Wan
14. Singing voice
16. Garland
17. Frenchman's cap
18. Gnome
20. Festive
22. Regret
23. Tear
24. Examination
25. Again
27. Smeller
28. Handle
30. Sprite
31. Arid
32. Laborer
34. Ceremony
35. Hitch
37. Great in amount
38. Expire
39. Australian bird
40. Smooth
42. Fur scarf
44. Solitary
46. Commotion
48. Rants
51. Truth
52. Animal collection
53. Harvest
54. Couple
55. Hankering
56. Pen

DOWN

1. Still
2. Mimic
3. Coin
4. Inmate's room
5. Metal-bearing mineral
6. Proper
7. Cautious
8. Beer's darker kin
9. Gel
11. Faraway journalist
13. Vertical
15. Stir
17. Edge
19. Rent
21. Time period
24. Large volumes
26. Value
27. Bite
29. So long, for short
33. Innocent
34. Unverified story
36. Golly!
37. Ran into
40. Crazy
41. Idle
42. Anon
43. Nights before events
44. Stern
45. Rule
47. Bambi's mom
49. Dine
50. Undercover agent

Starting box on page 562

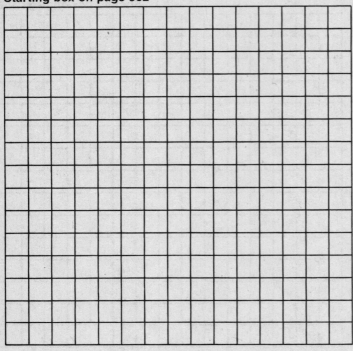

PUZZLE 71

QUOTAGRAM

Fill in the answers to the clues below. Then transfer the letters to the correspondingly numbered squares in the diagram. The completed diagram will contain a quotation.

1. Corporeal

$\overline{1}$ $\overline{50}$ $\overline{47}$ $\overline{30}$ $\overline{12}$ $\overline{57}$

2. Name as a candidate

$\overline{51}$ $\overline{9}$ $\overline{23}$ $\overline{4}$ $\overline{46}$ $\overline{28}$ $\overline{21}$ $\overline{55}$

3. Capable of being shaped

$\overline{56}$ $\overline{33}$ $\overline{11}$ $\overline{19}$ $\overline{40}$ $\overline{24}$ $\overline{18}$ $\overline{7}$ $\overline{2}$

4. Breakfast appliance: 2 wds.

$\overline{35}$ $\overline{10}$ $\overline{27}$ $\overline{39}$ $\overline{31}$ $\overline{52}$ $\overline{44}$ $\overline{43}$ $\overline{22}$ $\overline{54}$

5. Blackjack: hyph.

$\overline{8}$ $\overline{41}$ $\overline{45}$ $\overline{62}$ $\overline{37}$ $\overline{26}$ $\overline{61}$ $\overline{25}$ $\overline{53}$

6. Summoning

$\overline{20}$ $\overline{5}$ $\overline{14}$ $\overline{3}$ $\overline{17}$ $\overline{58}$ $\overline{32}$ $\overline{49}$ $\overline{60}$

7. Impishness

$\overline{29}$ $\overline{36}$ $\overline{13}$ $\overline{15}$ $\overline{38}$ $\overline{6}$ $\overline{63}$ $\overline{42}$

8. Brawl

$\overline{34}$ $\overline{16}$ $\overline{59}$ $\overline{48}$

1	2		3	4	5	6	7		8	9		10	11	12		13	14	15	16
17	18	19	20		21	22		23	24	25	26		27	28	29	30	31	32	33
34		35	36	37	38		39	40	41		42	43	44	45	46	47		48	49
	50	51	52		53	54	55	56	57		58	59		60	61	62	63		

ACROSS

1. Boat
5. Backbones
7. Kings' homes
9. Hemingway sobriquet
12. German emperor
13. European country
16. Fast plane
17. Walker
20. I smell ___
21. Short swim
23. Author Levin
24. Seine
25. To shelter
27. Sultan's home
29. Snake
31. Put away
32. Sample
36. Low island
38. Large homes
39. Belgrade denizen
42. Deep hole
43. Comedian Knotts
44. Also
45. Locale
46. Consumed
47. ___ longa, vita brevis
50. Speakers
52. Knocks lightly
54. French river
55. Swiss homes
58. U.S. sections
59. British gun

DOWN

1. Health resort
2. Belonging to that man
3. Division word
4. Skins
5. Scrutinize carefully
6. Places
8. Tippler
9. Baby food
10. She loves: Latin
11. Dab of butter
13. Western homes
14. Miss Lupino
15. Feel pain
17. Mouth parts
18. Part of QED
19. Large party
22. Green vegetable
26. Vast homes
28. Inquire
30. Greek god
33. Fountain drink
34. Horse's pace
35. Serf
37. Up to now
38. Bishop's hat
40. Poppycock
41. Constricting snake
42. Pastries
45. Snow glider
47. Circle part
48. College cheers
49. Shoe covers
51. Deprivation
53. Thin board
56. French summer
57. Sawbuck

Starting box on page 562

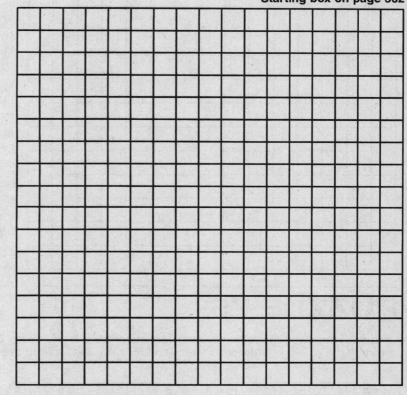

CHANGAWORD PUZZLE 73

Can you change the top word into the bottom word (in each column) in the number of steps indicated in parentheses? Do not change the order of the letters, and change only 1 letter at a time. Proper names, slang, and obsolete words are not allowed.

1. FACE (4 steps) **2. BASE** (4 steps) **3. CALM** (5 steps) **4. GOLD** (5 steps)

LIFT RUNS SEAS LINK

PUZZLE 74

ACROSS

1. Competent
5. Pillowcase
9. Precipitate
10. Employ
11. Be obedient
12. Leave unmentioned
13. Slumber
15. Iron
16. Beaver's barrier
18. Broadway success
19. Bark shrilly
21. Young child
22. Ship's helmsman
24. Writing tablet
25. Stately
27. That man's
28. Affirmative answer
30. Paper sack
31. Waiter's reward
33. Tale
36. Walks with measured tread
40. Sweetheart
41. Uncommon
42. Region
43. Spooky-sounding lake
44. Curve
45. Transmit

DOWN

1. Upper limbs
2. Lade water
3. Fishing cord
4. Concluded
5. Brief
6. Lemon's companion
7. Eye part
8. Birds and dogs
14. Wage
15. Deep hole
17. Tourist's need
18. Very warm
20. Rigid tubings
21. In the present
23. Fall behind
25. Provide with equipment
26. Allow
27. Dobbin's food
29. Drink slowly
30. Staff of life
32. Removes rind from
33. Thick slice
34. Ripped
35. Stove compartment
37. Be concerned
38. Actress Moran
39. Kernel

Starting box on page 562

Starting box on page 562

PUZZLE 75   WORD MATH

In these long-division problems, letters are substituted for numbers. Determine the value of each letter. Then arrange the letters in order from 0 to 9, and they will spell a word or phrase.

1 | 0 | 1 | 2 | 3 | 4 | 5 | 6 | 7 | 8 | 9 |

```
              T I N
      EASE  NATION
            I I N T
            O U E O
            N S I I
            U N L N
            U A T N
              L U G
```

2 | 0 | 1 | 2 | 3 | 4 | 5 | 6 | 7 | 8 | 9 |

```
              E A T
      NAP   SKATE
            N A P
            A W T T
            E P P T
            I P W E
            O N S A
            I W S
```

3 | 0 | 1 | 2 | 3 | 4 | 5 | 6 | 7 | 8 | 9 |

```
              V I E
      TAN   VANISH
            A N I M
            I S E S
            V E H S
            E V R H
            M S V M
            E E T
```

74

ACROSS
1. Constellation
4. Matterhorn, for one
7. Fish eater
8. Extinct bird
9. Luscious looker
13. Horse color
14. Can opener
17. Bank dividend: abbr.
20. Author Fleming
21. Shout of approval
22. Deer
23. Genetic inits.
24. Incubus
28. ____ Vegas
31. Baseball stat.
32. Old card game
34. Rodent
35. Have a nice night!: 2 wds.
40. Senate's concern
41. Lamprey
42. Mine output
43. Fleur-de-____
45. Baseless fancy: 2 wds.
51. Shade tree
54. Nest egg: abbr.
55. Weekday: abbr.
56. Tiny
57. Corral
58. Decade
59. Eye drop
60. Reveries
65. Certain ruler: abbr.
66. Observe
67. Expire
68. "Harper Valley ____"

DOWN
1. Guided
2. Sin
3. Individual
4. Sun god
5. Mauna ____
6. U.S. general
10. Parched
11. Voice pain
12. Trite
15. Muslim name
16. Implore
17. Writer Tarbell
18. Neither's partner
19. Palmer's mound
25. Queen of the gods
26. Streetcar
27. Area rugs
29. Pub quaff
30. Tippler
33. Offering by Keats
35. Blackthorn berry
36. Hospital room
37. Jug
38. Cousin: abbr.
39. Biblical judge
44. Ran up a dress
45. Lulu
46. Outrage
47. Forest god
48. Salamander
49. Exist
50. Cared
52. Shakespearean king
53. Simple
59. Elite or pica
61. Friend for Francois
62. Snake
63. Citi Field player
64. ____ of Marmara

PUZZLE 76

Starting box on page 562

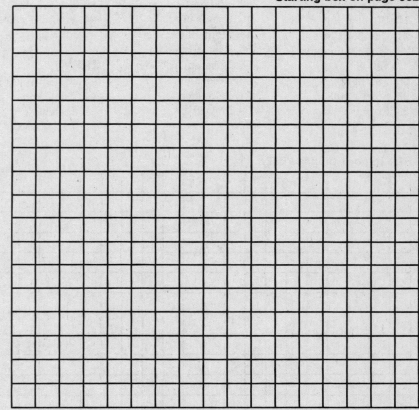

MOSAIC

PUZZLE 77

Place the twelve boxes, each containing two letters, into the empty diagram to form four 8-letter words reading across and down, as shown in the small example on the left.

Example:

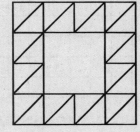

PUZZLE 78

ACROSS
1. Jacob's brother
5. Watering spot
8. Genie holder
9. Have a tendency
10. Go bad
12. Asian direction
13. Use scissors
15. Apply tempera
17. State firmly
19. Burden
21. Competition site
22. Make it snappy: 3 wds.
25. Partners
28. Scores 100 on
29. Promise
31. Manages
32. Don Juan's patter
33. Change
34. Annum
36. Gala affair
37. Shelley opus
38. ____ carte: 2 wds.
39. Escargots
41. Nature path
43. Elaborate
46. Crow's cry
49. Mont Blanc, e.g.
52. Corn concoction
54. Netman Wilander
56. Record for TV
57. Vein of ore
59. Moves
60. Pair
61. Kind of gem
62. Carriage's kin
64. Simply put: 3 wds.
66. Handle
67. Curved
68. Dispatch
69. Like a judge
72. Papa horse
74. Headland
75. Called
78. Kitchen appliance
79. Donate
80. Ink's mate
81. Hall-of-Famer Musial

DOWN
1. Mass transit RRs
2. Pushover
3. Baseballer ____ Otis
4. Riled: 3 wds.
5. Playwright O'Casey
6. Ago
7. Pismire
9. Oahu garland
11. Brown hue
14. Code or colony
15. Scapegoat
16. Trouble
18. Woody Allen's "____ Days"
19. From the area
20. Met musical
21. Top-drawer: 2 wds.
22. "____ Nagila"
23. Harvard vine
24. "On Your ____"
25. Slice
26. Football position
27. Catch sight of
30. Pale
31. Pine yield
35. Reagan's "Brother ____"
36. Erupt
40. Presses
42. On the ____ (running)
44. Young boy
45. Needlecase
46. Roasting bird
47. Separate
48. Actress Tuesday
49. Onager, e.g.
50. "____ It Be" (Beatles)
51. Elements
52. Rhymer
53. Above, to a bard
55. Male heir
56. Eiffel ____
58. Customs
59. Splashy clothes: 2 wds.
63. Famed revolutionary
65. Mr. Vigoda
69. Preserve
70. Unseal
71. Philly's Franklin
73. Radiate
74. Beat walker
76. Ms. Gabor
77. Bear's home

Starting box on page 562

★ **DIAGRAMLESS DEVOTEES!** *Delve into a special collection with loads of* ★
challenging puzzles in every volume of Selected Diagramless.
To order, see page 87.

76

ACROSS

1. Sleeping
5. Farm structures
7. Teacher
11. Power tools
13. Use a certain beam
14. Region
15. Medley
16. Young salmon
17. Design
18. Frets
20. Musical syllables
22. Horse
26. Wire measurements
28. Musical piece
32. 1966 French film
34. Hazy
35. Perfumed ointment
36. Prattles
37. New York team
39. Queen of _____
42. Deneb, for one
46. College subj.
47. Secrete
48. Majority
49. Ancient Syria
50. Posture
52. All females
54. Turn up one's nose
55. Fool

DOWN

1. Tennis champ
2. Life stories, for short
3. Rock group
4. Dash
6. Petite
7. Metric measures
8. Cleaning lady
9. Continent
10. Broadway's gas
11. Race parts
12. Smell _____
19. Goo
21. Generous piece
22. _____ operandi
23. Literary collections
24. Uncooked
25. Jacket
27. Warm and cozy
28. Elitist
29. Muslim leader
30. Face parts
31. TV's "Chico _____"
33. Words before carte
38. Back up
40. Pear
41. Start the poker game
42. Actress Rita _____
43. Novice
44. "Get Smart" actor
45. Send back
50. Straw beehive
51. Car part
53. Modern: pref.

Starting box on page 562

Mix 'Em Maxim

PUZZLE 80

Rearrange the letters in this silly sentence to spell out a familiar saying.

HE SAW TEAMS SKATE

Saying: ___ __ __ __ __   __ __ __ __ __   __ __ __ __ __ .

PUZZLE 81

ACROSS

1. Insult
5. Mouser
8. Land of Incas
9. Caste of India
10. "Lou Grant" photographer
13. Arty Roman emperor
14. Authenticate
16. Examination
17. Dismounted
18. Large hoglike animal
20. Abounding in bamboo
21. Unparalleled
23. Warbled
24. Curved to form a hollow for drinking
27. Roosted
28. Blackboard
31. Wrath
32. Highly spiced stew
34. Prohibited
35. Container
36. Declare openly
37. Roman road
38. Keystone State's founder
39. Withdrew from business
43. Lap (at)
47. Bantu native
48. Arab country
49. Sharp projection
52. Priest's white vestments
53. Telegraph
54. Age or cream
55. Cut of beef
56. Marble
57. Heavenly Twins
59. "____ Price Glory?"
61. Noses around
64. Lure
65. Apiary product
66. Take for a ____ (dupe)
67. TV's "The ____ Kids"
69. Lively
72. Dressing gown
73. Annul
74. Among
75. State as true
76. Cat or dog
77. FBI's Eliot

DOWN

1. Bracing with cross timbers
2. Gentleness
3. Very dry
4. Cougar
5. Restore to good spirits: 2 wds.
6. Manners
7. Dog's gait
9. Old
11. Aleutian island
12. Not fat
14. Annual time off
15. Comic King
19. Making of a book into a movie
22. Heroic
23. Healing ointment
25. Historic time
26. Cozy room
27. Washing compound
28. Agitate
29. Recent
30. Aid in crime
33. Possess
40. Precept
41. Napoleon's exile site
42. Twilight
43. Moo
44. Copied
45. Diamond weight
46. Recognized
49. Lively dance
50. High card
51. Jewels
55. Dozed
58. Suppress
59. Table attendants
60. Conceal
62. Bosc
63. "Auld Lang ____"
64. Stopping devices
67. Envelop
68. Residence
70. Russian czar
71. Take action

Starting box on page 562

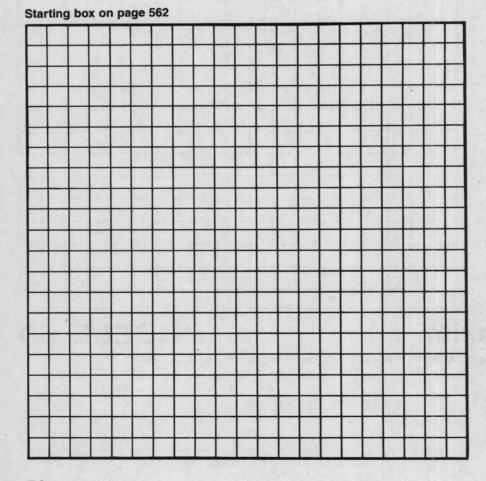

ACROSS

1. Do better than
4. ___ Paulo
7. Relocate
8. Vend
9. Bet
10. Unwritten
11. Opera hero
12. Network
15. African nation
17. Vandal
18. Worry
19. Macaw genus
20. "___ Misbehavin' "
21. Mobutu's land, formerly
22. "The ___ of Hoffmann"
25. Schuss
26. Post-marathon sounds
27. Prejudice
28. 100 centavos
30. Librarians' burdens
31. Pertain
33. Inlet
34. Actor Lowe
35. Place for suspects, on "Barney Miller"
36. Curved line
38. ___ go bragh
40. At all
41. Fizz water
43. Arab cloak
45. Fully mature
47. Kook
48. Start a poker pot
50. Refrain syllable
52. Ripens
53. Procured
54. ___ de France
56. Lovers
59. Dozen dozen
61. Quiche ingredients
63. Aroma
64. Recuperates
65. Sooner than, poetically
66. Creepy
68. African nation
69. Flourished
70. Cereal grain
71. Belligerent god
72. Illuminated
73. Prophet
76. Certainly!
77. Capital of Crete
80. Playwright Connelly
81. African nation
82. Therefore
83. Bedouin
84. Modern: prefix
85. Trinket

DOWN

1. African nation
2. Concluded
3. For each
4. Belgrade resident
5. Asian range
6. ___ podrida
7. Irish Sea isle
8. African nation
9. Departed
11. African nation
12. Bides time
13. Goofs
14. Stinger
15. Gangster's rod
16. Fit for farming
17. Appalachian Trail figure
18. Sugar source
20. Horned viper
21. African nation
23. Consume
24. Vane dir.
26. Indigent
29. Sculls
30. Pleasures
31. Hindu queen
32. African nation
35. Insert signs
37. African nation
39. Basketball group: abbr.
42. Club fees
44. African nation
46. Toledo's lake
49. Flip
51. African nation
52. Antenna
55. White heron
56. Fish eggs
57. Pindaric
58. African nation
59. Heredity units
60. Beams
62. Embroider
64. Present
67. Summer: Fr.
68. Writer Thompson
69. Guitarist Campbell
73. Portent
74. Unusual
75. Jason's ship
77. Remedy
78. "___ Bede"
79. Capture
81. Weaken

PUZZLE 82

• CONTINENT TOUR •

Starting box on page 562

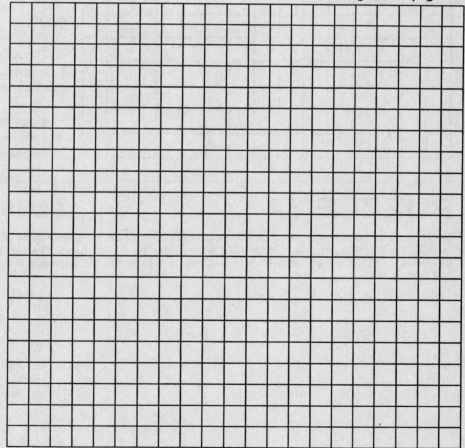

79

PUZZLE 83

ACROSS

1. Lean-to
5. Devoured
8. Horseback game
9. Merry
10. Evict
11. Theater box
12. Drill a hole
13. Droop
14. Biddies
15. Building site
16. Pod vegetables
17. Iterates
21. Coverlet
24. Humor
25. Cravat
26. Enamel
27. Flight record
28. Fur scarf
30. Upper limb
31. Storage drawer
32. Jumped
33. Snuggled
36. Chirp
37. Wheel track
38. Money house
39. Carpet
40. Hair divider
41. Despondent
43. Healthy
44. Help
45. Baking chamber
46. Ball peg
47. Occident

DOWN

1. Coffee stirrers
2. Clock numerals
3. Otherwise
4. Speck
5. Open-mouthed
6. Label
7. Organ of sight
11. Behind time
12. Necklace unit
13. Soak up
14. Warmth
15. Permit
16. Cage
17. Equipment
18. Upon
19. Vinyl square
20. Kernel
21. Bridge length
22. Remove rind
23. Edges
24. Took the cake
27. Cover
28. Look for
29. Faucet
31. Wager
32. Fasting period
34. Factual
35. Carry with effort
36. Natural guardian
38. Cotton bundles
39. Impolite
40. Prepare the way
41. Flying mammal
42. Falsehood
43. In what way

Starting box on page 562

PUZZLE 84

PLUS AND MINUS

Each group of numbers represents a 7-letter word. To decode them determine which letter is indicated by the question mark. The remaining letters are represented by a plus number (which comes after that letter in the alphabet) or a minus number (which comes before that letter). For example, if the question mark is F, then -1 is E and +5 is K.

A.	-2	-1	-3	-20	-1	?	-8
B.	+3	+4	+8	+14	?	+7	+1
C.	+14	?	-4	+1	+10	+10	-1
D.	+9	-5	+6	?	-9	+5	+5
E.	-11	+8	?	-4	-15	-7	-2
F.	+14	+20	+19	+17	?	+6	+4

PUZZLE 85

ACROSS
1. Edibles
5. Sound of laughter
9. Sailor's patron saint
10. Entertains
13. Winged
14. Grapple
15. Agitate
16. Gym pad
17. African nut
18. Dull pain
19. Extreme
20. Spanish ladies: abbr.
21. Pond growth
23. Greasy
24. Restaurant employee
26. None
27. Iowa or Idaho
29. Sault ____ Marie
30. Growing older
32. Spelling contest
35. Senior
37. Blunder
38. Ladies' man
40. Ship's personnel
42. Portents
43. Squash
47. Beneficial
48. Amend
49. Soothing plant
50. Jar cover
51. Was in debt
52. Sleeper car
54. Gorillas, e.g.
55. Happy looks
56. Adriatic seaport
57. Specks
58. Adamson's lioness

DOWN
1. Plumage
2. Stan's comic partner
3. Actor Sharif
4. June bug
5. Author Bret ____
6. Soul, in Paris
7. Corn wrappings
8. Fur trader John Jacob ____
11. Jazz's Fitzgerald
12. Black and Red
14. Watchful
15. Scram!
16. Wire measure
18. Nimble
19. Condensed
21. Barley heads
22. Cafe au ____
23. Kind of orange
25. Airport abbr.
28. Provide with an income
31. Obtain
32. Pierre's cap
33. ____ go bragh
34. Greek's Cupid
36. Zambia and Zimbabwe, formerly
39. Surrounded by
40. Nickel or dime
41. Fisherman's pole
43. Charts
44. University grad
45. Firm
46. Greeting word
47. Window material
48. Jugs
51. Milky gem
53. Encountered
54. Justice Fortas

Starting box on page 562

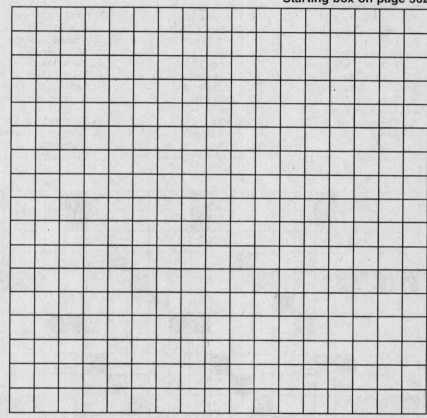

Changaword

PUZZLE 86

Can you change the top word into the bottom word in each column in the number of steps indicated in parentheses? Change only one letter at a time and do not change the order of the letters. Proper names, slang, and obsolete words are not allowed.

1. FORE (4 steps)   2. POST (4 steps)   3. LIFE (6 steps)   4. DRAW (7 steps)

CAST   MARK   BOAT   BACK

PUZZLE 87

• TRIPLETS •

ACROSS

1. Sure-handed
5. Pent
10. Cut drastically
15. Trudge
19. Chinese island
20. Surfaced
21. Tidal bore
22. Singer Abbe
23. Double-play combo
27. City officials
28. Some vines
29. Certain freighter
30. Magnetism unit
31. Leaflet
32. Tennis score
33. Prayer book
37. Seed covers
38. Ecclesiastical headwear
42. Singing group
43. Easily bruised items
44. Wings
45. Choose
46. Everyday trio, more formally
52. Excessively
53. Seal
54. Lariat
55. Laud
56. Regular
59. Reindeer herders
60. Ms. Dahl
61. Numskull
62. France's Hugh ____
63. Splitting knife
64. Ermines' kin
67. Wagner's Odin
68. See 9 Down
72. Hide
73. Scungilli
74. Islamic spirit
75. ____ Tse-tung
76. Dumas trio
81. Spoil
82. Water
83. Anthropoids
84. In re
85. Make clear in advance
88. Lost luster
90. Kicks off
91. Sea birds
92. 100%
93. Stadium sound
94. Kite
97. Celerity
98. Go through one's lines
103. Executive order?
106. Baseball's Moreno
107. Prosodic measures
108. Spud
109. Excited
110. Not any
111. Ranks, in tennis
112. Mouth: suffix
113. Gullets

DOWN

1. Information
2. Author Ludwig
3. Affectionate
4. Little one
5. Mayor Clint Eastwood's town
6. Russian cooperative
7. Thug
8. Linguistic suffix
9. Worthy of Beelzebub
10. Concatenation
11. CD player
12. Middlemen: abbr.
13. Bdwy. sign
14. Harassed
15. Celestial body
16. Rangy
17. As soon as
18. "The White ____" (Thurber)
24. Corrigenda
25. Malefic
26. Possess
31. Habit
32. Clinging plant
33. "Be prepared," e.g.
34. Ethereal fluid
35. Took a position
36. Ministry sch.
37. Nimble
38. Ovine laments
39. Rich cake
40. Stage part
41. Fashion
43. Poetry Muse
44. Go with the flow
47. Lots
48. Algonquian Indian
49. Mellow
50. Wading bird
51. With wheel shafts
57. Gem State
58. Memos
59. Secure with a hasp
60. NBA site
62. Short story
63. Locates
64. Rascal
65. Golden Horde member
66. British pigment
67. Poorer
68. Amerced
69. Always: Ger.
70. Sculptor ____-Gaudens
71. Legions
73. Scoters
74. Mocked
77. Apparitions
78. Battle-line bulges
79. Quite
80. Literary collection
86. Watchman
87. Weight allowance
88. Sheriffs' bands
89. Choir voice
90. Bogart film
92. ____ days
93. Edge again
94. Famous "playing fields" site
95. Asian holy man
96. Way off
97. Rent
98. Newspaper section, for short
99. "____ Bede"
100. Latvia's capital
101. Skier's thought
102. Ova
104. Sorrow
105. Make lace

PUZZLE 88

ACROSS
1. Title of respect
4. Tablet
7. Social division unit
12. Southern constellation
13. Hoosier humorist
14. Mountain nymph
15. Island wreath
16. Chess player's chortle
18. Actress Jillian
19. Strange
20. On ____ (next to bat)
22. Prepare flax
23. Prime the crime
27. Golf's Irwin
29. Stage callback
31. Hogback's kin
33. "As You Like It" forest
34. Most pleasing
36. Comply
37. Gossips
38. Subside
40. Battle mark
43. Holliman and Warren
45. Half of a bray
46. Equine control strap
50. Time period
51. Martinique spouter
52. Self-esteem
53. Op. ____ (footnote abbr.)
54. Ram constellation
55. Early day wetness
56. Mostly green parrot

DOWN
1. Potato or tuna
2. Goddess of peace
3. Ticket for a rescheduled event
4. Regulate
5. Stick
6. Farm implement name
7. Fuel
8. Branch
9. Yellow or Coral
10. Use a shuttle
11. Dutch commune
17. Ile de la ____
21. Smith and Jackson
23. Estate units
24. Hockey ploy
25. Prior to, to Keats
26. Countdown starter
28. Bandleader Brown
30. Arrest
31. At least one
32. Estuary
35. Rend
36. Compel
39. Class
41. Hawk's home
42. Rope
43. ____ out (makes with difficulty)
44. Winter whiteness
46. IRS form preparer, often
47. "And I Love ____"
48. Samuel's mentor
49. Third letter

PUZZLE 89

ACROSS
1. "For Me and My ____"
4. Kipling hero
7. "The Mystery of ____ Vep"
11. Actress Meyers
12. Metric land measure
13. Food regimen
14. Kisser
15. "The Fountainhead" author
17. Palindromic emperor
18. '80s TV adventure series
21. Poolside pursuit
22. Incensed
23. Bothersome one
25. Creative one
30. Layer's output
31. Goofed
32. Additionally
33. Star of 18 Across
35. Red ____
36. Gridiron's ump
37. Title for Guinness
38. Hero in 18 Across
44. Big Band singer Morse
45. Fly alone
46. Charged particle
48. Look
49. However
50. Hoopsters' gp.
51. Drags
52. Still
53. Acquire

DOWN
1. Herd of whales
2. In ____ (unchanging)
3. "When the ____ Down"
4. Singer Carpenter
5. Persian Gulf nation
6. Restaurant roster
7. Mary Martin stage vehicle
8. "Puttin' on the ____"
9. Distribute
10. "____, The Fighting Eagle"
16. Built like beavers
19. Lunch
20. Sgt. Friday's employer
23. Cathedral bench
24. Id's companion
25. Macrame and needlepoint
26. Bruin great
27. Oscar nominee for "The High and the Mighty"
28. Years and years
29. Balderdash
31. Widemouthed jug
34. Fleetwood Mac hit
35. Spy gp.
37. "Kenilworth" author
38. Musical pause
39. Vegetable oil product
40. Gusted
41. ____ Grape (rock band)
42. Evidence
43. Earring locale
47. "Unforgettable" King Cole

PUZZLE 90

Solve this puzzle as you would a regular crossword. Then read the circled letters from left to right, and they will reveal a quotation.

ACROSS

1. Exposed
6. Sanctuary
11. Storage buildings
16. Florida city
17. Aristocracy
18. Hag
19. Frosting ingredient
20. Permit
21. Actress Uta ____
22. Very loud
24. Accolades
25. Word of agreement
26. Icelandic literary work
27. Actor Wheaton
28. Opposite of NNW
29. Native mineral
30. Carson City native
34. Exhibits
37. Pungent
38. Author Jaffe and others
42. Cornet, e.g.
43. Kettle's output
44. Somewhat ancient
45. "Evening Shade" role
46. Tribulation
47. Capitol Hill negative
48. Compete
49. Keep
51. Routine
54. Give up
55. Raise
56. Unoriginal
57. Luncheonette
58. ____ of the absurd
60. Spearheaded
61. Dallas school: abbr.
64. Female fowl
65. Ridge of sand
67. Extinct bird
70. Sentinel
72. Torrid
75. Bay window
76. Tempers
77. Halt
78. Paid off
79. Historical ship
80. More manageable
81. Parts of hulls
82. Church recesses
83. Slashes

DOWN

1. Domineering
2. Severe
3. Storms
4. Vigor
5. Small perches
6. Was told
7. Coalition
8. TV host Bob ____
9. British school
10. Unused
11. Erudite
12. Teheran's nation
13. Trademarks
14. Pips
15. Awareness
23. Keats work
24. Camouflaged
27. Ball of cotton
29. Personal
31. Stat for Gooden
32. Pep
33. Approving gesture
34. Portion
35. Flutter
36. Declaim
37. Had a repast
39. Phileas Fogg portrayer
40. Remark to the audience
41. Transparent
43. Junior
44. Edible grain
46. Keeps back
47. Naught
50. Play section
51. Bonnet
52. Hydrocarbon suffix
53. Hair clasp
54. Spanish hero
56. Interdiction
57. Glitches
59. Snakelike fish
60. Rent
61. Scare
62. Actress Dressler
63. Functional
66. Lanchester and Martinelli
67. Orange Bowl site
68. Beginning
69. Ripening agents
71. Scottish dance
72. Cut
73. Triumphs
74. Heartfelt
76. Mineral spring

ACROSS

1. Actress Celeste ____
5. Stalks
10. Measures for Prudhomme: abbr.
14. Large continent
15. Mother of Tiberius
16. Bountiful's state
17. At that time
18. "Let's Make ____"
19. Darlings' dog
20. Relinquish
22. Prepared leather
24. Anthropoids
25. Done in
26. Greens stroke
28. Infer
31. Beach hills
32. Waves created by ships' courses
33. Federal program under Roosevelt: abbr.
34. Detroit innovator
35. Digs for ore
36. Wedding vows
37. Purpose
38. :
39. Council of ____
40. Hamlet's mother
42. Bring on staff
43. Glimmered
44. Baseball's "Country"
46. Unbroken
48. Pitching style
52. Tailor's concern
53. Spouse's kin
55. Othello, for one
56. Only
57. Prerequisites
58. Actors' organization: abbr.
59. They may be bitter
60. Like honey
61. Without dilution

DOWN

1. "Hell ____ no fury . . ."
2. Workplace watchdog group: abbr.
3. Mortgage
4. Orders
5. Drudge
6. "Prince of ____"
7. Fairy tale's penultimate word
8. Ms. Farrow
9. Crisp crackers
10. Burrower's trail
11. Carry the responsibility of
12. Window section
13. Food fish
21. Picks
23. Rainbows
25. Subway coin
26. Vital sign
27. Comprehend
28. Hiawatha's craft
29. Singsong
30. New England coast
31. Actor McClure
32. Playwright Oscar ____
35. Gem's setting
36. Dublin native
38. Gator's kin
39. God of thunder
41. London river
44. Skirt
45. Full of facts
46. ____ Royale
47. Broadway light
48. Dairy case choice
49. Super-duper
50. Part of NB
51. Mild epithet
54. Recent: pref.

PUZZLE 91

• FLIP-FLOP •

TOP TO BOTTOM

PUZZLE 92

Place the letters given below each diagram into the squares to form eight 4-letter words reading from top to bottom from square to connected square. The top letter is the first letter of all eight words, each letter in the second row is the second letter of four words, and so on.

Example:

Bare, Bark, Balk, Ball, Bulk, Bull, Burl, Burn

1.

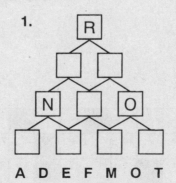

A D E F M O T

2.

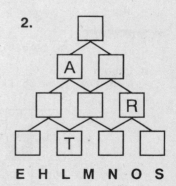

E H L M N O S

PUZZLE 93

ACROSS

1. Manner of running
5. Deserved

Starting box on page 562

7. Disparage
9. Teaches a dog obedience
10. Not fatty
13. Auto
14. Designer Christian
16. If not
20. "____ Irae"
22. More rational
24. Ocean
25. Owns
28. Musical sounds
30. N.Y. zone in summer: abbr.
31. Quick to learn
32. Female
34. Sports group
36. Ancient Italians
39. Wound mark
41. Tub
42. Sharp
44. Mend
47. To no extent
49. Magazine head
50. "Mine eyes have ____ ..."

DOWN

1. Put on weight
2. ____ and sciences
3. Loan rate: abbr.
4. Swiss archer
5. Actor Wallach
6. Property title
7. Grain husk
8. English counts
9. Fort Worth campus: abbr.
11. Help
12. Clamor
15. Hollow grass
17. Consume
18. White flakes
19. Mister: Sp.
21. Took a chair
23. San ____, Italy
25. Cap
26. Gorillas
27. Pile
29. Sleuth Spade
33. Part of USNA
35. Actress West
37. Spike
38. Liner: abbr.
40. Director Clair
43. Gives silent assent
44. Price per unit
45. English school
46. Golf norm
48. Make a knot

PUZZLE 94   QUOTAGRAM

FILL in the answers to the clues below. Then transfer the letters to the correspondingly numbered squares in the diagram. The completed diagram will contain a quotation.

1. Alamo name   ___ ___ ___ ___ ___
                 30 1   4 26 31

2. Nontalking Marx   ___ ___ ___ ___ ___
                      35 5 23 12 22

3. John or Tori   ___ ___ ___ ___
                   13 37 29 24

4. Pop-up appliance   ___ ___ ___ ___ ___ ___ ___
                       28 11 17 27   7 25 14

5. Bother   ___ ___ ___ ___ ___
             19   2 34   8 20

6. Children   ___ ___ ___ ___ ___ ___
                6 33 15 32 21   9

7. Heavy string   ___ ___ ___ ___ ___
                   10 18 36 16   3

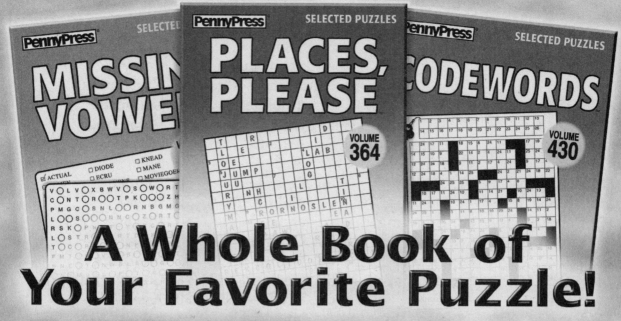
87

PUZZLE 95

ACROSS
1. Garret
5. ____ constrictor
8. Flying pro
11. Above
12. Carry with effort
13. Till
14. Arena receipts
15. Exist
16. "Saturday Night ____"
17. Mechanical flop
19. More orderly
21. Acorn tree
22. Attempt
23. Forewarned
27. Fire remains
31. Diaper fastener
32. Spinning toy
34. Ginger ____
35. Kind of bear
38. Pancake skillet
41. Shred
43. Metallic rock
44. Slander
47. Choppers
50. State positively
51. Night before a holiday
53. Incite
55. Aquatic bird
56. Female sibling, for short
57. Comfort
58. Before
59. Nosh
60. Bread and whiskey grains

DOWN
1. Fireplace item
2. Ellipse
3. Outdoor party
4. Earthquake
5. Comforter
6. Belonging to us
7. Spy
8. Landed
9. Inlet
10. Pitcher
13. Stage offerings
18. Cereal grain
20. Age
23. Likely
24. Be untruthful
25. Finish
26. Canine
28. Owned
29. Building addition
30. Espy
33. Object strongly
36. Attracted
37. Sweet potato
39. Anger
40. More profound
42. Silly ones
44. Court
45. Always
46. Golf cry
48. Serving platter
49. Watering tube
52. By way of
54. ____ Moines

PUZZLE 96

ACROSS

1. Mediterranean ____
4. Wind
8. "____ Get It for You Wholesale"
12. What a lobe is part of
13. Shaft
14. "Death on the ____"
15. Tennis point
16. Road distance
17. Fret
18. Softened
20. Black-eyed ____
21. "We ____ the World"
22. Container
25. Amphitheater
28. Uncooked
29. Writer Fleming
30. Strong wind
31. Glutton
32. Small lake
33. Before, in poetry
34. Aircraft engine housing
35. Dog treats
36. Concealed
38. Acquired
39. Chasing game
40. Reply
44. Tibia
46. Twirl
48. Actress Arden
49. Beep
50. Detest
51. Lamprey
52. Cravings
53. Person Friday: abbr.
54. Snoop

DOWN

1. Stock exchange membership
2. Apiece
3. Locality
4. Photographer's need
5. Oxygen compound
6. ____-advised
7. Stetson from "Scarecrow and Mrs. King"
8. Skirt panel
9. Summons
10. Malt drink
11. Unfamiliar
19. Recede
20. "Batman" interjection
22. Tote ____
23. Highway division
24. Concludes
25. Bronze and Stone, e.g.
26. Lightly cooked
27. Public vote
28. Playwright Serling
31. "Some Like It ____"
32. Kettles
34. Tent stake
35. Hat
37. Fumes
38. Strides
41. Blubber
42. At any time
43. Depend
44. Pig's digs
45. Weeding tool
46. ____ Na Na
47. Dance step

89

PUZZLE 97

ACROSS

1. Ginger drink
4. Rider's tool
8. Exchange
12. Half dozen
13. Employ
14. Pine nut
15. Vitality
16. Shangri-la
17. First-rate
18. General Robert ___
20. Penn and ___ (comedians)
22. Kitchen gadget
24. Rouse
25. Variety show segments
26. Fad
27. That girl
30. Small mounds
31. Self-importance
32. Portico
33. Total
34. Accessible
35. Quarter-back's play
36. Dolt
37. Bash
38. ___ and dryer
41. Apartment fee
42. Succulent plant
43. Minor
45. Not high
48. Rather's concern
49. Odd's opposite
50. Meadow mama
51. Try out
52. Trust
53. Fourth letter

DOWN

1. What bit Cleopatra
2. Prevaricate
3. Anticipated
4. Hurrah, e.g.
5. Go by car
6. Mine yield
7. Five-sided building
8. Dieter's aid
9. Lamb's fabric
10. Actress Archer
11. Gaze
19. Minus
21. Supplement
22. Facts and figures
23. Cooled
24. Conducted, as war
26. Lois Lane's profession
27. Surprised
28. Emcee
29. Simple as one, two, three
32. Stretch across
34. Corrida shout
36. Treasure ___
37. A ___ for your thoughts
38. Desire
39. In a sheltered direction
40. Female pigs
41. Lively dance
44. Preholiday night
46. Have creditors
47. Itty-bitty

ACROSS

1. Stable morsel
4. Heal
8. Thick slice
12. Wing
13. Again
14. Summon
15. Hearth
17. Regretted
18. Allow
19. Leans
20. Quiz choice
22. Highway
23. Smallest Greek letter
24. Most cherished
27. Singer Stevens
28. Squalid
30. Uncooked
31. Picked
33. Notation
34. Kind of ticket
35. Coast
37. Put to use
39. ___ Palmas
40. Sting
41. Boundary
46. Malevolent look
47. Overhang
48. Time of light
49. Whirlpool
50. "For Your ___ Only"
51. Metric measure

DOWN

1. Bumpkin
2. Boxing great
3. Sailor
4. Detective's projects
5. Merge
6. Scarlet
7. Mother sheep
8. Ranch
9. Washed
10. Matured
11. Garden plots
16. She, in Madrid
19. Actor Danza
20. Young horse
21. Tried
22. Curtain or lightning
23. Diamonds
24. Nourished
25. Identical
26. Pair
28. Corset bone
29. Snaky fish
32. Appetizer sticks
33. Thin fog
35. Mitten
36. Bowling alleys
37. Competent
38. "The ___ Piper"
41. Retainer
42. Sunbeam
43. Mont.'s neighbor
44. Play it by ___
45. Hearty bread

PUZZLE 99

• METALS •

ACROSS

1. ____-color (risque)
4. Burro
7. Spelling or quilting
8. Tide or key
9. Go over like a ____ (flop)
14. Abstain from food
15. Song from "A Chorus Line"
16. Elm or ash
18. Grotto
19. Sports building
21. Mend
23. Fragrance
25. Plated metal items
27. Stumbles
30. Bound
31. Beret's kin
32. Puma, e.g.
34. Edinburgh native
35. Gusto
36. Pork source
37. Tease
39. ____ lime pie
40. Profit
42. Not a soul
44. Public disturbance
45. Frozen precipitation
46. Ravel
47. European capital
48. Hawaiian wreath
50. Health spot
52. O'Keeffe's forte
53. Performed
56. District
58. Newt
60. Martini ingredient
61. Carte
62. Shouts
64. Metallic wrap
68. Frontiersman Daniel ____
69. Computer input
71. Montgomery heroine Rosa ____
72. Caution
73. Auction
75. Blemish
76. Iota
77. Retirees
80. Negative answer
81. "You ____ There"
82. Compass pt.
83. Place for flowers

DOWN

1. Corpulent
2. Stunt
3. Nourished
4. Entirely
5. Dirt
6. Saber
9. Etna's output
10. Nee
11. Again
12. Ms. Horne
13. Meticulous
14. Debbie Allen show
17. Transgresses
18. Magician David ____
19. Motive
20. Circle part
22. Jukebox of yore
23. Mountain
24. Fish spawn
25. Label
26. Musical sense
28. American poet
29. Hog enclosure
31. Type of old photograph
33. Gambler
36. Malayan boats
38. Crow
41. Atmosphere
43. Zilch
48. Deposit eggs

49. Before, to Keats
51. Astern
52. Hurt
54. Wayside stopover
55. Owing
57. Word of woe
59. Gratuity
60. Enlisted men: abbr.
61. Oliver's request
63. Without a date
65. Appoint
66. Friend of Kukla and Ollie
67. Podded vegetable
68. Cave dwellers
70. "Home ____"
72. Sent a telegram
74. Ardor
76. Mother, to Brigitte
78. Color
79. Chat

PUZZLE 100

ACROSS
1. Accomplish again
5. Temporary teacher, for short
8. Stage decor
12. British nobleman
13. La's cohort
14. Track shape
15. Eager
16. Picnic crasher
17. Ten cents
18. Rescind
20. Recuperated
22. Dish
24. Profession
28. Marathon participants
33. Fly alone
34. Mo. between Jan. and Mar.
35. Butter substitute
36. Movie fare
38. Teases
39. A new ____ on life
41. Kind of hound
45. Card suit
50. Start a poker hand
51. Also
53. Colt's mom
54. Put away
55. Goof
56. Great Lake
57. Haunches
58. Cub Scout group
59. Sign gas

DOWN
1. Hitchcock's "____ Window"
2. Roof edge
3. Faucet malfunction
4. Ye ____ Shoppe
5. Delay
6. Footed vase
7. Shower site, perhaps
8. Soft drink
9. Harmful
10. Not wild
11. Winter toy
19. Big monkey
21. Still, in poems
23. Sports palace
24. Recipe amt.
25. Kanga's baby
26. High mountain
27. "What's up, ____?"
29. Right this minute
30. Mr. Yale
31. Collecting a pension: abbr.
32. Mayday!
34. Worried
37. Corrida cheer
38. Wooden peg
40. Defleeced
41. Wild party
42. Against: prep.
43. Halt
44. Uses needle and thread
46. Prayer ending
47. Scarce
48. Small combo
49. Observed
52. Pay dirt

ACROSS

1. Selfish person
4. Lacerated
8. Breathe audibly
12. Fruit beverage
13. Similar
14. Repeat
15. Decade number
16. Moniker
17. Gas used in lights
18. Tense
20. Lifted
22. Contrite
24. Fairy tale heavy
25. "Long ago and far ____ . . ."
26. Do the dog paddle
27. Frying utensil
30. Thicken
31. Flogs
32. Chop
33. Burro
34. Porters
35. Birds of prey
36. In ____ your head
37. Jamie Lee's mom
38. Extras
41. Red planet
42. Fat
43. Temper
45. Sorceress
48. Helm position
49. Further
50. Mineral
51. Bruin
52. Remainders after deductions
53. Rock or peeve

DOWN

1. Stetson
2. Pastoral poem
3. Army officers
4. Pungent
5. All right
6. Elevated border
7. Efforts
8. Lamp spirit
9. Experts
10. Wingtip
11. "On Golden ____"
19. Not sweet, in wine
21. "Farewell to ____"
22. Hero's tale
23. Has debts
24. Proprietor
26. Clerks
27. Place to hock valuables
28. Spindle
29. Brood's home
31. Grotto
35. Row
36. Law and ____
37. Tires
38. Hunk
39. Faintly colored
40. Space
41. Majority
44. Shout to a bullfighter
46. Metric measure
47. Comprehend

PUZZLE 101

PUZZLE 102

ACROSS
1. Walking
6. Viewed
9. Fire residue
12. Army topkick, for short
13. Lace up
14. Trouble
15. Not fresh
16. Weirdo
18. Irritate
20. Saharalike
21. Dusting cloth
23. Garden tool
24. Inspired wonder
25. Table spread
27. Foothill
29. Want
31. Begs
35. Thrust
37. Let fall
38. Metal wedge
40. Author Levin
42. Ocean
43. Rotated
44. Baby's bed
46. Matted
48. Dug for ore
51. Actor Carney
52. Lemon or lime drink
53. Likeness
54. Approval answer
55. Each
56. Claw

DOWN
1. Donkey
2. Overweight
3. Citrus fruits
4. Stare at
5. Molars, e.g.
6. Taken by thieves
7. Military assistant
8. Marry
9. In the know
10. Firm
11. Grasped
17. Cried loudly
19. Keepsake
21. Staff
22. Pub drink
24. "____ the President's Men"
26. Greasing
28. Musical drama
30. Molasses liquor
32. Supply of weapons
33. Female rabbit
34. Health club
36. Support beam
38. Extra tire
39. Searches
41. Own up to
43. Remain
44. Give in
45. Kind of bean
47. Racing circuit
49. Self
50. Boy Scout division

ACROSS

1. Agreement
5. Thick mist
8. Comedian Johnson
12. Scent
13. Actress Gardner
14. Ogle
15. Cupola
16. Six-shooter
18. Mast
20. Nevada resort
21. Provo's state
23. Alcohol lamps
27. Make lace
29. Joint
32. Baseball stat
33. Ginger ___
34. Nun's outfit
36. Come in first
37. Road ingredient
38. Singer Seeger
39. Downcast
40. Valuable item
43. Canvas cover, for short
45. Finger ornament
48. Cleaning need
50. Pirates seek it
54. Iridescent gem
56. Broadcasts
57. Morning moisture
58. Western lily
59. Departed
60. Needle's hole
61. Three, in cards

DOWN

1. Pea holder
2. Commotions
3. Some are laptop
4. Trick or ___
5. Distant
6. Finished
7. Donated
8. Dole out
9. Race in neutral
10. Golfer's prop
11. Goof
17. Dollar bill
19. Impulsive
22. Pile
24. Informative publication
25. Operatic solo
26. Beach shoe-filler
27. London goodbye
28. Alack's partner
30. Lincoln's nickname
31. Catcher's glove
35. Afternoon socials
41. Blot out
42. "My country, ___ of thee"
44. Perch
46. Artist's model, sometimes
47. Author Zane ___
49. Book part
50. Children's game
51. ___ Grande
52. Coastal eagle
53. Mother sheep
55. Actress Myrna ___

PUZZLE 104

ACROSS
1. Hazardous driving condition
4. Chilly
8. Scheme
12. Summer drink
13. Neighborhood
14. Rural road
15. Library of ____
17. Concerning
18. Actor Williams
19. Step up
21. Hits, as on the head
24. That thing
25. Cumberland ____
28. Presently
29. '70s music fad
33. Awestruck
35. Waiter's bonus
37. With it, man
38. Family car
40. Actor Mineo
42. Doze
43. Pepe ____ Pew
44. Did the backstroke
46. Stag's weapon
50. Indian corn
54. Scarlett's home
55. Protested
58. Ready for business
59. ____ Unit Zappa
60. Long time span
61. Convene
62. Carl Sandburg, for one
63. Apple pie maker

DOWN
1. As a matter of ____
2. Scent
3. Hackman or Kelly
4. Egg holder
5. Pay dirt
6. Bandleader Brown
7. Short race
8. Frisbee material
9. Endure
10. Poker stake
11. Broadway light
16. Chatter
20. Help
22. Houseplant's home
23. Holey cheese
25. Stove fuel
26. ____ of Aquarius
27. Pea holder
30. Beau or Jeff, to Lloyd
31. Dove's call
32. Ancient
34. Chivalrous
36. Fox foot
39. Previously named
41. Mourn over
45. Singer Davis
46. Tiny particle
47. Neck part
48. Oak or elm
49. Prance
51. Thing
52. ____ hour
53. Dutch cheese
56. Ghostly sound
57. Quarterback Montana

ACROSS

1. Walking stick
5. Sentry's command
9. Wrestling surface
12. Regretted
13. Great Salt Lake's site
14. Anger
15. Dry
16. Cornhusker State
18. Bundling hay
20. Joins with thread
21. Marshal Wyatt ___
23. Marry on the run
26. Agree secretly
30. Brought legal action
31. Period in history
32. David's weapon
34. Cloth scrap
35. Computer input
37. California national park
39. Select
41. Gambling city
42. Electrical unit
44. Awards
48. Beef cut
51. Discharge
52. Stable morsel
53. Telephone
54. 18-wheeler
55. For what reason
56. Small child
57. Former Russian ruler

DOWN

1. Fiddler or horseshoe
2. Distinctive air
3. Singer Diamond
4. Whirlpools
5. With an appetite
6. Dined
7. Research rooms
8. Trio
9. Show Me State
10. Noah's vessel
11. Orange pekoe, e.g.
17. Piercing tools
19. Dozes
22. Preceding
24. Bog fuel
25. Boundary
26. Yield
27. Spoken
28. Birth
29. Entire collection
33. Unit of heredity
36. Molecule component
38. Humble
40. Choose
43. Waiter's aid
45. Iowa college town
46. Peru's capital
47. Mix
48. Explosive noise
49. Cheer
50. Sort

PUZZLE 105

PUZZLE 106

ACROSS

1. "Arabian Nights" name
4. Uppity one
8. Misplace
12. Lair
13. Sioux City's locale
14. Vicinity
15. Abandoned
17. Track transactions
18. Corner
19. Untidy
20. Chinese
22. Off base illegally: abbr.
24. Makes leather
25. Actor Thicke
26. Paddock mom
29. Fairy-tale beginning
32. Was introduced to
33. Lady's escort, for short
34. On the briny
35. You are something ___!
36. Perspective
37. Tired
40. Witnesses
41. Too
42. Loathed
46. Skidded
47. Like the desert
48. Actress Gabor
49. Window portion
50. Prohibits
51. Comic Buttons

DOWN

1. Tack on
2. Actress Ruta ___
3. Animal's guide
4. Temptress
5. B flat, e.g.
6. Have creditors
7. Misbehaving
8. Tab
9. Mined finds
10. Establishes
11. Simple
16. Wipe the slate clean
19. "___ Lisa"
20. Tiny energy source
21. Sensible
22. In solitude
23. Desire
25. Mimics
26. Catastrophe
27. Prayer ending
28. Veal, e.g.
30. Unsightly
31. Stories
35. Wear down
36. Plants-to-be
37. Stinging insect
38. Singer Fitzgerald
39. Z ___ zebra
40. Recipe word
42. Small portion
43. Historic period
44. Actress Arden
45. Pop

CODEWORD

Codeword is a special crossword puzzle in which conventional clues are omitted. Instead, answer words in the diagram are represented by numbers. Each number represents a different letter of the alphabet, and all of the letters of the alphabet are used. When you are sure of a letter, put it in the code key chart and cross it off in the Alphabet Box. A group of letters has been inserted to start you off.

1	2	3	4	5	6	7 Q	8	9	10	11	12	13 T
14	15 I	16	17	18	19	20	21	22 U	23	24	25	26

10	1	23	2	■	■	11	23	15	1	■	4	23	10	18
23	15	24	26	■	6	22	11	11	12	■	23	1	9	26
3	23	17	26	■	23	1	15	18	26	■	5	15	13	26
8	11	26	8	23	11	26	24	■	■	6	9	13	26	1
■	■	■	1	26	24	■	16	8	23	13	■	■	■	■
■	3	23	13	26	16	■	7	22	15	17	■	13	23	3
10	9	11	26	■	8	22	11	19	26	■	23	19	9	■
26	14	26	21	13	■	23	15	1	■	1	23	25	26	11
24	26	21	■	23	1	1	26	12	■	2	15	21	26	■
26	11	23	■	3	26	26	13	■	7 Q	22	26	16	13	■
■	■	6	26	23	24	■	20	22 U	11	■	■	■	■	■
20	23	14	9	11	■	3	23	15 I	21	16	13	23	12	■
26	25	23	3	■	26	4	26	10	13 T	■	1	9	5	26
26	1	16	26	■	14	9	13	26	16	■	23	21	26	2
24	26	26	11	■	26	12	26	24	■	5	26	13	16	

Alphabet Box

A B C D E F G H / J K L M N O P Ǫ R S / Ʋ V W X Y Z

101

PUZZLE 108

ACROSS

1. Father
5. Cleo's snake
8. Applications
12. Century plant
13. Female ruff
14. ____ Wolfe
15. Energetic
17. Slammer
18. ____ day now
19. Hardened
21. Delight
24. Experts
25. Maine tree
26. Emits sparks
30. June vow: 2 wds.
31. Celebrities
32. Fish eggs
33. Plot
35. Bye-bye: hyph.
36. Retained
37. Twangy
38. Colorful march
41. Petroleum
42. Adjoin
43. Shuns
48. Faction
49. Women's org.
50. Chimney dust
51. Germ
52. Sault ____ Marie
53. Finishes

DOWN

1. Dance step
2. Swiss mountain
3. Taro product
4. Charge with air
5. Bohemian
6. Notice
7. Toenail job
8. Not fair
9. Scorch
10. Great Lake
11. Peddled
16. Like: suff.
20. Ensnares
21. Heroic poem
22. Venice resort
23. Ever and ____
24. Separated
26. Salaries
27. Epochs
28. Church tribunal
29. Close tightly
31. Drove too fast
34. Glided on ice
35. Writer Gay
37. Nothing
38. Overtake
39. He loved a Rose
40. Cheeky
41. Fairy-tale monster
44. Devour
45. Bamboozle
46. Ivy clump
47. City roads: abbr.

ACROSS

1. Gasp
5. "—— to Billy Joe"
8. Get taller
12. Turn over —— leaf: 2 wds.
13. —— Vegas
14. Lounger's wear
15. Fruit center
16. Curved letter
17. Medicinal plant
18. Small, rounded hill
20. Dealt with
22. Flipper
24. "—— Are My Sunshine"
25. Put here and there
29. Late for class
33. Pained sound
34. Even score
36. Ocean movement
37. Release: 2 wds.
39. Des ——, Illinois
41. Cheerleader's yell
43. To and ——
44. Sooner ——: 2 wds.
48. Work dough
52. Lumber
53. Actor Majors
55. Challenge
56. Zero
57. Chemistry classroom, for short
58. Away from shore
59. Use a wooden spoon
60. Sphere
61. January to December

DOWN

1. Fill a suitcase
2. Soon
3. Sleuth Wolfe
4. High school senior: 2 wds.
5. Spanish cheer
6. Tiny bit, in cooking
7. Work by Elia
8. June event: 2 wds.
9. Somersault
10. Woodwind instrument
11. Unwanted plant
19. Ignited
21. "To Have and Have ——"
23. Volleyball essential
25. After fa
26. Billiards stick
27. Emulate Olivier
28. Tear
30. —— Tin Tin
31. Ike's monogram
32. Affirmative reply
35. Santa's helper
38. Cereal grain
40. Noah's boat
42. Greeting
44. Possesses
45. Origin
46. Actress Anderson
47. Bring up
49. Alleviate
50. Region
51. Cherished one
54. Flow back, as the tide

PUZZLE 110

ACROSS

1. Cicatrix
5. Flit
9. Actor Everett
13. Came to rest
17. Actress Lange
18. Succulent plant
19. Titanic
20. ____ jerk
21. Ed the singer
22. Part of HOMES: 2 wds.
24. Seasoning
25. Rhine tributary
27. Mouth-puckering
28. English waterway
30. Napoleonic marshal
31. Buzzer
32. Chop ____
33. Party ticket
36. After-dinner drink
37. Pencil tops
41. Dutch painter
42. Panel trucks
43. Jimmied
45. Spanish waterway
46. Castor ____

47. "Show Boat" composer
48. Take it on the ____
49. Difficulty
50. Islands of the Pacific
52. Authored
53. Bobbysoxers
54. Country-singer Campbell
55. French waterway
56. Face-powder ingredient
57. Nevada resort
59. Irish waterway
60. Argentine seaport: 2 wds.
63. Again
64. Separate
65. Tiresome one
66. As good as ____
67. Lodge
68. Wine-growing region
70. Toe ailment
71. Motivator Carnegie
72. Arranges: 2 wds.
74. Wire fastener

75. Knocks down
76. Augments
77. ____ of clay
78. Johnson or Knotts
79. Scottish chiefs
82. ____ rags
83. French waterway
87. To the ____ (completely)
88. Mississippi tributary: 2 wds.
91. Water bird
92. German waterway
93. "Death on the ____"
94. Floor covering
95. Wicked
96. Durante feature
97. Pirates' places
98. Lip
99. Spanish room

DOWN

1. Pretense
2. Italian body of water
3. Tarzan's friends
4. Begrudges
5. Linger idly
6. Winglike parts
7. Seoul soldier

8. Seesaws
9. Surly person
10. Damage
11. Past
12. Set of teeth
13. Analyzes
14. Rich soil
15. Unemployed
16. Makes lace
23. Interrupt
26. FFV name
29. Boss man
31. Rhine city
32. French waterway
33. Get out!
34. Secular
35. Pennsylvania waterway
36. Arm of the Amazon
38. "Clinton's Ditch": 2 wds.
39. Fruit covering
40. Does lawn work
42. Mineral deposit
43. Dial
44. Religious ceremony
47. Wounded ____
48. Aged woman
49. Cotton unit
51. Near the deck, matey!

52. "Rooster
    Cogburn"
    actor
53. Canaveral or
    May
55. Presently
56. Mountain
    pool
57. Shadow
58. Siam visitor
59. Smudges
60. Nobleman
61. Swiss hero

62. Impresses
65. Ferry
68. Heckled
69. ____ Bay
    Company
70. Collegian's
    concern
71. Identifies
73. Carolina
    waterway
74. Utah
    waterway
75. Pro

77. Glacier
    fragments
78. Challenges
79. "____ Came
    Bronson"
80. Hawaiian port
81. Priestly
    vestments
82. Arizona
    waterway

83. Sets
84. Russian
    waterway
85. Catch a thief
86. Singer
    Fitzgerald
89. Go quickly
90. By way of

PUZZLE 111

ACROSS

1. Wheelbarrow
5. Smell
10. Autocratic rulers
15. Cherished one
18. To the protected side
19. Sofa
20. Kukla and Fran's pal
21. Jai ____
22. Government concerns: 2 wds.
24. Teacher's critique: 2 wds.
26. Candle
27. Timberland
29. Useless
30. Declares
33. Inclines
34. Circulars
35. Faulty: pref.
36. Novel
37. Formerly
38. Primer, for one
39. Ump's call
40. Reaches agreement: 3 wds.
44. "Harper Valley ____"
47. Mild oath
48. Yarn spinner
49. Grub
50. Bridge term
51. Thrice: pref.
52. Hot-dog topping
54. ____ Crucis
55. "300" spoiler
56. Miner's tool
58. Athlete Jesse
60. Actress Ross
61. Scurried
63. Milky gems
64. Yields
65. "Where ____ Dare"
66. British river
67. Isolated hills
68. West Indian shrubs
69. Prejudice
70. Clown props
72. Ms. Dawber
75. Trudge
76. Sentry's order
77. German donkey
78. Solitary
79. But, to Caesar
80. Spring promenade: 2 wds.
84. Ring letters
85. Reclines
86. Shade makers
87. Stadium
88. Work unit
91. Government agcy.
92. Elf
93. Puppet holders
95. Stockade
97. Dull finish
98. Brew, as tea
99. Magical command: 2 wds.
101. Criticizes: 2 wds.
106. Lamb locales
107. More rational
108. T.S. ____
109. Bacchanal's cry
110. Superlative suffix
111. ____ cheese
112. Coarse files
113. Appointment

DOWN

1. Garfield or Felix
2. Wing
3. Actor Harrison
4. Swayed
5. Adjust
6. Teases
7. Above
8. Scratch
9. Fills in a test
10. Ontario's capital
11. Huskies' burdens
12. High mountains
13. Spanish river
14. Bondages
15. Tartan
16. Before the bell
17. Currents
21. Officiate
23. Differ
25. Ivory sources
28. Oven
30. Useful thing
31. Phase in life
32. OK at this time: 4 wds.
33. Ogles
34. Main artery
38. Flogs
40. Anne of ____
41. Greased
42. Post
43. Number endings
44. Frank: hyph.
45. Type of card
46. Hymn endings
50. Shopping binge
52. Fixed routines
53. Wishes
54. Sashes
55. Seasons
57. ____ up (hid)
59. Sickly

60. Spirit
61. Trickles
62. Knitting pattern
63. Sermonize
64. Reigned
66. Angles
67. African antelope
69. Diamond markers
71. Concise
73. Beside

74. Tablelands
76. Bald
78. Exposed
80. Inventor Howe
81. Lessees
82. Scheme
83. Current measurer
87. Square feet
88. French school
89. Show one the ____

90. Immense
92. Fun's partner
93. Sharpen
94. Tries out
96. Hosp. workers
97. "The ____ Love": 2 wds.
98. Ancient Egyptian city

100. Cutting tool
102. Guido's note
103. Actress Gardner
104. Balderdash!
105. Popular shirt

PUZZLE 111

PUZZLE 112

ACROSS
1. Young cow
5. Hindu king
10. Cease
14. Ron Howard role
15. Friend: Sp.
16. Vinyl square
17. 1960 VP candidate: 3 wds.
20. Table scrap
21. Slimy soil
22. Gayomart
23. Actress Louise
24. Apply concrete
26. Irony
29. Persian religion
30. —— carte: 2 wds.
33. Arabian gulf
34. April sign
35. Move the tail
36. Daydreams: 4 wds.
40. Strike
41. Meek
42. Fork prong
43. Hydrocarbon suffix
44. Broad
45. S.C. river
47. Skillful
48. So. Amer. plant cutter
49. VP Agnew
52. Agatha Christie's title
53. Chum
56. TV variety series, with "The": 2 wds.
60. Heraldic band
61. Nonpareil
62. Monster
63. Adolescent
64. Earth: Fr.
65. Lager

DOWN
1. Small salmon
2. Impressionist
3. Carpet fluff
4. Chemin de ——
5. Wisconsin city
6. Iraqi town
7. Agree
8. Past
9. Torrid
10. Supermarket
11. Neat
12. Gymnast Korbut
13. Ball-—— hammer
18. Rime-cold giant
19. Profuse
23. Dye
24. "Common Sense" author
25. Encourage
26. Chinese city
27. Mightily
28. Discrimination
29. Salt water
30. Expect
31. Singer Frankie
32. Give consent
34. All kidding ——
37. Chest of drawers
38. Machiavellian
39. Lab burner
45. Specimen
46. Space
47. "Over the Rainbow" composer
48. Speed check
49. Fired a gun
50. Skin opening
51. "Winnie —— Pu"
52. Activist
53. Book leaf
54. "God's Little ——"
55. Ogle
57. Humor
58. Poetic work
59. Tennis stroke

ACROSS
1. Track
5. Doc for Mr. Ed
8. Divorce city
12. Not working
13. In the past
14. Zone
15. Beer ingredient
16. Sidewalk fixture
18. Flightless bird
19. Trundle ____
20. Shopping reminders
21. Edible flesh
23. Passing fancy
24. Make block letters
26. Twenty-four hours
27. Secret agent
30. Sunder
31. Pelt
32. Place for a patch
33. "____ on a Grecian Urn"
34. Box top
35. Valentine shape
36. Rowing blade
37. Baseball hit
38. Dalmatian markings
41. After Fri.
42. ____ like a baby
45. Brightening
47. Sandal
48. Away from the weather
49. Female deer
50. Unskilled laborer
51. Gaze narrowly
52. It gives a hoot
53. Music and painting

DOWN
1. Clock
2. Rocker Ant
3. Make bright
4. "____ It Be"
5. Gentleman's gentleman
6. Old oath
7. Male turkey
8. Speedy
9. Greek god of love
10. Bird's home
11. Horse fodder
17. Stage drama
19. Baseball stick
22. Terminate
23. Distant
24. Golf teach
25. Scarlet
26. Defective bomb
27. Grabber
28. For each
29. Still
31. Evergreen tree
32. Barbie's boy friend
34. Prevail
35. Hovel
36. Different
37. Deli roll
38. Attack
39. Heap
40. Curved molding
41. Miss White of fairy tales
43. Underground plant part
44. Strong desires
46. Bride's response
47. Health resort

PUZZLE 113

PUZZLE 114

ACROSS

1. Padlock
5. Gash
8. Bring to a stop
12. Golf club
13. "___ Step Beyond"
14. Butter sub
15. Sour
16. Male horse
18. Part of G.B.
19. Put in reserve
20. Snares
22. Affront
26. Torrid
28. ___ of the line
29. And not
30. Actor Carney et al.
31. Kind of doll
32. Grow weary
33. Slave Turner
34. Tippler
35. States of mind
36. Deceitful
38. High time
39. Crown
41. Tie-up
44. Sewing-machine parts
47. Compliment
48. Traipse
49. Asian holiday
50. Frosts
51. Melodies
52. Solar and lunar: abbr.
53. Gumbo ingredient

DOWN

1. Mouthful
2. Algerian seaport
3. Opera glasses
4. Explosive abbr.
5. Expenses
6. "Do ___ others . . ."
7. Splitting
8. Grips
9. ___ Baba
10. Mr. Durocher
11. Heavy weight
17. Impart
19. Farm area
21. Hesitation sounds
23. British flag: 2 wds.
24. Lady's mate
25. ___ bien
26. Rooters
27. Moslem country
28. Corrode
31. Patent-holder's due
32. Also
34. Sideslip
35. "Mr. ___"
37. Washington's successor
38. Aeries
40. Buck or doe
42. Speak up
43. Tableland
44. Musical syllable
45. King: Fr.
46. Corn spike
47. Senor's river

PUZZLE 115

ACROSS

1. Kind of tide
4. Belgian resort
7. Food fish
11. Fibs
13. Mat
14. Tortoise's rival
15. Average
17. Feed the kitty
18. Geologic time periods
19. Church official
20. Aid
22. Giants
24. General Bradley
25. Privy to
26. ____ Aviv
29. Thicker
31. Partial refund
33. Terminate
34. Bette Midler role
36. Upon
37. Tilt
39. Manufactured
40. Daisy part
42. One who mimicks
44. Mideastern nation
45. Rises
49. Baseball team
50. Snaky fish
51. Quench
52. Koppel and Kennedy
53. Summer beverage
54. Cozy room

DOWN

1. Overhead trains
2. Bridle part
3. Actress Arthur
4. Bridge
5. Clergy member
6. Tack on
7. Oil-bearing rock
8. Tumbler's feat
9. Funnyman Johnson
10. Forest ruminant
12. Ridicules
16. Polka ____
19. Marine eagle
20. Final word in church
21. Orchestra's platform
23. Clinton's veep
24. Lyric poem
25. Treat pleats
27. Diminutive suffix
28. Zodiac sign
30. Of an age
32. Gets on a plane
35. Said
38. Rural roads
39. Fellows
40. Pub order
41. Buffalo's lake
43. Wan
45. Large body of water
46. Unhappy
47. Colorado Indian
48. Sty

PUZZLE 116

ACROSS

1. "___ in Space"
5. Neptune's kingdom
8. Derive
12. Smell
13. Place for experiments
14. Beige
15. Big-hearted
17. Talk
18. Wager
19. Edible bulbs
21. Youngster
24. Ink spot
25. Shoestring
26. Dark-haired woman
30. Had a snack
31. Shipping box
32. Victory
33. Uninhabited
35. Fruit peel
36. Skillets
37. Musical sounds
38. Rely
41. Sun god
42. Oast
43. French emperor
48. Fatigue
49. Night of a vigil
50. Aquatic eagle
51. Insult
52. Tie the knot
53. Actor Oliver ___

DOWN

1. Nautical record
2. Poem of exaltation
3. Male descendant
4. High voice range
5. Narrow groove
6. ___ de Cologne
7. Definite
8. Orate
9. Repeat
10. Irish island group
11. Deposits
16. ___ herring
20. ___ of the above
21. Garbed
22. Despise
23. Frozen treats
24. Annoying children
26. Completely fresh
27. Double
28. Fork part
29. Purposes
31. Scottish family
34. First game in a series
35. Paint applicator
37. Also
38. Speckles
39. Wicked
40. Lima's location
41. Made haste
44. Boulevard
45. Able was I ___ . . .
46. "___ Foot in Heaven"
47. Actor Beatty

PUZZLE 117

ACROSS

1. Prisoners
5. Aged
8. Fix the road
12. Component
13. A long way
14. Large continent
15. Diamond figure
18. Vend
19. Chocolate cream ___
20. Can covers
23. Report
27. Defused, as a bomb
30. False statement
31. Shake up
32. Always, to a bard
33. Music, for one
34. ___ carte
35. Gulps
38. Flinch
40. Pack of paper
41. Curve
43. Humble
46. Baseball position
52. Lotion ingredient
53. Noah's ___
54. Ireland
55. "Designing Women" actor
56. A Stooge
57. Baby-sit

DOWN

1. Mongrel
2. Wallet bills
3. Moses's river
4. Single photographs
5. ___ the wall
6. Track circuit
7. Dribble
8. Steps
9. Burned remainder
10. Compete
11. In one ___ and out the other
16. Director Kazan
17. Bound
21. Traced
22. Smudge
24. Cabbage dish
25. Vents
26. As of now
27. Spanish painter Salvador ___
28. Mideast land
29. First name in mystery
31. Glass ___
35. Scorched
36. Gold fabric
37. Egg dish
39. Provide food
42. Stuff
44. Entertainer Adams
45. Composer Jerome ___
46. Vehicle for hire
47. Guido's high note
48. "Neither snow, ___ rain . . ."
49. To and ___
50. Eisenhower's nickname
51. Scarlet

113

PUZZLE 118

ACROSS
1. Temperate ____
5. Time gone by
9. Sugar ____ Leonard
12. Equal
13. Defame
14. Metallic rock
15. Hollow stalk
16. Annual reference books
18. Methodical
20. Flop
21. Purpose
22. Felt
25. Allure
28. Sable or mink
29. Dried grass
30. Beer ingredient
31. Is able to
32. Apple center
33. Horned viper
34. Light brown
35. Chessmen
36. Butter or gallery
38. Tree fluid
39. Director Reiner
40. Screenplays
44. Musical
47. Implement
48. Hit the jackpot
49. Spool of film
50. Too
51. Court divider
52. Identical
53. "____ in Yonkers"

DOWN
1. "Less than ____"
2. Finished
3. Deficiency
4. Makes beloved
5. Sacred song
6. Confederate
7. Total
8. Merchant
9. Touring play
10. Circle part
11. Certainly!
17. "The Flying ____"
19. Edge
22. Energy source
23. Procure
24. Colors
25. Fellow
26. Stockings
27. Evident
28. Kind of club
31. Tabby
32. Funds
34. Potatoes, e.g.
35. Golf standard
37. Neither's partner
38. Climb
40. Flower part
41. Mallet game
42. Throw
43. Coin opening
44. "My ____ Private Idaho"
45. Bakery offering
46. Hot brew

ACROSS

1. Obstacle
4. Wooded valley
8. "The Tell-Tale Heart" author
11. Employ
12. Song for Pavarotti
13. Hat part
14. Antique firearms
17. Encounter
18. Small cut
19. Appoints
22. Out of the wind
23. Holy image
24. Contrary
27. Baseball's Durocher
28. Desire
29. Gielgud, for one
31. Prowler
33. Beak covering
34. Swing around a mast
35. Gave medicine to
36. Commotion
37. Tiny particle
39. Go for broke
44. Writing tools
45. Long time periods
46. Positive vote
47. Summer cooler
48. Unit of force
49. Finish

DOWN

1. Public transport
2. Pulverized lava
3. ___ Speedwagon
4. Social engagements
5. Great Lake
6. Fuzz
7. Fall behind
8. Handles according to routine
9. Swine sound
10. Printing measures
13. Prickly plant
15. Warning sign
16. Fjord
19. Zip
20. Cards with one pip
21. Opalescent gem
22. State positively
24. Twine
25. Preceding period
26. Ireland
28. Woo
30. Primary color
32. Mixtures
33. Singer Perry ___
35. Search with a divining rod
36. Cast off
37. Naval greeting
38. Nashville's state: abbr.
39. Mineral spring
40. Baseball's Williams
41. Cereal grain
42. Actor Berry
43. Unhappy

PUZZLE 119

PUZZLE 120

ACROSS

1. Palmer's game
5. Mae ____
9. Small rug
12. False deity
13. Poker stake
14. Rapper ____ - T
15. Cast or close
16. Emphasized
18. Oak and elm
20. Destroys
21. Overpriced
23. Empty
26. Viper
29. "Norma ____"
30. Wild card
31. Chief
33. Donkeys
34. Bow and ____
35. Play on words
36. Squid squirt
37. Actress Young
38. Domesticated
40. Shape dough
42. Caesar or Greek
46. Beast
49. Floor piece
50. Vote
51. Unlock
52. You are something ____!
53. Wager
54. G-man Eliot ____
55. Traffic sign

DOWN

1. Present
2. Smell
3. Knowledge
4. Escapes
5. Used to be
6. Meal course
7. Leather thong
8. Casual shirts
9. Jefferson City state
10. Expert aviator
11. Mr. Turner
17. Divide
19. Disperse
22. Auricle
24. Religious image
25. Office feature
26. Alack
27. Withered
28. Long-tailed bird
30. Sand hills
32. Singer Summer
33. Tramp
35. San Diego nine
38. Brownish gray
39. Appointments
41. Jacket or collar
43. Rhythm
44. Plus
45. Profound
46. Mr. Calloway
47. Deli bread
48. Type measures

ACROSS

1. Actor Alan ___
5. Salve
9. Trade
13. Jai ___
14. Pond growths
15. Refuse, of old
16. Male heirs
17. Shore
18. See from afar
19. Vegetable melange
21. Min. divisions
22. Pindaric
23. Acquire
24. Greek liqueur
25. Nourished
26. Filtered
30. Worship
33. Type of wheat
34. Glide on snow
35. Risque
36. Morning paper
37. Hurried
38. Pismire
39. Actress Blair
40. Musical movement
41. Big cats
43. Gang
44. Treaty
45. Snack
46. Mystery writer
49. Ottoman
50. Fireworks component
53. Sunbathe
54. Dens
55. Tennis star Sampras
56. Sky bear
57. Come to terms
58. Solar disk
59. Those opposed
60. Essence
61. Ointment

DOWN

1. Lariat
2. Audibly
3. Ball
4. ___ jockey
5. Swell
6. Muslim officials
7. Whip
8. Encountered
9. Kerchoo
10. Madison's locale
11. Swiss peaks
12. Thickness
14. Performed
20. Pointed arch
21. Beef fat
24. Paris airport
25. Saute
26. Eavesdrops
27. Welshman
28. Made do
29. Queen of Carthage
30. Asian sea
31. Jutlander
32. 007 flick
33. Grit
36. Pub missile
37. Goblin
39. Actor Lemmon
40. Repetition
42. Winter jackets
43. Clergy residence
45. Wading bird
46. Michelangelo masterpiece
47. ___ space
48. Revise
49. Scarlett's home
50. Biblical trio
51. Melodies
52. Reach
53. Roll
54. Delay

PUZZLE 121

117

PUZZLE 122

ACROSS

1. Cove
4. Concerning
9. Bit
12. Self
13. Rental agreement
14. Bemoan
15. Movie bargain
18. Cereal grass
19. Culture medium
20. Pertain
23. Farm buildings
26. Lawn problem
27. Not foreign
30. Keep one's ____ to the ground
31. Shawls
32. Miner's goal
33. Moves like a snake
35. Raised
36. Reveals
37. Glove leather
38. Gait
40. Excavated
41. When most convenient
48. Burst
49. Safe
50. Swine
51. Chimpanzee, e.g.
52. Borders
53. Decline

DOWN

1. Sleeping spot
2. Past
3. "Embraceable ____"
4. Soothe
5. Sugar source
6. Clod
7. Take advantage of
8. Oolong, e.g.
9. Pharmacy
10. Distinctive air
11. Tavern drink
16. Daring
17. Sunbathes
20. Overwhelms
21. Toll
22. Submarine's viewer
23. Wild hogs
24. Stereo system components
25. Thing, in law
27. Sketched
28. Incensed
29. Give up
31. "____ Can It Be Now?"
34. At that time
35. Insects
37. Befits
38. Father
39. On
40. Opposite of stet
42. First lady
43. Sorrowful
44. Carry
45. ____ and downs
46. Small inlet
47. Incite

ACROSS

1. Father, in Hebrew
5. Puncture
9. Poem type
12. Seasoning
13. Comfort
14. "The Raven" author
15. Talks idly
18. Wallet fillers
19. Nuisances
20. Ski resort
22. Greek porch
24. Marvin and Majors
25. Played a banjo
29. Deface
30. Fortune-telling card
31. Egg cells
32. Mixed
34. Dill
35. Prez's underling
36. Likely
37. Zones
40. Datum
41. Directs
46. One before tee
47. Iroquoian Indian
48. Space chimp
49. Witness
50. Drinks
51. Charter

DOWN

1. Mule
2. Humbug!
3. Blunders
4. Makes amends
5. Fewer
6. Nosh
7. Fire residue
8. No trespassing
9. Literary composition
10. Blockhead
11. Lampreys
16. Decade
17. Rafter
20. ____ mater
21. Red and Coral
22. Throat infection
23. Stomped
25. Cloy
26. Without pitch variation
27. Level
28. Calendar item
30. Locks of hair
33. Ellipse
34. William Tell, e.g.
36. Faux ____ (blunder)
37. King toppers
38. Demolish
39. Different
40. Lawyers' charges
42. ____-state area
43. Chic
44. Heavy weight
45. Concorde, for short

PUZZLE 123

PUZZLE 124

ACROSS
1. Sulk
5. Kneel down
8. Develop
12. Swear
13. Andy Capp's drink
14. Nevada city
15. Relied
17. Kitchen feature
18. Before, poetically
19. Gone by
20. Avoid
21. Deli bread
22. Row
23. Have the ___ touch
26. U.S. Uncle
27. Elevated trains
30. Once again
31. Bottle top
32. Make a sweater
33. Sleep
34. Horse feed
35. Spiteful
36. Rex or Donna
38. Actor O'Brien
39. Frighten
41. Deface
42. Go schussing
45. Volcano flow
46. Harm
48. Iowa college town
49. Picnic spoiler
50. Engagement
51. Marquis de ___
52. Golf peg
53. Flower holder

DOWN
1. Contrived
2. Finished
3. Vatican leader
4. Sheep
5. Emblem
6. Muffin topping
7. United
8. Thicket
9. Deeply respectful
10. Unusual thing
11. Habit
16. Certain votes
20. Purpose
21. Rarer than rare
22. Faucet
23. Operate
24. ___ nutshell
25. Corrupt
26. Utter
28. Fired up
29. Dirty place
31. Bounder
32. Cartoon's Krazy ___
34. ___ and haw
35. Grocery wagon
37. Obliterate
38. Glue
39. Sorrowful cry
40. Eastern priest
41. Belonging to me
42. Ticket-holder's claim
43. Actress Capshaw
44. News paragraph
46. Welcome ___
47. Streets: abbr.

ACROSS

1. Mama's mate
5. Golf standard
8. Leave out
12. Beer's cousins
13. Exist
14. Took the bus
15. At a ____ for words
16. Small taste
17. Football's Sayers
18. Gauges
20. Spoke pompously
22. Scottish negative
23. Director Howard
24. Glued
27. Examiner
31. "Much ____ About Nothing"
32. Saver's fund: abbr.
33. Cowardly
37. Inventor's protection
40. Epoch
41. Colorado Indian
42. Spock or Dolittle
45. Thawed
49. Adjoin
50. Quick swim
52. Abide
53. Greater amount
54. Poet's before
55. ____ go bragh
56. Equal
57. Beatty or Buntline
58. Depend

DOWN

1. Hand part
2. Medicinal plant
3. Bother
4. Approval
5. Went by
6. Jackie O's second
7. Book ____ (school assignment)
8. Church instruments
9. Castle ditch
10. Inactive
11. ____ off (irate)
19. Actress Dawn Chong
21. Fish eggs
24. Wages
25. Fruit drink
26. Fa follower
28. Lace
29. Sea eagle
30. Squealer
34. Epistle
35. Spanish gold
36. Prison head
37. ____ iron (worked out)
38. Consumed
39. Bank employee
42. Moist
43. Reed instrument
44. Heal
46. Grow weary
47. Wicked
48. Gainsay
51. Wrath

121

PUZZLE 126

• HOW MANY? •

ACROSS

1. Type of rain
5. Harassed
9. Flat bean
13. Worms, to fishermen
17. Skin opening
18. Thirst quenchers
19. Smallest particle
20. Funnyman Johnson
21. ____ gun salute
23. "At ____" (Janis Ian song)
25. Spooky
26. Waiter's handout
27. Had a pizza
29. Taxi
32. Physician, for short
35. Blues
37. Facilitates
39. Legislate
42. Dist.
43. "____ Cents" (1913 hit)
45. Jacob's twin
46. Curved molding
47. Opposite of WSW
48. Society page word
49. Experienced
50. Merit
53. Testament
56. Had bills
57. Kind of gin
58. Surrender
59. Cat talk
60. Tumble
63. Type of whiskey
66. Haggard novel
68. River to the Baltic
72. Bread spread
73. Sweet ____
75. Clamping tool
76. Hacienda
78. Cake unit
79. Taut
80. Mask or lift
81. Make a doily
82. Miner's yield
83. Facts and figures
87. Mend socks
90. "My ____" (MacMurray sitcom)
95. Three hundred ____ days a year
100. Peruse
101. Eartha ____ of song
102. Legend
103. He raised Cain
104. Music and literature
105. Smite, romantically
106. Pub potables
107. Aykroyd and Rather

DOWN

1. Ordinarily disposed
2. Female elephant
3. Hard feelings
4. TV room
5. Martha ____ of comedy
6. Olfactory stimulus
7. Contradict
8. Opposite of WNW
9. Tired, for Pierre
10. News brief
11. Relocate
12. Prayer response
13. Flying mouse
14. Live
15. Resident: suff.
16. Lacrosse team number
22. Golf pegs
24. Undressed
27. Swiss river
28. "____ in the Morning" (song)
29. Bistro
30. Nova Scotia's hourly syst.
31. Existed
33. "____ the Cuckoo's Nest"
34. Instance
35. "Taking Care of Business" gp.
36. Journey section
37. One, to Helmut
38. Watch
40. Coolidge's moniker
41. Egyptian king, for short
43. Car parts
44. Correspondents
51. Reverent fear
52. Stop light color
54. Small French land mass

122

55. WC
60. Not against
61. Neighbor of Miss.
62. Camera eye
64. Sharp yelp
65. Theater sign
66. Religious denomination
67. Haw's partner

69. Eat well
70. Kind of curve
71. Female ruff
74. Reception
77. Conceal
79. Theater award
84. Invites
85. Labor
86. Rectangular column
87. Phone part

88. Pivot
89. Hwy. choices
90. Refrain syllable
91. That girl
92. Squealer
93. Begley and Wynn
94. Pen

95. Terminal: abbr.
96. Trendy movement
97. Ms. Lupino
98. Moving truck
99. Printing measures

PUZZLE 127

ACROSS

1. Leap
5. Shakespearean king
9. "___ Eyre"
13. Of an epoch
14. Blockade
15. Author Haley
16. Good-bye, in Leeds
17. Became wan
18. Dunce-cap shape
19. Defames
21. Loves too much
22. Half ems
23. Dull looking
25. Babbled on
29. Accomplishment
30. Gym mat
33. Hollywood's Turner
34. Dish
35. ___ Khan
36. Sports site
38. Feel poorly
39. Hinder
41. Buddhist sect
42. Infect
44. Philosopher Descartes
45. Singer Garfunkel
46. Hue
47. Musical dramas
49. Segment
50. Lex. or Mad.
51. Amend
54. Miser Scrooge
59. Pod legumes
60. Pate ingredient
62. Rural road
63. Submerged
64. Refine metal
65. Sulawesi ox
66. Nervous
67. Story
68. Actress Carter

DOWN

1. Some planes
2. Russia's ___ Mountains
3. ___ Hari
4. Blueprint
5. Falsifiers
6. Congers, e.g.
7. Mature
8. Eric the ___
9. Son of Isaac
10. Thanks ___!
11. Hawaiian goose
12. Former spouses
14. Pay out
20. Ruby or Sandra
21. Outmoded
23. Distributed
24. Pier rodent
25. Public square
26. More scarce
27. Concerning
28. Sunbather's goal
29. Fire-starting stone
30. Father, to Caesar
31. Rocket stage
32. Takes a chance
34. Emulate Monet
37. Rose essence
40. Before, to Keats
43. Into thin ___
47. In the open
48. Farm enclosure
49. Bothersome
50. Certain poplar
51. Church recess
52. Go in front
53. Sharp taste
54. Stunt man Knievel
55. Spirit
56. Writer Grey
57. Chemical compound
58. Authentic
60. Mil. vessel
61. "___ Believer"

PUZZLE 128   Detection

For each clue, place an appropriate 7-letter word over the dashes. Spell this word with seven of the eight letters given on that line. Place the eighth, or extra, letter under the arrow in the last column. When you've finished, the letters in the last column will spell out the name of a mythical beast.

↓

	Clue		Letters	
1.	Fortress	_ _ _ _ _ _ _	L C E T P A I D	_
2.	Display	_ _ _ _ _ _ _	T E B I H E X I	_
3.	Recital	_ _ _ _ _ _ _	T E C G N O C R	_
4.	Wood eater	_ _ _ _ _ _ _	E R A T I E M T	_
5.	Work device	_ _ _ _ _ _ _	S N A H C I M E	_
6.	Pilot's place	_ _ _ _ _ _ _	T K I O C P C U	_
7.	Miami player	_ _ _ _ _ _ _	O H P D S L N I	_

ACROSS

1. Female horse
5. Go by horseback
9. Water pitcher
13. I smell ____
14. Beauty shop
15. Miner's quest
16. American poplar
18. Meat cut
19. Snout beetle
20. Ebbed
22. Parts of psyches
23. English composer Thomas ____
24. Native of Stockholm
27. Whittle
29. Hoop org.
32. Scat!
33. Free-for-all
34. ____ Francisco
35. Aquatic bird
36. Like a lion
37. Leg part
38. "Hansel ____ Gretel"
39. Swiss capital
40. Ripped
41. Vigor
42. Friendly nation
43. Primp
45. Actor Jannings
47. Southern constellation
48. Dye again
51. More moist
55. Inquires
56. Actor/director/ clarinetist
59. Suffix for natives
60. Santa's helpers
61. Thicke of TV
62. Not one
63. Peruse
64. Ivy League school

DOWN

1. Singer Davis
2. Lined up
3. Evaluate
4. Diminutive suffix
5. Singer Lou ____
6. UN agency
7. Portal
8. Made beloved
9. Barkin or Burstyn
10. Sabot
11. Singer Brickell
12. Cleave
14. Like a catty remark
17. Roman poet
21. Algonquian Indian
24. Glistened
25. Insect-eating bird
26. Long, long time
27. Cent
28. Toward shelter
30. Highland child
31. Queen Boleyn
32. Hit
33. Crumbly soil
36. Softer in tone
37. Sault ____ Marie
39. Bucket handle
43. Beseeches
44. Hindu deity
46. Like some stones
47. Did sums
48. Precipitation
49. Como ____ usted?
50. Function
52. Romp
53. Actress Raines
54. Actual
57. Eggs
58. Opposite of SSW

• TIMBER •

Fitting Description

PUZZLE 130

Fill in the blanks to complete a Fitting Description of a famous person. Place the letters you have added into their corresponding boxes to form the name of that person.

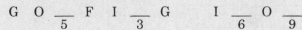

125

PUZZLE 131

ACROSS
1. Land measurement
5. Short sleeps
9. Respectful fear
12. Adversaries
13. Milky gem
14. Baltic or Adriatic
15. Actor Baldwin
16. More stringent
18. "M*A*S*H" character
20. Mountain refrain
21. Football throw
24. Queens' husbands, usually
27. Asphalt
31. African river
32. First number
33. Kilt feature
35. "Here Comes the ____"
36. Court dividers
38. Extremely hungry
40. Reside
42. Sharp
43. Train's track
45. Lavishes love (on)
49. Mulch material
53. Metal thread
54. Large vase
55. Notion
56. Red-pencil copy
57. Cooking fuel
58. Camper's shelter
59. Tints

DOWN
1. From a distance
2. Soft-drink flavor
3. Marsh grass
4. Flee
5. Negative votes
6. Suitable
7. Remove rind from
8. Smooth and glossy
9. Amaze
10. Tiny
11. Hearing organ
17. Goatee's locale
19. Sloping walkway
22. Personality
23. Slink
25. Adhesive substance
26. Dispatch
27. "On Golden ____"
28. Once more
29. Old soldiers
30. Not wild
34. Fastened with string
37. Wooden strip
39. Fell, as frozen flakes
41. Quota
44. Metallic vein
46. Neat
47. New York canal
48. Matched pairs
49. Wrinkle-faced dog
50. Historic period
51. Japanese monetary unit
52. Took a chair

PUZZLE 132

ACROSS
1. "Oh, Pretty ____"
6. Soft minerals
11. Worshiped
13. African expedition
14. Air-conditioner part
15. Tooth covering
16. Tyke
17. Song for two
19. Genuine
20. Brought legal action against
22. Partner
24. Pig's abode
25. Obstacle
27. Distant
29. Foot digit
31. Curved bone
32. Shoulder wraps
35. Oolong and Earl Grey
38. Do the slalom
39. Playwright Coward
41. Christmastime
43. Narrow walkway
45. Quick look
47. Grand Coulee, e.g.
48. Fancy apparel
50. Salad green
52. Stank
53. Hollowing tool
54. Made a mistake
55. Domineering

DOWN
1. Carries lightly
2. Hateful
3. Like lava, e.g.
4. Actor Carney
5. Require
6. Light brown
7. At a distance
8. Most inadequate
9. Make
10. Foolish
12. Bongo, e.g.
13. Hunting dog
18. Lend an ____
21. Information
23. Give off
26. Full-length dress
28. Heed
30. Married on the sly
32. Katarina Witt, e.g.
33. Player up at bat
34. Observe
36. Financial examinations
37. Bond servants
38. Extra
40. Suggestive look
42. ____ board (nail file)
44. Long walk
46. Rounded lump
49. Mr. Buttons
51. Pair

ACROSS

1. East Indian palm
5. Hairstyle
9. Ancient
12. Country plots
17. Anagram of veer
18. Shakespearean king
19. So-so grade
20. Pellets
21. Singer meets songwriter?
24. French artist Claude ____
25. Type measures
26. Butter portion
27. Poetic 17 Across
28. Tom Jones hit "____ a Lady"
29. Sawbuck
30. Not this
32. Cowboy's rope
35. Exchange premium
38. Milwaukee's specialty
39. Challenge
40. Event of 1812
43. "Giant" star meets "Matt Helm" star?
47. Exist
48. Pub serving
49. River isles
50. Indigence
51. French cheese
52. Soak flax
53. Drenched
54. Cheerio
56. Award
57. Baseball star meets comedienne?
61. "____ Moon"
64. Clumsy crafts
65. Opposite of pro
66. Pugilist's blow
69. Harbinger
70. Ali ____
72. Sabot, for one
73. Eggs for Caesar
74. "____ Smart"
75. Actress meets jazz trumpeter?
79. Single
80. I smell ____
81. Lupino and others
82. Yield
83. Of the kidneys
85. Use the scissors
86. Aaron's club
88. Blyth and Landers
90. Dance step
91. Male offspring
92. Ruff's mate
95. Della of song
97. Comedian meets comedian?
101. Biblical weeds
102. Hardwood tree
103. Famous canal
104. Malicious
105. Gravel
106. Vocalized hesitations
107. Makes lace
108. Church service

DOWN

1. Hawaiian goose
2. Lendl
3. Favorites
4. Circle part
5. Poe's middle name
6. Walkers
7. Chat, informally
8. Gold, in La Paz
9. Musical group
10. Glance askance
11. "____ Rosenkavalier"
12. Nav. rank
13. Intersect
14. Ely meets Cosell?
15. Fencer's sword
16. Concordes
22. Poet's unlock
23. Replenish the arsenal
29. Water tester
30. Oolong and pekoe
31. Layer
32. Tardy
33. Desertlike
34. Japanese coin
35. Slightly open
36. Windstorm
37. "____ a man with seven wives . . ."
38. Midler or Davis
39. Reverie
41. Pavarotti forte
42. Lively dance
44. Lumbermill worker
45. Count calories
46. Pot builders
51. Spelling match
54. Pentateuch
55. Query
56. Emulated a forty-niner
57. Quill
58. Cleric's garment
59. Dull pains
60. Australian hoppers, for short
61. Walt Kelly character
62. Church response word
63. Fonda meets Wolfe?
66. Jupiter's other name
67. Eager
68. Vile
70. Actress Theda ____
71. Asian sea
72. Rebuff
75. ____ Jose
76. Belorussian city
77. Amin
78. Deed
84. German industrial region
85. Plunders
86. Skeletal parts
87. Unspecified amount
88. ____ and crafts
89. Tidy
90. Former emcee
91. In a ____
92. ____ Ridge
93. Yalies
94. House wings
96. Wind dir.
97. Namath
98. Wager
99. Historical period
100. Garment edge

• FAMOUS MERGERS •

PUZZLE 134

• RINGSIDE •

ACROSS

1. Type of house foundation
5. Considerably
8. Wood sorrels
12. Clay-footed one
16. Italian lake
17. Wait
18. Guantanamo's locale
19. Actress Talbot
20. In a jiffy
21. Eurasian mountain range
22. Lope
23. Concordes
24. Throws in the towel
26. Taking the plunge words
28. Swathes
30. Ringing
34. Lamb Chop's manipulator
36. Half of Peter Pan's land
37. Spider's invite site
39. "7 Faces of Dr. ___"
40. Fewer
42. Celtic
44. Commensurate
45. Green with ___
47. Road or young ending
49. Stone Age tools
52. Urban trains
53. Fits to ___
54. Plowed land
57. Princess provoker
58. Hemingway novel
66. New Haven tree
67. Venetian red
68. Vista
69. Lacking effectiveness
72. Confrere
74. ___-dry
76. Peace Nobelist Myrdal
77. Actress Markey
79. Vatican City site

82. With regard to
84. Decade number
85. Rank
88. Pertaining to a division of Franks
90. Expunge
92. Perilous question?
95. Entire
96. Certain game's middle name
97. Pays heed
101. Above
103. Minute skin opening
105. Dan Blocker role
107. Division
108. Actor Edmund ___
109. Old French coins
110. Peter Gunn's love
111. Not a soul
112. Intrepid
113. On the cutting ___
114. Witness
115. Gusto

DOWN

1. Cicatrix
2. Ranger or wolf
3. Biblical prophet
4. Actress Granville
5. Type of aid?
6. Ohio college town
7. Repair a topcoat
8. Autumn month
9. Mongrel
10. "Life Is Just ___ of Cherries"
11. Subordinate ruler
12. Motivate
13. Melt
14. Giants great
15. Refrain syllables
17. Baby rabbits
25. Colleen
27. TV host Garroway
29. ___ loss
31. Panel
32. Sky bear
33. Actor Harrison
34. ___ Domingo
35. Flit
38. Care givers: abbr.
39. Frond
41. Hem and haw
43. Elucidate
46. Evergreen
48. Stadium sounds
50. Conger
51. Occupied a bench
55. ___ gratia
56. Sawing wood?
59. With it, once
60. Violinist Bull
61. Lard
62. Reproductive cells
63. Happy songs
64. Quay
65. Adult cygnet
69. Meld
70. Recently
71. Late-evening dynamo
73. Abie's sweetheart
75. Meticulous
78. Sagged
80. "The ___ Falcon"
81. Big Band singer Morse
83. Significant times
86. Young pig
87. Slip by
89. Yearns
91. Bring into accord
93. Heritage
94. Impressionist Janis
98. Chemical compound
99. 1492 vessel
100. "Nana" actress
101. Priestly garb
102. Overly
104. Toupee
106. Sonnet's relative

ACROSS

1. Food fish
5. Curtail
9. Dolt
13. Pool-table fabric
18. Revoke, legally
20. Hacienda house
21. Eskimo house
22. Title holder
23. Vaquero's rope
24. All: prefix
25. Will he, ___ he
26. European liquor
27. Strauss opera
31. Lots of laughs
32. Achy
33. Brains, of yore
37. Don Ameche film
40. Journal
42. Game on horseback
43. High, in music
44. Crack pilots
45. 1947 Nobelist
46. Friml operetta
48. Waller song
53. Tardy
54. Elected ones
55. She, in Paree
56. Inclination
57. Improve upon
59. French season
60. Spotted
61. Like Leroy Brown
62. Galena or bauxite
63. Magnani film, with "The"
67. Former football Giant great
73. "My Name Is Asher ___"
74. Mormon: abbr.
76. Inter ___
77. Wind direction: abbr.
78. "The ___ Strikes Back"
81. Hawaiian town
82. Famed caricaturist
83. "___ the season . . ."
84. Tobacco or Burma
85. Glynis Johns film, with "The"
89. William Starke ___
92. Easy's partner
93. Heraldic border
94. Small whale
95. Mr. Brinker
96. Islamic month
98. Kept to a Lenten diet
100. Tried anew
102. French city
103. Staff member
104. Betty Grable film
109. Widened at the top
112. Land of leprechauns
113. Pay a visit
114. En ___ (as a group)
117. Cowboy movie
118. Half-moon figure
119. ___ of heaven
120. Glossy
121. Actress Anna and kin
122. Vaticinator
123. Niche
124. White-tailed bird

DOWN

1. Vehicle
2. Lemon drink
3. Enjoy a tome
4. Former Cincinnati player
5. Dart
6. Scottish caps
7. Medieval laborer
8. Sloop propeller
9. Of 0's and 1's
10. Pointed arch
11. Earthen jar
12. Rounded corner
13. Ennui
14. Prize
15. Squid's weapon
16. Last letter
17. Before, in poems
19. Singer Lanza
28. Rum, in Spain
29. Ancient Hebrew measure
30. Daughter of Eurytus
34. Indonesian island
35. Choice
36. Range rangers
37. Proceedings report
38. River to Green Bay
39. Perfumes
40. Museum guide
41. Provoke
42. Station
45. Gem face
46. Musical piece
47. Tailor
49. Previous to this: prefix
50. Silk filament
51. Recede
52. Echelon or guard
57. Youthful
58. Worker ant
64. Omit
65. Hodgepodges
66. German river
68. Carpenter's tool
69. Fill with pride
70. Twist inward
71. Isolate
72. Plant anew
75. Sorrowful
78. Typo
79. TV's Garry
80. Passover
81. Grain beards
85. Burrowing fish
86. Distresses
87. Blue Eagle letters
88. Mississippi city
90. Certain tobacco fanciers, in certain areas
91. Like a day in June
96. Oklahoman
97. From, in Bonn
98. Balsam, e.g.
99. "The ___ Chronicles"
101. City in Germany
102. Threefold
103. Shoelace tag
105. "___ Grit"
106. Aristocrat
107. Butter's stand-in
108. North Sea feeder
109. Greek Aurora
110. Cauldron
111. Noshed
115. D.C. VIP
116. Stretch

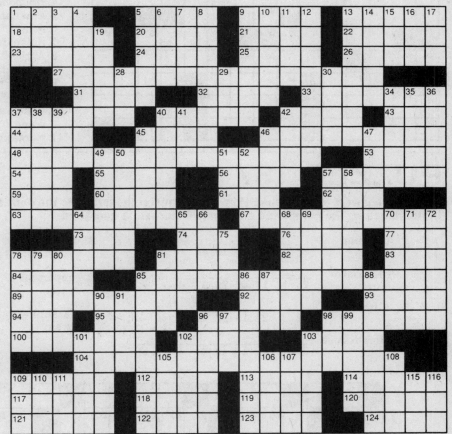

Note to Solvers: This Crossword does not have hints such as "2 wds." and "hyph."

PUZZLE 136

ACROSS

1. Bucket
4. Plateau
8. Pastimes
13. Domicile
14. Bitter: Fr.
15. New England's Island
16. Kind of armadillo
17. Eastern gulf
18. Positive terminal
19. Autumn sight
22. Downy coating
23. Album holder
24. Hindu melodies
26. This, to Juanita
29. Peevish
32. Artful Dodger, for one
36. Differently: abbr.
38. Art colony
39. Unnamed: abbr.
40. More forward
41. Vaulted recess
42. Portico
43. Source of energy
44. Actor Dabbs ___
45. Washed, searching for gold
47. Irani coin
49. Sparked again
51. Frank
56. Naples's st.
58. 1969 event
61. Greek liqueur
63. Have on
64. Stockholm canal
65. Muslim leader
66. Geraint's wife
67. Dark
68. Fibers
69. Beatty film
70. Moisture

DOWN

1. Resin
2. To love: It.
3. Courage
4. Hoi polloi
5. Emanate
6. Joint
7. Suit of mail
8. Agricultural association
9. Actor Philip of "Kung Fu"
10. Observatory scene
11. Norse poetry
12. Trickle
13. Interjections
20. Tied
21. John Wayne flick, e.g.
25. Floral oil
27. ___ a fait
28. Vitality
30. Flexible tube
31. WWI battle river
32. Inhale harshly
33. Rectangular pier
34. Simpleton
35. Illogical
37. Gloss starter
40. "Talk ___"
44. Basketball's Davis
46. Fudd and Gantry
48. Endows
50. Dominate
52. Hemmed
53. Mythical weeping stone
54. Under one's wings
55. Actor Richard ___
56. Brawl
57. Tibetan monk
59. Hilo bird
60. Put down
62. Poetic yet

PUZZLE 137   Quotagram

Fill in the answers to the clues below. Then transfer the letters to the correspondingly numbered squares in the diagram. The completed diagram will contain a quotation.

1. Lineman
$\overline{33}\ \overline{45}\ \overline{38}\ \overline{10}\ \overline{19}\ \overline{43}$

2. Channel or horn
$\overline{25}\ \overline{11}\ \overline{17}\ \overline{42}\ \overline{29}\ \overline{27}\ \overline{6}$

3. Alfresco
$\overline{12}\ \overline{5}\ \overline{21}\ \overline{16}\ \overline{22}\ \overline{4}\ \overline{37}\ \overline{44}$

4. More robust
$\overline{31}\ \overline{9}\ \overline{39}\ \overline{14}\ \overline{48}\ \overline{24}\ \overline{1}\ \overline{18}\ \overline{26}$

5. Level
$\overline{2}\ \overline{28}\ \overline{7}\ \overline{32}\ \overline{46}\ \overline{15}\ \overline{40}$

6. Important
$\overline{13}\ \overline{20}\ \overline{36}\ \overline{30}\ \overline{34}\ \overline{23}\ \overline{3}$

7. Jackknife or swan
$\overline{41}\ \overline{47}\ \overline{8}\ \overline{35}$

DOUBLE TROUBLE   PUZZLE 138

Not really double trouble, but double fun! Solve this puzzle as you would a regular crossword, EXCEPT place one, two, or three letters in each box. The number of letters in each answer is shown in parentheses after its clue.

ACROSS

1. Legal thing (3)
3. Ranch employee (7)
7. Light meal (6)
10. Pretense (4)
11. Bigger (6)
12. Mix (4)
13. Constantinople (8)
15. Peruse (4)
16. Sulks (5)
17. Whet (7)
19. Steamboat inventor (6)
21. Chewy candy (7)
23. Stogie (5)
25. Roved (8)
28. Steal from (3)
29. Satiating (7)
31. Fishing pole (3)
32. End of the line (8)
34. Cake decorator (4)
35. Singer Osmond (5)
36. Beer mug (5)
38. Ripped (4)
40. Sugar tree (5)

42. Sports group (4)
44. Attic window (6)
47. Gold paint (4)
48. Supplant (7)
50. Dog's wagger (4)
51. Indian boat (5)
52. Navigates (6)
53. Conducted (3)

DOWN

1. Withstand (6)
2. Medicine man (6)
3. Neckline fold (6)
4. Armed conflict (3)
5. Garment holder (6)
6. Horrible (8)
7. Answer a request (7)
8. Terrace (5)
9. Swaggers (6)
14. Four pecks (6)
18. Lead writer (6)
20. Nasal accent (5)
21. Orange root vegetable (6)
22. Caution light (5)
24. Pungent bulb (6)
26. Mistake (5)
27. Actor Murphy (5)
29. Closing musical number (6)
30. Lifeless (5)
33. Kissing plant (9)
35. Estate house (5)
37. Money earned on money (8)
39. Commands (6)
40. Sorcery (5)
41. Blueprint (4)
43. Sufficient (5)
45. Solid element (5)
46. Annoyed (5)
49. High card (3)

Crossout Quote   PUZZLE 139

Cross out one letter in each box so that the remaining letters spell out a humorous quotation.

131

PUZZLE 140

ACROSS
1. Actress Britt
4. Seedy nightspot
8. Cougar
12. Summer beverage
13. Singles
14. Particle
15. Turkey cookers
17. Steak order
18. Grates
19. Pains
20. Baby elephant
22. Train
24. Sigorney Weaver film
26. Pose
27. Choreographer Fosse
30. Fifth U.S. president
32. Part of a century
34. Tee
35. Wily
37. Medicinal portions
38. Allude
40. "Gorillas in the ____"
41. Presents
44. Tag
46. Original garden
47. Playing the coquette
50. Want
51. Mrs. Kennedy
52. Dove's comment
53. Corn units
54. Had debts
55. In the past

DOWN
1. Deface
2. Commotion
3. Young horse
4. Periods
5. Incompetent
6. Poet's outputs
7. Double curve
8. Dry
9. Beehive State
10. Extra
11. Iowa city
16. More protected
19. Played the part
20. Recreation area
21. Century plant
23. Assist
25. Meddles
27. Cathedral
28. Pindarics
29. "____ Friends"
31. Gnome
33. Kohoutek, for one
36. "The ____ Wallpaper"
38. Splits
39. Hoist
41. Hackman or Wilder
42. Notion
43. Swerve
45. Reared
47. Away
48. Holiday potion
49. Infant's sound

PUZZLE 141

ACROSS
1. Mrs. Sprat's preference
4. Bric-a-____
8. Deep cut
12. Actor Ferrigno
13. "In ____ Land We Trust"
14. Caron role
15. On a winning streak
17. Redolence
18. Borscht ingredients
19. Mother ____
21. Fitting
23. Actor Wallach
24. Hotel employee
28. 1991 Super Bowl site
32. Era
33. Computer key
35. Limo, for one
36. Kind of pole
38. Greed
40. Ump's kin
42. Nationality suffix
43. Improved, weatherwise
47. Overweight
51. Decomposes
52. Ends
54. Lily plant
55. Asian range
56. "Alley ____"
57. Musical group
58. Secular
59. Utter

DOWN
1. Botch
2. Perfect
3. Cylinder
4. Profane person
5. Snitch
6. Actor Baldwin
7. Hiawatha's transport
8. Singer Estefan
9. Verdi opus
10. Plod slowly
11. Take on
16. List ender
20. Of a high frequency
22. Truck weight
24. Night flier
25. Self
26. Charter
27. Harper Valley gp.
29. 1101, to Caesar
30. ____-10 football
31. Exist
34. Night
37. Got the lead out
39. Singer McEntire
41. Wild
43. Seafood offering
44. "Damn Yankees" vamp
45. School on the Thames
46. Oscar ____ Renta
48. Sonny Shroyer role
49. Portico
50. Catch sight of
53. ____ tai

ACROSS

1. Ulster
5. Vapor
10. "Call Me ___"
15. Laundry
19. Wheel rod
20. Marsupial
21. "A Bell for ___"
22. Expressive dance
23. Actor in "The Birds"?
25. Singer in "Dames at Sea"?
27. Puts into office
28. Then: Fr.
30. Shoo!
31. Desire
32. Boutique
33. Siouan Indian
34. Love song
38. Boxing brothers
39. Inhabitant
43. Sky hunter
44. Employed
45. Duos
47. Hebrew judge
48. Greek contest
49. Adriatic wind
50. Mountain lakes
51. Scottish port
52. Jog
53. Songstress in "Cats"?
56. Author of "On the Beach"
57. Type of pie
59. Berets' locales
60. Greek philosopher
61. Longest French river
62. Playwright Joseph
63. Illinois city
64. Spread rumors
66. Cathay
67. Violent downpours
70. Banish
71. Lyricist for "Bambi"?
73. Baby food
74. Elmer's tormentor
75. Figure of speech
77. ___ does it!
78. "City of Kings"
79. Pindaric
80. Ushers
81. Flight path
83. Breadmaker
84. False testimony
86. Unreliable people
87. Nosy Parkers
88. Taj Mahal site
89. Spanish cloak
90. Monk's title
91. Mideast peninsula
93. Alaska town
94. Disliked people
99. Actor in "The Birds"?
101. Actress in "Duck Soup"?
103. Leave in print
104. River to the Rhone
105. Rent
106. About
107. Highland wear
108. Make as net
109. Moth larva
110. Summit

DOWN

1. Moslem judge
2. Draft beasts
3. Lackaday!
4. Pavilion
5. Glided on ice
6. Actress Marta
7. Dines
8. "The Greatest"
9. Sea cow
10. Big leagues
11. Worship
12. Morse code words
13. Dancer Miller
14. Ogres
15. ". . . that ___ am, there ye may be also"
16. Emanation
17. Bridge coup
18. Dried grass
24. Yucatan Indian
26. Church pictures
29. Master
32. Abraham's wife
33. Wotan
34. Plank
35. Debate
36. Anthropologist in "The Blackboard Jungle"?
37. Actor Chaney
38. Nativity
40. Explorer in "The Sea Gypsies"?
41. Cheer up
42. Dressed to the ___
44. Charger
45. Eucharist plate
46. Crafts
49. Puppeteer Bil
50. Reddish-brown
51. Large airport
53. Roman official
54. Garb
55. N.H. city
56. Chemise
58. Combines resources
60. Linger
62. Looks for bargains
63. Beach
64. Early jazz
65. Ooze out
66. Coagulate
67. Massenet opera
68. Lion trainer
69. Shadowboxes
72. Football referee
75. Extraordinary
76. Christian under Ottoman rule
78. Minstrel's song
80. Sweetener
81. Farm sound
82. Subject to taxation, in Britain
83. Trademark
85. Gaynor and Lennon
86. Foam
87. Supplication
89. Small metric lengths
90. Moat
91. Bristle
92. Thing
93. Snick-a-___
94. All-male
95. Brew coffee
96. Compos mentis
97. Gumbo
98. Look for
99. Seattle's zone: abbr.
100. Small land mass: abbr.
102. Med. test

PUZZLE 142

• ZOO'S WHO! •

PUZZLE 143   NUTTY

Here is a puzzle with more than the expected crossword challenge—and rewards. Each clue involves a pun or some form of nuttiness. Look out for traps! With a little practice you will soon catch on to these tricky clues and enjoy the extra challenge.

ACROSS

1. Use your head fore this
5. Who's where?
10. It can really tie you down
14. L of a way to go
15. And Latin monkey?
16. Poet Black
17. The rest of Gen. Robert E. Lee
18. Back beer for "The Student Prince"
19. We hope you don't
20. Like the seven-footer to the six-footer
22. They vant to be alone!
24. The tale of money
26. Eastern soldiers take responsibility
27. Sen. Kennedy's campaign slogan?
31. No! No! A thousand times no!
35. Be sad for Pearls
36. You don't believe I do
38. From sand bars to sushi bars
39. Aware of victory?
40. It's in your blood
41. Yard goods for a grass skirt
42. Employ ewes
43. Pays for
44. Lo-caleries
45. Darling, what a bore!
47. A rush of elephant jokes
49. Nine men on the ball
51. Lays the table with knife and spoon on the left and the fork on the right
52. Umpire made sick?
56. Anesthetic to a T
60. Pre-Marxist Red
61. Line for the aides
63. Conceited Greek
64. Ow! It's supposed to be soft
65. Something to remember money by
66. It's down the drain
67. ''
68. It's quite correct, in a literary sense
69. Knows Barbie's friend's Scottish

DOWN

1. It's blushing to its root
2. Avis tries harder—a rare bird!
3. Egghead in good shape
4. No sick party this (that's rich)
5. He's in the rat race
6. He follows you home
7. What all the fuss is about
8. Narrowly avoid a strike
9. It came in under the wire
10. Concerning a girl who's been careless about getting married
11. The beginning of the end
12. Pat-a-cake
13. Finnish tables?
21. Sounds corny!
23. How you carry on
25. Repel back
27. Regarding one boxing match
28. Uncommonly common horse
29. Up to here
30. Threatens and reads
32. Surrounded by incense
33. What the grain was before it growed
34. Grammar gets on one's nerves
37. Winds blew away part of the visitors
40. Let's not and say we did
41. What your wife red about your night out with the boys
43. Bobby was a mere shell of a man
44. Seem like a duck
46. Muddler for a frozen daiquiri
48. Oh, come now!
50. Make a clean sweep
52. Agents for the GOP
53. As Sam would say, he's a worm
54. It's pretty as a picture
55. Dam your finger, little boy
57. There's nothing, but it sounds complete
58. We've heard what goes on on those playing fields
59. Starting point on the road to riches
62. Iniquitous locale

The directions for solving are on page 26.

Key (Puzzle 144):

#		#	
1	O	14	
2		15	
3		16	
4	W	17	
5		18	
6		19	
7		20	
8		21	
9		22	
10		23	
11		24	
12	N	25	
13		26	

Grid (Puzzle 144):

1	17	10	6	7	26	■	1	18	25	26	15	19
16	■	22	■	17	■	14	■	26	■	23	■	11
16	11	1	■	1 O	4 W	12 N	26	3	■	26	24	26
14	■	12	■	12	■	19	■	11	■	11	■	12
15	13	14	17	■	11	26	20	1	8	19	26	3
26	■	9	■	16	■	11	■	1	■	■	■	5
■	11	26	6	7	14	11	26	2	26	12	19	■
18	■	■	8	■	7	■	21	■	26	■	9	
1	20	26	11	8	10	17	21	■	26	15	13	1
23	■	12	■	12	■	19	■	14	■	24	■	1
14	15	26	■	26	25	26	15	19	■	19	10	2
12	■	2	■	21	■	3	■	15	■	14	■	26
22	10	5	26	21	19	■	21	13	11	26	4	3

Key (Puzzle 145):

#		#	
1		14	
2		15	
3		16	
4		17	
5		18	
6	A	19	
7		20	
8		21	
9	X	22	
10		23	
11		24	
12		25	
13		26	

Grid (Puzzle 145):

24	6	19 A	16	24	20	3	■	11	23	19	26	20
26	■	9 X	■	3	■	6	20	23	■	12	■	3
12	4	3	20	20	■	8	■	19	5	23	6	3
■	14	■	■	8	20	3	1	10	■	20	■	6
17	3	22	14	6	■	17	■	3	■	17	14	7
4	■	14	■	7	26	3	20	12	■	13	■	■
14	10	6	19	■	1	■	3	■	19	25	19	6
■	26	■	■	1	3	22	17	15	■	19	■	26
19	12	5	■	18	■	14	■	17	14	4	3	12
21	■	14	■	26	13	14	6	7	■	■	2	■
19	6	16	3	12	■	12	■	20	19	6	2	3
6	■	24	■	3	20	20	■	3	■	19	■	22
17	6	26	21	15	■	3	22	15	26	2	22	15

PUZZLE 146

ACROSS

1. Gold leaf
5. Convulsive breath
9. Assist
13. Chance
17. Aroma
18. October gem
19. Butter substitute
20. Opera highlight
21. Not any
22. Actor Lugosi
23. Outfits
24. "___ Tread on Me"
25. Shine
27. Infernal potentate
29. Peculiar
31. Playwright Stoppard
33. ___ Plaines
34. Deface
35. More precipitous
39. Round Table title
41. "L.A. ___"
42. Coach Shula
45. Frigid
46. Bath vessel
48. Four-door auto
50. Yearn
51. First floating zoo
52. Science room
54. Bounder
55. Fragment
56. Cozy home
58. Chastised
60. Stopped marching
61. At any time
63. Jar cover
64. Gambler's destination
65. Formed
68. Pullman car
70. Tip
74. Boundary
75. River, in Tijuana
76. Short swim
77. Spanish aunt
78. Like the Gobi
79. May or June
81. Baseball's Williams
83. Camping shelter
84. Join in matrimony
85. In what way?
86. America's uncle
88. Peas and beans
90. Vitality
91. ___ Angeles
93. Pallid
94. Said a poem
98. Redolent wood
100. Even
104. Astronaut Shepard
105. Suddenly brighter star
107. Wicked
109. Lose color
110. Deep mud
111. Snare
112. Bicarbonate of ___
113. Takes advantage of
114. Sajak and Summerall
115. Lucid
116. Three, at cards
117. Camera eye

DOWN

1. Oriental bell
2. Graven image
3. Solitary
4. Negotiated
5. Lump
6. Imitates
7. Mixed greens
8. Dishes
9. Antler
10. Actor Wallach
11. Lower limbs
12. "The ___ Always Rings Twice"
13. Navigational device
14. Potential steel
15. Croon
16. Actress Jackson
26. Floor washer
28. In its present condition
30. Uncooked
32. Encountered
35. Read quickly
36. Wrenched
37. Some lodge members
38. Governor
40. Ebbed
41. Stripling
42. Food regimen
43. Single time
44. Require
47. Saloon
49. Mom and ___
50. Barnstormer
53. Votes
55. "Peter ___"
57. Lukewarm
58. Garden plot
59. Make a knot in
60. "And I Love ___"
62. Horse doctor
64. Drive away
65. Cabbage dish, for short
66. "This Gun for ___"
67. In the center of
68. Moral lapse
69. Cherry stone
71. List entry
72. Queue
73. Makes lace
75. Tier of seats
79. Seconds
80. Golfer Irwin
82. Morning moisture
83. Melodic
85. Strike
87. Humble
89. "My ___ Sal"
90. Grape plants
92. Enjoy the taste of
94. Inclined walkway
95. Lamb's pen name
96. Shopping basket
97. "I Married ___"
98. Sleeveless coat
99. Be carried
101. Flower jar
102. Actress Barbara ___
103. Not as much
106. Moving truck
108. Deposit, as eggs

PUZZLE 147

ACROSS
1. Sauna
5. Work hard
9. Far down
12. ___ Minor
13. Govern
14. In the past
15. One from Providence
18. European capital
19. Looked at
20. Log abodes
23. Scarlet
25. Diva's song
26. Dog or cat
27. For
30. Pittsburgh native
34. Doleful
35. Render money
36. Stake
37. Infant food
38. "My ___ Sam"
40. Food-stealing bird
43. Breathe heavily
44. Those from Madison
50. Broke bread
51. Leather strap
52. Sea eagle
53. Cot
54. Defeat
55. Carnival attraction

DOWN
1. Saloon
2. Hardwood
3. Spanish uncle
4. Roman emperor
5. Cuts
6. Yorkshire river
7. Under the weather
8. Meadow
9. Woman
10. Double curve
11. Sentence component
16. Very long time
17. Mr. Buntline
20. Tams
21. Region
22. Restrict
23. Accelerate
24. Greek letter
26. Work busily
27. Liquid measure
28. Appraise
29. Unique thing
31. Health resort
32. Snappish bark
33. More disagreeable
37. Footwear
38. Pious person
39. Tourist haven
40. Use a mop
41. High flier
42. Owned previously
43. Greek letters
45. Sphere
46. Born
47. Three: prefix
48. Gridiron man
49. Perceive

PUZZLE 148

ACROSS
1. Graduate's gown
5. Landers and Sheridan
9. Be in debt
12. "Roots" author Haley
13. Expression of disdain
14. Pod seed
15. Cleaning brush
18. Actor Harrison
19. Elephants' great teeth
20. Imposter
23. Dock
25. Bit of information
26. ___ as pie
27. Lyricist Gershwin
30. Sanitation worker
33. Sunbather's aim
34. Go to the polls
35. Long hike
36. Itches
37. Lean-tos
38. Remove fleece from
41. Become semisolid
42. Housekeeper's machine
48. ___ aboard!
49. Hurting
50. So long
51. Foot part
52. Identical
53. Dutch cheese

DOWN
1. English WWII heroes: abbr.
2. Comedian Olsen
3. Actress Arthur
4. Ultra
5. Highest point
6. Neither's partner
7. Give a head signal
8. Sleep, slangily
9. Chooses
10. Paycheck period, for some
11. Rabbit's big features
16. That woman
17. California's Big ___
20. Boxer's weapon
21. ___ boy!
22. Songwriter Jerome
23. Treaties
24. Key
26. College on the Thames
27. Concerning
28. Actress Donna
29. Flat-bottomed boats
31. Himalayan peak
32. Olympics entrant
36. Chatter
37. Notice
38. Beat it!
39. Saint's aura
40. Author Gardner
41. Actress Verdon
43. Haul
44. ___ Lanka
45. Flat
46. Greek letter
47. Ewe's mate

PUZZLE 149

• TOUR JAPAN •

ACROSS
1. "Peanuts" expletive
5. Hurled
9. Poet
13. Close forcefully
17. Vim
18. Baseball's Matty
19. Akron's state
20. Cylinder
21. Two-wheeler
22. Couple
23. Beverages
24. Burden
25. Oriental rite
28. Petty quarrels
29. Nanny's child
30. Be in debt
31. "___ Are There"
32. Louvre, e.g.: Fr.
35. Oriental sites for rites
42. State firmly
43. October's gemstone
44. Field mouse
45. Medical gp.
46. Jacket type
47. Lendl of tennis
48. Conch
50. Switchblade
51. Nara lute
53. Seaside
54. French square
55. Hubbub
56. Tangle
57. Chatter
58. Actress Lisa ____
61. Flies high
62. Feudal warrior of Japan
66. African succulent
67. Frankie of song
68. Soccer star
69. Monterey Bay fort
70. Long, narrow inlet
71. Outwit
72. Classify
73. Type of wrestling
74. Tokyo stage show
78. Surfeits
79. Pro
80. Electrically charged atom
81. Carney
82. Interlace
85. Charmers of the Ginza
90. Marriage symbol
91. Lather
93. Emanation
94. Polly, to Tom Sawyer
96. "___ in Love with Amy"
97. Frontiersman Wyatt
98. Trim
99. Malay sailing boat
100. Rend
101. Ontario Indian
102. Cabbagelike plant
103. Stitched down

DOWN
1. Historic Johnny
2. Dismounted
3. Appropriate
4. Stealthy one
5. Wearing a mantle
6. Wing-shaped
7. French silk
8. Confusion
9. ". . . your old gray ___ . . ."
10. Nautical call
11. Apparatus
12. Two, in Toluca
13. Plug
14. Moon goddess
15. Border on
16. Jumble
26. French business: abbr.
27. Admit
28. "___ Enchanted Evening"
31. Holler
32. Charts
33. Eye part
34. Joint
35. Overpass
36. Chinese dynasty
37. Open to view
38. Tinware
39. "Cowardly Lion" man
40. Arab potentate
41. Be thrifty
43. Hot spot
47. "___ True?" (Brenda Lee song)
48. English county
49. "Bonanza" character
50. "Elephant Boy" star
52. French thought
53. Stately bird
54. Arrived
56. Linen
57. High wind
58. Hayloft site
59. Potpourri
60. Actor Beery
61. Levantine ketch
62. Bristle
63. Overwhelm
64. Henri's weapon
65. Solemn vows
67. Solitary
68. Actress Dawber
71. Clock dial
72. Search feverishly
73. Old Persian despots
75. Warning sign
76. French seaport
77. Louis XIV
78. ___ Lanka
81. Wide open
82. Run about busily
83. Chardonnay
84. Ancient Peruvian
85. Keen, to a Scot
86. Sinuous dance
87. Seed covering
88. Beguile
89. Aspen's delight
91. Dry, as rose
92. Gondolier's need
95. Sunbathe

138

PUZZLE 150

ACROSS

1. Road distance
5. Avoid
9. Pardon me!
13. Leave stranded
17. Qatar native
18. Apple center
19. Conservative
20. Redolence
21. Unbeliever
24. Leander's love
25. Terminus
26. Roused
27. Strong brew
28. Lessee
30. Badge metal
31. Brad
33. Legume
34. Author Anya ___
37. Mix
38. Stage successfully
42. First-rate
43. Shade tree
44. Quite a few
45. ___ Khayyam
46. Secondhand
47. Look here!
48. Work crew
49. Derogatory
50. Scorned
52. Slithered
53. Elegant sofa
54. Billiards stick
55. Prickly
56. I told you so!
57. Peeled in chips
60. Periodic current
61. Site of Arthur's court
65. Rustic
66. Birthday sweet
67. Female pig
68. Rational
69. Actress Moran
70. Strop
71. Chill
72. Seasoning
73. Worthless things
75. Oaf
76. Actress Sophia ___
77. Corridor
78. Sect
79. Excavation
80. Sickness
83. The ___ of 1812
84. Shape
86. Dawdle
89. Done
90. Liquor personified
94. Fibber
95. Hodgepodge
96. Remove
97. Floundering
98. Small whirlpool
99. Rim
100. College official
101. Bog fuel

DOWN

1. Created
2. Press
3. Praise
4. Flow away
5. Descendant
6. Toot
7. With pressing need
8. Fishing snare
9. Coral island
10. Domicile
11. Important age
12. Whodunit
13. Opportunity seizer
14. Thought
15. Bereft
16. Run briskly
22. String
23. Filament
29. Listener
30. Everyone
32. Goal
33. Shot sound
34. Tater
35. Gaelic
36. Stadium layer
37. Germ
38. Confection
39. Exclude
40. Grow dim
41. Without charge
44. Pine Tree State
47. Pay attention
48. Dance well
49. Joint
51. Affair of honor
52. Large nail
53. "Pygmalion" playwright
55. Be upright
57. Mr. Flintstone
58. Bait
59. Recital selection
61. Open to both sexes
62. Den of thieves
63. Formerly
64. Adolescent
66. Indifferent
67. Unpunished
70. Chaplain
71. Sick
72. Slick with mud
74. Roll of money
75. Street side
78. Indian boat
79. Clean feathers
80. Burrowing animal
81. Eager
82. Show the way
83. Liberal
85. Spanish jar
86. Misplace
87. Territory
88. Pesky insect
91. Ancient
92. Say further
93. Bottle top

PUZZLE 151

• FAMOUS AMERICANS •

ACROSS

1. Tamarisk
5. Dried up
10. Singer Campbell
14. Char
15. Winged
16. Anchor line
17. Nixon's 1960 running mate: 3 wds.
20. And so forth: abbr.
21. Sea eagle
22. More facile
23. Like some peanuts
25. Bible book
26. Antiquity, of yore
27. Danube feeder
28. ___ a girl!
31. Daniel of the frontier
34. Pintail duck
35. Greek portico
36. American composer: 2 wds.
39. Drysdale and Knotts
40. I'm all ___!
41. Cotton thread
42. Grads-to-be: abbr.
43. "___ Dalloway" (Woolf)
44. Fr. pronoun
45. Mine entrance
47. Crowed
51. Like some staircases
54. Salamander
55. Coach Parseghian
56. "Evangeline" poet: 2 wds.
60. Silver-screen dog
61. Tennessee ___ Ford
62. Otherwise
63. Meadow sounds
64. Act portion
65. Watches

DOWN

1. Fire residue
2. Canines
3. Jousting weapon
4. Prove human
5. Hallowed
6. African antelope
7. Mortar beater
8. WWII region
9. Sensed
10. Net's source
11. New Jersey town
12. Rim
13. ___-do-well
18. "Old ___"
19. Indian column
24. Horne and others
25. Templeton and Waugh
27. Moreno and Khayyam
28. Followers: suffix
29. Ring
30. Tag or white
31. Garden spots
32. Fragrance
33. Admits
34. Chic
35. From Uri, e.g.
37. Agnes and Cecil B.
38. Certain ester
44. Colombian export
45. Tapestry
46. Sandra ___ O'Connor
47. Start
48. Running total
49. Irregularly notched
50. V.P. Charles G. ___
51. Fake
52. Mexican currency
53. Division word
57. Grampus
58. Wind pt.
59. Singer Peggy

PUZZLE 152   CHAIN WORDS

Join the 12 words given below into a chain. Pick one word to start; the word that follows will do one of the following: 1. rhyme with it, 2. have the same meaning, 3. be an anagram of it (same letters in a different order), or 4. have one different letter. Work forward and backward to complete the chain. The first and last words will not connect. For example, the following is a chain: State, Great, Large, Lager, Later.

Cling	Truck	Write
Stick	Lower	Tower
Thing	Truce	Night
Cruet	Stuck	Wrote

ACROSS

1. Opera song
5. Mighty particle
9. Selects
13. Eye part
14. Make merry
16. Comedian Wilson
17. Tennis-ace Wilander
18. Exchange
19. Docile
20. Pitcher part
22. Pickens et al.
24. X
25. Anger
27. Competition
29. Orb
32. Here's partner
33. Stout
34. Grin
38. Type of beer
42. Hop
44. Pilot
46. Shower-wall piece
47. Adhesive strips
49. Goes it alone
51. Train part
52. Was ahead
54. Barrels
56. Nuns
60. College official
61. Explosive material: abbr.
62. Serenity
64. Pilfered
68. At a distance
70. Position
72. Sacred figure
73. Depend
74. Judgment
75. Stomped
76. Place for clothes?
77. Fume
78. Barks

DOWN

1. Gifts to the poor
2. Gather in
3. Toward the middle of
4. Convince
5. Creative work
6. Succinct
7. Track-shaped
8. Doc
9. Frequently, to a writer
10. Dish
11. Clocks
12. Depleted
15. Yellow color
21. Repairs a roof
23. Snooty one
26. Precious ones
28. Taunt
29. Experienced sailor
30. Excuse
31. Pile
35. "___ a Small World"
36. Lion constellation
37. Conger
39. Wedding missiles
40. Attired
41. Towel word
43. Animal skin
45. Came to one's feet
48. Percolate
50. Mineral springs
53. Treat with medication
55. Thing
56. Set out
57. Deduce
58. Trite
59. Satiates
60. Thickly populated
63. Is unable to
65. Gumbo
66. Ring
67. Completes
69. Bread grain
71. ___ point

Escalator

Place the answer to clue 1 in the first space, drop a letter, and arrange the remaining letters to answer clue 2. Drop another letter and arrange the remaining letters to answer clue 3. The first dropped letter goes into the box to the left of space 1, and the second dropped letter goes into the box to the right of space 3. Follow this pattern for each row in the diagram. When completed, the letters on the left and right, reading down, will spell related words or a phrase.

1. Trolls
2. Presages
3. Billfold items
4. Grab
5. Kind of train
6. Summon
7. Records
8. Leases
9. Take five
10. Self-defense method
11. Collector
12. Lachrymose drop
13. Fight back
14. Sacraments
15. Agitate
16. Bakers' needs
17. Corset parts
18. Russian news agency

PUZZLE 155

ACROSS
1. Append
4. Nearly: abbr.
7. Tour arranger's group: abbr.
11. Fourth planet
13. Golf score
14. Dance part
15. Norse god
16. Game bird
18. Uncover
20. Spy
21. French fashion magazine
22. Yards needed for a first down
23. Sobs
25. Oater
29. Female gametes
30. Pop
31. Durocher or Tolstoy
32. Firsts of the month?
35. Arab ruler
37. Chunk of eternity
38. King of Norway
39. Heavenly bread
41. Narrate
44. Beauty pageants, e.g.
46. Harrow's rival
47. Comic Johnson
48. In addition
49. Lily type
50. Ownership paper
51. Japanese coin
52. Author John ____ Passos

DOWN
1. Roman god of love
2. Miami's county
3. Road to the garage
4. Jonathan or Idared
5. Scrooge's word
6. Administered to
7. Agree
8. Kenton or Getz
9. Canvas shelter
10. Liable
12. Fishhook adjunct
17. Bronze and stone, e.g.
19. Oerter and Jolson
23. Type of jazz
24. Fred Astaire's daughter
25. Used to be
26. Raised
27. Ruff's mate
28. Neither's partner
30. Linda Evans series
33. Made an impression on
34. Top-drawer
35. Pub drink
36. Cobs and drakes
38. Actor Welles
39. Song from "Mondo Cane"
40. Prefix for before
42. Take-out words
43. Son of Seth
44. Heel
45. Foot digit

PUZZLE 156

ACROSS
1. Congeals
5. Had obligations
9. Talk session
12. Coagulate
13. "Mask" actress
14. ____ Marie Saint
15. Medicinal plant
16. Huge
18. Kind of split
20. Chimney dirt
21. Disorder
23. Whittled
26. Oversight
30. "Kiss Me, ____"
31. Edge
32. Up to this point
34. Call ____ day
35. Tattle
37. Pertaining to a country
39. Long tales
41. Convenes
42. "____ the Woods"
44. Improvised
48. Play about Siam, with "The"
51. Ballet dancer Spessivtseva
52. Actress Plumb
53. Opposite of dele
54. Close-by
55. Actor Beatty
56. ____ Roman Empire
57. Florida county

DOWN
1. Strikebreaker
2. Actress Logan
3. Footballer Al ____
4. Gives off vapors
5. Event
6. Thing Horton heard
7. Snaky fish
8. Sag
9. Hold back
10. Actress Haddad
11. Chum
17. Drench
19. Certain Scottish lake
22. Divans
24. Singer James
25. Bargain
26. Spheres
27. "____ 18" (Uris novel)
28. Fantasized
29. Christmas scene
33. Actress Moreno
36. Gun sound
38. Donny or Marie
40. Stow
43. Aware of
45. Petition
46. Hoople's oath
47. Venture
48. Boxer Norton
49. "____ Got No Strings"
50. Singer Shannon

ACROSS
1. "Moonstruck" star
5. Ego
9. Seaweed
13. Cicatrix
17. Ali ____
18. Seed covering
19. Oceans
20. Affectation
21. Baker's bit of monkey business?
25. Concerning
26. Brother of Eris
27. Heaps
28. Islet
29. Thunderstrikes
30. Cooling device
31. Start of a magical phrase
34. Cabbage salad
35. First fratricide
37. Double curve
40. Cupid
41. Clever
42. Mountain pools
43. Misfortune
44. Grow drowsy
45. Lots
46. Boston athlete
47. Composer Bartok
48. Reduce the severity of
50. Spanker et al.
51. Nero's alleged crime
52. Wyeth's forte
53. Treat for Fido's birthday?
55. Seance sound
56. Yorkshire pals
58. Mr. Flynn
59. Falsehood
62. Feel yesterday's exercise
63. Actress Uta
64. Chow
66. Swee' ____
67. Anger
68. Fracas
69. Honey-tongued
70. Assembly
71. French sea
72. Magnetite et al.
73. Zip
74. Certain coifs, for short
75. Greek vowel
76. Buck
77. Lend an ____
78. "Batman" actor
80. Tater
81. Eatery
84. Feature film for Miss Piggy?
90. Giant
91. Three-banded armadillo
92. Asian range
93. One
94. Junior-high graduate
95. Record
96. Tardy
97. Sawbucks

DOWN
1. Toronto network
2. Sunk fence: hyph.
3. Bard's black
4. Mangy grayhound?
5. Like brine
6. Age
7. Ignited
8. Road leading to Rover?
9. Hearth residue
10. Island garlands
11. Actress Rita
12. Viper
13. Utensil
14. Codger
15. Inquires
16. King of Spain
22. Munson et al.
23. Sloop hands
24. Tribes
29. Political partner
30. Huckleberry
31. Skater Brinker
32. Melville work
33. Role for Marlin Brando?
34. Moral transgression
35. Make watertight
36. Surface
37. Publication for Lamb Chop?
38. By oneself
39. Dramatist O'Casey
41. Pale
42. Court scene
45. New York nine
46. Philosopher Francis
47. Fiber food
49. Corner
50. Toot
51. Omani, e.g.
53. Famous positive thinker
54. Yens
56. Mangle
57. Land measure
59. Elsa's offspring
60. Paper measure
61. Weirs
63. Zeus's Mrs.
64. Pleased
65. Rend
68. "Be prepared," e.g.
69. Bargain in antelopes?
70. Sea swallow gathering?
73. Astound
74. Twosome
75. Ruhr Valley city
76. Steeple
77. Singer Rabbitt
78. Carry on
79. Rochester's Jane
80. Exchange
82. Anglo-Saxon drudge
83. Horse leash
84. Speck
85. Jack Sprat's no-no
86. Health club
87. Neighbor of Tenn.: abbr.
88. Styron's Turner
89. Rds.: abbr.

PUZZLE 158

ACROSS

1. Emily or Wiley
5. Certain trains
8. Trepidation
12. Bang
16. Eternally
17. Embouchure
18. Relative by marriage
20. Actress Yothers
21. Nirvana
23. Imaginary
25. Coasters
26. Canal or hat
28. Charged particle
29. Coin for Louis IX
31. Depend
32. Uncertain
36. Game fish
39. Breaker
41. Magistrate of Venice
42. Formerly named
43. Old English letter
44. St. Peter's portals
46. Actor/dancer Dailey
47. According to
48. Salamanders
49. Esau's grandson
50. Annoyance
51. Egyptian monarch, for short
53. Wears out
55. Classifies
56. Damsel
57. Woes
58. Dory
59. Slow musical movement
61. Part of NOW
62. Capital of Marne
65. Eye part
66. Distort
67. Heavyweight boxer
68. Ova
69. ____ Amarna
70. Songwriter's district
73. Abraham's nephew
74. Greek's seventh letter
75. Wallet stuffers
76. Grownup
77. Actress May Oliver
78. Echo
80. Military assistant
81. Tippler
83. Map abbr.
84. Governor Ella ____
86. "____ Life Is It Anyway?"
90. Alice's reverie
94. Green-flash time
96. ____ Morrow Lindbergh
97. Composer Erik ____
98. Still, poetically
99. "Pinocchio" goldfish
100. Achiever
101. The birds and the ____
102. Members of AMA
103. Playwright O'Casey

DOWN

1. Invigorates, with up
2. Elliptical
3. Dry
4. Certain winds
5. Hebrew judge
6. Mispronounce
7. Certain fishermen
8. At last!
9. Adversary
10. Peace nobelist Myrdal (1982)
11. Actress Dawn Chong
12. Prefix for close
13. Actress Ullmann
14. Actress Sue ____ Langdon
15. Blemish
19. Old washer adjunct
22. Milit. award
24. Lymph ____
27. Dudley Do-Right's love
30. Handy
32. Specks
33. Hades
34. Monster
35. Camp sights
36. Nib
37. King of the Huns
38. Utopias
40. Scottish inventor
41. "____ at Sea"
44. Prefix for rock
45. Bridge expert
50. Natatorium
52. Jazz bookings
53. Florida seaport
54. Wrath
55. Frightful
57. Body of troops
58. Ropes attached to clews
59. Metric quart
60. Mountain ridge
61. Ebbed
62. Summon
63. Showdown time
64. Bristle
66. Victors
67. Forage grass
70. All, to Monique
71. Water nymphs
72. Appends
77. Business standards
79. Law's partner
80. Attorney Becker on "L.A. Law"
82. Hooter
84. Event's total receipts
85. Had creditors
87. Leer
88. Mets' stadium, once
89. Harrow's rival
90. Roll of money
91. Lennon's wife
92. Opposite of SSW
93. Science workshop, for short
95. Officeholders

ACROSS

1. Clasp hard
5. Old saying
10. "Hot ___" Houlihan
14. Cager Archibald and others
16. Eliot's Marner
17. Takes the rind off
18. Spoil a plan: 3 wds.
21. Kind of bread
22. Singleton
23. Peachlike fruit
29. Prevaricator
33. Nose type
34. Spanish painter
38. Hawkeye's portrayer
39. Soft-drink source: 2 wds.
41. Kiln
42. Cots
43. Cool drink
44. Made a lap
46. Parade unit
47. Jack who ate no fat
50. Of birth
52. Theda of the silents
53. Singer Campbell
54. Take up again
55. Fitzgerald and Raines
57. Endure
59. Honest president
61. Singer Torme
63. Snout
66. Mideast ruler
67. Thick-skinned fruit
70. Greek war god
71. In a fitting manner
72. Gladden
73. Hospital shout
74. Make believe
76. Greek letter
78. First mom
81. Some golden-haired gals: 2 wds.
92. Lion's family
93. Knot again
94. Rope loop
95. Assists
96. Clever
97. Fret

DOWN

1. African antelope
2. Chat
3. "___ Magic"
4. Equal
5. Bat wood
6. Gambler's cube
7. Chicken ___ king: 2 wds.
8. Open space
9. Sixth sense
10. Frothy fabric
11. Mr. Gershwin
12. Each
13. Fast flier
15. Miss Piggy's home
17. Write
19. Oolong, e.g.
20. Building site
24. Urge
25. Play part
26. "___ Believer" (Monkees): 2 wds.
27. Put up fruit
28. Burden
29. Chemist's place
30. Seine sight
31. Tots up
32. Bronx cheer
34. Flip one's lid: 2 wds.
35. Egg-shaped
36. Itch
37. Also
39. American grape
40. Hybrid citrus fruit
45. Lofty
48. Operated
49. Zone
51. ___ Aviv
54. Train track
56. Kind
57. Evil
58. Ostrich's cousin
60. At any time
61. Chum
62. First garden
64. Briny
65. Superlative suffix
68. Bullring shout
69. Feline
74. British bar
75. Dolores ___ Rio
76. Little boys
77. Reverence
79. Wernher ___ Braun
80. Son of Seth
81. Health resort
82. Three: prefix
83. Free of
84. Historic time
85. Crimson
86. Map abbr.
87. Sharp bark
88. Play the ponies
89. Period
90. Wind direction: abbr.
91. Stitch

PUZZLE 160

ACROSS

1. Cheese eaters
5. Winged
10. Deadly snakes
14. Culture medium
15. North African capital
16. Spanish soprano Lucrezia ___
17. Lug
18. Wagner specialty
19. Border
20. Bauxite, e.g.
21. Skips
22. Derogatory
23. ___ Heights
25. Assaulted
26. Uses a ladder to wed
28. Cereal-grain husk
30. Japanese temple entrance
31. Presently
32. Stirs
36. Precipitate heavily
39. Quality of being: suff.
40. Bigwig
41. Synonym man
42. College building, for short
43. Greek messenger of the gods
44. Mint's cousin
48. Old Testament prophet
49. Wall hanging
50. Disagreements
52. Male feline
55. Bar order
56. Abash
57. South American marmoset
58. To ___ (exactly)
59. Of punishment
60. Punta del ___
61. Smaller
62. Words for hymns
63. Old Testament prophet

DOWN

1. ___ Grosso
2. "Young Frankenstein" character
3. Explicit
4. Before, to bards
5. Odors
6. Rabbit fur
7. Aid in wrongdoing
8. Gobs
9. Greek letter
10. Get ___ out of
11. Ferber novel
12. Overly proper person
13. Located
21. Obtained from oil
22. Heat producer
24. Suppose
25. German novelist Thomas ___
26. Raison d'___
27. Bank offering
28. Bust
29. Reddish color
31. Move
32. Worship
33. Assertion without proof
34. Kind of molding
35. Fast transports
37. Off-balance
38. Garb
42. Negative prefix
43. Hilton and Hyatt, e.g.
44. Junta
45. Narrow mountain ridge
46. Baobab et al.
47. Face part
48. Biblical villain
50. Son of Noah
51. Window part
53. "Beetle Bailey" dog
54. Van der Rohe
56. Mineral spring
57. Oolong

PUZZLE 161   SPINWHEEL

This puzzle works two ways, outward and inward. Place the answers to the clues in the diagram beginning at the corresponding numbers.

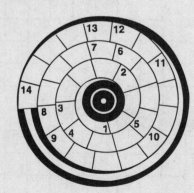

OUTWARD

1. Blew one's top
3. Land measure
5. Sailfish's pride
6. The main
8. Making sense
10. In the company of
12. Good-natured

INWARD

14. Reclined
13. Breakfast food
11. Like gypsies
9. Arm bones
7. Evergreen
4. Annapolis student
2. Chaste

146

ACROSS

1. Wine-press residue
5. Ditto
9. ___ van der Rohe
13. Chicago team
18. Electric lamp inspector
19. Copied
20. Crush
21. Arabian gazelle
22. Judy's wonderful mother?
26. Shipwreck recovery
27. Port in Egypt
28. Pompous
29. Columnist Landers
30. ___ and feathered
32. Twelvemonth
33. Wander
37. Epoch
38. Take care of
42. Corrode
43. Loni's VCR collection?
49. Favorable
50. Mania of the '60s
51. Pelt
52. Chemical prefix
53. ___-ling
55. Great times
57. Minus
59. Certain boat: abbr.
60. Steep slope
62. ___-Magnon
63. Cozily warm
65. Alejandro, crossing the Rio Mississippi?
72. Snigglers
73. Tantrum
74. Ace place
75. Bertha Cool and Donald ___
78. Amino acid
79. Do a party
81. Sea birds
82. Porter
83. Brown tint
85. Son of Uranus
88. Metaphysical being
89. Mae's courtship?
93. Golly!
94. U.S. Grant's opponent
95. "___ will be..."
96. River barges
99. Town in New Hampshire
102. Wages
105. Craggy hill
106. Believing
109. Fix
110. Subtlety
114. Jane's swingers?
117. Town in British Columbia
118. Needle case
119. Reagan's Attorney General
120. Verve
121. Thin, crisp fabric
122. 5-time presidential candidate
123. Let it stand
124. Long narrative

DOWN

1. Tatamis
2. Turkish title
3. Spool
4. Neckpiece
5. Dimensions
6. "___ Blue"
7. Intelligent group
8. Mystery writer's award
9. Medea, e.g.
10. Officeholders
11. Old English letters
12. ___ tern
13. Stabilizer
14. Province of Ethiopia
15. Candy striper
16. Study
17. Artful
19. Industry bigwig
23. "The ___ Love"
24. Stuck in mud
25. Position of a golf ball
30. Effective provisions of a law
31. Tapering seam
33. Seven musicians
34. Louisiana county
35. Posthaste
36. Arabic letter
39. Heroic poetry
40. Scriptures passage
41. Eskers
44. "___ Restaurant"
45. Argentine river
46. Legislator
47. McEnroe's ex
48. Centaur slain by Hercules
50. Excluded
54. Actor Kaplan
56. Missing labor leader
58. Steps over fences
61. Furry
63. Spuds
64. Belgian river
66. American orator
67. Muscat
68. Town in Alaska
69. Misplay, at cards
70. Sander
71. Agreements
75. Actor Bert
76. Century plant
77. Whimper
79. Letting it all hang out
80. Boisterous
84. Practitioners: suffix
86. And not
87. Former
90. Wired messages
91. Times of success
92. Actress Gretchen
97. Cooked
98. Diving birds
100. Crew
101. Signed off
103. "___ Rib"
104. Thesaurus compiler
106. Talon
107. Italian artist
108. Head: Fr.
110. Symbol of power
111. Room: Sp.
112. Hitch
113. Writer Ferber
114. Satisfied sounds
115. Massage
116. Plumbing joint

PUZZLE 162

• FILM DISCOVERY •

PUZZLE 163

ACROSS
1. Studio stand
6. Uncooked
9. Frighten
10. Get to
12. Dried plum
13. Chosen few
14. Urge
15. Untidy
16. Smile upon
20. Depart
21. Hang
23. Write, in a way
25. Kid
28. Pouncing jump
29. Stop
31. Worry's yield
32. Nimble
33. Understand
34. ____ up on (reviews)

DOWN
1. Catch sight of
2. Farm measure
3. Finnish bath
4. White-tailed eagle
5. Actor Marvin
6. Lift
7. Behaves
8. Curds and ____
10. Take away
11. Football team
17. Dive
18. Hound
19. Criticism
21. Because
22. Exhaust
23. And
24. Hold sway
26. Small landmass
27. Busy insects
29. Taxi
30. Conceit

PUZZLE 164

ACROSS
1. Baseball club
4. Thick slice
8. Texas city
12. Honest ____ Lincoln
13. Poi source
14. Scent
15. Congeal
16. ____ impasse: 2 wds.
17. Dressing gown
18. Winter tinkler: 2 wds.
21. Fourth letter
22. Sun-dried brick
26. Clock reading
29. Steals from
32. Fishing pole
33. Greek god of love
34. Opposite of WSW
35. House cleaner
36. I love: Latin
37. False god
38. Confederate
39. Estate house
41. Follower: suffix
43. Woodworkers
49. Bed board
52. Roof edge
53. Atlas chart
54. Doughnut center
55. Region
56. Skating surface
57. Aid (a criminal)
58. Make coffee, e.g.
59. Sen. Kennedy's nickname

DOWN
1. Purses
2. Cain's brother
3. Part of TV
4. Theater platform
5. Soaped
6. Desert dweller
7. Skeleton part
8. "The ____ According to Garp"
9. Commotion
10. Corn center
11. Native metal
19. March date
20. ____ Vegas
23. Evangelist Roberts
24. Seethe
25. Small whirlpool
26. Sports group
27. "____ la Douce"
28. Earth's satellite
30. Yoko ____
31. Person of faith
35. Marshal Dillon
37. Writer Levin
40. Eight musicians
42. Move furtively
44. Gather a crop
45. Remove peel
46. Give off
47. Marathon
48. Went fast
49. ____ Na Na
50. Tennis stroke
51. Strong beer

148

ACROSS

1. Like some chances
5. Compulsions
10. In a bad mood
15. On ____ (without client commitment)
19. Famous spy
20. E.T.'s word
21. Comedian Jack ____
22. Burrito's kin
23. Revival meeting word
24. Scans
25. Timepiece
27. Distributes
29. Crosses
31. Firebug's crime
32. Not very often
33. Layers
34. Artist Chagall
36. Break a fast
37. Wide
38. P.T. Barnum's find
42. Gambol
45. Indistinct
46. Grows weary
47. ". . . ____ gloom of night"
48. Electrified particles
49. Sidewalk edges
50. Cats' sounds
51. Father
52. "____ Kapital"
53. Bizarre
54. Caregiver
55. Wild ____ chase
56. Stealthily
58. Numbers game
59. Rotated
60. Harness part
61. Actress Davis
62. Price
63. King's chair
66. Breath fresheners
67. Pace
71. Downpours
72. Sailor blouse
73. Mrs. Phil Donahue
74. Is in possession of
75. Tacks on
76. Weathercocks
77. Baseball's Ernie ____
78. Porgy's love
79. Wheel part
80. Alluring woman
81. Rural buildings
82. Driving hazard
83. Catcher's equipment
85. Worthless
86. Big bird
87. Leslie Caron role
88. Faxes
89. Decanters
92. "____ Is Born"
95. Anorak
96. Accused of a crime
98. Heraldry interest
101. School rank
103. Bigfoot's kin?
104. Fashion magazine
105. Pueblo material
106. Places for icicles
107. Author Hunter
108. Vended
109. ____, Jose!
110. Don Adams role
111. Storage tower

DOWN

1. Pahlavi, for one
2. Fernando or Lorenzo
3. Goddess of peace
4. Unthinking
5. Remove from home
6. Catarrh
7. Mohair source
8. Movie's last word
9. Meetings
10. In the direction of
11. Gets wages
12. Slaloms
13. Scale notes
14. Thus far
15. Shirt stiffener
16. Sajak and Caddell
17. There: It.
18. Actress Mindy ____
26. Toad features
28. Wyoming's neighbor: abbr.
30. ____ moss
33. Clan
34. Dudley or Marianne
35. Ohms' cousins
37. Wilkes-____
38. Trunk
39. Grant's army
40. "How to Succeed . . ." star
41. Propagate
42. Dog's name
43. Mottled steed
44. Part of MIT: abbr.
45. Japanese mat
46. Cleanse
49. Adorable one
50. Fourth-down kicks, often
51. Kinds
53. Matches for Hogan
54. ____ Gritty Dirt Band
55. Zeal
57. 1990 Oscar winner
58. Divers' concerns
59. Drives
61. Former Delaware Senator
62. Plugs
63. Pursue
64. Wore
65. Riva ____
66. Collieries
67. Comedienne Brice
68. Quaker pronoun
69. Slacken
70. Sound for attention
72. Tuesday: Fr.
73. Imprints
76. Laboratory container
77. Wraps
78. Ol' ____ (Sinatra)
80. Vice President Agnew
81. Hockum
82. Self-satisfied
84. On cloud nine
85. Close-fitting shirt
86. A Gallo
88. Bossa nova's kin
89. Apple drink
90. Roman fountain
91. Of bristles
92. Crack pilots
93. Robert Vaughn part
94. Like some tales
95. Stem
96. Kind of bean
97. Flintstones' pet
99. Rooter
100. Hurly-burly
102. Butt

PUZZLE 166

Diagramless crosswords are solved by using clues and their numbers to fill in the answer words and the arrangement of black squares. Insert the number of each clue with the first letter of its answer, across and down. Fill in a black square at the end of each word. Every black square must have a corresponding black square on the opposite side of the diagram to form a diagonally symmetrical pattern.

ACROSS

1. To the rear
4. Distress signal
7. That woman

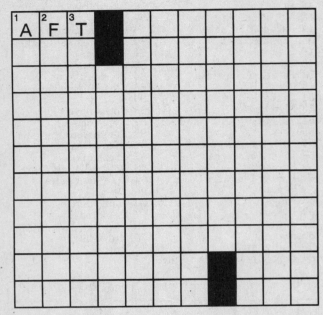

10. Falsehood
11. Statute
12. Dairy animal
13. Make ready
15. Copy
16. Bug
18. Woo
21. Lugs
24. Musical governess
25. Sassy
26. Traveler's way
28. Atomizer
29. Calm
31. Ostrich's kin
33. Par
37. Meadow
38. Notice
39. Singer Doris ____
40. Sick
41. Make a mistake
42. Lyric poem

DOWN

1. High mountain
2. Evergreen
3. Golf mound
4. Slope
5. Paddles
6. Sugary
7. Strew
8. School dance
9. Mama sheep
14. Brigand
17. Penny metal
18. Auto
19. Yoko ____
20. Strange
22. Epoch
23. Filthy place
27. Rub out
28. Scornful smile
30. Always
31. Inventor Whitney
32. Singer Tillis
34. Fuss
35. Wander aimlessly
36. Watch

PUZZLE 167

ACROSS

1. Swine
4. Boast
8. Long story

9. Collar fabric
10. Shrewd
11. Place for a posy
12. Choir voice
13. Shy
14. Gleeful
16. Grass stalk
17. Annually
20. Damp
22. Pin
25. Girl
28. Clutch
31. Whole range
32. Fencer's sword
33. Knave
34. Slim candle
35. Singles
36. Article
37. "The Way We ____"
38. Write

DOWN

1. Larder
2. Disregard
3. Carefree
4. Find fault with
5. Swift
6. Served perfectly
7. Set
8. Bargain event
10. Machine part
11. Fib
13. Meeting
15. Sweet potato
18. Cook in the oven
19. Illuminated
21. Label
23. Invent
24. Occur
25. Beer type
26. Entertain
27. Litigate
29. Appear
30. Each
31. Departed
33. Tier
34. Point

150

PUZZLE 168

ACROSS

1. Antique
4. Health resort
7. French chanteuse
9. Humor
10. Sailors' patron saint
11. Lion's neck hair
12. Weep
13. "Down Home" actress
15. Feather scarf
16. Large
17. Curtsy
18. Ginger drink
19. Eureka!
22. Central point
24. Preferential tournament status
25. Young boy
26. Desertlike
27. Sorrow
28. Porgy's love
29. Play on words
30. Elbow poke
31. Wealthy
32. Newsman Koppel
33. Careless
34. Torrid
35. Varnish ingredient
36. Gist
37. Corn wrapper
38. Newton fruit
39. Banner
41. Heroic poem
43. Kindled
44. Quality of sound
45. Booms
46. For each

DOWN

1. Musical drama
2. Easter flower
3. River barrier
4. Influence
5. Brooch
6. Took food
8. Minor character flaw
11. One of the "Little Women"
12. Dairy animal
14. Compete
15. Carton
17. Unopened flower
18. Affirmative vote
19. Actor Baldwin
20. Leftover meat dish
21. Classified items
22. Rock band Motley ____
23. Cheese skin
24. Dunk for apples
26. Likely
27. Floor polish
28. Took the bait
30. Coat
31. Steal from
33. ____ Vegas
34. Embrace
35. Carry with effort
36. More agreeable
37. Headgear
38. Delicate
39. Winter ill
40. Pitcher spout
42. Explode

Starting box on page 562

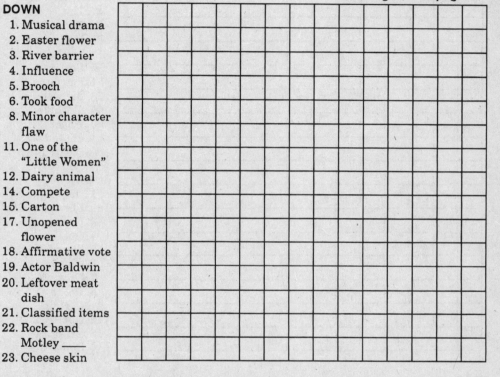

HONEYCOMB

The small arrows indicate the beginning of each 6-letter answer, which will circle its number in either a clockwise or counterclockwise direction.

1. Individualistic
2. Water
3. Beau
4. Restricted
5. Eye part
6. Young cat
7. Shooting star
8. Spanish fleet
9. Capital of Spain
10. Artist's workshop
11. Dairy spread
12. Save

PUZZLE 169

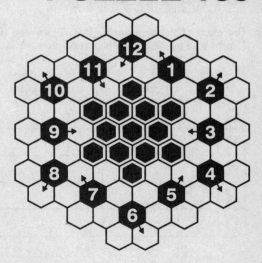

151

PUZZLE 170

ACROSS
1. Startle
6. Decay
9. Eagle's nest
10. Monkey
11. Tree fluid
14. Grill
15. Dare
17. Mix
19. Noise
20. Colored eye part
21. First home
23. Tidy
24. Be sympathetic
26. Likely winner
29. Precious
33. Banish
34. Circle segment
36. Small donkey
37. Distribute cards
38. Ponder
40. Nonagenarian's age
41. Canvas shelter
45. Poker stake
46. African lily
47. Tint
48. Swamp
53. Mail-order brochure
55. Destined
57. Singleton
58. Bat wood
59. Sky blue
60. Wager
61. Extend a subscription

DOWN
1. Droop
2. Flavoring plant
3. Unwritten
4. Quote
5. Sharp
6. Gulch
7. Unwrap
8. Decade
11. Certain
12. Opera solo
13. Nuisance
16. Badge metal
18. Sandwich store
19. Resolve
22. Facts and figures
24. Bun
25. Before, poetically
26. Nourished
27. Chopping tool
28. By way of
29. Responsibility
30. Historical period
31. Skill
32. Fish eggs
35. Penny
36. Morsel
39. Consider
40. Zero
41. Mexican sandwich
42. Verve
43. Memo
44. English beverage
47. Stockings
49. From a distance
50. Demolish
51. Daze
52. In this place
54. Science workroom
56. Morning moisture

Starting box on page 562

PUZZLE 171   Categories

For each of the categories listed can you think of a word or phrase beginning with each letter on the left?
Count one point for each correct answer. A score of 15 is good, and 21 is excellent.

	DOGS	FAMOUS JOHNS	UNITED NATIONS	SOUTHERN CITIES	FLOWERS
G					
R					
A					
N					
D					

PUZZLE 172

ACROSS
1. Lodgings, informally
5. Quagmire
8. Southern nut
9. Soloist at the Met
10. Solitary
11. Ultimate
12. Pang
13. Obstacle
14. Block
16. Perch
18. Medley
20. Snug
21. Heavenly body
22. Aid a felon
24. Flatfish
25. Meadow
26. Peruse
30. Claim
31. Vatican resident
32. Crustacean
34. Toward shelter
35. Eagle's nest
37. Peculiar
38. Plump
41. Young boy's title
46. Stop, on the sea
47. Student
48. Only
49. Hoodwink
50. Golf instructor
51. New Englander

DOWN
1. Place for a hero
2. Sacred picture
3. Squad
4. Mock
5. Tie
6. Elliptical
7. Wind gust
8. Feline foot
9. Soiled
11. To-do
12. Courtroom activity
13. Owl's cry
14. Foreman
15. Low female voice
17. Sea
19. Miner's quest
22. Excuse
23. Honey maker
26. Resort, of sorts
27. Tint
28. Imitated
29. Require
30. Hog fat
32. Motive
33. Lease
36. Without contents
38. Incline
39. Culminated
40. Edible root
42. Atmosphere
43. Twirl
44. Clock noise
45. Moose

Starting box on page 562

All Mixed Up

PUZZLE 173

Unscramble the letters in each line to find European capitals and their countries.

1. N A R C A R F S P E I _____

2. D A M I A N I P R S D _____

3. A P S O W A D A N L W R _____

4. M Y R L O E A I T _____

5. T E C H E A R N G E S E _____

6. I R V T A N E U A S N A I _____

7. O N R S L O W A O Y _____

8. W L A E S N B R E R T D I Z N _____

153

PUZZLE 174

ACROSS

1. Resorts of sorts
5. Citrus beverage
8. Actress Myrna ____
11. Zhivago's love
12. In addition to
13. Knight's attendant
14. Incensed
15. Astronomer's instruments
17. Coach
19. Or ____!
20. Beheld
21. Medicinal plant
22. Raging flood
26. Rule
27. In favor of
28. Honored
30. Actress Ellen ____
32. Perry Mason portrayer
34. Long periods of time
37. Daddy
38. Very difficult
41. Field glasses
45. Hindu queen
46. Enthusiasm
47. Religious group
48. Comic sketch
49. Solidify
50. Take food
51. Italian family

DOWN

1. Narrow cut
2. Young salmon
3. Regions
4. Miss Hawkins
5. Everything
6. Owing
7. Double curve
8. Pause
9. Type of molding
10. Affirmative
12. Part of MPH
13. Prince Charles's game
15. Choir member
16. Highland Scot
18. Clear
21. Ms. Landers
23. Apply
24. Mob disturbances
25. Heron
28. Mink or sable
29. Tinters
30. Bric-a-____
31. Doze off
32. Trite
33. Atop
35. Doctor's assistant
36. Saturates
37. Heap
38. Sculpture or dance
39. One
40. Location
41. Plead
42. Utilize
43. Meadow
44. Perform a part

Starting box on page 562

PUZZLE 175   Escalator

Place the answer to clue 1 in the first space, drop a letter and arrange the remaining letters to answer clue 2. Drop another letter and arrange the remaining letters to answer clue 3. The first dropped letter goes into the box to the left of space 1 and the second dropped letter goes into the box to the right of space 3. Follow this pattern for each row in the diagram. When completed, the letters on the left and right, reading down, will spell related words or a phrase.

	1		2		3	
	4		5		6	
	7		8		9	
	10		11		12	
	13		14		15	
	16		17		18	
	19		20		21	

1. Annul
2. Neat and tidy
3. Tie
4. Orion
5. Television knob
6. Charter
7. Goliath et al.
8. Annoying insects
9. Mr. Laurel
10. Adorned
11. Test score
12. Beloved
13. Pastry makers
14. Cavalry sword
15. Bans
16. Names
17. Slants
18. Categorize
19. Join the military
20. Small island
21. Roof piece

154

PUZZLE 176

ACROSS
1. Stockings
5. Chomping at the bit
6. Troubadour's instrument
7. Yearning
11. Correct
13. Whittle
15. Dreadful
17. Fades
18. Monastery quarters
20. Timbre
21. Vegas machine
23. Cry of regret
27. Watchband
30. Emanated
32. Powder ingredient
33. Succulent
35. Pry
38. Lubricated
40. Cash and ___
41. Lyric poem
42. Recumbent
43. Steed
44. Arrow poison
45. Type of journalism
47. Lawn tool
51. Stingy
52. Shut loudly
53. Parched
55. Dye plant
57. Reasoning
59. Away from the wind
61. Sun-dried brick
62. Pulls quickly
65. Highlands language
66. Actor Carvey
67. Type of collar
68. Tidings

DOWN
1. Sound
2. Egg
3. Positioned
4. Like Paradise
7. Horned viper
8. Brief discussion
9. Nimbi
10. Happening
12. Of formal attire
14. Danish weight units
16. Building additions
19. Animal parasite
22. Bowling need
23. Sleep like ___
24. Den
25. Metal compound
26. Public displays
28. Cracked open
29. Track prize
30. Frigid
31. Blackmore's "Lorna ___"
34. Infuriated
36. Greek theaters
37. Nobleman
39. Perry Mason's Street
40. Dairy animal
43. Moral lecture
46. Actress Wood
48. Celebration
49. Wear away
50. Austerity
54. Claim of possession
56. Sluggish
58. Average grade
60. Growing out
63. Be cognizant of
64. Without

Starting box on page 562

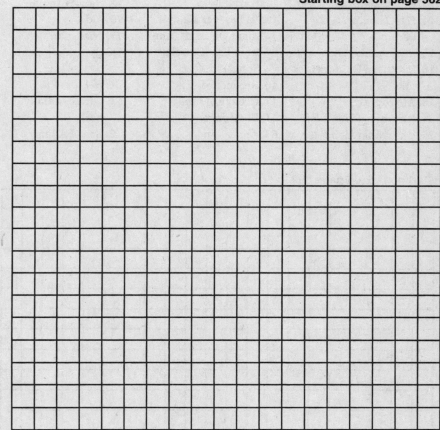

ROLL OF THE DICE   PUZZLE 177

The six dice are actually the same die shown from six different positions. What 6-letter word is formed by the letters on the six bottom faces, reading from left to right?

PUZZLE 178

ACROSS

1. Fault-finding food fish?
5. Perpendicular to a ship
10. Orchestra member
11. Muse
13. Enlist again
14. Kay Thompson heroine
15. Michigan or Ohio city
16. Southern California lake
18. Ate rapidly
21. Members of families
25. Baseballer Gonzalez
26. Muslim leader
27. Place
31. Verne's captain
32. Wine bottle
35. Kitchen appliance
37. Metric weight
38. Surround
40. Heraldic
42. "Wherever I may roam, on ____" (line from the "Caisson Song")
46. Reconciles
47. Groups of nine
51. Book page
54. Apportion
55. Paradisiacal
56. Nobleman
57. Sun. discourses
58. Scarlett's home
59. Synthetic fabric
61. British gun
62. Gushed forth
64. The world's oceans
70. Tropical mammal
73. ____ d'hotel
74. She, in Paris
75. Dakota Indian
76. Alda
77. Wise man
78. Gym equipment

DOWN

1. Parsley-family herb
2. Son of Adam
3. Rake
4. ____ up (invigorates)
5. Primates
6. Cowboy's weapon
7. Chemical compound
8. Mine entrance
9. Intermediate: pref.
12. Rip
15. U.S. section
17. Bribe
19. Bombeck
20. Fate
21. Rodents
22. Muscat's land
23. Chagall
24. Little
27. Main and Elm
28. Arizona Indians
29. Melville novel
30. Puerto Rico, e.g.
33. Tiarella cordifolia
34. Laborer
36. Widespread
39. Icelandic writing
40. U.S. financier
41. Tops
43. Lubricates
44. Chest sound
45. Athletic events
48. Med. school subj.
49. Dreadful
50. Read hurriedly
51. Tolstoy et al.
52. Name in the old West
53. Certain Frenchmen
60. Reno's st.
63. Not-for-sale model, for short
65. Worn-out horses
66. Missile's home
67. And others
68. Guthrie
69. Connery
70. Crew
71. Nazimova
72. Area of land

Starting box on page 562

ACROSS

1. Vagabond
5. Pig's digs
8. Scent
10. Uncommon
11. Natural gift
13. Spirit
14. Softened
16. Space
17. Timber
19. Wanderer
21. "___ Which Way You Can"
22. General Bradley
23. Raise
25. Tear
26. Fewer
29. Ooze
31. Ditto
33. Dreary
36. Symmetrical
37. Frozen water
38. ___ and butter
39. Apportion
40. Accelerate sharply
41. Sold to consumers
46. Undiluted
47. Evening meal
48. Previously owned
49. Flower leaf
50. Household animal
51. Roused from sleep

DOWN

1. Despised
2. Unwritten
3. Tree trunk
4. Sign of the future
5. Tossed greens
6. Snare
7. Longing
9. Army insect
10. Considered
12. Choir voice
14. Shade of blue
15. Rounded roofs
17. Armed conflict
18. Single
20. Lion's neck hair
24. Restrained
27. Rescue
28. Smudge
30. Snooped
32. Finished
34. Play division
35. Busy insect
38. French cap
39. Singer Haggard
40. Trick
42. Waiter's gratuity
43. Again
44. Division word
45. Security problem
46. Young dog

PUZZLE 179

Starting box on page 562

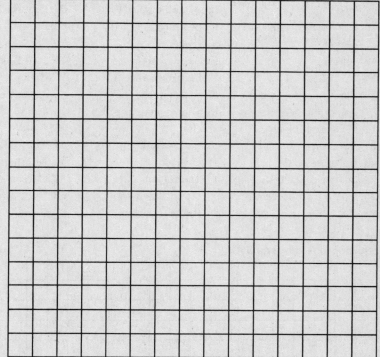

Word Math

PUZZLE 180

In these long-division problems letters are substituted for numbers. Determine the value of each letter. Then arrange the letters in order from 0 to 9, and they will spell a word or phrase.

1 | 0 | 1 | 2 | 3 | 4 | 5 | 6 | 7 | 8 | 9 |

```
              OWED
DEAR | DARKEST
       DEAR
       RDOES
       ROSSS
        KRFWT
        RAKFW
         DRET
```

2 | 0 | 1 | 2 | 3 | 4 | 5 | 6 | 7 | 8 | 9 |

```
              ONE
ROAD | ENGAGED
       EEUAG
       GUSSE
       GGDRF
        FSRAD
        AONRU
         EOOF
```

3 | 0 | 1 | 2 | 3 | 4 | 5 | 6 | 7 | 8 | 9 |

```
             LOU
DUO | LADLES
      AISA
      OLEE
      LIES
       ODUS
       OKKJ
        EIS
```

157

PUZZLE 181

ACROSS

1. Artist Chagall
5. "Remote Control" host
6. Venerable monk
7. Arrest
10. Jokester
14. "___ Rose"
16. Corrida cry
17. Vegetable gelatin
18. Mills and Reed
22. Hwy. sign
23. Imogene ___
24. Scotch or duct
25. North Carolina county
28. Cut
29. Sportscaster Allen
30. Western state
31. Author Fleming
32. 35mm, e.g.
35. Sea birds
36. Uplift
40. Sally in space
41. City in France
42. Space inits.
43. South American city
48. Battle souvenir
51. Overlook
52. Tennis star Mandlikova
53. Plane lanes
55. In the thick of
56. Author du Maurier
59. Soft drink
62. Verne captain
63. Actress Kaminska
64. El ___, Texas
65. Fisherman
67. Poetess Teasdale
69. Clumsy vessels
70. Scrooge's word
71. ___ Lake, Oregon
74. RBI, e.g.
75. Argentine Peron
76. Jug
78. Sailors
79. Rorqual
80. Oklahoma town
82. Carson's successor
83. "___ and the Swan"

DOWN

1. "Married to the ___"
2. Producer Rudy ___
3. Made over
4. Belief
7. German Ocean, now
8. Tall, in Tijuana
9. Has-___
10. Saguaro, et al.
11. Marketplace
12. Wisconsin city
13. Liquid measure
15. Pismire
19. Appoint
20. Parrot
21. Actress Ward
25. Breed of cattle
26. Heart chambers
27. "White ___"
32. French city
33. ___ time (never)
34. Handel composition
37. Canadian peninsula
38. Ratite bird
39. Compete
44. Opposed to
45. Concerning
46. Fracas
47. Baseball stat
48. "___ Surprise"
49. Ship of the desert
50. Tree resin
54. Greek city
56. Record
57. Hebrew month
58. Brazilian state
60. Actor Werner
61. Newels
64. Bygone
65. Burrows and Vigoda
66. Wheel hub
68. Chowed
72. Actor Tom ___
73. Actress Adoree
77. Cheese skin
81. Dennis Quaid film

Starting box on page 562

PUZZLE 182

ACROSS
1. Weeps
5. Gentle touch
8. Roundabout route
10. Robin Cook book
11. Gasoline component
12. Kitchen or den
13. Notable period
14. Goes bad
16. Hems a skirt
18. ____ Vegas
19. Mandarin
23. Eternity
24. Pretzel seasoning
26. Boor
29. Cravat
30. Gee ____!
31. Descendant of Shem
33. Camouflage
34. Paradise
35. Single
36. Stains

DOWN
1. Mystery
2. Canadian city
3. Feathered scarf
4. Tans
5. Billiards
6. Biblical prophet
7. Cap
8. Performs
9. Fill again
10. Catastrophe
15. Paddle
17. Kerchoo!
20. Obtained
21. "____ Son"
22. Type and class
25. High school student
26. Facial feature
27. Take a bus
28. Lack
30. Which person?
32. Spring month

PUZZLE 183

ACROSS
1. Mr. Vereen
4. "For ____ the Bell Tolls"
8. Secure
12. Untruth
13. The Corn State
14. Recreation
15. Crumb
16. Pure
18. Harass
20. Visit
21. Sagacious
24. Footlocker
28. With zeal
32. Great Lake
33. Lobster coral
34. African republic
36. Some
37. Actress Freeman
39. "____ in the Mist"
41. Flair
43. "____ in the Money"
44. Snoop
46. Uncertain
50. Cajun locale
55. Impressionist's work
56. Acquire
57. Strategy
58. Japanese board game
59. River in Normandy
60. Napoleon's island
61. X

DOWN
1. Globule
2. Emerald Isle
3. Profit gains
4. Drooping
5. ____ polloi
6. Hoot ____
7. Baseballer Willie ____
8. Globe
9. Boxing great
10. Chubby
11. Look at
17. Rainy
19. Member of a fold
22. Without a date
23. Body joint
25. Russian river
26. Al Hirschfeld's daughter
27. Low islands
28. Branches
29. ____ beer
30. Disclaim
31. Long ago
35. Rapture
38. Of high mountains
40. Meadow
42. Speakers' stumbles
45. Cry of surprise
47. Canter or gallop
48. Provoke
49. Jacket type
50. Mr. Durocher
51. Rowing item
52. Vase
53. Everything
54. Seize

159

PUZZLE 184

ACROSS
1. Rabid
4. Young woman
8. Kind of tide
12. Actress Arden
13. Catch sight of
14. Capable of
15. Agra landmark
17. Golfers' pegs
18. Effortless
19. Mourn
21. Aunt's husband
23. Singer Jerry ____
24. Singer Seeger
25. Winter toy
29. Billy ____ Williams
30. Craftiness
31. Spanish river
32. Artillery
34. Skater Brinker
35. Egg on
36. Not lean, as meat
37. Hobos
40. Spiritual leader
41. Metrical foot
42. Actor
46. Spooky-sounding lake
47. Ireland
48. ____ la la
49. Forest creature
50. Require
51. Even now

DOWN
1. Ran into
2. Actress Gardner
3. Sad
4. Landlord's contract
5. Pale
6. Health resort
7. Word part
8. Spice
9. Weapon
10. "____ o'clock scholar"
11. Mail
16. Boy
20. Century plant
21. Hair style
22. ____-do-well
23. Utter
25. Atomic No. 74
26. Tip
27. "____ Misbehavin'"
28. Curious
30. "The World According to ____"
33. One or two
34. Stringed instrument
36. Blended together
37. Even
38. Uncommon
39. French girlfriend
40. "An Officer and a Gentleman" actor
43. Hasten
44. Exist
45. ____ King Cole

PUZZLE 185

ACROSS
1. Applaud
5. Finished a cake
9. Wisecracker
12. Leslie Caron film
13. Title
14. Tavern drink
15. "The Wizard ____"
16. Scare
18. Eccentric old man
20. Faithful
21. Like the Sahara
23. Strange
26. Theater balcony
30. 56, to Cato
31. From ____
32. Golly!
33. Fly high
34. Old card game
35. Bullhorn
37. Diary item
39. Shield border
40. Passable
42. Stockings
46. Window-washer's item
49. Hammer or saw
50. French affirmative
51. Minus
52. Poet Pound
53. Negative word
54. Actor Parker
55. Gather crops

DOWN
1. Stop up, as a sink
2. Existence
3. Agave's kin
4. Vigor
5. Trespass
6. Sedan
7. Send out
8. Intensity
9. Disastrous loss
10. French land mass
11. X
17. Color
19. Notable time
22. San ____ Zoo
24. Terrible ruler
25. Ireland
26. Masculine
27. Harrow's rival
28. "The ____ Murders"
29. Intimacy
33. Refuge
35. Me, ____, and I
36. Employ busily
38. Fish eggs
41. Curved molding
43. Seep
44. Ibsen heroine
45. Strike
46. Family member
47. Status ____
48. Curve

PUZZLE 186

ACROSS

1. Excellent
6. Knit one, ____ one
10. Sloping walkway
14. Blockhead
17. Rock formation
18. Largest continent
19. Fragrance
20. ____ de Janeiro
21. Madden
22. Fake
23. Vail's state
25. Female deer
26. Chess threat
28. Paid athlete
30. Gave temporarily
31. Windshield cleaner
32. Pretend
34. Dried fruit
35. Told
38. Larva's envelope
41. Sand hill
44. Hammed it up
45. In the dumps
46. And not
48. Fiddle
49. Plunge
50. Coarse
51. Revolve
53. Strict
55. Suggestion
56. Predetermined
58. Unselfish
60. Shooting star
61. Quince yellow
64. Gray wolf
65. Put the cork back on
69. Says
70. Navigational system
71. Identical
72. Fib
73. Poke fun at
75. Culture medium
76. Paying guest
78. "My Two ____"
80. Burrow
82. Plague
83. Kettle
85. Three-way joint
86. Shadow
87. Doorbells
90. Kind of curve
92. There is no place like it
93. Feminists' gp.
96. Revoked
98. Poker holding
100. French river
102. Bauxite, e.g.
103. Make well
104. Grandma Moses
105. "Days of Our ____"
106. ____ capita
107. Obey
108. River of Hades
109. Dough raiser

DOWN

1. Pleased
2. "Biggest Little City"
3. "The Razor's ____"
4. Birthday number
5. Wood eater
6. Glued
7. Wedding member
8. Small inlet
9. Illuminating device
10. Artistic style
11. Hoopla
12. Girlfriend
13. Evidence
14. Gorilla's cousin
15. Assistant
16. Victuals
24. Foray
27. Copied
29. Regattas, e.g.
31. Child's squirting pistol
33. 2,000 pounds
35. Beatty film
36. Send out
37. Devotion
38. Trolley's sound
39. Evict
40. Viking
42. Musical symbol
43. Ogled
45. Saline solution
47. Helicopter part
50. Facial feature
52. Vexatious
54. More pleasant
56. Exclude
57. English town
59. Social call
60. Fable message
61. Lacking heat
62. Capital of Western Samoa
63. Rat charmer
64. Theater section
66. "It ____ Upon the Midnight Clear"
67. So be it!
68. Saucy
70. Reporter Lois et al.
74. However
76. Meander
77. Hospital attendant
79. Several
81. Required
82. Human chest
84. Educate
86. Glossy
87. Yield
88. Not there
89. Swing around
91. Resorts
93. Exploding star
94. Wallet items
95. Toward the setting sun
97. Prior to
99. Army insect
101. Hurry

161

PUZZLE 187

ACROSS

1. Irk
5. Thick slice
9. Dab
12. Conception
13. Void
14. Flurry
15. Serving aid
17. Compose
18. Chow
19. "White ___"
20. Holds
23. Australian bird
25. Tune
26. Wipes out
29. Multiple-yarn maker
34. Director May
35. Draw
36. Kind
37. Guides
40. Wooded valley
43. Stem
44. Tangy drink
45. "Long ___"
50. Hamilton bill
51. African shrub
52. Hart or roe
53. Hill builder
54. Understands
55. Groups

DOWN

1. Wire measure
2. Apple-cider girl
3. Egyptian cap
4. Grant and Dunaway
5. Closes
6. Defeat
7. Neighbor of Fla.
8. Actor Kingsley
9. Dad
10. Arabian gulf
11. Chinese society
16. Exhaust
19. Join together
20. Argon, e.g.
21. Primed
22. Seed covering
23. Energy unit
24. Rank for an off.
26. Cincinnati-to-New York dir.
27. Within: pref.
28. Tizzy
30. Fastener
31. Zip
32. Sign
33. Word of agreement
37. Blanches
38. Powerful people
39. Takes the point
40. Facts
41. British prime minister
42. Liturgical season
43. Lump
45. Children's game
46. Bar order
47. Playwright Blessings
48. Rent
49. 12-mo. periods

PUZZLE 188

ACROSS

1. Actor Pitt
5. Decorative case
9. Coliseums
11. With hand on hip
13. Attorney general, for one
15. Iranian currency
16. Sudden assault
17. Pitcher's numbers
18. Follower: suff.
19. Huddle
20. Beam
21. Intensifies
23. Tableland
24. New Guinea port
25. Brooch
26. Sean Connery, for one
28. Pertaining to a belief
32. Gruff
33. French bread
34. Nuptial vow
35. Mouths
36. Small islands
37. Bacchanalian cry
38. Public servants
41. Hunting dog
42. Sounds
43. Tints
44. Lawyers: abbr.

DOWN

1. Slowly cook
2. Money back
3. Deep blue
4. Actor Dailey
5. Meted
6. Actor Curry
7. Brown pigments
8. European peninsula
9. Bitter
10. Composed
11. Throughout the course of
12. Algerian city
14. Smears
19. Toast
20. Actress Tierney
22. Story
23. Air
25. Brig
26. Rode the waves
27. Shrewd
28. Major religion: abbr.
29. Sell off
30. Loves
31. Loamy deposit
32. Murmurs
33. Dock
36. Serves perfectly
37. Compile
39. Native: suff.
40. Mauna ___

162

MOVIES & TELEVISION

ACROSS

1. Leading
6. Gaming cubes
10. Thompson of "Howards End"
14. Film villain Peter ____
15. Erin ____ of "Happy Days"
16. Reeves of "Bram Stoker's Dracula"
18. Accumulate
19. Oscar or Emmy, e.g.
20. New York island
21. Tennis court divider
22. "The ____ Man"
24. Army chow hall
26. Consumed
27. "The Mouse That ____"
29. "Ebb ____"
30. Small nail
31. Comedian Louis ____
32. Actor Chaney
33. Very small
35. Orderly Ortiz on "Nurses"
38. Copenhagen native
39. "Full ____ Jacket"
43. Ken ____ of "thirtysomething"
44. Actor Grant
45. Buccaneer
46. Ullmann of films
47. Hollywood's Turner
48. Max ____ of "Barney Miller"
50. Pull along
51. Lou Grant's job
53. Store event
54. Paul ____ of "Scarface"
55. Beauty shop
56. "____ Time, Next Year"
57. Singing brothers
58. Actor/comedian Taylor
60. "____ Got a Secret"
61. Attention-getting sound
63. "____ House"
66. Soothe
68. "A ____ of Time"
71. "____ Max"
72. Twisted
73. "Little Man ____"
74. "The ____ Vegas Story"
76. Stand up
78. "The ____ and Daniel Webster"
80. Miss ____ of "Dallas"
82. Ceremonies
83. Actress Dunne
84. Della ____ of "The Royal Family"
85. "____ Having a Baby"
86. This, in Barcelona
87. Fathered

DOWN

1. Mr. Alda
2. Father on "The Simpsons"
3. Muse of poetry
4. "____ longa . . ."
5. "____ Rides Again"
6. "Way ____ East"
7. Lyricist Gershwin
8. Shade of red
9. Finished
10. ____ out (make with difficulty)
11. Gibson of "Lethal Weapon"
12. Of the cheek
13. Singer Baker
15. Hazel's job
17. Not new
23. "____ Haw"
25. Use needle and thread
28. Author unknown: abbr.
29. Danza of "Who's the Boss?"
30. Frothy beverage
32. Dr. Zhivago's love
34. "____ and the Detectives"
35. Warsaw natives
36. Italian actress Valli
37. Polite
38. Comedian Aykroyd
40. Ryan's daughter
41. Make amends
42. "Parker ____ Can't Lose"
44. "My Mother the ____"
45. Fruited pastry
47. Actress Anderson
48. "The Most Dangerous ____"
49. Pub brew
52. Shredded
53. Rescue
54. Dillon of "Gunsmoke"
56. Nuns
59. ____ Dee River
61. Host Sajak
62. Guides
63. Mr. Sharif
64. "April in ____"
65. Mrs. Bunker in "All in the Family"
67. MacDowell of "Green Card"
68. "The ____ Animal"
69. Aunt ____ of "Oklahoma!"
70. "____ the Titanic!"
72. "Porgy and ____"
73. Louise or Turner
75. "The Bad ____"
77. "____ No Evil, Hear No Evil"
79. Kitty's doc
81. Honolulu garland

PUZZLE 190

• SLIP ME SOME! •

ACROSS

1. Wolfe and Wicker
5. Jeweled coronet
10. Secretary's sub
14. She loved Narcissus
18. Biblical commander
19. Indochinese region
20. Philologist Aasen
21. Cat's-paw
22. Valuable violin
23. Big deal to a dermatologist?
26. Explodes
28. Prevalent
29. Opinions
30. Nigerian city
31. ___ Scott
32. Flag maker
33. Utter joy
34. Oracle
35. Match
36. Like some dorms
37. African tea
40. Glues
43. Auto pioneer
44. Light carriage
45. Baseball's Carty
46. Successful
47. Mr. Redding
48. Extinct birds
49. French psychologist
50. Bypass
51. Football action
52. Standstill
53. Magician's word
54. Chinese river
55. Clink
56. Alone, to Octavia
57. Spree
58. Dermatologist's serenade?
63. Hammer part
64. Legumes
65. Roman ruins site
66. Nuclear power org.
69. Irreligious people
72. Chief
73. Cookie maker's name
74. Tropical nut
75. Convex molding
76. Frog's home
77. English town
78. A Guggenheim
79. Pastures
80. Chalcedony
81. Small deer
82. Coils of yarn
83. Trickery
84. Rattles
85. Descartes
86. Fence part
87. Pluck
89. Wails
90. Neighbor of Wis.
91. Tolkien creature
94. Inviting
96. Official records
97. Philip II's realm
99. Narrow margin for a dermatologist?
102. Fantasies
103. Hair dye
104. Ruler of the Aesir
105. Gladden
106. Short-tailed rodents
107. Thessalian summit
108. Breathing sound
109. Allots
110. Historic times

DOWN

1. Made dull
2. Harangue
3. ___ Grosso do Sul
4. Beauty to a dermatologist?
5. Wine expert
6. Signed
7. Tropical cuckoos
8. Flowed
9. Passionate
10. Spats
11. Reveler's cry
12. Boy, eventually
13. "Roustabout" actor
14. Alcohol lamps
15. Dermatologists' caps?
16. Moderator
17. Corrida cheers
18. Directed
24. Ring weapon
25. Skidded
27. Son of Hera
32. Sticks
33. Stoles
34. Prevent
35. Brief interruption
36. Eurasian songbird
38. Vinegar: pref.
39. Dorothy's pet
40. Elegant
41. "Diana" crooner
42. Soak
43. Japanese city
44. Kind of energy
45. Composer Vittorio ___
47. Salad ingredient
48. Guys
49. Destitute
51. Hordeola
52. Surfer wannabe
53. Military stations
55. Dictation taker
56. Golfing great
57. Cicely or Mike
59. Silicon stones
60. Affect drastically
61. Office messages
62. Model Campbell
67. Carolina college
68. Sacks
69. Actress Negri
70. Assert
71. Dermatologists' wine holders?
72. ___ concours
73. To ___ (exactly)
74. German city
76. Picnic locale
77. Milleniums
78. Dermatologist's swim?
80. "I Never ___ My Father"
81. Discounted
82. Rational
84. Roman goddess
85. Spoils
86. Lucre
88. 1492 vessel
89. Picture
90. Photo finish
91. First name in planes
92. Chicago suburb
93. Soviet bureau
94. Regarding
95. Alpine equipment
96. Indigo
97. Repast
98. Stench
100. Seraglio chamber
101. Rock letters

164

ACROSS

1. Derek and Peep
4. Barber's word
7. Drummer before Starr
11. Colombian coffee city
15. Clay by another name
16. Norse explorer-outlaw
18. Waxes eloquent
20. In the company of
22. Determined by the stars
24. Phenomena first seen by Galileo
26. City near Madrid
27. Spanish pronoun
29. ____-earth element
30. "____ a Job" (rock song)
31. Cuff or missing
32. Crows
33. U.S. writer (1924-84)
35. Child's game
36. Outstanding
37. "L'etat," to Louis XIV
38. "A ____ of bread . . ."
42. Cowl like headdress
44. "Buddenbrooks" author
45. Iced drink
47. ____-faire (tact)
49. Prosecutor Jaworski
51. Spaceship to Venus
52. Space rock
53. One of nine
55. Eterne
56. Decorate
57. Esau feature
58. Piano-maker's wood
60. Little: Fr.
63. Go berserk
64. Goes hungry
65. New or X
66. Charity
67. Compass pt.
68. Discretion
69. Bollixes up
70. Ignition item
71. River island
72. Space station
75. Prepared a hook
76. First U.S. space program
80. Plant part
81. Spaceship
82. Warns
83. Bees followers
85. Think up
87. Italian resort
88. Earth offering
89. Make books
90. Calif. time
93. Feeling empathy
97. Drew a bead
98. Early American
99. Court
102. Hindu queen
103. Spiffy!
104. Heap of stones
105. Visitor for 1985 or 6
109. Great cover-ups
112. Hunter of the stars
113. Peruvian port
114. Plant foundation
115. United
116. Chimney dirt
117. Musical Horne
118. Ocean inlet
119. Little Edward

DOWN

1. Crystallized lava
2. "Twelfth Night" countess
3. Railroad part
4. Evening, to Loren
5. Dudgeon
6. ____ Juana
7. Copper-zinc alloy
8. Mama's word
9. Actor Gilliam
10. Land
11. Proofreading mark
12. "What a good boy ____"
13. New York island
14. Playwright William
17. Priest
18. American Indian
19. Breakfast sound
21. London's time: abbr.
23. Antlered animal
25. Angel's favorite sign
28. Sputnik and Explorer
32. Becloud
33. Lifer
34. Ardor
36. Moslem ruler
37. Horse hair
39. Ajar to Keats
40. Kim Hunter role
41. ____-de-lance
42. Prevent
43. Wading bird
44. Day: abbr.
45. Demon
46. Calhoun of filmdom
47. Site of Napoleon's capture
48. Compensate
50. Listeners
51. Unskilled laborers
52. ____ Frigoris (moon plain)
53. History
54. Solid ground
57. Impetuous
59. Spear part
60. Caterer's unit
61. Ant
62. Like most antiques
64. County events
65. Composer Bartok
66. Of a kind
68. Tight
70. Datum
73. "Taking a line for a walk" artist
74. Sycophant's word
75. Gravy or Love
76. ____ de mer
77. New Haven student
78. Stop light
79. Gater's kin
81. Rip
83. Like a dunce cap
84. Work unit
86. Food-conscious one
89. Michelangelo work
90. The Rock, e.g.
91. Calm
92. Became nervous
94. Negative contraction
95. Alpha, e.g.
96. Place of educ.
97. The end of ____
98. Oil-well stopper
99. Reporter's question
100. Rowers
101. Medley
104. New York ____
106. Old card game
107. Violinist Bull
108. Homo sapiens
110. Cos ____, Conn.
111. Mauna ____

PUZZLE 191

• STAR SEARCH •

PUZZLE 192

• CLOCK AND CALENDAR •

ACROSS
1. Camel's-hair coat
4. Mexican shawl
10. Lamp condensers
15. Water pitcher
19. ___ excellence
20. Iago's wife
21. Prepare a new itinerary
22. City on the Truckee
23. Buck
24. Milestone celebrated by Chicago in 1933-34
27. Singer Vic
29. "___ the Time to Fall in Love"
30. Important period
31. N.Z. parrot
32. ___ order
33. "Totem and Taboo" author
35. Shout of approval
37. "Go ___ out the window"
38. Mamie ___ Eisenhower
39. Black
41. Ring-necked duck
42. "Dies Irae"
44. Spanish town
45. Absconded
46. Laughing
47. Lutheran hymn
49. Moon vehicle
52. Whack
55. Reverie
57. Dishevel
58. Queen of heaven
59. "Give peace in our time, ___" (Book of Common Prayer)
61. Hydrocarbon suffix
62. Calendar abbr.
63. South Pacific islanders
65. Mexican dish
67. Canine mother
69. Recto page: abbr.
71. Deciphers
72. Delirium ___
74. Carpet pile
76. High mountain
78. Georgia ___ Clark
79. Actress Turner
80. Morality
82. French revolutionary
84. Messy home
85. Salamander
86. Accept
87. Feathery
89. Fragrance
91. Govt. agents
92. Billy Joel's "___ a Fantasy"
96. Underworld group
98. Committed perjury
99. Clod
100. Think
101. ___ well
103. Dutch cheeses
105. Blot
106. Saul's grandfather
107. Explosive: abbr.
108. Roman 1102
109. Ideal spot
110. Start of a famous address
115. Train systs.
117. Turkish village
118. Young
119. Not mailed
120. Seraglio room
121. Cheers
122. A votre ___
123. Soft soap ingredient
124. Snare

DOWN
1. GI's address
2. Cowboy's wear
3. Cellar entrance
4. Underling
5. Correct a text
6. Russian hemp
7. High, in music
8. More, in music
9. Deserved
10. "One ___ of glorious life" (Mordaunt)
11. Football officials, for short
12. Little devil
13. Heel over
14. Characteristic of fern seeds: suffix
15. Blunder
16. Respites from army life
17. Place on a throne
18. Prayer beads
25. Rita Coolidge hit song
26. Distort
28. Estate house
32. Top
33. ___-mouth disease
34. Pirate's drink
35. Frosts
36. Shade
38. Beneficiary
40. Closed carriage
43. ___ es Salaam
44. Official proceedings
45. Circus performers
48. Danish island
50. Composer Bloch
51. Lincoln portrayer
52. Carafe
53. Moslem limbo
54. Crisis
56. Interim
58. Cavity
60. Avatar of Vishnu
64. Type of short-term lease
66. Communist Hoxha
68. 1890s
70. Ski races
73. Incite a dog
75. Hammer head
77. Dress up
81. Repair a roof
83. Years of life
86. Cooks
88. Spotted sandpiper
90. Stamping tool
92. Total
93. Number 2 golf club
94. Fencing start
95. Bishopric
96. "A ___ All Seasons"
97. Small interstice
98. Mother of Apollo
99. Incapacitated
102. Ear anvil
104. Cacophony
105. British guns
108. Defrost
109. Eye tunic
111. Varangian tribe
112. Actor Ely
113. ___-cat tractor
114. Is: Latin
116. Met in session

WORDBENDERS

The answers for this crossword puzzle might be just around the bend! Solve the puzzle as you would a regular crossword. The clues for the words which bend in the diagram are listed under the heading BENDERS.

BENDERS

1. Surgical bandages
2. Rim
8. **Asian nanny**
9. Disgusting
17. Ferretlike animal
18. Stimulate
28. Weighted cord: 2 wds.
29. Clergyman's cap
30. Bone injury
32. Rash
43. Ancient Peruvian
49. Eye rudely

ACROSS

1. Slumber number
6. Camel's cousin
10. Cure-all
13. Forehead feature
14. Took a chair
19. ___ Grande
21. Knight's title
22. Sea eagle
23. Goof
24. Reflections
25. Cured herring
26. Unwell
33. Shoshone
34. Personal identity
36. Caustic wit
38. Honey-maker

39. Dandy
40. Wine barrel
41. Boy
42. Australian bird
44. Petition
50. Simon Peter, for one
51. Glorify
52. Leg joints

DOWN

3. Mimic
4. Spring month
5. Chat
6. Zodiac sign
7. Statute
11. Downfall
12. Make wrinkly
15. Goal
16. Interchanged
19. Redundant
20. Anger
27. Allowed to remain
29. Bison
31. Esteem
35. Affirmative vote
37. Papa sheep
44. "My Gal ___"
45. Choose
46. Doctrine
47. Category
48. Cardinal number

PUZZLE 194

• CHEMISTRY BASICS •

ACROSS

1. "____ the season . . ."
4. Sargasso ____
7. Fire a gun
9. Indonesian island chain
11. Easels, e.g.
12. Most ancient
14. Frying utensil
15. Golfer Woosnam
17. Santa's helper
18. Depot: abbr.
19. "____-Hur"
20. Certain
21. Part of speech
23. Venomous viper
25. Daughter's brother
26. Electricity measure
27. Victory sign
29. Road map abbr.
31. Foot part
33. Antiseptic element
35. Make a mistake
36. Balloon gas
38. Shorthand specialist
39. Light bulb gas
41. Suggestive grins
42. Mrs., in Spain
43. Naughty
45. Have creditors
48. Physicians: abbr.
49. Building addition
50. Fifth month
51. Dehydrate
54. "Agnus ____"
55. Exist
56. TV spots
59. ____ of the crop
61. Nonmetallic element
65. Michelangelo statue
67. Wire and pipe metal
69. Sought election
70. Diamond substance
71. ____ de France
72. Be victorious
74. French friend
75. Squealer
76. Sculpture, e.g.
77. Attorney's concern
79. Money mill
81. Evangelist Roberts
83. Mao ____-tung
84. Scientist's room
86. Third letter
87. Head gesture
88. Before, in poems
89. Reeks
91. Cold season
93. Maple and fir
94. Cheerful
95. Marina ____ Rey
96. ____ culpa

DOWN

1. Holier-____-thou
2. Charged particle
3. ____ chloride (salt)
4. Flammable yellow element
5. Terminate
6. Citrus coolers
7. Comedian Laurel
8. Russian ruler
9. Fly alone
10. Famous movie dog
11. Money user
13. More savory
16. At no time
17. January, in Madrid
19. "Puss in ____"
20. That woman
22. ____ degree (ultimate degree)
24. Serves wine
25. Bro's sibling
26. Yoko ____
28. Unit of work
30. Moray or conger
32. Typesetter's measures
34. One ____ million
37. Went in front
39. Improvise
40. "____ is an island"
43. Canopy or fourposter
44. Beer's cousin
46. Armed conflict
47. Organ of sight

51. Oddly amusing
52. Officially revokes
53. Jabber
56. Melody
57. One who devalues
58. Boutique, e.g.
59. 201, to Caesar
60. Cat's cry
62. Give a speech
63. Male sheep
64. Scallion's kin
65. TV host Sajak
66. Hill insect
68. Outer edge
70. Coolidge's nickname
73. Coin metal
75. Curies' discovery
78. Electrical power unit
80. Loch ____ monster
82. Tiers
83. Three, in cards
85. Feathery flier
88. Sicilian volcano
90. Formerly named
92. Opposite of SSW

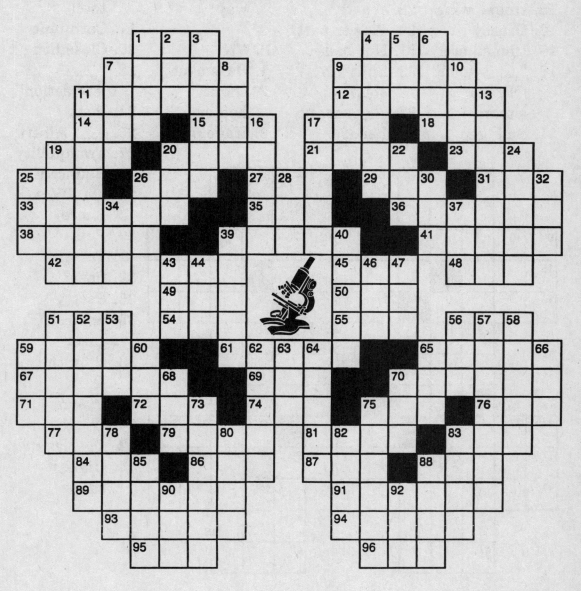

PUZZLE 195

ACROSS

1. Heifer
4. Animal foot
7. Female sheep
8. Mine output
9. Love song
12. New York Indian
15. House wing
16. Grassy
18. Immediately
19. "____ John" (Hirsch sitcom)
21. Smidgen
22. "I ____ Pretty" from "West Side Story"
23. Sports car
25. Distant
26. Paving liquid
27. Mrs. Nixon
28. Wager
29. Flower part
31. Not bad
33. Split ____ soup
34. ____ ma, no hands!
37. Bustle
38. Section
40. Clay, presently
41. Decide
43. Shunned
45. Time period
46. Hockey surface
47. Night and ____
48. Showed the way

DOWN

1. Basement
2. Night hooter
3. Have on
4. Child's steed
5. Exist
6. Hot dog
9. ____ of roses
10. Beer's cousin
11. Discourage
12. Bizarre
13. Female deer
14. Piercing tool
17. Corn unit
20. Classified
22. "____ Attraction"
24. Puss
25. ____ Albert
27. Tranquillity
28. Bounced
29. ____ Wee Reese
30. Full
31. Petrol
32. Poem
33. Pastry
35. Spanish cheer
36. Billy the ____
38. Drama
39. Wicked
42. ____ la la
44. Highest card

ACROSS

1. Dabs
5. Dried grass
8. Willing's partner
12. Range
13. Third person singular pronoun
14. Divulge
15. Handbills
17. Labyrinth
18. Man Friday
19. Canons
20. Twenty
23. "Peter ____"
24. Judd Hirsch series
25. Waned
30. Metallic dirt
31. Downpours
32. Actress Plumb
33. Pittsburgh skaters
35. Dominant
36. Notices
37. Wistfully
38. Dark fur
41. Casanova
43. Evangelist Roberts
44. Encourages
48. Huron, e.g.
49. "Gunga ____" (Grant film)
50. Colt's mom
51. Command to a child
52. Choose
53. Foil's kin

DOWN

1. Cohort
2. "You ____ My Sunshine"
3. Afternoon beverage
4. African hunting expedition
5. Weeded
6. Before: pref.
7. Certainly!
8. Nut type
9. Rosary part
10. Lounge
11. Just manages to earn
16. Fib
19. Tins
20. Traffic sign
21. Be concerned
22. Yoked animals
23. On ____ and needles
25. Soapbox
26. Triumph
27. Starring role
28. Sinister
29. Refuse
31. Ill-mannered
34. Ship's kitchen
35. French lady
37. Amount
38. Fly alone
39. Regal steed
40. Make cookies
41. Trim
42. Shade of color
44. "Much ____ About Nothing"
45. Draw on
46. Before, to poets
47. Admit as a visitor

171

PUZZLE 197

ACROSS
1. Wonder
4. Cross one
8. Hit sharply
12. Chum
13. Misplace
14. Ring of light
15. Ogle
16. Comfort
17. Again
18. Scheme
20. Become solid
22. Pale
24. ___ of day
25. Gab
26. Lay macadam
27. Narrow opening
30. Heavy weight
31. Strange
32. Prospector's find
33. Matched group
34. Camera part
35. State
36. Deed
37. Pick up the tab
38. Go around
41. Active person
42. Pack up
43. Single thing
45. Snooze
48. A Great Lake
49. ___ and shine!
50. "___ to Billy Joe"
51. Fuse together
52. Large deer
53. Tier

DOWN
1. Big monkey
2. Path
3. Dumbo, for one
4. Not dirty
5. Bay horse
6. Donkey
7. Busy places
8. Be generous
9. Fairy's baton
10. Toward the sheltered side
11. City
19. ___ the good times roll
21. Hymn ending
22. Performs
23. Sandal
24. Poison
26. Enjoyment
27. Head of state
28. Neighborhood
29. Saucy
31. Ginger drinks
35. Exist
36. Lost color
37. Carries
38. Huffed and puffed
39. Long ago
40. Bucket
41. Computer storage platter
44. Nothing
46. Fuss
47. Church bench

ACROSS

1. Deposit
4. On top of
8. Drill
12. "____ on a Grecian Urn"
13. Claudius's successor
14. Brainstorm
15. Large snake
16. Adolescent
17. "My Three ____"
18. Banister
20. Dashing
22. Extent
24. Bridle strap
25. Toledo's lake
26. Penalty
27. Escorted
30. Mail
31. Snake shape
32. Not taped
33. Chasing game
34. Swipe
35. Candid
36. Inquisitive
37. Like a tree-trunk growth
38. First aid for a broken bone
41. Kick
42. Bark
43. Blue bloom
45. Little demon
48. Cousin's mother
49. Egypt's river
50. Automobile
51. Hunted animal
52. There's ____ in them thar hills!
53. Lock opener

DOWN

1. Arched toss
2. Flurry
3. Hankering
4. Loosen
5. Fruit skin
6. Unrefined mineral
7. Gobbledy-gook
8. Shaggy bovine
9. Scent
10. Apartment fee
11. Uncompli-cated
19. Ripened
21. Pizza
22. Relax
23. Territory
24. "____ Business" (Cruise film)
26. Dining
27. Cosmetic item
28. Arden and namesakes
29. Refuse
32. Diving bird
34. 2,000 pounds
36. Excellent
37. Pondered
38. Exchange
39. Rain hard
40. Sole
41. Tablet
44. ____ de Janeiro
46. Actress West
47. Snoop

PUZZLE 199

• BACK IN THE SADDLE •

ACROSS
1. Feud
4. Father
7. Young dog
10. To's mate
13. Chicken ____ king
14. Ethan Allen's brother
15. GI's address
16. ____ Palmas
17. Gary Cooper film, with "The"
21. Buttermilk's rider
25. Huron's neighbor
26. This, in Barcelona
27. Gave temporarily
30. Type of cross
35. Living room
39. Shade trees
40. Avoid
41. Days gone by
42. Peak on Crete
43. Silver's rider
48. Squealer
49. Titled
52. Foreigner
54. Wiped
55. Actor Clark ____
56. Columnist Landers
57. Tom Hanks film
58. Ties
61. Base
63. Sierra ____
64. French income
65. M.D.'s group
67. "____ or Alive" (TV series)
73. Sullivan and Ames
76. Champlain or Tahoe
78. Zodiac ram
79. Premed course: abbr.
80. Producer Spielberg
83. Ruffs
84. Barkin and Burstyn
86. English school
88. Stomped
89. Trigger's rider
94. "Stagecoach" star
99. Fruit beverage
100. Small taste
101. ____ Jima
102. Affirmative vote
103. Take nourishment
104. Kind of bean or sauce
105. Sea, in Sevres
106. Actor Brooks

DOWN
1. Inexperienced
2. Bullfight cheer
3. Had being
4. Sup
5. "You ____ My Sunshine"
6. Patriotic group: abbr.
7. Apartment
8. ____ tree (stumped)
9. Fishing rod
10. Sunshine State: abbr.
11. Scurried
12. WWII intelligence group: abbr.
18. Hamilton bills
19. Before, to a poet
20. Disencumber
22. Sixth sense: abbr.
23. Delphi letter
24. Deviate
27. Hawaiian necklace
28. Antique
29. Miss Kitty of "Gunsmoke"
30. Write
31. "____ Maria"
32. Golf standard
33. Nabokov novel
34. Writer Deighton
36. "Bonanza" star
37. "____ pro nobis"
38. Soak flax
43. Pinky ____
44. Weird
45. Wisecrack
46. Musical note
47. Hair adornment
50. Attorney Becker on "L.A. Law"
51. Small fish
53. Author George ____
59. Genetic factor: abbr.
60. Member of Congress: abbr.

61. Brother's title
62. Guided
65. Jolson and Capone
66. Rug
68. Beret's kin
69. Historic time
70. Noise
71. Poor grade
72. Lion or baron suffix
74. Newsman Rather
75. Avenues: abbr.
77. Continuously
79. Actor Alan ____
81. DDE's command
82. Eggy drink
84. Sea bird
85. Base
87. Loch ____ monster
88. Norse god of thunder
89. Actress ____ Dawn Chong
90. Harem room
91. Up until now
92. ____ de Janeiro
93. Secret agent
94. "Jules and ____"
95. Have an obligation to
96. Southern potato
97. Comedian Louis ____
98. Lamprey

PUZZLE 200

ACROSS
1. Employer
5. Ocean vessel
9. Make happy
14. Prepare for publication
15. Couldn't ___ less
16. Instruct
17. Ripped
18. Location
19. Hag
20. Prize
22. Plot
24. Spelling contest
25. Was ahead
26. Olympic trophy
30. Swift
33. Weasel sound
36. Martini garnishes
38. Be untruthful
39. ___ the slate clean
40. Single
41. Frequently
43. Descended
44. Copier
45. Regret
46. King's seat
48. ___ in the face
49. Cheerful
51. Come in
52. "The Night ___ a Thousand Eyes"
53. Make a blunder
55. Explosions
58. Hook and ___
62. Banquet
63. Lounge around
65. Enjoy a book
67. Cream of the crop
68. Adored one
69. Military division
70. Senior
71. Moist
72. Use a keyboard

DOWN
1. Gamble
2. Smell
3. Father
4. Fret
5. Frighten
6. More difficult
7. Anger
8. Like two ___ in a pod
9. Engraved
10. Enticed
11. Nuclear particle
12. Musical pitch
13. Before, in poetry
21. Competent
23. Customer
26. Tooth
27. Wed on the run
28. Ate
29. State
31. Change
32. Pumpkin dessert
33. Aviator
34. Say
35. Singer Cetera of "Chicago"
37. Most tender
39. Alert
42. Mink, for one
47. Cattle group
49. Expert
50. Lemon color
52. Speed
54. Pep gathering
55. Saved by the ___
56. Put down
57. Slipped
59. Mild oath
60. Strange
61. Incline
62. Cover charge
64. "___ to Billy Joe"
66. Add color to

ACROSS

1. Grant
5. Performed
10. Equal to the task
14. In the midst of
15. Credulous
16. Table game
17. Best man's concern
18. Inexperienced
19. Playground
20. Belfries
22. Joshes
24. Went first
25. "___ M for Murder"
26. Fragrances
30. Snuggled
33. "Little ___"
34. Frequently
35. River bottom
37. Alter
38. Saute
39. "And Then There Were ___"
40. Clique
41. Feline animal
42. Taut
43. Two-toed flightless bird
46. Attorney
47. Uncle's wife
48. Hiatus
49. Vitamin C source
52. Love ballad
57. Anguish
58. Prospected
60. Environs
61. Stream
62. "___ by any other name . . ."
63. Partiality
64. Toboggan
65. City drain
66. Rational

DOWN

1. Sedans and coupes
2. Give off
3. Take a meal
4. Periphery
5. Obtuse and acute
6. Worried
7. Ascots
8. Dusk
9. Molar man
10. Dismay
11. Feathery stoles
12. Folk mythology
13. Lodge members
21. Blueprint
23. Nosh
25. Challenge
26. Overwhelms
27. Cowboy contest
28. Fails to mention
29. Was introduced to
30. Actor Jay ___ (Dennis the Menace)
31. "___ and Ivory" (Wonder song)
32. Thick
36. Stag or roe
38. Truth
39. Novel
41. Movie houses
42. Record
44. Sunbathed
45. Carpet
46. Pantry
48. Honking birds
49. Picks
50. Complain bitterly
51. Helper
52. Singer Phoebe ___
53. Arrests
54. Scotto song
55. College official
56. Alleviate
59. Choler

PUZZLE 202

ACROSS
1. Random try
5. Toward the stern
8. Breaches
12. Summon
13. Lobster eggs
14. Solo for Sills
15. "____ Graffiti"
17. Restrain
18. Change
19. Parking site
21. Poet's before
22. "____ Little Indians"
24. Crowd noise
26. Playmate
29. Wet dirt
31. Jot down
34. Fast horse
36. Every ____ and then
38. Quick-witted
39. Nary a once
41. Forty winks
43. Downcast
44. Well-known garden
46. ____ whiz!
48. Tin container
50. Solemn promise
52. Sports palace
56. Ungracious
58. Improved
60. Locale
61. Grant's foe
62. Point out
63. Shopping center
64. Piece out
65. Kinski film

DOWN
1. Ship's mast
2. Unexciting
3. "Rock of ____"
4. French hat
5. Rainbow
6. Colt
7. Pavarotti, e.g.
8. Car fuel
9. Blood carriers
10. Wharf
11. Identical
16. Bit of gossip
20. Pull behind
23. Type of buoy
25. "Raiders of the Lost ____"
26. Skillet
27. Have being
28. Lilac
30. Singer Henley
32. Reception
33. Finale
35. Fourposter, e.g.
37. Move back and forth
40. Race
42. Bog fuel
45. Princely
47. Assemble
48. Study for finals
49. Distinctive air
51. Seven days
53. Pennsylvania port
54. Profits
55. Thirst quenchers
57. Have a snack
59. To a ____

ACROSS

1. Eroded
4. Food fish
7. Garden tool
12. Floor-shiner
13. Mickey's ex
14. TV host Funt
15. Was
17. Carried
18. Nanny
19. Quote
20. Tennis star Ashe
22. Johnny ____
25. Hurls
28. Raw metal
29. Dander
30. To the sheltered side
31. Copycat
32. Tizzy
33. Map abbr.
34. Falsehood
35. Storms
36. Author Tolstoy
37. Reply
39. Sleep
41. Provokes
45. Steer
47. Playing marble
48. Fall bloomer
49. Wooden nail
50. Actress Bartok
51. Pinto and lima
52. Metric land unit
53. Sniggler's quarry

DOWN

1. Impresses deeply
2. Cab
3. Way out
4. Furnishes the food
5. Obvious
6. June honoree
7. Wit
8. Scheme
9. Changing
10. Ruby or Sandra
11. Wrap up
16. Ohio or Utah
19. Heal
21. Wishes
23. Famous canal
24. Wagers
25. Phone
26. Soothing plant
27. Spanish miss
31. "____ She Sweet"
32. Beetle Bailey character
34. Beams of light
35. Go back on one's word
38. Thirst quencher
40. Serene spot
42. General Robert ____
43. Split
44. Playful sea creature
45. Chat
46. Apply
47. Workout site

PUZZLE 203

PUZZLE 204

ACROSS

1. First woman
4. Health resort
7. ___ voyage
10. Food for an aardvark
13. Fall behind
14. Long ___ Sally
16. Destiny
17. Weeding tool
18. Place for petunias
21. Till
23. Grower
24. Baltimore bird
25. Workout locales
26. Expressions of surprise
28. Opposite of NNW
29. Neither's partner
31. Santa ___ Race Track
33. Sunbeam
36. Ginger drink
37. Carrot or cucumber
41. Native metal
42. Hive dweller
43. Orange drink
44. Goddess of the dawn
45. Collection of dishes
46. Leek's kin
49. Shovel
52. Foot digit
53. Dust cloth
54. Feels sore
57. "This Is ___ Tap"
60. Flightless bird
62. Walking on ___
64. Mauna ___
65. Fishing pole
67. Male sheep
68. Lawn weed
72. Expire
73. Director Reiner
74. Oaks and elms
75. Curvy letter
76. "___ a Living"
79. Chicken ___ king
80. Cereal grain
83. Transplants
86. Sell to consumers
89. Edible spear
92. Plant beginnings
96. Caribbean, for one
97. Sediment
98. Storm
99. Cookie grain
100. Household animal
101. Opposite of WSW
102. Scarlet
103. Not wet

DOWN

1. Santa's helper
2. Actor Kilmer
3. Self
4. Water vapor
5. Capital of France
6. Linen vestments
7. Indonesian island
8. German kings
9. Singers Young and Sedaka
10. Cry of triumph
11. Forget-me-___
12. Kind of summer shirt
15. Confederate general
16. Animal hair
19. Twisted
20. Humming sound
21. ___ Rica
22. Victory sign
25. Talent for growing plants
27. ___ the road
29. Capture
30. Bread spread
31. Become older
32. Lincoln's nickname
33. "I Never Promised You a ___"
34. "Butterflies ___ Free"
35. Still
37. Moving truck
38. McMahon and Asner
39. ___ Alamos
40. Sixth sense: abbr.
47. Memo of a debt
48. "___ the land of the free"
50. Hero of "Exodus"
51. Newsman Rather
55. Tic- ___ -toe
56. Knight's title

57. Call for help, on the ocean
58. Dads
59. Actress Nettleton
60. Go wrong
61. ____ Tse-tung
63. Large rodent
64. ____ Vegas
66. ____ Moines
69. Knuckles or ring
70. Congeal
71. Brings up
76. Writer Levin
77. Concise
78. Neighbor of Portugal
80. Policeman's emblem
81. Irked
82. Actress MacGraw
84. Flirt with the eyes
85. Egyptian king, for short
87. Always, in poems
88. Salty drop
89. Cleopatra's snake
90. Look at
91. Square of butter
93. Auction signal
94. Needlefish
95. Hog's haven

PUZZLE 205

ACROSS

1. Actor Pendleton
4. Babble
8. Actress Raines
12. Clockmaker Terry
13. Body of knowledge
14. Advertising light
15. Took nourishment
16. Caretaker
18. Emulated Cindy Crawford
20. Lower digit
21. Marsh plant
24. Seasons
28. Fare
31. Linen, e.g.
33. Long, long ____
34. Nibbles
35. Hollywood's Farrow
36. Makes proportional
38. Kind of tree
39. Gluts
40. Marquee name
42. Veggie
44. Noise
48. Take back
53. Black or Yellow
54. Atop
55. Singer Seeger
56. Be mistaken
57. Left
58. Blind part
59. "Native ____"

DOWN

1. Kind of tide
2. Tall, in Tijuana
3. TV's "Family ____"
4. Ice-skate feature
5. Homesite
6. Sculpture, e.g.
7. Root vegetable
8. Make esteemed
9. Meadow
10. Silent screen's Chaney
11. Picnic invader
17. Pries
19. Bard's before
22. Discharge
23. Appointments
25. Kind of bean
26. Follow
27. Bridge triumph
28. Yaks
29. Taj Mahal site
30. Horn's contribution
32. Examination
34. Army posts
37. Manuscript
38. Master
41. Resource
43. Cobras
45. Exploits
46. Famous fiddler
47. Mild oath
48. Tier
49. Genesis name
50. Enclosure
51. Slippery one
52. Depot: abbr.

PUZZLE 206

ACROSS

1. Neighbor of Cambodia
5. Electrical units
9. Thread's cylinder
14. Greek peak
15. Capricorn
16. Intertwine
17. B ____ Baker: 2 wds.
18. Freedom from anxiety
19. Gray
20. With one's ____ (in a practical stance): 4 wds.
23. Abandon
24. Styptic
25. Mr. Fleming
27. Slanting
32. Texas shrine
36. River to the Severn
39. Lupino and Tarbell
40. Stand fast: 4 wds.
43. College subject: abbr.
44. Sheer cotton
45. Songstress Lena
46. Type of floss
48. Honest ____
50. Wagers
53. Biceps band
58. Put a ____ (commit a faux pas): 4 wds.
63. Readied a printing press
64. At any ____
65. Borodin's prince
66. Uproar
67. Works at a cannery
68. Coty or Descartes
69. Kind of rehearsal
70. Bed support
71. Gaelic

DOWN

1. Lolls
2. Plus
3. Basket willow
4. ____ Barbara
5. Planned actions
6. Castle defense
7. Turkish bigwig
8. Stainless ____
9. Teems
10. 100 centavos
11. Hawaiian island
12. Range part
13. Furnish
21. Edible bulb
22. Type of fertilizer
26. Astronauts' org.: abbr.
28. Venice resort
29. Redolence
30. Chessman
31. Serf
32. Echoed
33. Magazine publisher Henry
34. Like ____ of bricks: 2 wds.
35. Neighbor of Wyo.
37. Ex-solders' group: abbr.
38. ____ Chaplin
41. Author Glasgow
42. Heat unit
47. Bears
49. Lowest
51. Civil wrongs
52. Garden pest
54. Watered silk
55. German gun
56. Certain collars
57. ____ on a match
58. Come upon
59. ____ about: 2 wds.
60. Dust Bowl victim
61. Hardy girl
62. Sicilian sight

ACROSS

1. Nimbus
5. Source of starch
9. Swap
14. Indigo dye
15. ____ Gemayel of Lebanon
16. Lofty nest
17. Cut into small pieces
18. Story
19. Commenced
20. Musical starring Judy Garland: 4 wds.
23. Yoko ____
24. Misfortune
25. Upright or grand
29. Alaskan town
32. Smears
36. Done
37. Passes
39. Depression-era agency: abbr.
40. Fairy-tale dwarf
44. Silkworm
45. Earthen wall
46. Sublease
47. Series
49. Actress Naldi
51. "Carmen," e.g.
52. Went first
54. Sun
56. Musical musical: 3 wds.
63. Raise
64. Dill seed
65. Apex
67. Decipher
68. Row
69. How ____ you!

70. Composers of commercials
71. Army command: abbr.
72. Paris airport

DOWN

1. Rhine feeder
2. Entity
3. Wealthy
4. Protected at sea
5. Glossy fabric
6. S.American river
7. Large lizard
8. Unique person
9. Prohibition
10. Shortened sail
11. Jason's ship
12. Portuguese navigator
13. Yet, to poets
21. Forested
22. Reside
25. Fathers: Fr.
26. Accustom
27. Acknowledge
28. Catnip
30. Group of eight
31. Miss Piggy's word
33. Place for a bracelet
34. Bramble
35. Father Christmas
38. Meander
41. Actress Evans of "Dynasty"

42. Glide on snow
43. Flower part: abbr.
48. Arm covering
50. Rise
53. German city
55. Customarily
56. Stomped
57. Rudder
58. Holiday
59. Monogram unit: abbr.
60. Piled hair style
61. Rive
62. Nobleman
63. Lad's group: abbr.
66. Door opener

185

PUZZLE 208

ACROSS

1. Cheat
5. Viper
8. Roman patriot
12. Toledo's lake
13. Indian dry spot
14. Imbecile
15. Chap
16. Champion
17. Likeness
18. See 38 Across: 4 wds.
21. Pestered
22. Transgress
23. Space initials
26. Gobi, e.g.
31. Port-au-Prince locale
35. Son of Judah
37. Perfume: var.
38. (With 18 Across) "___ boards shall reach from end to end." (Exodus 26:28): 5 wds.
41. Comfort
42. Corrida cheers
43. Songstress Della
44. Postal needs
46. South African town
48. Roman bronze
50. Rented
55. "And it came ___ days..." (I Kings 18:1): 4 wds.
61. Shepard and Paton
62. Ogle
63. Before: prefix
64. French river
65. Final
66. Type of silver: abbr.
67. Snick and ___
68. Time units: abbr.
69. Sunday talks: abbr.

DOWN

1. " . . . and Irad ___ Mehujael . . ." (Gen. 4:18)
2. Actress Dunne
3. Actress Lavin
4. Etta et al.
5. Attention-getting sound
6. Madras dress
7. Goads
8. Arrive
9. Noble horse
10. Roman wear
11. Individual
13. Vamp Bara
14. Pooh's creator
19. Skater Sonja
20. "We ___ Start the Fire" (Billy Joel song)
24. Dirt
25. South American range
27. Strongbox
28. Feminine suffix
29. College cheers
30. Elm or ash
31. Hurries
32. Biology course: abbr.
33. ___ boy!: 2 wds.
34. Other people
36. Aide: abbr.
39. Son of Amram
40. Law and ___
45. Dated
47. Warn
49. Actress Field
51. Pile up
52. A votre ___
53. Register
54. Color changers
55. Flat hats
56. "Good Earth" heroine: hyph.
57. Shave
58. Diarist Frank
59. Doubt
60. "___ of the D'Urbervilles"

186

ACROSS

1. Singer Cass
5. Father of Enos
9. Having an alkaline reaction
10. Met solos
12. Showing signs of age
13. Supple
15. Baseball deal
16. Bob Crane's TV role
19. Here, to Monique
20. Fashion vogue
21. Ran at an easy gait
22. Footprint
23. Anagram of tea
24. Rugged guys: hyph.
25. Tint
26. Keep at it
28. Made of cereal
29. In the first place
31. Sink
34. Reverting to type
38. One of the Horae
39. Caused to soar
40. Last queen of Spain
41. Donated
42. Fields of granular snow
43. Occident
44. Coastal state: abbr.
45. Revealed
46. Anthem
47. Bull's-eye
49. Servant's uniform
50. Contaminate
51. Sluggish
52. "___ Be Good"
53. Disavow

DOWN

1. Administrator
2. Digression
3. 1760 yards
4. Point-making tennis serve
5. Caesar or Waldorf
6. Ireland, to poets
7. Actor Conway
8. Natural site
9. Scold
11. Withdraw
12. Subway handhold
14. Mellow
16. Household engineer
17. Detective
18. Produced
21. Jacob's third son
22. Insurrection leader Daniel
24. City in the Ruhr
25. Sturdy
27. Part of a book
30. Currier's partner
31. Intolerant person
32. Landing place for Noah's ark
33. More than a couple
35. Unstable
36. Newspaper extra
37. Malicious
42. Smart, as in dress
43. Like loomed fabric
45. Curve
46. "___ eyes have seen . . ."
48. Actress Scala
49. Plug

PUZZLE 209

PUZZLE 210

ACROSS
1. Blockhead
5. Creature of ____
10. Swat
14. Othello's foe
15. City in Japan
16. Small monkey
17. Punishes severely: 4 wds.
20. Ancient ascetics
21. Dessert store
22. Needlefish
23. Grecian instrument
24. Snake's weapons
27. Raincoats
28. Speculate
31. Arabian gazelle
32. Time: Sp.
33. Painted metalware
34. Slept fitfully: 3 wds.
37. Morays
38. Crumbs
39. Adolescents
40. Opposite of NNW
41. Helm position
42. Terra ____
43. Hat edge
44. Outline
45. Good-luck charm
48. Actress Hartley
53. Fires: 4 wds.
55. Solar disk
56. Phonies
57. Dash
58. Scan
59. Feudal workers
60. Current events

DOWN
1. Mention
2. Actor Bert
3. Fairy tale heavy
4. Fate
5. Asian lilies
6. Star flower
7. Words for Scrooge
8. Alibi ____
9. Brindled pet: 2 wds.
10. Tend the furnace
11. Find agreeable
12. Perfume: var.
13. Feel for
18. Zigzag quickly
19. Boat blades
23. Inserts fat
24. Cleaving tools
25. Theater passage
26. Loch ____ monster
27. ____ Carlo
28. Actress Lisa ____
29. Actress Verdugo
30. Spreads hay
31. Sweetsop
32. Seraglio
33. Waste allowance
35. Rex Harrison role
36. Paradise
41. Son of Zeus
42. Love pat
43. Mixture
44. Skier Phil
45. Chinese gelatin
46. Small insect
47. Eye part
48. Stingy
49. Parallel
50. Far: pref.
51. Defrost
52. Time periods
54. That boy's

ACROSS

1. Trout's cousin
6. Allows
10. Hang around
14. Slugger Rod
15. Mine entrance
16. General's helper
17. Skirt style: hyph.
18. Wharf
19. Till the soil
20. Lessee
22. Song syllable
23. Withered
24. Kind of code
26. Cop's prey
28. Censored
33. Tablet
34. "On a ___ Day . . ."
35. Circus worker
37. Steal
40. Em, to Dorothy
41. Detested
42. Record
43. Nan's twin
44. Punt pusher
45. Dice throw
46. Total
47. Pro rata share
49. Throw about
53. "___ Who Dared"
54. Salary
55. ___ sister
57. Catch
62. Sea eagle
63. Chaste
65. Jagged
66. Ripe
67. Applies
68. "___ 66"
69. Drags
70. ___, weather, and sports
71. T-bone, e.g.

DOWN

1. War memento
2. "The ___ Animal"
3. Actress Moran
4. Fast time
5. Plucking tool
6. Circuit
7. Prepare copy
8. Banks
9. Short of money
10. Fell back
11. Greased
12. Love a lot
13. Less
21. ___ Tin Tin
25. Flower part
27. Hearing organ
28. Read quickly
29. Hint
30. Split
31. Have lunch
32. Passe
36. Kind of badge
37. Carry on
38. Doing business
39. Flex
41. Rustic
42. Actor Danson
44. Lay
45. Saints and ___
46. Spirited horses
48. Victory sign
49. Exude moisture
50. Freight
51. Spiro ___
52. Waken
56. Make coffee
58. Jog
59. Rake
60. Movie mutt
61. Quick look
64. Curvy letter

PUZZLE 212

ACROSS

1. Runner or pay
5. Head part
10. Culture medium
14. Counselor: abbr.
15. Bower
16. Inspire
17. Geranium nursery
19. Plant start
20. Horse command
21. Orient
22. Stumpers
24. Barking puppies
26. Street urchin
27. Ohio town
28. Essence
29. Rock group ____ Speedwagon
32. Teed off
35. Recruit
37. Papa in "Mama"
38. Decompose
39. Tops: 2 wds.
40. Prime meridian site
43. Suit of mail
44. Yes
45. Mine finds
46. Prior, in poetry
47. Lowest point
49. Weather
53. ____ Island, N.Y.
55. Scottish hillside
56. Sprinted
57. Principles
58. Go-ahead: 2 wds.
61. "Dies ____"
62. Auriculate
63. Queen of Jordan
64. Hindu illusion
65. Sunders
66. ____ -slapper

DOWN

1. Loose-fitting
2. "____ Grows in Brooklyn": 2 wds.
3. Stainless ____
4. Hurricane center
5. African desert
6. Traverse
7. Border on
8. ____ Alamos
9. Get ready
10. Too: Fr.
11. Theater lounge
12. Curing chemical
13. Cincinnati team
18. Poor
23. Sign of the future
25. Analyze grammatically
26. "Pride ____ before a fall"
28. Gators' cousins
30. Inventor Rubik
31. Lulu
32. Seaweed
33. Not any
34. English illustrator
35. Actor Rosey
36. Sultan's wives
41. Stem joint
42. Laundry squeezer
43. "Tempest" spirit
46. Antelopes
48. Lost: 2 wds.
49. Code
50. Inert gas
51. Western resort
52. ____ nous
53. Svelte
54. Home of Irish kings
55. Swiss capital
59. Actress Charlotte
60. Writing liquid

190

ACROSS

1. Rhythm
6. Exec's deg.
9. Unusual
13. Oak nut
14. Scottish port
15. Measuring device
16. Fabled swine: 3 wds.
19. Long periods
20. French article
21. Certain penguin
22. Piercing tool
24. Restricts
25. Stetson: 2 wds.
30. Gazelle
31. Little while, to a Scot
32. Joint
36. Spasm
37. Soup kitchen workers
40. Spanish uncle
41. Singer Paul ____
43. Competitor
44. Houston player
46. Girl's special age: 2 wds.
49. Antics
51. Thrice: prefix
52. Multitudes
53. Motorists' gp.
55. "____ each life . . ."
59. Lucky charms: 2 wds.
62. Tricks
63. Humbug!
64. Staircase post
65. Unlocks, in poems
66. Bard's before
67. Bone: pref.

DOWN

1. London gallery
2. Vibrate
3. "September ____"
4. Foretell
5. Countdown ending
6. Principal
7. Computer unit
8. Aptitude
9. Is contrite
10. Inclined
11. TV host Philbin
12. Highlander talk
15. Radio and TV
17. Soothe
18. Shaving foam
23. Mural location
24. Smirks
25. So long: hyph.
26. Paddy's land
27. Actor Nolte
28. Dames
29. Young hooter
33. Imitation: suff.
34. River to the Ouse
35. "____ Mullins"
38. Hesitant
39. ____ -Coburg- Gotha
42. Is ambitious
45. Tries for
47. Fish traps
48. Type type: abbr.
49. Horse's rump
50. Charm
52. Hair style
53. At a distance
54. Pain
56. Eft
57. Hatrack
58. Norway's capital
60. Director Burrows
61. Yoko ____

PUZZLE 213

191

PUZZLE 214

ACROSS

1. Male singer
5. Separate the wheat from the ——
10. Stuff full
14. Contribute a tenth
15. Excessive: Fr.
16. Flowering shrub
18. Give permission
19. Staff of life
20. Think
21. It's served at a luau
22. Saucy
24. Debatable
26. Nothing
27. Endurance
29. Supple
30. Repast
31. In addition
32. Form of rummy
34. Squeeze out water
37. Ballad
38. Goal
42. Lightly cooked
43. Golfer's cry
44. Thoughtful
45. Director Burrows
46. Fashion
47. Tined utensil
48. Moving truck
49. First woman of mythology
51. Snake sound
52. Rubies
53. Takes by theft
54. Transmitted
55. Thick soup
56. Attained
58. Small portion
59. Desire
62. Cooking fat
63. Periods of decline
67. Commotion
68. Persian fairy
69. Location
70. Kindled
71. Skiing hill
73. Egg-shaped
75. Moslem virgin
77. Evergreen trees
78. Cantaloupe, e.g.
79. Senior
80. Flog
81. Slumbered
82. Clarinet mouthpiece

DOWN

1. Intolerant person
2. Courtyards
3. That woman
4. Oozing
5. Hooded snake
6. Injure
7. Consumed
8. Concocting evidence against
9. Soft felt hat
10. Congeal
11. Shred
12. Straighten
13. Excessive excitement
14. Faucets
17. Prison room
23. Terminate
25. —— Rockefeller
28. Lion's neck hair
29. Ebb
30. Damages
32. Apple center
33. Armored vehicle
34. Encloses
35. Capital of Morocco
36. Goddess of peace
37. Bicarbonate of ——
39. Donor
40. Avoid
41. Uptight
43. Realty sign: 2 wds.
44. Pillar
46. Burrowing animal
47. Discover

50. Small arrow
51. Pay attention
52. Massages
54. Dry up
55. Black leopard
57. Billiards rebounds
58. Pair
59. Stinging insect
60. Speak off the cuff: hyph.
61. Not a soul: 2 wds.
63. Forked out
64. Shake a tail
65. Exhausted
66. Agitate
68. Nuisance
69. Come to a halt
72. Coal size
74. Strong beer
76. Bullfight cheer

PUZZLE 214

PUZZLE 215

• ARTFUL •

ACROSS

1. Blemish
4. Distort
8. Layer
11. In the style of
12. Winged
13. "Norma ____"
14. Celebrates wildly
21. ____ gin fizz
22. Weeps
23. Significant period
24. Pointless
27. Greek letter
28. Give off
29. Without doubt
31. Car for hire
34. Mineral fuel
36. Sediment
37. Yale students
38. Caviar
41. Barley bristle
42. Shopping center
43. "One ____ Beyond"
45. Vase
46. Embankment
48. Destroys: Brit.
50. Actor Carney
51. Wood for baseball bats
52. Sheriff's band
54. Bicuspids, e.g.
57. Overhead trains
58. Muddy
62. "Dies ____"
65. Rightful
66. Summer beverage
67. Previously owned
69. Coil
70. Pipe
71. More briny
74. Cover
76. Aerie
77. Lyricist Gershwin
79. Redact
80. First woman
81. Astronaut Shepard
82. Female horse
85. Very successfully
91. Wrath
92. Taboo
93. False statement
94. Seedcase
95. Chow
96. Meadow

DOWN

1. Chart
2. Expression of regret
3. Train track
4. Had been
5. Ht.
6. College cheer
7. Gift
8. Type of court
9. Legislative acts
10. Longing
15. "Of Mice and Men," e.g.
16. Rip
17. Toddler
18. Give up a claim to
19. Actor Idle
20. Facts
25. "____ Living"
26. Carpenter's need
28. Way out
29. Solicits votes from
30. Adverse
32. Jolson and Hirt
33. Refreshed one's knowledge of
34. Baseball's Ripken, Jr.
35. Be beholden to
39. Unrefined metal
40. USN officer
42. Unit of length
44. Chatter
47. Sounds of hesitation
49. Enzyme suffix

52. Green vegetable
53. Ancient
55. Bath
56. "____ Haw"
59. Beginning
60. "____ True?" (Brenda Lee song)
61. Actor Majors
62. Charged particle
63. Ramble
64. Mimicked
68. Made a hole
69. Tilting
70. Sum
72. Fresh
73. One of Jacob's sons
75. Chauffeured vehicle
78. Beam of light
81. Hair style
83. Tumble
84. Great Lake
86. Trendy
87. Neither's partner
88. African antelope
89. Ear of corn
90. Baltic, e.g.

PUZZLE 216

ACROSS

1. Gabor and Marie Saint
5. Summit
9. Sahara native
13. Went away
17. Johann Sebastian ___
18. Film ___
19. Anger
20. Assam silkworm
21. Cognizant of
22. He has his day
24. Lubricates
25. Snuggled
27. Author of "The Gold Bug"
28. Pointed beards
30. Lass
31. Hinder the growth of
33. For future broadcast: abbr.
34. Audibly
37. Bird dog
39. Bower
43. Fabricate
44. Flies alone
45. Ostrichlike bird
47. Noah's scout
48. Stop spot
49. Plant product
50. Hammett's hero
52. Belfry denizen
53. Delayed
55. Moist
56. Says slowly
58. Objects to
59. Ribbon
60. Rubbish
61. Reluctant
63. Piping god
64. Salad sauce
67. Fiver
68. Baseball misplay
70. "Archie" role
71. Driving site
72. Emmets
74. Have dinner
75. Attends
76. Paper quantity
77. Music pauses
79. Thinks of
81. Bothers
82. "Brother ___"
84. Unhappily
85. Fall behind
86. Cure-all
90. Teachers' org.
91. Reindeer's kin
95. Warning
96. Nut gatherers
99. Paddles
100. Lou or Rex
101. Divert
102. Minced oath
103. Cairo's river
104. Finishes
105. Mentally sound
106. Devitalizes
107. Snow coaster

DOWN

1. Black
2. Wind indicator
3. Plays a part
4. ___ wedding
5. Kind person
6. Wood unit
7. "O Sole ___"
8. Outburst
9. Fervent
10. Stadium cry
11. Excited
12. Sired
13. Dancer's garb
14. Buffalo's lake
15. Police report
16. Russian press group
23. People, places, or things
26. Young boy
29. Camel's-hair coat
31. Financially sound
32. Entice
34. Liquid with a low pH
35. The ___ Ranger
36. Salves
37. Holds a stance
38. Kiwi bird
40. Quails
41. ___ Office
42. Soaks flax
44. Transmitters

196

46. Formal speech
49. Wash lightly
50. Darn
51. Efface
54. Essence
55. Got a gold
57. Onager
59. Pub
60. Hurries
61. Long off
62. Tarzan's transport
63. Pius and Paul
64. Small, lacy mat
65. Organized
66. Prized ones
69. Capek play
70. Ducks
73. Leaves high and dry
75. Water walker
76. Sections
78. Pouch
80. Dog
81. Golf goal
83. Midterms
85. Endures
86. Skin opening
87. Prayer closer
88. Want
89. Bluish-green
91. Applaud
92. Dip out
93. Shield rim
94. Car sign
97. Large vase
98. Age

PUZZLE 217

ACROSS

1. Mountain cat
5. Dove's nest
9. Arrayed
13. Beyond
17. Modern Persia
18. Cheers
19. Grass skirt
20. Wilderness walk
21. Boxer's punch
22. Polynesian instruments
23. Isaac's son
24. Norse god
25. "Batman" butler
27. Part of the parade
30. Country roads
32. Wild ox
33. Mai ____ cocktail
34. Volumes
36. Coop sound
38. Copies
43. Moos
44. Poke
45. Songbirds
46. Snack
47. Barcelona bravo
48. Small change
49. Sandal
50. Byron poem
51. African swine
53. Demon
54. Not flat
55. Brynner of films
56. Nanny and billy
57. Heflin or Johnson
58. Cloudburst
61. Time measures
62. Summer cooler
66. Secret writing
67. Yogi ____
68. Oceans
69. Ancient vessel
70. Flying saucer
71. Preserves
72. Ring
73. Mild oath
74. Spoke softly
76. Mandibles
77. Slights
78. ____ in a day's work
79. Holbrook or Linden
80. Praises
82. Doris Day film
88. Lose one's balance
91. Well-behaved
92. Snigglers' catch
93. Flood survivor
95. Revere's journey
96. Or ____!
97. Scandal-sheet's specialty
98. Contest
99. Lady in King Arthur's court
100. Discovered
101. Large book
102. Mast
103. Accomplishment

DOWN

1. Tailless mammal
2. Eurasian range
3. Standish's vessel
4. Parkas
5. Rough
6. Cabinet wood
7. Those guys
8. Tried
9. Bill
10. Luxuriant
11. Asian range
12. Formidable
13. Fear
14. Opera role
15. Epidermis
16. Lean toward
26. Naval off.
28. Converse, slangily
29. Hoods' guns
31. Parsley unit
34. Boxing punch
35. Alley Oop's girl
37. Chunk of eternity
38. Actor Jeremy ____
39. Patch
40. Greenish blue
41. James ____ Carter
42. Postpone
44. Combine
45. Excites
48. Buddy
49. Princess's headwear
50. Sales pitch
52. Phoenician port
53. Down on all ____
54. Airwave buffs
56. Done in by a bull

57. Glass bottle
58. Slimy stuff
59. Health food
60. Bloodhound's clue
61. Roll-call response
62. Fewest
63. Roman monk
64. Faded
65. Tackles' neighbors
67. Stoutest
68. Stitch
71. Pick over
72. Fence stakes
73. Stepped inside
75. Young lady of yore
76. Pickle container
77. Petition
79. Swiftness
81. Different
82. Gets on in years
83. Axis extremity
84. Kennedy matriarch
85. Nautilus's skipper
86. Bluish purple
87. Lather
89. Actress Adams
90. Actor Foxx
94. Japanese pearl diver

PUZZLE 218

ACROSS

1. Singer Gluck
5. Sunday speech: abbr.
8. Harvest goddess
11. English composer
15. Noose
16. "Graf ___"
17. Victory signs
19. Pribilof dweller
20. Spanish pot
21. Hurries
22. Epochal
23. Concordes
24. Voter's choice
26. Jerusalem's country: abbr.
28. Fracas
30. Streisand film-country singer
35. Abandon
38. Hindrance
39. Footballer Y.A. ___
40. "You ___ My Sunshine"
41. Fully developed
43. Oil cartel
45. Gash
46. Prima donna
48. Highlander talk
50. Mediocre
53. Dawn goddess
54. Soak through
55. Organic compound
58. Sundae toppings
60. MacDonald-Eddy film- "Paper Roses" singer
65. Sandwich store
66. First month, to Jose
67. Aloud
70. Head covering
73. Styptic
75. Evergreens
77. ___ and dine
78. Clarinet mouthpiece
80. Red planet
83. Baseballer Mel and kin
85. Spanish queen
86. Take into custody
89. Bumpkin
91. "Carmen" and "Aida"
93. Hepburn film- Gershwin song, with "Oh"
96. Tennessee ___ Ford
97. Society bud
98. Kind of illusion
102. Put punch in the punch
104. Liver spread
106. With regard to
108. Only
109. Crafts partner
110. For keeps
111. Necessity
112. Baking unit
113. Essence
114. Printers' measures
115. Rove
116. Cozy abode

DOWN

1. Lily plant
2. Loaf
3. Beauty mark
4. Geronimo, for one
5. Line
6. Shoebox trio
7. Inhabit
8. Bulge
9. ___ capita
10. Disreputable
11. Forces
12. Colonize again
13. "King" Cole
14. City trains
16. Sheep dog
18. Slumbered
25. Region: abbr.
27. Without a companion
29. Medieval lyric poem
31. Texas city
32. Caustic substances
33. Potpourri
34. Seines
35. Fathers
36. Perry's 1813 battle site
37. Cleave
42. Bonus
44. Companion
47. Footless
49. To be, in Toulouse
51. Total
52. Sioux
56. German article
57. Shoal
59. Cover for Rainier

61. Red or Black
62. Building wing
63. Baltimore player
64. Laundry aid
68. O'Neill's Christie
69. Grasslands
70. Pack full
71. Lofty home
72. Makes faultless
74. Yucatan Indian
76. Bent down
79. Most cherished
81. Hot ____ (speed demons)
82. Terrier type
84. Stain
87. Vice
88. Rubbish
90. Receding
92. Electrical wizard
94. Depart
95. Stabbed, in a corrida
99. Shoreline recess
100. Pub brews
101. Season before Easter
102. Dawdle
103. Tycoon Onassis
105. Bowling frames
107. Teachers' gp.

PUZZLE 219

ACROSS

1. Lams out
6. Conning-tower device
11. Postage item
16. Sweater size
17. Playing marble
18. Bock's kin
19. Labor group
20. Pollute
22. Chill
23. Bishop's domain
25. Younger son
26. Napoleonic marshal
27. Sweet course
29. Actress Gray
30. Scullers' needs
31. Scents
33. Does usher's work
35. Head honcho
38. Certain Amerinds
40. Abraded
44. Eureka!
45. Actress Rosemary: 2 wds.
47. "—— Onegin"
48. Cavalry sword
50. Wood knots
52. Lachrymal drops
53. Subtly satiric
55. Gutter
57. GI's '50s ally
58. Hunting dogs
60. O'Hara home
61. Troubles
62. Redacts
64. Goads
66. Cicatrix
69. Bristle
71. Floral shrubs
75. Highlands hat
76. Stairway post
77. Japanese coin
78. Baden-Baden, e.g.
79. Sol Hurok et al.
82. Complete
84. Take it easy
85. Musical show
86. Turn inside out
87. Was lost in slumber
88. Active ones
89. Pub missiles

DOWN

1. Liquid
2. Jousting weapon
3. Iroquoian Indians
4. Self
5. Intuited
6. Oval
7. Past
8. Reel or tarantella
9. Floral essences
10. Prepares
11. Skirt feature
12. August hue
13. Guam's capital
14. Measuring device
15. —— upon (hunts)
21. Threat
24. Irregularly notched
28. Mayday!
30. Kind of orange
32. Meager
34. Verity
35. Foundation
36. Chicago's airport
37. Wooden shoe
39. Chic
41. Actress White
42. Sign up
43. Office furniture
45. Desiccated

46. Malaysian boats
49. Ingress
51. Outshines
54. Emergencies
56. Bandage material
59. One in charge of the wine
61. Greenland, for one: abbr.
63. 3-D
65. Carried on
66. Rouses
67. Ship of the desert
68. Sufficient
70. Well's mate
72. Fragrant compound
73. Separated
74. Epsom ——
76. Waiting-room word
80. Like, orate
81. "—— Town" (Wilder)
83. Eggs

1	2	3	4	5	■	6	7	8	9	10	■	11	12	13	14	15
16						17							18			
19						20					21					
22			■	23	24			25					■	26		
27			28					29				■	30			
■			31				32		33			34			■	
35	36	37		■	38			39	■	40				41	42	43
44			■	45					46	■	47					
48			49		■	50				51	■	52				
53				■	54	■	55				56		■	57		
58					59	■	60					■	61			
■			62				63	■	64			65		■		
66	67	68		■	69			70	■	71			■	72	73	74
75			■	76						77			■	78		
79			80					81			■	82	83			
84				■	85					■	86					
87				■	88					■	89					

PUZZLE 220

ACROSS

1. Wild attempt
5. Red planet
9. Hops kiln
13. Protective covering
17. Capture
18. Actor Guinness
19. London district
20. Follow
21. Director Kazan
22. Roman's warning
24. Kind of pressure
25. Speak of
27. African river
28. Actress Sommer
29. Character in "Prince Valiant"
30. Holiday
31. Sunbathe
34. "The Lone Ranger" star
37. Lacerated
38. Bakery offerings
42. Wheel shaft
43. Nautical greeting
44. "The Singing Cowboy"
46. Prune
47. Hesitated
49. Grove
50. Honey factory
51. Oslo's locale
52. Ornamental stone
53. Made like a sheep
54. Lamprey
55. Lone Ranger's pal
56. Old French coin
57. Empty
60. Skeleton part
61. Titans
64. Stop
65. Bother
67. Cow type
69. Physician's org.
70. Icebergs
71. Bargain
72. Covet
73. Malocclusion expert
75. Young beef
76. North African antelope
77. English horn
78. Southpaw's hand
79. Elec. measure
80. Eliminates
83. Cabaret
85. Steered
89. Untouchable serves
90. Most routine
92. Pakistan's language
93. Function
94. Completed
95. Sputter
96. Plant
97. Oklahoma town
98. Slalom necessity
99. Simple
100. Bronte's governess

DOWN

1. Goblet feature
2. Invention
3. Like
4. Withdraw
5. Georgia city
6. Lyricist Lerner
7. Race the engine
8. Vista
9. Missouri river
10. First-rate
11. Fruit ices
12. Comedian Smothers
13. Kansas capital
14. Cain's brother
15. Stink
16. Bonfire
23. Charge
26. Indignation
30. Cuisine
32. Israeli port
33. Foxy
34. Coaster
35. Yaks
36. Dairy-case purchase
37. Those people
39. Hip bones
40. Explore
41. Went over the limit
43. Inland sea
44. Major artery
45. Hair style
48. Pitcher
49. Shrewd
50. Creepy place
52. Arias

53. Elegant accessories
55. Melody
56. Threshold
57. African lake
58. Cloth of gold
59. Verve
61. Hockey target
62. Watch over
63. Hindu deity
65. Ditto

66. Reporter's pad
67. Cook
68. Goddess of night
70. White lie
71. Fortification
74. Flipped
75. Forbid
76. Leather worker's tool

78. Citrus fruits
79. Miss ____ of "Gunsmoke"
80. Seldom seen
81. Sacred image
82. Sandwich shop
84. All: pref.
85. Greek letters

86. Low card
87. River in Germany
88. Tenderfoot
90. Today's re- cordings: abbr.
91. Govt. agency

PUZZLE 221

ACROSS

1. Seeger
5. Copied
9. Type of roast
13. City on the Tevere
17. Comedian King
18. Audition aim
19. Silkworm
20. Black, to a bard
21. Pilot error: 2 wds.
24. Sediment
25. Cat or wool type
26. Century plant
27. Takes out
29. Bell sound
31. Gush out
33. Steely ____ (rock group)
34. Showed affection
38. Actor Jannings
40. Gaze
44. Hail!
45. Lotus-____
47. Uppity one
49. Little cut
50. Disencumbers
52. Morning sight
54. Type of bag
56. Stubbed item
57. Figure out
59. Heaps
61. Hoist
63. Church part
65. Leaks through
67. Animal shelter
68. Firefighting equipment
71. Worn out
73. Right page
76. Dos Passos work
77. Confirmation, e.g.
79. Winter wear
81. ____-fry
82. Prong
84. Underground chamber
86. Alley term
88. Chemical suffix
89. Fragrant compound
91. Trust
93. Picturesque
95. Muffler mangler
97. ____-do-well
99. Bonds
100. Like most fuels
104. Narrow valley
106. Searches blindly
110. Away from wind
111. Study of clairvoyance
114. Desserts
115. Mesabi Range ore
116. Student's bane
117. Setters
118. Popcorn seasoning
119. Small nick
120. Bus stops: abbr.
121. Once

DOWN

1. " ____ Don't Preach"
2. Verve
3. Chinese dynasty
4. Put into cipher
5. Little Rock locale
6. Mystery author
7. Actress Raines
8. Transactions
9. Saves
10. Swiss canton
11. Intellect
12. Called to the phone
13. Shows umbrage
14. Newspaper notice, for short
15. Lawn pest
16. Aardvarks' treats
22. Come into being
23. Negative reply
28. ____ Vegas
30. Outfit
32. Plane part
34. Mind
35. Like some fans
36. Wordy
37. French saint
39. Knowledge
41. ____ Circle
42. Fracas
43. Fencing sword
46. Partner of regulations
48. Club or park
51. Fish
53. Nest sounds
55. Kind of hug
58. ____ and anon

60. Glasses, for short
62. Contends
64. Actor Blore
66. Walkaways
68. Stringed instrument
69. Sale condition: 2 wds.
70. Nova
72. Land stretch
74. Miss Louise
75. Hershiser of baseball
78. Plumb
80. Some trains
83. Most strange
85. Plush
87. January, in Madrid
90. Operate
92. Kennel sound
94. Tristan's love
96. Lukewarm
98. Musical stops
100. Shoots the breeze
101. Lamb
102. Perceive
103. Be bold
105. Moscow negative
107. Needy
108. Hen grenades
109. Method: abbr.
112. Darling of baseball
113. Jefferson Davis's group: abbr.

PUZZLE 222

• A BIT OF KNAVERY •

ACROSS

1. Ship's movement
4. Move quickly
8. Split
13. Marathon unit
17. Lacquered metal
18. Riyadh resident
19. De Mille ballet
20. Horatian creations
21. Author James ___
22. Cooking pots
23. Enthusiastic
24. Rattletrap
25. Busy knave?
28. Harsh
29. Zounds!
30. Vientiane's land
31. Crow's call
32. Dillon portrayer
34. Knaves' fashion statements?
41. Semivowel
42. Choice
44. Uplift
45. Conger
46. Outfits
47. Long-billed sandpiper
49. Actress Janis ___
50. Celestial bear
51. Pass with flying colors
52. Aggravate
53. Baptismal receptacles
54. Concord
55. Stinging knaves?
58. Cloaks
59. Manipulated
60. Lennon's love
61. Diner card
62. Married
64. Knaves' light sources?
70. Harassed
71. Cetus
73. Dancer Shearer
74. Triumphant cry
75. Humanities
76. ___ facie
77. Comedienne Brice
78. Maui goose
79. Engraved stamp
80. Physicist Galvani
81. Absent
82. Anything
83. Trapped knave?

86. Shoddy
88. Increases
89. Wading bird
91. Course
92. Runs
95. Preachy knave?
102. Julie Christie role
103. Money
104. Disintegrate
105. Actress Martinelli
106. Oppositionist
107. Playful mammal
108. Calcutta garments
109. Mississippi mud
110. Stork's seat
111. Affirmative replies
112. Short gaiter
113. Bishopric

DOWN

1. System of exercises
2. Herring sauce
3. Relaxation times
4. Potato dishes
5. Gather
6. Former Secretary of the Interior
7. Aversion
8. Fold
9. Shipment
10. Brink
11. Charges
12. Craggy peak

13. Punk hairdo
14. March date
15. Vault
16. Discern
17. Muslim cap
18. Divans
26. Double curve
27. Libertine
28. Suggestive
31. Cabaret
32. Restaurant owner of song
33. Star in Orion
35. Campus figures
36. Modify
37. Lively dances
38. Weird
39. Finals
40. Destroy
41. Dreary
42. "___ Zapata!"
43. Oil letters
47. Stitched
48. Arabian region
49. Novelist Chaim ___
50. Excessive
52. Put forward
53. Neutral perch
54. ___ Mountains (Utah range)
56. Sitars
57. Australian animal
58. English king
61. Chief
62. Diva Callas
63. Nahuatl
64. Actor Farr
65. Yemen's neighbor
66. Single
67. Ratite birds
68. Nursery worker
69. "___ Got a Way"
70. Mecca pilgrimage: var.
71. Court document
72. Exalted
76. Groaners
77. Guile
78. Unnecessary
80. Rims
81. Asian desert
82. Dandy
84. Mideastern capital
85. Cyclists
86. Attribute
87. Desires
90. Looped band
92. Tartlike pastry
93. Swimmer's path
94. Food scraps
95. Burlap fiber
96. Deeds
97. Algonquian language
98. Israeli dance
99. Ballet bend
100. ___ Royale
101. Make a doily
103. "The Thin Man" actress

ACROSS

1. Clemens's nom de plume
6. Spellbound
10. Greek war god
14. Barriers
19. Female vampire
20. Or ____!
21. Dawdles
22. Mature
23. Circus performer
24. Home, in Veracruz
25. Skier's delight
26. Longest European river
27. October custom
30. Halloween sprite
31. "____ Are So Beautiful"
32. Killer whales
33. With a triangular sail
34. Went by train
38. Italian dessert
41. Ilk
42. Sacred Egyptian bull
43. Alaskan city
44. Person in an animal's form
49. Spook
51. Candlenut trees
52. Fresh flower
54. Iranian coin
55. Diving duck
56. Chemist's lair
57. Quizzes
58. Bandleader Count ____
59. Makes a boot repair
61. Epochs in history
62. Trust
63. Halloween decorations
67. Goes diving
71. Beams
72. Hates
76. Eagle's weapon
77. Reaches
79. Heating fuel
80. Watering places
82. Large vases
83. Modify
84. Speed
85. Sorceress
86. Symbol of bad luck
88. "Kon-____"
89. Apollo's mother
90. Sins
91. Pistol holder
94. Irish
95. Bull's-eye
98. Umps
99. Youngster
101. Halloween demons
102. Scary place
108. Throng
109. Servant
111. Soften
112. Window covering
114. Change
115. Lucid
116. Sprints
117. Rangy
118. Splits
119. Tool building
120. Proofreader's mark
121. Geena Davis film

DOWN

1. Thoughtful help letters
2. Cartoonist Kelly
3. Cupid
4. Honeycreeper
5. Actress Kulp
6. Gain back
7. Like a wing
8. Furtive whisper
9. Cafes
10. French region
11. Blusters
12. Self
13. Compass pt.
14. Old French dance
15. Sand brick
16. Rayon fabric
17. Basketball's Baylor
18. Ollie's partner
28. Greek island
29. Coastal eagle
30. Director Marshall
33. Loamy soil
34. Fad
35. Land of Solomon's time
36. Electron tube
37. Hairpin curves
39. Reveal
40. Ancient Dead Sea kingdom
41. "M*A*S*H" actress
45. Stole
46. Seine feeder
47. Rested
48. Absconded
50. Hector, for one
51. Actor Guinness
52. Faculty heads
53. Cong. aide
57. Cafeteria items
58. Give
60. ____ Palmas
61. Spiral-horned animal
62. Genetic letters
64. Algerian port
65. Draw forth
66. Part
67. End
68. Psychologist Jung
69. Arm bone
70. Pear variety
73. Ethiopia's Selassie
74. Organic compound
75. Religious groups
77. Astute
78. Strokes gently
79. Sturdy trees
81. Boot
83. Farm measures
84. Lagers
87. Bowlers
88. Soy product
91. Pointed
92. Firstborn
93. Cheer
95. Oar fulcrum
96. Major artery
97. More curt
98. German river
100. Old Spanish coin
101. Indian river steps
103. Tense
104. Serf
105. ____ Bator
106. Croon
107. Sumerian water god
109. Authors' drafts
110. Sigh of satisfaction
113. Pigment

PUZZLE 224

DOUBLE TROUBLE

Not really double trouble, but double fun! Solve this puzzle as you would a regular crossword, EXCEPT place one, two, or three letters in each box. The number of letters in each answer is shown in parentheses after its clue.

ACROSS

1. Tins (4)
3. Turkish title (5)
6. Molded again (6)
9. Flower holder (4)
10. Radio noise (6)
12. More arid (5)
13. Cuts (6)
15. Insult (7)
16. Dog types (6)
17. Ask (7)
19. Cut of beef (8)
21. Undecided (10)
24. Cure (4)
26. Having the same direction (8)
28. Tidy (4)
29. Bright chatter (8)
30. Ponti's wife (5)
31. Chic (11)
33. Reddish purple (7)
34. Guess (8)
37. Flower dealer (7)
39. Ravings (7)
42. Protection (4)
43. Exterior (5)
44. Tennessee city (7)
46. Take-home pay (3)
47. List of candidates (5)
48. Twosomes (5)
49. Carol (4)

DOWN

1. Polltaker (9)
2. Harsh (6)
3. Italian staple (5)
4. Employees (5)
5. Head cover (4)
6. Robin (9)
7. Sobbed (5)
8. Michaelmas daisies (6)
11. Donation (12)
14. Nut collector (8)
18. ___ Park, Colorado (5)
20. Mechanical routine (4)
22. Singly (10)
23. Whip (4)
24. Core (5)
25. To the calm side (4)
26. Sitting room (6)
27. Director Woody ___ (5)
29. Full (7)
31. Bog (3)
32. Actor Vigoda et al. (4)
33. Judicial officer (10)
35. Forms a mental picture (8)
36. Trying out (7)
37. Treats with disdain (6)
38. Russian city (4)
40. Inclined way (4)
41. Lose hope (7)
45. Show disapproval (4)

PUZZLE 225

FIVE SHIFTS

Slide each horizontal strip left or right up to four spaces so that five common 5-letter words read through the windows, from top to bottom.

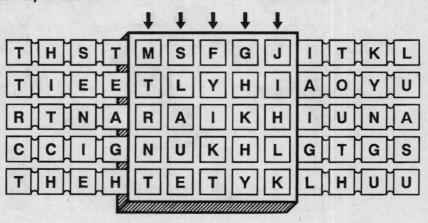

• FLOWERY WORDS •

ACROSS
1. Actress Thompson
5. Bunyan's blue ox
9. Rug type
13. Stored until ready
14. Assumed name
16. Alaskan seaport
17. Li'l Abner's mom
19. Mimic
20. Crafty
21. Topnotch
22. Mountainous
24. Verified
25. ___ Scott decision
26. Certain necklaces
29. Irrigated
32. Chimes
33. Morsel
34. Slept like ___
36. Normandy river
37. Fisherman, sometimes
38. Impart
39. Gaze
40. Elevs.
41. Tribal emblem
42. Samson's nemesis
44. Goofs
45. Inactively
46. Pelts
47. Garden flower
50. Poor box donations
51. Fruity drink
54. Jai ___
55. Cornflower
58. Port
59. Bumpkin
60. Sooner St.
61. Badgers
62. African fox
63. Dog's wagger

DOWN
1. Tree fluids
2. "I've Got ___ in Kalamazoo"
3. Withhold
4. Paid notices
5. Backwaters
6. Unescorted
7. Two-wheeler
8. ___ Claire, Wisconsin
9. Spiky flowers
10. Arizona Indian
11. Last word in prayer
12. Actor Richard ___
15. Wiser
18. Knitters' threads
23. Marvin or Remick
24. Orange and black flowers
25. Social engagements
26. Trim, as a photo
27. Employed
28. Year, to Pierre
29. Dimension
30. Upper class
31. City in Delaware
33. Asian peninsula
35. Emeralds and rubies
37. Small kangaroo
41. Body
43. Amin of Uganda
44. Botch
46. Runs away
47. Sunrise
48. Inter ___
49. Dangle
50. Northern Hemisphere birds
51. Musician Paul ___
52. Cold-cut mart
53. Kin of etc.
56. Mauna ___
57. Touch-me-___

Blockbuilders

Fit the letter blocks into the diagram to spell out the name of a famous tourist attraction.

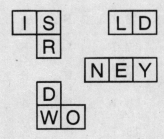

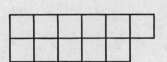

PUZZLE 228

CLUES IN TWOS

ACROSS
1. ____ weevil
5. Go up to the plate
8. Club
12. Island feast
13. Broadcast
14. Johnson of "Laugh-In"
15. Branch of math
16. JFK's predecessor
17. French river
18. ⎤
20. ⎦ Nick
22. Go lower
23. ____-Magnon
24. ⎤
27. ⎦ Season
31. Free ____ bird
32. ____ Jima
33. ⎤
37. ⎦ Brood
40. Fish eggs
41. Fury
42. ⎤
44. ⎦ Tone
47. Concluding passage
48. Diving bird
50. Skier's delight
52. Arabian gulf
53. National abbr.
54. Director Preminger
55. ⎤
56. ⎦ Spar
57. Win by a ____

DOWN
1. Sandwich initials
2. Belonging to us
3. Secular
4. Actor Bela ____
5. Mean person
6. Assistance
7. Ditch
8. Actress Elizabeth ____
9. Formerly
10. Fit to ____
11. Sea: Fr.
19. Fled
21. Mouths
24. Actor Mineo
25. Greek letter
26. Stool pigeon
28. Accomplished
29. Lamb's mother
30. Neither's companion
34. Absent
35. Extremely long time
36. Smear again
37. Digging tool
38. Spanish gold
39. Singer Ricky ____
42. Pop
43. Poems of praise
45. Aware
46. Decomposes
47. Machine part
49. Mil. entertainment group
51. Anguish

PUZZLE 229

Drop-Ins

Using only the letters given in the box, fill in all the dashes to form 8-letter words. Each letter is used only once.

```
AAA  C  DDD  EEEEEE  G  I  K  LL  MM
NNNNN  OOO  P  Q  RR  S  TTTT  U  YY
```

1. S _ T _ R _ A _
2. B _ S _ M _ N _
3. P _ O _ O _ E _
4. U _ I _ U _ L _
5. N _ T _ B _ O _
6. C _ N _ A _ O _
7. F _ I _ H _ E _
8. C _ V _ R _ E _
9. A _ I _ A _ E _
10. B _ O _ K _ D _

212

ACROSS

1. Hit's counterpart
5. Stick-on
10. Venomous snakes
14. Opposed
15. Marry on the run
16. "Sultan of ___" (Babe Ruth)
17. African nation
19. "Citizen ___"
20. Landers or Miller
21. Compasses
22. 1923 Derby winner
23. Group
24. Divest
25. Store away
28. Woodland deity
29. Test
30. Slightly open
33. Window part
36. Hermits and horseshoes
39. African nation
41. Remorse
42. African nation
43. Type of nut
44. Administer to
46. Utopia
47. Ice-cream treats
49. French connections
51. Hungarian cavalry member
53. In the fashion of
54. Spanish lady's title: abbr.
57. Blackbird
58. Of the mind
61. Metal
62. Spiel
64. African nation
66. Cornelia ___ Skinner
67. First word of choice rhyme
68. Away from the wind
69. The Seven ___
70. "Slammin' Sammy"
71. Parry

DOWN

1. Maternal parents
2. Silly
3. Caper
4. Title of respect
5. Stops
6. Antelope
7. Hill body: abbr.
8. Cap-___ (head to foot)
9. Apartment dweller
10. Inquire
11. African nation
12. Jury
13. Actor McQueen
18. Babylonian war god
26. Actor Mancuso
27. Hindu garments
28. Selling schemes
29. Formerly
30. Ten-percenter: abbr.
31. Container
32. Former African nation
34. Liberal ___
35. Take to court
37. So long
38. ___ Juan
40. Nothing, in Seville
45. Held up
48. Military units
50. Powder ingredient
51. Auras
52. Weld
53. Indoor courts
54. Trite
55. Gone up
56. Chipped in chips
59. Tied
60. Zip
63. Are follower
65. Lummox

Everything's Relative

PUZZLE 231

Find the word that precedes or follows four of the five words in each group below. Then, find the bonus word that precedes or follows the five words you've eliminated.

1. HORN	DIVIDE	HOUSE	TEA	CARD
2. KICK	OUT	ROLL	GUNS	HALF
3. DREAM	BED	APE	ROOM	BREAK
4. CAT	BUGLE	LAKES	OVER	CURTAIN
5. SAIL	ROW	LIFE	GRAVY	COAT

BONUS: _____

PUZZLE 232

• PLEASING PALETTE •

ACROSS

1. Viewpoint
6. Footless creature
10. Church tribunal
14. Japanese women divers
18. Maltese money
19. Singer Vikki ___
20. Poisonous plant
21. Vegetation
22. Jam fruit
24. Certain detectives
26. Rocker Stone
27. Bridge position
28. Hide's partner
29. English author et al.
30. Daybreak, to a poet
32. "___ to bury Caesar"
35. Father: pref.
36. Webb and Sues
38. Baseballer Herb ___
39. Stolen goods
41. Catch
44. Riga native
45. Certain evergreen
47. Chest wood
49. London farewell
50. City on the Oka
51. Topaz hummingbird
52. Reason
53. Burdensome
55. Sprung forth
58. Odysseys
59. Groove
60. Some are golden
61. First name in architecture
62. Spy group: abbr.
63. South African province
68. Squadron's home: abbr.
71. Type of machine
72. Moon depression
73. Fairs
77. Glanced off
79. Unfashionable
80. Check
82. Deteriorates
83. Hardwood
84. Single: pref.
86. Lion portrayer
87. Comedian Dan ___
88. Army Special Forces member
91. Not scheduled: Scot.
92. Actor Vereen
93. Adriatic wind
94. Hoopster Danny ___
95. Killed time
96. Tampa's neighbor
99. 1492 transport
100. Of late
101. Star-shaped
103. Part of a track
105. Part of N.B.
107. Owl sound
110. River of song
112. False bait
115. Awaits
116. Pianist Templeton
117. Proper's companion
118. Complete
119. Irving and Tan
120. French head
121. Murray and Marsh
122. Foolish people

DOWN

1. Priestly wear
2. Reject, of old
3. Brain
4. Fond du ___
5. Gravel ridges
6. Top performers
7. Iota
8. Hockey great
9. Sec
10. Indian money
11. Humorist Read
12. Water tower
13. Invite
14. Sacred table
15. Ellington song
16. British composer
17. Lip
21. Use worry beads
23. Outlaw
25. He was: Lat.
28. Duck
31. Canadian lake
33. Artwork technique
34. ___ y plata
35. "Ligeia" poet
36. Certain voices
37. Sloped
38. Indian weights
39. Not taped
40. Actress Munson
42. Icicle sites
43. Curl
45. Pronoun
46. Groups
47. Wolflike animals
48. Station term: abbr.
52. Metrical unit
54. Bireme team
56. Encircle again
57. Blue flag
58. Fido's doc
60. Promoter: abbr.
61. Compass point: abbr.
64. Brews
65. Wynken's shipmate
66. Component
67. Rupture
68. Bitter
69. Danish island group
70. Concentration
74. Pioneer actress
75. Iron oxide
76. Amati's kin
78. Harem room
79. Earnest request
80. Arrow poison
81. Negative word
83. Go wrong
85. Transparent fabric
88. Gunk's kin
89. Cloth unit, of old
90. Receptacle
93. Composer Bartok
95. ... as a bug ___
97. Corners
98. Striplings
99. Soldier's rifle
100. Anagram for tea
101. Rabbi Silver
102. Small
103. Regulation
104. Egg on
106. Electrical units
108. Small bills
109. Fairy tale baddie
111. Composer Ayer
112. Record speed: abbr.
113. Significant time
114. 66, e.g.: abbr.

ACROSS

1. Swiss vegetables
7. Smell ____
11. Egyptian wader
15. Chart
18. Like ancestors
19. Journalist's activity
21. Wings
23. Last month
24. ACTH recorded in history
26. "____ Care of My Baby"
28. U.S. playwright
29. Shabby condition
30. TV star Richard ____
31. Actress Salome
32. Actress Stevens
33. Defamation
37. Accustomed
38. French station
41. Foursome
42. Witticism
43. Moved fast
47. Mr. T's series
48. Walking stick
49. Brought to maturity
50. Emphatic type: abbr.
51. Spanish cough
52. Husk
53. Pens
55. General course
56. One form of geometry
58. Port on the Adriatic
59. Reproductive cell
60. Look again for the patio chef?
66. Fly in an aircraft
67. Paper factory
68. Eucharistic tray
69. Hobgoblin
70. Malice
72. Yawn
73. Magnon precedent
76. Eisenhower and Turner
77. Repast
78. Rodents
79. Draw off gradually
81. Vagrants
83. Base
84. Sowed
85. Skins
86. Bigwig on campus
87. Fixed in position
88. Book of the Bible
91. Fasten
92. Knight wear
93. Ones in arrears
94. Emanations
96. Whine
100. Single luminary legislator
103. Scribe
105. Ms. Moore
106. Up and down transits
107. Ethnic designation
108. Roman goddess
109. Irritated
110. Duel tool
111. Helen Gurley Brown, e.g.

DOWN

1. Actor Gulager
2. Dagger handle
3. Rectangular pilaster
4. U.S. psychologist and author
5. Noble cheese?
6. Plodded heavily
7. Hot felony
8. Emeritus: abbr.
9. Military correspondence letters
10. Plague
11. Gossip topics
12. Tarry
13. MIT element: abbr.
14. Rank above corporal: abbr.
15. Navy fliers?
16. "____ Comes Mary"
17. Satchel ____
20. Cheerful
22. German river
25. Mrs. Bunker
27. Dory stick
31. Singer Feliciano
33. Now!, to a doctor
34. Apollo's mom
35. Chemical endings
36. Gun group: inits.
37. Pursue (one's way)
38. Use the beeper
39. Verse forms
40. But, in Latin
42. Ms. Reno
43. One of the Johnsons
44. Bum ____
45. French relative
46. Church official
48. Motion picture
52. Regatta
53. Frankie ____ (bandleader)
54. Sea north of Iran
55. Certain art museum
56. Extol Iran, formerly
57. Tardy
58. U.K. subject
59. Fence opening
60. Violently intense
61. Elicit
62. Striped feline
63. Jannings and Ludwig
64. Solar-lunar year difference
65. Headland
70. Denomination
71. Light touches
72. ____ Carlo Menotti
73. Muslim judge
74. Cambodia's dollar
75. French wave
77. Wire thickness
78. U.S. anthropologist
79. Sell Pb
80. Confederate soldier
82. Minimum
83. Feeling
84. Paint with dots
86. Wonder Woman's alias
87. American uncle
88. Car part
89. Had possession
90. "Come up and ____ sometime"
91. Pronunciation mark
92. Code inventor
94. A Guthrie
95. Manipulator
96. Heart
97. Oppositionist
98. Not original: abbr.
99. One billionth: pref.
101. Loser to DDE
102. Apogee
104. And not

PUZZLE 234

ACROSS

1. "____ Girl Friday"
4. Vault
8. Lips
12. Smell
14. Tied
15. Danger
16. "The Way We ____"
17. Peruse
18. Without company
19. Tardy
20. Makes mistakes
21. Flogged
22. Fiber bits
24. Place
25. View
27. Camp bed
29. Always
33. Stupid ones
34. Opera song
36. Anger
37. Clear (of)
38. Standard time, in New York
41. Unhappy
42. Top card
43. Woody plant
44. Estimate
46. Disorder
48. Corn unit
49. Uptight
50. Afternoon party
52. Spherical object
53. Musical drama
56. Woe is me!
58. Every
62. Valleys
63. Harbor
64. Sandal
65. School theme
66. Brink
67. Vend
68. Flower part
69. Feat
70. Chart

DOWN

1. Wolf cry
2. Thought
3. Kind
4. Calm
5. Turn away
6. Fright
7. Finishes
8. Tell
9. Press
10. Belonging to me
11. Snow vehicle
13. Wound up
15. Step
23. Part of 70 Across
24. Mix
25. Portion, as of bread
26. Signal systems
27. Provide food to
28. Mine find
30. Clamps
31. Wipe out
32. Scarlet and rose
33. Stuff
35. Heavenly being
39. Zone
40. Ocean
45. Except
47. Steady flow
49. Sampled
51. Uncomplicated
52. Large boat
53. Poems
54. Ago
55. Otherwise
56. Copied
57. Loggins and Messina's "Mother ____"
59. Attention-getter
60. Soft drink
61. Aid

PUZZLE 235   Whirly Words

This diagram has been divided into sections, numbered 1 to 6. Each section contains spaces for four letters. The answer to each clue is a 4-letter word whose letters fit into the corresponding section so that the outer ring, middle ring, and inner ring all spell words reading clockwise beginning in section 1.

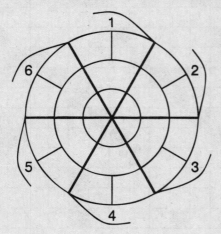

CLUES

Section 1: Senior member

Section 2: Weathercock

Section 3: Temporary structure

Section 4: Matured

Section 5: Character

Section 6: Applications

Outer Ring: Worthwhile

Middle Ring: Inserts

Inner Ring: Tease

ACROSS
1. Miffed
5. John Jacob or Mary
10. Dogger of Mary's footsteps
14. Not thick
15. Frighten
16. Avow
17. Relaxation
18. Eagle's claw
19. Deep mud
20. Rather than
21. Roll-call response
22. Avoided
24. Astaire, for one
26. E.C. ___ (Popeye's creator)
28. Has
30. Tell
34. Praises
37. Golfer's assistant
39. Add filler to
40. Otherwise
41. Plains dwelling
42. Renee's papa
43. Broke bread
44. Devilfish
45. Auto-body type
46. Abandon
48. Regatta
50. Lock of hair
52. Seldom
56. Fireplace area
59. Lively
61. Recline
62. Opera highlight
63. Ms. Oyl
65. Fish for salads
66. ___ of the valley
67. Horse and lion features
68. European river
69. D'Urberville female
70. Put forth
71. Seabird

DOWN
1. Spirited horse
2. Miss Scarlett
3. Ascended
4. Compass pt.
5. Aft
6. Wound remembrance
7. Stories
8. Spanish gold
9. Turncoat
10. Actress Hedy
11. Eager
12. Nothing more than
13. Born's partner
21. Fells with an ax
23. Differ
25. Morse ___
27. Make beloved
29. Play parts
31. Was imitative
32. Home to 2 Down
33. Genesis garden
34. Plant part
35. Glee-club member
36. Employer
38. Fitting
41. ___ pay (net pay): hyph.
42. Equal
44. Emporium
45. Order to Kitty
47. Leaves the straight and narrow
49. Take into custody
51. Porcupine's weapon
53. Dodge
54. Steamship
55. Long (for)
56. Stop
57. One of the Great Lakes
58. Feels unwell
60. Always
64. Slack
65. Toddler

1	2	3	4		5	6	7	8	9		10	11	12	13
14					15						16			
17					18						19			
20					21					22	23			
24			25				26	27						
			28			29		30				31	32	33
34	35	36				37	38				39			
40				41						42				
43				44					45					
46			47				48	49						
			50			51		52			53	54	55	
56	57	58				59	60				61			
62				63	64					65				
66				67						68				
69				70						71				

TWO BY TWO

Fill in the 6-letter answers to the clues using all the 2-letter pieces shown in the box below. When the puzzle is completed, the first letters of the answers, reading down, will spell out another 6-letter word.

AR	AS	BA	DS	EA	EC	ER	ES	IC
IN	IR	IS	KN	LA	OM	RA	SP	TT

1. Mixture for cake
2. Good smells
3. Manipulates dough
4. French pastry
5. Dried grape
6. Food flavorings

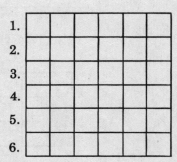

1.
2.
3.
4.
5.
6.

PUZZLE 238

ACROSS
1. Shopping place
5. Ridge
9. Dud
13. New York canal
14. Flower part
15. Balm
16. Plant starter
17. Prophecy
19. Suspend
20. "The Hunt for ___ October"
21. Ally
22. The Gay Nineties, e.g.
24. Not coarse
25. ___ Na Na
28. Overwhelm
30. That thing's
31. Smack
34. British flying machine
37. Library worker
38. Fire-starting stone
39. "___ the season . . ."
40. Legend
41. Otherwise
42. Bribery
44. Shad delicacy
45. Saloon
47. Woodsman's tool
48. Plaything
49. Nosegay
50. Mediterranean hat
52. Lose
55. Self-conceit
57. Rim
61. Trespasser
63. Actor Dillman
64. Strike-breaker
65. Turn over
66. Law
67. Weight allowance
68. Encounter
69. Church corner

DOWN
1. Net
2. Neighborhood
3. Claim
4. Rock formation
5. "___ in the Money"
6. Copied
7. Youth
8. Extract
9. Wash up
10. Medley
11. Anchor
12. Crooked
14. Spread out
18. Deceives
23. Engrossed
24. Spanish gala
25. Journalist Morley ___
26. Greeting
27. Come up
29. Diner
31. Nun's garment
32. Snow building
33. Minute
35. Individual
36. Negate
37. Singer Boone
40. Liberate
43. English school
45. Hog
46. Haven
49. Freshman
51. Zoo animal
52. Haze
53. Peruvian Indian
54. Heavenly body
55. "En garde" weapon
56. Chap
58. Bongo, e.g.
59. Actor Gordon
60. Paradise
62. Unclose, poetically

PUZZLE 239 Quotagram

Fill in the answers to the clues. Then transfer the letters to the correspondingly numbered squares in the diagram. The completed diagram will contain a quotation.

1. ___ of clay
   — — — —
   1 20 31 10

2. Be relevant
   — — — — — — —
   24 7 26 15 2 28 32

3. Coast
   — — — —
   27 21 8 4

4. Sit
   — — — —
   13 17 29 25

5. Bunch
   — — — — — — —
   33 19 5 9 23 34 6

6. Belief in God
   — — — — —
   18 14 3 30 11

7. That girl, subjectively
   — — —
   22 16 12

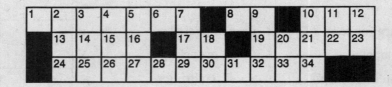

218

BRICK BY BRICK

Rearrange this stack of bricks to form a crossword puzzle. The clues will help you fit the bricks into their correct places. Row 1 has been filled in for you. Use the bricks to fill in the remaining spaces.

ACROSS

1. Clown
   Panel grooves
   Sews an edge
2. Served well
   Eldritch
   Mr. Clapton
3. Unisex
   Persons
   Quechua
4. Attractive
   Greek sea
5. Corn spikes
   Indian nurse
6. Atelier
   Conspirators
7. Decimal unit
   Lumpy
   Calyx part
8. Current units
   Broad cut
   Pleasant
9. Zest
   Attempt
   Born
10. Apis mellifera
    Backslide
11. Of low tides
    Nimbus
12. Wanderers
    Unfaithful
13. Arab prince
    Cilia
    Glen
14. Hindu queen
    Roast host
    Mine yields
15. Atop
    Activists
    Pindarics

DOWN

1. Nutmeg spice
   Secret store
   Sleuth Wolfe
2. Sacred image
   Musical speed
   Arab gulf
3. Convene
   Loosen
   Coin
4. Swirled
   Plot outline
5. Genesis exile
   Ogled
6. Hungry
   Beat up
7. Eternities
   TV excision
   I love: Lat.
8. Medicine
   Degrade
   Gaming cubes
9. Petroleum
   Bottomless pit
   Employer
10. Cracker seeds
    Torments
11. Devours
    Scream
12. Intensify
    Sorcery
13. Sea eagle
    Think out loud
    Three feet
14. Isinglass
    Sports car
    Sheltered
15. Read quickly
    Frozen rain
    Minus

BRICKS

E E	A D S	I C E	■ D I	N O M
S ■ I	R ■ H	N E E	A I R	E M I

| O R S | ■ A B | R E S | R E V | I C I |
| P A L | B B Y | D E S | A L O | E A R |

| D ■ E | E R T | N G ■ | R I C | L A S |
| D ■ S | ■ ■ ■ | S ■ A | N C A | E S S |

| E ■ O | A C E | E R I | E N T | E A N |
| S ■ O | C O E | O U L | ■ ■ ■ | ■ ■ ■ |

| S ■ S | Y A L | E Y B | I ■ E | H O N |
| C E ■ | A L E | N E A | O ■ D | ■ ■ ■ |

| A M P | E T T | A E G | E E ■ | H ■ N |
| S P I | ■ S E | M A H | P ■ H | A Y ■ |

| R A N | S L O | D I O | S T U | M C E |
| O N T | S ■ D | ■ N U | T E N | O E R |

DIAGRAM

	1	2	3	4	5	6	7	8	9	10	11	12	13	14	15
1	M	I	M	E	■	D	A	D	O	S	■	H	E	M	S
2															
3															
4															
5															
6															
7															
8															
9															
10															
11															
12															
13															
14															
15															

PUZZLE 241

Codeword is a special crossword puzzle in which conventional clues are omitted. Instead, answer words in the diagram are represented by numbers. Each number represents a different letter of the alphabet, and all of the letters of the alphabet are used. When you are sure of a letter, put it in the code key chart and cross it off in the alphabet box. A group of letters has been inserted to start you off.

Code key chart

1	14		
2 (O)	15		
3	16		
4 (F)	17		
5	18		
6	19		
7	20		
8	21		
9	22		
10	23		
11	24		
12 (R)	25		
13	26		

Alphabet box

A N~~O~~
B P
C Q
D R̶
E̶ S
F̶ T
G U
H V
I W
J X
K Y
L Z
M

Diagram

12	20	26	19	■	20	5	19	3	■	12	19	20	16	18
20	3	20	10	■	6	20	4	20	■	19	24	22	13	25
6	20	11	19	■	15	13	5	23	■	6	22	5	1	19
20	12	19	■	7	22	9	20	■	18	22	13	4	19	6
12	19	6	12	19	18	18	■	17 (F)	20	1	4	■		
■			2	20	4	■		2 (O)	21	19	10	19	6	
15	2	8	19	12	■	26	2	12 (R)	19	■	3	13	26	
13	12	19	■	6	2	9	20	■	12	18	■	19	8	19
21	19	19	■	21	2	6	10	■	7	20	12	19	16	
■	18	5	13	25	19	12	■	17	2	23	■			
■		1	2	18	10	■	12	13	14	19	4	19	12	
12	19	14	13	18	19	■	14	20	5	19	■	2	5	19
19	23	20	1	4	■	18	13	11	19	■	20	24	22	20
14	13	9	9	20	■	22	18	19	12	■	25	22	12	9
18	4	19	19	9	■	19	20	18	10	■	4	19	19	16

PUZZLE 242   Insert-A-Word

Insert a word from Group B into a word from Group A to form a longer word. Each word is used only once. For example, if the word FAR appeared in Group A and THE appeared in Group B, the answer would be FATHER (FA-THE-R).

GROUP A	GROUP B	
1. FISH	RAN	1. _____
2. BOON	ARM	2. _____
3. PAT	ARK	3. _____
4. STING	EVER	4. _____
5. LED	RAG	5. _____
6. CURT	ALL	6. _____
7. MET	NIT	7. _____
8. MOOR	AND	8. _____
9. GENT	EARN	9. _____
10. FOE	TEN	10. _____

PUZZLE 243

ACROSS

1. Selves
5. "___ Flubber"
10. Mind
14. Island near Java
15. Rhyme scheme
16. Jerk
17. Ship's slammer
18. Bean Town airport
19. Street urchin
20. Depression Era crime duo
23. Martin or McShane
24. Diving bird
25. Eeyore's friend
28. Window section
30. Tennis-star Shriver
33. Greek end
34. Famous marionette-maker
35. Actress Kedrova
36. Biblical foes
39. Opposed to
40. Claudius's successor
41. Circle or sanctum
42. French negative
43. Crooked
44. Bengali poet
45. Con's companion
46. Kansas City-to-Boston dir.

47. Comedy team
55. Florence's flower
56. Venerate
57. Flag
59. Journalist/ reformer Jacob ___
60. Merlin's nemesis
61. Mane site
62. Smith of song
63. Fronts
64. Cagney film

DOWN

1. Time of receding current
2. Clothing
3. Melange
4. Action on "What's My Line?"
5. Brine
6. Mitch Miller's instrument
7. Cobra
8. Scottish resort
9. Spanish dance
10. Billiards accessory
11. Treetop nursery
12. Interpret
13. Czech river
21. Spring nymph
22. Stage prompt
25. Pagan chief-god
26. Adult insect

27. Composer Ethelbert ___
28. San Diego player
29. Jason's craft
30. Soft, in music
31. Vary
32. Olympic-skier Phil ___
34. Snick's partner
35. Hanging around
37. Zambians' neighbors

38. Jungle vine
43. "You ___ Love"
44. Sounds of laughter
45. Novel text
47. Caper
48. Bjorling solo
49. Division
50. Tram passage

51. City saved by Balto
52. Tambour
53. Liquid measure
54. Pound sound
58. Kyoto coin

Across and Down

PUZZLE 244

Place the answers to the clues into the word squares so that the same words read both Across and Down.

A

1. Speedy
2. Loathe
3. Snapshot
4. Jots
5. Waste matter

1. Beginning
2. Habituate
3. Money unit of India
4. Stair part
5. Pays attention

B

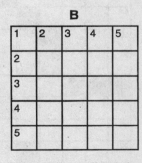

PUZZLE 245

• FAST TALK •

ACROSS

1. Freeway exit
5. Cauchos
9. Trade center
13. True
17. Wings, to Ovid
18. ____ contendere
19. English rock group
20. Mother Bloor
21. Chews the fat
22. Tear up the track
25. Cleared
27. Brent Spiner role
28. Ragged
29. Group of elephants
30. Subtle
31. Singer Coolidge
33. Horrifying
35. Used a spade's relative
36. Fidelity
40. Russian news agency
41. ____ beer
42. Cargo mover
43. ____-Magnon
44. Tate offering
45. Earth
46. Camera-inventor and family
47. Harmonize
48. Discerned
50. Paw
51. Relaxes
52. Burn the breeze
56. Worthless
59. Porters
60. Moves in volleyball
64. Bank of seats
65. Clothes-drying frame
67. Otiose
68. Hurry
69. Tumult
70. ____ on a match
71. Algonquian language
72. Debbie Allen show
73. Curb
75. "Moonstruck" actress
76. Fire iron
77. Centers
78. Adversaries
79. Steak order
80. Author of "The Moffats"
83. Shade of green
84. Human
86. Like a shot
90. German lancer
92. Type of mine
93. Fiji's capital
94. Mansard-roof feature
95. Island bird
96. Sevres seasons
97. Ship's stabilizer
98. Exploit
99. Mild oath

DOWN

1. Hint
2. Actor Webb
3. Hustle
4. Bedevils
5. Not nourished
6. Raucous
7. Pipe joint
8. Trooper
9. Dull finish
10. Addled
11. Creek
12. Beret's kin
13. Warm up again
14. Gen. Robert ____
15. "When I was ____"
16. Matron
23. Ocean liner?
24. Famed furrier
26. Subject to strain
30. Filly or colt
31. Comedian Foxx
32. "As I was going to St. ____"
33. Hart
34. Author Sagan
35. Children's classic
36. Italian poet
37. Cold desserts
38. Heraldic gearing
39. Beckons
41. Actor Harrison
42. Slats
45. Fairy-tale's White
46. Liquid measure
47. Arabian watercourse
49. Seaweed product
50. Skirmish
51. Massachusetts motto's first word
53. Burmese people
54. Fisherman, sometimes
55. Cay
56. Luminary
57. Spring or neap
58. Vintage cars
61. Make haste
62. Use a stopwatch
63. Visionary
65. Fictional whale-hunter
66. Rainbow
67. Incenses
70. Certain fund
71. Gladdened
72. Luck
74. Larcenies
75. Drink flavoring
76. Golfer's aim
78. Concluding
79. Quarreled noisily
80. Existence, to Virgil
81. Whack
82. Roof piece
83. Basilica feature
84. Change residence
85. Actress Turner
87. Entreat
88. Author Grafton
89. Arctic explorer John ____
91. "____ Kelly" (1970 film)

222

DOUBLE TROUBLE

Not really double trouble, but double fun! Solve this puzzle as you would a regular crossword, EXCEPT place one, two, or three letters in each box. The number of letters in each answer is shown in parentheses after its clue.

ACROSS

1. Endorse (7)
4. Begot (4)
6. Out of (4)
8. Trolley (4)
11. Phoneys (5)
12. Pliable (9)
14. Reply (6)
15. Interrogator (10)
17. Fish-eating bird (7)
18. Cower (6)
19. Celestial body (8)
21. Cleanse (5)
23. Enjoyments (9)
26. Watering holes (4)
28. Lea (6)
31. Fasten (6)
32. Meddle (6)
34. Postpone (5)
36. Singer Torme (3)
37. Hunting dog (9)
39. Instant (9)
41. Respond (5)
42. Outlets (5)
43. Finish (3)
44. Mangle (4)
46. Amuse (6)
48. Age (3)
50. Wild animal collection (9)
52. Tart (5)
54. Chatter (7)
56. Swiss district (6)
58. Joy (7)
60. Beach (8)
64. Mountain crest (5)
65. Gastronome (9)
67. Part of speech (4)
68. Object (5)
69. Mule of song (3)
70. Depart (5)
71. Say (5)

DOWN

1. Stitched-on decoration (8)
2. Bake (5)
3. Account (7)
4. Staff of life (5)
5. Spiffy (6)
6. Cavort (6)
7. Wherewithal (5)
8. Type shorthand notes (10)
9. Bristle (3)
10. Combine (5)
13. Sensational papers (8)
16. Deletion (7)
20. Will (9)
22. Crushed (8)
23. Entreaty (4)
24. Comely (10)
25. Perfumed bag (6)
27. Hobby (7)
29. Novice (7)
30. Wooden peg (5)
33. Obstinate (8)
35. Document rider (9)
38. Rosie, e.g. (7)
40. Reflection (5)
41. Carmine (3)
45. Recline (3)
47. Storyteller (9)
49. Bliss (7)
51. Malt liquors (4)
53. Warning sounds (5)
55. Explanation of reasons (9)
56. False story (6)
57. Abound (4)
59. Not of the cloth (6)
61. Roof edges (5)
62. Brief (5)
63. Refund (6)
66. Church part (4)

★ *LOOKING FOR DOUBLE TROUBLE? You've found it! Treat yourself to* ★
special collections of your favorite puzzles—over 50 in each!
To order, see page 87.

PUZZLE 247

• RIFTS AND SPLITS •

ACROSS
1. Complain bitterly
5. ___ Alegre
10. Short form of a wd.
14. One, in Hamburg
15. Outsider
16. Low cart
17. Becomes inoperative
19. "___ Cruz"
20. Bishopric
21. Applications
22. Mountain nymphs
24. Abner's father
25. Reeked
26. Eggs on
29. Being frugal
32. Magna ___
33. Gap
34. Teachers' gp.
35. Field of study
36. That place
37. Shot in the dark
38. Mauna ___
39. Trawler's net
40. Wooden baskets
41. Desk item
43. Baseball's Domingo ___
44. Unpleasant
45. Sun. lecture
46. Certain cutters
48. WWII battlefield
49. Harbors: abbr.
52. Touched down
53. Rest
56. Wood strip
57. Turn outward
58. City on the Adriatic
59. Tennis great
60. Saree wearer
61. Niblick

DOWN
1. CSA soldiers
2. Yorkshire river
3. Curare's kin
4. Grazing ground
5. Mountain gaps
6. More mature
7. Bravo and Grande
8. Knead leather
9. Put ___ (warn)
10. Arrival
11. Divide sharply
12. Keats or Pope
13. Scandinavian rugs
18. Kinte of "Roots"
23. Mystical verse
25. Rubberneck
26. Slugger Henry ___
27. Separates from
28. Greek vowel
29. Exhaust
30. Football's Anderson et al.
31. Chews the fat
32. Colombian city
33. Glittery
36. Truck driver
37. Malone of "Cheers"
39. Rigel, e.g.
40. Chocolate substitute
42. Boil
43. Connect
45. Cubic meter
46. Room in a casa
47. Cry for Yorick
48. Squint, in London
49. Bosc
50. Poi root
51. Epidermis
54. Haddad of films
55. Batter's stat

PUZZLE 248   Crisscross

Beside each diagram are six groups of scrambled letters. Rearrange each group of letters to form a word, and then fit the words into the diagrams to read across or down in crossword fashion.

1.

CEKATR
UHENGO
TROMEE
RAWROM
CICURS
DEURGT

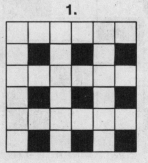

2.

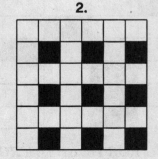

NALYTI
RATETI
SCVANA
HTRSCA
COSEAL
LRCARO

WORDBENDERS

The answers for this crossword puzzle might be just around the bend! Solve the puzzle as you would a regular crossword. The clues for the words which bend in the diagram are listed under the heading BENDERS.

BENDERS

1. Gurney
2. Allege
8. Religious statue
9. Iffy
17. Eavesdropper
18. Garden tools
28. Aversion
29. Ta ta
30. Earlier
32. Villainous
43. Nero's garb
49. Prima donna

ACROSS

1. Phase
6. Bounce
10. Raise
13. Sea cow
14. Cousin of et al.
19. Speedy transport
21. In addition
22. Reverential fear
23. Pedro's aunt
24. Core
25. Most modern
26. Gallivant
33. Yum-Yum's accessory
34. Trainee
36. Atelier
38. American poet
39. Stag's mate

40. The Roaring Twenties, e.g.
41. Append
42. Sun. lecture
44. Tautness
50. Lasagna seasoning
51. Hanker
52. Hepburn's costar

DOWN

3. Columbia, in song

4. Guido's note
5. Female gametes
6. Simone's summer
7. Goose formation
11. Expand
12. Serves
15. Hallux
16. Differentiated
19. Dock workers
20. Family member, for short

27. Regal steed
29. Overlook
31. Lagos locale
35. Bow
37. Prior to, to Shelley
44. Craggy hill
45. Marine raptor
46. Snorkel et al.
47. Canadian prov.
48. Negative conjunction

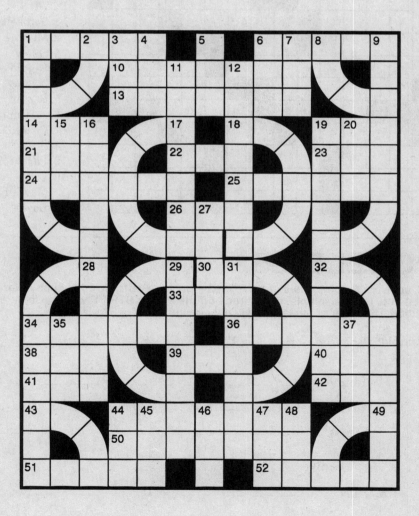

PUZZLE 250

ACROSS
1. Solemn
6. Liquefy
10. Smack
14. Existing
15. Go by car
16. Story
17. Locations
18. Worshipped object
19. Brainchild
20. Garden tool
21. Family chart
23. Untrue
25. Lumber
26. Playwright Moss ——
27. Grammar part
30. Out of bed
33. Charter
34. Was lavish with praise
36. Quiet
38. Seasoning
39. Freezer cubes
40. Volcano discharge
41. "A Chorus Line" song
42. Bed sheets
44. Provide with liquid
45. Sturdy
47. Not pretty
48. Dines
49. Combustion
50. Blind
52. Elephant's feature
53. Likely
56. Lass
57. Leaves
59. Gold digger
61. Monster
62. Ages
63. Sports palace
64. Equal
65. Depend
66. Full of items

DOWN
1. Soft belt
2. Mixture
3. Gnaw
4. Night before a holiday
5. Repair
6. Attempted
7. Conceal
8. Stir
9. Part of HEW
10. Lofty playthings
11. Boys
12. Out of the weather
13. Green vegetable
22. A Reiner
24. Sere
25. Go ——, young man
26. Safe place
27. Too
28. College officials
29. Gentleman's servant
31. Gladden
32. Unusual
34. Wedding items
35. Expert
37. Cautious
40. Type of excuse
42. Burden
43. Whole number
44. Laborer
46. School primer
47. Towel word
49. Finicky
50. Wise
51. Employ
52. River duck
53. Over again
54. Writing implements
55. Cafeteria item
56. Swab
58. Mine lode
60. Anger

PUZZLE 251   TRADE-OFF

The answers to the 2 clues in each line below are 6-letter words which differ by only 1 letter, which we have given you. In the example, if you trade off the P from STRIPE with the letter K, in the same position, you get STRIKE. The order of the letters will not change.

Example: Chevron S T R I P E   S T R I K E Hit

1. Hound   — — — S — —   — — — K — — Fruit container

2. Crude   C — — — — —   H — — — — — Husky

3. Stress   — — — — N —   — — — — P — Receive

4. Walk spiritedly   — — A — — —   — — — I — — Royal male

5. Hurl   — — — — L —   — — — — — R Correct

226

ACROSS

1. Circle segment
4. Trail behind
7. Plaything
10. Girl
11. Soda flavoring
12. Uncovered
13. Make into law
16. Tubas
19. Scatter
20. Slanderous statement
21. Circus animal
22. Wedding response
23. Dated
25. Choir voice
29. Diminish
31. Groups of seven
33. Nevada city
34. Exist
35. Gorilla
36. Society page word
38. Had bills
39. ____ as a fiddle
40. Boy
41. Grain beard
42. Loafer decoration
45. Taxi
48. Shoshonean
49. Lyric poem
50. Old horse
51. Entertain royally
55. Caviar
58. Observe
60. Milk provider
61. Musical close
65. Belonging to us
66. Overhead railways
67. Billiard stick
68. Finished
69. Kettledrums
73. Scads
74. Father Christmas
76. Metal fasteners
77. Ventilate
78. Thought
81. Dagger of old
82. Shelf
85. Double-reed players
89. Expression
90. Encourage
91. Pleasant
92. Japanese sash
93. Rodent
94. Cunning
95. Louse egg

DOWN

1. Grows older
2. Rave's partner
3. Reed instruments
4. ____ Angeles
5. Alack's partner
6. Hang open
7. Beige
8. Mineral deposit
9. Affirmative
11. Swear
12. Lively musical piece
14. Yield
15. Duo
16. Hit with an open hand
17. Evict
18. Fedora or sombrero
20. Haste
24. Lab burner
26. Novel
27. Unity
28. Reel's companion
29. Float
30. Operatic solo
31. Fitness center
32. Stitch
35. Fast, musically
37. Curtain calls
43. Earth's star
44. Greek letter
46. Summer drink
47. Plead
52. Squeezebox
53. Clumsy fellow
54. Flock females
56. Not in
57. Ireland
58. Feel
59. Actor Wallach
61. Type of lettuce
62. Eggs
63. Lair
64. Virtuoso
70. Billiard shot
71. Half quart
72. Tavern treats
73. Told a whopper
75. Fuss
77. The Greatest
79. Eternities
80. Dye plant
83. Mongolian desert
84. Give off
85. ____ and grill
86. Arabian coat
87. Matched group
88. Slippery

• STRIKE UP THE BAND •

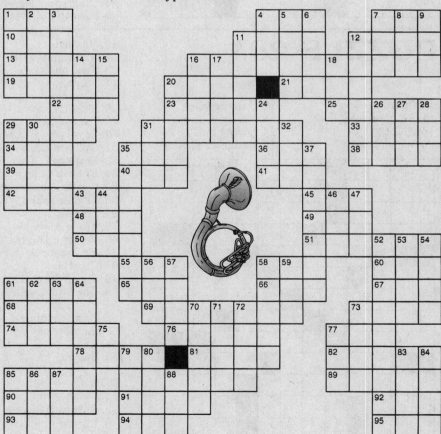

PUZZLE 253

ACROSS
1. Plaything
4. Gusto
8. Fighter Spinks
12. Harem room
13. Cooking pot
14. Early church desk
15. Actor Holt
16. Smear
17. Wading bird
18. Coming after
20. Book of anecdotes
21. Fashion
22. Jerks
25. Kind of committee
28. Retainer
29. Singer Carnes
30. Contends
31. Surface measure
32. Bistro card
33. Eggs
34. Newscaster Lindstrom
35. Central point
36. Rolled tightly
38. "2001" computer
39. Parking space
40. Venetian transport
44. Bucket
46. Farm structure
47. Dawdle
48. Teen's bane
49. Vaulted recess
50. Hydrocarbon suffix
51. Poverty
52. Certain ruminant
53. Behold

DOWN
1. Type of bag
2. Wotan
3. Sweet potatoes
4. Diagram of signs
5. African antelope
6. Punch
7. Check
8. "Moonlight Gambler" crooner
9. Left
10. Geisha's belt
11. Negative replies
19. Alien craft: abbr.
20. Cow
22. Pipe joint
23. Wrestling feats
24. Plant disease
25. Acknowledge
26. Opera singer
27. Be the star
28. Italian monk's title
31. Support
32. Bland
34. Indulge
35. Mode of action
37. Meted
38. Nag
40. Yawn
41. Mexican shouts
42. Swimmer's path
43. "A Death in the Family" author
44. God of shepherds
45. Master
46. Immoral

PUZZLE 254

ACROSS
1. Snug retreat
5. Fight
9. Welsh river
12. Singing voice
13. Malarial fever
14. Diving bird
15. Radar screen dot
16. Disturb
18. Abraham's wife
20. Send out
21. Piquant
23. Mine car
26. Mug
29. Deception
30. Royal
31. Obliterated
33. Emptiest
34. English county
35. "Cheers" bartender
36. Female rabbit
37. Stared at
38. Apple drink
40. Roger or Dudley
42. Mr. Warbucks
46. Crystal
49. Singer Irene ____
50. One billion years
51. Poet Pound
52. Was acquainted with
53. Small house
54. Char
55. Basted

DOWN
1. Catches
2. Governor Grasso
3. Excite
4. November gem
5. Greek letter
6. Light
7. Hard to please
8. Gratuities
9. Sleeper's amenity
10. Actor Brynner
11. Enlarge, of old
17. Private teacher
19. Journalist Thomas
22. "____ and Nancy"
24. In addition
25. Dole
26. Yield
27. Chemist Harold ____
28. Asphalt
30. Called
32. Biblical city
33. Rotten
35. ____ Madre
38. Rage
39. Book holders
41. Is indebted to
43. Hans Christian Andersen, e.g.
44. Attracted
45. Gape
46. Dry, as wine
47. Moreover
48. Attention

PUZZLE 255

ACROSS
1. Factory
5. Gratuity
8. Cummerbund
12. Operatic air
13. Undivided
14. Rapier's kin
15. Save
17. Deviate
18. Hit with the patella
19. Or ___!
21. Hairpieces
23. Collide
27. Mass
30. Feline
31. Ergo
32. Lager's relative
33. Wait
35. Pitch
36. Cook in an oven
38. Ramble
39. Anger
40. Free-for-all
41. Border
43. Amend
45. After some time
49. Petty quarrel
52. Edgeways
54. Every's partner
55. Actor Gossett, Jr.
56. Bowline
57. Poker bet
58. Termination
59. Bastes

DOWN
1. "___ the Knife"
2. Steel component
3. Spiel
4. Surgical beam
5. Crag
6. Research
7. Rind
8. Harsh
9. Simian
10. Witness
11. "Take ___, She's Mine"
16. Learned
20. Agenda
22. Chat
24. Opposed to
25. Battle mark
26. This place
27. Tepid
28. Sunburn soother
29. Pact
34. Touch lightly
37. Boil
42. Negotiations
44. Capri or Man
46. Phone noise
47. ". . . were Paradise ___!"
48. Army gps.
49. Briny body
50. Give a bad review
51. Legislation
53. Unexploded bomb

PUZZLE 256

ACROSS
1. Join
4. Shiny cloth
8. British nobleman
12. Japanese sash
13. Put-in-Bay's lake
14. Pump or brogan
15. Antiquated
17. Ice-cream treat
18. Quiet
19. Used a rosary
21. Short play
23. Test
25. Writing fluid
26. Wildebeest
27. Publish
31. Peg for Palmer
32. Boundaries
34. Tavern
35. Family car
37. Maven
38. Performed
39. Oyster's treasure
41. Drenches
42. Urge
45. Biblical prophet
47. "A Bronx ___"
48. From the East
52. Hero's story
53. Folk knowledge
54. Self-conceit
55. Distribute
56. "___ we forget . . ."
57. Fondle

DOWN
1. Court
2. Subside
3. Felt antipathy for
4. Hawk
5. Hibernia
6. Ignited
7. Salts away
8. Themes
9. Nautical greeting
10. Anchor line
11. Heavy metal
16. Three strikes
20. Lift
21. Makes a lap
22. Leg joint
24. Fructose, e.g.
26. Wilder and Hackman
28. Dodge
29. Segment
30. Conclusions
33. Filled pastries
36. ___ of the action
40. Coral reef
41. Succeeded
42. Thing
43. Scruff
44. Skirt feature
46. Encounter
49. Fish eggs
50. The ___ of Aquarius
51. Fate

PUZZLE 257

ACROSS
1. Party givers
6. Hermit
11. Worship
12. Musical drama
13. Aladdin's benefactor
14. Very small
15. Intellect
17. Top of the head
20. Bulletin-board sign
24. Become older
25. Sprinted
26. "____ Got Sixpence"
27. Casual shoe
29. Rosary item
30. Sooner or ____
32. Mixed greens
35. Cowboy circus
39. Similar
40. Make amends
41. Broader
42. Transparent

DOWN
1. Crone
2. "____ on a Grecian Urn"
3. Male child
4. Indian group
5. Prophet
6. Hand cream
7. Unlocks
8. Born
9. Sea eagle
10. Sunbeam
16. Separate
17. Chum
18. In the past
19. Afternoon beverage
21. Make a knot
22. Actress Gabor
23. Scarlet
25. Library patron
28. Snow unit
29. Thin soup
31. Periods in history
32. Cutting tool
33. ____ Baba
34. Box top
36. Female deer
37. Opposite of WSW
38. "____ the ramparts . . ."

PUZZLE 258

ACROSS
1. Lyric poems
5. Egyptian snakes
9. Purse
12. Horseback game
13. Slanting type: abbr.
14. Strong beer
15. "I met ____ with seven wives": 2 wds.
16. Songstress Cantrell
17. Allow
18. Communist hero
20. Irritate
22. Heavy string
24. Always, in poems
25. TV extraterrestrial
28. Guided trip
30. Decays
33. Weaverbirds: 2 wds.
36. Atmosphere
37. Peak
38. One of the Stooges
39. "Treasure Island" author's initials
41. Unwrap
43. Batman's city
45. Portals
49. ____ and arrow
50. Like the desert
52. Notion
53. Single thing
54. Corruption
55. Cleanser
56. Sleeping place
57. Comfort
58. Makes a mistake

DOWN
1. Milky gem
2. Rounded roof
3. Verve
4. Of sound
5. Be sick
6. Night-club entertainers: 2 wds.
7. Window glass
8. Blackboard
9. Place to dance
10. Away from the weather
11. Obtain
19. Memo
21. Region: abbr.
23. Diva Ponselle
25. Cry of triumph
26. Baseballer Gehrig
27. Wrinkled
29. Sloping walkway
31. Pair
32. Compass point: abbr.
34. Seasoning
35. Clarinet mouthpiece
40. Use a razor
42. Clamor
43. Departed
44. Opera solo
46. Scent
47. Back end
48. Drains of strength
49. Comedian Hope
51. Fourth letter

ACROSS

1. "____ Miserables" (1935 film)
4. "____ for All Seasons" (1966 film): 2 wds.
8. Bikini top
11. "Crash ____" (1943 film)
12. "Susan ____" (1961 film)
13. Paddle
14. Clifton Davis TV series
15. "____ Wave" (1975 film)
16. "Another ____ of the Forest" (1948 film)
17. The Fonz's put-down word
18. "____ in the Hole" (1951 film)
19. "United ____" (TV series)
21. "Make ____ Mink" (1960 film)
23. Raitt or Ritter
24. "My ____ Irma" (1949 film)
27. "The ____ Only" (1978 film): 2 wds.
30. "____ Force" (1943 film)
31. Fleur-____: hyph.
34. Only
36. Actor Burl
38. "Sweet ____ O'Grady" (1943 film)
40. Eager
41. French director Clair
42. Donna and Pamela
44. "____ Knew Her Apples" (1945 film)
45. "A ____ to Live" (1985 TV film)
48. Actor Beatty
50. "Fail ____" (1964 film)
51. TV's "The ____ of the Game"
52. "Little Women" author
55. Sea, to Bardot
56. "They ____ Him a Gun" (1937 film)
60. Farm structure
61. Greek epic
63. Singer Campbell
64. DDE's command
65. Gangsters' gals
66. TV's "____ Living": 2 wds.
67. Actor Ayres
68. "The ____ of Laura Mars" (1978 film)

69. "Please Don't ____ the Daisies"

DOWN

1. "____ Street" (TV series)
2. "____ in My Heart" (1933 film)
3. "____ No Flowers" (1964 film): 2 wds.
4. Linda Lavin TV role
5. "____ for Each Other" (1939 film)
6. 1961 Susan Hayward role
7. Gene or Ozzie
8. TV's "The Love ____"
9. "A ____ Breed" (1981 film)
10. Carney and Garfunkel
11. Blocker who played Hoss
12. Lionel of "Hart to Hart"
16. "____ Hattie" (1942 film)
20. Definite article
22. Neither Dem. nor Rep.
23. "The Ballad of ____" (1968 film)
24. "State ____" (1945 film)
25. "____ of No Return" (1954 film)

26. Cara or Dunne
28. "____ on Sunday" (1960 film)
29. "They ____ by Night" (1940 film)
32. Actor Greene
33. Function: suffix
35. Actress Barbara
37. "____ of Passion" (1961 film)
39. Actor Vince
43. ____ Malone of "Cheers"
46. Took a pew
47. "A Matter ____" (1976 film): 2 wds.
49. ____ Van Gleason III
51. Patricia and Tom
52. Actor Walter
53. "The ____ Show" (1977 film)
54. "I Gotta ____" (song from "Peter Pan")
55. "The Last ____" (1959 film)
57. Utah resort
58. Sleeveless garment
59. Spanish queen
62. Actress Myrna

PUZZLE 260

ACROSS

1. Holiday of deliverance
6. Egyptian skink
10. Criticize scathingly
14. Satire
15. Karate blow
16. River to the Rhine
17. Dromedary
18. Debutantes' ball
20. Poet Barrett Browning
22. Broad necktie
23. Marquis de ____
24. City on the Black Sea
25. Fray
28. Chap
29. Side dishes
30. "Kind Hearts and ____"
35. "____ Like It"
36. Cereal grain
37. Deadly
38. Mealtime bugle
40. Fish hawk
41. Secreted
42. Close behind
43. Penny metal
47. Vegetable amino acid
48. Rich tapestry
49. "____ the Crimson Petal"
54. Is cautious
56. Lowest deck
57. Capital of Italy
58. Greek god of love
59. Diacritical mark
60. ____ de panier
61. Confidential: abbr.
62. Twit

DOWN

1. Old Indian coin
2. River to the Caspian
3. Gypsy matron
4. Don Juan's mother
5. Browning poem
6. Give consent
7. Table ____
8. "How ____ the little crocodile . . ."
9. Bee: prefix
10. Untrue
11. Laymen
12. Irish exclamations
13. Busybody
19. Tennyson poem, with "The"
21. Formal dances: Fr.
24. "____ Town"
25. Foundation
26. Khan et al.
27. New Mexico resort
28. Obtained
29. Actor Waterston
30. Coolidge's nickname
31. Back of the neck
32. Raison d'____
33. Asian weight
34. Crafty
36. Antique
39. Atmosphere
40. Butterfingers' word
42. Spires
43. Director Frank
44. Synthetic fiber
45. English baby carriages
46. Person to whom a check is made
47. Take care of
49. Nominate
50. Great Lake
51. Songstress Fitzgerald
52. Seed containers
53. "Graf ____"
55. Tree juice

PUZZLE 261   Keyword

To find the KEYWORD fill in the blanks in words 1 through 10 with the correct missing letters and transfer those letters to the correspondingly numbered squares in the diagram. Approach with care—this puzzle is not as simple as it first appears.

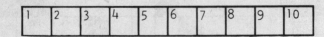

| 1 | 2 | 3 | 4 | 5 | 6 | 7 | 8 | 9 | 10 |

1. _ A P E R
2. C _ A M P
3. S T _ R K
4. P H O N _
5. B L O _ S

6. _ E A C H
7. T _ M E S
8. F L I N _
9. M U S _ Y
10. W A _ E R

ACROSS
1. Retains
4. Mineral springs
8. Cerise
11. Circle part
12. Temporary shelter
13. Cartoonist Larson
14. ___ Grande
15. Gambling city
16. Irk
17. Substance
19. Broached
21. Actress Thompson
22. Quarrel
23. Consumed
25. City in Israel
29. Charged particle
30. Flit
31. Plan for svgs.
32. Related to health
35. Woven fabric
37. Direction indicator
38. "___ for My Baby"
39. Notation
42. Sausage, in London
45. Scent
46. Parched
48. Lager
49. Gainsay
50. Delayed
51. Narrow inlet
52. Printers' measures
53. Nourish
54. Tropical tuber

DOWN
1. Damage
2. Song for Sills
3. Loch Ness country
4. "Silver ___"
5. Equal
6. Sheridan or Sothern
7. Bent over
8. Drizzle
9. Author Gardner
10. Tinted
13. Actress Scacchi
18. Perfect number
20. Buddy
22. Banal
23. Faded
24. Fish eggs
26. Sour
27. Dander
28. Pianist Cliburn
30. Tolkien's wizard
33. Yellowish white
34. Auto
35. Filled
36. Stopping place
39. Badgered
40. Actress Barbara ___
41. Dupes
42. Nip
43. Director Kazan
44. Paper quantity
47. Actress Dawn Chong

ACROSS
1. Glide
5. Tramp
8. President and chief justice
12. Formerly
13. Noshed
14. District
15. Gave an address
17. Sprightly tune
18. Gallery offerings
19. Principles
21. Wilkes-___
23. English school
24. Astronaut Sally ___
25. Rattles
29. Fruit drink
30. Schedule
31. Baltic, e.g.
32. Devote
34. Get out!
35. Pry
36. Day's march
37. Swindles
40. Flutter
41. Jai ___
42. Pester
46. Department
47. Enemy
48. Famous garden
49. Ornamental fabric
50. Thus far
51. Accomplishment

DOWN
1. Sun
2. "___ Step Beyond"
3. Bestowed
4. Go to bed
5. Prohibits
6. Colorado Indian
7. Think deeply
8. Aptitude
9. Opera highlight
10. Tumbled
11. Uses a shuttle
16. Diminutive suffix
20. Bestow excessive affection
21. Small nail
22. Assistant
23. Delight
25. Categorize
26. Prank
27. Derive
28. Satisfy
30. Highlander
33. Foment
34. Expressed
36. Inventor Whitney
37. Manhandle
38. Forearm bone
39. Secular
40. Worry
43. Eggs
44. Three-way pipe joint
45. Finale

PUZZLE 264

ACROSS
1. Vampire ____
4. Scoop out water
8. Reed instrument
12. Unrefined metal
13. Eye flirtatiously
14. Proofreader's mark
15. Maiden-name indicator
16. Similar to
17. Above
18. Maiden
20. Color
21. Great fury
22. Large keg
25. The same
28. Proper
29. "Much ____ About Nothing"
30. Land measure
31. Firearm
32. Grows older
33. Crossed letter
34. Golf average
35. Used money
36. Traditional sayings
38. Wide shoe size
39. Solar body
40. Reply
44. Adhesive
46. Stable grains
48. "We ____ the World"
49. Ventilates
50. Run away
51. Disencumber
52. Honey makers
53. Take care of
54. Conclusion

DOWN
1. James ____ (007)
2. Region
3. Abound
4. Waist-length jacket
5. Quick on one's feet
6. Type
7. Robert E. ____
8. Aroma, in London
9. Drink
10. Bullring cheer
11. Always, poetically
19. Location
20. Head covering
22. Storage box
23. Genesis garden
24. "____ in Space"
25. Facts and figures
26. ____ tea
27. Pirate's hoard
28. Cat's coat
31. Auto fuel
32. Gorillas, e.g.
34. Ink writer
35. Detected
37. Conjecture
38. Devoured
41. Merchandise item
42. ____ go bragh
43. Comedian Foxx
44. Jabber
45. Fib
46. Frequently, to poets
47. Beer's cousin

PUZZLE 265

ACROSS
1. Poodle, e.g.
4. Grotto
8. Massachusetts cape
11. Plunged headfirst
12. Unlock
13. Reverent fear
14. Biblical garden
15. Nuisance
16. Church bench
17. Long-plumed heron
19. Try out
21. Favorite beast
22. Very long time
25. Red cosmetic
28. Station ____ (car)
30. Of the mouth
31. Up to the job
34. ____ de Janeiro
35. "____ of the D'Urbervilles"
36. For both sexes
37. College paper
39. Latin-American dance
41. Snakelike fish
42. Small flap
45. Unpaid bill
47. Big
49. Weeding tool
51. Acorn trees
54. Cooking fat
55. Miscalculate
56. Fencing sword
57. Cravats
58. Affirmative word
59. Dispatched
60. Bullfight shout

DOWN
1. Elude
2. Not secret
3. Actor Hackman
4. Beat walker
5. Orangutan, e.g.
6. Sleeveless garment
7. Go in
8. Take prisoner
9. Have creditors
10. Morning moisture
11. Profound
18. Chamomile drink
20. Grimy
23. Fairy-tale monster
24. Sound
26. Oxygen or neon
27. Raised trains
28. Pie-piece shape
29. Facial feature
31. Play division
32. Squeezing snake
33. Those who loan
38. "____ My Children"
40. Certain woodwinds
42. Path
43. Concur
44. Fourposters, e.g.
46. Record on cassette
48. Palo ____
49. "____ Jude"
50. Raw metal
52. Barbie's man
53. Matched group

ACROSS

1. Some charts
5. Pasture
8. Cope's cousin
11. Sleuth Nancy ____
15. Printing process
16. Survey
17. Mined fuel
19. Roof part
20. Molecule part
21. Agitate
22. Soda flavoring
23. Decree
24. Handles
26. Sioux Indian
28. Author Gertrude ____
30. Song of Hawaii
34. Hun king
37. Unanimously
38. Metric volumes
40. Barnyard sound
41. Company
43. Shoshoneans
45. Mrs. Copperfield
46. Author Seton
48. Mariner Ericson
50. Location
53. Rock or peeve
54. Traffic sign
55. Garment fasteners
58. Amend copy
60. Song of Hawaii
67. Like some cream
68. Uprisings
69. Arm bone
70. Get it wrong
73. Glacial snowfield
75. Summers, on the Seine
77. Spat
78. Complaint
80. Ernie's wife
83. Opera composer Thomas ____
85. Poor grade
86. "Sleeping Beauty," e.g.
89. Garret
91. Western flicks
93. Song of Hawaii, with "The"
96. ____ del Sol
97. Hasty escape
98. Clap
102. "Tobacco ____"
104. Small case
106. Drill
108. Other
109. Johnson of "Laugh-In"
110. Night, in Milano
111. Cake froster
112. Denials
113. Must have
114. Racket
115. Bounder
116. Ankara native

DOWN

1. Baby buggy
2. Speck
3. Harrow's rival
4. Mogadishu native
5. Untethered
6. Yalie
7. Amalgams
8. Narrative
9. Old card game
10. Lightweight wood
11. Specified
12. Precipitation unit
13. Argentine Peron
14. Damp
16. Be widespread
18. Slats
25. Faldo's game
27. "____ shalt not . . ."
29. Have a repast
31. Thin layer
32. Dregs
33. Parched
34. Accumulate
35. Jay Silverheels's role
36. "Happy birthday ____ . . ."
39. Made a lap
42. Set aside
44. Poet Edmund ____
47. Rental units: abbr.
49. Comely
51. Eccentric
52. Lyricist Rice
56. Greek letter
57. Cordial flavoring
59. High-strung
61. Title of respect: abbr.
62. "Curly ____"
63. Onslaught
64. Sail smoothly
65. Surmise
66. Bistros
70. Certain tide
71. Widen, as a hole
72. Move
74. Waxed cheese
76. Nosy one
79. Inundated
81. Native of Florence
82. Sicilian volcano
84. Lawman Wyatt ____
87. Printers' measures
88. Hauls
90. Of a poetic foot
92. Ancient weight unit
94. Destined
95. Sculled
99. Baseball family name
100. Consumer
101. Work station
102. Operated
103. Mesabi find
105. Swiss canton
107. Wood sorrel

• THE CALL OF HAWAII •

PUZZLE 267

• TODAY'S ANTIQUES •

ACROSS

1. Valenciennes or Brussels
5. Skyline object
10. Booty
14. Load
18. Tanning substance
19. Argentine leader
20. Buffalo's lake
21. Norman or Rembrandt
22. Furnace's forerunner?
25. Pyromaniac's crime
26. Boats for cars
27. Came to the rescue of
28. Tracks
29. Daze
30. Jousted
32. Cuttlefish pigment
33. Bee follower
34. Sculpt
35. More certain
36. Poet Alexander ____
39. 3-D movie's forerunner?
43. Frequently, to a writer
46. "____, Babylon"
47. Dock denizen
48. Horatian works
49. Leg joint
50. Charter
51. Game fish
52. Parrot
54. Desires
55. Adventure
58. Multi-masted square-rigger
59. Sell
60. Emperor Selassie
61. Auditoriums
62. Saguaros
63. Long-tailed finch
65. Atop
66. Be overly friendly
69. English horns
70. Oppressively humid
72. Unit of heredity
73. Deceive
74. Encircle
75. Alley Oop's girl
76. ____ of Aquarius
77. The Venerable ____
78. Implore
79. Uzi's forerunner?
84. List extender: abbr.
85. Noiseless
88. Semisynthetic fabric
89. Lamprey
91. Easter symbol
92. Tot
94. Think up
97. Idle and Ambler
98. Group of cranes
99. Famous stone
100. Delicate fabric
101. Flashlight's forerunner?
105. Choral ensemble
106. Connecticut town
107. Muscle
108. Track feature
109. Scottish lake
110. Toe counts
111. Trudges
112. Threatening word

DOWN

1. Lick
2. Airborne
3. More appealing
4. Encompasses
5. Joins
6. Martinique spouter
7. Blue flag
8. Eurasian deer
9. Terminus
10. Small sizes
11. Molder
12. Dwelt
13. Stoke
14. Mexican shawl
15. Electric frypan's forerunner?
16. Welcome, in Molokai
17. Studies
21. Report
23. Either of two Irish lakes
24. Cannon fire
30. Queen of Hearts's creations
31. Choler
32. Lyon and Langdon
34. Halt
35. Discharge
36. Ash-colored
37. Rolvaag and Olsen
38. Electric blankets' forerunners?
40. Exchange
41. Chanticleers
42. Harem room
44. Banquet
45. Experiment
49. Masur and Vonnegut
51. Bundle
52. Beerlike
53. Woody's scion
54. Shortage
56. Exclaimed delight
57. Slapstick missiles
58. Forehead-covering hair
59. Spice
61. Navajo home
62. Staffs
63. Roman garment
64. Sashes for Yum-Yum
66. Under way
67. Love of Radames
68. Strip
70. Shed
71. Eskimo knife
72. Star of "Green Acres"
75. Submit
77. Take down a peg
80. Puff and Draco
81. Roof parts
82. Certain liquor
83. Vacillates
86. First cousins' fathers
87. Map corner feature, often
90. Neck and neck
91. Comedian Lenny ____
92. Strainer
93. Long-legged bird
94. Dealt
95. Baseball feat
96. Receives wages
97. School on the Thames
98. 3-handed card game
99. Sweeney of "Anything Goes"
102. Sixth sense letters
103. Zip
104. Formerly called

ACROSS

1. Air passage
6. Very small
12. Discordant
17. "Prizzi's ___"
18. Recount
19. Banish
20. "Don Pasquale," for one
21. Pogo
22. Crowbar
23. Chapel seat
24. Entitled
26. "Let's Make ___"
28. Barnyard mama
29. "Hollywood ___"
31. Provide with money
33. Seize for evidence
36. Broadway musical
38. Makes free of
42. Recluse
43. Catlike mammal
45. Famous fabulist
46. Spinning
47. Seer's card
48. Old TV western
50. "The Comeback Kid" actress
51. Fragrant wood
52. Aggressive person
53. Pale yellow
55. Fireside
56. Tactful person
59. Bizarre
60. Conrad's "Lord ___"
63. Twines together
64. Stiff
65. "The ___ Mutiny"
67. Sassy
68. Man's man
69. Spanish explorer
70. Informal affirmative
71. Marry on the lam
73. Genesis charmer
74. Bumpkin
76. Two-edged swords
79. Vietnam holiday
82. Wooden barrier
84. Leslie Caron film
85. Chew the fat
88. Standoffish
90. "Dirty ___"
92. Sky blue
94. Airport sight
95. Approve
96. Solitary person
97. Diner patron
98. "60 Minutes" commentator
99. Unbound

DOWN

1. Boutique
2. Famous diamond
3. Once more
4. "___ the Love of Benji"
5. Calm
6. Slender candle
7. Wash away
8. Bitter vetch
9. Astronaut's agcy.
10. Pupil
11. Aden native
12. "___ Dolly"
13. Hatchet
14. Tear apart
15. Killed
16. Present!
18. Wanderer
25. "Travels With My ___"
27. Hot-weather drink
29. Several
30. Enjoy the taste of
32. Christmas garland
33. "If ___ a hammer..."
34. Only
35. Victim
37. Profit
39. "___ It Romantic?"
40. Slumber
41. Practice fisticuffs
43. Academy member
44. Neighbor of Afghanistan
45. Dill
47. Baylor U.'s state
48. Kind of game
49. Hideous giant
51. Arrived
52. Understand
53. Gaudy
54. Lake, in the Highlands
55. Tremendous
56. Resist
57. Concerning
58. Entreaty
59. Fuel ship
60. Be in harmony
61. A part of
62. Entree dish
64. Penal sentence
65. Large bag
66. European mountains
68. Mount St. Helens, e.g.
69. "So long, it's ___ good..."
71. Make do
72. Pawnbroker
73. Burn slightly
75. Bid
77. Burning
78. Spring flower
79. Cassette
80. Singer Fitzgerald
81. Suit ___
83. Within: pref.
85. Wife of Jupiter
86. God of war
87. "The Way We ___"
89. Loneliest number?
91. Against
93. Menagerie

PUZZLE 269

• AROUND THE WORLD •

ACROSS

1. Papa's better half
5. Roman statesman
9. Bay of ____
15. Dart
19. Cheers
20. Overwhelmed
21. On terra firma
22. Attract
23. Quiet rooms
24. Window glass
25. Oil kingdom
27. South American republic
29. Jupiter or Ra
30. Shades
31. Mail
32. Cats
33. Soon
35. Pursue
38. Actress Bernhardt
39. Money makers
43. Clear
44. Made on a loom
45. Rack
47. Caesar's twelve
48. Lebanese president Gemayel
49. More desolate
50. Land of the Maori
52. Baseball's Darling
53. Author Andre ____
54. Chemist Marie ____
55. Alternatively
56. Patagonia's locale
59. Cut out
60. Tangled
62. Aberdeen miss
63. Buy off
65. "Star Trek" navigator
66. Soundness of judgment
69. Leather
70. Island republic, or island capital
75. Tart
76. Gripes
77. Balthasar and Melchior
78. Musical notes
79. Grand duchy
82. Content
84. Inventor Elisha ____
85. Eroded
86. Having handles
87. Goes bankrupt
88. Where the game is played
89. Quits
91. Shyly
92. Violet
93. Glut
94. Challenges
95. Aid
97. Messy one
99. Apples and quinces
100. Tangier's locale
104. Archipelago nation
107. Mongolian desert
109. Castle, in chess
110. Cargo
111. Accompany
112. December 24 and 31
113. Hawkeye State
114. Days of ____
115. Queens' crowns
116. Former filly
117. Exclusively

DOWN

1. Fashion
2. Writer Waugh
3. Bill of fare
4. Back stabber
5. Chicken entree
6. Grant
7. Decade
8. Poem
9. First, second, or third
10. Biblical prophet
11. Closes
12. Buffalo Bill
13. TV actress Meyers
14. Indeed
15. Show off
16. Oil job
17. Rainbow
18. Oolong
26. "Help Me, ____"
28. Act
29. Painter Albrecht ____
32. Blacktop
33. Astonish
34. Baseball team
35. "Nutcracker" girl
36. Wit
37. Doing very well
38. Kierkegaard
40. Glorify
41. Sluice
42. ____ with (supported)
44. Gullies
45. String
46. Taunt
49. "Itsy-____ teenie-weenie . . ."
50. Without sensation
51. Pause
53. Bug
54. Invents
57. Slur over
58. All ____!
60. Humid
61. Turkish regiment
64. Called
65. Crackles
66. Greek, for one
67. Sudden
68. Vetoes
69. Debauchee
71. Hint
72. Habitually
73. Downpours
74. Trial
76. Kind of code
80. Iron-rich range
81. Piece of wool
82. Actress Helen ____
83. Anagram for sail
84. Handel piece
87. Sherwood and Black
88. Copycat
90. Tristam's beloved
91. 35mm, e.g.
94. Contributor
95. Fossil resin
96. ____ City, Oklahoma
97. Scat!
98. Deceiver
99. Type size
101. Furry bandit
102. Hood
103. Approval
104. Wield
105. Caress
106. Greek letter
107. Muffin
108. Lobster spawn

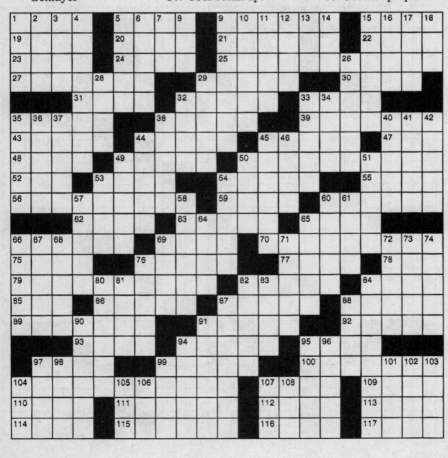

PUZZLE 270

• NICKEL AND DIME •

ACROSS

1. Food fish
6. Michelle Phillips, e.g.
10. Medley: abbr.
14. Secret society
19. Calamata, e.g.
20. Wild goat
21. Cake decorator
22. "A Bell for ____"
23. Cahn song worth a nickel?
26. Small finch
27. Declare
28. Streisand film
29. Safe measure from a dime?
31. Puts back
33. Some dogs
34. Ilk
35. "____ a Song Go Out of My Heart"
36. Charged atoms
37. TV clown
38. Rock or peeve
41. Performance at the Met
44. Revise copy
45. Computer unit
46. Skirt type
47. Virginia creeper worth a nickel?
50. Study hard
51. Esther's foe
52. Small French land masses
53. Clothing
54. Stepped
55. Practice of Jacob
56. Pitch
57. Sandal
58. Mist
59. Farm building
60. Nickel-and-dime shop?
66. Single time
67. Abominate
68. Food scraps
69. Petroleum
71. Basin
74. Verdi character
75. Swine
76. Car race
77. New York town
78. French river
79. Ladyfish worth a dime?
81. Carry
82. Shipshape, in London
83. Long-running musical
84. Tally
85. Hebrew "mother"
86. Deposited
87. Writer Alexander ____
88. Brit. cur.
90. "I Got You, ____"
91. "____ Kleine Nachtmusik"
92. Rapid spread
96. Nickel rummy?
100. ". . . what is ____?"
101. Talking bird
102. Muse for love sonnets
103. Precepts worth a dime?
106. Colorist
107. To shelter
108. Table d'____
109. Still
110. Anoint
111. Smaller
112. Bauxite et al.
113. Porticos

DOWN

1. Up to now
2. Critic Barnes
3. Splits
4. Exhausts
5. Pol. party
6. Stately dance
7. Borders on
8. New York team
9. Chop
10. Copiers
11. Images
12. Vassal
13. Wood preservative
14. Cuban leader
15. Skillful
16. Pressure: pref.
17. Blue dye
18. Companionless
24. Concerning
25. Trick
30. Seep
32. Norway's patron saint
33. Rope fiber
36. Caesar's date
37. Polar explorer
38. Arizona Indian
39. Dutch town
40. Little
41. Make the most ____
42. Rice dish
43. "If ____ Would Leave You"
44. ____ on (instigated)
45. Daniel or Pat
46. Myopic Mr.
48. Cornell's locale
49. "____ Is to Blame"
50. "The ____ Is Right"
51. Handles
54. Egyptian city
55. Cafe
57. Medicinal plant
58. Author Charles ____
59. Band
61. Alto, e.g.
62. Article
63. Middays
64. Musical form
65. Downy duck
70. Stringed instrument
71. Italian conductor
72. Molecule
73. Beatles' meter maid
74. Dry
75. ____ noire
76. Addition
78. Eastern
79. Adhesive
80. Like some cars
82. Forbidden
83. Co-op
86. Pakistani city
87. "I Fall to ____"
88. Backbones
89. Even
90. Tropical nut
91. Shore eagles
92. Gratify
93. Sal of "Exodus"
94. Within: pref.
95. Class
96. Greek cheese
97. Press
98. Weathercock
99. Take out
100. Love, in Peru
104. Unit of electricity
105. Wrong: pref.

PUZZLE 271

ACROSS
1. Timber cutter
5. Carson's predecessor
9. Flatfish
13. Tibetan monk
17. Stroller
18. Roof overhang
19. Writer Haley
20. Bedouin
21. Caught some rays
23. Place for dancing
25. Comes forth
26. Antic
28. Baltimore player
29. Rower's need
30. Metropolis
31. Small songbird
32. ___ lazuli
35. Overseer
36. Class
40. Evangelist Roberts
41. German composer
42. Masqueraded
43. Below average grade
44. Storage place
45. Caribbean nation
46. Imposing
47. Threshold
48. Enthusiastically
50. Breakfast bread
51. Phonograph record substance
52. Yak
53. Main force
54. Permit
55. Expression of disbelief
58. Rhett portrayer
59. Pillage
63. Burden
64. Tartan
65. By ___ of (force)
66. ___ Beta Kappa
67. Musical sense
68. Ground grain
69. Bishop of Rome
70. Mend
71. Obvious
73. Weeds
74. Baseball's Guerrero
75. Vessel
76. Caps
77. Broadcast
78. Downhill race
81. House, in Toledo
82. Swell
86. Salad vegetables
88. Jazz style
90. Polynesian instruments
91. Raid
92. Historical periods
93. Pull
94. Fit together
95. Behold
96. Identical
97. Jade

DOWN
1. Basilica section
2. Tom-tom, for one
3. Western writer Grey
4. Involve in conflict
5. Actor Ustinov
6. Exclamations of delight
7. Blvd.
8. Like Mars
9. Little Orphan Annie's companion
10. Spanish stew
11. Table support
12. Implored
13. Drawing together
14. Woody's son
15. Paw
16. French cleric
22. Turkish officials
24. Cornered
27. "___ So Easy"
30. "Your Show of Shows" costar
31. "___ That a Time!"
32. Leaf division
33. Song for Battle
34. Twinge
35. Newborn
36. Move with no effort
37. Norse god
38. Depend confidently
39. Shout
41. Flower starter
42. Trick
45. Animal stomach
46. Calabash, e.g.
47. Occupies a position
49. Goodness!
50. Quality
51. Outlet
53. Explosion
54. Highway division
55. Appeal
56. Cleanser
57. Large stringed instrument
58. Country singer Black
59. Rends
60. Acted like
61. Scorch
62. Mass unit, for short
64. Introduction
65. Accomplishes
68. Make neat
69. Hair ointments
70. Messengers
72. Turning pink
73. Retains
74. Stack
76. Scrumptious
77. Licoricelike flavor
78. Pond cover
79. Actor Perry
80. Fighter pilots
81. Cut short
82. Test
83. ___ avis
84. Small insect
85. Border
87. Greek dawn goddess
89. Writer Levin

240

PUZZLE 272

ACROSS

1. Herman's Hermits, e.g.
5. Fires
9. Stand
13. Feed some medicine
17. Soothing plant
18. Milky gem
19. Smell
20. At any time
21. China sea republic
23. Woolly northern animal
25. Stellar
26. "____ Without a Cause"
28. Aches
29. Average grade
30. Manages
31. Trust
33. Husband or wife
35. Cut wood
36. Place for a dance
37. Omelet item
40. Black cuckoo
41. Agog
42. Maxim
43. Feel poorly
44. Complicated
46. Pooh's quest
47. First name in mysteries
48. Knitter's requirements
49. Smoothed for travel
50. Soup spoon
51. Accomplished
52. Slim candle
53. Morass
54. "Valley of the ____"
57. ____ de ballet
58. Romantic composition
62. Out of the house
63. Saline
64. Yelled
65. Bo's number
66. Peace prize winner Brandt
67. Legends
68. Bit of cloth
69. Say further
70. "____ and the Man"
71. Jimmied
72. Party misfit
73. Moles
75. Boscs
76. Low evergreen
77. Ties up
79. Trouble for Pauline
80. Slued
83. As is
86. Kind of rock
88. Retained
89. Nimbus
90. Son of Seth
91. Copper water pot
92. Female sheep
93. Stagger
94. Liability
95. British school

DOWN

1. Lowest male voice
2. Dismounted
3. Idle
4. Collegian's goal
5. Fax
6. GI's address
7. Restricted
8. Woody Allen film
9. Hawsers
10. Loved one
11. The sun
12. Noted period
13. First entrance
14. Eavesdropped
15. Bench
16. Makes a boo-boo
22. Exist
24. African animal
27. Cot
30. Aviary enclosures
31. Doomed
32. Bohemian
33. Primary
34. Actress Archer
35. Squirreled away
36. Blooper
38. Fish feature
39. Merriment
41. New York island
42. Stirs
45. In a peculiar manner
46. Glad
47. "The ____ Has Landed"
49. Liberal, for one
50. Flops about
52. Highway charges
53. Packed cotton
54. Computer food
55. Was in arrears
56. Painting subject
57. Soothes
58. Tree trunks
59. Nutritious starch
60. Beloved
61. Brink
63. Father
64. Worry for many men
66. Place for a sash
67. Dawdled behind
71. ____ diem
72. Scarab
74. Throws things
75. Foot lever
76. Affirmative
77. Gospel writer
78. Over again
79. Father, to Francois
80. Suit part
81. Within: pref.
82. Actor Stockwell
84. Listener
85. Regret
87. Unruly crowd

PUZZLE 273

ACROSS

1. Exchange
5. Weather prediction
9. Unfermented grape juice
13. Ceremony
17. ___ Islands
18. ___ homo
19. Leaning tower city
20. Revise
21. This: Sp.
22. Capricious
24. Large party
25. Bar order
27. Paints
28. Eskimo homes
30. Broadcast
31. Woodworking tool
32. Monster
33. Hinder the growth of
36. On the house
37. Carbon ___
41. Pinball machine sign
42. Orange skin
43. Nods off
44. Autumn month: abbr.
45. Social insect
46. Legislators: abbr.
47. Moderated
48. South African fox
49. Prevailed
51. Counsels
52. Hail
53. Might's partner
54. Sired
55. Beethoven's birthplace
56. Munch noisily
58. Tablelands
59. Type of mushroom
62. There are six per inning
63. Brother of Moses
64. Auction
65. Confusion
66. Australian bird
67. Moved on a curved path
68. Scandinavian
69. Recipe instruction
70. Party member
72. Right's partner
73. Metric measure
74. Concoct
75. "It's a Wonderful ___"
76. By means of
77. Points of view
80. Verdi opera
81. Sons of the soil
85. Russian river
86. Octopus's arms
89. Object
90. Whack
91. "If ___ I Should Leave You"
92. Facility
93. Nuzzle
94. German river
95. Deserve
96. Hardens
97. Poker term

DOWN

1. Large quantity
2. Aspiration
3. Contrary
4. Agricultural laborer
5. Less
6. Requiring aspirin
7. Here, in Chantilly
8. Make over
9. Sap spout
10. Facial muscular contractions
11. UN member
12. Defamed
13. Involuntary response
14. Idea: pref.
15. A Jackson brother
16. Summers, in Nantes
23. Dimension
26. Frontiersman Carson
29. ___ point (embroidery stitch)
31. Greek god
32. Seeps
33. Celebrity
34. Fork part
35. Uncompromising demand
36. Ward off
37. Unaccompanied choral composition
38. Brutal
39. Quantity of medicine
40. Newt
42. Hammer part
43. Pedestal parts
46. Impudent one
47. Initiated
48. Writer Bontemps
50. Legs
51. Repair the lawn
52. Matador's wound
54. Green ___
55. Bundle
56. Certain college student
57. Scottish philosopher
58. Kind of parrot
59. Gasp for air
60. Baltic river
61. Loose gait
63. Lawman, often
64. Pete box
67. Israeli city
68. Mars
69. Staying power
71. Monastery resident
72. "___ Rose"
73. Galahad, for one
75. British measure
76. Flower holders
77. Too
78. Tidings
79. Small fly
80. Dill
81. Song follower
82. Type of collar
83. Remaining part
84. Pintail duck
87. Entertainer Tanguay
88. New Guinea seaport

PUZZLE 274

• JUICY FRUIT •

ACROSS

1. Spar
5. Spats
10. Merited
15. African land
19. Nora's pet
20. Eskimo
21. Ms. Massey
22. Abhor
23. Duck-walker
25. Darryl
27. Guards
28. Ponds
30. Skin layer
31. Burden
32. Spanish o.k.
33. Drama
34. Mount St. ____
37. German state
38. Unmindful
42. Rub out
43. Holly
45. Inlet
46. Flag
47. Molts
48. Tubs
49. Stew
50. Mom's boy
51. Ecstasy
52. Plantar regions
54. Treasure find
55. Vine frame
57. ____-ski
58. Bore a colt
59. Jim's pal
63. Solvent
66. Wheel rods
67. Legislated
71. Careening
72. Chopped
73. Hourly
75. Tongue suffix
76. Filament
77. Study
78. Oyster gem
79. Key letter
80. Scottish uncle
81. Myrtle
84. Provide food
85. DOD fields
87. Neck hair
88. Laves
89. Gaelic
90. Small parts
91. Swiss river
92. Exodus hurdle
95. Magna ____
97. Projection

101. Honeysuckle
103. Kiwi
105. Decree
106. Treeless plain
107. Proprietor
108. Stingy
109. Utters
110. Rims
111. Aeries
112. Record

DOWN

1. Raincoats
2. Tennis star
3. Daze
4. Undiplomatic
5. Shinbones
6. "____ You Now"
7. Minks
8. Evergreen
9. Hairdressers
10. Less safe
11. German oldster
12. Rocky peaks
13. Bambi's aunt
14. Laggards
15. Ms. Ladd
16. Injure
17. Italian town
18. Tunis rulers
24. Danish coin
26. Round and shiny
29. African fox
32. Mails
33. Brews
34. Burglary
35. Miscalculation
36. Frankie ____
37. Scoots
38. Dissension
39. Mr. Flynn
40. Sifter
41. Glutted
43. Egg whipper
44. Bundler
47. Carve
49. Swiss coin
51. Dull
52. Tempo
53. Hockey great's family

54. Of sound
56. Capital of Tibet
57. Competent
58. Crucial exam
60. Landed Scots
61. Surpass
62. Riverboat
63. Capital of Crete
64. Fragrant resin
65. Clock
68. Molars
69. Ms. Lauder
70. Beloveds
72. Recipient
73. Toast start
74. Sculls
77. So-so
78. DOD
79. Cellar

81. Concerned person
82. Beginnings
83. Lure
84. Antilles Indian
86. Attacks
88. Irrigates
91. Resource
92. Umps
93. Lamb
94. WWII date
95. Jutting rock
96. "Judith" composer
97. Long ages
98. Zone
99. Snare
100. "Jane ____"
102. Yore
104. Have debts

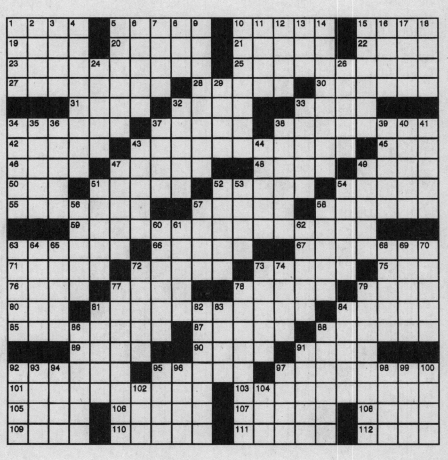

243

PUZZLE 275

• BASTING BEE •

ACROSS

1. Celt
5. Swimmer's problem
10. "Chariots of ___"
14. Cut in two
19. Harbin's continent
20. Of the ear
21. Doctorow's "___ Lake"
22. Secret reserve
23. Shabby
25. Laughing like mad
27. Watch
28. Ball position, in golf
29. Sourish
31. Thrice: pref.
32. Social occasions
33. La ___, Bolivia
34. Tiny arachnid
35. Electrical unit
37. Silas Marner, for one
40. Lamb's cry
41. High-school student
43. Cuddle
48. Early Peruvian
49. Perfectly fashioned
52. Singer/songwriter Leonard ___
53. Mai ___ cocktail
54. "___ street"
55. Rock musical
56. Loving
58. Catch
60. Datum
61. Beseech
62. ___-sahib
63. Live
64. Feathered missile
65. Hold it!
66. With competence
67. Wedded
68. Israeli dance
69. Crib
70. Mountain pass
71. Get along
73. TV's "Matt ___"
74. Sordino
75. Upright
78. Wagon-___
79. Reached
80. Bore
81. Collapsed
82. Ordinarily
84. Store's ___ leader
85. "The Purple ___ of Cairo"
86. House extension
87. More cunning
88. Gar
91. Snowfield
92. Assisted
94. Assistant
95. German exclamation
96. Bill attachment
97. Waste matter
99. Israeli port
101. Tool for Wade Boggs
102. HQ
106. Citrus drink
107. Stench
108. Mont Blanc, e.g.
109. Comedienne Charlotte
112. In the bag
115. Comic Oscar winner
118. Pomp
119. Broadway Tommy
120. Cadet
121. On the peak
122. Hailey novel
123. Stretch of time
124. Winter hazard
125. Refuse

DOWN

1. Portal
2. White-faced
3. Ireland
4. New Guinea port
5. Port of Spain
6. Hick
7. Coach Parseghian
8. ___ arts
9. Fold
10. Skim along
11. Charged particle
12. Cyrano's creator
13. Register
14. Behave
15. Understanding
16. Pain
17. Flightless bird
18. Kinski film
24. Winged
26. Qum's country
30. Take back
33. Black-eyed veggie
34. Post
35. "___ of Flying"
36. Rot
37. Bishop's headdress
38. Silly
39. Flycatcher
40. Bundle
42. Throw out
44. Drunkard
45. Anemone
46. Speak honestly
47. Foe
49. Biblical weed
50. "Butterfield 8" author
51. Confederate general
54. Plow (through)
57. Pad
59. Baseball team
60. "Animal ___"
61. Window glass
64. Senator from Kansas
65. Table d'___
66. First-rate
68. Macho guys
69. Handbag
70. Mrs. Fletcher's Cabot ___
71. Gordon of the comics
72. Theater divider
73. Director Prince
74. Deceive
75. Mishmash
76. Ointment
77. 10th president
79. Made well
80. Producer Mike
81. I'll be darned!
83. Necktie fabric
84. Honolulu garlands
85. Playwright Elmer ___
89. Lessened
90. Dancer Suzanne ___
91. Insect egg
93. Limn
96. Transported
98. "Awake and Sing" playwright
100. Army unit
101. Cornflower
102. Large party
103. Singing voice
104. Louver
105. Princely Italian family
107. Undo
108. French priest
109. Dull learning system
110. Soon
111. Catch sight of
113. Moray
114. Actress Merkel
116. Billy ___ Williams
117. Boy

PUZZLE 276

ACROSS
1. Duo
5. Shoo!
9. Pop's mate
12. Monster
13. Stillness
14. Respectful fear
15. Swarm
16. Failures to attend
18. Diving seabirds
20. Sustains
21. Skimpy
24. Ingested
25. Identical
26. Casual greetings
27. Fresh
30. Needlefish
31. Primary color
32. Walk in water
33. At least one
34. Showy actor
35. Naval jails
36. Price marker
37. Hole for a rope
38. Defeated side
41. December 24 and 31
42. Pronghorn
44. Platter
48. Slippery surface
49. Paradise
50. Tie together
51. Ground moisture
52. Encounter
53. Rams' mates

DOWN
1. Cooking vessel
2. Period in history
3. Make indignant
4. Comments
5. Jiggle
6. Young mammals
7. Pack animal
8. Larcenies
9. Medieval weapon
10. Had borrowed from
11. Disorder
17. Formerly named
19. Function
21. Legend
22. Strategy
23. Drafty
24. Give assistance to
26. Speak hesitantly
27. Brad
28. "The ___ of Night"
29. Actor Adam ___
31. Shred of cloth
32. Tussle
34. Manhattan section
35. So long
36. Kicker's stand
37. Happening
38. Positioned
39. Previously
40. Fret
41. Fencer's weapon
43. Pindaric poem
45. Uncooked
46. Topnotch
47. Response of
    agreement

PUZZLE 277

ACROSS
1. Slightly open
5. Spider's trap
8. Conger
11. Valley
12. Pub specialty
13. Commanded
14. Mr. Hyde's other side
16. Arden and Plumb
17. "___ to Billy Joe"
18. Beers
20. Actor Linden
22. Growing ashen
25. Curvy letter
26. Duo
27. Forbidden
31. Antique cars
33. Wane
35. Space
36. Destructive things
38. Yet, in poetry
40. Submachine gun
41. Israelite crossing spot
43. Vietnamese New Year
44. Gauguin's island
    home
47. Hawaiian dish
49. Lotion ingredient
50. Build
55. Flag maker
56. "The Raven" author
57. Opulent
58. Had lunch
59. Bark sharply
60. Views

DOWN
1. Append
2. Shock
3. "The Jazz Singer"
   star
4. Actor Oliver ___
5. Manner
6. Building annex
7. Casus ___ (reason for
   war)
8. Roof overhang
9. German river
10. Minus
13. Mendicant
15. Retained
19. Pismire
20. Tarragon, e.g.
21. Completely lost
23. Astonish
24. Earring locations
28. Small shop
29. Seep
30. Pass over
32. Sequence
34. Social work gathering
37. Backdrop
39. Dozes
42. Goofy
44. Mitchell plantation
45. Thanks ___!
46. Gardener's aid
48. Lubricates
51. ___ polloi
52. Slangy affirmative
53. Application
54. Questioning sounds

PUZZLE 278

ACROSS

1. Troublesome tot
5. Bath, e.g.
8. Unit of work
11. Comic Laurel
15. Subtle emanation
16. Galley blade
17. Grasshopper ____
18. Flavor
19. Caesar's fateful date
20. Exact
22. Decomposes
23. Tries
25. Greek letter
26. Inheritances
28. Dine on
30. Type measures
32. Vast time
33. Helmet
36. Coffee cup
38. Fruit seed
40. Eyed amorously
44. Culture medium
46. Redford film, with "The"
49. Not difficult
50. Italian seaport
52. Thing, at law
53. Danger color
55. Horse command
56. Porcelain
58. Model Koo ____
60. IRS mo.
63. Ring notable
64. Victimize
65. Crave
69. Secular
71. Attempted
74. Adhesive substance
75. Hawaiian greeting
77. Barnyard fowl
78. Area or scatter
80. Social gathering
81. Floating menagerie
83. Increase
85. Quick plunge
87. Rubber band
91. Spanish gold
93. Keen enjoyment
97. Pats
98. Cary Grant film
101. Translate
102. Ornamental case
103. Family connection
104. Lock opener
105. Hourglass contents
106. Realizes
107. Double agent
108. Bard's before
109. Antlered animals

DOWN

1. Lure
2. Discourteous
3. Metric land measures
4. Fondness
5. Drench
6. Skin
7. Mountain ridge
8. Spire ornament
9. Commence
10. Web-footed birds
11. Unfamiliar
12. Horn sound
13. Poker term
14. Promontory
21. College grounds
24. Americans' uncle
27. Excessively
29. Wine cask
31. Knight's title
33. Witch
34. Lifetime
35. Light brown
37. Embellish
39. Colleague
41. Dawdle
42. Native of: suff.
43. Coloring substance
45. Charles Dutton's sitcom
47. Steward's offering
48. Grassland
51. Cry of triumph
54. Thirsty
57. Island: Fr.
58. Oriental sauce

59. Small barrel
60. ___ mode
61. Schoolmate
62. ___ de Janeiro
64. Frankness
66. Priest's robe
67. Cry over
68. Society-page word
70. Car frame
72. Neptune's domain
73. Flop
76. Craft
79. Musician's engagement
82. Punts
84. Male duck
86. Pocketbook
87. Adam's address
88. Overdue
89. Border on
90. Poker counter
92. River in Europe
94. Secure
95. Combat vehicle
96. By all ___
99. Some
100. Perception

PUZZLE 279

ACROSS

1. Pie nut
6. Help
12. Lightweight wood
17. Proverb
18. Biased
20. Type size
21. Dawdles
22. Eventually: 3 wds.
24. Nothing
25. Waste allowance
27. Attempted, in Scotland
28. Inventor Whitney
29. Bristle
31. Garden flower
34. Work unit
35. "A ___ Grows in Brooklyn"
36. Grand Ol' ___
38. Big pitcher
40. Indian dress
42. Comfort
43. Rot
45. Deadly
49. Views
52. Bruises
54. Rasher
55. And so on: abbr.
56. Trolley
58. Info agencies
60. Sundance's gal
61. Greek letters
63. Rushed headlong
65. Shock
66. Gender: abbr.
67. Weird
68. Aces
70. Possesses
71. Heat lamps
73. Mends
75. Deer horn
77. Bird dog
79. Seed covering
81. "I Love ___"
82. Test
84. Emblem
85. Cupola
86. Blocks
89. Catch some Z's
91. Wading bird
93. Tablet
96. Sleeveless garment
97. Ohio city
99. ___ julep
101. Grassland
102. Without sincerity: 3 wds.
106. Homer's epic
108. Iroquoians
109. Aerial
110. Wash
111. Begin
112. Things of value
113. Borders

DOWN

1. Aches
2. Albert or Fisher
3. Reprimand: 3 wds.
4. Mature
5. Egg site
6. Beasts of burden
7. Grooved
8. ___ Paulo
9. Motel
10. Footprint
11. ___ Haute
12. Bare
13. Moslem title
14. Subsequently
15. Monument
16. Eagle's spot
19. Activists
23. Stately
26. Streak
30. Church section
32. Rams' pals
33. Pays
35. Headings
37. Schism
39. Street show
41. Legal matter
42. Art lover
44. Tokyo
46. Lose one's temper: 3 wds.
47. Insurance calculator
48. Sways
50. Manx
51. Glutted
53. Tuscany city
55. Sea birds

248

57. French Revolution leader
59. Yemen seaport
62. Iowa and Idaho
64. Bogs
69. WWII French city: 2 wds.

72. Gender
74. ____ Kenton
76. Dollop
78. Indian queen
80. Food
83. ____ Shriver
85. Hideaway
86. Arabic fruits
87. Cancel
88. Craze

90. Bird feather
92. Conies
94. Rental period
95. Bails
97. Statue
98. Play parts
100. Overwork

PUZZLE 279

103. Eur. lang.
104. "____ a jolly good fellow"
105. Philly to Boston: abbr.
107. Top

1	2	3	4	5		6	7	8	9	10	11			12	13	14	15	16
17						18					19		20					
21						22					23							
24			25	26				27						28				
29		30		31		32	33		34				35					
	36		37		38			39		40		41						
42					43				44		45				46	47	48	
49			50	51		52				53		54						
55			56			57		58				59		60				
61		62		63		64								65				
66			67					68				69		70				
71			72		73			74		75			76					
77				78		79			80			81						
		82			83		84				85							
86	87	88		89		90		91		92			93		94	95		
96				97			98		99			100		101				
102			103				104	105				106	107					
108					109							110						
111						112						113						

PUZZLE 280

ACROSS

1. Intrigue
5. Boor
9. Chemical spray
13. Warm-up
17. "___ Window"
18. Dad
19. Poet's black
20. Actress Albright
21. Wise
22. Exceeds
24. Jug
25. Tribal emblem
27. Taken ___
28. "The Raven" author
29. Sol or space prefix
30. Violet
32. Neck parts
35. One fourth: abbr.
36. Ford
37. Cheers for a matador
38. After Mon.
39. Chalcedony
45. Motorists' gp.
46. Laments
47. Antlers
48. Flu
49. Shaggy
51. Papal name
52. Tea cake
53. Astounded
57. Willow
60. Cathedral part
61. Odd
65. Explorer Heyerdahl
66. Rock fracture
68. In the center of
69. Eavesdrop
70. Ontario port
72. Ante
73. Fortuneteller
74. Encourage
75. Barbarian
76. Out-of-date
77. Spaghetti-sauce herb
81. Reporter's question
83. Chewing substance
84. Behind bars
85. Jove's weapon
89. Govt. agent
90. Specify
92. Pompous
94. Staff member
95. Once around the sun
96. Boleyn
97. High point
98. Minus
99. Makes a mistake
100. Comedian Laurel
101. Sax mouthpiece

DOWN

1. In favor of
2. Extended credit
3. Pledge
4. Traveling actors
5. Fine chinaware
6. Bathe
7. Runs
8. "The ___ of Seville"
9. Paris subway
10. Still snoozing
11. Dirty Harry, for one
12. Naval off.
13. West Point freshman
14. Mountain ash
15. Choose
16. Winter jacket
23. Knight's title
26. Those against
27. Writer James ___
30. Horace or Thomas
31. Tacks on
32. Biblical boatbuilder
33. Turkish regiment
34. Summer fruit
35. Freddie Mercury's group
36. Sausage
38. "Swan Lake" costume
39. Dry
40. Residence
41. Stands
42. Freudian subject
43. Rifle
44. Command to a mule
46. German industrial area
50. Bow's opposite
51. Flounces
52. Move swiftly, as clouds
54. Stewed meat
55. Cow's stomach

56. One
57. Baseballer Mel ___
58. Quiet!
59. Debt letters
62. Exploits
63. Gorillas
64. Stringed instrument
66. Apartment plant
67. Jason's ship
68. Plentiful
71. Couple
73. Russian teakettle
75. Reddish-brown colors
76. Grogshop
77. Computer number system
78. Fiber plant
79. Drat!
80. Wilder and Hackman
81. Hums
82. Bear ___
83. Wet behind the ears
85. Russian ruler
86. Alcohol lamp
87. Open fabric
88. Clock
90. Pigment
91. Poet's always
93. Writer Buntline

PUZZLE 281

ACROSS

1. Scold
7. French friend
10. Surrounded by
14. World's highest mountain
16. Heir
17. "David Copperfield" girl
18. Popular liqueur
19. The sun
20. Elliptical
21. Fish secretion
22. Hinged fastener
24. Cravat fabric
26. "I Like ——"
27. Employ
28. Kind of drum
30. Docile
32. Bean variety
33. Before, in verse
34. Electric unit
36. Fumble the job
39. Opponent
41. Initiate
43. Agitate
44. Bat wood
46. Male singer
47. Grotto
48. "Got —— of living . . .": 2 wds.
51. Macaw
53. Candlenut
54. Asian sea
55. Russian river
56. Assailed: 2 wds.
58. Chum
60. Want
61. Old-womanish
62. Trumpet sound
66. Mistake
68. Persian rose
69. Filch
71. Punta —— Este
72. Without moisture
74. Wretched-ness
76. Gums
77. —— de Triomphe
79. Catch
81. Variable star
82. Level
83. Greek letter
85. Instantly
87. Able to read
89. Garden herb
90. Part of a brogan
91. Was a hog
92. Icelandic classic
93. Dutch city
94. Redacted

DOWN

1. Blessing
2. Dreaded glance: 2 wds.
3. What's left
4. Exist
5. Restraining influence
6. Social standing
7. Ninny
8. Othello, e.g.
9. Sheltered bay
10. Commotion
11. Hollywood personage: 2 wds.
12. Neighbor of Turkey
13. Mrs. Roy Rogers
15. Trial run
18. Entertain
23. Serving dish
25. Ms. Dawber
28. Solutions
29. Spring
31. Name wrongly
35. School dance
37. Prima donna
38. Russian city
40. Bullfighter
41. Sports setting
42. Snare

45. Laughing sound: hyph.
48. —— of Cleves
49. Ogle
50. Hammed it up
52. Resounded
57. Exhausted: 2 wds.
59. "Dear ——"
63. Admire servilely
64. Akin
65. Bring joy to
67. Tease
69. Restore
70. Spoke
73. Italian poet
75. Unaccompanied
77. Competent
78. Hollow stalk
80. Commendable
82. College gp.
84. Alias initials
86. Undersized
88. Silkworm of Assam

PUZZLE 282

ACROSS

1. Glue
6. Cattle pen
12. Certainty
16. Sacrificial platform
17. Each
18. ___ podrida
19. Slant
20. Abate
21. Iranian money
22. Aching
23. Water lily painter
24. Tablecloth fabric
26. Wide-spouted pitcher
27. Native mineral
28. Browse
30. Timid
31. Elevator alternative
34. Melville's captain
36. Southern constellation
39. Feasted
40. Nickname for Hemingway
42. Whiplike movement
46. Trite
48. Closely trimmed
50. Fit of fever
51. Viewpoints
53. Summer treat
54. Mar
56. Germ
57. Spelunkers
60. Mountainous country
61. "___ Comes the Sun"
62. United States: abbr.
63. Mouse's foe
65. Sounds of uncertainty
66. Extraordinary
68. Belgrade's locale
71. Links score
74. Pre-Easter period
76. By birth
77. Couch
81. Mocking
83. Valuable thing
85. "Annie ___"
86. Ear part
87. "For fools ___ ..."
89. Complete
90. Skip over
91. Shop sign
92. Sports building
93. Sunbathes
94. Did a gardening chore
95. Alert

DOWN

1. Outdated
2. Permit
3. Supermarket
4. Slender candles
5. Before, to a poet
6. Dietary units
7. Kitchen device
8. Get up
9. Takes a nap
10. Top flier
11. Give help
12. Shape
13. Assumed name
14. Disagree
15. Garrulous
23. Castle ditch
25. Collection of sayings
29. Garb for Batman
32. Chaucer creation
33. Typewriter keys
35. Hold responsible
36. Disconcert
37. Indian princess
38. Fury
41. Declare positively
43. Wide open
44. Coffee additive
45. High shoes
47. Birch's cousin

49. Honey factory
52. "___ and Mrs. King"
55. Against: pref.
58. Sunday response
59. Filtered
64. Encourage
67. Actress MacGraw
69. Make into green fodder
70. On the beach
71. Airline employee
72. Scent
73. Spring bird
75. Cup, in Cannes
78. Horse opera
79. Cut of meat
80. Alleviate
82. Hair holders
84. Herringlike fish
88. One, to Pierre
89. Kind of dance

PUZZLE 283

ACROSS

1. Laughter sounds
5. Ringer
9. "___ Cotton" (1897 Sousa work)
13. French priest
17. Spanish eyes
18. American Indian
19. Realm
20. Kind of camp
21. 1889 Sousa work
25. Unmasks
26. Parts of speech
27. Forearm bones
28. Tattle
29. Catcher's need
30. Doctrine
31. Perplexed
34. German article
35. "...nobody ___ but you"
37. Spread hay
40. Siesta
41. Musical group led by Sousa
44. Numero ___
45. "Flower ___ Song"
47. Golly!
48. Touch on
49. Woodwind
50. Musical composition
52. Deceived
54. Orchestra section
55. 1888 Sousa work
59. Wind instrument
62. Turns pages
63. Atlantic island group
67. Charged atoms
68. Scorch
69. 1004, to Pliny
71. St. Petersburg's river
72. Trend
73. Sousa works
77. Husband
78. Tokyo, formerly
79. Desire
80. Kitchen worker
81. "Marching ___"
83. Short hairdo
84. Hold
85. Bath or Vichy
86. Crowbar
89. Higher
91. Unfeelingly
95. Military men whose motto is 55 Across
98. Horn sound
99. Stingy
100. Like lemons
101. Sea eagle
102. She, in Paris
103. Tennis's Arthur ___
104. Pulls
105. Nurture

DOWN

1. Julia Ward ___
2. Trojan War hero
3. Doctor's domain: abbr.
4. On land
5. "John Brown's Body" poet
6. Work units
7. Ignited
8. Of a big cat
9. Done for
10. Golf club
11. Role in "The Untouch- ables"
12. Thug's gun
13. "There Is ___ in Gilead"
14. Created
15. ___ Raton, Florida
16. Old English letters
22. Abraham's son
23. Perceiver
24. Pondered
29. Mickey and Minnie
30. "___ It Romantic?"
31. Joining words
32. Poi source
33. Rotated
34. Opposite of WSW
35. Declined
36. Magna cum ___
37. Sousaphone
38. Son of Seth
39. Deer
42. Old Irish alphabet
43. N.Y.C. sights
46. Upright poles
49. Mr. Welles
51. Links gadget
52. Swiss coin
53. Switch position
54. Show ___
56. Chubby
57. Uncanny
58. Volcano output

59. Higher-pitched version of 59 Across
60. Burden
61. Loosen
64. San ____, Italy
65. Author Hunter
66. Warbled
68. Dunce
69. Cat's comment
70. Bother
73. Task
74. Group of eight
75. Least rich
76. Flavor
82. Poet Sidney ____
83. Davis or Midler
84. Extra
85. "The ____ and Stripes Forever"
86. Pear-shaped instrument
87. Organic compound
88. Bowed instrument
89. Exploits
90. Egyptian god
91. Complacent
92. About
93. Singer Horne
94. Belgian river
96. Genetic material
97. Former French coin

PUZZLE 284

ACROSS

1. Prejudice
5. "____ Loves You"
8. Spoil
11. Ovine mothers
15. Coalesce
16. Bee product
17. Corrida sound
18. Wireless
20. Pact
22. Accompanying
24. CLXVII x VI
25. Chop or loin
26. Alleviate
27. ____ Aviv
28. Pay to play
30. Done
32. Slips up
33. Sit
34. Altar constellation
36. Manufactured
38. Lend an ____
39. Form of humor
42. "____ Racer"
43. Chevron
46. Exact
48. Metaphysical being
49. Hold
50. "____, Giorgio" (Pavarotti film)
51. Emphasize
53. Festive
54. Supervised
55. Dismounted
56. Eagle type
57. Sward
60. Bridge
61. Dog breed
63. Psychic letters
66. Barrier
68. Lawyers, as a whole
69. Brings to a conclusion
71. Odors
72. Servants
74. Perches
75. Famous opera house, for short
76. Shakespearean works
78. TV's man on the street?
79. Candid
81. Ornamental nail
82. "The ____ Thing"
84. Mop
87. "Major ____"
88. Fix socks
89. Holiday forerunners
91. Tone
92. Remove completely
95. Therapy
97. Whistle
98. Decimal unit
99. Poetic contraction
100. Soil
101. "Auld Lang ____"
102. "Another World" role
103. Magazine features
104. Books of ecclesiastical rules

DOWN

1. Commence
2. Annoys
3. Lifetime
4. Discharge
5. Turn suddenly
6. Longs (for)
7. Annex: abbr.
8. New Zealand bird
9. Adjusted
10. Hold back
11. Sea eagle
12. Clump
13. Opinionated newspaper article
14. Math terms
15. Baby's word
19. Flirtatious glance
21. Cow's sound
23. 19th letter
29. Norse explorer
31. Feel contrite
32. Certain seasons, in Burgundy
33. Component
35. "Aida" highlight
37. Not a red ____
38. European volcano
39. Snoop
40. Metric measure
41. Getaways
43. Military member
44. Shoo-fly ____
45. Objective
47. Brilliance
49. Summons
52. One, in Berlin
53. Lass
56. Verge

258

57. Saratoga Springs, e.g.
58. Propeller
59. Camel type
60. Tiff
61. Biblical brother
62. Kind of collar
63. "St. ____"
64. Backdrop
65. Letter extenders: abbr.

67. Hemsley series
68. The Rolling Stones, e.g.
70. Playthings
72. Prepared to ride
73. Directed
76. Layers
77. Hoarders
79. Pindaric verses

80. Plaster of ____
81. Algonquian-speaking Indian
83. Field
85. Relatives
86. Jo's sister
88. Have fine cuisine

90. Stage
93. Leo's home
94. Spanish queen
95. Afternoon social
96. New Jersey cape

259

PUZZLE 285

ACROSS

1. Good-bye
5. "My country, ___ of thee"
8. Gulf of ___
12. Freeway exit
16. Sleep like ___
17. Doggie delight
18. Corrupt
19. Son of Isaac
20. Ibsen woman
21. Ascend
22. Windstorm
23. Memo to a printer
24. Refined
26. Musical syllable
28. Sharp crest
30. Prevail
34. Wrinkle
37. Reform
38. To be continued
40. Scurried
41. Ms. Place (Sundance's girlfriend)
43. Polish river
45. Princely family
46. Nullify
48. Persuasion
50. Bristle
53. Barrel
54. The cat's ___ (something terrific)
55. Listened to
58. Equine sport
60. Hug a belief
67. Stag
68. Grain elevators
69. Cleveland's waterfront
70. Building annex
73. Jacob's wife
75. Arden and Brent
77. Auction
78. Debatable
80. Salamander
83. Of an epic
85. Actor Knight
86. Shrub of the rose family
89. Harbinger of spring
91. Metric units
93. Obdurate
96. Coal
97. Surgeons: abbr.
98. Essay
102. Stringed instrument
104. Swimmer's place
106. Exhort
108. Bull: Sp.
109. Out of the weather
110. Elbe tributary
111. Eternities
112. Greek love god
113. Bitter
114. Stiffens
115. Vast amount
116. Scarlet colors

DOWN

1. Pungency
2. Lily plant
3. Lacerated
4. Writer Christie
5. Sheer linen
6. Winners
7. Fume
8. Entertained
9. Yellow bugle
10. Large lizards
11. Warns
12. Refinish
13. Star
14. Actress Marsh
15. Lay
17. Military commissions
25. Relax
27. Splitsville
29. Cote dweller
31. Sketched
32. Astonishes
33. Palm fruit
34. Fragment
35. Hindu queen
36. Bestow
39. Table part
42. Iran's capital
44. One at rest
47. Was obligated to
49. Uses a shuttle
51. Spinning toy
52. Potent pugilist
56. King: Fr.
57. Miss Evans
59. Individuals

61. Dolores ____ Rio
62. Billy ____ Williams
63. Catholic devotion
64. Choleric
65. Tanker
66. Necessities
70. German spa
71. Droops

72. Dawdler
74. Sir: Ger.
76. Greets, in the military
79. Bugle
81. Marvels
82. Ski lift component
84. Happy song
87. Decline
88. White poplars

90. Discharges
92. Seesaw
94. Storm, in Sevres
95. ____ Graecia
99. Religious writer Hannah ____

100. Goad
101. Throw
102. Baseball or cowboy
103. Wing
105. Profit
107. Shad's output

PUZZLE 286

ACROSS

1. Zip
5. Actor Cronyn and namesakes
10. System of laws
14. ___ up (admits)
18. Papal cape
19. Clio's sister
20. Yemen seaport
21. Bloke
22. Optimistic belief
25. Colombian Indian tribe
26. Compass dir.
27. Tension
28. Type measures
29. Preached with passion
31. Job-seekers' aids
33. Stir
34. Allow (for)
35. Fuzzy texture
36. Avid fan's purchase
40. Font
43. Top banana
44. Roadways: abbr.
45. Iowa Indian
48. Within: pref.
49. Flat's counterpart
50. Bar chair
52. Festive
53. Guidelines
55. British advisor
57. Thrice: pref.
58. Steinbeck character
59. Meager
61. Removes
62. Redeems
64. Silica gemstones
65. Supreme Ross
67. Wall Street item
69. Author Bret ___
70. Designation
71. ___ George
74. Pitch in
77. Resolutions
79. Rooney of "60 Minutes"
80. Scandinavian
81. Suit and top
82. Uncalled for
83. In medias ___
84. Indian tribes
85. Drays
86. Irrigate
87. Hollywood recruiters
91. Washed out
92. Exchanges
94. Alehouse
95. Finally achieves success
99. Blue-penciller
100. Table crumb
101. Dealer
104. Historic time
105. Easy gait
106. Bias-free
110. Mine shipments
111. Unskilled worker
112. Washington sound
113. Niblick numbers
114. Bridge position
115. Small pie
116. Slants
117. Hardy heroine

DOWN

1. Uneven
2. Strike locales
3. Bar drink
4. Peter Jennings, for one
5. Legatees
6. Major or Minor
7. Balthazar, Caspar, and Melchior
8. Town on the Thames
9. ___ Canals
10. Howitzer
11. Horatian works
12. Scotch whisky
13. Bewitches
14. Musical span
15. Reason
16. Christened
17. Hammett's Sam
18. Humdinger
23. Footfall
24. Spanish finger
30. Korean GIs
32. Partnership
33. Cleo's way out
34. Climber's peg
36. Window cover
37. Sensory organs
38. Rocker's equipment
39. Rainbow fish
40. Blue-ribbon winner
41. Poker chip-in
42. Old Glory
43. Singer Montez
46. Shampoo ingredient
47. Certain classics
49. Ginza drink
50. Bathroom item
51. Heavy weight
52. Watkins ___
54. White Cliffs site
56. Town and cheese
59. Bender
60. Persian or Siamese

63. Pretentious
64. Feel one's ___
65. Ship levels
66. Blue flag
67. Battle souvenir
68. Put an edge on
69. "Back Street" author
70. Homes away from home
72. Wave: Fr.
73. French river
75. Cut in
76. Blessings
77. Scoot
78. Teheran resident
81. Greek letter
84. Bread spread
85. Corn holder
86. Guarantee
88. Swear (to)
89. Short race
90. Disconnects
91. Small bird
92. Downwards
93. Prize
95. Mine entrances
96. Leaf features
97. White-tailed seabirds
98. Droops
100. Skunk's defense
101. Quiz answer
102. Latvian capital
103. Congregation's response
107. Teachers gp.
108. Mil. rank
109. Reason for sudden death

PUZZLE 286

PUZZLE 287

ACROSS

1. Noggin
5. Lesion adhesion
9. Delighted
13. Maltese and manx
17. Diva Gluck
18. Rock's Jethro ___
19. Bacteriologist Dubos
20. Stratford-on-___
21. By the ___ of one's teeth
22. Century plant
23. Truck-stop sign
24. Longest river
25. Bookkeeper, for one
28. Equestrian's equipment
30. Compass pt.
31. Roost
32. Naysay
33. Violin virtuoso
36. "That's one small ___ for a man . . ."
38. Dutch scholar
42. Pitch in
43. Cornered
45. Cartoonist Disney
47. Shredded
48. Tizzy
50. Galena, e.g.
51. Minstrel's lay
52. Latest thing
53. Belfry
55. Sleigh jockey
56. Restaurant
57. Naught
58. Actress Hunt
59. Skip and jump's tagalong
60. Outline
63. Ritzy
64. Melodious
68. Carroll's March creature
69. Clare Boothe ___
70. Botch
71. Incense
72. Above
73. "Smooth Operator" singer
74. Lindsay and Lowell
76. Genetic abbr.
77. Mr. Chips, e.g.
79. Patton's vehicle
80. Mountain nymph
82. Icicle's site
83. Actor Gerard
84. Top of Guido's scale
85. Settle a score
88. Mechanic
94. Football's Starr
95. Assigned part
97. Sleuth Wolfe
98. Sports attendance
99. ___ est percipi
100. Opposite of aweather
101. Mass
102. Charo's this
103. Sidelong glance
104. Property
105. Besides
106. Rank below vice-admiral

DOWN

1. Latch
2. Sommer of films
3. ___ Gemayel
4. Hoofer
5. Like old bread
6. "I Spy" star
7. Baseball brothers
8. Hallowed
9. Welcome
10. Shakespearean king
11. Hymenopter
12. Dinner finale
13. Hospital aide
14. Gung-ho
15. Turnpike fee
16. Dagger
26. "___ It a Pity"
27. Ball-and-socket joint
29. Collection of sayings
32. Actress Burke
33. Boldness
34. Hue
35. Plimpton book
36. Parched
37. Palmer's peg
39. Bewail
40. Coax
41. Diviner
44. Tumble
45. Blustery
46. Utah resort
49. Agent
51. Javelin
54. Peach or pumpkin
55. Because

56. Johnson or Knotts
58. Acclaim
59. Harm
60. Effort
61. Contain
62. Region
63. Emergency signal
64. Odyssey
65. Discharge
66. Elbow-wrist connection
67. Guide
70. Long geological period
73. More than two
74. "City Slickers" actor
75. Han ____ of "Star Wars"
78. Xanthippe, e.g.
79. Ascot
81. New York hockey player
83. Selfishness
84. Sentimental- ize
85. First shepherd
86. Amphora
87. Gaelic
88. Watkins ____
89. Peddle
90. Louisiana town
91. Cheese: Ger.
92. Singer James
93. Fifty-two weeks
96. Writer Hansson

PUZZLE 288

ACROSS

1. More difficult to find
6. Provide refreshments
11. Gravy holders
16. Mistreat
17. Alienated
18. Flynn of films
19. Plaudits
21. Finnish bath
22. Tokyo, formerly
23. Off the deep ____
24. Japanese shoes
26. Make a stake
27. Agitates
30. Turncoat
32. Smell
34. Ten cents
35. Evolve
38. Grid official
40. Eye parts
44. Pitcher's stat
45. Lasting
48. Backward: pref.
49. Opera feature
51. Please the cook
52. Turkish title
54. Home of the O'Haras
55. Musical composition
57. ____ size
60. Ribbed fabric
61. Pinches
63. Shrew
64. Facial growths
66. Sullen
68. Shut again noisily
70. Showed up
74. Avoiding, as an issue
78. Gin mill
79. Long-necked bird
81. Expand: abbr.
82. Tibetan antelope
83. Maine town
85. Those not qualified
88. Snake poison
89. Italian city
90. Not any person
91. Plant disease
92. Pull out all the ____
93. Merchandise

DOWN

1. Competed in the Indy 500
2. Dwelling
3. Scuttlebutt
4. Psi power
5. Submitted
6. New Jersey city
7. Strong beer
8. Chinese society
9. "____ Laughing"
10. Took a break
11. Steel name
12. Mouths: pref.
13. Antilles island
14. Tinted
15. Blackboard material
20. Role for an actress
25. Blue dye
28. Horned viper
29. Pocket the cue ball
31. French playwright
33. New Testament bk.
35. "Magic Man" rock group
36. Tell's missile
37. American patriot
39. Wheel rims
41. Drummer Ringo ____
42. Did wrong
43. TV serials, informally

46. Actress Dawn Chong
47. Easily bruised item
50. Cliche
53. Walking leisurely
56. Sooner State
58. Sculler's need
59. Young animal
62. Fail-safe
65. Quantity: abbr.
67. Is worthy of
69. Coils of yarn
70. Overhead
71. Peeled
72. Likely
73. Sinker
75. Nanook's home
76. Phrase describing a limitless amount
77. Vapors
80. Roman emperor
84. ____ de plume
86. Mouth part
87. Scare word

PUZZLE 289

ACROSS

1. Store
5. Calligrapher's tool
8. N.Y. summer hours: abbr.
11. Cheerful
15. Animated
16. Unadorned
17. Affirmative
18. "En garde" weapon
19. State positively
20. "Essays of ___"
21. Sailor's patron saint
22. Certain two-digit numbers' suffix
23. Relevant
25. Electrical unit
27. Walking ___
29. Start of a college song
34. Industrialist Samuel ___
37. Argentina's former dictator
38. Boil
39. Roman 149
40. Type of tide
42. Has title to
44. Move about
45. Djibouti inhabitant
47. Coaster
49. Mast
52. Actress Sheridan
53. Ancient people of Gaul
54. Scottish landowner
57. Part of QED
59. More of the college song
66. Outdoor winter covering
67. Valuable violin
68. Large bodies of water: Fr.
69. Mountain
72. Wielded
74. Those people
76. Author Hunter
77. Ancient city in Asia Minor
79. Furniture piece
82. Niblick
84. Enlarge
85. Grain beard
88. Bide time
90. More beloved
92. End of the college song
95. Tidal bore
96. Zodiac sign
97. ___ and white (colors of the 59 Across school)
101. Notice: abbr.
103. Of a period
105. Dream: Fr.
107. Needle case
108. Female soldier of WWII
109. Knights' titles
110. Was in debt
111. Lopez theme song
112. Racing vehicle
113. ___ and haw
114. Such: Fr.
115. Narrate

DOWN

1. Scoria
2. Apian abode
3. In excess of
4. Pompano
5. More ashen
6. Silkworm
7. "Be ___ when my light is low . . ." (Tennyson)
8. Long fish
9. ___ and Pythias
10. Quirts
11. Steps aside
12. Short play set to music
13. Understand
14. Hankering
16. Varanasi
17. Cowardly
24. Last word
26. Longest river in Spain
28. Reverent fear
30. Emerge
31. Motels
32. Goatee's site
33. Composer Jerome ___
34. Muffler
35. Long-term prisoner
36. San Antonio shrine
41. Tolerated
43. Racer
46. Edges
48. Excavates
50. Parabola
51. Cheer
55. Becoming slower, musically
56. Missile
58. Subdue

60. Antelope
61. Dawn goddess
62. Gauguin's place of self-exile
63. No!
64. Ancient cannon
65. Actor Ed ____
69. Asian nursemaid
70. Stringed instrument of old
71. Label displaying cost
73. College official
75. Sang as the Swiss do
78. Sidewise
80. Billows
81. "Citizen ____"
83. Requirement
86. Coat
87. Anew
89. Native of Luzon
91. Silvery
93. Penthouse
94. New and different
98. Indian
99. Soothe
100. "____ M for Murder"
101. Boring tool
102. Greek letter
104. Limb
106. Bleater

PUZZLE 290

ACROSS
1. Oak, e.g.
5. ___ on the back
8. Spanish cheer
11. ___-de-camp
12. Uprising
14. Green vegetable
15. Joy
16. Decoration
18. Smidgen
20. New York team
21. Dinosaur bone
24. Tricky
25. Historic time
26. Chess pieces
28. Firm
32. Overhang
34. Enraged
36. Traveled by horseback
37. Sleighs
39. Lamb's cry
41. Actor Silver
42. "___ Smart"
44. With delight
46. Emerge
49. Yak
50. Dew
52. Baseball's Ruth
56. Addition to a house
57. Insult
58. Psyche components
59. Glimpse
60. "___, Giorgio"
61. Votes in favor

DOWN
1. Move back and forth
2. Petroleum
3. Keats composition
4. Property documents
5. Difficulty
6. Broadcast
7. Picking-up tool
8. Frank
9. Church season
10. Chow
13. Opposite of heads
17. Civic official
19. Goal
21. Charges
22. Evangelist Roberts
23. Set aside
27. Collar
29. Nobleman
30. Matinee ___
31. Reject
33. Borders
35. Knives
38. Chairs
40. In the style of
43. Sincerely
45. Monastery
46. Singer Ed ___
47. Arctic site
48. Mound
51. Deplore
53. "The ___ of Innocence"
54. Scarf
55. Double curve

PUZZLE 291

ACROSS
1. Female voice
5. Tropical snake
8. Sometime
12. College football game
13. Snack on
14. Molten rock
15. Cleveland's lake
16. Creative
18. Tennis call
19. Jazz, e.g.
20. Foxy
21. "___ Girl"
23. Priest's title: abbr.
25. Consistent
27. Possible to consume
31. Contented noise
32. Meets with
33. Not there
36. Mediterranean fruit
38. Ruin
39. Singer Smith
40. Sham
43. Daddies
45. Leader of the flock
48. Awkwardly
50. Heavenly headgear
51. Make sharp
52. Plumbing joint
53. Epochs
54. Paradise
55. Melancholy
56. Examination

DOWN
1. Biblical brother
2. Knowledge
3. Cheeps
4. Corrida shout
5. "___ and the Beast"
6. Rowing needs
7. Garb
8. Overhead trains
9. Tanks
10. Malicious
11. Risque
17. Chilled
19. "___ About You"
22. Seraglio
24. Stopover
25. Baden-Baden, e.g.
26. Old boat
28. Drink
29. Golf's Trevino
30. Curve
34. Dozes
35. Qualities
36. Approved
37. ___ Vegas
40. Yearn
41. Oaf
42. Melody
44. Petition
46. Pub potables
47. Maximum
49. Crew
50. Stetson, e.g.

PUZZLE 292

ACROSS

1. Beaver and Wally's dad
5. Vise
10. Farm structure
14. Clinton's canal
15. Edmonton player
16. Sea east of the Caspian
17. Lamprey and moray
18. Mail distributor
20. Golden horse
22. Twits
23. Dregs
24. Equipment
25. Church tables
28. Cooking styles
32. Highway
33. Fire starter
34. Hard wood
35. Burrowing mammal
36. Laments
37. Plateau
38. Curve shape
39. Puerto Rico port
40. Manservant
41. Tie
43. Bother
44. Depend
45. Heart of the matter
46. Contradiction
49. Gave
53. Names
55. Baseball's Murphy
56. Humble
57. Efface
58. Eye
59. Motives
60. Thorny flowers
61. Approach

DOWN

1. Cry
2. Zone
3. Creek
4. Uninhabited
5. Duplicates
6. Large cats
7. Plus
8. Came across
9. Necessary nutrients
10. Expedition
11. Rainbow
12. Decorative fabric
13. Spanish shouts
19. Holy day
21. Pond
24. Trickery
25. Supplied
26. Unfettered
27. Oklahoma city
28. Begin to make sense
29. Carols
30. Stand
31. Glide
33. Liking
36. Fuzzier
37. Elephantlike animal
39. Fold
40. Expansive
42. Beverages
43. Razzes
45. Migratory birds
46. Small change
47. Eve's garden
48. Requirement
49. Favoritism
50. Pay
51. Jazz's Fitzgerald
52. Bambi, e.g.
54. To and ____

Successorgrams

PUZZLE 293

Rearrange the letters in each pair of words below to make one 8-letter word. The last letter of each word will be the first letter of the following word. The last letter of the last word will be the first letter of the first word.

1. CLAN + DEAR _____

2. VANE + ROTE _____

3. MITE + SEAT _____

4. RAVE + NODE _____

5. SIRE + RANT _____

6. TINT + RUNE _____

7. RAGE + MELT _____

8. CRAM + THEN _____

9. DASH + UNTO _____

10. COST + DIME _____

PUZZLE 294

ACROSS
1. Arrive
5. Nebraska city
10. Persian ruler
14. Thought
15. "___ at Sea"
16. Pipe
17. Afternoon gatherings
18. Unwraps
19. Singer Fitzgerald
20. Respect
22. Sank
24. Caustic solutions
26. Cenozoic and Mesozoic
27. High voice
31. Time periods
35. Self-regard
36. Trades
38. Pry
39. Teheran's nation
41. Equestrian
43. Blemish
44. Trait carriers
46. Dressed to the ___
48. Mineral
49. Settled down
51. Adventure
53. Conflicts
55. Noble rank
56. Lodes
60. Responsible
64. Concluded
65. Urgent
67. Navigate
68. Look for
69. Leave to marry
70. Type of fur
71. Blunders
72. Stitched
73. Beers

DOWN
1. Quote
2. Lyric poems
3. Main part
4. Painting stands
5. Mileage gauge
6. Chart
7. Iowa college site
8. Therefore
9. Guarantee
10. Broad-brimmed hats
11. Shell
12. Adept
13. Chief
21. Watched
23. Hits lightly
25. Discolor
27. Pretend
28. Concur
29. Bank transactions
30. Classic song
32. Winter drink
33. Stash
34. Binge
37. Feel
40. Broadcasting companies
42. Brought to mind
45. Black and Red
47. Indian garment
50. Golf shots
52. Blood fluid
54. Window sash part
56. Medicine amount
57. At any time
58. Colleague
59. Place in storage
61. Empty water from
62. Sequence
63. Lodge members
66. Act like

PUZZLE 295   Keyword

To find the Keyword fill in the blanks in words 1 through 10 with the correct missing letters. Transfer those letters to the correspondingly numbered squares in the diagram. Approach with care—this puzzle is not as simple as it first appears.

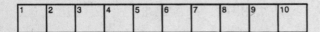

1. C L O ___ E
2. R O U G ___
3. ___ R A I N
4. B ___ A R S
5. S T U N ___
6. S H ___ F T
7. F L I N ___
8. G ___ A N T
9. C H ___ I R
10. ___ A V E L

272

ACROSS

1. Final
5. Marten
10. Jab
14. Inscribe
15. Nearer the facts
16. Idyllic spot
17. Fly high
18. Perfume ingredient
19. ____ the line (conformed)
20. Coils
22. Rules
24. Contend
25. More undiluted
26. Bird's sound
29. Pub specialty
30. Aeries
34. Hems and ____
35. Wildebeest
36. Astrologer's concern
37. Cheer for a toreador
38. Domain
40. ____ Grande
41. Seoul resident
43. Gunk
44. Assist
45. Attempt
46. Golf mound
47. Outlaw James
48. Evaluated
50. Support
51. Nome native
54. Gluttonous
58. German composer
59. Tortes
61. At rest
62. Do ____ others . . .
63. Bow down
64. Close at hand
65. Experiment
66. Fashion
67. Contest

DOWN

1. Without
2. Above
3. Mark
4. Flourishes
5. Actor's arena
6. ____ and letters
7. However
8. Athletic group
9. Mistake
10. ____ out (dwindled)
11. Redolence
12. Sharp
13. Purposes
21. Small drink
23. Poison
25. Promoted
26. Clog
27. Rings of light
28. Pitchers
29. Actress Jillian
31. Begets
32. Follows
33. Breadth
35. Juniper liquor
36. Menagerie
38. Eskimo canoe
39. Female deer
42. Range of hearing
44. Equivocating
46. Apartment resident
47. Lively dance
49. Small nails
50. Passageway
51. Adjoin
52. Kent's coworker
53. Deeds
54. Rind
55. Opinion
56. Hit hard
57. Roll call response
60. Small island

Build-A-Pyramid

Use all the jumbled letters to build a pyramid so that each word contains all the letters of the word above it plus one additional letter. A starting letter has been set in the top square of the diagram.

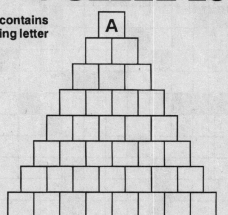

PUZZLE 298

ACROSS
1. Peter or Paul
5. To's companion
8. Couch
12. Turquoise's relative
13. Paddle
14. Augury
15. Oxidation
16. Narrow inlet
17. Cummerbund
18. Tit for ___
19. Bread spread
21. "___ Abner"
22. Biblical lion
23. Actress Brenner
24. Singer Cara
26. Continued, as a subscription
28. Cafe patron
29. ___ capita
30. Freddy's street
31. Painter's need
34. Young frog
38. Fall flower
39. Mature
40. Raced
41. Health spot
42. Harnessed, as oxen
44. Deed
45. Cultivate
47. "And I Love ___"
48. Agitate
49. First name in mystery
50. Wire measure
51. Quality of sound
52. Take five
53. Pig's home
54. Goad

DOWN
1. Cream of ___
2. Cube's face
3. Texas capital
4. Fink
5. Eternally
6. Complained violently
7. Type of exam
8. Weep convulsively
9. Egg dish
10. Cat
11. Horn
19. Trinkets
20. Produced
25. Highway exit
27. Fencing blade
30. With enthusiasm
31. Spring holiday
32. Strive
33. Stable compartments
34. ___ to heart: 2 wds.
35. Haranguer
36. Adding liquor to
37. Main course
43. Electric units
46. Lease
48. Actor Erwin

PUZZLE 299

ACROSS
1. Respond
6. Collapsible bed
9. ___ Vegas
12. Disagree
13. French friend
14. Building extension
15. "I ___ Symphony": 2 wds.
16. Grown boys
17. Oppose
18. Jerusalem's country
20. Profound
21. Actress Allyson
23. Patronize
25. Onager
26. ___ of Liberty
27. Bind again
29. Rome's country
33. Withdraw
37. Command to a horse
38. Summer cooler
41. Billboard
42. White House office shape
43. Rabbit, e.g.
45. ___ on your life!
46. Combat
47. Vaults
50. Supplement
51. Lyric poem
52. Pause
53. Legal thing
54. Sparks or Beatty
55. Stadium

DOWN
1. Cheerleader's word
2. Sooner than, poetically
3. Con
4. Swear
5. Lachrymose drop
6. Shutterbug's device
7. Egg dish
8. Sn
9. Quay
10. ALF or E.T.
11. Caught some Z's
19. Toward the stern
20. Song for two
21. Container
22. Consume
24. Cease
26. Observed
28. Baal, e.g.
30. Incite
31. Lower limb
32. Strong desire
34. "Easter ___"
35. Loved
36. Cerise
38. Solitary person
39. Call forth
40. Companions
41. Grimace
44. Singer Fitzgerald
46. Came in first
48. Witty remark?
49. Saratoga Springs, e.g.

274

PUZZLE 300

ACROSS

1. "A ____ December"
5. A Simpson
9. "____ Hungry"
13. Zodiacal sign
15. Cyprinoid fish
16. "In ____ Only"
17. 1947 Hepburn film
19. Native metals
20. "The Egg ____ I"
21. Diamond ____ (Mae West role)
22. 1956 Kelly film, with "The"
23. "The Red ____"
24. Willard's family
26. 1987 Ameche film
28. Adore to excess
29. Exclamation of contempt
32. Silent star Negri
33. Giver
34. Actress Alicia
35. 1945 Muni/Oberon film
39. Place for Arnold of "Green Acres"
40. Actress Adoree
41. "The ____ Is Silence"
42. "You ____ What You Eat"
43. Thicke or Arkin
44. "____ Boy"
45. Dill
46. Flock
48. "____ and Pepper"
50. Meadow mower
51. Actress Peeples
54. Director Reiner
55. 1970 film about footballer Piccolo
59. Toward shelter
60. Yours and mine
61. Burn
62. Actor Orson ____
63. Red vegetable
64. "China ____"

DOWN

1. "I ____ Male War Bride"
2. Actor Kincaid
3. Grapefruit skin
4. Actress Ryan
5. Comedian Crystal
6. ____ Annie of "Oklahoma!"
7. Gun an engine
8. Literary monogram
9. "The ____ of Kilimanjaro"
10. Scarlett's home
11. Sherman Hemsley TV series
12. "____, Giorgio"
14. Han and kin
18. Flipper
22. Cubic meter
23. "____ 9 from Outer Space"
24. Actress Blakely of "Nashville"
25. "____ Age Vampire"
26. Stumper
27. Song from "A Night at the Opera"
28. Mamie Van ____
29. "____ in Toyland"
30. "____ of Robins"
31. Emcee Mary ____ of "Entertainment Tonight"
32. Judson Laire TV character
33. Robert ____ of "Goodbye, Mr. Chips"
36. Asner's TV role
37. Vision or phone starter
38. TV horse show
44. "____ the Beasts and Children"
45. Woody or Steve
46. Holiday meal
47. Possess
48. "____ of the Century"
49. Zone
51. "____ Shall Escape"
52. Actress Swenson
53. Matures
54. Musician Calloway
55. Newhart or Hoskins
56. "The Murders in the ____ Morgue"
57. Choler
58. "____ Hopkins"

PUZZLE 301

ACROSS
1. Roster
5. Pulls
9. Sprays lightly
14. Involved with
15. PDQ's relative
16. Loosen, as a knot
17. Thanks ____!
18. Fertilizing substance
19. Hackneyed
20. Title again
22. Pummeled
24. Fashionable
26. Adolescent
27. ERA, e.g.
29. Painter, e.g.
33. Clapton and Sevareid
37. Nest egg plans: abbr.
39. Words of understanding
40. Dorothy's dog
41. Clan
42. Bullring cheers
43. Unlock
44. Church song
45. Clumsy
46. Settle snugly
48. Faction
50. Ewes' mates
52. Indy 500 vehicle
57. With great adornment
61. Royal chair
62. Arrive at
63. Assistant
65. Skin problem
66. Class division
67. Ship's boom
68. Slip
69. Collect
70. Skirt edges
71. Sight organs

DOWN
1. Untruthful ones
2. Bay
3. Rocky
4. Entire
5. Most docile
6. Made in the ____
7. Clothing
8. Wet sound
9. Assemble troops
10. Purpose
11. Heavenly light
12. Mosaic piece
13. Plant starter
21. Hit or ____
23. Taunt
25. Furry
28. Decorates, as a tree
30. ____ of Wight
31. Ooze
32. Large quiz
33. English school
34. Heavy cord
35. Suffix for inhabitants
36. Legal agreements
38. Civil War's Doubleday
41. Essay
45. Prickling sensation
47. Wood-turning tools
49. Provides food
51. Cut wildly
53. Wipe out
54. Arrogant
55. "Little Orphan ____"
56. Marsh plants
57. Killer whale
58. Paper amount
59. Rocket program inits.
60. Word of fright
64. River barrier

PUZZLE 302 — Alpha Quotes

Reveal the quotes by eliminating the letters of the alphabet that are not part of the quotes. The unused letters go in alphabetical order from A to Z.

1. I A T S B I C M P D O E S S I F B G L H E T I O J M K E
   N L D M A N F O E N P C E Q I R F S Y O T U R E U S V I
   T T W I N X G O Y N Z I T.

2. L A O B G C I C I S D A E N Y F L I G N H E O I F J R E
   K A S O L N M I N G N T H O A P T Q P R O R V E S Y S O
   T U A U R V E W R X I G Y H Z T.

276

ACROSS

1. Tree's fluid
4. Tin containers
8. Distant
12. Sporting event
13. Playing marble
15. Wash
16. Level
17. Batman's sidekick
18. Frosted
19. Repaired
21. Tranquilizes
23. Go by yawl
25. Matched group
26. Tavern bill
29. Hosiery mishap
31. Rationed
35. Hubbub
36. Unspoken
38. Men or boys
40. Rich soil
42. Embankment
44. Broad valley
45. Goofed
47. Considers
49. Roofing material
50. Sidled
52. Break suddenly
53. Needle hole
54. Taproom
56. Cut, as with scissors
58. One who supports
62. ___ computer
66. Zone
67. Put into effect
69. Lemon's kin
70. Fibber
71. Musical production
72. Radiate
73. Writing tablets
74. Unwanted plant
75. I-topper

DOWN

1. Rescue
2. Hymn closer
3. Remains unsettled
4. St. Louis baseballer
5. In the past
6. Arrests
7. Swine pens
8. Came to ground
9. Turn toward
10. Park and Fifth: abbr.
11. Funnyman Skelton
12. Valuable stone
14. Finished
20. "___ of Eden"
22. Molecule component
24. Tied, as shoes
26. Story
27. Worship
28. Plank
30. Donates
32. Young fellow
33. Make overjoyed
34. Postpone
37. Youthful years
39. Withered
41. Actress Ryan
43. Issued forth
46. Unpaid bill
48. Revolve
51. Librarian's stamp
55. Subscribe again
57. Became wan
58. Diva's specialty
59. Rosary unit
60. Hearing organs
61. Speak wildly
63. Bigwig's car
64. Overlook
65. Achieve
66. Swiss peak
68. Billiard stick

Drop-Outs PUZZLE 304

The answer to each clue is the name of a famous person whose initials in the clue have been replaced with asterisks. For example, base*all g*eat (baseBall gReat, initials BR) is Babe Ruth.

1. Norwegian *kating c*ampion _____

2. Aut*or of "*oby Dick" _____

3. President o* *uba _____

4. "M*d Magazin*" represe*tative _____

5. Britis* *aval hero _____

6. "The buck stops *ere" pre*iden* _____

7. Americ*n marksw*man _____

8. *enowned da*cer _____

9. Vaudeville *tage sensa*ion _____

10. *ead figure in "*tar Wars" _____

PUZZLE 305

ACROSS
1. Tabby
4. Ray
8. Butt
11. Parched
13. Soup server
14. Again
16. Row
17. Get up
18. Cast a ballot
19. Stuff
21. Young child
22. Roman date
23. Cloth for cleaning
24. Not moving
25. Oils
29. Lay macadam
31. An ____ of prevention
32. Late
34. Wedge tightly
37. Came down to earth
38. Terrace
39. Deceive
40. Was ahead
41. ____ the music
42. Broader
43. Depository
44. Serial segment
46. Baseball or hockey
49. Astern
50. Seep
51. Noise
54. Used a harvester
58. Huff and puff
59. Take as one's own
61. Church part
62. Rational
63. Moola
64. Lumber source
65. Scarlet
66. Entreaty
67. Conclusion

DOWN
1. Serene
2. Operatic solo
3. Hue
4. Ban
5. Blue-pencil
6. In addition
7. Encounter
8. Gulley
9. Battery terminal
10. Parking timer
12. Take away
13. Clothing size
15. Sunset direction
20. Comfort
24. ____ League
25. Aim
26. Reign
27. Arthurian lady
28. Pile
29. Self-respect
30. Fuss
33. Dined
34. Self-defense art
35. Parroted
36. Only
38. Pot
39. Far away
41. Overweight
42. Spouse
43. Made beer
45. Political group
46. Cries noisily
47. Kind of bear
48. Form of oxygen
51. Moist
52. Hero
53. Not any
55. Whittle
56. Tied
57. Feat
60. Soup vegetable

(Crossword grid with numbered cells 1–67)

PUZZLE 306   TIE-IN

Place a 3-letter word on the dashes to complete a word on the left and to begin another word on the right. For example, HEN between EART and NA would complete EARTHEN and begin HENNA.

R E G ___ ___ ___ R T   S C ___ ___ ___ I N E

S E V ___ ___ ___ C T   I M P ___ ___ ___ I V E

M U F ___ ___ ___ I S H   E L ___ ___ ___ L E R

T A T ___ ___ ___ T H   F A T ___ ___ ___ A L D

S A ___ ___ ___ S E L   H U ___ ___ ___ A G E

278

ACROSS

1. Garfield, e.g.
4. "Sanford and ____"
7. Atlas feature
10. Vigoda of "Fish"
11. Parisian's affirmative
12. Stuffing herb
13. Jelly's counterpart
16. Attempt
17. Require
18. Study
20. Quick swim
21. Tavern
24. Chat
27. Big ____, California
29. Hodgepodge
31. Exercise
32. Ostrich's kin
33. Paid athlete
34. Style
37. Metal container
38. Kindled
39. Van Winkle of literature
40. Peeper
41. Tier
43. Small amount
44. Mai ____ (cocktail)
46. Worship
48. First woman
49. Paddle
50. Relaxes
53. Color
54. Water barrier
56. Neckwear
57. Emulate Hammer
60. "____ and Away" (Cruise film)
62. Father
65. Jackie's second husband
66. "Absence of ____"
68. ____ Jima
69. News agency: abbr.
70. Diamond gal
71. Wager
72. Morning moisture
73. Writing implement
74. Wild ox
75. Append
76. Beer barrel
78. "The ____-Tale Heart"
80. Golly
82. Ice-cream topping
87. "____ the Fire"
88. ____ de Cologne
89. Afore
90. Afternoon social
91. Speck
92. Press for payment

DOWN

1. Tam
2. Help
3. Sign of sorrow
4. Old French coin
5. "Down and ____ in Beverly Hills"
6. Pointed end
7. Partner
8. Seasoned
9. ____ capita
12. Pace
14. Comedian Louis ____
15. Federation
19. Alaskan town
20. Eat
21. Flattered
22. Large continent
23. Break
24. Solidify
25. "____ Blue"
26. Dairy product
27. Most agile
28. Psychic Geller
30. Place
35. Epoch
36. Reel's companion
42. President Wilson
45. "____ Maria"
47. Beam
51. Conway of comedy
52. Ocean
54. Tyne of "Cagney and Lacey"
55. Diva's song
57. Lemon peel
58. Perform
59. Glimpse
60. Twitched
61. Reverence
63. Mimic
64. Noise
67. Soup scoop
75. Low voice
77. Self
78. Melody
79. James of jazz
81. Beige
82. Drill attachment
83. Crimson
84. ____ Paulo, Brazil
85. Trim
86. Female chicken

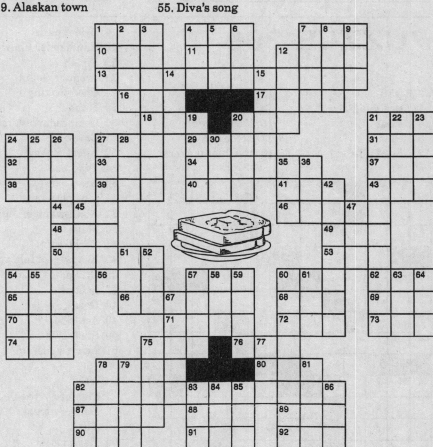

PUZZLE 308

ACROSS
1. Hones
6. Shy
11. Pay up
12. Worship
13. Isolated
14. Relating to birth
15. Kettle
16. Dwelling place
18. French summer
19. Afternoon get-together
21. ___ of the ball
23. Folklore dwarf
25. Ox
27. Beret
30. Doctors' org.
31. American Indian
33. Received
35. Crochet stitch
37. Student's rank
39. Slur over
40. Granted as true
41. Discourage
42. Silvery foodfish

DOWN
1. Shawl
2. Serf
3. Ham it up
4. Metallic element
5. Stair
6. Bicycle for two
7. Mountain in Crete
8. Overnight stop
9. Furious
10. Printer's direction
17. Terminate
20. Ripen
22. Permit
24. Gender
25. Facial expression
26. Implied
28. Desert plant
29. Cindy Crawford, e.g.
30. Imitated
32. Roe
34. Temporary shelter
36. Lyric poem
38. Outer edge

PUZZLE 309

ACROSS
1. Zsa Zsa's sister
4. Smear
8. Peasant
12. Roll of bills
13. Soar
14. Jacob's son
15. Made lovable
17. Actor Arkin
18. Mischief-makers
19. Bridal path
20. Bandleader Shaw
22. Finish
23. Premier Golda
24. Good-looking
29. Hubbub
30. Composer Anderson
31. Crazy
32. Sweet melon
34. Type size
35. Have a go at
36. ___ pole
37. Actress/singer Jones
40. Mailed
41. Reckless
42. Keeps from falling
46. Dull pain
47. Is in debt
48. Doze
49. Act
50. Roof style
51. Actress Jasmine ___

DOWN
1. Member of the flock
2. Delivery truck
3. Ell
4. Hang loosely
5. Melodies
6. Purpose
7. Cot
8. Tartans
9. Congers
10. Egg-shaped
11. Diamond team
16. Arab dignitary
19. Artist Warhol
20. Asian nurse
21. Update
22. Poet's sufficiency
24. Actress Lamarr
25. "You ___ There"
26. Leaving out
27. Apple-pie spice
28. Mild cheese
30. Stringed instrument
33. Inscribed
34. Frogs' haunt
36. Tantalize
37. Degree holder
38. 10K, for one
39. Netman Arthur ___
40. Appear
42. Land
43. Pair
44. Grenoble water
45. Mata Hari, e.g.

PUZZLE 310

ACROSS
1. Masculine
5. Coat with metal
10. Frighten
12. Artist's stand
13. "The Mark of ___"
14. Backbone
15. The Queen's language: abbr.
16. Small child
18. What's up, ___?
19. Units of inheritance
21. Sassy
22. Worrier's complaint
24. Caution
27. Take as one's own
30. Hubbub
31. Three: prefix
32. Bend one's ___
34. Serious
36. Very small amount
38. Self-esteem
39. Anklets, e.g.
40. Rhyme and reason
41. Exam

DOWN
1. Labyrinth
2. ___ for the ride
3. Size
4. Be human
5. Annoying one
6. Track loop
7. Stage direction
8. Pavarotti, for one
9. Chosen few
11. Roadside inn
17. Film award
20. Convent member
21. Golf teacher
23. Prepares for publication
24. Yellowjackets, e.g.
25. Worship
26. Archer Hood
28. Tranquility
29. Approaches
31. Oak or elm
33. Remainder
35. Asner et al
37. Corrupt

PUZZLE 311

ACROSS
1. Touch down
5. Kind of year
9. Ocean
12. Aroma
13. Singer Guthrie
14. Law's is long
15. Miffed
16. Sham
18. Ripens
20. Pilgrim John
21. Saddle part
24. Thoroughfares: abbr.
25. Cease! asea
26. Capital of 33 Across
30. "___ o' My Heart"
31. Golly
32. Galley propeller
33. Grand Canyon State
36. Heavenly food
38. Debtor's letters
39. Denial of orthodoxy
40. Chan portrayer
43. Tardy
44. Novelist Lewis
46. Keen!
50. Tennis call
51. Sea eagle
52. Palo ___, Calif.
53. ___ to a customer
54. Goblet part
55. Seattle ___

DOWN
1. ___ Alamos
2. Commotion
3. Likewise not
4. Fantasies
5. Coat feature
6. Goes wrong
7. Pub drink
8. ___ salad
9. Hourglass contents
10. Gaelic
11. So be it!
17. Otherwise
19. Obtain
21. Mama's mate
22. More than
23. Creche figures
24. That girl
26. Shade of green
27. "___ but the Brave"
28. Fleming and Smith
29. Physician's photo: hyph.
31. African antelope
34. Metallic element
35. Lots and lots
36. Assembled
37. Sports buildings
39. Seraglio
40. Norway's capital
41. Property bond
42. Poker stake
43. Lothario's come-on
45. Mr. Carney
47. Building wing
48. Had a bite
49. Pull

281

PUZZLE 312

ACROSS

1. Groove
4. By
7. Torpid
10. Dry
12. Gold digger
13. Flutter
15. Carry
16. Ginger drink
17. Wipe out
19. Luge
20. Key
22. Prom dress
25. Primary
28. Roe
29. Be overly indulgent
30. Sire
33. Smooths
35. PBS series
36. Drive back
37. Seine
38. Piggery

DOWN

1. Brink
2. Wed
3. Singing voice
4. Foot
5. Epoch
6. Competitor
8. Save
9. Ringlet
11. Cancel
14. Crimson
18. Gnome
19. Tried
21. Duck down
22. Lump
23. Baker's need
24. Cart
26. Stairs
27. Doctrine
31. Night before
32. Make lace
34. Cunning

PUZZLE 313

ACROSS

1. Freeway
5. Barrel
9. Everyone
12. Egg on
13. Dash
14. Easy as
15. Electronic reminder
16. Palm fruit
17. Garden dweller
18. Paradise
20. Snake
22. Straightened
25. Lyric poem
26. Cheryl and Diane
27. Esteem
31. Cruising
32. That woman
33. Con man
34. Gored
36. Trojan _____
37. Order's partner
38. Tapering at both ends
39. Broaden
42. Papa's better half
43. Bustle
44. _____ tide
46. Smear
50. Suffering
51. Sea eagle
52. Path
53. Allow
54. Beams
55. Fencer's need

DOWN

1. Massage
2. Mine find
3. Grow old
4. Reliable
5. Yielded
6. Mr. Arkin
7. Perched
8. Works dough
9. Copied
10. "Saturday Night _____"
11. Ogle
19. _____ Moines
21. Horrendous
22. Sad cry
23. Endure
24. Brainstorm
25. Above, poetically
27. Scarlet
28. Ireland
29. Hurl
30. Spruce or willow
32. Chop
35. Flag
36. Restrain
38. Binds
39. Cry
40. Not working
41. Oaf
42. Scads
45. Time period
47. Circuit
48. Unit
49. Casual shirt

PUZZLE 314

ACROSS
1. Neap, e.g.
5. Lyric poem
8. Youngster
9. Carry on
11. Smooth talk
12. Opposed
13. ____ of Capri
14. Worry's supposed yield
15. Insulated bottle
18. Before, poetically
19. More novel
21. Droop
24. Put up with
28. Mature
30. Kind of skirt
31. Notion
32. Linen item
34. Rolltop, for one
35. Young hooter
36. Map abbr.
37. Garden intruder

DOWN
1. Book name
2. Young doctor
3. She-deer
4. Go wrong
5. Spoken
6. Do the tango, e.g.
7. Come in
8. Alda TV series
10. Weary
11. Fruit stone
14. Employed
16. Encounter
17. Possess
20. Wrinkle
21. Stated
22. Poisonous snake
23. Hotel visitor
25. Did autumn work
26. Go out
27. Clangor
29. Actress Veronica
32. This instant
33. Wonder

PUZZLE 315

ACROSS
1. Practice boxing
5. Actor Vigoda
8. Mr. Preminger
12. Prince Charles's sport
13. Write
14. "____ Here to Eternity"
15. Self: prefix
16. Tablet
17. Domesticated
18. Raceway horse
20. "The Magnificent ____"
21. Ocean
22. Singleton
23. Boohoo
26. Straight flier
29. Statute
32. Lyricist Gershwin
33. Grain unit
34. Actress Arden
35. Each
36. ____ Allan Poe
38. Comic Skelton
39. Car fuel
41. Vat
43. Looks over
45. Meeting records
49. Deposited
50. Summer sign
51. Sped
52. Ms. Boleyn
53. Motel's forebear
54. Story
55. GI's dining room
56. Ralph Kramden's vehicle
57. Paradise

DOWN
1. Tiff
2. Decant
3. Palo ____
4. Haley work
5. Seemed
6. Endure
7. Conclude
8. Frequently
9. One on the road
10. Weighty work
11. Portent
19. Pekoe, e.g.
20. Plant
23. Small drink
24. Mined find
25. Buying opportunities
27. Cloth scrap
28. Speeches
30. "____ Maria"
31. Join
36. Kind of curve
37. Operate
40. S. Amer. mountains
42. Montana city
43. Close noisily
44. Sugar source
45. Bill of fare
46. Frog's kin
47. ____ Stanley Gardner
48. Observed
50. Women's ____

283

PUZZLE 316

ACROSS

1. Mischievous
4. Emanation
8. Acquire
11. George Washington
12. Actor's aid
13. Space or station start
14. Bumpkin
15. "____ each life . . ."
16. Seethe
17. Harsh
19. Appeared
21. Sorry mount
22. Aver
23. "Father Knows ____"
25. Lash wound
26. Father's Day gift
29. Shoe width
30. Recoils
31. Disagreeably damp
32. Completely
33. On ____ and needles
34. Long
35. Clear the tape
37. Curve part
38. Pitch in
40. Slightest
43. Writer Macdonald
44. Behindhand
47. Yarn measure
48. Useless
49. Constantly
50. On the ____
51. Singer Dennis
52. Take a flat
53. Time periods: abbr.

DOWN

1. Sounds of disapproval
2. Med. subj.
3. Without protection
4. Imitating
5. Samovar
6. Corrupt
7. Peter and Paul, e.g.
8. In Euclidean fashion
9. Toledo's lake
10. Narrated
13. Aid a criminal
18. Squeal
20. Beanery offerings
22. Left Bank's river
23. Ms. Arthur
24. Moray or conger
25. American painter
27. Mr. Fleming
28. She-sheep
30. Resorts
34. Ante
36. Ascend
37. On the ball
38. Saharalike
39. Pop
41. Char
42. Highland headwear
45. Hail, to Pliny
46. Hamilton bill

PUZZLE 317

ACROSS

1. One of Goldilocks's bears
5. Aspirations
9. Shoemaker's tool
12. Astronaut Shepard
13. Gossip bit
14. Born
15. Relax
16. Highway section
17. Butterfly catcher
18. Withdraw
20. Appointment
22. Feel concern
24. Domain
27. Box or side
30. Water game
32. Healing plant
33. "You ____ What You Eat"
34. Marsh bird
36. Topsy's friend
37. Stingy
39. Rung
40. Study
41. Relieved
43. Pennsylvania port
45. Sonnets' relatives
47. Insight
51. Veto
53. Play's players
55. Knowledge
56. Hoosier humorist
57. Bread spread
58. Lamb's pen name
59. Wand
60. Type of admiral
61. Chasm

DOWN

1. Young salmon
2. Toward shelter
3. Time gone by
4. Caper
5. Wing controls
6. Call ____ day
7. Fix
8. Defame
9. Tempered
10. Minuscule
11. Permit
19. Sentences
21. Afternoon custom
23. Type face
25. Treasure
26. Intend
27. Staff
28. Region
29. Deliberated
31. Agent
35. Saga
38. Embarrassed
42. Room ornamentation
44. Swiss mathematician
46. Bargain event
48. Burrowing rodent
49. The Emerald Isle
50. Undiluted
51. Tavern
52. Stir
54. Body of water

PUZZLE 318

ACROSS
1. Football term
5. Everyone
8. Uses oars
12. Got down
13. Bambi's mom
14. Bad
15. Explode
17. Actor Barry
18. Male sheep
19. Peeled
20. Use a broom
23. Dictator
25. Amphibian
26. Rudolph, for one
30. Sin
31. Stove
32. "You ____ There"
33. Five-sided shape
35. Large continent
36. Consumer
37. Prohibitive, as cost
38. Acute
41. Make lace
42. Ripped
43. Groundskeeper
48. Toward shelter
49. "____ Life to Live"
50. Withered
51. Peruse
52. Good-____
53. Care for

DOWN
1. Cushion
2. Pub drink
3. Use a chair
4. Put in a warehouse
5. First man
6. Parcel of land
7. Actor Majors
8. Affection
9. On top of
10. Claret or sherry
11. Snow vehicle
16. Snooze
19. Window glass
20. Stair
21. Had on
22. Merit
23. Singing voice
24. Omen
26. Fury
27. Comfort
28. Pennsylvania port
29. Harvest
31. File
34. Rotated
35. Swear to
37. Unhappy
38. Asterisk
39. Pit
40. Locale
41. Timber source
43. Mass or lump
44. Some
45. Born
46. Sea eagle
47. Crimson

PUZZLE 319

ACROSS
1. Matterhorn, e.g.
4. Competent
8. Flower of love
12. Anguish
13. Sketch
14. At any time
15. Assess
17. Anxiety
18. Plunge
19. Harbors
20. Remove from print
23. Long way off
24. Regions
25. Suffering
29. Cravat
30. Amend
31. Female deer
32. Like some exercise
35. Songs for two
37. Raced
38. Large wasp
39. One from the Himalayas
42. Farm laborer
43. Thickened lump
44. Ship's steerer
48. Carry
49. Small land mass
50. Bullfight shout
51. Oceans
52. Emotional state
53. Moist

DOWN
1. Wonder
2. ____ Angeles
3. Animal companion
4. Confesses
5. Courageous
6. Tardy
7. Female sheep
8. Change for the better
9. Above
10. Chair
11. Makes a mistake
16. Concept
19. Equality in value
20. Information collected
21. Sandusky's waterfront
22. Sly look
23. Sly dog
25. Twitch
26. Paradise
27. Memo
28. Exam
30. Fish part
33. Speaks
34. Outlaw
35. Destined
36. Vases
38. Telephone greeting
39. Performs
40. Fruit of the blackthorn
41. Very small quantity
42. Mexican money
44. That man
45. Cut grass
46. Malt drink
47. Profit

PUZZLE 320

ACROSS

1. Hemingway
5. Methods
10. Eats late
14. Fail to include
15. Slur over
16. Rope fastening
17. Dryer residue
18. Flax cloth
19. Doing nothing
20. Margin
21. Occurrences
23. Scrape by
24. Navigate
26. Of the ear
28. List of candidates
31. Composition
33. Negligent
34. Deli bread
37. Army commander
41. Feel poorly
42. Propel a boat
43. Permit
44. Rage
45. Make ready
47. Sooner than, in a poem
48. Formerly named
49. Sherbets
50. Speed detector
52. Dish
55. Accumulate
58. Scarlet
59. Forms
62. Mop
66. Swellheads
68. Wide-awake
69. English count
70. King's title
71. Phase
72. Small combo
73. Fret
74. Card game
75. Sofa

DOWN

1. Flag holder
2. Among
3. Engine sound
4. Bear witness to
5. Free-for-all
6. Ms. Oyl
7. Greasy spoon
8. First garden
9. Dispatched
10. Schuss
11. Beneath
12. Bohemian dance
13. Tempered iron
22. Strolls
25. Tiers of gardens
27. Employ
28. Direct affront
29. Lion's den
30. Wheel rod
31. Gape at
32. Look closely
35. Olden days
36. Sheep mothers
38. Fruit skin
39. Region
40. Grin nastily
46. Hole in the ground
51. Resources
52. Journalists
53. On the up and up
54. Idolize
55. Nearly vertical
56. Unite
57. Fall flower
60. Hinged fastener
61. Female singer
63. Item for sale
64. Opera highlight
65. Ink stain
67. Stitch

PUZZLE 321   Pairs

Place the same pair of letters onto both sets of dashes to complete a common word. The pair of letters will be different for each answer.

1. H __ __ D G __ __ R

2. __ __ U R __ __

3. __ __ P E N __ __ N T

4. P __ __ H __ __ D L E

5. __ __ T I __ __ __

6. S E __ __ S U C K __ __ __

7. __ __ D E F __ __ __ I T E

8. __ __ R N U __ __ __ P I A

ACROSS

1. Begone!
5. Without bubbles
9. Door handle
13. Shovel
14. Molten rock
15. Bright star
16. Fluorescent tube gas
17. At any time
18. Iridescent gem
19. View
20. Make an effort
21. Convent room
22. Prime time
25. Question
27. Becoming visible
31. Feather scarf
34. Victor
37. Very long time
38. Long for
40. Vagabond
41. Slice
42. Darn!
43. Portents
45. Citrus beverage
46. Theater passage
47. Sopping
48. Obvious
51. Hooting bird
52. Condense in a layer
56. Action word
59. Following
63. Menagerie
64. Pennsylvania port
65. Stop
66. Love affair
68. Hen products
69. Take apart
70. Cookstove
71. National flower
72. Adam's home
73. Coatrack

DOWN

1. Shopping binge
2. Sly
3. Fuss
4. Decimal unit
5. Bend
6. Wash
7. Declare
8. Plaid
9. Rap
10. Nothing doing
11. White House office
12. Bouncing toy
13. Cummerbund
20. Organ of sight
23. Evil sprite
24. Electric unit
26. Pigpen
28. Summarize
29. Dutch cheese
30. Come in
31. Taverns
32. Spoken
33. Feed the kitty
34. Food
35. Residence
36. Be an accomplice
39. Prepares for print
44. Carpenter's cutter
46. Too
49. Commemorative tablet
50. Cup handle
51. Overweight
53. Atmosphere layer
54. Blusher
55. Drill
56. Swerve
57. Hence
58. Equips
60. Available money
61. Ocean motion
62. British school
66. Craft
67. Cause a blemish

Escalator

Place the answer to clue 1 in the first space, drop a letter, and arrange the remaining letters to answer clue 2. Drop another letter and arrange the remaining letters to answer clue 3. The first dropped letter goes into the box to the left of space 1, and the second dropped letter goes into the box to the right of space 3. Follow this pattern for each row in the diagram. When completed, the letters on the left and right, reading down, will spell related words or a phrase.

1. Fluffier
2. Stash
3. Way of learning
4. Office clip
5. Glue
6. Ladder rung
7. Young folk
8. Bridge position
9. Injection
10. Bug
11. Petty coins
12. Decades
13. Respond
14. Vow
15. Conflicts
16. Yawners
17. Lance
18. Church recess

PUZZLE 324

ACROSS
1. Urban pall
5. Tooth's pal
9. Baseball club
12. Ring
13. Assistant
14. Mineral source
15. Against
16. Makes good as new
18. Pair
20. Actor Williams
21. Most recent
24. Wager
25. Clean the slate
26. Prom gift
30. Purpose
31. "Sweet and ___"
32. Ordinance
33. Gratified
36. Hang loosely
38. Ship's diary
39. Puzzling problem
40. Colorado resort
43. Tree part
44. Went quickly
46. Gravy dish
50. Swee' ___
51. Fork prong
52. Division word
53. Foreign agent
54. Leaf cutters
55. Abound

DOWN
1. Belgian resort
2. Brando film, with "The"
3. Cereal grass
4. Soars
5. Jeweler's measure
6. Made like Pinocchio
7. Commercials
8. More saturated
9. Tiresome type
10. Length x width
11. Assay
17. Leftovers
19. Employ
21. Hurdle
22. Seed covering
23. Bring to heel
24. Debut
26. Provincetown's cape
27. Woeful word
28. Stare
29. Pitcher
31. Triangle side
34. Downwind
35. "Moonlight ___"
36. Political party: abbr.
37. Brer or Peter
39. Ebb and neap
40. African cobras
41. ___ lively!
42. Beseech
43. Ash Wednesday's time
45. Relatives
47. George Washington
48. Lunched
49. ___ Thumb

PUZZLE 325

ACROSS
1. Crucifix
5. Overhead trains
8. Thwarts at bridge
12. ___ en point
13. River: Sp.
14. Land east of the Urals
15. Crucial trial: 2 wds.
17. Cake decorator
18. Happen again
19. Actor Michael
21. World or Davis
23. Chicago area
24. Post exchange
28. Speak publicly
31. Past
32. Small stream
34. Comedian Knotts
35. Jury
37. Raceway figures
39. Like a bug in a rug
41. Black cuckoo
42. On the scene
45. Conditions
49. Japanese aborigine
50. One of Jason's men
52. Church area
53. Tiny, to Burns
54. Shade of green
55. Cane
56. Behold
57. Yemen's capital

DOWN
1. Admiral or echelon
2. Fairy-tale beginning
3. Auricular
4. Subtract
5. Before, to Byron
6. Mispronounce
7. Yuccalike plant
8. Tar
9. Adventure
10. Row of seats
11. Variety of chalcedony
16. Very faithful: hyph.
20. Investigate: 2 wds.
22. Via
24. ___ d'Antibes
25. ___ Khan
26. Bosh
27. It was east of Eden
29. "High ___"
30. O'Toole's rank: abbr.
33. Anglo-Saxon money
36. Followed, as a result
38. Strauss's city
40. Chews
42. TV's Jack
43. Mature
44. Ash or elm
46. Foray
47. Ass-horse offspring
48. British gun
51. Golly

288

PUZZLE 326

ACROSS
1. Actor Carney
4. Went swiftly
8. Prehistoric home
12. Vehicle
13. Whimper
14. Reed instrument
15. Novel by 25 Across
18. Prophets
19. Golf norm
20. Had a snack
21. Meager
25. With 35 Across, American novelist
28. Charge
29. Ages and ages
30. Greek war god
31. Monk's title
32. Cowboy's comrade
33. Actress Farrow
34. Heavy barge
35. See 25 Across
36. Hunting dog
38. In favor of
39. Have being
40. Strong thread
43. Novel by 25 Across
48. British count
49. Become fatigued
50. Foot part
51. Out of the wind
52. Burn
53. Female sheep

DOWN
1. Behave
2. Stadium sounds
3. Component of 31 Down
4. Flashy
5. Regular throbbing
6. Yore
7. Type of fishing
8. Savage snake
9. Blood group system
10. Solemn promise
11. Electric fish
16. Speed regulators
17. Back of the neck
22. Paper measure
23. Tender
24. Pass catchers
25. Atrocious actors
26. Pennsylvania port
27. Tidy
28. Cook bacon
31. Timberlands
32. Indian Zoroastrian
34. Brave man
35. Member of many clubs
37. Dining board
38. Plant life
41. Tardy
42. Sufficient, in poetry
43. British beverage
44. Actor Holbrook
45. Sooner than
46. Fasten
47. Perceive

PUZZLE 327

ACROSS
1. Shark movie
5. Forbid
8. Gelatin cup
12. Estrange
14. African lily
15. With flags
16. Dancer Kelly
17. Prepare a hide
18. Packed groceries
20. Begin
23. Hindu queen
24. Cheap cigar, slangily
25. Supporting beams
28. Breeze
29. Royal house of Italy
30. Bullfight cry
32. Ease, as a burden
34. Theater piece
35. Weeder
36. Thin pancake
37. Dozing
40. Zodiac Lion
41. Plunder
42. Like a cocktail sandwich
47. Haze
48. Guard
49. Female singer
50. Small child
51. Binds

DOWN
1. Poke with the elbow
2. ____ carte
3. Triumph
4. Guard
5. Farm building
6. Devoured
7. Snoopy's enemy
8. Jiggs's wife
9. Designer Cassini
10. Solitary
11. Feat
13. Orderly
19. Singer Williams
20. Depot: abbr.
21. Work
22. Dugout
23. Large stream
25. Fence section
26. Actor's part
27. Strike
29. Nursery rhyme home
31. In a pig's ___!
33. "In the ___" (Presley song)
34. Gain
36. Penny
37. ____ mater
38. Dirt
39. Misplaced
40. Give temporarily
43. Pod vegetable
44. Black cuckoo
45. After bee
46. Overhead railroads

PUZZLE 328

ACROSS

1. Stag, e.g.
5. Wound mark
9. Playing group
13. Historic periods
14. Patriot Nathan ___
15. Minuet, e.g.
16. Queens nine
17. Great Lake
18. Blacksmith's implement
19. Indefinite pronoun
20. Wager
21. Period
23. Gridiron measures: abbr.
24. Avenues
26. Basketball official, for short
28. ___ sirree!
29. Taxi
31. Persia today
35. Writing material
38. Sandwich shop, for short
39. Soldiers' home
40. Spanish cheer
41. Gentleman's man
42. Cravat
43. Cease
45. "___ Well That Ends Well"
46. Daily food
48. Musical sound
49. Zodiacal Lion
50. Observe
51. Tiny
53. Follows closely
57. And so on: abbr.
60. Fire residue
62. Brooch
63. ___ a la mode
64. Lee's foe
66. Finished
68. Sea swallow
69. Desert spots
70. Departed
71. Mine products
72. Raced
73. "___ Fall in Love"
74. Facility

DOWN

1. Short messages
2. "___ We All?"
3. Anon
4. Kind of curve
5. Bed linens
6. Two-wheeled wagons
7. ___ Baba
8. Actress Donna
9. Beach color
10. Jealousy
11. Caustic substance
12. Torme and Brooks
15. Social engagement
20. Alcoholic brew
22. Planet's path
25. Storm center
27. White lie
29. Violin's cousin
30. Pub brews
32. Grade
33. Largest continent
34. Require
35. Mail
36. Choir voice
37. Laborer
38. Roy's wife
41. Lowlands
44. Church seat
46. Pinto or kidney
47. Primary color
50. Some are short-sleeved
52. Consumes
53. Exhausted
54. "Aida" or "Othello"
55. Cables
56. Sight, e.g.
57. Selves
58. Snare
59. Container
61. Wolf's cry
65. Actor Sparks
67. Victory letter
68. ___ the line (behave)

PUZZLE 329 **JOINERS**

Arrange the 13 letters in the word ARITHMETICIAN to form four overlapping 4-letter words. The words join with the circled letters in the bottom diagram, the last letter of each word becoming the first letter of the next. Use all the letters of the given word once. Be sure to cross out the letters already placed in the diagram for you.

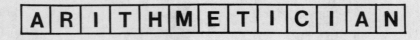

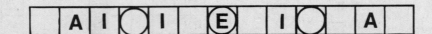

290

ACROSS

1. Final
5. Not cloudy
10. Takes a chair
14. Away from the wind
15. Multitude
16. Concerning
17. Bit of gossip
18. Be of use
19. British gun
20. Write music
22. Crept silently
24. Cake layers
26. Sooner than, to poets
27. Complains unnecessarily
30. Vacillating
35. Extreme stress
36. Unpredictable
37. Fish eggs
38. Fake coin
39. Talks wildly
40. Shabby
41. Private eye
42. Warps
43. Parson's house
44. Heavenly
46. Elevates
47. Sprinted
48. Choose by vote
50. Babies
54. Normal
58. Autos
59. Cream of the crop
61. Wickedness
62. Fencing sword
63. Horseman
64. Cries noisily
65. Fortune-teller
66. Supermarket
67. Large knife, of old

DOWN

1. Secular
2. Female singer
3. Appear
4. Enticing
5. Pursues
6. Sweetheart
7. Historical period
8. Mine entrance
9. Eases
10. Nun
11. Division preposition
12. Woody plant
13. Transmit
21. Greasy
23. Hunted animal
25. Defraud
27. Indian social group
28. Shoelace tip
29. Provide proof
31. Performs on stage
32. Presses
33. Scandinavian
34. Heredity units
36. Actress Wynter
39. Goes in again
40. Restaurant server
42. Grain husk
43. Ceremonial club
45. Pencil rubber
46. Venerate
49. Not now
50. Frosts a cake
51. Back of the neck
52. Without charge
53. Narrow cut
55. Shakespeare's river
56. Taunting remark
57. Otherwise
60. Wedding response

Three to One

Starting with each word in Column A, add a word from Column B and then one from Column C to build eight longer words. For example, CORN plus ERST plus ONE is CORNERSTONE. Each small word will be used only once.

	A	B	C		
1.	ELECT	AT	MA	1.	_____
2.	DIP	I	RENT	2.	_____
3.	TEST	OR	ME	3.	_____
4.	CON	SO	TRY	4.	_____
5.	PIT	LO	TIC	5.	_____
6.	ERR	AN	OR	6.	_____
7.	WIN	A	ATE	7.	_____
8.	PLEAS	CUR	LESS	8.	_____

PUZZLE 332

ACROSS
1. Dread
5. "____ the Woods"
9. Downturn
12. Sea eagle
13. Shortcoming
14. Actress Meyers
15. Surround
16. Small nail
17. Wire measure
18. Close
19. Actor Morrow
20. Church recess
21. Look at
23. TV spots
25. Diminished
28. Poured
32. Nation south of Sicily
33. Light brown
34. Help
36. Biblical strong man
37. Utmost
38. Tip
39. Tory's opponent
42. Antique auto
44. Trim
48. Long time
49. Contented sound
50. Chilled
51. Wapiti
52. ____ of Man
53. Earth goddess
54. Crucial
55. Molted
56. Appear

DOWN
1. House plant
2. Toledo's lake
3. Tolstoy heroine
4. Feeling sorrow for
5. Deeply instilled
6. Roman emperor
7. Oolong portion
8. Uncanny
9. Moist
10. Rainbow
11. Heap
20. Legislatures
22. Leaven
24. Arabian emirate
25. "I ____ Camera"
26. ____-relief
27. Molinaro and Hirt
29. "____ Girl Friday"
30. Self-image
31. Study
35. Songbird
36. Sawed logs
39. "That Was the ____ That Was"
40. Cavity
41. Very dark
43. Perry's creator
45. Quantity of land
46. Grant
47. Dutch cheese
49. Circle ratios

PUZZLE 333

ACROSS
1. Desire
5. Recite
9. Watch steadily
12. Culture medium
13. Actor Robert ____
14. Common
15. Blood fluids
16. Extremely narrow
18. Salon specialties
20. "____ but the Brave"
21. Plant parasites
23. Sandwich shop
27. Soaked
29. O'Neill and Flanders
30. Stared at
31. Wears away
33. Record envelope
34. Maple product
35. Succor
36. By way of
37. Hardy heroine
38. Sierra Leone's location
40. Basketball's Malone
42. Ingested
45. Infancy
49. Circular vault
50. Period of history
51. Isaac's son
52. Author Bombeck
53. Court divider
54. Distribute
55. Nicholas, for one

DOWN
1. Yellow jacket
2. Author/critic James ____
3. Storytellers
4. Walk heavily
5. Cheer
6. African antelopes
7. See you later
8. Mend
9. Yale grad
10. Over there
11. Ram's mate
17. Shelf
19. Flock member
22. Drivers' licenses, e.g.
24. Lifts
25. Tribe of Israel
26. Notion
27. "My Little Chickadee" star
28. Clinton's canal
30. Classic tune
32. Dim
33. Respectful title
35. Riding the waves
38. Transpired
39. Military student
41. Attention getter
43. Flaubert's heroine
44. Proximate
45. Actor Kingsley
46. Exist
47. Nocturnal creature
48. Expected

PUZZLE 334

ACROSS
1. Ten cent piece
5. Qualified
9. Sheep's cry
12. Bloodhound's enticer
13. Horse color
14. Elderly
15. Be afraid of
16. Jeer
17. Fisherman's pole
18. Decisively important
20. Buried explosives
22. Poorly lit
23. Exercise place
24. Deuce
27. Impart
29. Bowsprit locale
33. Paddles
35. Formerly named
36. Mentally healthy
37. Type of high school
38. Adolescent
40. Favorite animal
41. Donkey
43. Pelt
45. Used money
48. Leaf-raking seasons
52. Small mass
53. "The Duke of ____"
55. Ring
56. ____ in the hole
57. Malevolent
58. Or ____!
59. Adult males
60. Noblewoman
61. Kernel

DOWN
1. Remove, as a hat
2. Concept
3. Castle ditch
4. Got it wrong
5. Disputes
6. Seethe
7. Chemist's workplace
8. Foe
9. Brought into life
10. Soothing plant
11. Sums up
19. ____ as a fiddle
21. Small demons
23. With exultation
24. Spinning toy
25. Armed conflict
26. Prospector's find
28. Actor Van Cleef
30. Seance sound
31. Individual
32. Drenched
34. Bridge
39. Brazil or filbert
42. Iron alloy
44. Guidelines
45. Did the crawl
46. Rate of walking
47. Genesis garden
48. Desert-dry
49. Burrowing mammal
50. Snout
51. Went too fast
54. Frank's ex

PUZZLE 335

ACROSS
1. Back talk
5. Cooking vessel
8. Utter
11. Aviator
12. Commotion
13. Go with haste
14. Dote on
15. Muses
17. Antlered animal
18. North Dakota city
19. Moray, e.g.
21. Sketch
25. Iced
29. Silly fowl
30. Fabulous bird
31. Pigs
33. Easy as ____
34. Dwelling
36. Nitwit
38. "____ Lisa"
39. Born
40. Baseball's Pee Wee ____
44. Saharalike
48. Fragile
51. Dress style
52. Boat propeller
53. Corrida cheer
54. Gives temporarily
55. Had a meal
56. Short sleep
57. Nervous

DOWN
1. Flank
2. ____ vera
3. Reddish-brown horse
4. Sault ____ Marie
5. Mama's partner
6. Smell
7. Chinese association
8. That woman
9. Atmosphere
10. Of course!
11. Writing tablet
16. Extinct bird
18. Soared
20. Alternatively
22. Heavy cord
23. Largest continent
24. Unwanted plant
25. Stuff
26. Tramp
27. Religious image
28. Immerse
29. Cowboy Autry
32. Lineup number
35. Pub missile
37. Cured
41. English school
42. Jazz's Fitzgerald
43. Ooze
45. Finger ornament
46. ____ 500 (car race)
47. ____ Moines, Iowa
48. Constricting snake
49. Ship deserter
50. Great anger
51. Ginger ____

293

PUZZLE 336

ACROSS
1. Knife, to a hood
5. Oak's beginning
10. Messy one
14. Sharpen
15. Light boat
16. Honey factory
17. New Year's Day game
19. Prayer response
20. Discussion group
21. Envelope addressee, sometimes
23. Female prophet
26. Gives out sparingly
27. Concerning
29. Homesteader
32. Electrical unit
35. Criticize
37. Crude metal
38. Cosmetic ingredient
39. Courtroom event
41. Presently
42. Drink through a straw
43. Lab burner
44. Excelling all others
45. ____ corpus
49. Rewrites copy
51. Miss by ____
53. Gymnast
57. Large stone column
60. Cooking smell
61. Coup d'____
62. Firecracker
65. Trig function
66. Uncanny
67. Catchall phrase
68. Large number
69. Fear
70. Unit of force

DOWN
1. Hunts for bargains
2. Goddesses of the seasons
3. Wacky
4. Admire
5. Sleeve lurker
6. Car for hire
7. ____ about
8. Used oars
9. Wrestling hold
10. Sunglasses
11. Sedimentary rock
12. Pizzeria fixture
13. Crooked
18. Secluded valley
22. ____ de France
24. Cult
25. Capture
28. Hackneyed
30. Greek love god
31. Tenant's expense
32. Bathe
33. Inter ____
34. Lead comedian
36. Bearlike animal
40. Secular
41. Soaked up
46. Behaved theatrically
47. Be sickly
48. Carved
50. Waiter's receptacle
52. The heavens
54. Plunder
55. Capital of Jordan
56. Postpone
57. Military meal
58. Of the ear
59. Roll-call response
63. Estuary
64. Maple or herring

Codeword is a special crossword puzzle in which conventional clues are omitted. Instead, answer words in the diagram are represented by numbers. Each number represents a different letter of the alphabet, and all the letters of the alphabet are used. When you are sure of a letter, put it in the code key chart and cross it off in the Alphabet Box. A group of letters has been inserted to start you off.

Code Key Chart:

1	2	3	4	5	6 L	7	8	9	10	11	12	13
14	15	16	17	18	19	20 I	21	22	23	24	25	26 E

Grid:

	12	9	24	▪		14	9	13	26	▪	14	9	14	3	26
7	20	8	26	▪		9	25	20	11	▪	9	6	6	9	10
9	2	15	9	▪		18	26	19	18		8	6 L	9	22	26
21	15	11	4	26	18		23	26	24	▪	20 I	23	26	11	
8	26	26	▪	9	6	12	▪	1	9	17	26 E	▪			
▪		17	1	26	9	18	▪	18	9	11	18	26	1		
23	16	22	26	19	▪	5	16	18	26	23	▪	9	5	26	
9	6	20	18	▪	13	26	24	26	1	▪	16	25	26	19	
11	20	12	▪	24	9	1	19	11	▪	18	3	20	1	23	
3	16	11	18	26	23	▪	11	18	26	9	21	▪			
▪		16	8	26	10	▪	11	9	14	▪	26	6	13		
7	16	10	11	▪	11	16	12	▪	18	16	1	2	15	26	
9	1	16	11	26	▪	23	15	4	26	▪	16	15	11	18	
21	9	4	26	11	▪	26	21	20	1	▪	21	9	18	26	
11	6	26	23	11	▪	6	9	23	11	▪	12	6	10	▪	

ALPHABET BOX

A B C D E̶ F G H I̶ J K L̶ M N O P Q R S T U V W X Y Z

PUZZLE 338

ACROSS

1. —— Flat, Arkansas
4. Marching musicians
8. Gaunt
12. Sward
15. West Virginia town
16. Mother of Romulus and Remus
17. Double-curved arch
18. Heavy book
19. Japanese aborigine
20. Gulf of Mexico resort
22. Georgia town
23. —— -Salem
25. Rages
26. Natives of Dallas
28. Tyke
29. Autocrat
30. Sect
31. Georgia city
34. Pedal digits
35. Rooster
36. Mont Blanc
39. "One Day in the Life of —— Denisovich"
40. Pasture sounds
41. First Family from Tennessee
42. One —— customer: 2 wds.
43. Saul's uncle
44. Playground
45. Arkansas town
46. Tennessee county
47. Nurserymen
49. Individual character
50. Scottish families
51. Civil War battle site: 2 wds.
55. Descendant
57. Soaks up
58. Circled around
61. Swindles
62. Ways and ——
64. Cote sounds
65. Chimpanzee
66. Wood sorrel
67. Black-smith's workshop
68. Actors in a play
69. Leg joint
70. Existed
71. Brink
72. Window glass
73. Skinflint
74. French holy women: abbr.
75. King's title
76. Animal pouch
77. President from Georgia
80. Baylor University site
81. Capital of Mississippi
85. Malarial fever
86. Native of Mobile
89. Georgia town
90. Coconut tree
91. Effect of the moon on earth
92. Blue-pencil
93. Destroy
94. Before, poetically
95. At any time
96. Walter —— Mare: 2 wds.
97. Admit (a visitor)

DOWN

1. Polynesian chief
2. —— Fein
3. Astrodome site
4. Prejudiced person
5. Chester —— Arthur
6. Naught
7. Confederate First Family
8. Defeated person
9. Represen-tatives: abbr.
10. Modern: prefix
11. Bluegrass State
12. Soft drink
13. Sign of the future
14. Scout groups
15. Raven's cry
18. Schoolbook
21. Distinctive times
24. 2,000 pounds
27. The BPOE
29. Captured
30. Unheated
31. —— the Merciless of "Flash Gordon"
32. State positively
33. Piedmont region
34. Body trunk
35. Greek island
36. Peachtree Street residents
37. Bank grant
38. Settles (a bill)
40. Grade
41. Columbus's starting point
44. Unskilled laborer
45. Rope fibers
46. Roman 152
48. Courts
49. Mississippi county
50. Hackneys
52. Custom
53. Lasso loop
54. Gait between a walk and a run

55. Barge
56. Actress Imogene
59. Three-sided rapier
60. Antlered animal
62. Not excessive
63. Energy units
64. Walking stick
67. Garden party

68. Rebounded
69. Punters
72. Type size
73. Certain apple, for short
74. Check
75. Cavalry sword
76. —— Rosa County, Florida
77. Sleeveless coat

78. Chinese gelatin
79. Precept
80. Walk in water
81. Prison
82. Swing around
83. Migrant worker

84. —— compos mentis
87. 54
88. Cyprinoid fish

PUZZLE 339

ACROSS

1. —— facto
5. Asian nurse
9. Question's start
13. Music symbol
17. College official
18. Uh-uh
19. Tresses
20. Pit
21. Fasting time
22. Christmas carol
23. Subtle quality
24. African fox
25. Occupied
27. Lounge
29. Poems
31. Actor Harrison
32. Conceal
33. Wampum
34. Unspoken
37. Robin of Sherwood
38. Diminished
42. Play's star
43. Jungle king
44. "Divine Comedy" author
45. Reverence
46. Exist
47. Stinging insect
48. Social gathering
49. Presage
50. In the direction of
52. Russian antelope
53. All
54. —— Vegas
55. Church steeple
56. Miss West
57. Belt
60. Glossy
61. Hide
65. Claim on property
66. Tilt
67. Platter
68. Sea eagle
69. Anglo-Saxon coin
70. Supposes
71. Rugs
72. Czech, Serb, or Croat
73. Greets
75. Mah-jongg piece
76. Filmy
77. Dis-mounted
78. Oliver's request
79. Home-radio operator
80. Occur
83. Vasco da ——
84. Solemn
88. Way out
89. All: prefix
91. Important point
93. Sour fruit
94. Choir section
95. Burden
96. Traditional learning
97. Duke of ——
98. Rip
99. Dines
100. Scrutinized
101. Indian peasant

DOWN

1. Sluggish
2. Hammer head
3. Warbled
4. Its capital is Toronto
5. Addition
6. State of mind
7. Jungle creature
8. Rowdy child
9. Orca, e.g.
10. Drag
11. Ventilate
12. Mockery
13. Accusation
14. Defeat
15. Otherwise
16. Profes-sional charges
26. Acquire
28. Strange
30. Comfort
32. Hula ——
33. Five: prefix
34. "—— Girl"
35. Of flying
36. Ship's company
37. Snake's sound
38. Big
39. Title
40. Jug
41. Declare untrue
43. Boys
44. Milk store
47. Cloak
48. Enamel, e.g.
49. Finished
51. Actor Mowbray
52. Rotates
53. Apiece
55. Pretends
56. Naval meal
57. Lacking speed
58. Grow weary

59. Genuine
60. Freezing rain
61. Location
62. Morays
63. Snare
64. Begrudge
66. Florida Indian
67. Glen
70. Deal out sparingly
71. Supernatural event
72. Almost the same
74. One who confines
75. Actor Cruise
76. Conflict
78. Female servants
79. Jinxed
80. Warmth
81. Wheel shaft
82. Flat bread
83. Pesky fly
84. Positive
85. Greasy
86. Shield boss
87. Chair
90. Extinct bird
92. Cowboy Rogers

PUZZLE 340

ACROSS

1. Pastry shell
6. Biblical righteous one
11. Turnpikes
16. Awn
17. Angry
18. Attacks
20. Out of this world
22. Mars, for one
23. Hasten
24. Hawthorne's birthplace
25. Follow orders
27. Are you a man —— mouse?: 2 wds.
28. Being: Latin
30. Roam aimlessly
31. Carried on
33. Portent
34. Pioneer
36. Dike
37. Heaven on earth
38. Lean and strong
39. In the sack
40. Twinge
41. Church sections
44. Goad
45. Back lanes
48. Gem surface
49. —— in the ocean (card game)
50. Drag
51. Pekoe
52. Spanish aunts
53. School official
54. Steadfast
55. Crosby
56. Canad. prov.
57. Dock
58. Worry
59. Irregular
60. Baseball's Graig
62. Took wing
63. Conifer trees
64. Son of Aphrodite
65. Garden and sweet
66. Ran
68. Was concerned
70. Squeeze
71. Clergyman
75. French priest
76. Search for weapons
77. Four-in-hand
78. Trouble-maker on Olympus
79. Indian weight unit
80. Eternity
81. Betel palm
83. High in music
84. Actress Joyce
86. Very great
90. Beer mug
91. Burst forth
92. Columnist Westbrook
93. Winter precipitations
94. Perceive
95. Spud

DOWN

1. Sailing voyage
2. Most ready for harvest
3. Employ
4. Some boats: abbr.
5. Scarlet bird
6. Quoted
7. Taro plant
8. Roman household god
9. Greek letter
10. Treasured
11. Lassoed
12. Sole
13. King of Judah
14. Religious sect
15. Cubic meters
16. Fire residue
19. Kenton et al.
21. Of wings
26. Honey source
29. Small cases: var.
31. Disprove in debate
32. Assert
33. Hodgepodge
35. Catalogue
36. Rabbit fur
37. Unfurnished
40. Bier
41. Scottish river
42. "Common Sense" author
43. Giddy person
44. Dispute
45. Boxing match
46. Thick
47. Wise ones
49. Views
50. Concoction
53. Machine tool parts
54. Curl
55. Harness
57. Trudge

58. Flat bottle
59. Fencing sword
61. Clothes or shoe
62. Charges
65. William and Harry
66. Caught sight of
67. Doctrine
68. Lawsuits
69. White poplars
70. Palmer, for one
72. Suitable for plowing
73. Boat's steering handle
74. Silicate
76. Senses
77. Hackneyed
80. Again
81. Serpents
82. Space
85. Altar phrase: 2 wds.
87. Mineral find
88. Sister
89. Representative: abbr.

PUZZLE 340

PUZZLE 341

ACROSS

1. ____ -to-shore
5. Vega or Sirius
9. Theme: abbr.
13. Pedestal part
17. Japanese zither
18. Fountain drink
19. Turkish title
20. Of the mouth
21. Be an accomplice
22. Mexican fare
24. Island of Hawaii
25. Salad veggie
27. Edmonton athlete
28. With hands on hips
30. Indian weight
32. Galley blade
33. Read quickly
34. Grand Canyon's river
38. Suburban dwelling
43. Hawaiian assembly
44. Chinese, e.g.
46. Lorelei
47. This minute
48. Summit
50. Whole: Lat.
52. Women's group: abbr.
53. Delicate
54. Feather shaft
56. Kind of wheat
58. Sheen
59. Alliance
60. Exchange fees
61. Laborer
62. Cut
64. Used up
65. Wrinkled
68. Cover the exterior of
69. Clam genus
70. ____ distance
72. Siamese
73. Ornamental vase
74. Of apples
76. Perch
78. Wood sorrel
79. Project outline
82. Victories
84. Provo's state
85. Badger
87. ____ St. Vincent Millay
88. Paper wasp
91. Play the guitar
93. Egg or Island
97. "____ Three Lives"
98. ____ bridge
101. Nimbus
102. Burn
103. Garlic feature
104. Roll of cloth
105. Annoys
106. Marsh bird
107. TV staple
108. Chances
109. Comfort

DOWN

1. Card game
2. A road's scholar?
3. Columnist's entry
4. Maine product
5. Part of SAT
6. Also
7. Choir voice
8. Percentage
9. Tourists' trademarks
10. Esau's grandson
11. Wire measure
12. Clergyman
13. "The ____ Principle"
14. Ancient Syria
15. Smear
16. Potpourri
23. Winglike
26. African antelope
29. Actress Madeline ____
31. Pedro's good-by
33. Beat it!
34. Burn slightly
35. Painful word
36. Succotash ingredients
37. Cereal grain
39. Insect nest
40. Taft-Hartley concern
41. "____ and Lovers"
42. Woolly ones
45. Gentle push
49. Great success
51. Taking to court
53. Parade vehicle
55. Vertical's opp.
57. Copter blade
58. Turn right
60. ". . . to fetch ____ of water"

61. Johnson and Johnson, e.g.
62. Riffraff
63. Israeli dance
64. Airy sprite
65. Routine task
66. "To ___ His Own"
67. Buenos ___
69. Foot race
71. Babe
74. Distribute
75. Gallops easily
77. Sandwich filling
80. Treeless plain
81. Not any
83. Golf club
86. Thick soup
88. Serpent's sound
89. Croissant spread
90. Posterior
91. Cover for Rainier
92. State of mind
94. Mitchell plantation
95. BPOE members
96. U.S. national flower
99. Pindar poem
100. ___ hat

PUZZLE 341

303

PUZZLE 342

ACROSS

1. Inflexible
6. West Pointers
12. Scene of action
17. Mountain ridge
18. Pizza seasoning
20. Downy duck
21. Actress Wyman et al.
22. Air Force officer: 2 wds.
24. Corroded
25. Sherbets
27. Clemens's pen name
28. Take advantage of
29. Seasoning plant
31. Bay window
34. "—— walks in beauty . . ."
35. Hastened
36. In addition
38. River nymph
40. Body science: abbr.
42. Merriment
43. Welcome
45. Musical exercises
49. —— -camp: hyph.
52. Above: prefix
54. Debris
55. Military college: abbr.
56. Prima donna
58. Jeweled headpiece
60. Within: prefix
61. Musical pause
63. Noncommissioned officers
65. Dueling status symbol
66. Other things: Latin
67. Sing softly
68. Clockmaker Thomas
70. Summer: Fr.
71. Pace
73. Conductor Caldwell
75. Elongated fish
77. Self-preoccupation
79. Replenish
81. Some August people
82. Coral ridge
84. Hollywood luminary
85. Catherine ——
86. Dog's feet
89. Rarer than rare
91. Hit a golf ball poorly
93. Oil cartel: abbr.
96. Apple cider girl
97. "The Waste Land" poet
99. Sandwich fish
101. Bullfight cry
102. Equipment officer
106. Sensational
108. Stomach sore
109. Military action zones
110. Maternally related
111. "—— Dinsmore"
112. "But the dove found ——. . .": 2 wds.
113. Shoe bottoms

DOWN

1. Indian prince
2. Angered
3. Commander in chief
4. Native: suffix
5. Lucy's partner
6. Cringe
7. Ascending
8. Cub Scout unit
9. Souffle item
10. Diplomacy
11. Overwhelms, slangily
12. Actor Connery
13. Pewter ingredient
14. Total: 2 wds.
15. Honkers
16. Goofed
19. Nebraska city
23. Bearings
26. Bill and ——
30. Extorted money from
32. The walls have ——
33. Commissioned officers
35. Rubbernecks
37. "The Bad ——"
39. Dark brown pigment
41. Tread the boards
42. Drop-leaf table
44. Across: prefix
46. Marine Corps enlisted man: 2 wds.
47. Country properties
48. Prop up
50. Record
51. Tinker to —— to Chance
53. Russian co-op
55. Make a public speech
57. Howling

59. "Thin Man" dog
62. S. Amer. mammals
64. Skirt panels
69. Wahine dance
72. Carbohydrate suffix
74. Cure
76. Roman fiddler
78. Actress Oberon
80. Authors
83. Bazaars
85. Female swan
86. Irritate
87. " . . . makes Jack —— boy": 2 wds.
88. Early female soldiers
90. Ladies
92. Damned
94. Type size
95. Yields
97. Raison d'——
98. Mexican sandwich
100. Porters
103. Defendants
104. Cruise ship: abbr.
105. Foot digit
107. Numero ——

PUZZLE 343

ACROSS

1. Foundation
5. Grand Canyon State: abbr.
9. Pierce
13. Slammer
17. Muscat's land
18. Pizarro's prize
19. Actress Williams
20. Major or Minor
21. FDR's mother
22. Actor McCowen
23. Nutmeg covering
24. ___ of Gilead
25. Coffee additive
27. Muskmelons
30. Small bird
31. Close
32. Hockey idol
33. Jaclyn Smith, once
36. Legatee
37. Turnip's cousin
42. A friend in ___ ...
43. Van Cliburn's instrument
44. Made do
45. Studio decor
46. Be human
47. ___ of the Covenant
48. Smoothed
50. October gem
51. Love apples
54. Copy
55. Merchandise
56. "Thy will be done ___ ...": 2 wds.
58. More appealing
62. Bombast
64. Cushion or pocket
66. Norm
69. Sad word
70. 39th President
73. Food particle
74. Horse command
75. Scatter rug
76. Chaste
77. Sea birds
79. Pretty
80. Foretells
82. Roles
83. Kind of beam
84. Peleg's son
85. Party cheese
86. Weep
87. Large fruits
92. Pie plant
96. Silkworm
97. Cereal husk
98. ___ of duty
100. Exchange premium
101. Sow
102. Olden slave
103. Soothe
104. Multiply
105. Sailors
106. "___ Window"
107. Sleuth Nancy
108. Munchies

DOWN

1. Pear
2. Hong Kong nanny
3. Hindu dress
4. Passed, as law
5. Individually
6. Depend
7. Anger
8. Squash
9. Meager
10. Small pie
11. Song
12. Voted
13. Scarsdale to NYC
14. "The Tender ___"
15. Man or Wight
16. Farm butters
26. "___ the ramparts..."
28. Dawn
29. To the mouth
31. "The ___-Wolf"
33. Dill
34. Pianist Peter
35. Sprout
36. Backpacker
37. Subscribes again
38. Maui instrument, for short
39. Spring veggie
40. Clothing
41. Tamarisk
43. Malay outrigger
47. Noshed
49. Goddess of plenty
50. Was in arrears
52. "B.C." insects
53. Fixed looks
57. Triple, for one
59. Short jackets
60. Jug handles
61. Explosive: abbr.
62. Walkway
63. Winged

65. "The ____ of the Native"
67. Network
68. Cervus
70. Pickle's beginning
71. Craft
72. Withstood
76. Wharf
78. Caddoan Indian
79. Slaw need
81. Fears
83. Baseballer Gehrig
85. Mistake
86. Mouselike rodent
87. "Batman" actor
88. Region
89. Row
90. Celtic
91. Singer Cantrell
92. Stratagem
93. Taj Mahal site
94. Mob scene
95. Submits
99. Boat propeller

PUZZLE 344

Diagramless crosswords are solved by using the clues and their numbers to fill in the answer words and the arrangement of black squares. Insert the number of each clue with the first letter of its answer, across and down. Fill in a black square at the end of each word. Every black square must have a corresponding black square on the opposite side of the diagram to form a diagonally symmetrical pattern.

ACROSS
1. Consumed
4. Horseshoe ___
8. Shovels' kin

11. Comedian Bob ___
12. Basketball players
13. Otherwise
14. "___ Day Will Come"
15. Teases
17. Applies
19. Blue
20. Lively dances
22. Speed check
26. Type of meal
28. Thespian's part
29. Totter
33. Heavy weight
34. City in Peru
35. Rat
37. Press
38. Grows, as crops
39. GI's meal
40. Work unit

DOWN
1. Citrus beverage
2. Sea swallow
3. Curvy letters
4. Sharp cheese
5. Bakery product
6. Church part
7. Spelling contests
8. Scrub
9. Take a break
10. Assent
16. Pitcher part
18. Phrases
21. Droop
23. Bestows excessive fondness
24. Solo
25. Leases
27. ___ Haute, Indiana
29. Actor Pickens
30. Radial, e.g.
31. Cookie man
32. Bellow
36. Use a shovel

PUZZLE 345

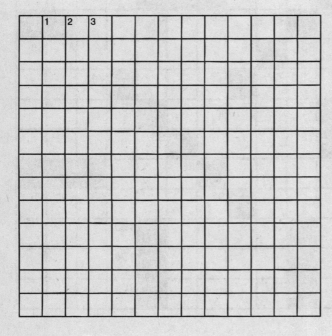

ACROSS
1. Ram's mate
4. Traveler's aid
7. Ward off
9. "God's Little ___"
11. Type of acid
13. Actor Estrada
14. Lofty trains
15. Historic time
17. Washington bill
18. Baseball's Bando
19. Expansive
21. Sees
23. Charge
25. Golfer's gadget
26. Vulture
28. Coaster
29. Favorite
31. Feminine pronoun
32. Camomile drink
33. Bustle
36. Roof edge
38. Journey
40. Playing card
41. Style
42. Bard's before
43. Wrath

DOWN
1. Corrupt
2. Saturates
3. Blunder
4. Fannie ___
5. Crossword direction
6. Publish
7. King's superior
8. Cravats
10. Supplement
12. Coveted
16. "The Greatest"
19. Compete
20. Had a snack
22. Thoroughfare
23. Enemy
24. Conclude
26. Witty
27. Choose
28. Portion
30. Pie's kin
31. Harden
33. Attest to
34. Low hill
35. Ancient
37. Storm center
39. Jackie's second

PUZZLE 346

ACROSS

1. Gorilla
4. Hemingway's nickname
8. Vex
10. Persia
11. Winter flakes
12. Wooden nails
13. Fruit drink
16. Casino cube
17. Greek vowel
18. Location
20. Donkey
21. Tear apart
23. Summer TV show
24. Exist
25. Oak nut
27. Needlefish
29. Log float
30. Diaper fasteners
31. Assam silkworm
32. Poem division
33. Cushion
35. Barter
37. Memorandum
41. "Ben ___"
42. The ___ of time
43. Tear
44. Gold: Sp.
45. Merry
46. Unemployed
47. Potato
49. Ancient Persian
50. Otherwise
51. Greek Mars
52. Snakelike fish

DOWN

1. ___ gratia artis
2. Greek lyric poet
3. Kay Thompson heroine
4. "The Pied ___"
5. Mountain crest
6. Heathen
7. Reply: abbr.
9. Rams' mates
13. Wide-awake
14. Mend socks
15. Former French coin
18. Benefits
19. Motors
22. Ventured
24. Criminal burning
26. Auto
28. Picnic pest
30. Rice field
32. Site of the first miracle
33. Royal color
34. Awaken
36. Dust cloth
38. Command
39. Diacritical mark
40. Fencing foils
41. Watering tube
46. "___ Yankee Doodle Dandy"
48. Punta ___ Este

Starting box on page 562

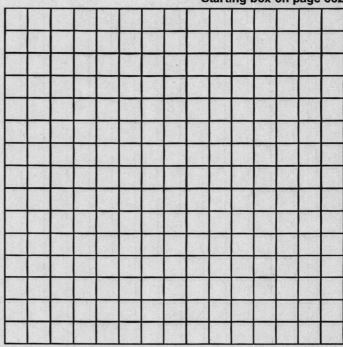

WORD MATH

PUZZLE 347

In these long-division problems, letters are substituted for numbers. Determine the value of each letter. Then arrange the letters in order from 0 to 9, and they will spell a word or phrase.

1

0	1	2	3	4	5	6	7	8	9

```
                MIL
      ERIE | FLOWER
             FTML
              LELE
              ERIE
              BFOTR
              BWIIM
               BRFB
```

2

0	1	2	3	4	5	6	7	8	9

```
                MOE
      PULL | BATTLE
             AEBA
              ABEL
              PULL
              PPOCE
              POPEM
               OBOB
```

3

0	1	2	3	4	5	6	7	8	9

```
                RID
      GIRL | STOOPS
             GIRL
              PPDTP
              POIHD
               IRPS
```

PUZZLE 348

ACROSS

1. Smoked pork
4. The one there
8. Bedouin
10. Tracks down
12. Sum
14. Tourist
16. Rouse
17. Military assistant
18. Snub-nosed dog
20. Lion's home
21. Author of "The Purloined Letter"
22. Counterfeit
24. ___ pro nobis
25. Happiness
26. Anchors a ship
28. Traffic tie-up
29. Public vehicle
30. Striped cat
32. However
33. Ewe's mate
34. Cavalry sword
36. Dog's hand
39. Period in history
40. Silent
41. Nota ___
42. Mix
44. Produce electricity
47. Unspoken
49. Works of fiction
50. Back of the neck
51. Ford a stream
52. Once named

DOWN

1. Topper
2. "And pretty maids all in ___"
3. Bullfighters
4. Barter
5. Possess
6. Flying hero
7. ___ Aviv
9. Muffin makers
10. Three musicians
11. Soldier of India
13. Songstress Horne
14. Faucet
15. Carpet
19. Chewable sweet
22. Explosives
23. Abstinent
25. Poke with the elbow
27. Not at home
28. West Indian
30. Plaid
31. Sweet potato
32. Arabian country
33. Take a breather
35. Insect
36. Norman Vincent ___
37. Social insects
38. Tiny
41. Raised cattle
43. Ready for picking
45. Present time
46. Actress Gabor
48. Golf gadget

Starting box on page 562

PUZZLE 349   QUOTAGRAM

Fill in the answers to the clues below. Then transfer the letters to the correspondingly numbered squares in the diagram. The completed diagram will contain a quotation.

1. English furniture style $\overline{19}\ \overline{42}\ \overline{3}\ \overline{16}\ \overline{34}\ \overline{13}\ \overline{28}\ \overline{46}\ \overline{39}\ \overline{24}\ \overline{20}$

2. Finger joints $\overline{12}\ \overline{43}\ \overline{15}\ \overline{36}\ \overline{37}\ \overline{41}\ \overline{7}\ \overline{14}$

3. Kidnap a sailor $\overline{9}\ \overline{23}\ \overline{30}\ \overline{40}\ \overline{44}\ \overline{1}\ \overline{35}\ \overline{32}$

4. Be an artist $\overline{4}\ \overline{11}\ \overline{17}\ \overline{6}\ \overline{33}$

5. Slightly damp $\overline{10}\ \overline{26}\ \overline{21}\ \overline{38}\ \overline{31}$

6. Elevator column $\overline{8}\ \overline{29}\ \overline{2}\ \overline{25}\ \overline{45}$

7. Marriage symbol $\overline{27}\ \overline{5}\ \overline{18}\ \overline{22}$

1	2	3	4	5	6	7	8	9	■	10	11	12	13	14	■	15	16
17	18	■	19	20	21	22	23	24	■	25	26	27	■	28	29	30	31
32	33	■	34	35	36	37	38	■	39	40	■	41	42	43	44	45	46

ACROSS

1. Wild plum
5. Set down
9. Colony of bees
10. Fed the kitty
12. New
13. Long-billed sandpiper
14. Subsequent
15. In unison
17. Failure
18. Shredded
20. False name
23. Actor on "The A-Team"
26. Foil material
27. Donkey
28. Toupee
31. Amuse
33. "The Glass ___"
36. Anesthetic
40. Epoch
41. Stag's mate
42. Awaken
43. Outstanding
45. Angry
46. Excludes
49. Marshy inlet
52. Aggravated
54. Surgeon's beam
55. At no time
56. Pen name of Charles Lamb
57. Tidings
58. Beloved

DOWN

1. Chance
2. Dwell
3. Completed
4. Elongated fish
5. ___ Cruces
6. Dancer Pavlova
7. "___ No Secret"
8. Bus station
11. Indicate
12. Lowest point
14. Humdinger
16. Football's Dickerson
17. Pat gently
19. Opposite of WSW
21. Territory
22. Tune
23. Donny's sister
24. Religious ceremony
25. ___ la la
28. Protagonist
29. Wharf
30. Toward
32. Emcee Mack
33. Encountered
34. God of love
35. Diner's cloth
37. Wit
38. Biblical twin
39. Blushing
44. Warning device
47. Cover with concrete
48. Brood
49. Bundle of cotton
50. Largest continent
51. Century component
53. Hesitant sounds
54. Guided

Starting box on page 562

YOU KNOW THE ODDS

Six football terms are spelled below, but they are missing every other letter. Can you fill in the missing letters? It shouldn't be too difficult to fill in the even-positioned letters once You Know the Odds!

1. C _ N _ E _ S _ O _ S

2. Q _ A _ T _ R _ A _ K

3. O _ F _ C _ A _ T _ M _ O _ T

4. L _ N _ O _ S _ R _ M _ A _ E

5. G _ A _ P _ S _ S

6. T _ I _ D _ O _ N

PUZZLE 352

ACROSS
1. Lobo
5. Grate
9. Circa
11. Bread spread
12. Knotted rope
13. Space
15. Rely
17. Command
19. Tier
21. Drip
24. Groupie
25. Peel
26. Contradict
28. Moral wrong
29. Library
30. Total
32. Shell
33. Hog
34. Sink
36. Merit
38. Profit
39. Appeal
40. Yes
41. Weary
44. Tidbit
50. Citrus fruit
52. Depart
53. Parent
54. Challenges
55. Cypress
56. Brooches

DOWN
1. Baton
2. Woodwind
3. Circle
4. Meld
5. Steal
6. Permit
7. Burn
8. "On Golden ____"
10. X
14. Seaweed
16. Lackluster
18. Cause
20. Responsibility
22. Dry
23. Knowledge
24. Marsh
26. Rue
27. Cistern
29. Radio tuner
31. Numerous
32. Hole
33. Zip
35. Look
37. Brad
40. Cherish
42. Remainder
43. Arab chieftain
45. Aged
46. Harvest
47. Indian robe
48. Tied
49. "____ Than Zero"
51. Formerly named

Starting box on page 562

PUZZLE 353 — Quotagram

Fill in the answers to the clues. Then transfer the letters to the correspondingly numbered squares in the diagram. The completed diagram will contain a quotation.

1. Entertain
$\overline{16}\ \overline{22}\ \overline{30}\ \overline{9}\ \overline{14}$

2. Parcel
$\overline{33}\ \overline{28}\ \overline{1}\ \overline{13}\ \overline{32}\ \overline{17}\ \overline{10}$

3. Looking glass
$\overline{3}\ \overline{8}\ \overline{36}\ \overline{24}\ \overline{19}\ \overline{5}$

4. Matterhorn, e.g.
$\overline{12}\ \overline{27}\ \overline{4}$

5. Blossom
$\overline{23}\ \overline{26}\ \overline{34}\ \overline{39}\ \overline{11}$

6. Rodent
$\overline{7}\ \overline{38}\ \overline{21}\ \overline{15}\ \overline{25}$

7. Unit of length
$\overline{40}\ \overline{35}\ \overline{6}\ \overline{31}$

8. Worry
$\overline{29}\ \overline{37}\ \overline{2}\ \overline{18}\ \overline{20}$

1	2	3	4	5	6	7	8	9	10		11	12	13	14	15
	16		17	18	19	20		21	22	23	24	25	26	27	28
	29	30	31		32		33	34	35	36		37	38	39	40

ACROSS

1. Ruinous
6. Swimsuit part
9. Caustic
10. Sweat of one's ___
11. Hollywood hopeful
12. South Korean city
13. Violent spasm
14. Thunder sound
18. Intone
19. Gear for a horse
20. Tendency
22. Indian tribe
23. Ms. Landers
24. Code
25. Miniature car
26. Temple
29. Ceremonial drink
31. Restaurant list
33. Speedy
34. Set in a row
36. Early man
39. Mrs. Reagan
40. Stands up
42. Tibetan language of the Sherpas
43. Leg joint
44. Gloomy
48. Barb
49. Ancient Greek cynic
52. To wit
56. German wife
57. Small insect
59. Overstate
60. Condemns
61. He could eat no fat
62. Plant bristle
63. Morsel
64. Forbidden
65. Novelist Alexandre ___
66. Large bird
67. Chemical ingredient
69. Journalist Whitelaw ___
70. Study of plants
71. Craving
72. Dormant

DOWN

1. Erupting
2. Ohio city
3. Legend
4. Beverage
5. Chinese nut
6. New York zoo site
7. Defeat
8. Leather tool
9. Peace goddess
10. Whopper
11. Fasten
12. Clipped
15. Northern Scandinavian
16. Detest
17. Noted sculpture
18. Italian farewell
21. Pitfall
22. On a slide
24. Dog or wolf
27. Muscat and ___
28. Postpone
30. Head ornament
32. Oily
35. Viewing
37. Appealing
38. ___ toast
41. Appear
45. Grant and Majors
46. Not appropriate
47. ___ firma
49. Valence's land
50. Poetry unit
51. Clean the floor
53. Oxygen or iron
54. Enumeration
55. Bread's need
56. Located
58. Pianist Jose ___
60. Deplete
62. Cane or beet
63. Indian tribe
65. Suitor
66. Exclamation
68. Long time

Starting box on page 562

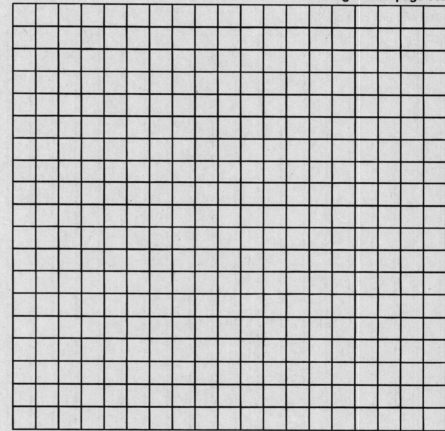

Tiles

Imagine that these tiles are on a table, each showing a 2-letter combination. Can you rearrange these tiles visually to form a 10-letter word?

PUZZLE 356

ACROSS

1. Irish poet
6. Eskimo boot
7. Worry
11. Paint board
12. Corpulent
14. Observe
15. Brick carrier
16. Wood varnish
18. "___ Miserables"
19. Prophetic
23. Spring month
24. Eye nerve
27. Contribute
28. ___-Columbian
29. Australian city
30. Faucet problem
31. Machine guns
33. Uneven
34. Permits
35. Fosters
36. "___ Fan Tutte"
39. Pear variety
41. Pakistani title
42. Onion's kin
43. Crooned
44. "Against All ___"
45. Filament
47. Campus military org.
50. Notices
55. Reddish dye
56. Out of control
57. Seething
58. Actor Byrnes
59. Antacid, for short
61. Bet
62. In the past
63. Musical introduction
66. "Bali ___"
67. Retaliation
70. Boston's Red ___
71. Historic period
72. Sequence
73. Ms. Weld
76. Depend
77. Delineated
78. Fix a seam

DOWN

1. Actor Brynner
2. Enlarge, of old
3. Even if, briefly
4. Private teacher
5. Running away
6. Eminent composer
7. Sudden blaze
8. ___ room
9. Lawyer's abbr.
10. Struck heavily
11. Certain frog
12. London apartment
13. Hungers
14. Ski resort feature
17. Cereal grasses
20. Center
21. Single thing
22. Track circuits
25. "___ My Party"
26. Registers
31. Established
32. Chinese vehicle
37. Mitchell's heroine
38. ___ Diego
39. Smash hit
40. Reference book letters
45. Rows of bushes
46. Massachusetts city
47. Marathon, e.g.
48. General Bradley
49. Civil wrong
51. Spanish queen
52. Intellectual
53. Dismal
54. Site of Damascus
55. Discover
59. Ghost
60. Currier's partner
64. Road
65. Business bigwigs
68. Prior to, in poems
69. Zilch
74. Haggard novel
75. Morning dampness

Starting box on page 562

PUZZLE 357   Mix 'Em Maxim

Rearrange the letters in this silly sentence to spell out a familiar phrase.

CAT SUES TUNA BOAT

Saying: ___ ___   ___ ___ ___ ___ ___   ___ ___   ___ ___ ___ ___ ___ ___ ___

314

ACROSS

1. Speed contest
5. Knock
8. At a distance
9. Pindaric work
10. No more than
11. Lose brightness
12. Sleep vision
15. Meadow sound
18. Antlered animal
19. Dessert dish
21. At rest
22. Fuss
23. 2,000 pounds
25. Singer Campbell
26. Flirtatious gesture
27. Unadulterated
30. ____ mode
33. Took the bus
34. Dye plant
35. Narrow opening
36. Arrived
37. Deep hole
38. Surrender
39. Grow older
40. Apportion
41. Charged atoms
42. London's Big ____
43. Mineral deposits
44. Apartment
45. Pack
48. Each and every
49. Old witch
50. Give off
53. Slip up
54. Delivery truck
55. Decade
57. Helsinki natives
59. Egg-shaped
61. Corrosive liquid
65. Forget-me-____
66. Openwork fabric
67. Lamb's dam
68. Biblical garden

DOWN

1. Zodiac's Aries
2. Amazement
3. Automobile
4. Looked at
5. Wander
6. Append
7. Rind
11. Counterfeit
13. Crimson
14. Building extension
16. Milky gem
17. Broad
20. Very long time
21. Printing fluid
23. Ocean movement
24. Washington bill
25. Colloid
26. Ladies
27. News sheet
28. Join together
29. Ceremonies
30. Representative
31. Boys
32. Mimic
33. Tantrum
36. Musician Calloway
38. Solid fuel
40. Cut the grass
41. Under the weather
44. Obese
45. That girl
46. Piquant
47. Fairy-tale monster
50. Devilish
51. Adult male
52. Wayside respite
56. "____ But the Brave"
57. Destiny
58. Bargain event
60. Promise
62. Rogue
63. Frozen water
64. Cozy place

Starting box on page 562

MIX 'EM MAXIM

PUZZLE 359

Rearrange the letters in this silly phrase to spell out a familiar saying.

NATE WATTS ON TOWN

Saying: __ __ __ __ __   __ __ __ ,   __ __ __ __ __   __ __ __ .

PUZZLE 360

ACROSS

1. Shut loudly
5. Yugoslav president
6. Ages
8. Back talk
12. Honorariums
17. Ballerina's garment
18. Designate
19. Long ago
20. Machine suffix
21. Whole
22. Algerian seaport
23. Silly behavior
25. Geometric figure: abbr.
26. Scrape
30. Kind of whale
31. Singer Nelson ___
32. Epochal
33. Cowgirl's rope
36. Mart event
38. Actress Turner
39. Plant stalk
40. Son of Daedalus
43. Boca ___, Fla.
44. A ___ are soon parted
47. Miller's salesman
50. Purloined
51. College instructor, for short
52. Mine access
53. The Venerable ___
54. English county
56. Mouselike rodent
57. Biblical book
59. Comedian Leon ___
62. War god
63. "And giving ___ . . ."
64. Turns a profit
69. Very small
70. Arkin and Bates
71. Church section
72. Wool weights
73. South American monkey
74. "___ yellow ribbon . . ."
75. Not changed
78. Mineral sources
79. Lad
80. Bone: pref.
81. Guide

DOWN

1. Tritely
2. Stead
3. Speck
4. Payment means
7. Sawed wood
8. Immediately, to a doctor
9. Cars
10. Trample
11. Wave rider
12. Organic compound
13. Spouse
14. Poet Khayyam
15. Tennis player Austin
16. Mailed
21. Part of BLT
24. Prayer
26. Pass on
27. Smell ___
28. Heal: Lat.
29. Blueprint
31. Comedienne May
34. Archaeological mounds
35. Amo, amas, ___
36. Moves sideways
37. Longed
41. Baseball officials, for short
42. Marsh bird
43. Improvement
44. Goddesses of destiny
45. Be ___ (be shrewd)
46. Just as much
47. Molten rock
48. Fragrance
49. Unit of distance
55. Right away
57. Negative particle
58. Workweek starter
60. Walking ___ (happy)
61. Embankment
63. Aleutian island
64. Equaled
65. Dismounted
66. "Kiss Me, ___"
67. Author Bagnold
68. Pro votes
76. Melt
77. Kett of comics

Starting box on page 562

316

ACROSS

1. Consumes
5. Certain hairstyle
6. Play a part
9. Ship's canvas
10. Word before bean or sauce
11. Game fish
13. Cease
14. Designate
16. Opted
17. Baseball pitch
20. Sped
21. Dayton's state
22. Evening bugle call
25. Garden bloom
27. Table utensil
28. Farm building
29. Finest
30. Quaker William ——
31. Order's companion
32. Compassionate
34. French capital
36. Forbid
37. Press
38. Finger
42. Brewed beverage
43. Alan or Robert
44. Down in the dumps
45. Movie spool
46. Bargain

DOWN

1. Sunrise direction
2. Off yonder
3. Group of three
4. Answer
6. Bewilder
7. Dove sounds
8. Category
12. Little bit
13. Fair portion
15. Acquires
16. Baby's bed
17. Glowed
18. Jungle beast
19. Transportation mode
21. Unblock
23. Ordinary
24. Seeds
26. Pencil end
27. Madrid native
33. Zany
34. Cherry stones
35. Section
39. Delight
40. Inspiration
41. "Walking ——"

PUZZLE 361

Starting box on page 562

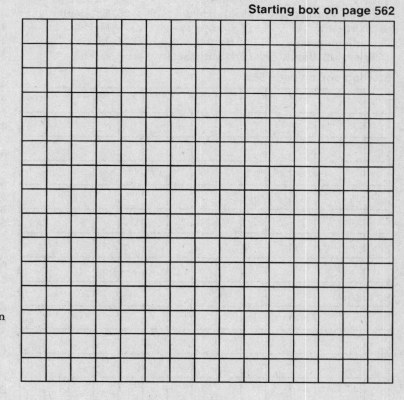

Word Math

PUZZLE 362

In these long-division problems letters are substituted for numbers. Determine the value of each letter. Then arrange the letters in order from 0 to 9, and they will spell a word or phrase.

1 | 0 | 1 | 2 | 3 | 4 | 5 | 6 | 7 | 8 | 9 |

```
              O D D
MISS | N O I S I E R
         N N Z S I
         A S R R E
         A Z R S Z
         A S A A R
         A Z R S Z
           N R A D
```

2 | 0 | 1 | 2 | 3 | 4 | 5 | 6 | 7 | 8 | 9 |

```
                I O N
PACE | A M E N D E D
         A H C P C
         A E M D E
         A I A P E
         M H I C D
         A D P I O
           A C I M
```

3 | 0 | 1 | 2 | 3 | 4 | 5 | 6 | 7 | 8 | 9 |

```
                I C Y
HILL | L I N I N G
         G Y K S
         N O I N
         K G N K
         H K Y O G
         H K O Y O
           N C I
```

317

PUZZLE 363

ACROSS
1. City transportation
4. Short swim
7. Gardening tool
8. Prior to, to Byron
9. Red, powdery spice
13. Marched
18. Composer Harold
19. Health facility
21. Fur scarf
22. "From —— shining . . ."
23. Rocky hill
24. Bald or golden
25. —— Diego
26. Baseballer Mel ——
28. Jackie's second
29. Delivery person
33. Romaine
36. "Top ——" (Cruise film)
37. Before this time
38. Negative vote
39. Pirate's drink
40. —— foo yung
41. Bicker
43. Summer, to Pierre
44. Fruit drink
45. Tooth doctor's org.
46. Pertaining to the pope
51. "It —— to Be You"
53. Croc's cousin
55. Exhibition site
56. Crude metal
57. Make amends
58. North American reindeer
60. Provided food
62. Chicago railways
63. "—— Maria"
64. Jamie —— Curtis
65. "Viva —— Vegas"

DOWN
1. Twilled cotton cloth
2. Thumbs up!
3. —— of burden
4. Leaving
5. Savings plan
6. A Gershwin
9. Rite of ——
10. Partial floor covering
11. Smoothing wood
12. Prepare flax
14. —— loss (perplexed)
15. Man's best friend
16. House wing
17. Billy —— Williams
20. Lacking money
27. Wild duck
29. Crow's comment
30. Taj Mahal's site
31. Tavern
32. Hearty bread
33. Originator
34. Surpassed
35. Smudged
42. Not far
46. ——-Man (video game)
47. Coach Parseghian
48. Part of MPG
49. Black cuckoo
50. Price tag
52. Stick-on design
53. Fence openings
54. Lunched
59. Mexican "Rah!"
61. Ms. Gardner

Starting box on page 562

PUZZLE 364   Disco

Each numbered disc has a 5-letter answer (Clue A) and a 4-letter answer (Clue B) reading in a clockwise direction. Enter the first letter of each 5-letter answer in the circle in the preceding disc. For example, in disc 1: E + QUIP = EQUIP.

A	B
1. Furnish	1. Witty remark
2. Perfect model	2. Distribute cards
3. Oak nut	3. Maize
4. Stretch	4. Apiece
5. Ascend	5. Branch
6. Fable message	6. Type of exam
7. Severe	7. Pretty
8. Woolen fabric	8. Garden nuisance

PUZZLE 365

ACROSS

1. Female knight
5. Prayer ending
6. Except
9. Travel units
11. Bat wood
12. With a rounded roof
14. Fiddling emperor
16. Stocking fiber
18. Inside information
20. Fatless
22. Successive one in sequence
24. Assumed name
28. Downcast
30. Foyer
32. Price
33. Commotion
34. Great Lake
35. Sample food
37. Permit
38. Make suitable
39. Affair of honor
40. Genuine
42. Terminates
44. TV knobs
47. Precious
49. Reverie
51. Blue above us
52. Spouses
54. Cravat
55. Ten cents
56. TV interference

DOWN

1. Water barrier
2. In with
3. Cantaloupe
4. Foe
6. Prohibit
7. Secondhand
8. Royal seat
10. Vends
13. Female deer
15. Started the bidding
17. Twangy
19. Supplemental
21. Consumer advocate
23. Journey
24. Drama division
25. Freight
26. Point in dispute
27. Be in the audience
29. Loved to excess
31. And still
36. Firstborn
38. Morning ringer
41. Assistance
43. H.H. Munro
45. Goes in front
46. Shiny fabric
48. Dark bread
50. Office note
53. Take stitches

Starting box on page 562

North and South   PUZZLE 366

Place the listed words in the numbered columns, some up and some down, to form five new words across.

1.
ALIVE
DELTA
LAVES
PARED
TRADE

2.
ANGEL
ARROW
MOUSE
PRESS
SCADS

319

PUZZLE 367

ACROSS

1. "How to Beat the High —— of Living"
5. Pigmented eye part
6. With competence
10. "—— Name: Emerald"
14. Farm buildings
16. "—— Grass of Kentucky"
17. Neighborhood
18. Arrange in a straight row
19. Streisand film
20. Barely as much as indicated
21. Weary from too much walking
24. Breathes heavily
25. Male swine
26. Sound-recording technique
29. Type of grass
31. Carbonated beverage
32. "—— Lampoon's European Vacation"
35. Educator/writer W.E.B. Du ——
36. Expression of sorrow
37. —— hour (last possible moment)
39. German article
42. Have a compelling desire
43. Step on the —— (hurry)
44. Shopping-center happening
45. His wife turned to salt
46. Prepare for conflict
51. Amend a manuscript
52. Credit-union transaction
53. Antiquated table-covering
55. Type of brake or camera
56. Dieter's aid
57. Gracefully slender
59. Black waist-length coat
60. Sky-supporting Titan
62. Bowling game
66. Constructed
67. Says as a greeting
68. Trace of contamination
71. Reverse
72. Toward the sheltered side
73. Large diving duck
74. Lee Trevino, at times
75. The Grateful ——
76. African lily plant
77. Withhold the possession of

DOWN

1. Caribbean island
2. President's —— Office
3. Typographical feature
4. Latin-American ballroom dance
6. Deviating from a standard
7. Obscure by smearing
8. Ancient stringed instrument
9. "——, Sir, That's My Baby"
10. Tropical evergreen tree
11. Long-armed ape, for short
12. Fender imperfection
13. Has boeuf bourguignon
15. Supercilious
20. Hanks/Hannah comedy
22. Bull, in Estremadura
23. French river
26. Fibrous mineral
27. Lunchtime, for many
28. Mine entrance
30. Luxurious quality
32. Carpenter's necessity
33. Soprano's counterpart
34. Skill in dealing with a difficult situation
38. Wine-storage container
39. Rectangular board section
40. Descended from a truck
41. Third son of Adam
44. Type of gypsum
46. Firstborn
47. Work hard
48. Woody fiber
49. Given authority
50. Make extremely happy
54. Horseshoe sound
57. Move in contact with a smooth surface
58. Determination in facing danger
60. Touch at the border
61. "—— in Tomorrow . . ."
62. Cleopatra's river
63. Theory
64. Water nymph
65. Move sideways
67. "The —— News Bears"
69. Illuminated sign
70. Three-spot playing card

Starting box on page 562

320

PUZZLE 368

ACROSS

1. Coach Shula
4. Cut wildly
9. Gourd, e.g.
10. Game fish
12. Vector mosquito
13. Hires
15. Bar Harbor's state
16. ——-Darwinism
17. Pallid
18. Parabola
19. Have being
20. Sharp comment
22. Pool shot
24. Brief attempt
26. Resistance measure
29. Impetuous
30. Compass point: abbr.
31. Harvesters
33. Puritanical
36. Fall back
37. Guitarist Clark
39. Fortune
40. Scandinavian rug
41. Halluces
43. Convinces
45. Gym pads
47. Glengarry, e.g.
48. Pier rodent
49. Yuck!
50. Sigma follower
53. Thought purchaser
55. Seesaws
57. Linda Lavin role
58. Sault —— Marie
59. Spiel
60. Forestall
61. Taste enhancer: abbr.

DOWN

1. Devote
2. Forthright
3. Sniffer
4. British gun
5. Country road
6. Jason's vessel
7. Bath or Vichy
8. Poppycock
9. Oyster products
11. Approaches
12. Latin I word
14. Snick or ——
21. Poor reviews
22. Artist Chagall
23. Declare
25. Double-cross
26. Give an address
27. Legatee
28. Mother, to Livy
29. Noosed rope
32. Frolic
34. Prepares flax
35. Condemn
38. Hankering
39. Fool
42. Posture
43. Seal
44. Pay
46. Ocular ailment
50. Portable shelter
51. Comic Johnson
52. Consumer
53. Hand part
54. Yale and Terry
56. Dead heat

Starting box on page 562

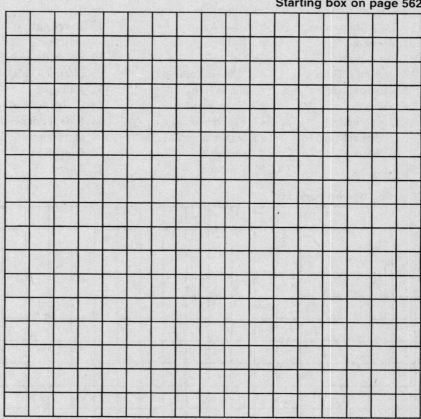

End of the Line   PUZZLE 369

For each of the categories listed, can you think of a word or phrase ending with each letter on the right? Count one point for each correct answer. A score of 12 is good, and 16 is excellent.

FOOTBALL TERMS	U.S. ASTRONAUTS	SECTIONS OF A BOOK	MALE GOLF GREATS	GAMES	
					R
					E
					N
					D

321

PUZZLE 370

ACROSS

1. Cabbage dish
5. Rental agreements
7. Sunday tollers
12. Unique chap
16. Actress Hope ——
17. "—— Magnolias"
18. Metes out
20. Encourage
21. Designer Klein
22. Muse of lyric poetry
23. Hive dweller
24. Cathedral topper, perhaps
28. Sesame
29. Kind of review
30. Compass pt.
31. Historic age
32. Jeweler's weight
33. Fireman's need, at times
36. American Indian
37. —— Walter Raleigh
38. Gnats, e.g.
41. "Like a Rolling Stone" singer
45. Narrow inlet
47. Floe material
48. Natural water source
51. Rescued
53. Ginger drink
54. —— Amin
57. Thunderstruck
58. Fail to keep up
59. Chimes for callers
62. Haul
65. "—— of Two Cities"
67. Disney or Whitman
68. Wander
69. Takes out, in printing
70. Related on one's mother's side
72. Add up
73. Go in quest of
74. Independence Hall attraction
76. Drenched
77. Raced

DOWN

1. Suit fabric
2. "Arsenic and Old ——"
3. Fire remnant
4. Arachnids' traps
5. Fencing move
6. Bristlelike
7. Social organization
8. Tortoise's opponent
9. Fasting season
10. Fabrics of a certain weave
11. Large quantities
12. European river
13. Neither's correlative
14. Thrilled
15. Hit the hay
19. Type of energy
24. Uncovers
25. A Gabor
26. "—— It Be"
27. Slithery swimmers
29. Evaluate
32. Saucer's companion
34. Lend a hand
35. Like the Sahara
39. ——-state area
40. Moral wrong
42. "Days of Our ——"
43. Hit a hole in one
44. Actor Sparks
46. Exchange premium
48. Dinner course
49. Table-setting items
50. Entertain lavishly
51. Song gal
52. Piercing tool
55. Wooden pin
56. Teheran native
59. Secretary's station
60. Spill the beans
61. Diminutive suffixes
62. Lugged
63. Egg shape
64. Artesian or oil
66. Sheltered side
68. Clad like a judge
71. God of love
72. Youngster
75. Knock gently

Starting box on page 562

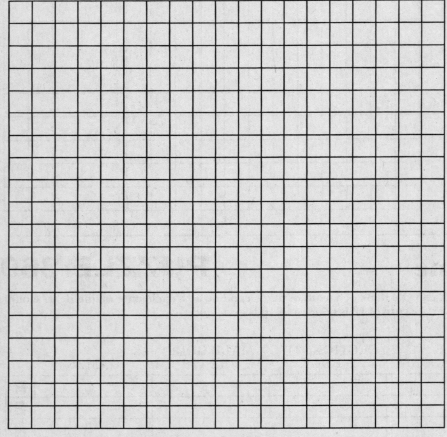

ACROSS

1. Decay
4. Pinta's companion
5. Chilled
8. Fast
9. Leg joint
10. Damp
11. Summons
12. Wheel and ——
13. Inn
14. —— and crafts
15. Soft cap
16. Wave peaks
18. "Seek, and ye shall ——"
19. Baby's cry
20. Landscaping material
22. Scientist's workplace
25. Ripened
26. Before the appointed time
28. Highway behemoth
29. Carmine
30. Belief
32. Reimbursed
33. Low card
35. In the direction of
37. Tire surface
39. Leading
40. Fetch
41. Endorse
42. Long Island ——
43. Pine Tree State
45. Miner's tool
46. African river
47. Pub order
48. Sworn promise
49. Singleton

DOWN

1. Tears
2. You have my word ——
3. Small amount
4. Carpenter's fastener
5. Small bay
6. Jailhouse room
7. Affirmative response
8. Ridicules
9. "Kiss Me, ——"
10. New York nine
11. Heavy string
12. Fear
13. Female chicken
14. Equipped with weapons
15. Holy book
16. Enclosure
17. Female pronoun
18. Hairy
19. Blemish
21. Hurried
22. Acquire knowledge
23. Amongst
24. Auction action
27. However
28. Iberian country
31. Game tile
33. Look after
34. Small cloth
36. Earnings
37. Cease-fire
38. Skating arena
40. Seethe
41. Lament
42. Recreation spot
43. Ghost's noise
44. Poker bet
46. Bill and ——

PUZZLE 371

Starting box on page 562

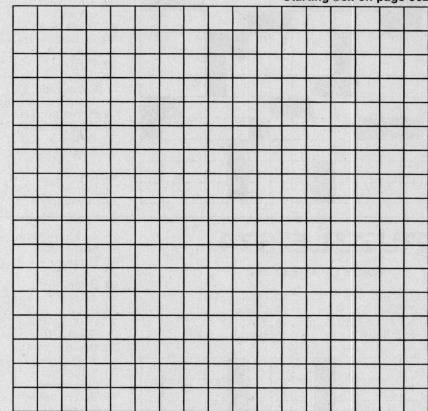

Changaword

PUZZLE 372

Can you change the top word into the bottom word in each column in the number of steps indicated in parentheses? Change only one letter at a time and do not change the order of the letters. Proper names, slang, and obsolete words are not allowed.

1. BURN (4 steps)   2. BOAT (5 steps)   3. CAMP (5 steps)   4. HIKE (6 steps)

WOOD   LAKE   TENT   PEAK

PUZZLE 373

• SEEING DOUBLE •

ACROSS
1. Taxis
5. Drenched
8. Without
12. On the water
13. "What Kind of Fool ____"
14. Part of a whole
15. Petty quarrel
16. Without warning
18. Coal or gas
20. Sow
21. Dull
23. Bird beds
27. Father
29. Retained
32. Hurry
33. Sick
34. Artist's prop
36. Southwestern Indian
37. Summer drink
38. Vex
39. Author John ____ Passos
40. Lariat
43. Diane or Alan
45. Republic of Ireland
48. Female deer
50. Trivial
54. Darn
56. Conception
57. "Annabel Lee" author
58. Hereditary factor
59. Hospital garb
60. Concorde, e.g.
61. Famous garden

DOWN
1. Feline
2. Seemingly
3. Confuses
4. More secure
5. Had being
6. Down Under birds
7. Ocean motion
8. Shoe material
9. Actress Sothern
10. Nothing
11. Porky's pad
17. Cozy room
19. Huron, e.g.
22. Grizzly
24. Trembled
25. Yugoslavian leader
26. Perceives
27. Phone
28. "M*A*S*H" actor
30. Greek letter
31. Disclose
35. Heavy metal
41. Car model
42. Grease
44. Evade
46. Shreds
47. Abel's nephew
49. Rational
50. Hog
51. Groom's response
52. Morning mist
53. Obtain
55. Perfect number

PUZZLE 374

• BIRDS OF A FEATHER •

ACROSS
1. Vault
5. "What's up, ____?"
8. Trade
12. Great Lake
13. Cheer
14. Trim
15. Mountain lake
16. Jackie's second
17. Misfortunes
18. Hiatus
20. ____ clock
22. Guarantee
25. Actress Francis or Lenz
26. Braid
27. Part of MPG
28. Greek letter
31. Omen
32. Storage unit
33. Actor Penn
34. Lyric poem
35. Tavern order
36. Cognizant
37. Grippe
38. Forest openings
39. Baltimore athlete
42. Be unwell
43. Skirt type
44. ____ alai
46. Boys
50. Fruity drinks
51. Likely
52. Double-reed
    instrument
53. Take it easy
54. Affirmative answer
55. Proceeded

DOWN
1. Allow
2. Baseball stat.
3. Atmosphere
4. Batman's foe
5. Fall in folds
6. Paddle
7. Barnyard occupant
8. Tangy
9. Stroll
10. Woody's son
11. Mexican money
19. Actor Carney
21. Nasser's gp.
22. Lhasa ____
23. Slipped
24. Wise
27. Easy as ____
28. Scan
29. Tortoise's rival
30. Change for a five
32. Toronto athlete
33. Ingest
35. Everything
36. The Greatest
37. Impose fraudulently
38. Paces
39. Poet Khayyam
40. Astronaut Sally ____
41. March date
45. Primate
47. Lincoln's nickname
48. Put on
49. Matched group

CRYPTIC

British-style or cryptic crosswords are a great challenge for crossword fans. Each clue contains either a definition or direct reference to the answer, as well as a play on words. The numbers in parentheses indicate the number of letters in the answer word or words.

ACROSS

1. Spell nectar wrong (6)
4. Look at object boiling (8)
9. Saying what a cow says, about two times (5)
10. Bodily injured car-pooler (9)
11. Unassisted, capturing top gangster (8)
12. Arrest lunatic, or call (6)
14. Nautical speed puzzle (4)
15. Song of nutty Rhode Island lass (8)
19. Examiner agitated former serviceman (8)
20. Back news magazine issue (4)
23. One practicing medicine during winter nights (6)
25. Emphasized dinner sweets should be returned (8)
27. Get magazines regularly from ship writer (9)
28. Post office receives recently stolen picture (5)
29. Broadcasting one Bud ad was ample (8)
30. Answer about the Greek city (6)

DOWN

1. "Big" actor's polite remark about upcoming month (8)
2. Vegetable paintings I suppress (9)
3. Rough copy—pH changes (6)
5. Get near bananas (4)
6. Complete love in Norse god that's disgusting (8)
7. Perfect, I pass out the cards (5)
8. Georgia has folk tales aplenty (6)
10. Wild Etruscan horsemen (8)
13. Ms. Midler holds race with dark-haired lady (8)
16. Let in some punk rock (9)
17. A guy keeps Mr. Clapton in the U.S. (8)
18. Earnest ladies' man has debts (8)
21. Seat is rearranged for nap (6)
22. Pair of Democrats see tyrant (6)
24. Stick up hoops—that's not allowed (5)
26. Incorrectly file magazine (4)

PUZZLE 376

ACROSS

1. Mexican coin
5. Dawdling
9. Banner
13. Ice-cream thickener
14. Study hard
15. Certain Nicaraguans
17. Early Americans
19. Saunter
20. Query
21. Part of AD
22. Customs duty
23. French company: abbr.
24. Discussion group
26. Boston Tea Party, e.g.
29. Accuses of a crime
33. Saudis
34. Foretell
36. Surfeit
37. Fishhook part
38. Passover ritual
39. Lagomorph
40. Type of type: abbr.
41. _____ chic
42. Clear of the bottom
43. Bouquet
45. Primps
46. Needs of the "Mayflower"
48. Airport word: abbr.
49. Swallow
52. Juno's counterpart
54. Storage tank
57. Faint
58. Famous seamstress
60. Fishing net
61. Type of clarinet
62. Lamb's pen name
63. Winter toy
64. Author Paton
65. Decade unit

DOWN

1. South American rodent
2. Freudian selves
3. Vaccine doctor
4. Galleon's cargo
5. Type of harpsichord
6. Kind of shark
7. Lowest deck
8. Westrum or Craven
9. Mounted
10. City worker of yore
11. Early church desk
12. Dolls
16. Number unit
18. Fastens down
22. Circle or city beginner
23. Paving piece
25. Charges d'affaires
26. Israeli statesman
27. Shelley's Muse
28. Spanish lengths
30. Author Luce
31. Shroud of ____
32. "The Thirty-Nine ____"
34. Emerald
35. Keats work
38. Dye for wood
42. Regalia
44. Profited
45. Weems or Brown, e.g.
47. Conch
49. Writer's output: abbr.
50. Impresses deeply
51. Muddy
53. Singer James
54. Mouse's cousin
55. Area east of the Urals
56. Nicholas I
58. Cote sound
59. Spanish king

PUZZLE 377 — Slide-O-Gram

Place the seven words into the diagram, one word for each across line, so that one of the rows reading down will spell out a 7-letter word that is related to the others.

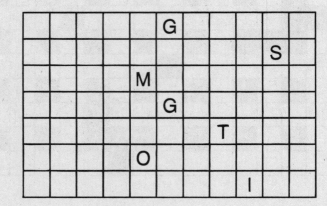

Colossal

Enormous

Giant

Gigantic

Huge

Mammoth

Towering

326

The diagram represents the sea which contains a crossword puzzle; the answer words are Battleships. The letter-number combination to the left of each clue indicates the location in the diagram where a Battleship has been hit (for example, A4 is in the first row, fourth column). A hit is any one of the letters in the answer word. Using this clue, you must determine the exact location of each answer and whether it is an across or a down word. Fill in black squares to separate words as in a regular crossword. We have filled in the answers to clues A1 and A4.

A1	Hindu garment	I10	Of the kidneys
A4	Drains	I13	Decade
A8	Frolic	I13	Fuming
A8	Intellect	J1	Older person
A12	Blemish	J9	Undersized ones
A12	Gather	J10	Paces
A14	Ponderous	J11	Not on tape
B3	Lily plant	J14	Removes from print
B6	Bad	K6	Black, to poets
B7	Eggs	K7	Nonpermanent resident
B11	Adjusted	K10	Rescue
B15	Waste time	K12	Pollute
C2	Grad	L1	Male turkey
C3	Fanfare	L3	Burrowing animal
C4	Certain liquors	L5	Most upstanding
C6	Rational	L6	Type of deer
C14	Rare gas	L8	Sayer and Genn
C15	"Auld Lang ____"	L13	Disfigure
D1	Hit with force		
D6	Renovates	L14	Layer
D10	Moist	M2	Rebelled
D13	Pond plant	M2	Spoken
D14	Astonishment	M8	Abbreviated skirt
E4	Bossy's sounds	M10	Heavenly place
E9	Implore	M13	Golf club
E11	Calendar item	M15	Remnants
E12	Time periods	N3	Gordon and Garnett
F3	Postulate	N4	Bishopric
F4	Til	N8	Tavern brews
F5	Composure	N9	Bottom line
F10	____ as a hatter	N12	Pb
F15	Ridicule	N13	Territory
G2	Palindromic sheep	O1	Touches
G6	Toggle	O1	Icy rain
G7	Cut off	O8	Missile housing
G13	Ventured	O9	Love excessively
H2	Once more than once	O14	Diner sign
H4	Car adjunct		
H4	Clinton's canal		
H9	Plan		
H14	Bargain event		
H15	First garden		
I1	Greek vowels		
I3	Wading bird		
I3	Oak starter		
I8	Gives		

	1	2	3	4	5	6	7	8	9	10	11	12	13	14	15
A	S	A	P	S	■										
B	A														
C	R														
D	I														
E	■														
F															
G															
H															
I															
J															
K															
L															
M															
N															
O															

PUZZLE 379

Not really double trouble, but double fun! Solve this puzzle as you would a regular crossword, EXCEPT place one, two, or three letters in each box. The number of letters in each answer is shown in parentheses after its clue.

ACROSS

1. Best qualified (6)
4. Zaire River, of yore (5)
7. Equals (7)
10. Prevaricator (4)
11. Stellar spectacular (4)
12. Anglo-Saxon drudge (4)
13. Hercules's ___ lion (6)
14. Court with song (8)
15. Stair part (5)
16. International city (6)
18. ___ floss (6)
20. Tease (4)
22. Craftsman (7)
24. Under the weather (6)
27. Faith (5)
29. Daub (5)
31. Enraptured (7)
32. Hold dear (7)
34. A ___ in time . . . (6)
36. Affirmative (3)
37. Movie houses (7)
39. Warming (7)
41. Tater type (7)
43. Plot (6)
45. Stew (6)
48. Backups (8)
49. Vinegary (6)
50. Wearying (6)
51. Intones (5)
52. Close firmly, anew (6)
53. Baltic people (5)

DOWN

1. Skirt style: hyph. (5)
2. Fault (5)
3. Alienate (8)
4. Tory creed (12)
5. Nine-day devotion (6)
6. Prodded (6)
7. Worldly doctrine (11)
8. Kasparov's game (5)
9. Derisive look (5)
17. Approach (4)
19. Involve (6)
20. Tic (6)
21. More accurate (5)
23. Most rational (6)
25. ___-gritty (5)
26. Hereditary units (5)
28. Tacky quality (10)
30. Of calculation (12)
33. Glisten (5)
35. Swindle (5)
38. Very one-sided contest (8)
40. Unappreciative ones (8)
41. Correction (7)
42. Food unit (7)
44. Model's word (6)
46. Circumference (5)
47. Day trips (7)

PUZZLE 380

Place the answer to clue 1 in the first space, drop a letter, and arrange the remaining letters to answer clue 2. Drop another letter and arrange the remaining letters to answer clue 3. The first dropped letter goes into the box to the left of space 1 and the second dropped letter goes into the box to the right of space 3. Follow this pattern for each row in the diagram. When completed, the letters on the left and right, reading down, will spell related words.

1. Lying flat
2. Candid
3. Long time
4. Greet
5. Slightest
6. Season
7. Chicken part
8. Long look
9. Take five
10. Angry lecture
11. Assessed
12. Palm fruit
13. Blackboard
14. Final
15. Posed
16. Smudges
17. Paper measures
18. Paddock mom

PUZZLE 381

• DRIVING START •

ACROSS

1. Diplomacy
5. Appetizer
9. Canadian ___
14. Culture medium
15. Melville work
16. Texas shrine
17. Stationary bells
19. Persian waterwheel
20. Audible acclaim
21. Thoroughly: 2 wds.
23. Rouen seasons
24. Wounded ___
25. Sibilant letter
26. Corner
29. Yemeni city
31. Oklahoma Indian
34. Seagoing brook trout
36. Solar disk
39. Color-play gem
41. Manchester measure
42. Complete: prefix
43. Assumed
44. Enjoy
46. Ride
47. Josip Broz
49. Princely Italian name
50. ESP gp.
52. Fruit drinks
54. Gets forty winks
58. Haughty one's creed
60. Scottish cake
63. Heavy gas
64. Pink
66. Metal bar
67. Redact
68. Successor of William and Mary
69. Senses
70. Advantage
71. Seethe

DOWN

1. Sonora snack
2. Sisal plant
3. 200 milligrams
4. Stale
5. Tommy Hitchcock's sport
6. Theban god
7. Style
8. Red dye
9. United
10. Liliaceous plant
11. Astronaut Scott
12. Skips
13. Webster et al.
18. Tilts
22. Dearest's kin
24. Ma and Pa of films
27. Gun cleaners
28. Gen. Robert ___: 2 wds.
30. Sup
31. She-swine
32. Milit. address
33. Charged shell
35. Ares's sister
37. Biblical judge
38. Beak
40. Waikiki wreath
45. Hair dye
48. Contaminates
50. Letter's cross stroke
51. Smoothing implement
53. Host
55. Architectural piers
56. Nub
57. High-tea biscuit
59. Hammer or sickle
60. Naval prison
61. Before: prefix
62. Was aware
65. Append

PYRAMID

PUZZLE 382

Here's a word pyramid you build by starting at the top. Each line across is a word in code, with the letters represented by symbols. Every word contains all the letters of the word in the line above it. One letter has been given to start you off.

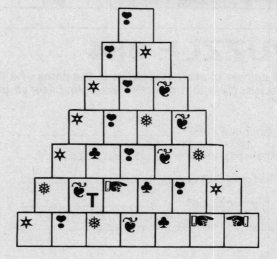

329

PUZZLE 383

ACROSS

1. Have feelings
5. Latin dance
10. Umpires' calls
14. Elevator man
15. TV's "F ___"
16. Cut
17. Price
18. Sun-dried brick
19. Notion
20. Telephone-company employees
22. Fortunetellers
23. Maple genus
24. Contented sound
25. Litters' littlest
27. Shows affection
31. Melodies
32. Snoops
33. Headwear
34. Undressed
35. In a happy way
36. Like an owl
37. Dined
38. Stories
39. "The Taming of the ___"
40. Goes onstage
42. Bides one's time
43. Carpentry tools
44. Crones
45. ___ America
47. Exaggerate
52. Actor Thicke
53. Fair-haired
54. Fibber
55. Mailed
56. Actress Faye
57. Author Ferber
58. Koppel and Turner
59. Burdened
60. From ___ to riches

DOWN

1. Ms. Chanel
2. Resting on
3. Shine's partner
4. Alienate
5. Texas and Utah
6. Passion
7. Strand
8. Newhart and Barker
9. Imitate
10. Willow trees
11. Chest covering
12. Row
13. Health resorts
21. Play parts
22. Takes to court
24. Victim
25. Path
26. Comprehend
27. Weeps
28. Is sick
29. Relaxes
30. Hearty meat dish
31. Ginger cookie
32. Florida tree
35. Long-nosed fish
36. Painter James
38. "Our ___"
39. Droops
41. Swoons
42. Prison figure
44. Therefore
45. Final
46. Toward shelter
47. Spanish pot
48. Null and ___
49. Verdi opera
50. Strong taste
51. Historical periods
53. French dance

PUZZLE 384   DROP-OUTS

The answer to each clue below is the name of a famous person whose initials have been replaced with asterisks (*) in that clue. For example: base*all g*eat (baseBall gReat) — Initials B.R. — is Babe Ruth.

1. Stumbling *omi* _____
2. H*wkeye portr*yer _____
3. Cha*pion he*vyweight _____
4. *-*ay command*r _____
5. Ameri*an *efense lawyer _____
6. *i* bandleader _____
7. He *ade "*lazing Saddles" _____
8. *artoon *oy _____
9. *uddled TV *ousewife _____
10. TV *ditor Lou Gr*nt _____

PUZZLE 385

• TWOSOMES •

ACROSS

1. Grates
6. Sorrow
9. Diva Nellie
14. "____ Ben Jonson!"
15. Annex
16. Neighborhoods
17. Biblical pair
20. Integral part
21. Vehement
22. Lowest RAF rank
23. Ten: prefix
24. Shadowbox
27. Cognizant
29. Malt drink
33. Hockey great
34. Persia, today
35. Ointment
36. Mythical pair
40. Decorate
41. Tragic king
42. Ike's monogram
43. Ilk
44. Lance
46. Convene
47. Char
48. Old car
50. Add sugar
54. 9 Across, e.g.
58. Fictional pair
60. Red dye
61. Extinct bird
62. Hindu social division
63. Hebrew months
64. ____ of the covenant
65. Kilmer poem

DOWN

1. Teased
2. Asian sea
3. Except
4. Schoolbook
5. Jewish feast
6. Poverty
7. Peculiar
8. More nervous
9. Mediterranean island
10. Buffalo's lake
11. Spare
12. Belfry residents
13. Tennis great
18. Capital of Turkey
19. Formerly
23. Baby bouncer
24. Fountain treats
25. Spanish national museum
26. Suit of mail
28. Pale
29. ____ humbug!
30. Skip over a vowel
31. Sidestep
32. Change an alarm
34. Motel
35. Liner abbr.

37. Food scrap
38. Coal size
39. River to the Tweed
44. Spots
45. Central American land
46. ____ and pestle
47. British guns
49. Difference between solar and lunar years
50. ____ butter
51. Actress Natalie
52. Actress Martinelli
53. Arab prince
54. Coyote State: abbr.
55. African fox
56. Musical symbol
57. "The Defiant ____"
59. And not

CRYPTO-LIMERICK

PUZZLE 386

To read this humorous verse, you must first decode it as you would a regular cryptogram (other letters are substituted for the correct ones).

```
SK WHYOLN, PRE'T I TROGROHN LISON TIS,

TCEBO I FETCBK KEALM GONYMHOON HIS;

    DAC TEEL RO PIT FIAMRC,

    ILN FRIHMOT POHO DHEAMRC

WEH CIVYLM I TROOG EL CRO BIS.
```

PUZZLE 387

ACROSS

1. "The World According to ___"
5. Lost color
10. Heehaw
14. Wings
15. Actress Ryan
16. Go afield
17. Touch down
18. Irish patriot Robert
19. Begin
20. Autumn flowers
22. Bucks
24. Building location
26. Exclamation of surprise
27. Summer game
31. Pantry
35. Hawaiian dances
36. Lugs
38. Actress Charlotte
39. List abbr.
40. Miser's joy
41. Canape item
42. "Daily" workers: abbr.
43. Domicile, for short
44. Clocked
45. Hearth tools
47. Cocktails
49. Proverbial seven
51. Do usher's work
52. Backpacker's abodes: 2 wds.
56. Makeup mistake
60. ___ Canal
61. Ruth's mother-in-law
63. Bagel, e.g.
64. Recede
65. Son of Jacob
66. Epochs
67. Close noisily
68. Sparkled
69. Actress Thompson

DOWN

1. Festive
2. Woeful word
3. Rave's mate
4. Idol's spot
5. Arizona bowl
6. Give weapons
7. Certain pols
8. Foe
9. Itemized
10. Wall Street worker
11. Lariat
12. Swear to
13. Cravings
21. Teases
23. Auditors: abbr.
25. Rock star John
27. Ewes
28. Surpass
29. Hip bottle
30. Packs
32. Stage play
33. Dinner guest
34. Rex and Willis
37. Three, to Pierre
40. Words of praise
41. Imagines
43. Montana Indian
44. Crew
46. High regard
48. Streetcar name
50. Secrete
52. Church benches
53. Russian mountain range
54. ___ colada
55. NYC area
57. Dumb ___
58. Delighted
59. Actress Lanchester
62. Brando film, with "The"

PUZZLE 388

ALL FOURS

How many 4-letter words can you find in the diagram by moving from letter to adjacent letter up, down, forward, backward, and diagonally? A letter may be used more than once in a word, but only after leaving it and coming back. Foreign words, abbreviations, and words beginning with a capital letter are not permitted.

YOUR WORD LIST

332

PUZZLE 389

ACROSS

1. Pueblo Indian
5. Pain
9. Italia's capital
13. Arabian gulf
14. Sketched
15. Cut apart
16. Tattled
17. Desert feature
18. Prevent
19. Held back
21. Goes to bed
23. Walking aids
25. Be under the weather
26. Oxidized
29. Heavy stream
33. Poker play
34. Scandinavian
35. Source of metal
37. Bound
38. Epoch
39. Among
40. Sault ____ Marie
41. Cuisine type
43. Speed contest
44. Obliterating
46. Prison official
48. Small amount
49. Make happy
51. Belittles
55. "____ Fidelis"
58. Strike out
59. Other
61. Beginner
63. Goes by taxi
64. Cake layer
65. Singer Adams
66. Loch ____ monster
67. Towel word
68. Antlered animal

DOWN

1. Tam or beret
2. Scent
3. Soccer great
4. Accused of a crime
5. Part of a sum
6. Rough
7. Barnyard sight
8. Pitcher
9. Speak abusively
10. Concluded
11. Scant
12. Music and painting
15. Parody
20. Highland negative
22. Corn units
24. Silo function
26. Rodents
27. Bring together
28. Guide
30. Algerian seaport
31. Rover
32. Moment
34. Berliner's no
36. First address
39. Stopped
41. Dramatic comments
42. Location
45. Awaits
46. They walk in water
47. Consumed
50. Light beam
51. "Family Plot" star Bruce ____
52. Nobelist Wiesel
53. Divests
54. Adam's third son
56. Ocean movement
57. Great Lake
60. Falsehood
62. Byron's above

Stars and Arrows

PUZZLE 390

Start at the square marked "S" and move through the diagram to the square marked "F." An arrow in a square indicates the direction you must take; a star allows you to move in any direction horizontally or vertically, but not diagonally. No turns are allowed in the blank squares. You do not have to pass through all the squares.

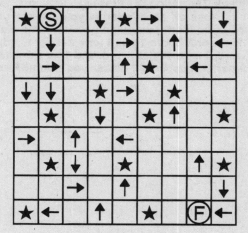

PUZZLE 391

ACROSS

1. Paw part
4. Haydn's sobriquet
8. Demonstration
12. "____ Day Will Come"
13. Happening
15. Charge
16. The Gay Nineties, e.g.
17. Soft, in music
18. Edmonton player
19. Vicki Lawrence part
21. Tow
22. Make amends
23. Informal language
25. Bridge feats
27. Nevertheless
29. River animals
34. Circle part
37. Jousting weapons
41. Auditorium sign
42. Move on wheels
44. Intended
45. Loosen
46. To shelter
47. Sell
49. Common gull
50. Prior to
52. Shrill bark
54. Cupid's weapon?
58. Divulges
62. Prestidigitation
66. Blue flag
68. Gather
69. Avoid
70. Whittles
72. Affirmative vote
73. Lawn pests
74. Harden oneself
75. Torrent
76. Has bills
77. Vortex
78. Behave humanly

DOWN

1. Verses
2. Pertaining to the ear
3. Serious theater
4. Vivacity
5. Eager
6. Certain cuts of gems
7. Record of a single year
8. Narrow cut
9. Aura
10. Harbinger
11. Existed
14. Roman dress
15. Crow
20. "____ Bonds Today"
24. Coagulate
26. Primarily
28. Fix
30. Football holder
31. Quiz
32. Get up
33. Goulash
34. Semite
35. Play part
36. Staff symbol
38. By birth
39. Bounder
40. Terminate
43. Lion constellation
48. Corrode
51. Tears
53. By means of
55. Van Winkle and Torn
56. Talk pompously
57. Telegraphed
59. Landlord's contract
60. Coat
61. Asparagus unit
62. Notice
63. Declare openly
64. Brisk wind
65. March date
67. Sow
71. Crafty

PUZZLE 392

Home Runs

Score Home Runs by forming 5-letter words starting and ending at home plate. Select a home-plate letter and write it over the first answer blank. Then choose a first-base letter for the second blank, and so on. Cross off each letter as you use it. If you can only form a 2-, 3-, or 4-letter word, go back to home plate and start your next word. Score 1 point for a 2-letter word, 2 for a 3-letter word, 3 for a 4-letter word, and 4 for a 5-letter Home Run. A perfect score of 20 makes you a Home Run champion.

HOME PLATE

334

CODEWORD

Codeword is a special crossword puzzle in which conventional clues are omitted. Instead, answer words in the diagram are represented by numbers. Each number represents a different letter of the alphabet, and all of the letters of the alphabet are used. When you are sure of a letter, put it in the code key chart for easy reference. Three letters have been given to start you off.

1	14
2	15
3 **A**	16
4	17
5	18
6	19
7	20
8	21
9	22 **M**
10	23
11	24
12	25
13	26 **N**

Puzzle 393 grid:

11	19	22 **M**	3 **A**	26 **N**		5	19	18	26	10	1	13
3			23			1		26		13		1
25	23	12	13	3	26	24		9	21	23	16	16
1		13		16				3		21		3
9	20	23	1	16	17		9	23	7	1		15
		1			19			17				1
8	18	14	14		1	2	1		11	23	26	17
20				6		16			22			
3		4	18	23	7		22	18	22	12	16	1
13		18		26				9		18		26
10	19	23	26	10		3	10	1	16	1	9	9
1		21		16		21			1			18
17	1	9	8	1	26	24		3	10	23	16	1

CODEWORD

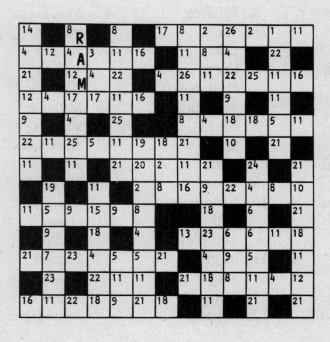

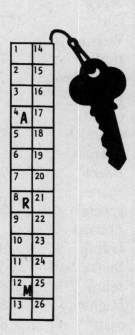

1	14
2	15
3	16
4 **A**	17
5	18
6	19
7	20
8 **R**	21
9	22
10	23
11	24
12 **M**	25
13	26

335

PUZZLE 395

ACROSS

1. Irish clan
5. Saunas
10. Before, at sea
15. —— the board
18. "—— Grows in Brooklyn": 2 wds.
19. Chutes
20. Magician's word
21. Tombstone
22. Wyoming mountains
23. Spoil a plan: 3 wds.
26. Gaelic
27. Sault —— Marie
28. Girl
29. Writing tablets
32. —— Deco
34. Paper quantity
36. A Smith
40. Actress Brent
41. Store special
43. Actress Irving
44. Basketball team
45. Highway-man
47. Musical composi-tion
51. Horse fathers
52. Chant
53. Waste allowance
54. Crab and monkey
56. Wilde, e.g.
57. Enjoy
59. California fort
60. Overflowed
64. Prong
65. Make a choice
69. Antoinette of France
70. Castle and Dunne
72. Shows scorn
73. Algerian city
74. Work at
75. Lithogra-pher James
77. Grassy place
78. Criminal group
79. Stout and porter
81. Actress Claire
82. Colorer
83. Of flying
85. Goddess of dawn
87. Fly high
90. Chance of a lifetime: 2 wds.
96. Something counted
97. Practical
98. Cubic meters
100. Special ability
101. Tears
102. Albania's capital
103. Kills
104. Precipitous
105. Method: abbr.

DOWN

1. Tree fluid
2. Beige
3. Kind of school
4. Pitches
5. Wild party
6. Certify
7. Halloween alternative
8. Right-hand man
9. Ooze
10. Guinness and Templeton
11. In great shape: 4 wds.
12. Aroma
13. Budget item
14. Kind of curve
16. Eng. money
17. Tipplers
19. Like a sauna
24. River duck
25. South American animals
29. Elfin being
30. Bard's river
31. IOU
33. Takes a breather
35. Consume
37. Dreadful
38. Declare to be true
39. Disarray
41. Feeble
42. Mountain ridge
46. Kegler's milieu: 2 wds.
48. Make a speech
49. American composer
50. Make amends
51. Noise makers?
55. Armed band
58. Varnish ingredient

60. Environmental woe
61. Medic or meter
62. Neighbor of Turkey
63. Marshal Matt
66. Slippery
67. Algonquian
68. Despot

71. Dark bread
74. Mom or Dad
76. Immense
80. Group of seven
81. Tristram's love
82. Laundry appliances
84. Paradises
86. Suppose

88. Eject
89. Against
90. Aim
91. Large-mouthed jar
92. Belonging to us
93. Individual: abbr.

94. Salver
95. Deep longings
96. Main ideas: abbr.
99. Convened

PUZZLE 396

ACROSS

1. Cut (off)
4. Hubbub
8. Pain
12. Stumble
16. Hearing organ
17. Silly
18. Deceive
19. Assistant
20. Salutations!
22. Gingko, e.g.
23. Flatfish
24. Leak
25. Mature
27. Expert
29. Motion picture
30. Speed-check device
31. Only
32. Trundle and bunk
33. Destined
34. Finish
38. Porter
39. Creates
40. Dixie
41. Negative vote
42. Johnson of "Miami Vice"
43. Chill
44. Astonishes
45. Shoot
46. Joined
48. Begin
49. Muffled
50. Mesh
51. Athletic game
52. Brooch
53. Nudges
56. Animated
57. Blame
61. Runs into
62. Jet
63. Tint
64. Bishop's domain
65. Anger
66. Jogs
67. Coarse grain
69. Stitch
70. Refers to
72. Snow vehicles
73. Allows
74. Selvage
75. Tantalize
76. Metal containers
77. Angle
80. Colossal
81. Mukluk or chukka
82. Greedy
83. Speck
85. Art Buchwald, for one
89. Spouse
90. Female horse
91. Wear away
92. Feasted
93. Implored
94. Hurried
95. Jells
96. Soap ingredient

DOWN

1. Limb
2. Paddle
3. George C. Scott TV role
4. Bit
5. Beach color
6. Unappreciative person
7. Dwells
8. Following
9. Maize
10. Garden tool
11. Wind and rain, e.g.
12. Pendant
13. Revelry
14. Dawdle
15. Equal
17. Detail
21. Congers
26. Tablet
28. Curved opening
29. Criminal
30. Did an autumn chore
31. Ascend
32. Commanded
33. Aspect
34. Tribunal
35. One
36. Venture
37. Watched
39. Bogs down
40. Glare
44. Heater
45. Resource
47. Terminates
48. Twirls
49. Coal pits
51. Louvers

52. Sulks
53. Prudish
54. Infrequent
55. Augury
56. Solitary
57. Reproach
58. Necessary
59. Contests
60. Current events

62. Agendas
66. Ocean movement
67. Glimpses
68. Rebuild
71. Cared for
72. Black or Red
73. Jungle king
75. Clocked

76. Volume
77. Bivouac
78. Egg-shaped
79. Ceremony
80. Gusset
81. Young flowers

84. Hit lightly
86. Parcel
87. Pigpen
88. Type of shirt

PUZZLE 396

PUZZLE 397

ACROSS

1. Straddled
7. German river
12. Minnow
18. Believe
19. Trickle
20. Harangue
21. Flower cluster
22. Textile fiber
23. Overjoyed
24. Brink
25. Rye disease
27. Prevent
29. Choler
30. Unites
32. Roman date
34. Andy Capp's order
35. Sacred
36. "____ With the Enemy"
38. Strokes
40. Indian princess
41. Grade
42. Roofing material
43. Exclamation of triumph
44. Breezy
47. Light
48. Expense
52. Help with the dishes
53. Biotic prefix
54. Gal of song
55. Ticket holder's guarantee
56. Salamander
57. Indemnification
61. RR stop
62. Lily genus
64. Guitarist Turner
65. Single
66. Mitosis structure
68. Performs
70. ____ accompli
71. Sulkers
72. Chemical suffix
73. Pitch
74. Reminder
75. Conspires
78. Fertilizer
79. Depressed pressers?
83. Sweetheart
84. Pale
85. Ukrainian seaport
87. Authentic
88. Snake
89. Deadly
91. Senses
93. Actor Holm
94. General Putnam
96. Islamic spirit
98. Mean
100. Tease
101. Turn inside out
102. Rap session?
103. Clandestine meetings
104. Formal procedures
105. Frame for stretching cloth

DOWN

1. Put the ____ on
2. Go abroad
3. Ebb
4. Pindaric work
5. Thin coin
6. Forever
7. Concentrated
8. Babble
9. Lip
10. English essayist
11. Raise
12. Cordwood measure
13. Sword handle
14. Babylonian war god
15. Country
16. Swimmer Gertrude ____
17. Rotgut
26. Ruined
28. Overhead railways
31. Slaves
33. Incorporeally
35. Sunken fences
37. Caesar's father
39. Nevada city
40. Zodiac sign
42. South American monkey
43. Nimbus
44. Dismal
45. Winchester, e.g.
46. Author Chekhov
47. Put into the pot
48. Irish house of Parliament
49. "Beau ____"
50. Restaurant patron
51. Excels
53. Inquires

54. Immediately, to Marcus Welby

58. Erin

59. Part

60. Ruth's mother-in-law

63. Corrects

67. Fun

69. Flanders and Platt

70. Coniferous tree

71. Olympic winner

73. Brightly colored bird

74. Pal

75. Grievance

76. Actress Louise ____

77. Fish hawk

78. Tangled mass

79. Icy rains

80. East

81. Shade

82. Mailer

84. Cambria, today

86. Conflagrant

89. Hat material

90. Claude ____-Strauss

92. Dirk

95. Public notices

97. Butterfly catcher

99. Beach shade

PUZZLE 398

ACROSS

1. Boston ____
5. Arab cloak
8. Half-pints
12. Gentle as ____
17. Throw off
18. Paving substance
19. Again
20. Hindu gown
21. Go up
22. Cereal grain
23. Greek meeting-place
24. Actor Daniel ____
25. Famous exhortation, with 80 Across
29. Bakery offerings
30. "____ Haw"
31. Singer Lesley ____
32. Stroke
35. Not high
36. Mister
37. Hairpiece
40. Skirt style
41. Auto
42. Brusque
43. ____ avis
44. 1977 AL MVP, with 71 Across
45. Reward
46. Back talk
47. Sand ridges
48. Small Old World ruminant
51. Classify
52. Curved bone
53. Source of 25 and 80 Across
58. Made of: suff.
59. Standard
60. Fog
62. ____ nova
65. Escapade
66. Singer Tillis
67. Call ____ day
68. Sooty
69. Red plant
70. Shooting marble
71. See 44 Across
73. Social
74. Actor Lahr
75. Singer Johnnie
76. Soup server
77. The Bee ____
78. Poetic contraction
79. Jetty
80. See 25 Across
87. Strange
88. Hardens
89. Tolkien creature
90. River deposit
92. Dentist's command
93. Ylang-ylang
94. Sault ____ Marie
95. Andrews Sisters, e.g.
96. Prodded
97. Congressmen: abbr.
98. Craggy hill
99. Fill up

DOWN

1. ____ annum
2. Leave out
3. Fiddlesticks!
4. Make more precipitous
5. Expiates
6. Idols
7. Showy
8. Nut
9. Loosen
10. Underling
11. Blusters
12. Declare
13. Shaping machine
14. ____ code
15. TV's Griffin
16. Part of NB
26. French city
27. Norse deity
28. Habit
32. Singer Vikki
33. Reserved
34. "Easy ____"
35. Deposit eggs
36. Energy
37. Having an unnatural pallor
38. Erin: abbr.
39. Empty talk
41. Rockabilly pioneer Perkins
42. Billiards shot
43. Country bumpkins
45. Short dog, for short
46. Regretful

47. Aria singer
49. Oxeye
50. Sicilian city
51. Snub
52. Virginia dance
54. Cove
55. Spurt forth
56. French river
57. Pupil given extra help
61. Hock
62. Tool for 44 Across
63. Full of: suff.
64. Wild sheep
65. Keeps trying
66. Spring month
69. Suds
70. O'Hara home
71. Pool tools
72. Nabs
74. Hit on the head
75. Della and Pee Wee
76. Giggle
77. Canadian flyers
78. Repeatedly
79. Horse
80. Cover
81. Hodgepodge
82. Rat
83. Withered
84. Sleep
85. Italian bread, once?
86. Dash
91. Hallux

PUZZLE 399

ACROSS

1. Engage-ments
6. "Saturday Night ——"
11. Kind of music
16. Chemical group prefix
17. Come up
18. Thespians
20. Star of 6 Across: 2 wds.
22. Harass
23. Cuckoo
24. Took long steps
25. Severinsen et al.
27. Geological period
28. Budget item
30. Before, in poems
31. Of great breadth
32. Sea birds
33. Cartoonist Gardner
34. Printers' measures
35. Music source
36. Free ticket
37. Russian river
39. "They're Playing Our ——"
40. Ital. island
41. Amaze
44. Rhythm
45. Lively one
49. Flings
50. Person on the move
51. Play a record
52. Actress Charlotte
53. Suit to ——: 2 wds.
54. Place to blend music: 2 wds.
56. Home of the Leaning Tower
57. Blue Eagle inits.
58. Speedy
59. Become limp
60. Located
61. —— it! (wake up!): 2 wds.
63. Pedestal part
64. "The ——" (Van McCoy tune)
65. Single
66. Stir up
67. Price
68. Seldom seen
70. Take a look
71. Explosive noise
72. Donkey
75. Interval
76. Tiny particle
77. Equip
78. Rung
80. Eggs
81. Military gp.
82. Escargots
85. Hail!
86. '60s dance
88. "Do the ——" (Rufus Thomas song): 2 wds.
91. Slanted
92. Banish
93. Laundromat equipment
94. Playground item
95. Rodeo performer
96. Kernels

DOWN

1. Hummer
2. Glowing
3. Perfect number
4. Tolkien creatures
5. Arrange
6. Indulges
7. Wear away
8. Nasty
9. Superlative ending
10. Pa. city
11. Emulate Patrick Swayze
12. Frosts a cake
13. Sault —— Marie
14. Cryptog-raphers
15. Synthetic fabrics
16. Slightly open
19. D.C. legislators
21. Stadium
26. Not even
29. Snarl
31. Desire
32. Work hard for
34. First lady
35. Atlantic City attraction
36. Ache
38. Overhead trains
39. Observed
40. Do the Australian crawl
41. Indian hemp plant
42. Bizarre
43. Terrific
44. Boxing match
45. Espy
46. Grain for the mill
47. Artist's tripod
48. Novelist Charles
50. Golly!
51. Han ——
54. Fill
55. Joy ——

56. Ziti and vermicelli
58. Excellent
60. "—— Stop"
62. Sported
63. Per ——
64. In what way
66. Present again
67. Jay Leno, e.g.
68. Competitors

69. Powerful explosive
70. School gp.
71. Entreaty
73. Put up the money
74. Cuts
75. Pulls
76. Stage direction
77. Foot part

79. Enclosures
81. Secondhand
82. Quick cut
83. Certain degs.
84. King's title
87. News

service: abbr.
89. Wifely prefix
90. Co., in Cannes

345

PUZZLE 400

ACROSS

1. Northern native
5. Bottle tops
9. Primrose ——
13. Penpoints
17. Befuddled
18. Newspaper column, for short
19. Molding
20. Siouan Indian
21. Encircled
22. Allot
23. Lasting
25. Petty ruler
27. Attempted
29. "The Night of the ——"
30. Wee bits
32. Dawn goddess
33. Greek letters
34. "The French ——"
37. Exhausted
41. Tarzan's companion
42. Short jackets
43. Get washed up
44. Possess, in Glasgow
45. Outlet
47. Brother-hood: abbr.
48. Former First Lady
49. Spanish abode
50. Door sign
52. Author Runyon
54. Like some animals
56. "Brave —— World"
58. Rooms in 49 Across
60. Unit of work
61. Squealer
65. Capital of Oregon
67. Like some music
71. Sightsee
72. In the future
74. —— de deux
76. Storm
77. Classifieds
78. Garden tool
79. GI locker item
81. Grab hold of
82. Soda-pop men
84. RR cargos: 2 wds.
86. River of England
87. Pedro's river
88. Concerning
89. Biblical strongman
92. Threadbare
94. Speaks
97. Life
99. Bambi et al.
101. Wings
102. She, in Paris
103. Official approval
104. Breaks bread
105. Stare open-mouthed
106. Rind
107. Places
108. Mild oath
109. Guesses at: abbr.

DOWN

1. Falls behind
2. —— Minor
3. Relevant
4. Theater angel
5. Some cars
6. Mr. Burrows
7. English statesman
8. Sound systems, for short
9. Paul and Pius
10. Like good cheese
11. Gerard —— Borch
12. Half a globe
13. Failure to utilize
14. Willow
15. German city on the Rhine
16. Bristle
24. Spry
26. To ——: 2 wds.
28. Charged particle
31. Tolerated
33. Small: Fr.
34. Spelunk-er's delight
35. Golf event
36. Ancient Peruvians
37. Stop up
38. Better late —— never
39. Relaxation
40. —— Sea
43. Trite
46. Choir member
48. Tooth
49. Stogy
51. Aunt or uncle: abbr.
53. Modern beam
55. Sculpture, for one
57. The frontier

59. Brown tint
61. Take a —— at
62. Fuss: hyph.
63. Eject
64. Tidal bore
66. Craze
68. Smoking items
69. Hoople's oath
70. Society girls
73. Your, in France
75. A.M. sight
78. Mary Ann Evans
79. Spurred
80. Agent's forte
83. Garment ornament
84. One kind of score
85. Electrical failure
87. Spins
89. Ooze
90. Car part
91. A —— a minute
92. Word to kitty
93. Calendar measure
95. Entranced
96. Bishoprics
98. Formerly named
100. Timetable abbr.

PUZZLE 401

ACROSS

1. Boat canvas, for short
5. Thunder sound
9. Cheshire Cat look
13. Greek portico
17. Double-reed instrument
18. Baltic port
19. Meander
20. Scorch
21. Kipling route: 3 wds.
24. Take five
25. "Hurry ——" (1967 film)
26. Mr. Sedaka
27. Out of sorts
28. Top
29. —— Fein
30. Infuse
32. Badger's kin
35. King's better
36. Pottery fragment
38. Noah's boat
41. Grunts
42. Line of cliffs
44. Bible book
45. "—— man can tether time or tide" (Burns)
46. Even score
47. Goblet part
48. Map addition
50. Eng. river
51. Indiana native
53. Tiff
54. Gretel's brother
56. Pina-colada base
57. The —— Pass
60. Old English letter
61. Vast plain
64. "Dies ——"
65. Sculler
69. Flight records
70. Tanning shrub
72. Weak
73. Dijon donkey
74. GI's address
75. To be, to Jean
76. Piano wood
78. Pear-shaped fruits
79. See 2 Down
80. English novelist
82. Conclusion
83. Czech patriot
84. Spin
86. Tea flower
88. Govt. agcy.
89. Discharges
91. Sulk
92. Tied
96. Bank deal
97. Hope-Crosby route: 3 wds.
100. Writer Bagnold
101. Clare Boothe ——
102. Telephone line
103. Spanish measure
104. Like a moray
105. Perches
106. Bandy words
107. Formerly, once

DOWN

1. Craggy hills
2. Hunt poem, with 79 Across and "Adhem"
3. Horse of a certain color
4. Sells
5. Throng
6. Depict
7. Moslem chief
8. Basket
9. Iotas
10. Bun
11. Marsh elder
12. French marshal
13. Fallen rock
14. Pirate route: 3 wds.
15. Hops drier
16. Affected
22. Travail
23. Bear's lair
27. Spreads to dry
29. Swindle
30. Ditto
31. Pledge
32. Dr. West-heimer
33. Exchange discount
34. Parkman's route: 3 wds.
35. Bitter
37. Speed
39. Seldom found
40. Hull part
42. Fr. holy woman: abbr.
43. Ship's boat
47. Dolt
49. Innings number
50. Workers
52. Dines
53. Antitoxins
55. High nest
58. Frosted
59. Circular

61. Chunk
62. Small shark
63. Fragrant compound
66. —— old thing
67. Orleans cherub
68. Headland
71. Asian river
72. Corn cake
75. Sister of Ares
77. Imparts
78. Gay
81. Eats away
83. Tito
85. "Peter Pan" girl
87. Absent
88. —— sanctum
89. Abscond
90. Glaucus's love
91. Covenant
92. Arctic Sea arm
93. Ski lift: hyph.
94. Otic organs
95. Mild expletive
97. Literary inits.
98. Arles affirmative
99. Vim

PUZZLE 402

ACROSS

1. Constrictors
5. Morning moisture
8. Nonsense
12. Writer Whitman
16. English queen
17. Nimbus
18. Jalopy
19. On the sheltered side
20. Anatomical canal
21. "Don Juan" writer: 2 wds.
23. Throw
24. "The Vision of Sir Launfal" writer
26. Aquatic mammal
27. Emily Dickinson, e.g.
29. Lunchtime
31. Stowe book
33. Kin: abbr.
34. Be a hostess
37. Irish parliament
39. Sierra ——
43. Danish island
44. At no time
47. Doctors' charges

49. Coagulate
50. Actor Murray
52. Emulate
54. Trusted
57. Scoff
59. More agreeable
61. Trusted
62. Sudden police visit
64. Jeans
66. Nashville's locale: abbr.
67. Prayer book
69. V-shaped fortification
71. Dollars and ——
74. Ransomed
76. Make merry
78. FDR's mother
79. —— Chech
80. Remitted
82. Calyx leaf
84. Do embroidery
85. "Mr. —— Goes to Town"
88. Raced
90. Disconcerts
92. Be under the weather
94. Potato
96. Sonnet subject
97. Neighbor of Germany

101. "A Narrative of Adventures in the South Seas"
103. Ebb
107. Mucilage
108. "Tristram of Lyonesse" writer
111. Wedding cake layer
112. Stunning blow
113. Frilly fabric
114. Germ
115. Evangelist Roberts
116. Mining tools
117. Potato buds
118. Nationality suffix
119. Director Clair

DOWN

1. Money for release
2. In the know about
3. Once more
4. Placid
5. Twosome
6. Sins
7. Got one's feet wet
8. Laurel herb: 2 wds.
9. "—— Mutual Friend"
10. Organ valve

11. Public esteem
12. Bird's double chin
13. Tropical lily
14. Minus
15. Hardy heroine
17. Everywhere: 2 wds.
22. Minstrel
25. Cut of pork
28. Lamprey
30. "The Rosary" composer
32. Came to an end
34. Pillages
35. "Exile of ——"
36. "Kubla Khan" writer
38. Suggestive look
40. "Reflections on an Icebreaker" writer: 2 wds.
41. Lack
42. Days of yore
45. Machiavellian
46. Fast snake
48. Small barracuda
51. Rent
53. Crowbar
55. Generated power: abbr.
56. Dressed to the ——

58. Diva Stevens
60. Carnival attractions
63. Soggy
65. Rescue
67. Pond
68. Grazing lands
70. Himalayan monarchy
72. Genealogy diagram
73. Proverbs
74. Vermilion
75. Pickpockets
77. Slaved
81. Testifies
83. Wash
86. Library stamps
87. Baronet's title
89. Stupid
91. Combat zone
93. Hosiery thread
95. Extinguish
97. Curious
98. Hypercoracoid bone
99. Took to court
100. Not at home
102. Smeltery raw materials
104. Irish newspaper
105. Doyen
106. First name in mysteries
109. Bar rocks
110. Wedding announcement word

PUZZLE 403

ACROSS

1. Stare blankly
5. Payment
8. Outdo
12. Pitcher
13. Generation
14. Healing plant
15. Small dogs
17. Money vault
18. Conjunction
19. Contaminates
21. Paddle
24. Shoemaker's tools
25. Firm
26. Criticize
27. Second son of Noah
30. Bright
31. One's equals
32. Took food
33. Author Talese
34. Fat
35. Masters
36. Stable youth
37. Abounds
38. Give away
41. Polite address
42. Chimps
43. Ghouls
48. Printed matter
49. Self-respect
50. Exclusive
51. Picnic spoilers
52. Lower limb
53. Weight

DOWN

1. Understand
2. Terrify
3. For each
4. Task
5. Nourish
6. Goof
7. Towards a certain direction
8. Foundation
9. Verve
10. Plush
11. Mounds
16. Printing liquid
20. Donations
21. Type of rug
22. Dad
23. Eccentric
24. Warning signal
26. Water surface position
27. Rabbit's relative
28. Small bit
29. Military meal
31. Conspiracy
35. Spoil
36. Flings
37. Point
38. Statistics
39. Candid
40. Afterward
41. Air problem
44. The ___ of Aquarius
45. Lobster spawn
46. Gnome
47. Duet

ACROSS

1. Risks money
5. Box
9. Ethical
10. Telegrams
12. Crave
13. Buck's feature
15. Classify
16. Dowel
18. Roof projection
19. Fuss
20. Platform
22. Bill's film buddy
23. Seat
25. Bank employees
27. Dory stick
29. Fish eggs
30. Dominate
34. Skins
38. Jackie's second husband
39. Dish
41. Bat wood
42. Untruths
44. Caustic substance
45. Contribute a share
46. Find
48. Sturdy
50. At no time
51. Beef animal
52. Adjusts
53. Rabbit ____ (antennae)

DOWN

1. Capital of Massachusetts
2. Cleveland's lake
3. Old salt
4. Dozed off
5. Strut
6. Fastener
7. Comedian Johnson
8. Tell
9. Union general
11. Cut off
12. Dreary
14. Cincinnati nine
17. Break a fast
20. Pointed
21. Wed in secret
24. Portable bed
26. Pasture
28. Skate wheels
30. Beckon
31. Hunter constellation
32. Female relatives
33. Place
35. Stoves
36. Chemical compound
37. Tool storage building
40. Concise
43. Preserve
45. Ripening agent
47. Asian holiday
49. Actress Hagen

PUZZLE 405

ACROSS
1. Encountered
4. Kind of race
8. Fellow
12. Monkey
13. Fence
14. Shoestring
15. Entertainer Liza ___
17. Hunch
18. Genuine
19. Cruise of "Rain Man"
21. Strive
22. Shelved
26. Not lean
29. Each
30. "___ Got Sixpence"
31. All right
32. Ingot
33. Understood
34. Provide with equipment
35. Feast on
36. Cautious
37. Naval rank
39. "___ Hur"
40. Angler's need
41. Dismiss from work temporarily
45. Prince Charles's sport
48. Cute
50. Middle Eastern country
51. Hired thug
52. Electric ___
53. Turner and Kennedy
54. Finishes
55. However

DOWN
1. "I Remember ___"
2. Narrative poem
3. Camper's shelter
4. Bleak
5. Revive, as spirits
6. Am sick
7. Twinkle
8. Ascend
9. Possessed
10. King beater
11. Round vegetable
16. Silly
20. Paddle
23. "What's My ___?"
24. At any time
25. Covered with moisture
26. ___ and aft
27. Similar
28. Labels
29. Sajak of "Wheel of Fortune"
32. Dressing for a cut
33. African nation
35. Self
36. Discovers
38. Smooths wrinkles
39. "First ___" (Stallone movie)
42. Follow directions
43. Escape
44. Sensed
45. "The ___ and the Pendulum"
46. Crude metal
47. Boy
49. Johnson or Ameche

PUZZLE 406

ACROSS

1. Bestow
6. Sight
11. Dawn
13. Mounted gun
14. Improve
15. Elaborately adorned
16. Generously
18. Pepe Le ____
19. Carried on
23. Legendary Baba
24. Perfume
25. Racket
26. According to
29. Least
32. Yuletide drink
34. Curvy letter
35. Road diagram
37. Previously
38. Chimpanzee
39. Douses
40. Suitable
43. Shovel
45. Mollify
47. Hesitant
52. Turned the soil
53. Light bulb inventor
54. Arias
55. Pace

DOWN

1. Yak
2. Mourn
3. Actor Carney
4. Wayne's word
5. Tire feature
6. Fluctuating
7. Lodge
8. Break suddenly
9. Carryall
10. Again
12. Upper limb
13. Lassie, for one
17. Bachelor's home
19. Type of model
20. Hubbubs
21. Oaths
22. Earlier than, in poems
26. "____ Karenina"
27. Bolt
28. "Rock of ____"
30. Tennis overhands
31. Knocked
33. Thick substance
36. Split ____ soup
39. Mails
40. Dangerous snakes
41. Type of shirt
42. Hammer or wrench
44. Expected to arrive
46. Couple
48. Small drink
49. Practice
50. Fish delicacy
51. Conclude

PUZZLE 407

ACROSS

1. Allow
4. Middle East native
8. Religious image
12. Unrefined metal
13. Corn bread
14. Back of the neck
15. Produce
17. Sketch
18. Cupola
19. Cultivates
20. Govern
23. Pitcher's stat
24. Assistant
25. Schedules
29. Outrage
30. Sheriff's star
32. Frozen cube
33. School assignments
35. Taxi fee
36. Painting or sculpture, e.g.
37. Did office work
38. Shovel
41. Free from dependence
43. Nation
44. Weight-room items
48. Adolescent skin problem
49. Malicious
50. Snack
51. High schooler
52. Actor Hackman
53. Actress Irving

DOWN

1. Fireplace wood
2. Before, poetically
3. Decade number
4. Cook's smock
5. Wander
6. Poker stake
7. Honey maker
8. Native American
9. Poet Sandburg
10. Milky gem
11. Current events
16. Boundary
19. Maple, e.g.
20. Train track
21. Republic of Ireland
22. Fateful March date
23. Quiche ingredient
25. Commercials
26. Gauge
27. Estate measure
28. Plant's beginning
30. Tiresome person
31. Hill-building insect
34. Dishearten
35. Monetary penalty
37. Legend
38. Bed support
39. Rate of speed
40. "____ of Green Gables"
41. Signal hello
42. Actress Moran
44. Plead
45. Meadow
46. On the ____ (fleeing)
47. Hog's home

ACROSS

1. Hang around
5. Not shallow
9. Steers
11. Tail
13. Be against
14. Out-of-the-way
15. Prone
16. Misfortunes
18. Cushion
19. Zodiac lion
20. Brush
21. Rents
22. New
24. Average
25. Assoc.
26. Fled
27. Walking stick
29. Least
32. Sunday service
33. Make the grade
34. Corn on the ___
36. Yellow Pgs.
37. Big sandwich
38. Astonish
39. Kitchen tool
41. Laughed heartily
44. Brook
45. Striped cats
46. Dance movement
47. Not as much

DOWN

1. Evening meal
2. Walk cautiously
3. Fuss
4. You bet!
5. Bucks' mates
6. Shade tree
7. Marries secretly
8. Starchy food
9. Target
10. Using a needle
11. Turn loose
12. Unites
17. Choose
20. Existed
21. Solitary
23. Debate sides
24. Cuts lumber
26. Spa
27. West Point students
28. Demand
29. Distant
30. Frightens
31. Skyscrapers
32. Atlas contents
33. Salon treatment, for short
35. Garden plots
37. Pile
40. Golfer Trevino
42. Lubricate
43. Grow older

PUZZLE 409

ACROSS
1. "The ____ of the Roses"
4. Hurt
8. Male foal
12. Rage
13. Release money
14. Telephone ____ code
15. Free
16. Chooses
17. Assemble
18. Painter's stand
20. Lamb's mother
22. Plate
25. Wear away
29. Cushion
32. Market
34. Eager
35. Tell a whopper
36. Knolls
38. "Car 54, Where ____ You?"
39. Lyric poems
41. Bog fuel
42. Football's Dawson
43. "____ of Endearment"
45. Glitch
47. Charged atom
49. Comedian Williams
53. Bucket
56. Taken by mouth
59. Frost
60. Land measure
61. Leisure
62. Foot part
63. Starring role
64. For fear that
65. Conclusion

DOWN
1. Telegram
2. "Tosca" solo, e.g.
3. Cincinnati team
4. Do away with
5. Baseball hat
6. Slap
7. Otherwise
8. Picture taker
9. Crude metal
10. Jamie ____ Curtis
11. Make lace
19. Actor Asner
21. "The Way ____ Were"
23. Boat
24. Golfer's goals
26. Egg-shaped
27. Terrible
28. First garden
29. Scheme
30. Helper
31. Forest creature
33. Blueprint
37. Young actress
40. Grinned
44. Therefore
46. Leave
48. Christmas
50. Mouthful
51. Religious image
52. Necessity
53. Buddy
54. Expert
55. Lyricist Gershwin
57. "Norma ____" (Field film)
58. Donkey

ACROSS

1. Exist
4. Lay down
7. Clean a fish
9. Washes down
11. Trouser part
13. Call off
14. Biblical boat
15. Tied
17. Some
18. Angler's tool
20. Sidekick
21. Undercover man
22. Flaps
24. Superior or Huron
26. ___ and behold
27. Waterloo's st.
28. Mend
30. Sculpture and music
32. Votes against
33. Purpose
35. Spike of corn
37. ___ close for comfort
38. Mock
40. By means of
42. Overseas
44. Daisy Duck's love
46. Fierce stare
47. Book parts
48. Look at
49. Fourposter

DOWN

1. Squirrel's meal
2. Tennis bat
3. Antlered deer
4. Opie, to Andy
5. Flee
6. Very small
7. Hot tub
8. Electric fish
9. Contained
10. Foxy
12. Knocks softly
13. Nun's room
16. Sacramento's st.
19. Stories
21. Glide on ice
23. Feather scarf
25. Melody
28. Stadium sound
29. Put
30. In the center of
31. Fierce
32. Majestic
34. "___ in the Mood for Love"
36. Aggravated
37. Follow
38. Actress West
39. Dirty Harry, for one
41. Classified items: abbr.
43. Mineral
45. Catch

PUZZLE 411

ACROSS

1. Swine
5. Butter serving
8. Fairy-tale beast
12. Baking chamber
13. Deception
14. Neighborhood
15. Window section
16. Pub drink
17. Stalemates
18. Drowsy
20. House of worship
22. Knock
23. Garden tool
24. Young boy
27. Allow
29. Nude
33. Corrosive substance
35. Negative word
37. Sour green fruit
38. Bicycle feature
40. At this time
42. Convent sister
43. Convened
45. Atmosphere
47. Picnic basket
50. Noisy sleeper
54. ____ vera
55. Play a part
57. Roast
58. Minus
59. Expected
60. Angers
61. Quiz
62. Go wrong
63. Tree house

DOWN

1. Jumps
2. Track shape
3. Actor/dancer Kelly
4. Scornful smirk
5. Baby's enclosure
6. Be sick
7. Dentist's concerns
8. Breakfast fare
9. Clutch
10. Film spool
11. Luxury
19. Sidekick
21. One billion years
24. Drink like a cat
25. King-topping card
26. Performed
28. Heavy weight
30. Relatives
31. Ostrich's relative
32. Animal's home
34. Wettest
36. Bread browner
39. Marvin or Majors
41. Victory
44. Swap
46. Red-breasted bird
47. Cease
48. Away from the wind
49. Forest-floor plant
51. Unusual
52. ____ out (barely makes)
53. Relaxation
56. Mutt

360

ACROSS
1. Skiff
5. Cumberland ____
8. Brought forth
12. Diva's song
13. Long, long ____
14. G.I. hooky
15. Call out
16. Grant's foe
17. Shoal
18. Needle hole
20. Label
22. Pursue
25. French river
29. Dinghy paddle
30. "____ John B"
34. Wail
35. Pub brew
36. In addition
37. Bro or sis
38. ____ of a gun
39. Fencing swords
41. Utilize
42. Russian emperors
44. Cornered
46. Slippery swimmer
48. Okay, to a sailor
49. Advantage
52. Tourist's stop
54. Largest continent
58. Rowdy
59. Forget-me- ____
60. Extended credit
61. Door openers
62. Female bighorn
63. Create

DOWN
1. Montego ____
2. Nev.'s neighbor
3. Be under the weather
4. Narratives
5. Storm
6. Ripen
7. Robert Frost, e.g.
8. Canal sight
9. Be indebted to
10. Fish beginnings
11. Pixie
19. Positive response
21. Snake
22. Seashore
23. Circles of light
24. Auditorium
26. Put forth
27. Unpleasant sound
28. Receded
31. Splash gently
32. First digit
33. "____ to the West Wind"
39. Opposite of WNW
40. Porker's pad
43. Slender grasses
45. Kingdom
47. ____ of scrimmage
48. Pot filler
49. Large deer
50. Gentle creature
51. Gal's date
53. At this time
55. "... from ____ to shining ..."
56. Pen's fluid
57. Consumed

PUZZLE 413

ACROSS

1. Gym pad
4. Dustcloth
7. Lincoln's nickname
10. Expert
11. Ripened
13. Lobster's pincer
14. That woman
15. Weekly newsmagazine
16. Knowledge
17. Dog's shelter
19. Little green men
21. "___ to Evening"
22. Police officer
23. Not spicy
26. Triumphed
27. Baseball stick
30. Mine yield
31. Rock
33. Organ of sight
34. Sleeping place
35. Reverence
36. Observed
37. ___ for the books
38. "We ___ the World"
40. Bleak
43. Sword or gun, e.g.
47. Desert dweller
48. Snare
50. Gorilla, e.g.
51. Hawaiian garlands
52. Bygone days
53. Gosh!
54. Boy
55. Moray or lamprey
56. Finish

DOWN

1. Costume part
2. Dull pain
3. Adolescent
4. Gave a PG to
5. Nimble
6. Diamond, e.g.
7. Medicinal plant
8. Cattle shed
9. Female sheep
12. Church officer
13. Trim
18. Gesture of agreement
20. Solitary
23. Unruly crowd
24. Wrath
25. Conducted
26. Sorrow
27. Hive builder
28. Yea
29. Twice five
31. Mentally healthy
32. A score
36. Body of water
37. Globes
38. Conscious
39. Fend off
40. Bouncing toy
41. Zone
42. Foray
44. Book leaf
45. Store sign
46. Poverty
49. Fish eggs

ACROSS

1. George Michael's group
5. ____ Triomphe
10. Wound memento
14. Scottish island
15. Smack again
16. Buckeye State
17. Light dessert
19. Modernize
20. Georgia product
21. Legal matter
22. Sugar vegetable
23. Writer Silverstein et al.
25. Egyptian god of music
26. Rapid
30. "Don't Bring Me Down" group
31. Discover
34. Fire remains
36. Spot
38. ____-Magnon
39. Oblong cream puff
42. Craggy peak
43. Comes in second
44. Long walks
45. Arrives
47. Singer Stewart
49. Mexican money
50. Wicked
51. Cheated
53. Poet Sandburg
55. ____ longa, vita brevis
56. Chewy candy
61. On the Caspian
62. Potluck dishes
64. Thailand, formerly
65. Arab prince
66. World: Ger.
67. "The King ____"
68. Demolishes
69. ____ majesty

DOWN

1. Delicate thing
2. Expectation
3. Sulawesi ox
4. Educator Horace ____
5. "We ____ World"
6. Kind of room, briefly
7. Creamy desserts
8. River embankments
9. Summers, in Paris
10. Frozen treat
11. Rich dessert
12. Nurse's helper
13. Plant anchor
18. Gloomy guy?
24. Actress Lanchester et al.
25. Park resting spot
26. Data
27. "...woman who lived in ____"
28. Butter cookie
29. Private eye
31. Gambler's cube
32. Weeps
33. Human trunk
35. Compact
37. Greek fabulist
40. Actor Chaney
41. Sass
46. Deli meat
48. Prevents
51. Stage play
52. European beetle
53. Spanish home
54. Z ____ zebra
55. Maple genus
57. Poultry
58. Escape
59. Snakelike fish
60. Roman ruins site
63. Witness

PUZZLE 414

PUZZLE 415

ACROSS
1. Time frames
5. Young lady
9. Sate
13. Nessie's nest et al.
15. Lowest female voice
16. Main role
17. French revolutionary
18. "____ M for Murder"
19. Consumes
20. Protestors
23. Dry
24. Packed performance initials
25. Fold flock
28. Danger
33. Painted, for one
35. Type size
36. Gemstone
38. Harvests
41. Thing
42. Primitive dwellings
43. Observe
45. Golfer Sammy ____
47. Spotted
48. Self-esteem
51. Canyon sound
54. Lettering pros
60. Verbally summon
61. Thanks ____: 2 wds.
62. Kind of room or noodle
64. Messes up
65. "Nautilus" captain
66. Steeple
67. Orderly
68. Cable car
69. As it was

DOWN
1. Tree species
2. Street
3. Lots of space
4. Disgrace
5. Boys
6. Landed
7. Celebrities
8. ____ eclipse
9. Singer Laine
10. Shakespearean king
11. Dobbin's dinner
12. Footballer's distances: abbr.
14. Shops
21. More recent
22. Summit
26. "Able was I ____ ..."
27. Actor Laurel et al.
29. Saga
30. Traditional practice
31. Drink cooler
32. On the ____ (escaping)
33. Social event
34. "Born Free" heroine
36. Exclamations of surprise
37. Humorous wordplay
39. "Tell-Tale Heart" author
40. Sharply inclined
44. Moves slowly
46. D.C. neighbor: abbr.
49. Jumbo
50. Flirter
52. Assists
53. Satellite's path
54. Worry
55. Taj Mahal site
56. That
57. Italia's capital
58. Nuclear concern
59. Tender
60. Animal enclosure
63. Moist

ACROSS

1. Noise
4. Quartet
8. Spouses
13. Correct
15. Alleviate
16. Motionless
17. Toward shelter
18. Phase
19. Actor's platform
20. New
22. Obligation
24. Cut the grass
25. Sell directly to the consumer
27. Negative words
29. Bee's abode
30. Discolor
34. Tit for ____
37. Express
39. Opera melody
40. Superior to
42. Weaken
44. Nautical direction
45. Delight
46. Cooking vessels
48. Society-page word
49. Calms
53. Spiral
55. Frolic
56. Trial
59. Flick
62. ____ moss
64. Purpose
66. Revere
68. Clock
70. Position
71. Of the sun
72. Adam's address
73. Head coverings
74. Shuts loudly
75. Dispatched
76. Forget-me-____

DOWN

1. Beloved
2. Lazy person
3. Eugenie, to Charles
4. Joyous
5. Cereal grain
6. Exploited
7. Regret
8. Man's title
9. Social insect
10. Sports group
11. Hence
12. Beef dish
14. Dentist's concern
21. Unsophisticated
23. ____ constrictor
26. Camera part
28. Break suddenly
31. Heavy metal
32. Father
33. Dislike
34. Designates
35. Competent
36. Three-____ sloth
38. Faucet
41. Wiener schnitzel meat
43. Somewhat, musically
44. Actor's whisper
47. Deluge
50. Slender candles
51. Before, poetically
52. Hockey players' needs
54. Collar attachment
57. Of a certain continent
58. Game of chance
59. Go by
60. Rocker Billy ____
61. Carbonated drink
63. High or low
65. Robin's home
67. Sheep
69. Males

PUZZLE 417

• SAILORS, AHOY! •

ACROSS

1. Night flier
4. Broadway musical
9. Pigpen
12. Turkish title
13. Lollobrigida et al.
14. Actor Marvin
15. Hold your position!
20. Actress Kendall
21. Also
22. Jolson and Hirt
25. Sailor's direction: abbr.
26. Old card game
29. The Matterhorn, e.g.
30. Teensy
33. Actress Ethel ____
35. Sharp remarks
37. Aft
39. Old stringed instrument
40. Canal transport
42. Ventilates
43. Sick
45. Operated
46. Australian bird
47. Ostrich's output
48. Sort
50. Mrs. Cantor
52. Four-oared craft
54. Strike
57. "Norma ____"
58. Modern
59. Tennyson's "Crossing the ____"
60. Fuss
61. Commercials
62. Building wing
63. Singleton
64. Negative word
65. Tax month: abbr.
67. Historic time
70. Meadow
72. Twitch
74. Blond
76. Dinghy
78. So
81. Most competent
84. Bread ingredient
85. Select
87. ____ Moines
88. Foot digit
90. Stain
91. Pair
92. Uncooked
93. Finale
94. Onassis, for short
95. Wealth arrives!
104. Armed conflict
105. Close, old style
106. Plaything
107. Bandleader Brown
108. Trap
109. Take to court

DOWN

1. Evil
2. Past
3. Merchant vessel
4. Self
5. London's Old ____
6. Writing fluid
7. Make lace
8. Cigar residue
9. Single-masted craft
10. "____ and Sympathy"
11. Still
16. Sunburns
17. Deli bread
18. Greek letter
19. Gaucho's weapon
22. Boring tool
23. Medieval song
24. Down with the jib and spinnaker!
26. Greensward
27. Sphere
28. Woodwind
30. Get under way!
31. Make a mistake
32. Printers' measures
34. Wiggly fish
35. Feather scarf
36. Detective Spade
38. Label
40. Fishing craft
41. Harbor craft
44. Ocean craft
47. Heron
48. Lyricist Gershwin
49. Boy
51. Dolores ____ Rio
53. Author Fleming
55. Wedding words
56. Child
66. Before: pref.
68. Baseball's Campanella
69. Thunderstruck
70. Misplace
71. Chow down
73. Japanese statesman
74. Passing fancy
75. Actor Vigoda
77. Large inlet
79. "Born in the ____"
80. Stitch
82. Pilots
83. Masses
85. Heal
86. Lifts
89. Asner and Begley
91. Water barrier
95. Night hooter
96. Scottish negative
97. Owns
98. Tavern
99. Green veggie
100. Auto
101. Mine output
102. Debt initials
103. Comic Louis

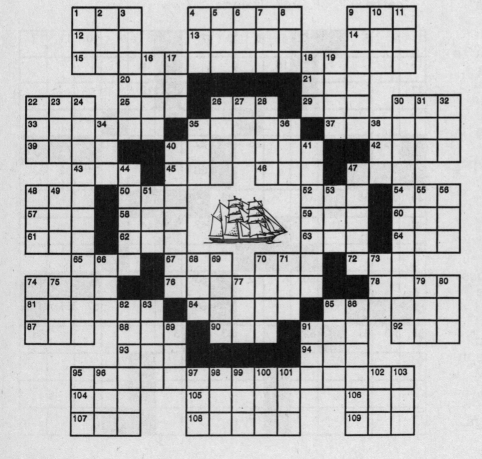

ACROSS

1. Overlook
5. Emulate a father-to-be
9. Frenzied
10. Spunk
11. Kitchen containers
13. Actress Peeples
14. Menorah fillers
18. "What's up, ___?"
21. Precise
22. Satisfy fully
24. Food fish
27. Singer Kabibble
28. Heap
29. Small pie
31. Orangutan, e.g.
32. Inventor Whitney
33. Building wing
34. ___ de Janeiro
35. A Bobbsey twin
36. Tame
38. Like a teddy bear
40. Businessman Onassis
41. Shy
42. Threat
45. French mathematician
48. Boulevard: abbr.
49. Biblical boat
51. Prohibit
52. Cry of discovery
53. Mal de ___
54. Nick's wife
56. Camera part
57. ___ de plume
58. Some
59. Sorrowful sound
61. Bench
62. Hurricane center
63. Chowder holder
65. Hive insect
66. Sea robber
72. India's continent
73. Oak or maple
74. Harvest
75. Vend

DOWN

1. Singer Davis
2. "___ Dreamer"
3. Male child
4. Lean
5. Daisy components
6. Strong beer
7. Freeway sight
8. Navy officer: abbr.
12. Comedian Caesar
14. Monastery room
15. Exist
16. Ingest
17. Night twinkler
18. Stopped, as a motor
19. Capital of Norway
20. Deception
21. Despicable
23. Skater Heiden
24. Christmas treat
25. Milky gem
26. Refute
28. Louisiana bird
30. Large-billed birds
37. Tax shelter: abbr.
39. Two, in Toledo
42. Papa's partner
43. Equal
44. Cupid
45. Gasp
46. Nautical shout
47. Like some excuses
50. Mr. Kristofferson
51. Lima or kidney
55. In the past
56. Pasture
60. Wheel ornament
61. Fragrances
64. Legume
66. Saloon
67. Function
68. Spy's letters
69. Before, poetically
70. Electric fish
71. Aunt or uncle: abbr.

PUZZLE 418

• CANNERY ROW •

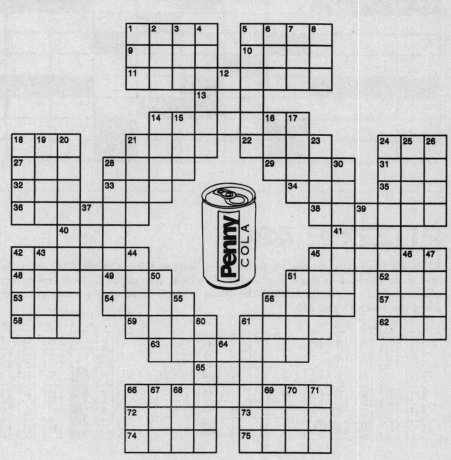

PUZZLE 419

Not really double trouble, but double fun! Solve this puzzle as you would a regular crossword, EXCEPT place one, two, or three letters in each box. The number of letters in each answer is shown in parentheses after its clue.

ACROSS

1. Search (5)
4. Superstar quality (8)
7. Figure in Greek tragedy (5)
10. Thespian (5)
11. Guide (5)
12. Jot (4)
13. Nucleus (6)
15. Juvenility (10)
17. Religious image (4)
19. Singing voice (4)
20. Retreat (9)
24. Hamper (6)
28. Pair (3)
29. Unsteady (7)
31. Tease (5)
32. Polite one (9)
34. Misers (10)
36. Playwright Neil (5)
38. Interstice (3)
39. Responses (9)
42. Resolute (10)
46. Sting (4)
47. Angler's quarry (5)
50. Merchant (6)
51. Examined (6)
52. Evicted (6)
53. Pung (4)

DOWN

1. Phony (5)
2. Organic compound (5)
3. Ripped (4)
4. Pure (6)
5. Ascend (4)
6. Xylophones' kin (8)
7. Pith (4)
8. Bypass (6)
9. Friendship (5)
14. Draw out (6)
16. Puree (4)
18. Wild ass (6)
20. Betting ploy (5)
21. Litter's wee one (4)
22. Garden pest (4)
23. Epochs (4)
25. Get (6)
26. Baseball ploy (4)
27. Permits (4)
30. Mattress casing (7)
33. Estate house (7)
35. Speakeasy girl (7)
37. Frightful (9)
39. Deny (5)
40. Farm measures (5)
41. Dyed (6)
43. Factions (5)
44. Play for time (5)
45. Came in (7)
48. Umpire's call (3)
49. Actor Danson (3)

PUZZLE 420

Fill in the diagrams below by putting the lines of letters VERTICALLY into their squares. The letters in each line must remain in the same order. The lines are given in jumbled order. When finished, you will be able to read a saying ACROSS the rows in each square. We have entered one line of letters in the first diagram to start you off.

1.

2.

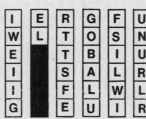
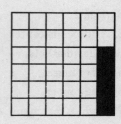

DOUBLE TROUBLE

Not really double trouble, but double fun! Solve this puzzle as you would a regular crossword, EXCEPT place one, two, or three letters in each box. The number of letters in each answer is shown in parentheses after its clue.

ACROSS

1. Those under age (6)
5. Take in (6)
9. Planet's kin (8)
11. Most sprightly (9)
12. That girl (3)
13. Audience members (9)
15. Actress Dawber (3)
16. Dross (4)
18. Agriculture goddess (5)
19. Snake (7)
20. Ritualistic (10)
22. Servants' wear (6)
23. Sinning (6)
24. Scouring rock (6)
25. Takes five (5)
26. Varying (10)
28. Silenced (5)
29. Fritter away (5)
30. Most insignificant (5)
32. Greek letter (3)
33. False show (8)
35. Quaker pronoun (4)
36. Relocate (8)
38. Kind of candle (5)
40. Meara's mate (7)
41. Brought up (6)

DOWN

1. Purees (6)
2. Weave (9)
3. Hockey-great Bobby (3)
4. Earth (4)
5. Louganis et al. (6)
6. Golly (3)
7. Like an eel (8)
8. Scriptures (9)
10. Perceptive (10)
11. Property attachments (5)
14. River duck (4)
17. Hailed (7)
19. Utilitarian (11)
21. Famed cat (6)
22. Key fruit (4)
24. Tangy (7)
25. Eating establishment (10)
26. Pure (6)
27. Mitt material (7)
28. Curs (5)
29. Tap yield (5)
31. Guided (7)
33. Lean toward (6)
34. Char (4)
37. Window part (4)
39. Pod veggie (3)

1	2	3	4			5	6	7	8
9				10	11				
12		13		14				15	
16		17		18			19		
	20		21			22			
		23			24				
	25			26				27	
28			29				30		31
32		33				34		35	
36		37			38		39		
40						41			

QUOTE FIND

Start at the circled letter and draw one continuous path moving from letter to adjacent letter, horizontally, vertically, and diagonally, to discover a humorous quotation. Each letter will be used once. The path does not cross itself.

Answer:

A	G	R	A	I	O
I	S	R	I	T	N
E	N	E	A	M	D
C	T	A	T	O	A
S	(D)	P	M	R	F
I	R	O	O	T	E

PUZZLE 423

ACROSS
1. Plant
4. Anti
7. Heroic poem
9. In the air
12. Impulsive
13. Confusion
15. Run away
16. Certain
17. Length times width
21. Heavy weight
22. Translate
25. Commotion
26. Info
27. Points
29. Flirt
33. 100 cents
36. Malevolence
37. Wee
38. Daft
39. Stain
40. Moist

DOWN
1. Vassal
2. Gem
3. Sage
4. Taxi
5. Corrida cheer
6. Silent acknowledgements
8. Swindle
10. Piccolo's kin
11. Seer's cards
14. Chess pieces
18. Crimson
19. Geologic period
20. Capable
22. Simpleton
23. Honorable
24. Fray
25. Too
28. Toboggan
30. Admit
31. Vermin
32. Scheme
34. Whichever
35. Grain

PUZZLE 424

ACROSS
1. Comedian Conway
4. Hemingway's nickname
8. Appendages
12. Distress
13. "Rock of ____"
14. Snout
15. Disorder
17. Large truck
18. Connection
19. Closed car
20. Arrange
23. Cliburn or Heflin
24. Toothed wheel
25. Throwing
29. New Haven tree
30. Cubicle
32. Brewed beverage
33. Kitchen cloth
35. Green veggies
36. Attention
37. Heat
39. Perspire
42. Fates, e.g.
43. Rend
44. Farm building
48. Orient
49. Stake
50. In the past
51. Target
52. Observes
53. "I ____ Rhythm"

DOWN
1. Couple
2. Obligation letters
3. Encountered
4. French capital
5. Delegate
6. Apex
7. Query
8. Not here
9. Oboe's need
10. One of Goldilocks's bears
11. Pelt
16. Smear
19. Window part
20. Venerable
21. Sandwich shop
22. Bottlenecks
23. Container
25. Carpentry joint
26. Unit
27. Tidy
28. Incision
30. Naughty child
31. Scull's adjunct
34. Robust
35. Experts
37. Composed
38. Helpers
39. Phase
40. Erode
41. Loosen
42. Musical sound
44. Had being
45. Crone
46. Id's kin
47. Speck

PUZZLE 425

ACROSS
1. Sail support
5. Coolidge's nickname
8. Lively party
12. Toward shelter
13. Exist
14. Pain
15. Sound a bell
16. Paid athlete
17. King of beasts
18. Classical language
20. Citrus coolers
21. Brick carrier
24. Pub
26. Commotion
27. Make a knot
28. Appeared in a play
32. Putrid
34. Fast
35. Primp
36. Dandy
37. Woman's secret
38. Helpful hint
40. Scarlet
41. Actor Baldwin
44. Slur over
46. Laundry
47. ____ de France
48. Nothing more than
52. Diminutive suffix
53. Give permission
54. News paragraph
55. Forest creature
56. Pigpen
57. Forbidden

DOWN
1. Road guide
2. Pub beverage
3. Ocean
4. Tattle
5. Ship's officer
6. Come
7. Sierra ____
8. Equilibrium
9. Etching fluid
10. Sandal
11. Biddies
19. Be present
21. Angel's instrument
22. Fragrance
23. Love unwisely
25. Knocked
29. Salty drop
30. Border
31. Colored the hair
33. Instructor
34. Fashionable group
36. Boneless cut of meat
39. Salome's costume
41. Overwhelmed
42. Tardy
43. Italian noble family
45. Radiate
49. Greek letter
50. Confederate soldier
51. Flightless bird

PUZZLE 426

ACROSS
1. Hog fat
5. Bombard with laser beams
8. Arrived
12. Woodwind instrument
13. Actor Wallach
14. Opera solo
15. Alack
16. Spires
18. Relic
20. Make amends
21. Beam of light
22. Golf instructor
23. Humorous
26. Dawn
30. Metallic rock
31. Triumphed
32. Actor Gibson
33. Walks like a duck
36. Settle a loan
38. Help
39. Folding bed
40. Salt water
43. Bowmen
47. Tongue
49. False god
50. Prod
51. Massachusetts cape
52. Quote
53. Back end
54. Vanity
55. Soupy meat dish

DOWN
1. Rich soil
2. Competent
3. Wander
4. Sandy wasteland
5. Flavorful
6. Choir voice
7. Pizza
8. Prisoner taker
9. Singer Guthrie
10. Demeanor
11. Facility
17. Merit
19. Negative vote
22. Play on words
23. Cry of wonder
24. George Gershwin's brother
25. Actor Danson
26. Distress signal
27. Little devil
28. Mediterranean ____
29. English cathedral town
31. Marry
34. Peril
35. Stead
36. Fabulous bird
37. Morals
39. Belief
40. Smudge
41. Scarce
42. Actress Swenson
43. Open-mouthed
44. Blue-pencil
45. Fixed routine
46. Killed
48. High card

PUZZLE 427

ACROSS

1. Twosome
5. Muslims' religion
10. Manner
14. Hautboy
15. Like potato texture
16. Eager
17. Fondles
18. Flute player
19. Lack
20. Depots
22. Score and a half
24. Different
25. Dog's pest
26. Outlaw
29. Long-distance access
33. Stir
34. Weird
36. Stunned
37. Rounded roof
39. Cast parts
41. Places
42. Government funding
44. Stateroom bed
46. Forget-me-____
47. Signed the back of a check
49. Downy ducks
51. Peruse
52. Yield
53. Heated
56. Bothered
60. Mountain: prefix
61. Tee off
63. Therefore
64. Place
65. Cruise ship
66. Civil disturbance
67. Passing fashions
68. Gives off
69. Flip

DOWN

1. Bursts
2. Aid in wrongdoing
3. Modicum
4. Took a break
5. Deceiver
6. French river
7. Drinks like a dog
8. Ginger drink
9. Flowering evergreen
10. Insanely zealous
11. Above
12. Food plan
13. Small whirlpool
21. Tennis star Nastase
23. Leader
25. Less restricted
26. Emblem of authority
27. Decorate
28. Wilderness wanderer
29. Felt poorly
30. Fresh air
31. Room scheme
32. Works on manuscripts
35. Clothed with authority
38. Huge
40. Pittsburgh footballers
43. Forest plant
45. Conceal
48. Cowboy's seat
50. Barren spot
52. Desire jealously
53. Wild canine
54. Diva's solo
55. Hollow grass
56. Short skirt
57. The Supremes
58. Swellheads
59. Specks
62. Circular edge

PUZZLE 428   Anagram Word Squares

A word square has the same words reading across and down. The first word across is also the first word down; the second word across is the second word down, etc. Can you form anagrams of the letter groups and place them in the diagrams to form word squares?

1. STEP
   SAGE
   PALE
   GEED

2. TIME
   METS
   MEET
   TEAM

3. MILE
   NEED
   SEAL
   DIVA

372

PUZZLE 429

• YOU RANG? •

ACROSS

1. Pesky insect
5. Birds' abodes
10. Swap
15. Book of maps
17. Notions
18. Circled high
19. "____, for me and my gal": 4 wds.
22. Actress Grant
23. ____ de France
24. Had dinner
25. Husband, to wife
28. Weightlifter's equipment
34. Boxing wonder
35. Derisive wit
36. Forbid
39. Sunbather's desire
40. Most primitive
42. Actress Gabor
43. Inquired
46. Cigar residue
49. Reclined
50. Ireland
52. Silent
54. Track events
56. Anwar
57. Sheep cry
58. Model again
59. Fruit drink
61. Health resort
62. Dampen once more
65. Become firm
66. To a large extent
73. Botch things up
74. House wing
75. More spooky
76. ____ de Janeiro
77. Combative
80. Not new, as a car
81. Actress Arden
84. Exist
85. Republican party initials
87. Wartime hit about a sailor: 2 wds.
97. Depends
98. Stranger
99. Kindled the fire again
100. Semiprecious stones
101. Cowboy's home
102. Neat

DOWN

1. Gangster's gun
2. To the ____ degree
3. Pub brew
4. Dining-room need
5. Nothing
6. Sullivan and Koch
7. Ocean
8. Paving material
9. Wind direction: abbr.
10. Sounds
11. Old cloth
12. Operatic solo
13. Fender-bender
14. Rim
16. Observe
18. Window ledge
20. Guided
21. Rouses
25. ____ Hari
26. Woe!
27. "Peter Pan" fairy
29. L.A. university: abbr.
30. Damage
31. Measure of cooling capacity: abbr.
32. Auction offer
33. Before, to a poet
36. Homes for carillons: 2 wds.

37. Actress Gardner
38. "No" vote
41. Russian news agency
44. Of an historic period
45. Cuts vegetables
47. Nova
48. One who conceals himself
51. Certain tide
53. Put on, as cargo
55. For men only
59. Grow old
60. Dolores ____ Rio
63. PA port
64. Walked on
67. Lease again
68. Conger
69. Onassis
70. Twitch
71. Zodiac sign
72. Many moons: abbr.

77. Little ones
78. Love god
79. Self
80. In a dither
81. Madrid's river
82. Al Gore, e.g.
83. Fitzgerald
86. "____ Town"
88. "____ Abner"
89. Make lace
90. Bullring cheer
91. Cookbook direction
92. "____ and Sympathy"
93. Hospital workers: abbr.
94. Inventor Whitney
95. Free from
96. Pigpen

373

PUZZLE 430

ACROSS
1. School of whales
4. Fling
8. Spill the beans
12. Self
13. Choir member
14. Grade
15. Seine
16. Once ____ . . .
17. Ajar
18. Paradises
20. Highest point
22. "____ the ramparts . . . "
24. Relieves
28. Full of folks
32. Oregon, for one
33. Secreted
34. ____-hard
36. Dove sound
37. Objects of worship
40. Deter
43. Dot
45. Ms. Gabor
46. Tree growth
48. Legate
52. Cager Chamberlain
55. "Our ____"
57. Mimic
58. Kind of eye
59. Pony's gait
60. ____ Remo
61. The Venerable ____
62. Evergreens
63. High trains

DOWN
1. TV's Rayburn
2. Old
3. Speck
4. Made happen
5. Swiss mountain
6. Hold it!
7. Musical sounds
8. Wall St. dealer
9. Place for a cat
10. Grazed
11. Actor Kingsley
19. Right away
21. Likely
23. ____ alert
25. Shoestring
26. Celebrity
27. Place for a coin
28. Golfer Beck
29. Take a cab
30. Scent
31. Immerse
35. Before
38. Small
39. Plant
41. Happenings
42. Actor Heflin
44. Simple song
47. Stab
49. Flower holder
50. Cloudy stone
51. Urges
52. Network
53. "____ Got a Secret"
54. Cover
56. Awesome!

PUZZLE 431

ACROSS
1. Existed
4. Pops
8. Dawber et al.
12. Flightless bird
13. Fencing weapon
14. Needlecase
15. Maine's symbol: 2 wds.
17. Terra firma
18. Seed covering
19. ____ State (Illinois)
21. Ave!
23. Thus
24. Muhammad ____
26. Bobbsey Twin
28. Quick
32. Fast time
34. ____ State (Mass.)
36. Moniker
37. Filch
39. ____ State (Idaho)
41. Records: abbr.
42. River: Sp.
44. Semester
46. Soaps up
50. Canadian official
53. Burn plant
54. Texas's symbol: 2 wds.
56. Halt
57. Mineral deposits
58. Sesame plant
59. Aloud
60. Salamander
61. Singleton

DOWN
1. Cried
2. Friend: Fr.
3. ____ State (Florida)
4. Hold
5. Spring mo.
6. Profound
7. Prophets
8. Louisiana's bird
9. Rose oil: var.
10. Actor Paul
11. Flank
16. Sked abbr.
20. Ventilate
22. Sci. room
24. Jolson et al.
25. Rent
27. Henpeck
29. ____ State (South Carolina)
30. Elf
31. ____ Moines
33. ____ State (North Carolina)
35. Nonetheless
38. Untruth
40. Least
43. Synthetic fabric
45. Thing, in law
46. French composer
47. Winged
48. '70s TV show
49. Angry
51. Conceited
52. ____ Stanley Gardner
55. Modern

374

ACROSS

1. Walkers
5. Supervisor
9. Flying mammal
12. Profess
13. Diva's solo
14. Lager
15. Food shop
16. Trey, e.g.
17. Can
18. Form of address
20. Dressing gown
21. Orb
24. Component
25. Vegetable
26. Come
30. Hill dweller
31. Coronet
32. Wagon
35. Gun
36. Frost
37. Divan
40. Refute
42. Atop
43. Increase in pay
45. ___ annum
46. Bath powder
47. Tide
51. Epoch
52. Range
53. Prod
54. Mr. Bolger
55. Pare
56. Winter white

DOWN

1. Craze
2. Night before
3. Squiggly fish
4. Commonplace
5. Germ
6. Verbal
7. Father
8. Woeful
9. Wand
10. Excuse
11. Belief
19. Angry
20. Be sorry
21. Resort
22. Sty
23. Topper
27. Music category
28. Satirical
29. Weathercocks
32. By way of
33. Perform
34. Formerly
    called
35. Pale
37. Extra
38. Musical drama
39. Defeat
41. Variety
43. Unusual
44. Toward shelter
46. Faucet
48. Coastal flyer
49. Past
50. Church bench

ACROSS

1. Detained
5. Church section
9. Rower's need
12. Fencing sword
13. Earth
14. ___ air mail
15. Circle
16. Musical composition
18. Vivid red
20. Portable bed
21. Small island
22. Rigid
25. Tolerate
28. ___ Moines
29. Bullfight shout
30. Spire
31. Grassland
32. African antelopes
33. Santa's helper
34. Sickly pale
35. Surround
36. Impassive
38. ___ Diego
39. Fish eggs
40. Brought into harmony
44. Finish
47. Very small quantity
48. Ms. Gardner
49. Let fall
50. Close
51. Buddy
52. Weakens
53. Other

DOWN

1. His and ___
2. Heroic poem
3. Singer Horne
4. Put down
5. Useful thing
6. Frost, for one
7. Knight's title
8. Chooses
9. Displays of approval
10. Help
11. "Norma ___"
17. Neither's partner
19. Tell a whopper
22. ___ of Tranquility
23. Tip
24. Exam
25. High cards
26. Exit hastily
27. Unofficial
28. Lair
31. Young man
32. Authentic
34. Handles
35. Club
37. Trim
38. Stairs
40. Above
41. Christmas season
42. Greek letters
43. Venture
44. Wind up
45. Female gametes
46. Historic period

PUZZLE 434

• MUSICAL TWOSOMES •

ACROSS
1. Worthless cloth
4. Take ____ from me
8. Cry of lament
12. Hail, Caesar!
13. Carry on

14. Pro
15. Paving material
16. Lennon and ____
18. Hole for a coin
20. Assistants
21. Additional
23. Landers et al.
25. Puppy feet
26. Excited
27. Wail
30. ____ Baba
31. Courageous
32. Psychic Geller
33. Football's Dawson
34. Edison's middle name
35. Tickled
36. Cosmetic ingredient
37. Divulges
38. Pile up
41. Trucker's rig
42. ____ and David
45. By way of
48. Fishing string
49. Woodwind
    instrument
50. Play a role
51. State of bliss
52. French head
53. Wedding
    announcement word

DOWN
1. Rodent
2. Ms. Gardner
3. George or Ira
4. Knight wear
5. Diplomacy
6. Ltd., in the USA
7. School org.
8. Basketball's Gilmore
9. Come to earth
10. To ____ (exactly)
11. Pronounces
17. Mountainous region
19. "____ Girls"
21. October birthstone
22. Yarn
23. Yucca, e.g.
24. ____ Scotia
26. Folksinger Guthrie
27. Gilbert and ____
28. Spoken exam
29. Opens, in bridge
31. Light wood
35. Jewel
36. Washed out
37. Kin of ha-ha
38. Having the
    necessary skill
39. ____ of Orleans
40. Skin condition
41. Highlander
43. Nonsense!
44. Author Kobo ____
46. Frozen water
47. Enjoyed a meal

PUZZLE 435

• VEGETABLE GARDEN •

ACROSS
1. Swiss peak
4. Sound loudeners
8. This one: Sp.
12. Hiss preceder
13. Welsh product

14. "Final Four" league
15. Cauliflower kin
17. Bombast
18. More uncanny
19. Calm under pressure
21. Football pts.
22. Wiped out
25. Gay ____
28. Torme or Tillis
29. ____ Perrot, PQ
30. Desert Storm missile
31. Equinox mo.
32. Songwriter Porter
33. What's in the Louvre
34. Dined
35. Like a window
36. Made fun of
38. Each
39. ____-Sadr
40. In a circle
44. Analyze poetry
46. Pre-pickled pickle
48. Really big
49. Mars, to the Greeks
50. Time period
51. 1/1000 milennium
52. Money in Milan, once
53. Reiner or Lowe

DOWN
1. French clergyman
2. Folk knowledge
3. Shoddy
4. Give one's okay
5. Heaths
6. Chum
7. Raingear
8. Sign up
9. Green onion
10. Sunbathe
11. Chew and swallow
16. Quoted
20. Vinegar's partner
23. Model MacPherson
24. Act
25. High-school exam
26. Land parcel
27. Hardy turnip
28. Satirical magazine
31. Curative
32. Rebound
34. Bog
35. Read carefully
37. More rational
38. Indiana cager
41. German
    preposition
42. Roman fiddler
43. Plain
44. Meek
45. Pool stick
47. William Tell's home

PUZZLE 436

ACROSS
1. Arm or leg
5. Jogger's distance
9. Wager
12. Region
13. Had debts
14. Pub staple
15. Refute
16. Blarney
18. Yoko ____
20. Watched over
21. Get
25. ____ Angeles
26. "____ Grant"
27. Heels
29. Cease
32. French friend
33. Behind the ____ ball
35. Exist
36. Bottle part
38. Grimace
39. ____ King Cole
40. Relatives
42. Spinning-wheel part
44. Went by
47. Gardener's tool
48. Restore the confidence of
50. Sleeveless garment
54. Sea bird
55. Rip
56. Pennsylvania port
57. Pea's home
58. Luge
59. Author Ayn ____

DOWN
1. Young boy
2. Anger
3. "Twelve Angry ____"
4. "Blue ____"
5. Disneyland ride
6. ____ Jima
7. Fasting season
8. Ford's lemon
9. Dick Clark's "American ____"
10. Otherwise
11. ____ off (angry)
17. Seth's son
19. Pleasingly acceptable
21. Actor Bates
22. Arrive
23. Dangerous ground
24. Borders
28. Sheep watcher
30. Spoken
31. Mr. Seeger
34. Small combo
37. Buss
41. Tree houses
43. Not once
44. Kind of school
45. Flying: pref.
46. Affair of honor
49. "Norma ____"
51. Notable time
52. Transgression
53. Actor Knight

PUZZLE 437

ACROSS
1. Chunk
5. Clever remark
9. Everything
12. Merry old king
13. Egg on
14. Sticky stuff
15. Affirm
16. Huge
18. School break
20. Fish eggs
21. Carry
23. Of ships
27. Church seat
30. Solid
32. Ripped
33. From ____ Z
34. Hues
36. Falsehood
37. Upon
39. Cleo's river
40. Pavement material
41. Speeder's bane
43. Always
45. Author Fleming
47. Removed wrinkles
51. Barbecue's need
55. Distribute
56. Mr. Torn
57. Wicked
58. American Indian
59. Besides
60. Uncommon
61. Actor Sharif

DOWN
1. Wound reminder
2. Adore
3. Actor Baldwin
4. Frenchman's hat
5. Inquiry
6. Footed vase
7. Composer Stravinsky
8. Former Argentine dictator
9. Past
10. Singer Reed
11. ____ Alamos
17. Pork
19. Cushy
22. Tennessee ____ Ford
24. Electric measuring unit
25. Opera highlight
26. Ogle
27. Former TV host
28. Ms. Kett
29. Oak
31. "Moby Dick" author
35. Prophet
38. Couple
42. Al Unser, for one
44. Cowboys' competition
46. PBS series
48. "Cheers" patron
49. Lamb's pen name
50. Forest creature
51. Shed tears
52. Hasten
53. Fitting
54. Broadcast

PUZZLE 438

ACROSS

1. Rainbows
5. Silver: Sp.
10. N.T. book
14. Part of TV
15. Hawsers
16. Single combat
17. Burden
18. Pointed arches
19. Sicilian volcano
20. Westminster Abbey area
23. Policeman
24. Have a bite
25. Nonrotating parts
27. Subway stops
32. Box cautiously
33. Emoter
34. "The Mystery of Edwin ____"
36. Hues
39. Mine products
41. Word in Psalms
43. Tilt
44. Puerto Rican city
46. Mislays
48. Baseball stat
49. Covers
51. Disturbs
53. Holding in reserve
56. Ten: Fr.
57. Atmosphere
58. Chief foundation
64. Declaim violently
66. Elevate
67. Mother of Zeus
68. Neighborhood
69. Careens
70. Goals
71. Angel's instrument
72. Frozen rain
73. Black dust

DOWN

1. Upon
2. Nevada city
3. Whodunit lead
4. Sonnet conclusion
5. Exam supervisors
6. Trademark
7. Mimic
8. Youthful years
9. Possessions
10. Citrus beverage
11. Economize
12. Male singer
13. Rebuffs
21. Uttered
22. Engrossed
26. Dog's wagger
27. "Little ____ of Horrors"
28. Poi source
29. Area for vocal worshipers
30. Playwright Coward
31. Concert selections
35. Short race
37. Forbidden
38. Small cut
40. Wound mark
42. Dentist's-chair support
45. Movie spectacular
47. Snow runners
50. Scoffs
52. Movie scene crowd
53. Actress Bernhardt
54. Coronet
55. Chalice
59. River at Cairo
60. Princely Italian family
61. Buckeye State
62. Captain of the "Nautilus"
63. Orient
65. Choose for membership

PUZZLE 439 — Crypto-Crostic

In this puzzle the answers to the CLUES and the TRIVIA DESCRIPTION have been disguised by the same simple substitution code (each letter represents a different letter). Answer CLUES and transfer the letters you have decoded to reveal other WORDS and the TRIVIA DESCRIPTION. When you have completed both parts of the puzzle, the answer to the TRIVIA DESCRIPTION will be spelled out by the initial letters of the decoded WORDS.

CLUES	WORDS
Inscrutable	D P C K A H X T B C
Added on	I S S A V E A E
Dogs	Q I V X V A C
Noisy fight	R H I N O

CLUES	WORDS
Tremor	A I H K L W B I U A
Pitched	K L H A N
Leftover meat dish	L I C L

TRIVIA DESCRIPTION

CLIUACSAIHAIV SOIP NXKL KLHAA NXKQLAC IVE

RIVWBT'C DBHEAH.

378

PUZZLE 440

ACROSS

1. Show happiness
6. Mother's sisters
11. Piano
12. Sidesteps
14. A.A. Milne character: 3 wds.
16. Sothern and Sheridan
17. European deer
18. Rubber tree
19. Once-named
20. Soon
21. Skilled
22. Slapping sound
24. Lease again
25. Indifferent to right and wrong
27. Femmes fatales
28. Fills
29. Flower
30. Ali, formerly
31. In ____ (bored): 2 wds.
32. Gobbled
35. Boor
36. Lava
37. Gumbo ingredient
38. Casey Jones was one: 2 wds.
41. Baby-____
42. Snare
43. Plus item
44. Perch

DOWN

1. Backbone
2. Famed pool hustler: 2 wds.
3. Hostels
4. Hawaiian garland
5. Lasting forever
6. Pale
7. Hawaiian instruments, for short
8. Bite
9. Agitators
10. Sweet yeast bread
11. Graceful bird
13. Trousseau items
15. Blow a horn
20. Dear me!
21. Air: prefix
23. Victim
24. Uproar
25. Scarves
26. Mosquito-caused disease
27. Mantle, for one
29. Grain
31. Give a warning
33. Pick up the tab
34. Frontiersman Wyatt
36. Snick and ____
37. Hep
39. "____ a Living"
40. Sea goddess

PUZZLE 441

ACROSS

1. Fiery particle
6. Puff up
11. Passionate
13. Polite word
14. Drowsy one
15. Spring festival
16. Roof edges
18. Reporter Donaldson
19. Wall painting
23. Masterpiece
24. Levin and Gershwin
25. Golf mound
26. TV commercials
29. Rowdiness
32. Nonsense
34. Overhead railroads
35. Immediately
37. Annoy
38. In addition
39. Made over
40. Existed
43. Wear away
45. Shout from the audience
47. Ethically neutral
52. Gazed fixedly
53. Make larger
54. Having prongs
55. Plains Indian tent

DOWN

1. ____ Francisco
2. In favor of
3. Find a sum
4. Stoplight shade
5. Take a prayerful position
6. Chargeman
7. Bandleader Brown
8. Dinner for Dobbin
9. On the ocean
10. Semester
12. ____ la la
13. Looked searchingly
17. Wine tank
19. Speechless actor
20. Asian river
21. Beams
22. Fireplace residue
26. Enthusiastic
27. Sandwich shop
28. Snow toy
30. Went in
31. Secured, as a boat
33. Fury
36. Court
39. Send payment
40. Actress Mae ____
41. Opposed to: pref.
42. Scrutinize
44. Mom's partner
46. Mine output
48. Spanish cheer
49. Knock lightly
50. Devoured
51. Golfer Trevino

379

PUZZLE 442

ACROSS

1. Poi source
5. Actor Nicholson
9. "Le ___ Goriot"
13. Astringent
14. African antelope
16. Baal
17. "Waiting for the ___"
19. Scottish loch
20. Inscribed pillar
21. Verbena plant
23. Muslim ruler
26. Unhearing
27. Nemo's craft
31. Wild croquet ball
35. Esse ___ percipi
36. Hue
37. Endeavor
38. "It's ___ to Tell a Lie"
40. Expiate
42. Goddess of discord
43. Insert new film
45. Breathe heavily
47. Printemps follower
48. Water vapor
49. Kern musical
51. Queen of heaven
54. Neighborhood
55. Getting ahead
58. Cosmetician Lauder
62. Mrs. Dithers
63. Drake's ship
66. Employer
67. Perfect
68. Ireland, to poets
69. Writing table
70. Very strange: var.
71. Baking ___

DOWN

1. Mariners
2. Thanks ___!
3. Hick
4. Brunch dish
5. Fast plane
6. Strong beer
7. Visit
8. Do a bakery job
9. "H.M.S. ___"
10. Genesis garden
11. Diva Ponselle
12. Overhead trains
15. English sand hill
18. Forgive
22. Small pie
24. Homer epic
25. Smallest of the litter
27. Approaches
28. Thing of value
29. Useful
30. Ceases
32. Small green bird
33. Sra. Peron
34. Change, as an alarm
37. ___ Wences
39. Biblical craft
41. Okinawa city
44. Iowa college town
46. Pre-adolescent
50. Lively parties
52. Swiss mountain
53. Battery terminal
55. Assumed attitude
56. Mars
57. Part song
59. Novice: var.
60. Geraint's wife
61. Actress Best
62. Cow's chew
64. ___ es Salaam
65. English cathedral town

1	2	3	4		5	6	7	8		9	10	11	12
13					14			15		16			
17			18							19			
20						21		22					
		23		24	25		26						
27	28	29				30			31		32	33	34
35				36				37					
38			39		40		41			42			
43				44		45			46		47		
48						49				50			
			51		52	53		54					
	55	56					57			58	59	60	61
62				63			64	65					
66				67						68			
69				70						71			

PUZZLE 443

Codebreaker

Each group of 5 letters listed below is a word in a simple substitution code (a different letter represents the real one). The same code is used throughout. The clue next to each group gives you one of the real letters. The 10 clues give you the 10 letters used to form all the words. As a starter, we'll tell you that V stands for the letter I in all words.

1. U X V B T — one letter is I
2. F O X C U — one letter is D
3. O V F V U — one letter is G
4. H X C B T — one letter is A
5. B H O V F — one letter is P

6. X B V U L — one letter is E
7. X C F O T — one letter is N
8. B C L L O — one letter is S
9. H X H L O — one letter is R
10. B H O X T — one letter is Y

380

PUZZLE 444

ACROSS

1. Ascend, as a mountain
6. Begone, kitty!
10. Hive dwellers
14. Street show
15. Roman emperor
16. "____ Camera": 3 wds.
17. Get up
18. Fairy-tale start
19. Rapid pace
20. Bath linen
22. Wharf
23. Light fog
24. Authentic, informally
25. Wagon
29. Jump the track
31. Hawaiian greeting
33. Veteran: hyph.
38. Flower part
39. Switch word
40. Give the slip
41. Putting out, as energy
43. Removed
44. Reluctant
47. Remit
48. Prey
52. Suit to ____: 2 wds.
54. Book of maps
55. Southern swampland tract
60. Pinball-machine word
61. Golda
62. Had a fit
63. Not aweather
64. Comic Johnson
65. Make corrections in
66. Tear apart
67. Child's toy: hyph.
68. Peevish

DOWN

1. Animal stomach
2. Dr. Zhivago's love
3. Garden flower
4. Netting
5. Nut tree
6. Short nap
7. Focal point: 3 wds.
8. Instep
9. Foot digit
10. Mouthfuls
11. Our planet
12. Overact
13. Woodland deity
21. Young boy
22. Shook
24. Baby goat
25. Sleeveless garment
26. Emcee Trebek
27. Repetition
28. ____ she blows!
30. TV alien
32. Church parts
34. Singer Burl
35. Man or boy
36. Paradise
37. Funnyman Foxx
39. Wallet bill
42. Wall plant
45. Record player
46. Always, to Keats
48. Doha's country
49. Useful
50. Gracie or Fred
51. Assessed
53. Snowy bird
55. Architect Saarinen
56. Shiny fabric
57. Grows older
58. Car boo-boo
59. Whirlpool
61. Spring month

PIECE BY PIECE

PUZZLE 445

A humorous quotation has been divided into 3-letter pieces. Spaces between words have been eliminated. Rearrange the 3-letter pieces shown in the box to reconstruct the quotation. The dashes below indicate the number of letters in each word.

AMI	BEL	EIN	ENT	EUN	EVE
GHO	ION	IEV	IFY	LYR	OAF
ONT	OUD	RBE	STS	VEN	YOU

— — — — — —   — — — — —   — — — — — — —   — — — —

— — — — — — ,   — — — — —   — — — — —   — — — —

— — — —   — — — — — — —   — — — .

PUZZLE 446

ACROSS

1. Skein
5. Recuperate
9. Fed
13. Hindu chiefs
18. Religious image
19. Osprey's abode
20. Branches
21. Build
22. Be impetuous
25. Likewise
26. Guards
27. Recent: suff.
28. Pericles's mistress
30. Coal by-products
31. Food fish
32. Word on a tote board
33. "___ for Sergeants"
36. Spiny fish
38. Cathedral
42. Fire remains
43. Jazz style
45. Actress Charlotte
46. Bakery employee
47. "Two Mules for Sister ___" (1970 Eastwood film)
48. Protection
49. Elevation
50. Rhine feeder
51. Type of rifle
55. Summoned
56. Small amounts
59. Alpine crest
60. Unaided
61. Astaire and Savage
62. Geometric solids
63. Hint
64. Brackish
66. 100%
67. Chained
70. Rectify
71. Emergency exit
73. To's mate
74. Domesticated
75. Scottish river
76. War god
77. Nuclear particle
78. Pitcher's stat
79. Clint Eastwood film
83. Deep voice
84. Hoofers
86. Make effervescent
87. Eddie or Carrie
88. 100 square meters
89. Paid attendance
90. Impudent
91. California town
95. Cripple
96. Larders
100. Pungent
101. Scott Baio TV sitcom
104. Stand out
105. Wife for a 13 Across
106. Elder girl: Fr.
107. Million: pref.
108. Wise lawgiver
109. Certain Shoshoneans
110. It's sometimes more
111. Pastoral poem

DOWN

1. Villain's greeting
2. Yearn (for)
3. Lunchtime
4. More puzzling
5. Start of a toast
6. Youngest Greek god
7. Goal
8. County in Kentucky
9. Beowulf's victim
10. Seychelles island
11. Pierre's pal
12. East Indian palm
13. Evergreen tree
14. Certain early Christians
15. Goes by Phantom
16. Play part
17. Greek portico
19. Conflagrant
23. British streetcars
24. Throw
29. Cheese or Guard
31. Glacial ice
33. Young dragonfly
34. Mr. Levant
35. Chuck Connors TV series
36. Admonishes
37. Scarlett's Butler et al.
38. Alaskan glacier
39. Oldwife
40. Atelier item
41. Thin
43. Provokes
44. Curved molding
47. Stockholm native
49. Scope
52. Non-Polynesian Hawaiian
53. Bert's buddy
54. Sows
55. Two cups
57. Pickling liquid

58. ____ an ear
60. Loci
62. Horn-shaped structures
63. Amerind abode
64. Replete
65. City in Iraq
66. Jewish nation
67. Travesty
68. Irregularly notched
69. Giver
71. Mists
72. ____ blanche
75. Had the effrontery
77. Deli offering
79. Town in Connecticut
80. Ancient Greek region
81. Delicate
82. Breakfast porridge
83. Nativity
85. Gambling room
87. Wield an epee
90. Window sections
91. Back talk
92. Lover of Narcissus
93. Seed integument
94. Beige
95. Long, thick hair
96. Brooches
97. Stirred up
98. Like a souffle
99. Otary, e.g.
102. Derby
103. You: Ger.

PUZZLE 446

PUZZLE 447

CODEWORD

Codeword is a special crossword puzzle in which conventional clues are omitted.
Instead, answer words in the diagram are represented by numbers. Each number
represents a different letter of the alphabet, and all the letters of the alphabet
are used. When you are sure of a letter, put it in the code key chart and cross
it off in the Alphabet Box. A group of letters has been inserted to start you off.

1	2	3 E	4	5	6	7	8	9	10	11	12	13 N
14	15	16	17	18 D	19	20	21	22	23	24	25	26

11	15	26	23	■	12	11	22	3	9	■	9	12	1	3
15	12	18	3	■	11	15	12	7	3	■	3	23	26	13
12	7	26	8	■	23	3	9	3	22	■	15	3 E	13 N	18 D
17	12	9	12	16	3	3	22	■	3	15	12	22	3	11
■	■	■	9	25	11	16	■	20	15	3	21	■	■	■
12	6	6	3	13	22	■	5	4	15	22	25	17	15	3
9	12	2	■	18	26	18	26	11	■	11	13	12	25	15
26	17	4	11	■	11	25	21	3	11	■	14	25	7	3
5	3	22	3	9	■	22	25	18	3	11	■	15	3	14
12	18	3	10	4	12	22	3	■	6	15	12	11	11	19
■	■	4	13	18	26	■	18	9	12	14	■	■	■	■
12	15	15	3	14	3	■	7	25	3	8	12	23	15	3
15	26	12	13	■	3	24	3	6	22	■	22	26	26	15
3	17	25	6	■	5	26	22	3	15	■	3	15	15	11
11	3	9	3	■	11	22	26	9	19	■	11	26	15	3

ALPHABET BOX

A B C D̸ E F G H I J K L M N̸ O P Q R S T U V W X Y Z

384

PUZZLE 448

ACROSS
1. Form of address
5. Malice
9. Government agents
14. Exile island
15. Below decks, nautically
16. Consumed
17. Jewish month
18. Bottom
19. Draft horse
20. Job
21. River through Connecticut
23. Not kosher
25. Large-mouthed fish
26. One who professes
29. Courts
31. Dawdle
32. Shrinks
37. Colombian city
38. Riverbank
39. "Duke of ____"
40. "An Unmarried Woman" actor
42. Hog
43. Yemen seaport
44. Charged
45. Vestal
49. Pedestal part
50. Consumer advocate
53. Takes a small bite
57. Stan's sidekick
58. Dry
59. David Copperfield's wife
60. More cunning
61. Dawber and Shriver
62. Mayberry's frequent jailbird
63. Pumpkins' beginnings
64. Stave
65. Pesters

DOWN
1. Butcher's ware
2. "California Suite" actor
3. Down with: Fr.
4. Aka Samuel Clemens
5. Waitress
6. Shy
7. Perfume resin
8. Ram's partners
9. Ilie ____ of tennis
10. Porthos's sidekick
11. Curbs
12. Nobel prize winners Marie or Pierre
13. Plans
22. Digs
24. Mystery-writer Stout
26. Spanish treasure chest
27. Wiener schnitzel ingredient
28. Iberian pot
29. Braided
30. Change back from a five
32. Badger gathering
33. Coast Guard Academy location
34. Jib, e.g.
35. Marine bird
36. Luge
38. Loaded
41. Beach frequenters
42. Comic Caesar
44. Baldest
45. Vexed
46. Leipzig's neighbor
47. Kate's roomie
48. Scouted
49. Skin
51. Vipers and cobras
52. Distribute
54. Bit
55. Bluenose
56. Rudeness

PUZZLE 449

ACROSS

1. Two pints
6. "___ Her Standing There"
10. Headlight
14. Mr. Heep
15. PBS science series
16. Kirghiz mountains
17. Consent
18. Act
20. Word a suitor seeks
21. Grimace
23. Fry or dressing
24. Halite
25. Imprison
26. Roof of the mouth
29. Singer Ives
30. Preserve food
33. Ike's excuse?
34. Markdown time
35. Marine bird
36. Act
39. Agent: suff.
40. Chicago attraction
41. Loafed
42. Strong desire
43. Set of three
44. Table linen
45. Chantilly
46. Tarzan's transportation?
47. View
50. "___ Go Near the Water"
51. ___-tac-toe
54. Acted
56. Foolish
58. By the ___ of your pants
59. Porky's comment
60. 37th president
61. TV award
62. ___ bene
63. Sparkle

DOWN

1. Stone wharf
2. Impulse
3. Melodies
4. "Norma ___"
5. Topical
6. Enter computer data
7. Solitary
8. "Showboat" actress
9. Traveler
10. Jacket feature
11. Author Paton
12. Artist Chagall
13. Heart
19. Seed coat
22. Cheer from Juan
24. Sword
25. Minty drink
26. Songstress Cline
27. Having wings
28. Compare
29. ___ Rouge
30. Fashion
31. Enrage
32. Destitute
34. Sleep noise
35. Bivouac
37. Atomic particle
38. Atilt
43. Mexican menu item
44. Author Anais
45. Southpaw
46. Russian spirit
47. Part of a cathedral
48. Appear to be
49. British baby carriage
50. Small depression
51. Hack
52. Aware of
53. Copper coin
55. My, in Milan
57. Zero

ACROSS

1. Garden implement
6. Diminish
11. Smear
14. Betting game
15. Town ____
16. Dined
17. Ruling class
18. Gary Burghoff role
19. Little piggy
20. Finished
21. ____ in the bag!
22. Adjust
24. Booted
27. Indefinite pronoun
28. Horse headgear
31. Bursts
36. Fermented drink
37. Modern
39. Frozen-yogurt holder
40. Stockpile
42. Grant
43. Leisure
44. Birch, e.g.
45. Beauty parlors
48. Failure
49. Beryls
51. Ribs
53. Frigid
54. Burn slightly
55. Capitulate
58. Obstruct
60. Worry
64. Hail!
65. Harangue
67. Put punch in the punch
68. Society-page word
69. Arias
70. Put money in the pot
71. Termination
72. Checks
73. Annoying

DOWN

1. Went quickly
2. Marco ____
3. Related to
4. Abhor
5. Sooner than, in verse
6. Bitter
7. Neighbor's child, perhaps
8. Assists
9. British beverage
10. Wayward
11. ____ base
12. Upon
13. Root vegetable
23. Tennis tie
25. That woman
26. Lode yield
27. Select
28. It makes waste
29. Frighten
30. River embankment
31. Spins
32. "Do ____ others . . ."
33. Thoroughfares
34. Follow
35. Plant embryos
38. Dressed
41. Spooky
45. Like a fox
46. Unspecified degree
47. Andaman, e.g.
50. On the other side
52. Secret
54. Salad plant
55. Copenhagen native
56. Divisible by two
57. Nourish
58. Buck or bull
59. Power source
61. Pretends
62. Smell
63. Whirlpool
66. Decompose
67. Race measure

PUZZLE 451

When you have solved this crossword puzzle, the tinted letters, reading from left to right, reveal a quotation.

ACROSS

1. ____ serif
5. Eggs
8. Hurried
12. Body of soldiers
13. Scoop
14. Gurus
16. Heavenly
18. Trill
19. Fish snares
20. Ruler of the Aesir
22. "A Shropshire ____"
23. Abraham's nephew
24. Self-satisfied
25. Phi ____ Kappa
26. Speakers' platform
28. Centers of activity
29. Females
30. Raises
31. Cotton machine
32. Canvas cover
34. Prevents
36. Cease
40. "Little ____ Marker"
42. Roofing metal
43. Recent: pref.
44. Writer Gertrude ____
47. Tightly drawn
49. Gait
50. Pleasure trip
51. Kind of sculpture
52. Service charge
53. Transgress
54. Safari
55. Be a good guest
58. Fields of conflict
60. Language study
62. Probable
63. Bother
64. Sign of measles
65. Social appointment
66. Still
67. Singing voice

DOWN

1. Litigates
2. Contribute to a fund
3. Ultimate skeptic
4. Pool members
5. Lyric poems
6. By way of
7. Poise
8. Graceful water bird
9. ____ excellence
10. Symbol
11. Expand
14. Drink heartily
15. Portable chair
17. Soak flax
21. Dirt particles
24. "The ____ Also Rises"
25. Smacks
26. Failure
27. Primate
28. Snake sound

PUZZLE 451

29. English architect
31. Big smile
33. Mine entrance
35. Descendant of Mohammad
37. Belonging to the whole
38. Bishopric
39. Summit
41. Daze
42. Expression of disapproval
44. Baseball ploy
45. Intensely hot
46. Hooray!
48. Wandering
49. Spanish wife
51. Industrious
52. Competent
54. Robust
55. Thaw
56. Shopping reminder
57. Reverberation
59. Amount after deductions
61. Hurry

PUZZLE 452

ACROSS

1. Spoiled child
5. Loathe
9. Singer Johnny ____
13. Burning
17. Italian money, once
18. Summer drinks
19. On vacation
20. Robert De ____
21. Declare positively
22. "____ Lisa"
23. Tennis's Sampras
24. Love god
25. Salad toppers
28. Captivate
30. Earl or viscount
31. Gravestone letters
33. Pub quaff
34. Clumsy
38. Demolished
40. Bad habits
44. Actress Belafonte et al.
45. Sovereign's deputy
47. Shift
48. Michael ____ of "A Fish Called Wanda"
49. Offered as an example
50. Corporate bigwig: abbr.
52. Author Deighton
53. Let it stand
54. Fashions
55. Basic
57. French schools
59. Having less money
60. Texas city
63. Find out
64. Winning serves
68. "Married to the ____"
69. Skater Babilonia
70. Sorrow
71. Home of the Dolphins
72. Element
74. Unmasks
76. Astringent compound
77. Loved excessively
79. Char
80. Gopher of "The Love Boat" et al.
81. "____ the season ..."
83. French resort
84. Flock
85. "____ and Old Lace"
89. Stars
95. Forbidden fruit
96. Sandwich shop
98. German river
99. Ellipse
100. Persian mathematician
101. Blue-pencil
102. Dullard
103. Donated
104. Sleeps
105. Refuse
106. Sugar apple
107. Again

DOWN

1. Tattle
2. Tear apart
3. District
4. Marine bird
5. Laundry holders
6. Put on a pedestal
7. Choir voice
8. Jacob's brother
9. Overturned
10. Reverent dread
11. Glut
12. Happy animal?
13. California city
14. Succotash ingredient
15. Household appliance
16. Civil wrong
26. Madrid's country
27. Copies
29. 155
32. Through: pref.
34. European vipers
35. "____ Price Glory?"
36. Cabbagelike plant
37. Author
38. Formal acts
39. Hospital employees
41. Fountain order
42. At all
43. Ship
45. Television
46. Long
49. Lassie et al.
51. "A Chorus Line" tune

54. Tooth
55. Flies high
56. Empties
58. Inhabitant: abbr.
59. Charles Willson ____
60. In the course of
61. Lorre role
62. Assist a criminal
63. Major or minor
65. Sugar source
66. Kuwaiti ruler
67. Errs
70. Persistence
71. ____ gras
73. Falling stars
75. Big shot
76. Towers
78. Clamor
80. Small stone
82. Paneled
84. Spartan serf
85. Shortly
86. "Arrivederci ____"
87. Cinch
88. Yield
90. Helen's mother
91. Robe of office
92. Scientist Pavlov
93. Roof part
94. Great number
97. Waterfall, in Scotland

1	2	3	4		5	6	7	8		9	10	11	12		13	14	15	16
17					18					19					20			
21					22					23					24			
25				26				27			28		29					
			30					31		32		33						
34	35	36	37				38				39		40		41	42	43	
44					45						46		47					
48					49					50		51		52				
53				54					55				56					
		57	58				59											
60	61	62					63						64	65	66	67		
68				69			70					71						
72			73		74		75				76							
77				78		79					80							
			81		82		83			84								
85	86	87				88		89		90				91	92	93	94	
95					96		97			98				99				
100					101					102				103				
104					105					106				107				

PUZZLE 453

ACROSS

1. "The Iliad,"
   e.g.
5. Catch
8. Small grip
11. Hit hard
15. Section
16. Cupidity
18. Fibs
20. Flat piece
21. Piece of
   drapery
22. Like a lamb
23. Shoshonean
24. Draw
26. Very early
27. Gutsier
28. Headland
30. Identify
33. Fling
35. Saberhagen's
   stat
36. Learns
39. Digit number
40. Mrs., in La
   Paz
41. Relaxed
44. Attitude
47. Cuts in three
49. Italian river
50. Supplants
54. Ironic
55. Trifle
56. Mat
57. Like neon
58. Squealer
59. C-in-C before
   DDE
60. Rider's
   direction
61. By means of
63. Neighbor to
   Swed.
64. Piece by
   Chopin
66. Preposterous
67. Flit about
68. Wrap
69. Knights'
   ladies
70. Henry's sixth
   wife
71. Copies
73. Feature
76. Light gesture
77. Stock value
79. Particle
80. Lost
82. Indian
   measure
83. Disagree-
   ments
85. Part of a
   pecan
86. Bulldog
   school
90. Kane and
   Lynley
92. ___ king
94. Social
   gathering
96. Lost color
97. Rank
98. Bridge
101. Harmonize
103. Series of
   songs
104. Opposite
105. Charges
106. Music stand
107. Compass pt.
108. Hurdle
109. Beholds

DOWN

1. Overjoy
2. Longs
3. Cool
4. Irish or Scot
5. Warning
6. Female cells
7. Fellow
8. Points
9. Lenient
10. Hive insect
11. Cache
12. Molten flow
13. Author Sacks
14. Biological
   categories
15. Like some
   silk or sugar
17. Crude
19. Italian
   evening
25. Arthropods
27. Part of N.B.
29. Success
31. Scruffy
32. "Able was I
   ___ ..."
34. Venice resort
37. Nibbled
38. Band
   instrument
40. Dazzle
41. Gaped
42. Corrective
   list
43. Pronounce-
   ment
45. Actual
46. Film ___
48. Child
51. Deliberative
   body
52. Figures of
   speech

53. Italicize
59. Command of old
60. Outfit
61. TV's Mindy
62. Impart
65. Precious
66. Asserts
67. Silly creatures
68. Slow
70. Malaysian sailboat
72. Medieval lyric poem
74. Guides
75. Actor Robbins
77. Sounded
78. Succeed
81. Final
82. Flaw
83. Smooth
84. Labor
87. Rugged crest
88. Corridors
89. Wraps up
91. Burden
93. Beverage
95. Fundamentals
98. Strive
99. City area
100. Civil War initials
102. Sham

PUZZLE 454

ACROSS

1. Congressional gofer
5. Jacob's son
10. Out-of-this-world sightings: abbr.
14. "Family Ties" son
15. Erupt
16. Polynesian god of fertility
17. Honshu city
18. Pork cuts
19. Employer
20. Nell Carter's sitcom
23. Hebrew letter
24. Type sizes
25. Agile
27. Run on
31. Ensilage
33. Field
34. Skin
35. Red, white, and black
38. Actress Perlman
39. Joined
40. ___ and hearty
41. Elegant wood
42. Rueful word
43. Variety of tea
44. Corn seed
46. California peak
47. Director Hitchcock
49. Parked it
50. Flightless bird
51. Prepare the way
58. Deck hand for the cap'n
60. Singer Ford
61. Suspension
62. This: Sp.
63. Point connectors
64. British boob tube
65. Balance
66. Not much
67. During

DOWN

1. Twinge
2. Asian mountain range
3. Origin
4. Midterm, e.g.
5. Eager
6. Boors
7. Kojak's lack
8. Coastal bird
9. Smoothed again
10. Sumerian sun god
11. Basketball ploys
12. Patrick or Ryan
13. Lend a hand
21. Electric fish
22. Goat's offspring
26. Hooks up
27. Simpson son
28. Suffix with head or back
29. Morning meals
30. Wide-mouthed glass
31. "___ Attraction"
32. Native minerals
34. Whiten
36. Spiny houseplant
37. Witnessed
39. Country-singer Barbara ___
43. Course
45. Confederate Johnny
46. Current
47. Resin color
48. Untied
49. Cloud carriers
52. One of five Greats
53. Actress Sten
54. This, in Seville
55. Feature
56. Columbian city
57. Wide- ___
59. Fish trap

ACROSS

1. Strike
5. Hawaiian hello
10. Beehive
14. Conifer
15. Not at any time
16. Broz
17. New York mountains
19. Atilt
20. Small horse
21. Scottish lake
23. Greek letter
26. ____ de la Cite
27. "Cheers" patron
28. Copies
30. Sail support
32. Finder's sound
35. Colorado resort
36. Icelandic tales
37. After gross
38. Sports-pg. number
39. Specks
40. Cracked
41. Lamprey
42. Land measures
43. Toil
44. Sp. lady
45. DDE and namesakes
46. Gazes fixedly
47. Muslim judge
49. School org.
50. Prov. of Canada
51. Receptacles
54. Greek magnate
55. Of the ear
56. Canadian mountain range
62. Close at hand
63. Famous cow
64. Robert or Alan
65. Sicilian volcano
66. It also rises
67. Patch of ground

DOWN

1. Place to get a workout
2. Put a ____ on it!
3. Bird of the cuckoo family
4. Each
5. Records
6. Shelf
7. An avis lays them
8. Mild oath
9. Home of the Ozarks
10. Footballer Bart ____
11. Tanzanian mountain
12. British school
13. Bishop of Rome
18. Hamburger garnish
22. Sandbox groupies
23. Obliterates
24. Bed canopy
25. North American trail or mountains
29. Steep flax
30. Partners
31. Birthday numbers
33. State of bliss
34. Idle
36. Loser or throat
39. Alaska mountain
40. According to
42. Verdi's opera
43. Mar
46. Mason's girl
48. Ghana's capital
49. "I Love ____"
51. Best
52. Printer's mark
53. Bargain-hunter's word
57. "Born in the ____"
58. Draw out
59. Not well
60. Confusion
61. ____ King Cole

PUZZLE 456

ACROSS

1. Enthusiasm
5. One-spots
9. Meerschaum
13. Big ____ Theory
17. Walking stick
18. Kewpie, e.g.
19. Plant part
20. Olive genus
21. Be exactly right: 6 wds.
25. Jacutinga, e.g.
26. Pongid
27. Play on words
28. Chooses
29. Table scrap
30. Mediterranean island
32. Crater edge
33. Overseas telegram
36. Dress fashion of 1947: 2 wds.
38. Lorelei
42. Greedy
43. Variety of ruby
44. Cartoonist Gardner
46. Subtle emanation
47. Encountered
48. Headlong
49. Fashion
51. Excavate
52. Gifts
54. ____ Na Na
55. Foreigners
57. Singer Nelson
58. Coquettish
59. Surrounded by
60. Kind of goose
63. Follower of Attila
64. Ceremonial etiquette
68. Parseghian
69. Concur
71. Self-esteem
72. Mature
73. Turnpike exit
75. Long period of time
76. Uneven
77. Woody plant
78. Entreat
80. Include
82. Measuring device
83. Min. part
85. Having wings
86. Conducted
87. Annoys persistently
91. Had lunch
92. Unit of measure
93. Little devil
96. Symbol of touchiness: 5 wds.
100. London streetcar
101. Hyde ____
102. Pedal digits
103. Otherwise
104. Gargantuan
105. Health resorts
106. Indefinite amount
107. Harvest

DOWN

1. Alpine sound
2. Lion's den
3. Cash for cards
4. Clear profit
5. Proficient
6. Strobile
7. Guido's high note
8. Depart unobtrusively: 2 wds.
9. Quickly
10. Electrified particle
11. Containers
12. Anesthetic
13. Arty area
14. Actor Guinness
15. Well-groomed
16. Moves restlessly
22. Leveret
23. Soothes
24. Yale students
29. Elderly
30. Thaws
31. Large artery
33. Tent city
34. Declare
35. Snack
36. Loathsome
37. Central
39. Impolite
40. Ms. Moran
41. Scolds
43. Surgical dressing
45. Apple pie ____: 3 wds.
48. Columnist Hopper
49. Modest
50. Choice
53. Andaman or Tasman
54. Male heir
56. Wedding response: 2 wds.

396

58. Billiards item
59. Get up
60. Find fault
61. Asian lake
62. Title
63. Hair dye
64. Ordinary writing
65. Low wagon
66. Curved molding
67. Suggestive grin
70. Fish eggs
71. Objects strongly
74. Diversion
76. Fill with joy
77. Tycoon Turner
79. Profound
81. Metallic sounds
82. Banquet fare
84. Riding whips
86. Type of ends
87. Footway
88. Neutral color
89. Type of carpet
90. Cold ___
92. Oates opus
93. Unoccupied
94. Tableland
95. Kind of school
97. ___ pro nobis
98. Michigan canals
99. Irish sea god

PUZZLE 457

ACROSS

1. Pianist Templeton
5. Name for a dog
9. Bath-powder ingredient
13. Webber show
17. Ballplayer Blue
18. Nondairy spread
19. Type of rug
20. Near the deck
21. Shoot forth
22. Member of the "Cheers" gang
23. Fishing need
24. Type of party wear
25. Tool
27. Lee or Ty
29. On the level
31. Auricle
32. Numerous
33. Actress Moore
34. Whips
37. Entertainment
38. Airplane launcher
42. Put aboard
43. Experts
44. Staller's word
45. Black, e.g.
46. Egg: pref.
47. Opinion
48. Monkee Tork
49. Yogi, e.g.
50. Feline
52. Lamb and veal
53. Houseplants
54. Poet's word
55. Prepared
56. By way of
57. Pub game
60. Glides
61. Snoozes
65. Outrages
66. Ages
67. Bath rugs
68. French map word
69. Tell a lie, e.g.
70. Steamers
71. Indy entries
72. Feline fingernail
73. Boos
75. Noggin
76. Continues
77. Primates
78. Satisfy
79. Iota
80. Gesture of respect
83. Gumbo ingredient
84. White wine
88. Molding edge
89. Matlock's concern
91. Genuine
93. Put
94. Gold coins of Latvia
95. Against
96. Lung sound
97. Story starter
98. Envelope part
99. "___ Wolf" (Fox movie)
100. Droning sounds
101. Horse directions

DOWN

1. With: Fr.
2. Peruvian city
3. Blue-pencil
4. Lustrous gem
5. Naval need
6. Deere item
7. Anthem word
8. Gibs
9. Striped feline
10. Nomad
11. Don Ho wear
12. Medical tube
13. A feline favorite
14. African plant
15. Clothes
16. Hit
26. Ballet step
28. Unified
30. Poet Khayyam
32. Sound from Morris
33. Appointments
34. Woolly substance
35. Volcano output
36. Mine passage
37. Unattached
38. Spiteful
39. Utilizer
40. Jack Sprat's fare
41. Mariners
43. Walleye
44. Directs
47. Big shots
48. Bosc and Anjou
49. String, e.g.
51. Production locales
52. Way
53. Tantrums
55. Living et al.
56. Casks
57. Compact ___

58. Sills song
59. Apartment fee
60. Closes
61. Concern
62. Is unwell
63. City map
64. Hems
66. Homeless feline
67. Spouse
70. Ammo for toy pistols
71. Throat ailment
72. Index
74. Condiment
75. Links goal
76. Ignited
78. Portion of yarn
79. Packages
80. Elsie's offspring
81. Russian mountains
82. "Rio ___"
83. Bone: pref.
84. Quiet
85. Opposite of wax
86. Copper blue or green
87. Lime drinks
90. Donkey: Fr.
92. ___ de Cologne

PUZZLE 458

ACROSS

1. Mandible
4. Piercing tool
7. Supplemented
11. Lyric poem
12. Placed
14. Electricity carrier
15. High-schooler
17. Vivacity
18. "Chances ___"
19. To the other side
21. Prospector's territory
24. "Rock of ___"
25. Put to sleep
26. Wearing footgear
27. Uncooked
30. Cereal grain
31. Play's setting
32. Woodchopper's implement
33. Pair
34. Pod vegetables
35. Lubricants
36. Fairy's scepter
37. Manservant
38. Hardening adhesive
41. Strike
42. Presidential office shape
43. Jungle trumpeter
48. Gentle
49. Urgent
50. Baltic or Adriatic
51. Bullfight cheers
52. Part of RPM
53. Ink writer

DOWN

1. Scribble hastily
2. Citrus beverage
3. ___ Willie Winkie
4. Frighten
5. Salary
6. Fib
7. Pitchers
8. Metric weight unit
9. Historic time periods
10. Lairs
13. Mythical fire-breathers
16. Carpenter's spike
20. Yield
21. Lump of earth
22. Hawaiian feast
23. Choir voice
24. In front
26. Aromatic
27. Banister
28. Wheel shaft
29. Sunset direction
31. Bridge
35. Pledge
36. Fuses together
37. Venomous serpent
38. Singer Perry ___
39. Malevolent
40. Stallion or buck, e.g.
41. This place
44. Fleshy mouth part
45. Cleopatra's snake
46. Born
47. Turn into leather

PUZZLE 459

ACROSS
1. Touched
5. Zoo enclosure
9. Soft hat
12. Vicinity
13. Engage
14. Actress MacGraw
15. Social standing
16. Charming
18. Regard highly
20. ___ rummy (card game)
21. Arrests
23. Trimmed
27. Machine part
30. Genuine
32. Days of old
33. Lyric poem
34. Uses a lever
36. Be victorious
37. Burden
39. Strip of wood
40. Mesh
41. Cupid's weapon
43. Bridge
45. ___ Cruces
47. Nation of De Gaulle
51. Makeup item
55. Lunch or dinner
56. Golly!
57. Singly
58. Miscalculates
59. Hooting bird
60. Thin stick
61. Prescribed amount

DOWN
1. Price of passage
2. Historic periods
3. Time before Easter
4. Removed
5. Judge's office
6. Help
7. Sailor's beverage
8. Spooky
9. Taxi
10. "___ in the Family"
11. Cherry or mince
17. Artist Warhol
19. Marshal Wyatt ___
22. Spinnakers, e.g.
24. Formal dress
25. Huron's neighbor
26. Dimple
27. Soft drink flavor
28. Smell
29. Equipment
31. Kids' jumping game
35. Celebrity
38. Raggedy Ann, e.g.
42. Torso's narrowest part
44. Called
46. Winter white stuff
48. Roman fiddler
49. Autos
50. What ___ is new?
51. Conceit
52. Longbow tree
53. Snaky fish
54. Inventor Whitney

401

PUZZLE 460

ACROSS
1. Faucet
4. Agt.
7. Make merry
9. Bravery award
11. Kitchen gadget
13. Gully
14. Big ___ (London landmark)
15. Character Pyle, played by Jim Nabors
17. Neckwear
18. Self
20. "The Old Man and the ___"
21. "What's up, ___?"
22. Make ___ meet
24. Gateway
26. ___ what?
27. Near
28. Governor Wilson
30. Soupy meat dish
32. Headgear
33. ___ mode
35. Pat gently
37. Male child
38. Collision
40. Comedian Skelton
42. General George S. ___
44. Ice cream concoction
46. Direction sign
47. Actor Wallace
48. Artificial coloring
49. Printers' letters

DOWN
1. Wigwam
2. Retaliate for
3. Ballpoint ___
4. Accelerate
5. Newspaper employee
6. Sudden fear
7. Mr. Petrie of "The Dick Van Dyke Show"
8. Break a ___!
9. Damage
10. Gypsy Rose ___
12. Flagmaker Betsy ___
13. Enjoy a book
16. "Love ___ Tender"
19. Beginning
21. Bestowed excessive love
23. Speck
25. Cereal grain
28. Food closet
29. Make money
30. Back talk
31. Prison official
32. Store up
34. "___ Law"
36. Chicago team
37. Health club
38. Elsie, e.g.
39. Core
41. Actress from 34 Down
43. Foot digit
45. Born

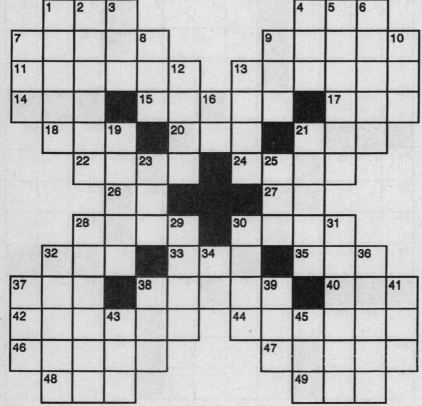

ACROSS

1. Shade tree
4. Fast plane
7. Transmitted
11. Paper measure
13. Mine yield
14. Defined space
15. Nevada resort
16. Egg layer
17. Linen fiber
18. Room for relaxation
20. Social equal
21. Notion
23. Reverent fear
25. Pastoral poem
26. Dutch bulb
28. Apple seed
31. Tavern drink
32. Turf
33. Baseball stat
34. Comedian Skelton
35. Subscribe again
37. Pull behind
38. Lemon refresher
39. Place for a roast
41. Failed play
44. Afternoon beverage
45. Encase
46. Chimpanzee, e.g.
48. Some resorts
52. Where the heart is
53. Untruth
54. Follow
55. Portent
56. Traveler's lodging
57. Attempt

DOWN

1. Be human
2. Confederate general
3. "The Invisible ___"
4. Everyman Doe
5. Sooner than, in poems
6. Decade number
7. Out of danger
8. Perry's creator Gardner
9. Close-by
10. Tariff
12. Style
19. Take nourishment
20. Vigor
21. Inactive
22. Feat
23. Solo
24. Broad
25. Rower's implement
27. Secondhand
28. Cartoon dragon's owner
29. Wrought ___
30. Fido's foot
35. Knock sharply
36. Sorrow
40. Extensive
41. ___ the heart (sincerely)
42. Limping
43. Accessible
44. Adolescent
45. Which person
46. Boxer Muhammad ___
47. Needle's cousin
49. Singer Boone
50. Ventilate
51. Cunning

PUZZLE 462

ACROSS

1. Blemish
5. To and ____
8. Criticizes
12. Huron, e.g.
13. Edge
14. Verbal
15. Land measure
16. Song of praise
17. "Better Luck Next ____"
18. Defeated
20. Packed
22. Derby, for one
23. Ingest
24. Tier
27. Footstool
31. Period in history
32. Oxygen or helium
33. Fuss
34. Beverage maker
37. Totaled
39. One billion years
40. Hot tub
41. Mechanic's place
44. State of mind
48. Porter and stout
49. Red deer
51. Small opening
52. Snout
53. Astonishment
54. Verve
55. Obtains
56. Conducted
57. Bird's home

DOWN

1. Thick slice
2. Walk impatiently
3. Gumbo ingredient
4. Cut a tooth
5. Facade
6. Disencumber
7. Egg dishes
8. Tuber
9. Very dry
10. Moniker
11. Winter vehicle
19. Lend an ____
21. Cereal grass
24. Testing place
25. In the past
26. Thus far
27. Sculler's need
28. Angry
29. Summer drink
30. Motion of agreement
32. Universal
35. Pokes fun at
36. Record
37. Mimic
38. Moisten
40. Horse
41. Group of bandits
42. ____ vera
43. Take five
45. Column
46. Cenozoic and Paleozoic
47. Let
50. Be indebted to

ACROSS

1. Snoop
4. ____ work and no play . . .
7. Feline sound
10. Casual shirts
12. TV's "____ John"
14. "____ Maria"
15. Spoken
16. Father, to the crib set
17. Illuminated
18. Undiluted
19. Prison chamber
21. Dawn to dusk
24. Spider's trap
25. Hi-fi component
28. Sandwich shop
30. Make ale
34. Distant
35. Ship's canvases
37. Time period
38. Leisurely gait
40. Fashion anew
41. ____ cleaning
42. Container
44. ____ of the line
46. Ruth the legend
48. Gambler's concern
52. Neither's companion
53. Small letter
57. Enthusiasm
58. Dine
59. Tuneful threesome
60. Singer Fitzgerald
61. Give it a whirl
62. Franklin, to friends
63. Keep a stiff upper ____

DOWN

1. Cease
2. Lima's land
3. Twelve months
4. Tack on
5. Meadow
6. Fellow
7. Shopping area
8. Wickedness
9. Sopping
11. Luge
13. Relay, for one
20. Wane
22. Madison Avenue products
23. Crave
24. Playwright Oscar ____
25. Rearward
26. Spoil
27. Sport instructor
29. Misrepresent
31. Angry color
32. Be inaccurate
33. Pave the ____ for
36. Alan, to Robert Alda
39. Bathing need
43. Monthly due
45. Slumber
46. Wild pig
47. Pretentious
49. Vale
50. Surrealist painter
51. Strike
52. Mesh
54. Globe
55. Cravat
56. Long time

PUZZLE 464

ACROSS

1. Flower holder
5. Kind of bed
9. Dove's sound
12. Concert solo
13. Unwrap
14. Wise bird
15. Camera eye
16. Agreed
18. Enthusiastic
20. Golf gadget
21. Recline
24. Tilts
28. What snowflakes are
32. Frog or year
33. "Flying Down to ___"
34. Examines by radar
36. Pub offering
37. " . . . three men in ___"
39. Imitated
41. Artist's cap
43. Matured
44. Minstrel's song
46. ___-case scenario
50. A fly in the ___
55. Raise
56. Fruit cooler
57. Cultivate
58. Boundary
59. Chubby
60. Choir member
61. Medicine unit

DOWN

1. Earthly life
2. Territory
3. Vocalize
4. Art stands
5. Feather scarf
6. ___ and downs
7. Sparrow's home
8. Genuflect
9. Folding bed
10. Feel obligated
11. Ancient
17. Singer Young
19. Spoils
22. Chantilly
23. Pack animal
25. Subway scarcity
26. Narrative
27. Drove too fast
28. Lobster's kin
29. Ritual
30. Thine
31. Cozy
35. Seattle ___
38. Waistband
40. Worshiped
42. City in western Florida
45. Holler
47. Make over
48. Stoops
49. Coatrack
50. Simpleton
51. Asian peak
52. Lacrosse goal
53. Wayne's word
54. Deuce

PUZZLE 465

ACROSS
1. Through
4. Bakes
9. Keats poem
12. Painting, for instance
13. Hangout
14. Neither's partner
15. Fate
16. Blunder
17. British beverage
18. Join together
20. Band instrument
22. Evaded
25. Fable message
28. Foot lever
30. Roomy
31. ____ and tonic
34. Imp
36. Out of the ordinary
37. Cracker-jacks
39. More congenial
41. Summits
43. Patterns
47. Wedding band
49. "Jack ____ could eat no fat"
50. Itty-bitty
52. Texas shrine
55. Blvd.
56. Overhead trains
57. Havana native
58. Golf gadget
59. Whit
60. Retains
61. Pipe joint

DOWN
1. Worth
2. Shackles
3. Garret
4. Chirped
5. Paddle
6. "____ Town"
7. Granny, for one
8. Play a guitar
9. Canadian province
10. Bambi's mom
11. Period
19. Knock
21. Hair decoration
23. Actress Barbara ____
24. Comedian Letterman
26. Append
27. Went in front
29. Parasites
31. Opening
32. Frost
33. ____ and dearest
35. Exercises
38. Winter transport
40. "____ Van Winkle"
42. Nibble
44. Bother
45. Orange type
46. Stainless ____
48. Paste
50. "Charlotte's ____"
51. Hebrew priest
53. Politician Ribicoff
54. Motorist's guide

407

PUZZLE 466

ACROSS

1. Bivouac
5. Additional
9. Cook in oil
12. Smell
13. Imitates
14. Pastureland
15. Dog's treat
16. Baby's powder
17. Unit of corn
18. Take advantage of
20. Large spotted cat
22. Maiden
25. Epoch
26. Mineral-bearing rock
27. Once around a track
29. Swap
33. Shade of color
35. Roll of cash
37. Stumble
38. Glossy fabric
40. Armed conflict
42. Command to a horse
43. Dawn dampness
45. Water down
47. Sticks
51. Beaver's construction
52. Golfer Trevino
53. Singer Jerry ____
55. Stingy
58. Rowboat propeller
59. Wicked
60. Poker starter
61. Last word
62. Matched groups
63. Ragout

DOWN

1. Corn on the ____
2. Commotion
3. Memorial structure
4. Push
5. Wrestling surface
6. October's stone
7. Confederate general's signature: abbr.
8. Accompany
9. Circus insect
10. Back side
11. Three feet
19. Moray, e.g.
21. Hair division
22. Morse code symbols
23. Opera solo
24. Attorney's subject
28. Animal foot
30. Dispute
31. Way to lose weight
32. Fencer's weapon
34. Moon's pull
36. Mom's spouse
39. You get on my ____!
41. Divest
44. Operate a loom
46. Tibetan monks
47. Succulent plant
48. College official
49. Group of cattle
50. Incision
54. Overhead trains
56. Dined
57. Turn over a ____ leaf

ACROSS

1. Decay
4. Price paid
8. Filled tortilla
12. Commotion
13. Head growth
14. Winter flakes
15. Euclid's field
17. ____ and now
18. Cigarette residue
19. Candle cores
20. Carries on
22. Rendered fat
23. Lawyer's assignment
24. Bugs Bunny's celluloid world
27. Singer Garfunkel
28. Long family quarrels
30. Fasten with a knot
31. The ____ State (Utah)
33. Touched
34. Ceremonial garment
35. Unsatisfactory
37. Pours down
39. Matador's cheer
40. You are something ____!
41. Interfering
46. Questions
47. Impulse
48. Pair
49. "____ Horizon"
50. Stag or roe
51. Red or carpenter

DOWN

1. Cloth shred
2. Type of poem
3. As well
4. Bureau
5. Promises
6. Knight's title
7. Attempt
8. Pullover
9. Amusing tales
10. Bottle stopper
11. Is in debt
16. Lion's head fur
19. Large conflicts
20. Hard to find
21. Printer's stars
22. Young fellow
23. Hired car
24. Billiards stick
25. Greasy
26. Tennis court divider
28. White lies
29. First woman
32. Truthful
33. Gasoline, e.g.
35. Hunter's cabin
36. More aged
37. Genuine
38. In addition
41. Wet dirt
42. Bard's before
43. Peak on Crete
44. Religious sister
45. Acquired

409

PUZZLE 468

ACROSS

1. Wipe
4. Forfeit
8. Acts
12. Cooling beverage
13. Sowing wild ____
14. Hamburger order
15. Steps
17. Gumbo ingredient
18. Requested
19. Texas city
21. Broad-antlered deer
23. Jabbered
27. Spaceship
30. Affirmative vote
32. Loom
33. Siestas
35. Bark
37. Nancy ____ (girl detective)
38. Standard of perfection
40. Trashy newspaper
42. Sample
43. Becker's game
45. Bear cave
47. Distribute cards
49. Titles
53. To ____ it may concern
56. Steelers' sport
58. Ames's state
59. Sinister
60. Need
61. Adolescent minor
62. Trust
63. Was in front

DOWN

1. ____ mia!
2. Lyric poems
3. Pikes ____
4. Noisily
5. Scull
6. Fret
7. School paper
8. Wilted
9. Kind of paneling
10. Make a gaffe
11. Body of water
16. Understand
20. Raucous cry
22. Crucial
24. Role
25. "If ____ I Would Leave You"
26. Moist
27. Component
28. Wash out
29. Store sign
31. Light breeze
34. Visitor who brings sleep
36. Writing tablet
39. Speak falsely
41. Daintily
44. More secure
46. Grab
48. "All You Need Is ____"
50. Manhandle
51. Alternative
52. Winter vehicle
53. Humor
54. Garden tool
55. Have creditors
57. Fossil fuel

ACROSS

1. Stroke
4. Swerve
7. Taken
10. Ultimate
12. Pennsylvania port
14. "The Greatest"
15. Ogle
16. Soothe
17. Staff
18. Arizona city
19. Huge pond
21. Certainly!
24. Cleopatra's viper
25. Belfry dweller
28. Vamoose!
30. Subdued
34. Cool drink
35. Apologetic
37. Non-professional
38. Went on horseback
40. Dog in "Our Gang"
41. Caustic
42. Bandleader Brown
44. Morsel for an aardvark
46. Resign
48. "God's Little ___"
52. Jog
53. Finished
57. Victuals
58. Roman three
59. Diamond number
60. Loyal
61. Select
62. Cooking direction
63. Room for relaxation

DOWN

1. What a psychic might read
2. Fencing sword
3. Plumbing joints
4. Last letter
5. Lyricist Gershwin
6. Dogfaces
7. Listen
8. Century plant
9. Acted
11. Doctor's picture
13. Morays
20. Suitable
22. Road curve
23. Stores
24. Main artery
25. Exclude
26. Bedlam
27. Senator Kennedy
29. Unrefined metal
31. Entirely
32. Mother ___ I? (child's game)
33. Storm center
36. Hankering
39. Inventor Whitney
43. Collar type
45. 27th president
46. Witticism
47. Squadron
49. Heavy string
50. Rake
51. First garden
52. ___ de Janeiro
54. By
55. Cease
56. Jazz pianist Garland

PUZZLE 470

• LEPRECHAUN LAND •

ACROSS

1. Toward the mouth
5. Pouch
8. Gifts from Oahu
12. Actress Francis
14. "___ Marner"
16. Tapestry
18. March 17th honoree: 2 wds.
20. Insinuating
21. Likely ___ (probably): 2 wds.
22. Biremes' needs
23. Listen here!
25. Envy, for one
26. Regrets
27. Three: pref.
28. Nice summer
29. Lean-to
30. Soul, in St. Lo
31. Docs
33. Ladies' soc.
36. Grand and little, in bridge
38. Bandleader Lanin
40. Ecology gp.
41. Laughs coarsely
44. Causes displeasure
46. Humane gp.
48. Wyoming range
49. Shipping channel
52. Penthouse
55. Greek porch
56. "___ Alte"
57. Hibernia: 2 wds.
60. Heart-machine reading: abbr.
61. To join, in France
63. Old defense org.
64. Onlookers
66. Murray and Meara
68. Unhurried
70. Tizzy
71. Beers
73. Botanist Gray
74. Metric unit of area
78. Forgets
80. Baseball's Bando
81. Letter additions: abbr.
82. Actor Ely
83. Declines
85. Corrida shout
87. La Brea Pits substance
89. Highlander
90. Ditty
91. Army acronym
92. Musical ending
93. Bridges
94. List of candidates
96. Cork's kissable rock: 2 wds.
99. English composer
100. Wise men
101. Musical studies
102. Get away!
103. Adage
104. Actor Auberjonois

DOWN

1. Potpourris
2. Overhead item
3. Formicary dweller
4. Stations
5. Lords
6. Actress MacGraw
7. Hidden store
8. "___ Train to Clarksville"
9. Coastal eagle
10. Hunting dog: 2 wds.
11. Miss Hawkins
12. Take for granted
13. Hindu queens
14. Takes long steps
15. Revue units
17. Force to go
19. Swiss river
21. Asian sea
24. Ego
29. Pintail ducks
31. Actress Oberon
32. Nightmares
34. Spotted horse
35. Entered the Indy
37. Height: abbr.
39. Spanish aunt
42. Chess pieces
43. Hitch
45. Dagger
47. Scientific suffix
49. Cassia product
50. Gaelic saying: 3 wds.
51. Pitchers' stats
53. Followers: suff.
54. African antelopes
56. Double
58. Strongman of myth
59. Algonquian Indians
62. Unicorns
65. And so on: abbr.
67. ___ Lanka
69. John-Boy and Erin, e.g.
72. Pack neatly
75. Secret
76. TV's Arledge et al.
77. Tolkien creatures
79. Messy ones
81. Orison
83. Comfort
84. Monthly notices
86. Modern name of Greece
88. Summer cooler
89. Fine china
91. Flying prefix
92. Boatmen
93. Amaze
95. Chinese way
97. ___ Khan
98. Sault ___ Marie

412

DOUBLE TROUBLE

PUZZLE 471

Not really double trouble, but double fun! Solve this puzzle as you would a regular crossword, EXCEPT place one, two, or three letters in each box. The number of letters in each answer is shown in parentheses after its clue.

ACROSS

1. Started (5)
4. Enthusiastic (4)
7. Quarrel (7)
10. Father (4)
11. Exposes (5)
12. Ripped (4)
13. Gently (10)
15. Corporal's superior (8)
17. "____ on Sunday" (5)
18. Zealous (7)
19. Quagmire (6)
21. Monk's room (4)
22. "No man is an ____" (6)
25. Invoice (4)
26. Tailing (9)
28. Summon (4)
29. Sunlight hours (7)
31. Avoid responsibility (5)
32. Deuce topper (4)
33. Hotel redcap (7)
35. Mauna ____ (3)
36. Divert attention (8)
38. Not vital (10)
41. Game fish (6)
42. Instill confidence (7)
44. Strike (5)
45. Ore vein (4)
46. Groggy (5)
47. Smidgens (4)

DOWN

1. Adjacent (6)
2. Cooking bulb (6)
3. Tidy condition (8)
4. In a deft manner (4)
5. By way of (3)
6. Bureau (7)
7. Warps (8)
8. Cleanse (5)
9. Renter (6)
14. Happily ____ after (4)
16. Twilight hours (7)
18. Guild (10)
19. Gruesome (6)
20. Soothe (5)
21. Scoundrel (3)
23. Spear (5)
24. Dawdle (5)
26. Varnish (7)
27. Anger (3)
30. Limit of tree growth (10)
32. Send (8)
34. Quick-tempered one (7)
35. Easy gait (4)
36. Bleak (6)
37. Stepped on (4)
38. Lengthen (6)
39. Facts (4)
40. Drains (6)
43. Demolish (4)

WHIRLY WORDS

PUZZLE 472

This diagram has been divided into sections, numbered 1 to 6, and each contains spaces for four letters. The answer to the clue for each section is a 4-letter word whose letters fit into the corresponding section so that the inner ring, middle ring, and outer ring all spell words reading clockwise beginning in section 1.

CLUES

Section 1: Bugle call

Section 2: Rip

Section 3: Jaw

Section 4: Compensated

Section 5: Merit

Section 6: Celebrity

Inner Ring: African desert

Middle Ring: Affectionate

Outer Ring: Players

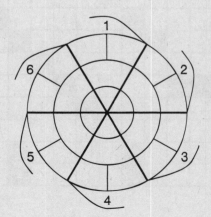

PUZZLE 473

• "MY KIND OF TOWN" •

ACROSS

1. Arizona river
5. Pack down
9. Bryce Canyon location
13. German philosopher
17. Door to ore
18. Hebrew zither
19. Space gr.
20. Fit to ___
21. Loyal
22. Home of NBA's Suns
25. Wyoming city
27. Egyptian pharaoh
28. Lodger
29. Conjunction
30. Greek letters
31. Italian resort
32. Oklahoma national park
35. Pirate's take
36. Current suppressor
40. Hawkeye State
41. Muslim spirit
42. Chaos
43. Caesar's salutation
44. Hydrocarbon suffix
45. Canine mothers
46. Expert
47. Solar disk
48. Missouri city
50. Split radially, as a log
51. Texas river
52. "Texas ___ Darlin'"
53. Top hats' accompaniers
54. Strong ale
55. Florida port
58. Home-run champ
59. Illinois city
63. RR car pullers
64. Not mounted
65. Shake
66. Nevada or Minnesota city
67. Theater sign
68. Ire
69. North Adriatic wind
70. Central Illinois city
71. Beehive State's flower
73. California wine valley
74. Calendar or numeral
75. Donate
76. Lichen's kin
77. Perch
78. Actress/singer Joyce
81. Housatonic River town
82. Phillips Academy city
86. Site of a U.S. mint
89. Arkansas resort city
90. Poison
91. Certain
92. The Buckeye State
93. Seed pod
94. Marbles
95. Gaelic
96. Breathe rapidly
97. European juniper

DOWN

1. Nerve
2. Brainstorm
3. Con man
4. Home of Emory University
5. Rhinoceros's kin
6. Davis Cup winner
7. Cow call
8. Star of "The Music Man"
9. School credits
10. Judd Hirsch vehicle
11. Botanist Gray
12. Ninth or twenty-third president
13. Toy instruments
14. Power source
15. Hawaiian bird
16. Eye drop
23. Straight-up
24. Kind of crystalline acid
26. Witty saying
30. Eternities
31. Ira or Meyer
32. Desserts
33. Solitary
34. Thunderstruck
35. City southwest of Toledo
36. Complimentary reviews
37. London good-bye
38. Range part
39. Gambling city
41. Hoosegow
42. New ___, Connecticut
45. 552, to Cato
46. North Dakota city
47. Michigan college city
49. Donations
50. More unusual
51. U.S. publisher
53. Radio's Kasem
54. ___ Verde National Park
55. Untidy mishmash
56. Concerning
57. Highly excited
58. Fish
59. Alabama town
60. Two horses
61. Arm bone
62. Tatum's dad
64. The cosmos
65. Severs
68. Type of dress
69. Louisiana city
70. Jefferson Memorial river view
72. Moldings
73. Admonition
74. Banish, of yore
76. Struggle
77. Durante feature
78. Redact
79. Russian river
80. Recently
81. Old Hebrew measures
82. Tennis score
83. Miles or Ellen
84. Oklahoma city
85. Respiratory sound
87. Mutt
88. Norwegian rock group

PUZZLE 474

The directions for solving are on page 101.

Key legend (left):

1	14		
2	15		
3	16	I	
4	17		
5	18		
6	19		
7	20	N	
8	21		
9	22		
10	23		
11	24		
12	25		
13	26		

Puzzle 474 grid:

25	4	20	13	16	17	11		21	20	7	16	20
4		12		7		20		4		10		7
16	7	8		9	20	21	5	23		26	20	14
17				4			16					16
19	24	24	19	12	3	19	23	6	19	7	6	19
		16		19		21			16			17
15	4	19		2	19	5	16	17		21	20	11
19		13			19		12		5			
16	7	2	4	23	17	12	16	20	13	16	18	19
1				20			22					21
15	10	26		3	20	1	4	19		20	23	22
17		16		19		20		18		12		17
23	16	17	19	2		23	8	19	17	6	15	11

(I N shown filled at positions 16 7 2 row)

Alphabet reference (right):

A · N
B · O
C · P
D · Q
E · R
F · S
G · T
H · U
I ✗ V
J · W
K · X
L · Y
M · Z

PUZZLE 475

Key legend (left):

1	14	T	
2	15		
3	16	I	
4	17		
5	18		
6	19		
7	20		
8	21		
9	22		
10	23		
11	24		
12	25		
13	26		

Puzzle 475 grid:

13	19	14	6	17	23	26		13	19	7	23	1
26		19		11		5				23		19
19	10	1	7	19	2	3	8	19	1	3	17	23
23		26				2				17		18
16	3	24		26	2	17	12	7	26	23	10	26
		26		22		4		16				15
17	18	18	3	1	9		14	20	3	1	26	16
24				24		16		26		19		
10	20	19	24	9	10	1	26	24		21	19	24
20		16				24				21		20
19	5	5	24	17	22	3	15	19	1	26	2	9
24		26				5		3		1		15
18	7	23	25	16		16	19	2	11	17	4	26

(I T shown filled at row 7)

Alphabet reference (right):

A · N
B · O
C · P
D · Q
E · R
F · S
G ✗ T
H · U
I ✗ V
J · W
K · X
L · Y
M · Z

PUZZLE 476

ACROSS

1. Magician's stick
5. Type of sink
9. Soft mineral
13. See to
17. Lotion ingredient
18. Time period
19. Thought
20. Sioux
21. Impudence
22. Wheels
23. Grate
24. Judge
25. Gift
27. Former coin of India
29. Track-event official
31. Certain palindrome's middle word
32. Legendary bird
33. Exploit
34. ___ cotta
37. Fails to win
39. Small explosive
43. Landed
44. Yield
45. Container weight allowance
47. Dull sound of impact
48. ___ Constitution
49. Greek letter
50. Hang gracefully
52. Opposite of WSW
53. Indian shelter
55. Church table
57. Sign
58. Too
60. Roman greeting
61. Russian news agcy.
63. Fleming's spy
66. Weighing device
68. Cuddle
72. Summer quaff
73. Brittle
75. Turkish general
76. Drivers' gr.
77. Star
79. Halo
80. American Beauty
82. Sediment
83. Chiffonier
85. Trembled
87. Strongman Charles ___
88. Hit-play sign
89. Viper
90. "To ___ with Love"
91. Bares
95. Mischievous child
96. Stillness
100. Declare
101. Smidgen
103. Common Latin abbr.: 2 wds.
105. Tattle
106. Joke
107. Shake ___ : 2 wds.
108. Phone
109. Stuff
110. Pismires
111. Taboo: hyph.
112. Canasta card
113. Beer-making ingredient

DOWN

1. Stinging insect
2. Winglike
3. Snoop
4. After-dinner treat
5. Alan Ladd role
6. Lummox
7. Ump's decision
8. Suggested
9. Fatigue
10. Ohio Northern University town
11. Fewer
12. Seizure
13. Stream
14. State, to Pierre
15. Musical symbol
16. Forest denizen
26. Baseball stat
28. Skating surface
30. Peer Gynt's mother
32. Reel's counterpart
34. Tense
35. Alternatively
36. Stand
37. Zodiac sign
38. Old hat
39. Wonderful
40. Attention-getter
41. Sand mound
42. Anthony or Barbara
44. Board game
46. Liable
49. Bro., for one
51. Carries on
54. Tablet
56. Scope
57. Forerunner of the CIA
59. Happen
60. Assumed name
62. Dead ___ Scrolls
63. Sousa's group
64. Scent
65. Granular snow
67. Timetable abbr.
69. Follow
70. Refrain syllables: 2 wds.
71. Diner sign
74. Future probability
75. Query
78. Postulates
79. Wind-borne
81. Alley ___ of the comics
82. Lengthen
84. Span. lady
86. Pig product
87. Feel poorly
90. Ridiculous
91. Hindu prince
92. Level
93. Waistcoat
94. Unaccompanied
95. Othello's foe
96. Bargain hunter's mecca
97. Roman emperor
98. Thunderous sound
99. Shade trees
102. Commandment number
104. Roofing material

DOUBLE TROUBLE

Not really double trouble, but double fun! Solve this puzzle as you would a regular crossword, EXCEPT place one, two, or three letters in each box. The number of letters in each answer is shown in parentheses after its clue.

• HIGHER EDUCATION •

ACROSS

1. Read (6)
4. Break a promise (6)
7. Sieve (6)
10. Fit (4)
11. Roman statesman (4)
12. One who sharpens (5)
13. Informative speech (7)
15. What-on-earth science (7)
17. Basketball's Thurmond (4)
18. Entranced (4)
19. Notwithstanding (7)
22. Of algebra, e.g.(10)
26. More contemptible (5)
27. Sore (4)
28. Ventured (5)
29. Tongues (9)
31. Let go (7)
32. Porcelain dynasty (4)
33. Obese (3)
34. Emulates Lewis and Clark (8)
37. Educational institution (10)

41. Good-natured (7)
42. Got off the fence (5)
44. Mountain crest (5)
45. Modern gas lights (5)
46. Airing (7)
47. "The Lord of the ____" (5)

DOWN

1. Bell sound (4)
2. Bumpkin (4)
3. Choose (6)
4. Establish anew (8)
5. Tidy (4)
6. Where-on-earth science (9)
7. "The ____ for Scandal" (6)
8. "Biggest little city" (4)
9. Force (6)
14. Bring together (5)
16. Summer in Paris (3)

19. Fiend (5)
20. Street argot (5)
21. Andes nation (4)
22. Equals (7)
23. Manufactured (4)
24. Crowns (6)
25. Yield (4)
27. Pushy (10)
30. Kind of acid (5)
31. Time, to Einstein (8)

33. Endowing (7)
34. Test (7)
35. Painter Picasso (5)
36. Optical glass (4)
38. More unusual (5)
39. ____ pretty (7)
40. ____ sirree! (3)
43. Impression (4)

CHANGAWORD

Can you change the top word into the bottom word (in each column) in the number of steps indicated in parentheses? Do not change the order of the letters, and change only one letter at a time. Proper names, slang, and obsolete words are not allowed.

1. PINK (4 steps)   2. LAST (5 steps)   3. WOLF (6 steps)   4. ACTS (7 steps)

ROSE   WORD   PACK   NICE

PUZZLE 479

ACROSS

1. Nursery bed
5. ____ de plume
8. Sallow
12. Metallic-threaded cloth
13. Imitate
14. Consumer
15. "If ____ the Circus"
16. Revere
18. Author Bracken
19. Coach
20. Pupil surrounder
22. Demand
26. Type of truck
28. ____ Alamos
29. First name in Chinese leadership
30. Mild expletive
31. Stocking mishap
32. Barbecue bar
33. Blunder
34. Total
35. Corridors
36. Disburse
38. Smidgen
39. Ruler
41. New Deal group: abbr.
44. Dampens
47. Roman way
48. Of flight: pref.
49. Shad delicacy
50. Stratum, as of coal
51. Paradise
52. Fast flier
53. ____-on favorite

DOWN

1. Fast pace
2. Seldom seen
3. Unreal
4. TV's Dr. Casey
5. Parts of churches
6. Ready for business
7. Brief reference
8. Feline sounds
9. Botanist Gray
10. "____ It Be"
11. Previous, to a poet
17. Ages and ages
19. Wire measure
21. Royal-carpet color
23. Embedded
24. Spinnaker
25. Small children
26. Quick look
27. Indian tourist town
28. Abner's partner
31. New Jersey university
32. Perched
34. Christmas-pudding ingredient
35. Torrid
37. Actor Welles
38. Patch
40. Son of Seth
42. Peruse
43. Branches
44. Actress West
45. British reference book: abbr.
46. Choler
47. Equal: pref.

PUZZLE 480

ACROSS

1. Actor Tamblyn
5. Sonnet's relative
8. Singer Redding
12. Module
13. Pandemonium
14. Large vases
15. Thought
16. Powerless
18. Small cup
20. Circuit
21. Nourished
22. "The ____" (Redford film)
26. Ancient Scandinavian
29. "____'clock scholar . . ."
30. Cuckoo
31. Buddies
33. Senator Symington
34. Refrigerated
36. Glowed
38. Part of FDIC
40. In the manner of
41. Doily
42. Shaded areas
45. Penny for your ____
49. Article
50. Clamor
51. Be obligated
52. Saint Philip ____
53. Oxen harness
54. Show assent
55. Redolence

DOWN

1. Bankrupt
2. Release
3. German legendary hero
4. Platforms
5. God of war
6. Obscure
7. Boarded, at an airport
8. Production
9. Three, to Sophia
10. Hostelry
11. Concorde, e.g.
17. Bit for Dobbin
19. Footnote word
22. Of birth
23. Commenced again
24. Chip in chips
25. Noisy
26. Unsophisticated
27. Fairy-tale beginner
28. Long-distance race
32. Where Anna taught
35. Affectedly modest
37. One with a pigmentation deficiency
39. Type of doll
42. Utilized
43. Prefix for dynamic or space
44. Moslem prince
45. Take to court
46. Hunting cry
47. Hardwood tree
48. "____ for the Seesaw"

418

PUZZLE 481

ACROSS

1. Hindu gown
5. Feeling his ____
9. Bath, e.g.
12. Golf club
13. Cowboy's rope
15. Refusing to listen
16. Touched
17. William Tell's missile
18. Andean Indian
19. Abilities
21. ____ of Paris
23. Sturgeon delicacy
24. Winter hazard
25. Narrow
28. Sultan's wives
32. Remind constantly
35. Imitates
36. "The ____ of Pauline"
37. Mongrel
38. Acidic
39. Train needs
40. Dog's name
41. Rainbow
42. It parted for Moses
43. Again
44. Abbreviated highway
45. Dangerous curves
46. Placards
47. Kind of jacket
49. Always, in poems
50. Colonized
54. Church leader
58. Mishmash
59. Adorer
61. Out of control
62. Jungle king?
63. Rock
64. Dreadful
65. TV's Rather
66. Transmit
67. Yearnings

DOWN

1. Uncake, in a way
2. Space
3. Rock's companion
4. Concern
5. Speak eloquently
6. Pretenses
7. Pitch
8. Cease
9. Judge's duty
10. Gait
11. Long way off
14. Carpenter's tool
15. Record
20. Likewise not
22. Goals
25. Mongolian tribesman
26. Asunder
27. Understanding
28. Chairs
29. Spring up
30. Angers
31. Actress Lanchester
33. "Look, Stranger" poet
34. Multiplies
36. Elected official: abbr.
40. "My ____" (Broadway hit)
42. Authentic
46. Visit
48. English public school
49. Misspoke
50. Vended
51. Lamb's pseudonym
52. Asner and McMahon
53. I-toppers
54. Sean or William
55. Pierre's female friend
56. Shredded
57. Makes do
60. Foot digit

Codebreaker

PUZZLE 482

Each group of five letters is a word in substitution code. The same code is used throughout. The clue next to each group gives you one of the real letters. The ten clues give you the ten letters used to form all the words. As a starter we'll tell you that D stands for L in all words.

1. G J F D V — one letter is L

2. J D F G M — one letter is C

3. G Y Z B L — one letter is S

4. M V F B Y — one letter is A

5. B F D D L — one letter is R

6. B Z Z G Y — one letter is O

7. Y V F J M — one letter is H

8. B V D F L — one letter is Y

9. M Z B G V — one letter is E

10. L V F G Y — one letter is T

PUZZLE 483

• NEW YORK, NEW YORK •

ACROSS

1. Upon
5. Newsman Koppel
8. Slang
13. Money, in Modena, once
14. Angelic instrument
16. Donny's sister
17. Divisions of time
18. Toledo's lake
19. Gems
20. City's greenery
23. Mesh
24. Routine
25. Piggery
26. Norm: abbr.
27. F. Lee Bailey, e.g.
30. Protection
32. Nest egg letters
33. Completes
37. Chorister
39. Score
42. Popeye's affirmative
43. Range
45. Glum
46. "Our Gang" dog
48. Spoil
49. Photocopy, for short
51. Established
54. Map abbr.
55. Corn unit
58. Asian holiday
59. Golf term
60. First Capitol
65. Actress Tatum ____
67. Emend
68. Author Wiesel
69. Vassal
70. French resort
71. Designer Ricci
72. Cosmetic queen Lauder
73. Two, in Toledo
74. Walk

DOWN

1. Actor Baldwin
2. Weary
3. Algerian port
4. Danish ____
5. Dramatic works, in London
6. Actor Holliman
7. Dribbles
8. Berserk
9. Chat
10. General's monument
11. Greased
12. Try out
15. Bog fuel
21. Bemoan
22. Grain
26. Mud
27. Inebriated
28. Bedouin
29. Financial area
31. Vapor
34. Siesta
35. Stain
36. Ready
38. Ellipse
40. Guitar's kin
41. Affirmative
44. Prior to
47. Manors
50. Game prop
52. ____ Aviv
53. European capital
54. Indian princesses
56. Gulf of ____
57. Fashioned anew
59. Staff
60. Exit hurriedly
61. Wealthy, to Juanita
62. Came to earth
63. Phone wire
64. ____ year
66. Mellow

PUZZLE 484   Mathboxes

Fill in the missing numbers across and down using only the digits given above the diagrams. Always perform the mathematical operations in order from left to right and from top to bottom.

1 1 2 3 3 5 7 8

A.
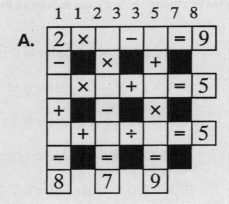

1 2 2 3 4 5 5 6

B.
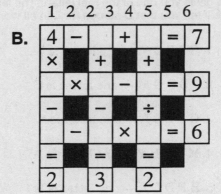

ACROSS

1. Chest bone
4. Upper limb
7. Thought
9. "My ___ Sal"
12. Classic car
13. ___ the Terrible
17. Frigid
18. Opera number
20. Shade of green
21. Biblical wise men
22. Great lady of jazz
25. Support
26. Some
27. "Norma ___"
28. Jovial
30. Accumulate
33. Office tables
35. Twosome
36. Young male horse
37. Pee Wee ___
38. Misfortunes
42. Little tyke
43. Dried grass
45. Cleopatra's snake
48. "Dies ___"
49. Milky gem
51. Foreshadow
53. Set ___ (reserve)
54. Nero, e.g.
55. Arguer
57. Border on
58. TV host Trebek
59. Pigpen
61. "The Catcher in the ___"
62. No ___, ands, or buts
65. Bandleader's stick
67. "Remember the ___"
71. Lagoon
72. Pea container
74. Italian city
75. Bees' product
76. Tatter
78. Singer Davis
79. Belonging to us
80. Director Preminger
82. "Satchmo" of jazz
89. Not fatty
90. Camper's shelter
91. Puny
92. Clothes presser
93. Social engagement
94. Onassis, to pals
95. Use a crowbar
96. Tableland
97. Speedy plane
98. Use needle and thread

DOWN

1. Paddy harvest
2. Object of worship
3. Chime
4. Vicinity
5. Domain
6. Shaped
8. Oklahoma city
9. Acquires
10. Affectedly Bohemian
11. Designer Claiborne
13. Playing off the cuff
14. Differ
15. Past
16. Small bite
19. Concur
20. Difficult journeys
23. Quick
24. Soothe
29. Feel remorse for
30. Pretended manner
31. Cow's call
32. Charlie Parker's instrument
33. Moistureless
34. Caribbean, e.g.
39. Iraq's neighbor
40. Dawdle
41. Behold
43. Greek underworld
44. Wide-awake
46. Sprinkle
47. Investigate
50. Peach stone
52. Ostrichlike bird
53. Assist in crime
55. Wipe gently
56. High note
60. Sweet potato
61. Actor/director Howard
63. Adversary
64. Cunning
66. Neither's partner
68. Boundary
69. Sorrowful word
70. Large parrot
71. Harbor
73. Greek letters
75. Eskimo dog
76. RBI, e.g.
77. Active ones
79. Sharif of films
80. Antique
81. Chamomile drink
83. Single entity
84. Agent: abbr.
85. Basketball-hoop part
86. Miner's finds
87. Facial feature
88. Munch

• ALL THAT JAZZ •

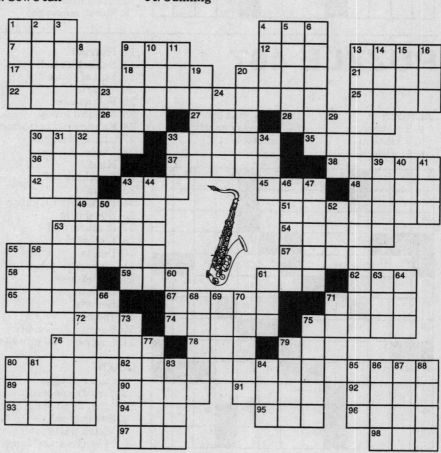

PUZZLE 486

ACROSS
1. Love to excess
5. Flock member
8. Snow toy
12. Finished
13. Jazz instrument
14. Patriot Nathan ____
15. Cowgirl Evans
16. Tot's vehicle
18. Spanish bravo
19. Cowboy's rope
20. Lend an ____
21. Biting bug
23. In addition
25. Rose Bowl event
27. Bares teeth
31. Test
32. Spinnaker
33. Solution
36. Sandy
38. "The Old Man and the ____"
39. Orient
40. Held
43. Congregation of insects
45. Research room
48. Soda can material
50. Missed by a ____
51. Gather leaves
52. Long time
53. Chip in chips
54. Recognized
55. Football's Marino
56. Easily bruised items

DOWN
1. Non-flying bird
2. ____ Office
3. Morse message
4. Bard's before
5. Manor
6. Armed conflicts
7. Lives
8. Timid
9. Pillowcase edging
10. She, to Juanita
11. Doe
17. Furry bandit
19. Shaver
22. Sue, John, and Dave, e.g.
24. Watering hole
25. Each
26. Hatchet
28. Clanking
29. Ignited
30. Stallone's nickname
34. Actor Arnaz
35. Gaped
36. Bonn native
37. Male sheep
40. Listen
41. Poet Seeger
42. John Wayne's nickname
44. Halo
46. Choir voice
47. Spelling contests
49. Small gull
50. Fannie ____

PUZZLE 487

ACROSS
1. Exclamation
4. First man
8. Stockings
12. Time gone by
13. Put away neatly
14. Imitated
15. Peak
17. Hurried
18. Snakelike fish
19. Full of rocks
20. Wharfs
22. Pollinators
23. Musical group
24. Baby grand performer
27. ____ and downs
28. Lures
30. Haul
31. Knocking softly
33. Naught
34. Pakistan's neighbor
35. '60s dance
37. Is concerned
39. Coffeepot
40. Delete
41. Fingernail job
46. Brand-new
47. Dark brews
48. Remote
49. Tense
50. Sunrise direction
51. Low cardinal number

DOWN
1. ____ and eggs
2. Freud's concern
3. "____ Send Me"
4. Subsequent
5. Watch parts
6. "The Greatest" boxer
7. Blokes
8. Rush
9. What black and white are
10. Detected
11. Swirl
16. A friend in ____ . . .
19. The Seven ____
20. "____ Was a Rolling Stone"
21. Impelling
22. Bridle part
23. However
24. Poke resident?
25. Categorize
26. Couple
28. Bent
29. Texas governor Richards
32. Beautiful
33. A metal
35. Melodies
36. Watch spot
37. Arrive
38. Surrounded by
41. Pearl ____ Bailey
42. According to
43. Alien vehicle
44. Jogged
45. Prior to

Rearrange this stack of bricks to form a crossword puzzle. The clues will help you fit the bricks into their correct places. Row 1 has been filled in for you. Use the bricks to fill in the remaining spaces.

ACROSS

1. Young lady
   Band
   Conversation
2. Encourage
   Calm
   Medicinal plant
3. Corner
   Torching
   Dwell
4. Lagomorphs
   Flowed
   Resting place
5. Clothes, in
   Madrid
   Golf club
6. Trig. function
   D.C. figure
   Brown-capped
   mushroom
   Knight's title
7. Fragrant
   Go to bed
8. Gray-haired, in
   Seville
   Positive pole
   Dash
9. Moorish drum
   Devote
10. Above, to a bard
    Jasper, e.g.
    Negative
    Baste
11. Counsel
    On the ocean
12. Liberated
    Police off.
    Example
13. Soil
    Lucy's brother
    Sitarist
    Shankar
14. Italian wine
    region
    Tally
    Streetcar
15. Nuisance
    Belfry
    Poet Akhmatova

DOWN

1. Strip of wood
   Chocolate source
   Flutter
2. Cove, in
   Barcelona
   Declaim
   "The ___ Tattoo"
3. Oracle
   Detection device
   Ingests
4. Guide
   Crowd
   Send
5. Small rail
   Grew older
6. Bath, e.g.
   Like a flower
   Mil. transport
7. Turtle
   Doc
8. Tabula ___
   Food fish
   Sufficient,
   poetically
9. Symbolic
   Deprive of
   natural
   qualities
10. Stall
    Altar screen
    Mil. branch
11. Expectation
    News report
12. Bird's claw
    Gumshoe
    Main artery
13. Got down
    "The Rise of ___
    Lapham"
    Mend
14. Fondness
    Incensed
    Author Hunter
15. Hull part
    Regenerate
    South American
    capital

BRICKS

T / E	P / A	M / E	N / A	SEW	SIR / IRE	OT / SEA
HO / RON	ES / ROP	COS / ARO	LOE / IVE	OER
I / T	S / T	MO / SR	E / R	T / A	HAR	RAM / NNA
COR / OWE	ED / ML	P / IC	C	DEL / AVI	LAN / ATE
CAN / ATA	EAC / RSO	O / BAL	A	FRE / LOA	TEL
DET / INU	AST / PES	RE / MAT	ABE / TRE	RAN / A I
EP / RET	NOD / DE	E / N	A / L	GE / RED	E / DIC

DIAGRAM

	1	2	3	4	5	6	7	8	9	10	11	12	13	14	15
1	L	A	S	S		S	T	R	I	P		T	A	L	K
2															
3															
4															
5															
6															
7															
8															
9															
10															
11															
12															
13															
14															
15															

★ **BRICK BY BRICK FANS!** *Get a ton of Brick by Bricks—over 50 fun puzzles in* ★
each of our special collections! To order, see page 87.

PUZZLE 489

ACROSS

1. Bed board
5. "Atlas Shrugged" author
9. Traverse
13. Head topping
14. ___ Haute
15. Canary's home
16. Mobile Bay hero
19. "___ a Tramp"
20. Savings programs
21. Harbingers
22. Saw-whet's call
23. Retail place
25. WWII Pacific commander
30. Carson's predecessor
31. Jug handles
32. Actor Torn
34. Moistureless
35. Raisin, formerly
37. Biblical wise men
38. Soggy
39. Seed part
40. "The ___ of Night"
41. "Bull" of Leyte Gulf
46. Food, informally
47. Essayist Lamb
48. Term of address
51. Tom-tom
52. Tennis shot
55. 25A's Japanese counterpart
59. Neighbor of Ken.
60. Racetracks
61. Chip in chips
62. Makes lace
63. Dune material
64. Fashion name

DOWN

1. Iranian bigwig, once
2. Take on cargo
3. Objectives
4. Threesome's prefix
5. Connect
6. Yips' cousins
7. New Deal gp.
8. Article of German
9. Shrimp dish
10. Summon
11. Son of ___
12. Captures
14. Seer's card
17. Rivers, in Barcelona
18. Quarters
22. Group of zebras
23. Easy job
24. Retain, as a lawyer
25. Baseball's Rod ___
26. Part of Hispaniola
27. Domain
28. Commerce
29. Bob Marley's son
30. Handle roughly
33. Comic missile
35. Pluck
36. Inlets
37. Plateau
39. San Antonio mission
42. Becomes aware of
43. Messenger
44. Grads
45. Certain bean
48. Bench's glove
49. Dazed
50. Forbidding word
51. Actress Cannon
52. TV's Anderson
53. Sarge's dog
54. South African settler
56. Boxing letters
57. Vine fruit, e.g.
58. Carroll's ___ Hatter

PUZZLE 490   Family Ties

Each group contains four unrelated words. Without rearranging the letters, change one letter in each of the words to form four related words.

Example: Rise, Lilt, Patsy, Ires (**Answers:** Rose, Lily, Pansy, Iris)

1. Finger _____	Basic _____	Dial _____	Same _____
2. Yummy _____	Poser _____	Wrist _____	Bridle _____
3. Vandal _____	Loot _____	Dump _____	Speaker _____
4. Silo _____	Rhino _____	Fool _____	Melt _____
5. Cruel _____	Veal _____	Bearer _____	Flank _____
6. Union _____	Leer _____	Chides _____	Shallow _____

424

ACROSS

1. "___ Side Story"
5. Location
10. "The Lady ___ Shanghai"
14. Declare openly
15. Second showing
16. Volcano's flow
17. Roller coaster, e.g.
18. Diner
19. Chilled
20. Plot
21. Weep
22. Unit of electrical current
24. At that time
26. Self
27. Remained
30. Evangelist
35. Glutton
36. Radio and television
38. Innocent
39. Absent
41. ___ and outs
42. Larch, for one
43. Fasten again
45. Quayle and Mondale, for short
48. Conclusion
49. Got ready
51. Broils
53. Auto
54. Fender mishap mark
55. Shining
59. "___ Girl Friday"
60. Milky gem
64. Mine vein
65. "You Only Live ___"
67. Lion's hair
68. Unwrap
69. Loaded
70. Golf club
71. Experiment
72. Put into action
73. Small coin

DOWN

1. Twist out of shape
2. Iniquity
3. Soft drink
4. Score
5. Go before
6. Discover
7. Theatrical
8. Billiard stick
9. Infuriate
10. Impertinent
11. Marathon
12. Done
13. Created
23. Lament
25. Garment edge
26. Wipe out
27. Acute
28. Turret
29. Playing marble
30. Yearned
31. Cougar, for one
32. Engages
33. Occurrence
34. Marsh grasses
37. Scuba user
40. Puppy's sound
44. Per
46. Gift
47. Male offspring
50. Baby's plaything
52. Nuclear
54. Chopping tool
55. Stain
56. Lariat
57. March date
58. Fellow
59. Conceal
61. Trim
62. Before long
63. Loaned
66. Polish

Crackerjacks

Find the answer to the riddle by filling in the center boxes with the letters needed to complete the words across and down. When you have filled in the Crackerjacks, the letters reading across the center boxes from left to right will spell out the riddle answer.

RIDDLE: What occurs once in every minute, twice in every moment, but not once in a thousand years?

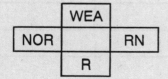

WEA
NOR | | RN
R

PA
STI | | TO
TE

IN
OU | | OST
IX

ANSWER: _____

PUZZLE 493

ACROSS
1. Ran away
5. Place firmly
10. Steals
14. In person
15. Bluish purple
16. Great Lake
17. Diva's forte
18. Llamas' home
19. Behind schedule
20. Theater section
22. Competed against
24. Eggs
25. Remove one's clothing
26. Dark-haired
30. Simpler
34. Broadcast
35. More recent
37. Rocky shelf
38. Fireplace fuel
40. More serious
42. Painful
43. Horse
45. Religious belief
47. Headed
48. Attack
50. Ones who perform alone
52. Pungs
54. Large tree
55. Student
58. Regal homes
62. Ache
63. Lounging garments
65. Strong wind
66. About
67. Slipknot
68. Poem
69. Deficiency
70. Small fights
71. Do an usher's job

DOWN
1. Unwanted fat
2. Money, in Malta, once
3. Corrupt
4. Church official
5. Originated
6. Oodles
7. Immature flower
8. Tennis star Chris ___
9. Want
10. Backslides
11. Mr. Roberts
12. Nip
13. Sow
21. Kitchen appliance
23. Bottle
25. Female prophet
26. Lightweight wood
27. Rampages
28. Goads
29. Taunt
31. False gods
32. Plumed bird
33. Marsh plants
36. Splitsville
39. Salted
41. Sets free
44. Anet
46. Bell's sound
49. Acquires knowledge
51. Pictures
53. Sag
55. Twirl
56. Staff
57. Employ
58. Nuisance
59. ___ May, New Jersey
60. Lamb
61. Cult
64. Feather scarf

PUZZLE 494

Categories

For each of the categories listed can you think of a word or phrase beginning with each letter on the left? Count one point for each correct answer. A score of 15 is good, and 21 is excellent.

	FISH	BIRDS	LANGUAGES	DOGS	AMERICAN CITIES
G					
R					
E					
A					
T					

ACROSS

1. "___ It Romantic"
5. Saw
10. Flat-bottomed boat
14. Room opening
15. Exclude
16. Possess
17. Actress Bonet
18. Alpha's antithesis
19. Addled
20. Conductors
22. "Show Boat" composer
23. Cookie containers
24. Take advantage of
26. Thespians
29. Titled lady
34. In that place
35. Acknowledged applause
36. By way of
37. Weighty units
38. Vetches
39. Natural
40. Roses ___ red
41. Flatfish
42. Snooped
43. Shop owner
45. Sheets
46. Indignation
47. Plant's beginning
48. Wheeled vehicles
51. Practicers
57. Wicked
58. Affirms
59. Flexible armor
60. Charity
61. Intestinal fortitude
62. Being, to Cassius
63. Fold members
64. Arboretum dwellers
65. Exigency

DOWN

1. Run in neutral
2. Dirt
3. Pry
4. Plow pullers
5. Bedecks
6. Items for show
7. Already retired
8. Indicator
9. Marks of eradication
10. Flustered
11. Docket item
12. In excess of
13. Free from dependence
21. Grow weary
25. Lay lawn
26. Fragrant floral oil
27. Duty
28. Doctrine
29. Hole-maker
30. Astonishes
31. Arouse
32. Warning device
33. Smooths wood
35. Cotton bundle
38. Broad-minded
39. Indentured servants
41. Masculine address
42. Quay's relative
44. Supermarket features
45. Some real estate papers
47. Tennis stroke
48. Give in
49. Declare openly
50. Make angry
52. Always
53. "___ We Go Again"
54. Ameliorate
55. Sun's morning activity
56. Winter transport

Crossblocks

Insert the letters and letter groups into each diagram to form words reading across which answer the clues on the left. A bonus word will read diagonally down in the tinted blocks.

1.

AY BI CO DI ECT HA ION
LL M NE OR R S T TA W

- Merge
- Corridor
- Play coach
- Depot

2.

AT C CH E ES FIN G GL
GO I LD MO NG ON R SC

- Lab eyewear
- Ogee
- Restrict
- Minor injury

427

PUZZLE 497

• NAUTICALLY SPEAKING •

ACROSS

1. Singer Davis
4. Flipper
7. Ball star
9. Italian port
11. Floating kitchen
12. Passenger ships
14. Antiquated
15. Circle part
17. Touring vehicle
18. Meadow
19. Ampersand
20. Above
21. Allows
23. Social insect
25. Assist
26. Owing
27. Large bird
29. Uh huh
31. Cozy room
33. Ranch worker
35. Light brown
36. Muslim headdress
38. Put off
39. Sailor's bed
41. Stage
42. Marino of football
43. Wildebeest
45. Axlike tool
48. Portland's locale: abbr.
49. Play it by ____
50. Bleat
51. Drink cubes
54. Moray
55. Little devil
56. Expert pilot
59. Derision
61. Luxury boat
65. Desert plant
67. Corner occupant
69. Take to court
70. Drive forward
71. Printing measures
72. Roll of money
74. Baste
75. Highlander's headgear
76. Sample
77. Tree fluid
79. Tableland
81. Gusto
83. 24 hours
84. ____-de-France
86. Shy
87. Comedian DeLuise
88. ____ Lanka
89. Ship's steering device
91. Far Eastern boat
93. Augusta's state
94. "Silas Marner" author
95. Was introduced to
96. Have a snack

DOWN

1. Blend
2. "____ in the Family"
3. Divide
4. Spunky
5. Lodging house
6. Mr. Coward
7. ____ eagle
8. Bronte heroine
9. Adhesive
10. Length x width
11. Venetian boat
13. Sailing hazard
16. Greek island
17. Dull
19. Televised
20. "____ Town"
22. Matched group
24. Taunt
25. Say further
26. Actress Susan ____
28. Ruin
30. Young dog
32. Opposite of SSW
34. Moving truck
37. Athens letter
39. Stout
40. Routine
43. Gosh!
44. Scottish refusal
46. River barrier
47. Shoot
51. Religious images
52. Fast pirate ship
53. Sea eagle
56. In the past
57. Sailor's boss
58. Each
59. That woman
60. Recent
62. Analyze
63. Billiards stick
64. Cut
65. Upper limb
66. Tarzan portrayer
68. Butt
70. Baking dish
73. Respectable
75. Mexican fare
78. Purple fruit
80. Aching
82. Misplace
83. Darn!
85. Dutch cheese
88. Blotch
90. Atlantic City cube
92. Actress Farrow

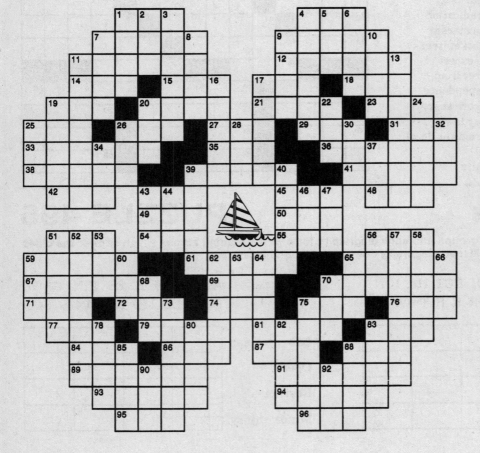

ACROSS

1. Oaf
5. Oxford, e.g.
9. Vigor
12. Comical scene
16. Staffer
17. Derive
18. Response at sea
19. Pepper, e.g.
20. Kept
22. Moved elsewhere
24. Section of writing
25. Curve
27. Like a rabbit
28. Night before a holiday
29. Scoff
31. Tattle
32. Portion
35. Entertains agreeably
37. Frenzy
41. Soldier's station
42. Victories for Kasparov
43. Poorly lit
45. Television science series
46. Befitting
47. Wrestler's pad
48. Gear for an angler
50. Singer Boone
52. Sunbathe
53. Wavered
56. None
58. Fiends
60. Dull routine
61. Delve
63. Old horse
65. Respectful title
66. Does penance
69. Duffer's objective
71. Commanders
75. Polynesian garland
76. Floor covering
78. Plot for flowers
80. Trifle
81. Breakfast grain
82. Finales
84. Actress West
86. Embankment
88. Bamboozle
89. Curvy letters
91. Indication of rank
93. Adjust
94. Circuit
96. Musk source
97. Objective
98. Like some peanuts
101. Army off.
102. Took for granted
106. Film showing
108. Urgent
110. Matches up
111. Fourth letter
112. Clinton's canal
113. Personality components
114. Connecting words
115. Peculiar
116. School official
117. Lemieux's milieu

DOWN

1. Dogpatch creator
2. Money, in Seina, once
3. Poems by Keats
4. Final course
5. Suit fabric
6. "I ___ Dreamed"
7. State neighboring Cal.
8. Put in peril
9. Piece of land
10. Aperture
11. Money of questionable source
12. Athenian's foe
13. High flyer
14. Cooled
15. Broadcasting's Turner
19. Remnant
21. Part of a roof
23. "___ House"
26. Logic
29. Determined
30. In the ___

32. Squabble
33. Aspiration
34. Small orbiting bodies
35. Gave a mark to
36. Drink
38. Scandalous
39. Tennis's Lendl
40. Containers
42. Tarnish
44. Cross
47. Gauge
49. Racket
51. Cranky
54. Large wine cask
55. Immerse briefly
57. Varnish ingredient
59. "Cara ___"
62. Yak
64. Portals
66. Aweather's opposite
67. Hamilton bills
68. Addition amount
70. Experience in memory
72. "Annabel Lee" poet

73. Neck's back
74. Direction on a manuscript
77. State of matter
79. Placed trust
83. "Being There" star
85. And so on
87. Canine doc
88. Less extroverted
90. Fills to excess
92. Outfitted
93. Move upward
95. Farm enclosure
97. Poplar
98. Peruse
99. Dry
100. Prank
102. Largest continent
103. Eastern visitors
104. Boys school
105. Office furniture
106. Bad Ems, e.g.
107. Author Buntline
109. Previously, to a bard

PUZZLE 499

ACROSS

1. Dinner course
6. Lengthwise threads in weaving
10. The Plow City
11. Food choppers
13. Prom bouquet
14. Chemical substance
16. Leftover
17. News stories
19. ____ Paulo
20. Cripple
22. Denim trousers
23. Albanian coins
24. Run, as colors
26. Gun a motor
27. Feasts
28. Road curves
30. Yields
32. Home of a popular diet
34. Tinseltown hopeful
36. Piece of pie
39. Composer Carmichael
40. Hebrew letter
42. Sudden swell
44. Weapon: Fr.
45. Capacious handbags
47. Comic strip possum
48. Refrain syllable
49. PTA members
51. Quill
52. Hit show
54. Chauffeurs
56. Memorizes
57. Consumers
58. Small barracuda
59. Foils

DOWN

1. Raids
2. Musicians Jolson and Hirt
3. Ananias
4. Cherub
5. More profound
6. Loses crispness
7. "Easy ____"
8. Radiation quantity
9. Gift
10. Esprit de corps
11. Inferred
12. Serpents
13. Rooster's crest
15. Prepare 1 Across
18. Exaggerate
21. Moral
23. Arranged to be available
25. Disparage
27. Removes from print
29. ____ volatile
31. Statute
33. Wisecracks
34. Oxalis
35. Mexican entree
37. Insecure seekers
38. Tent caterpillars
39. Chapeaux
41. Buyer
43. Ages and ages
45. Rub it in
46. Shoulder band
49. Skin opening
50. Scene
53. Sitter's creation
55. Neck style

PUZZLE 500   Dart Game

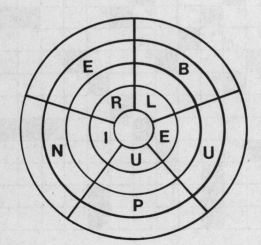

Form five words, reading from the center of the diagram outward, by adding the letters given below to complete the 5-letter words. Each letter will be used only once and each word begins with the center letter.

A E G L N O P S T U Y

ACROSS

1. Mediocre
5. Hot brew
8. Slews
13. Actress Berger
14. Singer Mel ___
16. "Kate & ___"
17. Actor Williams
18. TV character Felix ___
19. Director Sergio ___
20. "So ___ My Love"
21. Journalist Nellie ___
22. Hunters' gp.
24. Donkey, in Dijon
25. Actor Peter ___
27. "___ Twist"
29. Ryan or Tatum ___
31. Salt water
32. "Rio ___"
35. "Two ___ Kind"
37. Actress Judy ___
40. "___ in Heaven"
41. TV Actress West
44. "___ Time, Next Year"
46. "Mr. ___"
47. Walking pole
48. "___ That Uranium"
49. Longings
51. "___ Desqueyroux"
53. Actress Ward
54. "Brenda ___"
56. Soak, as flax
57. Approached
59. The Bumsteads' dog
61. "Maid of ___"
63. Remove from power
65. "The ___ Blade"
69. "___-Hoo" (Carmen Lombardo song)
70. Menial
72. Greek letter
73. Scruff
74. Benefits
76. Street show
78. "___ Grows in Brooklyn"
79. Kitchen appliance
80. "___ Laughing"
81. Flimsy
82. "___ of Love"
83. ___ el Amarna
84. "Raton ___"

DOWN

1. "In Which We ___"
2. Actress Tricia ___
3. Actor Sylvester ___
4. Stable morsel
5. Actor ___ Randall
6. Energy unit
7. Hemsley TV series
8. Actor Mineo
9. "Leave It to Beaver" family
10. "Home ___"
11. Barry Levinson film
12. "___ How She Runs"
13. French holy women: abbr.
14. Hayward/Preston film
15. "Margin for ___"
21. Actor Joe ___
23. Linda Lavin series
26. "Howards ___"
28. Balin or Claire
30. "The ___ Bride"
31. "Swan Lake" et al.
32. Erin or Linda
33. "A Day at the ___"
34. "Secret ___"
36. Laissez ___
38. Michael or George
39. "The Life of ___ Zola"
42. "___ Wednesday"
43. "___ a Living" (TV series)
45. Zounds!
50. "No ___ for Me"
51. Ford/McGuire film
52. Chou ___
53. "Bewitched" character
55. "Norma ___"
58. Always, to a bard
60. "The Big ___"
62. Actress Jane ___
63. German submarine
64. Peter of Herman's Hermits
66. Has concern
67. Dueling swords
68. ___-do-well
71. Deficiency
72. Emma ___
74. Bikini top
75. "The Desk ___"
77. Highway: abbr.
78. Viper

PUZZLE 502

ACROSS

1. Go away!
5. Leather strap
9. Helper: abbr.
13. Wan
14. Austen book
15. Dish
16. Poker bet
17. Fruit seeds
18. Gin and tonic garnishes
19. Foot part
20. Acreage
21. Common word
23. Printers' letters
24. Mistake
26. Time period
28. Garden flower
31. Gazes fixedly
35. Deep cut
38. Paradise
40. Selling place
41. Roadway: abbr.
42. Soars
44. Dessert
45. ___ Carlo
48. Mets, Jets, or Saints
49. Require
50. Whole
52. Barter
54. Prepare potatoes
56. Then
59. Concorde
62. Baden Baden, e.g.
63. Fielder's ball
64. Pirate's drink
66. Chicago airport
68. Meat order word
70. Opera song
71. Used a stopwatch
72. Holiday periods
73. "On Golden ___"
74. Raced
75. Mr. Dillon
76. Or ___! (threat)

DOWN

1. Small fight
2. Indian vessel
3. Change
4. Golf mound
5. Newspaper worker
6. Give out
7. Little prankster
8. Bad-tempered
9. "The Greatest"
10. Ditto
11. Plant part
12. Hardy girl
15. Material folds
20. ___ Angeles
22. "___ Just My Bill"
25. College cheer
27. Maze traveler
29. Prepare copy
30. Adjust anew
32. Lasso
33. Huron's neighbor
34. Pumpkin ___
35. "The Dating ___"
36. Shakespeare's river
37. Remitted
39. Close
43. Tiniest
46. "Tiny" singer
47. Obliterated
49. Mesh
51. Sixth sense letters
53. Dennis or Doris
55. Sultan's wives
57. Actor Flynn
58. Archaeologists' finds
59. Tipplers
60. Vessel
61. Subdued
63. Guitar part
65. Constructed
67. Primary color
69. Ms. Gardner
70. Mimic

PUZZLE 503   Keyword

To find the KEYWORD fill in the blanks in words 1 through 10 with the correct missing letters and transfer those letters to the correspondingly numbered squares in the diagram. Approach with care—this puzzle is not as simple as it first appears.

1	2	3	4	5	6	7	8	9	10

1. F L _ S H
2. D R O _ L
3. _ E G A L
4. M _ A N S
5. B R I N _

6. T R _ C K
7. G R E _ T
8. _ E R V E
9. S _ O U T
10. Q U O T _

432

CRYPTIC CROSSWORD

British-style or Cryptic Crosswords are a great challenge for crossword fans. Each clue contains either a definition or direct reference to the answer as well as a play on words. The numbers in parentheses indicate the number of letters in the answer word or words.

ACROSS

1. Sound of backyard barbecue in woods and lakes (5,8)
10. Wrong juice tins smashed (9)
11. Short-term office worker with love for rhythm (5)
12. Other names for one confused lassie (7)
13. Slipped south to be teased (7)
14. Tracks marsh birds (5)
15. Pamper me! A blemish is partly letting everything soak through! (9)
17. Mother peers about in journals (9)
19. Reverent addendum about debt (5)
20. Poker-faced college official holds classified page (7)
22. Study in bunk covered with crumbs (7)
24. I follow a glib, but not grand, excuse (5)
25. Ah! Well put! Crazy to distraction. (2,3,4)
26. Can schemer not disrupt invasions? (13)

DOWN

2. Jo surrounded by crushed ice in band celebration (9)
3. Helps fool on 'is way back (7)
4. Twist moist leaves out (5)
5. Lustre, a sure sign of hidden valuables (9)
6. Studio destroyed? Note exterior. (7)
7. Frosted? To some extent after I'm edited. (5)
8. #5 is a traveler's stamp (4)
9. Silent lineup of broken sleds (8)
14. Intended to fix telephone again around me (8)
15. For example, Florida nun is pale. That's odd! (9)
16. Announce brother before commercial actors (9)
18. More energetic private eye in prize mystery (7)
19. Go before "Crepe Mix" editor returns (7)
21. Stranger article about deception (5)
22. Make mess of both around first of century (5)
23. Toy baby left twice after party (4)

PUZZLE 505

ACROSS

1. Pads for gymnastics
5. Apiece
9. Work well together
14. Yearn
15. Abhorrent
16. Gaseous element
17. The Grateful ____
18. Notion
19. Northern abode
20. Playwright Albee
22. Extra weight
24. Hour, in New York
25. Negative responses
27. Long sandwiches
29. Agrees
33. Weak
37. Kimono sash
38. La ____
40. Challenger
41. Walden, e.g.
43. Author Jong
45. Narrow road
46. Backward: pref.
48. Provide for
50. Actor Tayback
51. On the beach
53. Become adjusted again
55. Tempo
57. Highlander
58. Lummox
61. Guantanamo locale
63. Yoga positions
67. Question severely
69. Droplet
71. Glittering fabric
72. Weird
73. Therefore
74. "Pumping ____"
75. Slackens
76. Achieves
77. Vesicle

DOWN

1. Fabricated
2. Received a top grade on
3. Melt
4. Family cars
5. Testimony
6. Lend a hand to
7. Staff symbol
8. Mends
9. Plagiarized
10. Fall behind
11. Actor Eric ____
12. Dove sounds
13. Marine speed unit
21. Small deer
23. ____ Wiedersehen
26. Sky lights
28. Insignia
29. Coconut meat
30. Woodwind instruments
31. Last inning
32. More clever
34. "____ New World"
35. Soviet leader
36. Standing up
39. Units of land
42. Decline
44. Fruit for guacamole
47. Seers
49. God of love
52. Common Market currency
54. Style of type
56. Subsided
58. Molding curve
59. Type of code
60. Conifers
62. Air: pref.
64. Not one
65. John ____ of "Good Times"
66. Posted
68. Fib
70. Become ripe

PUZZLE 506

LETTERGRAMS

Rearrange each line of letters to form a 6-letter word. Then rearrange the marked letters to reveal the name of a movie actor.

1. W A C H E S ___ ___ ___ ___ ___ ___

2. C E I T K T ___ ___ ___ ___ ___ ___

3. S C H U R O ___ ___ ___ ___ ___ ___

4. E L B E T E ___ ___ ___ ___ ___ ___

5. A P P O R L ___ ___ ___ ___ ___ ___

6. G T U N E G ___ ___ ___ ___ ___ ___

7. L E A C A P ___ ___ ___ ___ ___ ___

8. D O N M A R ___ ___ ___ ___ ___ ___

Movie actor: ___ ___ ___ ___ ___ ___ ___ ___ ___ ___

ACROSS

1. Polynesian dance
5. Basilica recesses
10. Quahog
14. From this time
15. Male duck
16. Tramp
17. Photosynthesis site
18. Excavation worker
19. Clinched
20. Quirks
22. Provoke
24. Breaks down
25. Quick glance
26. Arrangement
29. Overcame
33. Argentite, e.g.
34. Room style
36. Nighttime sound
37. Political contest
39. Deplete
41. Confident
42. Holding device
44. Result
46. Grass
47. Gives support to
49. Electromagnetic wave devices
51. Voyage
52. Cooking meas.
53. Craving
56. Covered with thin sheets
60. Resound
61. French river
63. Rich source
64. Emerald Isle
65. Succulent plants
66. Theater box
67. Operates
68. Loses strength
69. Dancer's movement

DOWN

1. Circle of light
2. Took advantage of
3. Cargo
4. Assert with confidence
5. Owned up to
6. Moves with a lever
7. Without
8. Add to
9. Sequence
10. Cowards
11. Sources of power
12. Support in wrongdoing
13. Manner
21. Tailless amphibian
23. Captures
25. City of Lights
26. Compulsion
27. Graduate exams
28. Summarize
29. Wails
30. Waken
31. Mistake
32. Actions
35. Stream
38. Feelings
40. Lack of sensation
43. Feline sound
45. Relaxation
48. Playground item
50. Incantations
52. Principle of belief
53. Forest animal
54. Very light brown
55. Leg part
56. Bowed musical instrument
57. Derivation
58. Perimeter
59. Heartfelt
62. Actor Wallach

PUZZLE 507

SHARE-A-LETTER

PUZZLE 508

Fill in each diagram with words that pertain to the subject. Letters in the larger areas will be shared by more than one word. Words read across only.

1. TREES

2. HORSE RACING

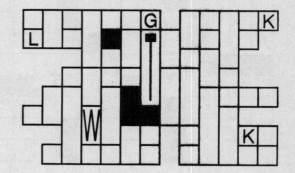

435

PUZZLE 509

ACROSS

1. Finance
5. Actor Lugosi
9. Bounding main
12. Emollient ingredient
13. Mild oath
14. Jungfrau, e.g.
15. Heroic activity
17. Cleverness
18. Dispatch
19. Writer Gardner
21. Orient
24. Consumer advocate
27. "Who's That ___?"
30. Actor Chaney, Jr.
32. Nap
33. Hubbub
34. Impersonate
35. Monk's title of address
36. Plod
38. By means of
39. In the distance
40. "___ Dragon"
42. Baby's bed
44. Complaint
46. Scolds
49. Single
51. Sweetheart
55. Sorrow
56. Southernmost Great Lake
57. Wicked
58. Transgress
59. Virginia dance
60. Jells

DOWN

1. Rotten
2. Pub offerings
3. Center
4. Nucleus
5. Actor Kingsley
6. Farm product
7. Load
8. Bedeck
9. Shortened at the end
10. Inventor Whitney
11. Apropos
16. Rhoda's TV mom
20. Boy
22. Russian, for example
23. Subject
25. Poet Pound
26. "___ Window"
27. Inhale quickly
28. Loafing
29. Soft drink
31. Close to
37. Equestrian's command
39. Wanes
41. Cut
43. Hostel
45. Cuisine
47. Bestow
48. Irritable mood
49. Be in arrears
50. Word accompanying neither
52. Golf ball's position
53. Sniggler's quarry
54. Chicago trains

PUZZLE 510

ACROSS

1. Pretend to be
4. Laboratory gel
8. Capsule
12. Female goat
13. Bundle
14. Territory
15. Persons of taste
17. Extended
18. Dislike strongly
19. Styles
21. Professional cooks
23. Infiltrate
24. "The Doctor" star
25. River crossing
26. "The ___ Patrol"
29. Stone or Bronze
30. Gambling machines
31. Self
32. Sea between Africa and Asia
33. Debit
34. Talon
35. Promote
36. Consecrate
37. Milwaukee player
40. Neighbor of Afghanistan
41. Stir up
42. Moved from the margin
46. Section of a church
47. Observed
48. Night of anticipation
49. Want
50. Temperature
51. Football's Marino

DOWN

1. Hoosier humorist
2. Romaine
3. On a leash
4. Encourages
5. Total receipts
6. Bar potable
7. Begins again
8. Turned white
9. Fetter
10. Allow the use of
11. Falls back
16. Knife handle
20. Disencumbers
21. Scorch
22. Immense
23. Perch
25. Grow vigorously
26. Let up
27. Turkish notables
28. Pulls behind
30. ___ gin fizz
34. Scottish family group
35. Wool fabric
36. Actor Spiner
37. Grain part
38. Matured
39. Otherwise
40. Theory
43. Wedding announcement word
44. Actress Marie Saint
45. Hiding place

436

ACROSS

1. Like The Hatter
4. Morse or zip
8. Road or gang suffix
12. ___ on (adores)
14. Tresses
15. Sandwich type
16. Hen's home
17. Spur on
18. Simply
19. Provide with weapons
20. Roman loans?
22. Sea birds
23. Cowboy movie
25. Excerpt
27. Age
28. Overcook
29. Baste
32. Turner and Cantrell
35. Showers
36. Depot: abbr.
37. Oblong circle
38. Bides one's time
39. Collections
40. Musician Paul
41. Quart sections
42. Take a nap
43. Fire remnant
44. Rental units: abbr.
45. ___ and crumpets
46. Barn toppers
48. Rivalry
52. Come up
54. Porkpies
55. Had dinner
56. Mineo and others
57. Night twinkler
59. Lets up
61. Pinball error
62. Wine variety
63. Winter forecast
64. Mexican cheers
65. Sweet potatoes
66. "___ the King's Men"

DOWN

1. Actress Mary Tyler
2. Small particles
3. French preposition
4. Make butter
5. Blades
6. Archaeological site
7. Bard's before
8. Without enough money
9. Volunteer State
10. ___ Stanley Gardner
11. Rogers and Clark
12. Inhale
13. Shepherds
21. Parseghian
22. Long time spans
24. Fresh-water duck
25. Throws in the towel
26. Coffee vessels
28. Lures
30. Diminutive suffix
31. Stinger
32. Actress Albright
33. Streets: abbr.
34. Capital of 9 Down
35. Blows one's top
38. Help with the dishes
39. Blind part
41. Window section
42. Sight, hearing, etc.
45. Small child
47. Aides: abbr.
48. Small wagons
49. Painter's stand
50. Shade of blue
51. Probe
52. Concerning: 2 wds.
53. Train-track part
54. Damage
57. Secret agent
58. Suit ___ tee: 2 wds.
60. Wing

PUZZLE 511

PUZZLE 512

ACROSS

1. Coins for 17 Across
5. Personnel
10. Norse god
14. Elevator name
15. Of sound
16. Chianti, e.g.
17. Italian painter: 3 wds.
20. ___ well
21. Coined
22. Secret agent
23. Location
24. Peps up
28. Italian volcano
29. River barrier
32. Seer's card
33. Obstacle
34. Divorce city
35. Italian physicist: 2 wds.
38. City in Ohio
39. Sludges
40. Actress Burstyn
41. Dutch commune
42. Boast
43. Works dough
44. "___ of Fools"
45. Baked dessert
46. Nuclear
49. Clasp
54. Italian dictator: 2 wds.
56. Lively dance
57. Slow: Fr.
58. Fleck
59. Concerning: 2 wds.
60. South American mountains
61. Relieve

DOWN

1. Actress Albright
2. Roman road
3. Uproar
4. Old laborer
5. Peels
6. Present time
7. Ever and ___
8. Fancy
9. "The ___ Kid"
10. String
11. Clue
12. Formerly
13. Wallace ___
18. Possessions
19. "La Dolce ___"
23. Luminaries
24. Venture
25. Whitened
26. Good-night girl
27. Expense
28. Furnish with money
29. ___ Robbia
30. Fed the kitty
31. Sad sounds
33. Nosy person
34. Character
36. Roman general
37. Italian region
42. Voucher
43. Candy drops
44. Grin
45. Glue
46. Dugout
47. Adolescent
48. Unique thing
49. Accumulation of money
50. Otherwise
51. Basketry palm
52. Son of Seth
53. Ceremony
55. Chess pieces

ACROSS

1. Barge
5. Bottles
9. Box-shaped
14. Actress Anderson
15. Director Kazan
16. Scene of action
17. In ____ (bored): 2 wds.
18. Four, at sea: 2 wds.
20. Faucet fittings
22. Dogpatch man, with 43 Across
23. Rent
24. Author Harte
25. Kickback
27. Illiterate
30. Discontinue
32. Ponds
33. Goad
34. Sheep meat
38. Turnpike fee
39. Straighten
40. Stead
41. "The Defiant ____"
42. Actress Remick et al.
43. See 22 Across
44. Movie award
46. Hollers
47. Untamed horse
50. Tiff
51. Air: pref.
52. Ab ____ (from the beginning)
54. Discarded
58. Flock leader
61. Popular gem
62. Don't tell ____: 2 wds.
63. Aquarium
64. Female horse
65. Italian painter's family
66. Is in debt
67. Exhibition

DOWN

1. Cabbage salad
2. Mrs. Dithers
3. Responsibility
4. Eagerly: 3 wds.
5. Ridiculed
6. Careening
7. Contraption
8. Comedian Mort
9. Metal ropes
10. English river
11. ____ Abzug
12. Cove
13. Social group
19. Harangue
21. Historic ages
26. Navy pants: hyph.
27. Until: 2 wds.
28. Lunchtime
29. Play part
30. Town ____
31. Ages and ages
33. Entreaty
35. Japanese native
36. Track event
37. Prickly cases
39. Recess
43. Shouts of surprise
45. Frowns
46. Flint flames
47. Fictional elephant
48. Pee Wee ____
49. Synthetic fiber
50. Vista
53. Mr. Preminger
55. Colorful fish
56. Gambler's game
57. Took wing
59. Him: It.
60. "Hee ____"

PUZZLE 514

ACROSS
1. Persian fairy
5. Emulates Newman
9. Display frame
13. Finished
14. Folk myth
15. Climber's spike
16. Trip on the Whip
17. Arid: 4 wds.
19. 7th Greek letter
20. Slight
21. Fabulous bird
22. Sunday seat
23. Coward
25. "Charlotte's ___"
27. Publicizes
28. Believable
33. Plant firmly
35. Filament
36. Pairs
37. Mother deer
38. Helots
39. Toper
40. Pindarics
42. Forest plant
43. Philippine island
45. Learned
47. Israeli dance
48. "Butterflies ___ Free"
49. Strips
52. Eggs
55. ___ Jima
57. United
58. Guggenheim display
59. Ill: 4 wds.
62. Tropical oil source
63. Hindu gowns
64. Ditty
65. Glacial snow
66. Danish measure
67. Mind
68. Profound

DOWN
1. Studied
2. Sra. Peron
3. Embarrassed: 4 wds.
4. Choler
5. Birches' cousins
6. With the center removed
7. Hear judicially
8. Char
9. Chest bone
10. Onto
11. String-holder shape
12. Recognized
15. Set the speed for
18. Planters
20. Actor Bond
24. Make a knot in
26. Offer
28. Was concerned
29. Widespread
30. Occupied: 4 wds.
31. Rob
32. Villa d'___
33. Demigod
34. Style
35. Present!
38. Scatters
41. RR locale: abbr.
43. "The ___ Boat"
44. Before, in verse
46. Silkworms
47. Depended
49. "Lorna ___"
50. Secret store
51. Brew
52. Thessalian peak
53. Small flask
54. Israeli port
56. Imprecation
60. Family
61. Outstanding
62. Knock off

ACROSS

1. Dreary
5. Come to a close
8. Regulations
12. Lasso
13. Recline
14. Yearn
15. Mischief-makers
16. Particular time
18. Each
19. Relieve
20. "Major ___"
21. Woodwind
23. Station break airings
25. Medal
27. Famous vampire
31. Texas town
32. Water tester
33. Impersonated
34. Show
36. Sinned
37. Went ahead
38. BLT dressing
39. Play division
42. "Li'l ___"
44. Meal starter
47. More delicate
49. Inscribe
50. Gumbo ingredient
51. Roofing material
52. No longer are
53. Ooze
54. Messy home
55. Heaven on earth

DOWN

1. Hold fast
2. Eternal City
3. Come close
4. Affirmative
5. Marry on the run
6. Pleasant
7. State
8. ___ Cruces
9. Corrosive
10. Halt!
11. Dispatch
17. "M*A*S*H" actor
19. Turf
22. Swelter
24. Frightening
25. Dazzle
26. Bee's product
27. Speck
28. Pulled out
29. Spike or Bruce
30. Cooking instruction
32. Morsels
35. Pound
36. Pitcher handle
38. Full of gaiety
39. Fusses
40. Piece of ___
41. Exhaust
43. Orderly
45. Farm measure
46. At that time
48. Siesta
49. Member of the flock

PUZZLE 515

441

PUZZLE 516

ACROSS

1. Thailand
5. Author Edna
9. African antelopes
13. Ms. Anderson
14. Chou ——: hyph.
16. Draw a line
17. Al fresco: hyph.
19. Colorado Indians
20. Frat letter
21. For fear that
22. Loathsome
24. Uncooked
25. Precipice
26. Knock down
29. Distend
31. Table protector
34. Awaken
35. Carries on
36. Yoko ——
37. Greek letter
38. "Beau ——"
39. F, D, or R, e.g.
40. Inner: prefix
41. Solution strength
42. Ms. Garbo
43. Dict. offering
44. Greek marketplace
45. Shade of blue
46. Fabric type
48. Bowler's target
49. Piercing
51. Pivot
53. Decline
56. Nothing, in Malaga
57. In the doghouse
60. Approval word
61. Scent
62. Dimension
63. Chipper
64. Affected
65. Cultivate

DOWN

1. Hog fare
2. Proofs of debt
3. Against
4. "O Sole ——"
5. Moisten
6. Adam's grandson
7. Vegas opening
8. Pave
9. Author Paul de ——
10. Broke: 3 wds.
11. Cordon ——
12. Meeting: abbr.
15. Quarantine
18. Blaze
23. Morse sounds
24. Artist Bonheur
25. Opposed: prefix
26. Cooked in fat
27. At large
28. On the blink: 3 wds.
29. Armorican
30. Cutting beam
32. Actress Morris
33. Add
38. Professional escorts
39. Cast or pig
41. Exaggerated
42. Sorrow
47. Cheerful
48. Swollen
49. Abrupt retort
50. Harness item
51. Agitate
52. Garret
53. Wicked
54. Nitwit
55. Ale, e.g.
58. Actress Merkel
59. Cleo's snake

ACROSS

1. Chinese fraternity
5. Fit for a king
10. Football Starr
14. Arab chief
15. Plant disease
16. Aroma
17. Vinous valley
18. Actor John
19. Actress Louise
20. Across: prefix
22. Shortchange a worker
24. Mr. Turner
25. Clamor
26. Enraged
30. Fretted
34. Actor's gp.
35. Spelling match
36. Stage ploy
37. African antelope
38. Kegs
41. Zip
42. Long: prefix
44. Cycle or pod lead-in
45. Adept
46. Inquiring
48. "I Only —— for You: 2 wds.
50. Dove's desire
52. Blue Eagle inits.
53. Swimming hazard
56. Ball
59. Equine hue
60. Teach
63. Labor
64. Axlike tool
65. Eagle's nest
66. Medieval laborer
67. Falsified
68. Consumers
69. Adjudge

DOWN

1. Bedouin dwelling
2. Actor Sharif
3. Very close: 3 wds.
4. Alhambra site
5. Cartoonist Gardner
6. Asner and Begley
7. Just make it: 4 wds.
8. Acid type
9. Kenesaw Mountain ——
10. Indian-fig sources: 2 wds.
11. Take —— (swim): 2 wds.
12. Ms. Barrett
13. Butler's burden
21. Jeanne d'Arc, e.g.: abbr.
23. These, in Toledo
26. Molten material
27. Indian coins
28. Cagers' group: abbr.
29. Always to a poet
31. Squeak to victory: 4 wds.
32. Roman magistrate
33. Erases
38. Blunder
39. Victorian ——
40. Actress Ullmann

43. Matured
45. Charged with gas
47. Parisian cake
49. Call it quits
51. Area and zip
53. Asian mountain range
54. Story complications
55. Bewilderment
57. Film
58. Basic: abbr.
61. Balsam
62. Affirmative

PUZZLE 517

PUZZLE 518

ACROSS
1. Pant
5. Forehead hair
10. Daze
14. "Rio ___"
15. ___ from the blue: 2 wds.
16. Surface
17. Greek war god
18. "Andrea ___"
19. Busy as ___: 2 wds.
20. WWII pinup: 2 wds.
23. Youngster
24. TV ___
25. Large pond
27. Tea expert
31. Flower arranger
34. Enroll
35. Actor James
36. Barbecue rod
38. Jazzman Getz
39. ___ -stitch
40. Ascend
41. Relatives
42. Singer Guthrie
43. Actress Dana
44. Scour
46. French sauce
47. Formerly, once
48. Took a chair
49. Buffet
51. "The House of the ___": 2 wds.
58. Town in Washington
60. Sped
61. Verdi opera
62. Speck
63. "___ Gay"
64. Washer cycle
65. Arabian port
66. Small valleys
67. City in Italy

DOWN
1. Snatch
2. River to the Ouse
3. Printer's direction
4. Ago
5. Annoy
6. End a mission
7. Nick and ___ Charles
8. Fluent
9. "Rambo" star
10. Ems, e.g.
11. Quantity of sugar
12. Tunic of the eye
13. Depend on
21. River to the North Sea
22. Corn unit
26. Face, slangily
27. Kinski role
28. Caper
29. Horse's companion
30. More uptight
31. Aesop story
32. French composer
33. Diadem
35. Recall subjects
37. Server
39. Galloped easily
43. Indian vessel
45. Donkey
46. A Gabor et al.
48. Fishhook tie
49. Capital of Italia
50. Among
52. Weathercock
53. Environment science: abbr.
54. Footing
55. Mouth parts
56. Revise copy
57. Rational
59. Actor Howard

ACROSS
1. Hairless
5. Wash
10. Applaud
14. Medley
15. Persian
16. Chinese: pref.
17. ____ dynasty
18. German pistol
19. Dove shelter
20. Apiaries
22. Bagpipes
24. Step ____!: 2 wds.
25. Rabbit tails
26. Counterfeit
29. Sand sculptures
32. Stockpile
33. Oleo, in England
35. Quantity: abbr.
36. Fury
37. "Robinson Crusoe" author
38. Trifle, of old
39. Body of land: abbr.
40. Grant
41. Kiln operator?
42. Protect
44. Actor Raymond
45. Roman dictator
46. Accompanying
47. Celery's kin
49. Porcine homes
53. Mr. Cassini
54. Hibernian
56. Farm unit
57. Soar
58. Nine-part song
59. "____ That Tune"
60. Queens nine
61. Social people
62. Abrupt blow

DOWN
1. Flop
2. "I cannot tell ____": 2 wds.
3. Points connector
4. Snoopy's home
5. "Pagliacci" character
6. Vinegar bottle
7. Tatters
8. One: Fr.
9. Home for Tweety Pie
10. Actor George: 2 wds.
11. Dens: 2 wds.
12. Chip in
13. "Raven" poet and family
21. Native Americans: abbr.
23. Trick
25. Young haddock
26. "I Love ____"
27. Shatter
28. Aerie: 2 wds.
30. TV host
31. Tale
33. Stiller's partner
34. Continent: abbr.
37. Residence
38. Home for guppies: 2 wds.
40. Tamarisk
41. Jazzman Waller
43. Thrusts forward
44. Strengths
46. Sadder but ____
47. Contour
48. Writer Wiesel
49. Yearn
50. "Yes ____": 2 wds.
51. Author Bombeck
52. Ooze
55. Pooh's pal

PUZZLE 520

ACROSS

1. '60s rock group
6. Have the lead
10. Trojan War hero
14. Boil ____: 2 wds.
15. Chrysalis
16. Not any
17. Book room
18. Opposed
19. Party to: 2 wds.
20. Junior
21. Palm fruit
23. Fats ____
25. Skeleton part
26. Greek queen of heaven
27. Tribute
30. Jefferson ____
34. All eyes
35. Tips off
37. "Pygmalion" playwright
38. Rarer than rare
39. Kindled
40. Keats poem
41. One who squeaks by
43. Explosion
45. Arab prince
46. Smokey Robinson's group
48. Glowing coals
50. Part of ASAP
51. Commoner
52. Lighthouse
55. At what time
56. Eggs
59. Molten rock
60. Dumb ____
62. Mr. Doubleday
64. Wicked
65. Eye center
66. Richest part of milk
67. Marries
68. Punta del ____
69. Ahead of time

DOWN

1. '70s rock group
2. Division word
3. Substantive
4. Baby goat
5. Roguish man: 2 wds.
6. Flood
7. Melody
8. Likely
9. Paul Revere and the ____
10. Eric Burdon's group
11. Songstress Mitchell
12. Ever and ____
13. Foreign: pref.
22. Over again
24. Fret, in Scotland
25. Purse
26. Clues
27. Sultan's wives
28. Japanese city
29. Grass cutter
30. Opera songs
31. "A House Is Not ____": 2 wds.
32. Lowest point
33. Pitchers
36. Ethan ____
42. Felix Cavaliere's group
43. Deborah Harry's group
44. Far: pref.
45. ____ and flow
47. Pigeon's sound
49. "Dennis the ____"
51. Stage
52. Huffed
53. Roof overhang
54. Keen
55. Legal order
56. Humdinger
57. Calf meat
58. Ground troops
61. Heraldic golds
63. Bikini top

ACROSS

1. Heavenly instrument
5. Adjust an alarm
10. Float on the breeze
14. Muffin topper
15. Axiom
16. War god
17. Asterisk
18. Gusto
19. Singer Coolidge
20. Harbor
21. Summer, in Paris
22. "___, She Wrote"
24. Vases
26. Experienced
27. River boats
30. Protected an invention
34. Perfect
35. Propounded
36. Ancient Burmese capital
37. Christmas song
38. Nuisances
39. Flaw
40. Physicians: abbr.
41. Blackboard
42. Berate
43. Tennis shoes
45. Warmed
46. Watch face
47. Half quart
48. Instigates
51. Play on words
52. Russian news agcy.
56. Wacky
57. Wide-awake
59. Wicked
60. Against
61. Slipknot
62. Actor's quest
63. Key ___
64. Adjusted a piano
65. Flurry

DOWN

1. Clinic: abbr.
2. Female singer
3. Tail end
4. Part of Iberia
5. Black birds
6. Prepares copy
7. Judicious man
8. Self
9. White ants
10. Actor Beatty
11. Bleak
12. Holiday
13. Autocratic ruler
23. Took advantage of
25. Family member: abbr.
26. Squander
27. Dilemmas
28. Decorate
29. Pee Wee ___
30. Masts
31. Unspoken
32. Elude
33. Challenged
35. Oyster gem
38. Agreeable
39. Smashes
41. Revue sketch
42. One hundred yrs.
44. Dexterous
45. Gave a clue
47. Handbag
48. Cabbage dish
49. Sound quality
50. Performs
51. Laborer
53. Shakespeare's river
54. Missile housing
55. Seattle ___
58. Singer Rawls

PUZZLE 522

ACROSS

1. Grackle's cackle
4. X, for one
9. October birthstone
13. Mr. Cassini
15. Lofty shelter
16. Extremely
17. Grinding device: 2 wds.
19. Fencing sword
20. Eulogized
21. Wild West name
23. Actor Barker
24. "The Immoralist" author
25. Strut
29. Made a commotion
33. Goudas' kin
34. Pews
35. Sea: Fr.
36. Building additions
37. Spear
38. Hara-____
39. Hanoi holiday
40. Reception
41. Figure-skating great
42. Piece of sacred music
44. "____ Wonderland"
45. Best man's concern
46. Sixty secs.
47. Alternatively
48. Lanky
53. Carillon
55. Handy dispenser
57. Coquettish look
58. Candidates' list
59. ____ Verde
60. Needy
61. Kind of berry
62. Pig's home

DOWN

1. Contend with
2. "Taxi" role
3. Bewailed
4. Soup ingredient
5. Quill feather
6. Like the Mojave
7. Naught
8. Deputy
9. Carry too far
10. Gum flavor
11. "Butterflies ____ Free"
12. Caustic substance
14. Mail abbr.
18. Raines and Cinders
22. Objectives
25. Take care of: 2 wds.
26. Author Luther
27. Italian dance
28. "____ Pinafore"
29. Literary patchwork
30. Weblike
31. Mysterious
32. Less humid
34. Rani's garb
37. Generosity
38. Barbie's friend
40. Operatic Lily
41. Part of an oyster shell
43. Rudder adjunct
44. Person whose foot has been trod on
46. Dull surface
48. Willing
49. Legal deg.
50. Land bits: Fr.
51. Political cartoonist
52. Confederate color
53. Jazz category
54. Self
56. "____ about Eve"

ACROSS

1. Tiny ____
4. Seance sound
7. Mineo
10. Historic time
11. "____ That Tune"
12. 5,280 feet
13. Author Zola
16. Bride's young attendants: 2 wds.
19. Consumerist Ralph ____
20. Be sick
21. Laurel or Musial
22. Pindaric poem
23. 1492 ship
25. Actor Falk
29. Light-switch position
31. Traditional brides' wear
33. Actress Hayworth
34. Stadium cheer
35. Make taboo
36. Coal measure
38. Unexpected problem
39. DDE's command
40. Superlative ending
41. Yale man
42. Spanish gentlemen
45. There ought to be ____!: 2 wds.
49. Step ____!: 2 wds.
50. Strong wind
51. Meander
52. Endures patiently
55. Mimic
58. Automobile
60. Weir
61. Young sheep
65. Teachers' gp.
66. ____ king: 2 wds.
67. "____ Got a Crush on You"
68. Ripener
69. "Oh, ____ Me"
73. Nuptial-notice word
74. Three-dimensional
76. Show to be true
77. Fall behind
79. Something owed
82. Buck's mate
83. Welles or Bean
86. Nuptial-band conveyors: 2 wds.
90. Chimney output
91. "Dies ____"
92. Having wings
93. New Deal agcy.
94. Baseball-player's need
95. Derek's number
96. Hood's gun

DOWN

1. High-school youngster
2. "____ La Douce"
3. Bride's attendant: 3 wds.
4. Uncooked
5. Brotherly quartet of the '50s
6. Bouncy
7. Title for Galahad
8. The entirety
9. "____ Miserables"
11. Actor Nick ____
12. Excavators
14. Guided
15. Before, to a bard
16. Unbiased
17. Fluffy bits of thread
18. Opening
23. Gasp for breath
24. TV comic Johnson
26. Soft, white metal
27. Greek vowel
28. Cleaning cloth
29. Native metals
30. Inevitable lot
31. Natural or synthetic fuel
32. The sun
35. Groom's attendant: 2 wds.
37. Honeymoon falls
43. Yoko ____
44. Inlet
46. Science workshop, for short
47. ____ MacGraw
48. 69 Across, e.g.: 2 wds.
53. Roof overhang
54. Pintail duck
56. Vim
57. O.K. Corral name
58. Instance
59. October brew
61. ____ Vegas
62. In the past
63. Tillis
64. Golden Gate ____
70. Command
71. Othello, for one
72. Actor Burl ____
75. Coming-out-party gal
77. ____ Alamos
78. Fortify
80. Thrash
81. Fable
84. Vegetable
85. Tidy
86. "Adam's ____"
87. Lyricist Gershwin
88. ____ King Cole
89. Operated

PUZZLE 523

• BELLS ARE RINGING •

PUZZLE 524

ACROSS

1. That woman
4. Automobile
7. Close securely
8. Unwrap
10. Gets close to
11. At no time
13. Church seat
14. Retained
16. Take a chair
18. Length times width
20. Crimson
22. As well
23. Body trunk
25. Unit
26. Pig's home
27. More intelligent
30. "____ De-Lovely"
33. Actress Lupino
34. Peels
38. Permit
39. Small child
40. Ocean swell
41. Hearing organ
42. Raise
45. Victory sign
46. Spokes
49. Curses
51. Alert
52. Level
53. "Little Women" character
54. Morning wetness

DOWN

1. Caspian or Sargasso
2. Listen!
3. Otherwise
4. Satisfied
5. Gorilla
6. Race, as an engine
7. Betsy Ross, e.g.
9. Treetop nurseries
10. Pianist Peter ____
12. Mob action
13. Tap
15. Apportion
17. Plaything
19. Mule's relative
21. Profound
24. Skip over
28. Worshiping
29. Rough
30. French land mass
31. Rip
32. "Turkey in the ____"
35. Poe's bird
36. Nights before
37. Behold
43. Still sleeping
44. Rant's partner
47. Water barrier
48. Anger
50. Recent

PUZZLE 525

ACROSS

1. Meat and vegetable dish
5. Kettle's relative
8. Bartok and Peron
12. Great Lake
13. A few
14. South of France
15. Avoid
17. Infamous tsar
18. Rewrite
19. Actress Samantha and kin
21. Dispute
23. Director
25. Neighbor of Miss.
26. Table scrap
27. Peevish
31. Naught
32. FDR agency
34. Private pension plan, for short
35. Subway coin
38. Wallach or Whitney
40. Press for payment
41. ". . . so ____ a day in June?"
43. "____ and Meek" (comic strip)
44. Prairie wolf
47. "Let's Make a ____"
49. Did a garden chore
50. Bosom buddy
54. "Bus Stop" author
55. Assam silkworm
56. Concerning
57. Picks on constantly
58. Ring count
59. The cat's ____

DOWN

1. "For ____ a jolly . . ."
2. Jackie's second
3. Superintendent or sale
4. Pay attention to
5. Design
6. "____ O'Clock Jump"
7. Did hunt-and-peck work
8. Expatriate
9. "____ Zapata!"
10. Hebrew month
11. Transgressions
16. Farm tower
20. "____ Smart"
21. Carry on
22. Mixture
24. "But only God can make ____"
28. Football field boundary
29. Loyal
30. Jerk
33. Magic lamp's owner
36. Deteriorates
37. ____ King Cole
39. Phrase of understanding
42. Bowling alley button
44. Vandyke locale
45. Charlie Chaplin's wife
46. Safecracker
48. Actor Tamiroff
51. Fury
52. ____-Magnon
53. London's ____ Gardens

PUZZLE 526

ACROSS
1. Lip
5. Face part
8. Two cups
12. Descended
13. Shoshonean Indian
14. ____ of March
15. Waiter's handout
16. Representative
18. Christmas drink
20. Actor Majors
21. Pack down
23. Faithful
27. Alphabet letter
30. School session
32. Title
33. Zodiac sign
34. Busybody
36. Meadow
37. Alan Alda show
39. Sandwich fish
40. Finish
41. Got up
43. Pub missile
45. Constrictor
47. Guide
51. Chinese seaport
55. Holy Father
56. Flying: pref.
57. Donkey
58. Level
59. Baby's bed
60. Sheep's cry
61. Marsh plant

DOWN
1. Identical
2. Shake ____
3. Warble
4. Unusual feat
5. Conclusion
6. Had brunch
7. Fountain
8. Park bird
9. Actress Lupino
10. Ensnare
11. Mao ____-tung
17. Snaky fish
19. Horse food
22. Haughty
24. New Haven university
25. Prayer ending
26. Command
27. Shady trees
28. Chair
29. Passable
31. Da Vinci painting
35. Shear
38. Associate on very friendly terms
42. Household pet
44. Candle
46. "Moby Dick" character
48. Bird of peace
49. Fencing sword
50. Tear apart
51. Pouch
52. That woman's
53. Jackie's second
54. ____ rule

PUZZLE 527

ACROSS
1. God of thunder
5. Poles
9. Door rug
12. Not run-of-the-mill
13. What's ____ for me?
14. ____ mode
15. White House office shape
16. Huge
18. Great pleasure
20. Honey maker
21. Dine
22. Warns
25. Meat sauce
28. Bind
29. Make angry
30. Solitary
31. Cushion
32. Sprinkle
33. Imitate
34. Carton
35. Jet flyer
36. Formal decision
38. Eternity
39. Period
40. Horse for Roy Rogers
44. Hinterland
47. Load with cargo
48. Morsel for Mr. Ed
49. Ireland
50. Robert ____
51. See you!
52. Orange skin
53. Aquarium

DOWN
1. Walked
2. Possess
3. Spoken
4. Ease
5. Correct
6. Step ____
7. Use a shovel
8. Farm building
9. Fabric
10. Actress MacGraw
11. Tic-____-toe
17. Born named
19. Merry
22. Assist
23. Small combo
24. Dispatched
25. Happy
26. Thick string
27. Short story
28. Assess
31. "Gold Bug" author
32. Curl
34. Good, ____, best
35. Hawaiian food
37. Actor Ely
38. Proved human
40. Sea bird
41. Festive
42. Paradise
43. Give off vapors
44. Watch pocket
45. Beam
46. Three, to Cato

PUZZLE 528

ACROSS

1. Boston team
7. Postponed
13. Planters
14. Scraped
16. Lunar or solar
17. Siege
18. Increase
19. Pursued
21. TV's "_____ Sharkey"
22. Ark builder
24. Target disk
25. Bee's relative
26. Inception
28. Auricle
29. Hall's singing partner
30. Scorched
32. Group of six
34. CEO, e.g.
35. Dog doc
36. Picturesque
39. Knock down
42. Ranges
43. Actress Hagen
45. Fished for congers
47. Golf goals
48. Like fresh lettuce
50. Prophet
51. Crude mineral
52. Natural breakfast
54. "Much _____ About Nothing"
55. Sugar producer
57. Connects
59. Rival
60. Draft regulators
61. Pleases
62. Rate

DOWN

1. Calls
2. Free
3. North Caucasian language
4. Little devils
5. Retreats
6. Slunk
7. Orators
8. Red as _____
9. Actor Davis
10. Trail
11. Teach
12. Like some eyes
13. "_____ evil, hear . . ."
15. Falls
20. Meadow
23. Sky
25. Fences
27. Triplets
29. Daisy
31. Outer: pref.
33. Zsa Zsa's sister
36. Keep it to yourself
37. Fastidious
38. Arrow poisons
39. Former Dodger manager
40. Acid esters
41. Garden workers
42. Germ
44. Sn
46. Residue
48. Mediterranean island
49. Requests
52. Bothersome fly
53. Charity
56. Nigerian town
58. Imitate

[crossword grid]

PUZZLE 529

QUOTAGRAM

Fill in the answers to the clues below. Then transfer the letters to the correspondingly numbered squares in the diagram. The completed diagram will contain a quotation.

1. Scare
 ___ ___ ___ ___ ___ ___
 14 33 25 41 13 8

2. Upper leg
 ___ ___ ___ ___ ___
 4 17 1 21 36

3. Whim
 ___ ___ ___ ___ ___ ___
 29 23 26 5 10 40

4. Sending a telegraph
 ___ ___ ___ ___ ___ ___
 31 3 24 27 20 16

5. _____ Sad, Serbia
 ___ ___ ___ ___
 7 32 38 19

6. Distort
 ___ ___ ___ ___ ___
 34 9 15 6 12

7. Float
 ___ ___ ___ ___
 11 37 22 18

8. Change
 ___ ___ ___ ___ ___
 28 35 39 2 30

[quotagram grid numbered 1-41]

ACROSS

1. Located visually
4. Check
7. Emmet
10. Melody
12. Kitchen gadget
14. Lots
15. Coin
16. "___ in Wonderland"
17. Cab
18. Ask with force
20. Vouch
22. Food scrap
23. Fade
24. Tan
26. Graceful tree
27. Chair
30. Run into
31. ___ mode
32. Expiated
34. Above, poetically
35. ___ stick
37. ___ nutshell
38. Helix
40. Dawn goddess
41. Plant part
42. Observed
43. To and ___
44. ___ the drum
45. Porticos
47. Owned
48. Talk like a bird
50. Exhibit
53. Unclean
54. Forty-___
56. Auto shoe
58. Throw off
59. Night sound
60. Wicked
61. Seine
62. African antelope
63. Squiggler

DOWN

1. "My Sister ___"
2. Lifeless
3. ___ and dine
4. Revealed
5. Actress Meyers
6. Soothe
7. Woe is me!
8. Barber's call
9. Prefix for light
11. To an extreme
12. Jargon
13. Network
14. Hi-fi
19. Noah's boat
21. Enjoy the flavor of
23. Jackets
24. Toots
25. Eagle's nest
26. Yalie
28. Writer Loos
29. Belief
30. Jan. and Sept.
31. Piercing tool
32. Capone and Pacino
33. Barrier
35. ___ Claus
36. Menagerie
39. Outcome
41. Calm
43. Playing possum
44. Tavern
46. Has
47. Rabbit
48. Any
49. Give up
50. Town in Indiana
51. Plunge
52. Pennsylvania lake
53. Marsh
55. Negative prefix
57. Annex

HIDDEN CITIES

Find the names of the 8 U.S. cities hidden in the sentences below. The letters of each city are in consecutive order.

Example: The festival will feature top com<u>bos</u> <u>ton</u>ight.

1. The butcher, the baker, the taco maker.
2. Those who knew have not been identified.
3. Jumbo is elephant-size.
4. "The Sun" is the best A.M. paper.
5. Many people report landings of spacecraft.
6. A carnivore keeps the den very hidden.
7. Prepare noodles per directions.
8. Disney World's construction was a boon for landowners.

PUZZLE 532

ACROSS

1. Ransack
6. Tiny particle
10. Rule
13. Moon of Uranus
14. Endure
15. Onassis
16. Elizabeth I: 2 wds.
18. Noise
19. Dogmas
20. Baseball inning components
21. Uses henna
22. Depot: abbr.
23. Blows one's own horn
25. Tell
29. San ____, Italy
31. By oneself
32. Drilled
33. Grand Coulee, for one
36. Sprightly
37. Loaded with cargo
38. Go by car
39. Kennedy or Danson
40. Worries
41. Rescues
42. Common
44. Fruit
45. Italian city
46. Spanish hero
47. ____ Stanley Gardner
48. Pain
50. Fast planes: abbr.
54. Neon or freon
55. Round Table member: 2 wds.
58. Marriage vow: 2 wds.
59. Constellation
60. Smell
61. Japanese coin
62. Pound
63. Subsequently

DOWN

1. Mr. Shankar
2. Eye part
3. Steady
4. "____ Diamond"
5. ____ Whitney
6. Touch at the border
7. Cravats
8. Poem
9. Males
10. Medieval rider: 2 wds.
11. Zodiac sign
12. Succeeds
14. Blue-green shade
17. Musical sound
21. Country-singer Seals
22. Sault ____ Marie
23. British gun
24. Do away with
25. Paying attention
26. Robert ____: 2 wds.
27. British hero: 2 wds.
28. Emmet
29. Representation
30. Greek god
32. Actress Theda
34. Yemen seaport
35. Arizona city
37. Tibetan monk
38. Sped
40. ____-Magnon
41. Down
43. Individual
44. Tres ____
45. School division
46. Movie-detective Charlie
47. Shield
48. Opera song
49. Blood accumulation
50. Evening: It.
51. Coin insert
52. Large book
53. Nova
55. Cry
56. Anger
57. Silent ____

PUZZLE 533

MYSTERY WORD

Can you find the 6-letter Mystery Word that is hidden in the diagram below in four minutes or less?

A	B	I	D	G	E
O	F	L	S	I	L
I	C	E	J	C	H
E	A	K	D	O	R
G	I	H	B	O	G
D	E	A	E	L	H

My first letter occurs only twice in the diagram, but not in the same row.

My second is at the end of a row which also includes three vowels, all different.

My third occurs exactly four times in the diagram.

My fourth is above my first.

My fifth occurs at the beginning and the end of one of the rows across.

My last letter is the only vowel occurring twice in a row across.

Mystery Word: __ __ __ __ __ __

454

ACROSS

1. Labyrinth
5. Chore
9. Kilns
11. Honshu's land
12. Rise up
13. Enough
14. Make a mistake
15. Sound receiver
17. Order's partner
18. Slender candle
20. Gave nourishment
21. "Aida," e.g.
23. Door rug
25. Hospital employee
28. Actor Holbrook
29. Friend
30. Scientist's workshop, for short
32. Get up
34. Make happy
36. Stream
37. Appraises
38. Hammer part
39. Sassy

DOWN

1. Additional
2. Ward off
3. Striped animal
4. Compass point: abbr.
5. Scottish cap
6. Golden delicious
7. Vegetable dish
8. Was aware
10. Siesta
11. Urn
16. Sports stadium
19. Poker kitty
20. Distant
22. King, e.g.
23. Singer Osmond
24. Breathing
26. List of candidates
27. Diner patron
28. Heavenly instrument
29. For each
31. Most suitable
33. Coin from 11 Across
35. Track unit

ACROSS

1. Taste liquid
4. Throb
8. Bogus
12. Mine product
13. Den
14. Roman garment
15. Minus
17. Base
18. Cowboy Autry
19. Shrubbery
20. Cling
23. Arthur of "The Golden Girls"
24. Observes
25. Depletes
29. Moray
30. Allow
32. Edgar Allan
33. Laborious
35. Cat sound
36. Bill denomination
37. Grooms
39. Converses casually
42. Cereal husk
43. Hearty
44. Acquires
48. Eternal
49. Comfort
50. Mr. Carney
51. Rates
52. Fruit drinks
53. Merry month

DOWN

1. Offspring
2. Anger
3. Clothespin
4. Change
5. "The ____ Mutiny"
6. Busy abode
7. Before, before
8. "Silver ____"
9. Car part
10. Eager
11. Spouse
16. Ripens
19. Warm up
20. On the ocean
21. Bambi
22. Clutched
23. "Gentle ____"
25. Existed
26. Fencing sword
27. Lunch hour
28. Uses needle and thread
30. Leaves
31. Jog
34. Speaks
35. Bill of fare
37. Nonpoetic language
38. Relays
39. Cook
40. Own
41. Sheltered from the wind
42. Nail
44. Small vegetable
45. Aries
46. Epoch
47. Pigpen

PUZZLE 536

ACROSS

1. Repeated, as a movie
6. Small quarrel
10. Moist and chilly
14. Actress Cara
15. Hue
16. Singer Adams
17. David's weapon
18. Feed the kitty
19. Not yours
20. Knowledge
21. Disembark
23. Flower part
24. Group of cows
25. Celebration
27. Choose
30. Geometrical figure
34. Warn
35. Temperamental
36. Shorten
37. Affection
38. Wait on customers
39. Small bay
40. Gorilla
41. List of candidates
42. More unhappy
43. Dainty
45. Singer Pearl
46. Military branch
47. Heavenly instrument
48. Vision
51. Sounded a bell
52. Black bird
55. Opera highlight
56. Incline
58. Was sick
60. Little brook
61. Eager
62. Perfect model
63. ___ of Man
64. Contradict
65. Mother-of-pearl

DOWN

1. Danger
2. Writer Gardner
3. Check
4. Raggedy doll
5. Disregard
6. Lose one's lap
7. Frog's home
8. Picnic pest
9. Golfer's peg
10. Humble
11. Mine entrance
12. Actress Foch
13. On an even ___
22. Museum pieces
23. Act the part
24. In this place
25. Orchard
26. Assistant
27. Veggie dish
28. Marry on the lam
29. Flat
30. Rich cake
31. Evil spirit
32. River embankment
33. Corundum
35. Pithy
38. Serb or Croat
39. Cut out, as coupons
41. Beat it, feline!
42. Buyer's delight
44. Take a breath
45. Prohibit
47. Convenient
48. Hindu garment
49. Eye part
50. Fish organ
51. Shower
52. Actor Guinness
53. Close by
54. Not working
56. Small boy
57. Adam's wife
59. Actress Lupino

PUZZLE 537   Escalator

Place the answer to clue 1 in the first space, drop a letter and arrange the remaining letters to answer clue 2. Drop another letter and arrange the remaining letters to answer clue 3. The first dropped letter goes into the box to the left of space 1 and the second dropped letter goes into the box to the right of space 3. Follow this pattern for each row in the diagram. When completed, the letters on the left and right, reading down, will spell related words or a phrase.

1. Instruction
2. Snouts
3. Dollars
4. Flattened at the poles
5. Sheep's cry
6. Sash
7. Mysterious
8. Hoisting device
9. Relay ___
10. Disagree
11. Shot (a gun)
12. Prevalent
13. Rents
14. Closes securely
15. Minus
16. Package
17. Location
18. ___ Cod

PUZZLE 538

ACROSS

1. Employed
6. Wound remainder
10. Ragout
14. Wear away
15. Ballerina's bend
16. Israeli folk dance
17. Suddenly, to Keats
18. Landlady's income
19. Singer Redding
20. Eliot's "Do I ____?": 5 wds.
23. Help a criminal
24. Kind of bet
25. Pamper
29. Workroom
30. Not aweather
31. Highway sight
34. "____ Teenage Werewolf": 3 wds.
39. Kind of complexion: 3 wds.
42. ____ dot
43. "____ My Heart": 2 wds.
44. Cartoonist Peter
45. Put down carpet
47. Two-edged sword
49. Christmas drink
53. Spoke
55. Certain cosmetics: 2 wds.
61. Terrible tsar
62. Seaweed extract
63. Synthetic fiber
64. Ocean bird
65. Angry
66. "____ Lucy": 2 wds.
67. Friendly nation
68. Elm
69. Indian abode

DOWN

1. Noggin
2. "____ La Douce"
3. Lion's sound
4. Actress Adams
5. ____ floss
6. Shopping binge
7. Sport-shoe feature
8. "____ Misbehavin'"
9. Use adhesive again
10. Blacksmith, at times
11. Add up
12. Author Jong
13. Wishy-____
21. Excessively fat
22. Sudden fear
25. Cartoonist Al
26. Dairy-case item
27. Bargain
28. Pack of cards
29. Bell sound
32. Catch sight of
33. Actress West
35. Cover, as a gift
36. Flying prefix
37. Rational
38. Love, to Pedro
40. Nimbi
41. Greek dialect
46. Terrified
48. Dexterous
49. Broadway hit
50. Judge's hammer
51. Make knotted
52. Dolt
53. Entrap
54. Concur
56. Composer Stravinsky
57. A Gardner
58. Drooping
59. Change locations
60. Snick and ____

FAMILY TIES
PUZZLE 539

Each group below contains four unrelated words. Without rearranging the letters, change one letter in each of the words to form four related words.

Example: Rise Lilt Patsy Ires (**Solution:** Rose, Lily, Pansy, Iris)

1. Poach _____
2. Might _____
3. Center _____
4. Barn _____
5. Cold _____
6. Marsh _____

Ample _____
Limp _____
Sun _____
Chap _____
Plead _____
Duly _____

Tango _____
Porch _____
Gallon _____
Soar _____
Grease _____
Map _____

Grace _____
Bulk _____
Lone _____
Since _____
Band _____
Dune _____

PUZZLE 540

FOUR-MOST

All of the 4-letter entries in this crossword puzzle are listed separately and are in alphabetical order. Use the numbered clues as solving aids to help you determine where each 4-letter entry goes in the diagram.

ACROSS

5. Rub
10. Place to rejuvenate
14. Assistants
17. Copy
20. Collection
21. Tillable
26. Ancient Greek city
29. Cut-out letter
32. Litigation
33. Come in
35. Pavarotti, e.g.
39. Detection device
42. ___ up (gets smart)
44. Sulks
46. Recent: pref.
47. Smash
49. Declare
53. Noble titles
56. To's partner
62. Claw
66. Obliterate
68. Attach
69. Escorted

DOWN

4. Bother
5. Rotating shafts
6. Employs
8. Swamp
9. Property
15. Reindeer name
24. Corroded
25. Thong
27. Plaster of ___
28. Covered with water
29. Mister, in Seville
30. Silly
31. Independent person
34. Thick books
38. Flares
40. Convinced
45. Opposite of NNW
48. Tried
50. Specimen
52. Ascended
63. Sky altar

4 LETTERS

ADIT	PLAN
AMEN	PRAY
ANNE	RAIN
ARAB	RANI
ARID	RANK
ASEA	RANT
BETA	RIND
CUES	RIOT
EATS	SLAB
ELKS	SLAW
ERIN	STAN
EVES	STEW
EYES	STUN
FLAT	SWAP
LANE	TAME
MORE	TINS
ORAL	WAVE
PAIL	WENT

PUZZLE 541

• WORDS OF A FEATHER •

ACROSS

1. No longer owed
5. ____ bien
9. "Who's the Boss?" character
13. Staked item
18. Therefore
19. The March King
20. Sere
21. "Too ____ Handle"
22. 5 site developments
26. Rocky hill
27. Feels poorly
28. Dobbin's favorites
29. Actress Joyce
30. Author Yutang
31. Astronaut's positive response
32. Rational
34. 4 words of a weather
45. Bridge seats
46. Haifa residents: abbr.
47. "____ Misbehavin'"
48. Medicinal plant
49. Mr. Johnson
50. Certain NCOs
51. Loco
52. Impersonating
53. 5 atmospheric words
58. Dealer buster
59. Kin of ltd.
60. Mulligan, e.g.
61. ____ Paulo
62. Enjoy
64. Appetizers
67. Hip or tip follower
69. Fitting
72. New York baseballers
74. UN division
75. Actor Guinness
77. 5 greasy words
85. ____ -gritty
86. Youngster
87. "Baby ____"
88. Wine town
89. Australian bird
90. Polly or Em
91. Biblical man
92. Stakes
93. 5 electrifying words
98. Mel of baseball and family
99. Smith and Capone
100. Goddess of fertility
101. Rouse to action
105. Caron role
107. Letters for MPs
109. Ad ____
112. 5 chilling words
117. Give a speech
118. Liberal or fine
119. Meathead's mother-in-law
120. So be it
121. Painter Max ____
122. El ____, Texas
123. Portnoy's creator
124. French department

DOWN

1. Nuisance
2. Guthrie
3. Prince of opera
4. Speck
5. Utensil
6. Grooves
7. Sixth sense
8. Bars
9. Dillon
10. Spheres
11. Nothing
12. Stir
13. Mountain home
14. Falana
15. Gudrun's husband
16. "Blame ____ Rio"
17. Another speck
19. David's weapon
23. Biblical murderer et al.
24. Acorns' yield
25. Volunteer St.
30. Word-for-word
31. Blimp
32. December personages
33. River island
34. Negotiate
35. ____ avis
36. "The Addams Family" star
37. Swiss peak
38. Stellar pref.
39. TV host Jack ____
40. Melodic phrase
41. Entranced
42. Other name
43. Land of Ephesus
44. Black, in Barcelona
50. One who fires?
51. Enunciation
52. "It Might ____ Be Spring"
54. With decorum
55. ____-Alicia
56. ____ in the bag
57. Not wholesale
63. Command for DDE
65. Inventor Whitney
66. Grande Armee men
68. Withdraws
69. Doubleday
70. ____ donna
71. Tribe emblem
73. Tummy exercises
76. ____ Rica
78. I've had ____ to here!
79. Camera part
80. Bristle
81. ____-in-hand
82. Stewpot
83. Agenda element
84. Mispronounce
90. Qty.
91. Movie-making machine
92. Delicious fruit
94. Phrase originator
95. Italian commune
96. Bamako's land
97. Sponge
101. Forehead
102. Republic of Ireland
103. Strikebreaker
104. Beret site
105. WWII craft
106. ____ facto
107. Mine entry
108. Accompanying
109. Star's car, for short
110. Bakery worker
111. Flex
113. Lid
114. Age
115. Tokyo, before
116. Singer Morrison

459

PUZZLE 542

• A WORLD OF COLORS •

ACROSS

1. Possession rights
5. Rose essence
10. Jungle creeper
15. Punches
19. Her, in Madrid
20. Innocent
21. Pianist Levant
22. Drive away
23. Disreputable kin
25. Some deer
27. Dry, as wine
28. Vientiane's site
29. Diamond girl
31. Hold back
32. Principle of life
33. J. Fonda film
35. Diabolical one
37. Early Egyptian citizen
39. Serpentine stone
41. Dusky, sly beast
43. Flaked down
46. Form into tight curls
47. Sulk
48. Wallaroo
50. Serious
51. Festive event
52. Existed
53. Somewhat moist
55. Dash
56. Suffer
57. Pacific gulf
59. Actress Johns
61. D-Day ship: abbr.
62. Diffident
64. Digress
66. Cuts into
68. Fed one's face
69. Durocher's nickname
70. Down for the count
71. Spider's works
75. Domesticates
77. Wastes
81. "___ Town"
82. Animates
84. Italian royalty
86. Danish money
87. Capital of Valais
89. Short barks
90. Lose energy
91. Coin opening
92. Actor Booth
94. Bye, in Kent
96. Price of passage
97. Cadet's counterpart
98. Hide worker
100. Motor City skater
102. Actor Gene ___
103. Economized
105. 2, 4, 6, etc.
106. Raccoonlike animal
107. Make a doily
109. Altar exchanges
111. Carole ___ White
112. Tropical tree
113. African grazer
116. Cattle breed
119. Bond's would-be nemesis
122. Indian coin
123. Ace Rickenbacker
124. Feudal lord
125. Legume seed
126. Asiatic deer
127. Actor Jack ___
128. Church official
129. Skills

DOWN

1. Society newcomers
2. That one, to Livy
3. Dakota mountains
4. Baglike structure
5. With a handle
6. Cal. lake
7. Deadlocks
8. Mad. or Lex.
9. Fix again into cloth folds
10. Degenerate
11. Pertaining to: suff.
12. Sour substance
13. Archibald and Thurmond
14. Sports sites
15. King of Judah
16. Fancy radials
17. "Copacabana" dancer
18. Middling
24. Blockhead
26. Binding
30. Columbia's league
34. Judy's daughter
35. Inebriates
36. Deafeningly
38. Sped
39. Gift ___ (eloquence)
40. Cape Verde capital
41. Proceeds
42. Roentgen's discovery
44. Wider at the top
45. Dings
47. Ring out
49. Everywhere: pref.
52. Gainsborough subject
54. Acute conjunctivitis
57. Following
58. Globe bearer
59. Yawns
60. Punts, e.g.
63. Teamster's order
65. Verge
67. "Rhoda" character
71. Math subgroup
72. Ramee's pen name
73. Urban dwelling
74. Fit
75. Student, often
76. Fiends
77. Tender
78. Forty-niner
79. Eat away
80. Woodland deity
83. Type of mineral
85. It borders Tenn.
88. Hirschfeld's daughter
91. Delta material
93. Composer Ethelbert ___
95. Counsels
96. Swindle
97. Florida city
99. Indian Ocean arm
101. Moisturize
102. Voracious eater
104. Old-fashioned
106. Beg
107. Lift in Aspen
108. Cartoonist Peter ___
110. Take a stand
112. Appealed
114. Spiffy
115. Samovars
117. Used to be
118. Kay's title
120. Slippery stuff
121. Hoop org.

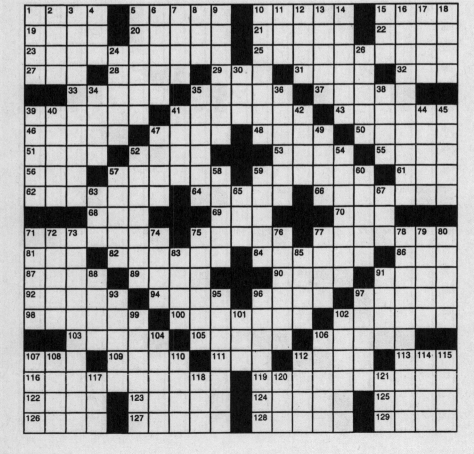

ACROSS

1. Crazes
5. Pianist Peter ____
9. Political monogram
12. Boards for plaster support
17. Guinness
18. Copycat
19. City of Iraq
21. Hunter in the sky
22. Timber wolf
23. Isinglass
24. Passageway
25. Actor DeVito
26. Blab
30. Fish
31. Neither's partner
32. Admit
33. Illumination
36. Certain infection
38. Gaelic
39. Church section
43. High card
44. Garlands
46. Sudden outbursts
48. Muzzle-loading item
50. Keeps
52. Soprano Lehmann
53. Nautical cord
54. Decorates
55. Spanish gentleman
56. Gain a profit
57. Levin or Gershwin
58. Scottish negative
59. Perched
60. Scandinavians
62. Legal thing
63. Goddess of the underworld
64. Boxing blow
66. Hodges of baseball
67. Mayday!
68. Give new strength to
69. "____ Vegas Story"
70. Bishopric
71. Wheel tooth
72. On the briny
73. Borough of England
75. Evolution theorist
78. Handsome young men
80. Ancient Persians' kin
81. Low cabinet
82. Chieftain
83. Do, re, mi, ____
84. Ballet costume
85. Meadow
86. B.A. word
87. Social affairs
89. Stare fiercely
91. Allude
93. Subjects
94. ____ la la
95. Antonio starter
96. Confront one's opponent bravely
105. Horror-movie actor
106. Of kidneys
107. Miscellaneous assortment
108. Congo river
109. Without help
110. Betel palm
111. Ms. Horne
112. Congers
113. Assumed a posture
114. Piggery
115. Mild expletive
116. Petty quarrel

DOWN

1. Season
2. Lily plant
3. Obligation
4. Whisky
5. Designated
6. "Iliad," e.g.
7. Withdraws a statement
8. Speaker
9. Pluck
10. Passe
11. Filches
12. Woolen cloth
13. Bedouin
14. Turner or Louise
15. ____ Kong
16. Bend in a ship's timber
19. ____ de Cologne
20. Latvians
27. Special telephone setup
28. Western state
29. High priest
33. Zhivago's love
34. Kind of tea
35. Be irritating
36. Bro's sib
37. Make a show of wealth
39. Actress Irving
40. Coyote
41. Reddish-brown horse
42. Icelandic literary works
45. Abstract being
47. Sharpening device
49. Landers and Sheridan
51. Inland sea
52. Have nothing to do with
53. Nonclerics
55. Israeli
56. Ferber and Best
59. Strongboxes
61. Governs
63. Barrel-making worker
64. Had recourse
65. British ____
66. Bacterium
67. La ____, Milan
68. Chest sound
70. Japanese military caste
74. ____-do (affluent)
75. Decimal point
76. ____ fixe
77. Close to
79. Mormon: abbr.
80. French composer
81. Hint
83. Sires
84. Home on wheels
88. Special newspaper edition
90. Palmer of golf
92. Follows immediately
93. Cornered
95. Young pig
96. Philippine knife
97. God of love
98. British composer
99. Like some dresses
100. Stevedores' gp.
101. Foch of films
102. Far down
103. Logan or Fitzgerald
104. Aerie
105. Track circuit

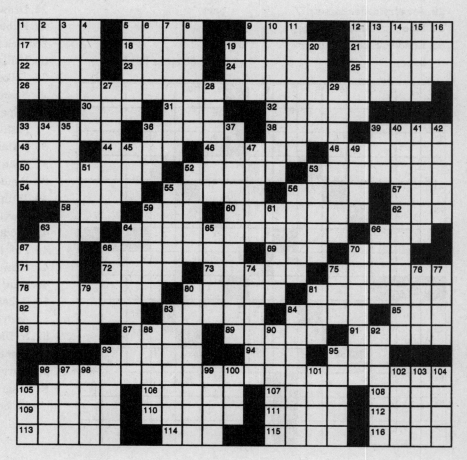

PUZZLE 544   PUNS AND ANAGRAMS

ACROSS

1. Our vines were a gift
9. Boasts about shoes
15. No, Ian, make changes with vet!
16. Remit to a Turkish inn
17. Deed on flat was reduced
18. Banker heard to go solo
19. Escapee without air conditioning
20. Crazy! Tut in New York?
22. Consumed tea
23. Takes a chair from 'er sister
24. See why doe is lure?
25. Old West dish
26. Allow rent
27. Win easy or wither
28. Swerve and leave 5 pitchers
29. Jewelry seller cometh?
31. I'd act to statements
33. Reader, each consumer bonds
35. He and Carol are singers
39. Trust a peacock
41. Ann, ade is Peruvian
42. Get home to ease a pet
45. Does nothing with tress
47. Redness becomes you, Dr.!
48. "B" as in "Birds"
49. Heartless parents have these clothes
50. Root for the bull
51. Sir, you're taxing!
52. The vale you had has worth
53. Remits no tea to hoarder
54. Hates 50 machines
56. Behold the greats at races
58. Narcissus goes it alone
59. Empty cave after you eat
60. Remove Ted and Lee
61. Seers met during school year part

DOWN

1. With 50 spies I'd skid
2. Triumphed with peace, I hear, in swimsuit
3. Loosen turf, teen
4. He loves rodents
5. Go back to save these women
6. Mr. Turner, an ant!
7. Tin zee in Bolivian river
8. You see, 500 deer cut back
9. Why is list full of lees?
10. Oh, May, an island!
11. Bleat Scrooge's word?
12. Fancy that atoner!
13. Waver about extraterrestrial tree
14. Without an A one rating, waitress scatters
21. Action left a shaken medicine
24. Restaurant was done in red
25. Draws back to turf
27. Rubbish! Me sweat?
28. Make stone collars
30. Utilizes 1,000 goddesses
32. Talks about satchel without the Spanish
34. Capek's play with Mr. Capp was rustic
36. Watch Etta soar in a balloon
37. Poet, you had real tea
38. Renders nothing to signer
40. Terms sure net
42. Pursued detail
43. Produce anger ere nag
44. Plot is about a gun
46. Stow TV's with ease
49. Glue a pest
50. Substitute left tubes to Andronicus
52. In Dave's t-shirt
53. Came to a club
55. Hurry a greeting?
57. Magnet, though repelling 10, held a leg

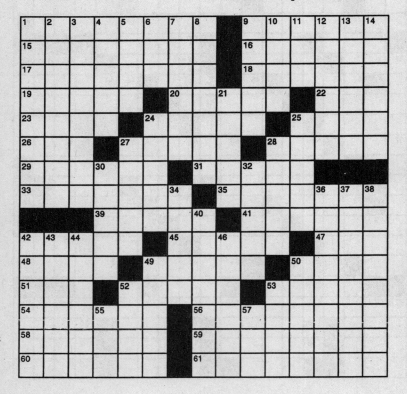

• TWO-TIMERS •

ACROSS
1. Beam
6. Movie lion
10. South American beast of burden
15. English theologian
19. Repent
20. Inner being
21. Watering holes
22. Angered
23. Actress Burke
24. Oriental weight measure
25. Soars
26. Roof segment
27. John John
30. Retires
32. Cowboy's headgear
33. Piano piece
34. Repulses
35. Country-singer Morgan
36. Blackthorn
37. Heep
39. Fuchsia
42. Alexander Alexandre
47. In the center of
48. Promises
49. Plaintive poem
50. Fall mo.
51. Write
52. Anonymous critic
55. Works the land
56. Alpine wind
57. Turtles, sometimes
59. Dark wood
61. Cultivate
63. Spree
64. ____-pros
65. Loafer's part
66. Dry gully
69. Theater ticket
71. Braggarts
75. ____ off
76. Three-____ Island
77. False: pref.
79. Chaney
80. Actress Munson
81. Shanghai resident
83. Spanish ladies: abbr.
84. Appointment
85. Mary Mary
88. Noun suffix
91. Gather together
92. Poetic nights
93. Rat-____
94. Porcelain worker
97. Guinness
98. Puts in a new round
102. Rest on one's ____
104. James James
107. Air: pref.
108. Renown
110. Ashen
111. Radioactive element
112. Essen no
113. "Sweet ____ O'Grady"
114. Winglike
115. Articles
116. Remnants
117. Shocks
118. Camera part
119. Create a pleasant aroma

DOWN
1. Cheryl and Alan
2. Aggravated profoundly
3. Decipher
4. Designated
5. Continues perusing
6. Mid-European country
7. Advance
8. Took to court
9. Steve Steve
10. Rhine temptress
11. Siberian dog
12. Nincompoop
13. Keep a rendezvous
14. Persuading
15. Dien ____
16. Obliterate
17. Imp
18. Actress Barbara and family
28. Ilk
29. Shares an apartment
31. Suitable
36. Pump
37. Newsman Garrick ____
38. Old World deer
39. Charts
40. Sermon finale
41. Lollobrigida
43. Uris
44. State of mind
45. Land unit
46. Musial
48. Execs
52. Neuter
53. Stout's Wolfe
54. Annoy
55. Victoria Victoria
56. Harte
58. Walk heavily
60. Snake
61. Incite
62. As well as
65. Not worth a ____
66. Upon
67. Bandit's town?
68. Harvest
69. Circle measurements: abbr.
70. Arm bone
71. Engineering degree: abbr.
72. Enthusiasm
73. Mil. student gp.
74. Relative of snick
76. Fail the mark
78. Without: Fr.
81. ____ Semple McPherson
82. Angry canines
83. Spirited horse
84. Set off an explosion
86. Sponsors
87. Has empathy
88. Money-makers
89. Flowered stalk
90. Of food energy
94. Flat surface
95. Of cereal
96. Distended
97. Vehemently
99. "Our Miss Brooks"
100. Condemns
101. Detect
103. Connery, for one
105. Retail event
106. "The Good Earth" character
109. Baton Rouge sch.

PUZZLE 546

• BY THE NUMBER •

ACROSS

1. Sternward
4. Pace
8. Shawn and Mack
12. Gambol
17. Girlfriend, for Pierre
18. Not as extroverted
19. Hit the tarmac
20. Hogback's kin
21. Snow field
22. Christie novel
25. More perspicacious
27. Bottle dweller
28. Hyson or oolong
29. Venetian blind part
30. "____ longa . . ."
31. Man in gray, for short
33. Map abbr.
34. Toots
36. Cloth component
39. Meander
43. Enclosure
44. St. Anthony's cross
45. Out producers
49. Rooter
52. Chuck or Ken
54. In shreds
55. Having prongs
56. Rail
57. Former Barbary st.
58. Welles and Bean
60. Merrie ____ England
61. A tiny Tom
62. Actress Jackson
64. OT book
66. Having less speed
68. Derisive smile
69. Bitter vetch
71. Actress Patricia and kin
73. Corby and Barkin
76. Cries of discovery
79. Breakfast fare
81. Young ladies
83. Aleutian island
86. Linked
88. Actress Haddad
89. Kaminska and May Park
90. Footprint
91. Sitcom producer
92. Locked chests
94. Colloid
95. Sinatra film
98. Alphabetic trio
99. Saloon
100. Author O'Faolain
101. Certain paint
103. Dilapidated
106. Quant.
109. Dutch settlement
110. Gold, to Pedro
113. Tien Shan Mountains part
114. Sols preceders
116. Spook
118. "____ Sang for My Father"
120. Yul Brynner film, with "The"
124. Pay for the use of
125. Spinning
126. Byron work
127. Sheeplike
128. Enrages
129. Having few words
130. Hart
131. Alexandria's river
132. Double curve

DOWN

1. Muslim ruler
2. Military bigwig
3. Youth
4. Haggard novel
5. High ringing sound
6. Elver catcher
7. Patterned cloth
8. London gallery
9. House wing
10. ____ of Worms
11. Durocs' digs
12. Unscrupulous man
13. Gone up
14. Norman Vincent ____
15. Lab burners
16. Remainder
17. "Diana" singer
18. Sesame or easy
23. Rows
24. Snoozed
26. Goof
32. Thai coins
35. Matter, in law
37. "Ben-____"
38. "The Mystery of Edwin ____"
40. Cartoonist Soglow
41. Seed covering
42. Obeys
44. Archer William and family
46. Irish lake
47. Come after
48. Sailboat feature
49. Good luck symbols
50. Supply with guns
51. Pinch
52. Take game
53. Sings, Tyrolean style
56. Cut wool
59. Hard to find
61. Suit fabrics
63. Carter and Gwyn
65. Refrain starter
67. Fairy tale opener
70. "We ____ Overcome"
72. Put away for a rainy day
74. Mane site
75. Meeting places for Zeno
77. Toward shelter
78. Helot
80. Soprano's syllables
81. Musician's job
82. Food fish
84. Pitch
85. ____ Major
87. Zeus's daughter
90. Neck area
93. Politician Beame
95. Stable morsel
96. Play, as a role
97. Author Gordimer
99. Part of LBJ
102. Chess pieces
103. Trumpet sound
104. Champing at the bit
105. Buckets
107. James or Pamela
108. Italian fountain
111. Coty and Cassin
112. Table leavings
113. He loves, to Ovid
115. Ella's forte
116. Hindrance
117. Malefic
119. Iroquoian
121. Seine sight
122. Baseball stat.
123. Chemical suffix

464

ACROSS

1. At that time
5. Bunks
9. Bird call
12. Equal
16. Atmosphere
17. Stratum
18. Past
19. Volcano output
20. Hollywood actor-American president
24. Pierce
25. Actress West
26. Tourist havens
27. Put out
30. Fuddled
32. Stretched
34. Approaches
35. Muddy
36. Aromatic
39. Arrived
40. Ice-cream holder
41. Spear
42. Broadcast
44. Matterhorn, for one
45. Bolt
46. Burn
47. Normandy town
48. Tease
49. Chinese chime
50. Destined
51. "Georgia on My Mind" singer-Midwest senator
55. Thunder sounds
57. Principal
58. Gone wild
59. Very dry
60. Go shopping
62. Hoosegow
63. Needle
66. ____ Vegas
67. Meager
68. Dart
69. Step
70. Fierce feline
72. Pod dwellers
73. Yelled
74. Cape Cod sight
75. Turnover
76. Establishes
77. River to the Baltic
79. For each
80. Planet
81. American president-tennis star
88. Feels ill
89. Ignited
90. By mouth
91. Perjurer
92. Actress Negri
93. Enemy
94. English river
95. Herb

DOWN

1. Little bit
2. Tint
3. Extermination
4. Edict city
5. Grouch
6. Blade
7. Powerful initials
8. Inconsequential
9. Grotto
10. Turkish title
11. Took the blue ribbon
12. Dive
13. Merit
14. Holiday times
15. Operated
21. Angry
22. Negative
23. Toot
27. Peruvian Indian
28. Logo
29. Indian hominy
30. Force
31. Mine find
32. Breather
33. Fairy-tale starter
35. River part
36. Throes
37. Dapper
38. Roofing material
40. Elegant
41. Sheets
43. Pole
45. Declares
46. Thick
47. Pouch
48. Hairless
49. Allow
50. Amphibian
51. Work reward
52. Alter
53. Trojan hero
54. Give forth
55. Buddy
56. Pertaining to a certain time
60. Peruse
61. Shear
62. Sheep's cry
63. Sprinkle
64. Frosted
65. Cradles
67. Discharge
68. ____-de-lance
69. Former North European state
71. Seaport in the South Ukraine
72. Imitate
73. Salmon colors
75. Oolong
76. Distant
77. Buckeye State
78. "The farmer in the ____"
79. Meat spread
80. Beast of burden
81. Hat
82. Imp
83. ____ Grande
84. Attempt
85. Chinese dynasty
86. Witch
87. Before, to bards

465

PUZZLE 548

• KUDOS •

ACROSS

1. Actor Idle
5. Ease up
10. Splash about
15. Journals, for short
19. Variable star
20. Young salmon
21. Main artery
22. Winglike structures
23. Goalie's goal
25. Physicist's motivation
27. Within: pref.
28. Isthmus
30. More mannerly
31. Deficit
34. Dagger handle
35. German industrial city
36. Make soaking wet
38. Sport groups
40. Keep
44. Enrage
45. Abrasions
48. Earthenware jar
50. Ladies, in Toledo: abbr.
51. "____ Grant"
52. Pace
54. Times past
56. Football's Cross
57. Tosses softly
59. Dreary song
61. Holmes's creator
63. Energy
64. Pours down ice
67. Myths
69. Fish-catching fence
70. Mormons: abbr.
71. Carpenters' needs
73. Buzzwords
75. Melt frost from
77. Part of a bathing suit
79. Cashews, e.g.
81. Food regimens
83. Answers in response
86. "A ____ Youth"
87. Build
89. Marshall Wyatt, et al.
91. Oak or cherry
92. Tooth-fixers' org.
93. Tartan
95. Western rope
97. Choose
98. Encircle in a band
100. New York island
102. Shucks
104. Neighbor of Minn.
105. Positions
107. Basil preparation
109. Show up for
111. Diving ducks
114. Wine container
116. Entry
117. Calm down
120. Long fruit
122. Excavations' goals
125. Musician's position
127. Fielders' honors
131. Amo, amas, ____
132. Propelled a rowboat
133. Famous cow
134. Radiation units
135. Runs into
136. Across: pref.
137. Incline
138. Tizzy

DOWN

1. Measures of type
2. Habit
3. Writer Turgenev
4. Product from tallow
5. Go ____ over
6. Bark
7. Segments of circles
8. Veracity
9. Wit
10. Hygienic
11. Booty
12. Ball
13. "The 39 ____"
14. Heavenly headgear
15. Leathernecks
16. Got off
17. Firm look
18. Wise man
24. Diving birds
26. Responded in court
29. Writer Waugh
32. Glaswegian, for one
33. Tear up
35. Reserved account
36. Dribble
37. Cartoonist's recognition
39. "In the ____"
41. Race horse's distinction
42. With handles
43. Invitation notations: abbr.
44. Problems
46. Send outward
47. Lean-eating Jack ____
49. Related
53. Stared at
55. Trickier
58. Briny deep
60. Bizarre
62. Albany's canal
65. Part of a fork
66. Drink noisily
68. Unproven charge
72. Pillar
74. Narrow piece
76. Jaguar, e.g.
77. Gloats
78. Half diameters
80. Sells for more
82. Predict, in Aberdeen
84. Barely warm
85. Movie backgrounds
88. Clay piece
90. Place
94. Tosses out
96. Singing range
99. Cannot stand
101. Jazz's Getz
103. Snitch
106. Position
108. Missouri Indians
110. Fielding mistakes
112. Neckwear
113. "The Merry Widow" composer
115. Mound
117. Off in the distance
118. Kind of cotton
119. British buggy
120. Tres ____
121. Additionally
123. Makes tied
124. Trucking rig
126. Southern constellation
128. Downturn
129. Go to the right
130. Fast plane: abbr.

466

Place the answer to each clue into the diagram beginning at the corresponding number. Words will overlap with other words.

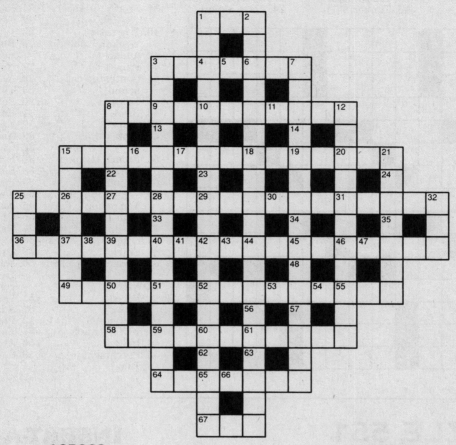

ACROSS

1. Fixed charge
3. Awaken
4. Employ
5. Bristle
8. Scottish Gaelic
9. Place after first
10. Large vulture
11. Flat-bottomed boat
15. Cart
16. ____ upon a time
17. Stop
18. Cloth joint
19. Astound
25. Hiding place
26. Play unfairly
27. Devoured
28. Singing voice
29. Norwegian
30. Grasslike plant

31. Water birds
36. Wash lightly
38. Be aware of
40. Ego
41. Fairylike
43. Last
45. Solo
47. Bird's home
49. Hope
50. Storage building
51. Dutch cheese
52. Entertain
53. European finch
54. Fruit peel
58. Exhaust
59. Restrain
61. German city
64. Fishing spool
65. Lamb
66. Prevaricator
67. Payable

DOWN

1. Man-goat
2. Always
3. Love symbol
4. Mom's brother
6. Author Hemingway
7. Fragrance
8. National bird
9. Legislature
10. Tidy
12. 365 days
13. Related on mother's side
14. Female horse
15. Texas city
18. Use great effort
19. Sports building
20. Jason's ship
21. Jar
22. Even
23. Old-womanish
24. Used to be
25. Auto
26. Ice-cream holder

28. Examine
29. Egypt's river
31. Pure
32. Newt
33. Chemical compound
34. Back of the neck
35. Tear roughly
37. Unused
39. Otherwise
42. Jump
44. Accustom
46. Norse god
48. Household animals
50. Place
51. Mistake
52. Tell's target
55. Motel
56. Send money
57. Russian ruler
60. Beg
62. Heavy metal
63. Tiny insect

PUZZLE 550

ACROSS

1. "Born Free" heroine
5. Scrutinize
9. Parcel
14. Favor
15. 152, in Rome
16. Tanker
17. Indonesian island
18. Pealed
19. Illumination
20. Randolph Scott romantic comedy: 3 wds.
23. Overhead trains
24. Actor Majors
25. "Lives of a ____ Lancer"
29. Walk in water
31. Fruit drink
34. Nebraska Indians
35. Confront
36. German river
37. Scott's "To the ____": 3 wds.
40. Trig ratio
41. Weekday: abbr.
42. Audacity
43. Expert
44. Contented-cat sound
45. Settings
46. Beige
47. Serpent
48. Scott's "Ride ____": 3 wds.
56. French sculptor
57. Merit
58. Conquer
60. "____ You Glad You're You"
61. Skin
62. ____ mater
63. Disguises
64. Singles
65. Decade component

DOWN

1. Recede
2. Lounge
3. Individual performance
4. Indigo
5. Parchment
6. Talons
7. "____ She Sweet"
8. Near, to poets
9. Candy
10. Moon valley
11. Wings
12. Wax
13. Waste allowance
21. Rent
22. Senior
25. ____ nova
26. Body of moral principles
27. Not a soul: 2 wds.
28. Actor Richard
29. Thin cookie
30. Performs
31. Embellish
32. Explore
33. American Indians
35. Quartet count
36. Fencer's weapon
38. Smarted
39. Peruvian
44. Watercolors
45. Noises
46. Opine
47. Narrow-minded
48. Mine car
49. Israeli dance
50. Yoruba city and Netherlands commune
51. Leander's love
52. Adam's son
53. Platter
54. Function
55. Arizona city
59. Sailor

PUZZLE 551

INSERT-A-WORD

Insert a word from Column B into a word from Column A to form a new, longer word. Each word is used only once. For example, if the word FAR appeared in Column A and THE appeared in Column B, the answer would be FATHER (FA-THE-R).

COLUMN A	COLUMN B	
1. Cup	Hop	_____
2. Ad	Own	_____
3. Deed	Peas	_____
4. Bade	All	_____
5. Show	Lean	_____
6. Abed	Era	_____
7. Brie	Shame	_____
8. Ape	Rig	_____
9. Sworn	Us	_____
10. Ate	Flat	_____

PUZZLE 552

ACROSS
1. Cereal holder
5. Faucet fault
9. Demure
12. Huron's neighbor
13. Assess
14. United
15. Working crew
16. Gives the once-over
17. ____ King Cole
18. Moves stealthily
20. Sad sound
22. Agenda
24. Rob
27. Burro
30. Close to
32. Beige
33. Dog's foot
34. Wipes, as dishes
36. Can
37. Nefarious
39. Cabbage dish
40. Droop
41. Discourage
43. Go away!
45. Fossil fuel
47. Nero, e.g.
51. Cigar residue
53. Nothing
55. Stravinsky
56. Regret
57. Above
58. Funny Johnson
59. Finale
60. Frees
61. Final

DOWN
1. Implores
2. Algerian seaport
3. Burgundy
4. Lawful
5. Bureaus
6. Actor Bolger
7. Particular
8. Mexican coins
9. Links
10. "Cat ____ Hot Tin Roof"
11. Still
19. Goodhearted
21. Devoured
23. Follows
25. Diva's selection
26. Breathing organ
27. Imitated
28. Conserve
29. Changed, as places
31. Nuclear devices
35. Influence
38. Mr. Durocher
42. Shaving apparatus
44. Error's partner
46. Tribe of Israel
48. Site of the Taj Mahal
49. Negatives
50. Weight allowance
51. Exist
52. Solar-system center
54. Crimson

PUZZLE 553

ACROSS
1. Game on horseback
5. Strike gently
8. Chime
12. Scottish resort town
13. Spanish gold
14. Arrow poison
15. Deteriorated badly
18. Bullring cheer
19. One of the Fords
20. After OPQ
21. In toto
22. Biblical kingdom
24. Oar
27. Ease, as a seam
30. Sulawesi ox
31. River near Rouen
32. Tattered
35. Short-legged hound
37. Soccer great
38. Superlative suffix
39. Street, in Rome
41. Glacial ice form
43. Baby food
46. Out of favor
49. ____ homo
50. Building annex
51. Judicial order
52. Comedian Mort
53. Scottish river
54. Camera part

DOWN
1. Cartoon possum
2. Old Greek coin
3. Pathway
4. Single person
5. Pampered pet
6. Companion of crafts
7. Close behind
8. Offer
9. Immense
10. Table supports
11. For fear that
16. Swiss archer
17. French female
21. Old saw
23. Nevada experiment
24. Average
25. Sayings
26. Li'l Abner's domain
28. Actress Mary
29. Vietnamese New Year
33. Otherwise
34. Legally conveyed
35. Small hound
36. Author Sholem
39. Competes
40. Old Peruvian ruler
42. Part
43. Unadulterated
44. A ____ apple
45. Favored ones
47. Norse goddess
48. Wise one

469

PUZZLE 554

ACROSS

1. Corded fabrics
5. Zodiacal sign
10. Cooled
14. Domain
15. Northern Eskimo
16. Flightless bird
17. Marry
19. Chute sled
20. Property
21. Religious candle bearer
23. Conducted
24. Sacred chest
25. Social groups
29. Rice wine
31. Algonquian
34. Elected
35. Trekked
36. "Ben ____"
37. Herring
38. Lowest point
39. Current
40. "____ My Baby Comes Home" (Vandross song)
41. Make broader
42. Photo toner
43. Lime or lemon
44. Mastered
45. Poet John Crowe ____
46. Erected
48. Sickness
49. Eliminating
52. Employ too much
57. Knows of, in Soho
58. Secret nuptials
60. Foil's kin
61. Number of movie brides or brothers
62. Spin like ____
63. Reprieve
64. Burns
65. Stupid

DOWN

1. Pro ____
2. Newsman Sevareid
3. "____ Gynt"
4. Fill
5. Feudal lords
6. Marked
7. Roll
8. Melee
9. Assailant
10. Dawdles
11. Dating stages
12. Advantage
13. Go-getter
18. Dragged
22. Having colorful patches
25. ____ Rica
26. Plant pest
27. Stand-offs
28. Danson of "Cheers"
29. Sympathized (with)
30. Similar
32. Kind of cassette
33. Heavy or light
35. Inclination
38. Politeness
39. Sawbuck
41. Arabian gulley
42. Oregon city
45. Poe's quoter et al.
47. Credit
48. Gloomy one
49. Water pitcher
50. Bridle
51. High-school club
53. Study
54. Do ____ others . . .
55. Period, in a telegram
56. Detect
59. Eggs

PUZZLE 555

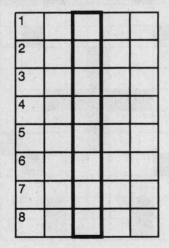

Hocus Pocus

Fill in the diagram with words formed by unscrambling the letters so that an 8-letter word will be revealed reading down the outlined column. This is a bit tricky since the scrambled letters may form more than one word.

1. A L M O R
2. E E H R T
3. A D I N V
4. A V O P R
5. A E S T T
6. A G N O R
7. D E I R R
8. A E L R Y

PUZZLE 556

ACROSS
1. Engrossed
5. Wager
8. Tony Orlando's backup group
12. Chills and fever
13. "Norma ____"
14. Director Kazan
15. Peddle
16. "____ People"
18. Rascal
20. Baseball teams
21. Arch
22. Actress Hagen
23. Russian rulers
25. Artist's studio
29. Fabulous bird
30. Copier need
32. Cow noise
33. Clumsy
35. Thicket
37. Picnic pest
38. Whet
39. Fundamental
42. Big hit?
45. Lingerer
47. Urgent
48. Poker stake
49. Vase
50. Profit
51. Root or birch
52. Stooge name
53. You are something ____!

DOWN
1. Hives
2. Author James ____
3. Retreat
4. Narrator
5. Worry
6. Merit
7. Broadcasting's Turner
8. Disavowal
9. King of comedy
10. Cable
11. Negative votes
17. Message transmitter
19. Case
22. Colorado Indian
23. ____-la-la
24. Plant
25. "Romeo ____ Juliet"
26. Regal
27. Goddess of daybreak
28. Caviar
31. Food scrap
34. Restaurant employee
36. Nervous
38. Lena of song
39. Spill the beans
40. Superior
41. Location
42. Superman, e.g.
43. "Trinity" author
44. Hawaiian goose
46. Mai tai ingredient

PUZZLE 557

ACROSS
1. Hope
5. Not high
8. ____ cents' worth
11. Hurt
12. Epoch
13. Unwritten
15. One-year old horse
17. Plateau
18. Snow or sweet
19. Snakelike fish
21. Help
22. Imitate
24. Tavern
26. Questions
28. Deal (out)
30. Verse
32. Hinder
34. Seer
38. Perfect
40. Yuletide
41. Large sandwich
43. Decade count
45. Ewe's mate
46. Cured salmon
47. Site
49. Blunder
51. Against
53. Maestro
57. Ragged
58. "We ____ the World"
59. ____ fixe
60. Operated
61. Directed
62. Close-at-hand

DOWN
1. Route
2. Frozen water
3. Svelte
4. Roll-call response
5. Hawaiian necklace
6. Stubborn
7. Salary
8. Turkey or cat
9. Inflict
10. Desert greenery
14. Kid
16. Research room, for short
20. Lion's home
22. Commercials, for short
23. Kettle
25. Toward the sheltered side
27. Peruse
29. Turkish ruler
31. Character
33. Revered one
35. Deteriorate
36. Grassland
37. "Nightmare on ____ Street"
39. Dress
41. Commend
42. Surplus
44. Fish snare
46. Rule
48. Elliptical
50. Spoil
52. Bed and breakfast
54. Scarlet
55. Ocean
56. "____ the ramparts..."

471

PUZZLE 558

ACROSS

1. Actress Dawber and others
5. Applaud
9. ____ Rica
14. Busy as ____: 2 wds.
15. Right-hand person
16. Up to the time that
17. Thanks ____!: 2 wds.
18. Rock cadence
19. Shore
20. Polish again
22. Halloween wear
24. Male sheep
27. Most relaxed
32. Fathers
34. Site
35. Nursery-school period
38. Catchall abbr.
39. Actor Connery
40. "One ____ at a Time"
41. Baseball team
42. Ranch worker
43. In Dreamland
46. Seas
49. Reasoning
50. Pie, e.g.
52. French refusal
53. Throw for a
55. Wine fruit
60. Feels yesterday's exercise
64. Feedbag grain
67. Racetrack
68. Baby grand
69. Weary
70. College building, for short
71. Consumed
72. Cole ____
73. She-sheep

DOWN

1. Jack of TV
2. Competent
3. Feline sound
4. ____ good example: 2 wds.
5. Taxi
6. Recline
7. Father of Cain
8. Flower part
9. Clock bird
10. Yoko ____
11. Train stop: abbr.
12. "____ the season . . ."
13. Height: abbr.
21. Medical picture: hyph.
23. Note after fa
25. Liable
26. "Upstairs, Downstairs" figures
28. Picturesque
29. Kind of kitchen: hyph.
30. Argot
31. Distant: prefix
32. Rare animals
33. Little
35. Serenity
36. Bowling alleys
37. Keep an ____ (watch): 2 wds.
39. Wearing footwear
44. Self
45. Table-tennis sound
47. Ozzie or Harriet
48. Hit-show letters
51. Horn sounds
54. Bucket
56. Went on horseback
57. Declare
58. Peel
59. Shade trees
60. Mimic
61. Wash. organization: abbr.
62. Derby or boater
63. Wind direction: abbr.
65. Refrain syllable
66. Use needle and thread

PUZZLE 559   A FEW CHOICE WORDS

Find the synonyms of the eight words listed below by selecting one letter from each of the eight letter-groups to the right of each word. For example, the answer to number 1 is PATERNAL.

1. Fatherly	*p*at	*h*ad	*t*er	*r*ed	*r*at	*n*ot	tea	yu*l*
2. Aromatic	aft	rot	rea	gar	ert	ear	hyn	ate
3. Foreigner	ask	toy	wre	ail	rnx	ugy	ear	orp
4. Move like a wave	uxc	rnt	aid	uym	elw	avx	ert	ieu
5. Small planet	yua	isl	xte	leg	urx	lob	uiv	edw
6. BBQ need	ycx	yuh	lag	rot	cut	yox	aby	yol
7. Make a hole	let	wxq	vcd	art	vet	iat	ton	ret
8. Have a premonition	fat	oar	ert	elh	jbx	uow	red	ety

PUZZLE 560

ACROSS
1. Locale
6. Not cooked
9. Rock
10. Feedback, of a sort
12. Bother
13. Urge
14. Choice word
15. Heavy metal
16. Late
20. Take to court
21. Disburse
23. Bygone
26. Open a little
30. Vicinity
31. Motion-picture theater
33. Untruthful one
34. Receive
35. Mr. Carney
36. Chick sounds

DOWN
1. Bell sound
2. Minus
3. Plus
4. Pres. Coolidge
5. Female sheep
6. Answer
7. Land measure
8. Rider's command
9. That girl
11. "The ___ Couple"
17. Serpent
18. Regret
19. Lion's lair
21. Begin
22. Frug or waltz
23. Chum
24. Song at the Met
25. Char
27. GI's vehicle
28. Elec. units
29. Squeal
31. Toy ammo
32. Skating surface

PUZZLE 561

ACROSS
1. ___ service
4. Squabble
8. Take's partner
12. Fuss
13. Coat or pony
14. Anytime
15. Space
16. Remove
18. October gem
20. Wrongs
21. Kind of charge
23. Lawyer's unit
25. Fresh way to start
26. Land of the Incas
27. Knock
30. Each
31. Make the scapegoat
32. Mr. Wallach
33. Curvy letter
34. At a ___
35. Actress Barbara
36. Stare open-mouthed
37. Streamlined
38. Line of stitches
40. For Pete's ___!
41. Made critical remarks
44. Mass of hair
47. "It's a sin to tell ___": 2 wds.
48. Corn Belt state
49. Flock parent
50. Fish snares
51. Brat
52. Retreat room

DOWN
1. Hang back
2. Rhoda's mom on "Rhoda"
3. Puffy muffins
4. Asparagus stalk
5. Public opinion sampling
6. Actress MacGraw
7. Fielding's Jones
8. Lamp spirit
9. Mr. Lendl
10. Old soldiers, for short
11. Sooner, to a poet
17. Publication
19. Bench
21. ___ Cod
22. Dollar bills
23. Discontinue
24. "A Farewell to ___"
26. Support
27. Saved
28. Out of the wind
29. Healthy hue
31. Fire
35. Large deer
36. Fun and ___
37. Nasser's successor
38. Flatfish
39. Radiate
40. Uses a needle
41. Is able to
42. Tuck's chum
43. Foot extremity
45. Be in debt
46. Writer's tool

PUZZLE 562

• CUP OF LIFE •

ACROSS
1. Crush
5. Ewes' mates
9. Hindu god
13. Grouch
17. Singing voice
18. One of a Latin trio
19. Arabian gulf
20. Sat astride
21. Asian weight
22. Carbonated beverage
23. Flintstone's pet
24. Leak
25. Much ado about nothing
29. Sword
30. Asian palm
31. Noted sailor
34. Phosphorescent mollusk
38. The two
40. In want
41. Glum
44. Tall grasses
46. Lemon skin
48. Control
49. Dusseldorf donkey
51. Coin-toss decision
53. Bit of liquid
55. Map abbr.
56. Reference book
58. Covers with plaster
60. Barn sounds
62. Benevolence
68. Small case
69. Be frugal
70. Anwar
71. Buddy
74. Bishoprics
76. Asparagus unit
78. Evergreen
79. Parrots
81. WWII landing craft
83. Western lilies
85. Sawbuck
86. Appraised
88. Work hard
90. Exclude
92. Red Bordeaux
94. Reimburses
96. Thing, in Spanish
99. Revelry trio
104. Italian island
106. Church area
107. Margarine
108. Sift through
110. Actual
111. Holiday nights
112. Employs
113. Jacaranda, e.g.
114. "Untouchable" man
115. British spare
116. Ripped
117. Origin

DOWN
1. Table-setting item
2. Winged
3. Brew
4. Doyle's sleuth
5. Triathlon, for one
6. Biblical prophet
7. Beer ingredient
8. Blot
9. Soft drink
10. Used as a model
11. Wind indicator
12. Sulawesi oxen
13. Bing, e.g.
14. Soft drink
15. Axlike tool
16. Drone
26. Fruit
27. Pen point
28. Jewelry piece
32. Mine entrance
33. Unit of force
35. Tennis call
36. Neatest
37. Farewell
39. Habitation of a recluse
41. Joint
42. Italian region
43. Vale
45. ____ down (loses weight)
47. Diving bird
50. "Swan ____"
52. Name for a skinny guy
54. Homes for peas
57. Tipplers
59. Cuts
61. Finger sound
63. Stoke
64. Kicked, in a way
65. Blue-pencil
66. Sound
67. '30s actress Anna
71. Playwright Connelly
72. Asian sea
73. Red grapes
75. Wayside inn, e.g.
77. Steal
80. Soaps, e.g.
82. Short-haired cat
84. Pouches
87. Family room
89. Soap ingredient
91. Perches
93. Belief
95. Muzzle
97. Night sound
98. Consent
100. Like tidal waters
101. In addition
102. ____-do-well
103. Medication serving
104. Fish-eating eagle
105. Actor Majors
109. Actor Knight

474

ACROSS

1. "___ Enchanted Evening"
5. Opera heavy
9. Woe is me!
13. Canvas cover, for short
17. And others: abbr.
18. Baseballer Matty
19. Markdown event
20. Fans' hero
21. "___ and Moonbeams"
23. Astaire-Rogers musical
25. Asian holiday
26. Stipend
27. Monkeys
29. Caused to lean
30. Prohibit
31. Fit of pique
32. Search for adventure
33. Truman's birthplace
36. Great ___
37. Inlet
38. Chem. class locale
41. Chinese gelatin
42. Clyde McCoy's theme song
44. ___ carte
45. Capek play
46. Singer Sonny
47. Eye suggestively
48. Princely Italian family
49. State
51. Unsullied
53. Thespian
54. Employ
55. Lift
56. "___ the Man Down"
57. Bus fare
59. Walking sticks
60. Wild duck
63. ___ Gemayel
64. "Parachutes and Kisses" author
65. Bakery products
66. Singer Peggy
67. Males
68. Early Technicolor musical, with "The"
71. Sicilian volcano
72. Chang's twin
73. Prayers
74. Roof edge
75. Twelve
76. Hunted animal
77. Rice wine
78. Sebaceous cyst
79. Rector
82. Ant genus
83. Nasser's group: abbr.
84. ___ Flores
87. "___ in Paris"
89. "It's Only ___"
92. Comic Johnson
93. Moon goddess
94. Scrabble piece
95. Forever ___ day
96. Headland
97. Make a sweater
98. Comedian King
99. Passion

DOWN

1. Scottish clan branch
2. Nebraska Indian
3. Germinated barley
4. Wapiti
5. German spa
6. ___ vera
7. Tippler
8. ___ and the Elders
9. Resource
10. Enactments
11. ___ Baba
12. Forwarded abroad
13. Name
14. Mine entrance
15. "By the Fountains of ___"
16. Entreated
22. At a distance
24. Donates
28. Wharf
30. Cocktail lounge
31. Palm starch
32. Capital of Seine-Maritime
33. Hog fat
34. Chills and fever
35. John Philip Sousa
36. Sand hill
37. Sports shoe nail
38. The Band's farewell concert film, with "The"
39. Palo ___
40. Boxer Max
42. Tender
43. Consecrate
46. Farm structure
48. Environmental sci.
50. Mortgage
51. African River
52. Untruth
53. TV's "___ Fair"
55. Suspends
56. Singer Joan
57. Not feral
58. Augury
59. NYC's ___ Island
60. Baseballer Johnny
61. M. Descartes
62. College head
64. Musician's slang
65. Prepare (the way)
68. European limestone plateau
69. Brave deed
70. Capital of Indonesia
71. Thousands of years
75. Bruce of films
76. Seeger and others
77. Summer ermine
78. Rouse
79. Blueprint
80. Lightly cooked
81. Doers: suffix
82. Fire god
83. Bruins' campus: abbr.
84. By itself
85. "M*A*S*H" star
86. Bed board
88. Religious sister
90. Petroleum
91. Hooray!

PUZZLE 563

• I GOT RHYTHM •

PUZZLE 564

ACROSS

1. Swindle
5. Sandwich store
9. Quick
14. You are something ___!
15. Hot and dry
16. Wipe out
17. "Let's ___ a Deal"
18. A la ___
19. Nimble
20. In place of
22. Guaranteed
24. Grow more mature
25. Sock front
26. Formulate
30. Regular
35. Lends a hand
36. October's gem
37. Mediter-ranean, e.g.
38. New York canal
39. Complain
40. Stereo
41. Sever
42. Paddles
43. Assistants
44. Desk opening
47. Blood vessel
48. Angry
49. Upper limb
50. Crime
54. Fine glassware
59. Eerie
60. Challenge
62. Part of TLC
63. Big
64. Former spouses
65. Hymn ender
66. Spirited horse
67. Swallow's home
68. Enjoy a book

DOWN

1. Trucker's rig
2. Family group
3. Inquires
4. Encounter
5. Harm
6. Deteriorate
7. Jar top
8. Concept
9. Purpose
10. Debated
11. Couple
12. ___ of Wight
13. Exploit
21. Has brunch
23. Old, as bread
26. Inspect
27. Summer TV fare
28. Cream of the crop
29. Orangutan, e.g.
30. Steeple
31. Knocks softly
32. Stage comment
33. Allude
34. "Driving Miss ___"
36. Spoken
39. Merchandise
40. Strike
43. Navy's cousin
45. Come forth
46. ___ over (delivered)
47. Place in custody
49. Real-estate units
50. Night birds
51. Accomplish-ment
52. Blaze
53. First garden
55. Wound mark
56. Domesticated
57. Vicinity
58. Advance, as money
61. Woodsman's tool

ACROSS

1. Food, slangily
5. Begin
10. Toward the bottom
14. Entice
15. Comedy
16. Region
17. Word of woe
18. Excuse
19. Action word
20. Sandwich source
21. Accomplished
22. Attains height
23. Profound
25. Frog's kin
27. Soak in liquid
30. Shoulder gesture
32. Golfer's peg
35. Certain throat node
37. Consume food
38. Owned
39. Fearful respect
40. Chewy candy
43. Hen product
44. Valuable stone
45. Saloon
46. Lottery
48. Cunning
49. Lifting device
51. Social engagements
52. Tattered
53. ____ and means
55. Spell of indulgence
58. Cover
59. Ocean movement
63. Slender
64. Rise from a seat
66. Garden of Paradise
67. Eye part
68. Fence of bushes
69. Plant starter
70. Type of ranch
71. Soothed
72. Paves, as a road

DOWN

1. Delighted
2. Regulation
3. Russian range
4. Furthermore
5. Hue
6. Dutch bulbs
7. Surrounded by
8. Actor/director Reiner
9. Prefix for three
10. Comedian Letterman
11. Raw metals
12. "The Way We ____"
13. Arrests
22. Scrap of cloth
24. Heroic poem
25. Streetcar
26. External
27. Does' mates
28. Absorbent cloth
29. Foe
31. Listens to
32. Crime of stealing
33. Large bird of prey
34. Sidles
36. Toil
41. Drizzle
42. Woman
47. Most swift
49. Gardener's tool
50. Pang
52. Rigid
54. Totaled up
55. Skidded
56. Lima's country
57. Sudden invasion
58. Young fellows
60. Thought
61. Forest creatures
62. Concludes
64. That girl
65. Afternoon social

PUZZLE 566

ACROSS
1. Go in front
5. Favorable reviews
10. Stain
14. Wheel shaft
15. Watchful
16. Cavern
17. Flooring material
18. Look at fixedly
19. Unlocked
20. Of a certain office worker
22. On a ship
24. Attention-getter
25. Auto
26. Applaud
27. Hair goo
28. Has a snack
29. Sandwich bread
32. Tire feature
35. Wash
36. Snakelike fish
37. Assists
38. Kindly forbearance
39. Sedate
40. Take advantage of
41. Molars, e.g.
42. Spheres
43. Decade number
44. Solemn promise
45. Cry convulsively
46. Night hooters
47. Relaxation room
48. Unruly crowd
51. Painter or sculptor
54. Sighting of shore
56. Anthracite
57. Some golf clubs
59. Actor Alan ____
60. ____ of Man
61. Chop finely
62. List entry
63. Tinted
64. Sidles
65. Unusual

DOWN
1. Gate fastener
2. Banishment
3. Passage between buildings
4. Doe, e.g.
5. Scoundrel
6. Sacrificial table
7. Schnitzel meat
8. Miscalculate
9. Sneaky
10. Ice-cream server
11. Mama's man
12. Higher than
13. Look after
21. Frozen
23. Foundation
26. Capture
27. Oxygen or neon
28. Our planet
29. Genuine
30. Shout
31. Shady trees
32. Rigid
33. Ascend
34. Biblical garden
35. Red vegetables
38. Dinner hour, e.g.
39. Taxi
41. Pulls behind
42. James ____ (007)
45. Touch and taste
46. Lubricated
47. Waltz or fox trot
48. Mediterra-nean island
49. More aged
50. Accuse
51. Corrosive substance
52. Optimistic
53. Story
54. Drawn-out
55. Unbiased
58. Disencumber

ACROSS

1. Large bag
5. Shoestrings
10. Gulp greedily
14. Zone
15. Likeness
16. Object of worship
17. Nanny or billy
18. Kitchen smock
19. Sound quality
20. Put together
22. Holy
24. Maiden-name word
25. Pub brew
26. Wealthy
27. Mine find
28. Unpaid bill
29. Prefix for three
32. Take it easy
35. Buckets
36. Have supper
37. ____ and above
38. Ravine
39. Huron or Superior
40. Big ____ (London bell)
41. Grass color
42. Seraglio
43. Finish
44. Batters
45. Ship's journal
46. Small amounts
47. Cow's comment
48. Comedian Conway
51. Burning
54. Library rack
56. Train track
57. Dix and Knox
59. Competent
60. Skin problem
61. Combine
62. Bed board
63. Hive dwellers
64. Tart fruit
65. ____ and haws

DOWN

1. Astronomer/writer Carl ____
2. Got up
3. Halt
4. "Kiss Me, ____"
5. Susceptible
6. Plenty
7. Be concerned
8. Self-esteem
9. Having good judgment
10. Sorceress
11. Aroma
12. "The ____ Ranger"
13. Ran away
21. Socialist Karl ____
23. Performs a role
26. Govern
27. Rower's need
28. Challenges
29. Drop of sorrow
30. Garden tool
31. List entry
32. Loose garment
33. Tied, as a score
34. ____ an ear (listen)
35. Verses
38. Appreciative
39. Fall behind
41. Sullen
42. ____ and eye (fastener)
45. Untie
46. Bundles
47. Slogan
48. ____ of contents
49. Muslim religion
50. Runs into
51. Saudi, e.g.
52. Turn toward
53. Queue
54. Hat edge
55. Ready money
58. Single thing

PUZZLE 568

ACROSS

1. Serene
5. Risk
9. Hurt
13. Ostrichlike birds
17. African lily
18. Eve's garden
19. Reclined
20. Passport endorsement
21. Heavenly body
22. Soft drink
23. ___ and crafts
24. Frozen fruit treats
25. Medicines
27. Wound mark
29. Triumph
31. Foot parts
33. Duration
35. Ingest
36. Pod vegetable
39. Clutch
41. Pork or beef, e.g.
43. Gas, brake, or clutch
47. Ornamental vase
48. Motionless
50. Bead of moisture
52. Valley
53. Ceremony
55. Tidy
57. Singer of "Fame"
59. Running game
60. Foe
62. Spin
64. Baby cats
66. Charged particle
68. Fish eggs
69. Gull's cry
70. Regulate
74. Daytime dramas
77. Producer on "Murphy Brown"
81. Metal-bearing rock
82. Cleveland's lake
84. Support
85. Bossa ___ (dance)
86. Church service
88. Relocate
90. Top compass point
93. Parachute cord
94. Tailor
96. Brooklyn team
98. Steak order
99. Subways' relatives
100. Food fish
102. Must-have
104. 365-day period
106. Titled commoner
110. Foray
112. Sports complexes
116. Religious image
117. Fiber source
119. Chair
121. Uncovered
122. Walked heavily
123. Ambiance
124. Cloak
125. Dueling sword
126. Collections
127. Spool
128. Toboggan
129. Starring role

DOWN

1. Playbill listing
2. Palo ___, California
3. Money advance
4. Worth
5. Final dinner course
6. Fuss
7. Scarlet and crimson
8. Pass into law
9. Frightened
10. Auto
11. Strikes
12. Follow
13. Kicked out
14. Small rodents
15. Purposes
16. Back talk
26. Gear teeth
28. Direct at a target
30. Baseball hat
32. Canonized person
34. "Duke of ___"
36. Unaltered
37. Ireland, poetically
38. Kitty contribution
40. Gusted
42. Removed
44. Appoint-ment
45. Actor Alda
46. Lower limbs

480

49. Animals' shelters
51. Prissy
54. Give off
56. Girl Scout group
58. Thing
61. Days of old
63. Gain knowledge
65. Identical one
67. Average
70. Robin Cook novel
71. Verbal
72. Bird's dwelling
73. Tawny cat
75. Destitute
76. Mist
78. Knowledge
79. Wicked
80. Weakens
83. Equal
87. Extra helpings
89. Everlasting
91. Doctored
92. Get word
95. Actor Ely or Silver
97. Red or Dead
101. Exclude
103. Platters
105. Mutiny
106. Fragments
107. Land measure
108. Tooth's anchor
109. Correct
111. Distribute, as cards
113. Back of the neck
114. Sector
115. Kernel
118. "Diamonds ___ Forever"
120. Orangutan, e.g.

PUZZLE 568

1	2	3	4		5	6	7	8		9	10	11	12		13	14	15	16
17					18					19					20			
21					22					23					24			
25				26			27		28			29		30				
			31			32		33			34		35					
36	37	38		39			40		41			42		43		44	45	46
47				48				49		50			51		52			
53			54			55			56		57			58		59		
60				61		62				63		64			65			
			66		67			68					69					
70	71	72				73		74			75	76		77		78	79	80
81				82			83		84						85			
86			87		88			89			90			91	92		93	
94				95		96			97		98						99	
			100		101		102			103		104			105			
106	107	108				109		110			111		112			113	114	115
116					117		118			119		120			121			
122					123					124					125			
126					127					128					129			

PUZZLE 569

ACROSS

1. Entire
4. News bit
8. Ripped
12. Stags' mates
14. Slangy negative
15. Archer's missile
16. Accomplished
17. Cut away excess from
18. Napped leather
19. Break sharply
20. Particular description
22. Building curve
24. In back of
28. Swagger
30. Wasteland
32. Maiden-name indicator
33. Streetcar
34. Papa's mate
35. Read quickly
36. Spoiled child
37. French cap
38. Harbor
39. In person
40. Make a living
41. Arrived
42. Cooling drink
43. Contradict
44. Solitary person
45. Conviction
47. Work crew
48. Wanted
51. Dawdles
55. Established
58. For both sexes
59. Radiate
60. Regions
61. Otherwise
62. Plunge headfirst
63. Control knob
64. Bambi, e.g.
65. A.M. moisture

DOWN

1. Totals up
2. Crazy as a ___
3. Singer Horne
4. Not broken up
5. Flaming light
6. Heroic poem
7. Brief note
8. "___ or Consequences"
9. Prospector's find
10. Reel's partner
11. Ram's mate
13. Not together
15. Ed ___ of "Lou Grant"
21. German submarine
23. Molasses liquor
25. ___ tax
26. Closer
27. Dimple
28. Take long steps
29. Go on a journey
30. Wed
31. Sign of the future
34. Intend
35. "The Star ___ Banner"
36. Tattle
37. Complains
41. Swindle
43. Exploits
44. Climbing aid
46. Image of perfection
47. Honking fowl
49. ___ tea
50. Actor's part
52. In the middle of
53. Donate
54. Soupy meat dish
55. Unfavorable
56. Jackie O's second
57. Baltic or Caspian

ACROSS
1. Cloth belt
5. Long feather
10. ___ gin
14. Small combo
15. The Ritz, e.g.
16. Former Italian money unit
17. Palo ___
18. Conscious
19. Singing brothers
20. Job supervisors
22. Intense delight
24. Example of perfection
27. Crossed letter
28. Loafers or pumps
31. By way of
33. President John Quincy ___
37. Type of frost
38. Hunting dog
40. Meadow
41. Possessive pronoun
42. Follower of Sun.
43. Owns
44. Unwell
45. Purpose
46. Rod and reel user
48. TV detective Houston
49. Roosevelt or bear
51. Very long time
52. Impudent
53. Decay
55. Sacred song
57. African expeditions
61. Representation
65. Encase
66. Dog's tether
69. Funnyman Johnson
70. Poker starter
71. Show host
72. Zodiac Leo
73. Foot digits
74. Ceremonies
75. Plant starter

DOWN
1. Pierce
2. Singer Guthrie
3. Uses a bench
4. Indiana native
5. Moon period
6. Close to the bottom
7. Actress Hagen
8. Only
9. Choose by vote
10. Scheduled
11. Peru's capital
12. Unrefined metals
13. Simple
21. Koch and Asner
23. Scorches
25. Retaliate for
26. Ignited
28. Yell
29. Dwelling
30. Rowed
32. Capital of Greece
34. Assumed name
35. Defrosts
36. Briny
38. Male child
39. Corn unit
42. City official
47. Cut off
48. Milk-producing vertebrates
50. Curtains
52. Cunning
54. Mosaic-maker
56. Fire remnants
57. Whack
58. Pisa's river
59. Destiny
60. Trucker's rig
62. Soft French cheese
63. Oklahoma Indian
64. Give temporarily
67. Play division
68. Witness

PUZZLE 570

PUZZLE 571

ACROSS

1. Fisherman's poles
5. Narrow band
10. Vocalized music
14. Heroic tale
15. Harmonizing group
16. Region
17. Apiece
18. Greeting word
19. Schnitzel meat
20. Run away
21. Olive or canola
22. Party, in Spain
24. Entryway
26. Pea containers
27. True
30. Tug along
31. Health resort
34. Blackboard adjunct
35. Pine Tree State
36. Possesses
37. Oriental staple
38. Discovered
39. Part of speech
40. Large deer
41. Nickel and dime
42. Gander, e.g.
43. Bro.'s sibling
44. Party-giver
45. Professional lender
46. Electrical unit
47. Commotion
48. Blot up
51. Droop
52. Otherwise
56. Bellow
57. Coral island
59. Dead to sensation
60. Weapons
61. Rent
62. Snooty one
63. Borscht vegetable
64. Large ponds
65. Omelet ingredients

DOWN

1. Great Barrier ____
2. October's stone
3. Gaming cubes
4. Timetable
5. Institute of learning
6. "____ Finest Hour"
7. Bun
8. Feel unwell
9. Deeply significant
10. Hoards
11. Raw metals
12. Orderly
13. Festive
23. Out of work
25. Hardwood tree
26. Causes suffering
27. Farm measures
28. ____ con carne
29. Short nails
30. Visit often
31. Rattled
32. Brief lull
33. Ed ____ of "Lou Grant"
35. Slightly wet
38. Autumn sport
39. Gibberish
41. Scorch
42. Auto fuel
45. Reveille instruments
46. Most terrible
47. Misleading
48. Saudi, e.g.
49. Tedious one
50. Alike
51. Drench
53. Breathing organ
54. Air pollution
55. Wanes, as the tide
58. Chamomile drink

ACROSS

1. Singer/mayor Sonny ___
5. Audible breath
9. Entitled
14. Higher than
15. Vicinity
16. Nimble
17. Filly's mom
18. Temporary gift
19. Rigid
20. Flower
22. Pulverizer
24. Refrain syllable
25. Very warm
26. Tollhouse ___ (dessert item)
30. Old maid
35. Change
36. Jaw part
37. Chopping tool
38. Feel sorry for
39. By oneself
40. Downhill runners
41. Woman of Eden
42. Military grade
43. Storage box
44. Lover's night music
47. Wave tops
48. Chemist's room
49. Prefix for three
50. Foreign mission
54. Trash
59. Circles
60. Grows older
62. Poker bet
63. Telegraph code
64. Refuses to
65. Plant stalk
66. Scornful look
67. Dozes off
68. Female pigs

DOWN

1. Explosive device
2. Egg-shaped
3. Infamous emperor
4. Mine yields
5. Aplenty
6. Fragrance
7. Mediterranean, e.g.
8. Twinge
9. Country
10. Representatives
11. Brain
12. What ___ is new?
13. Stag or doe
21. Mix
23. German river
26. Cod and Horn
27. Martini garnish
28. Aquatic mammal
29. Lock opener
30. Gleamed
31. Light red
32. Seizes
33. Have being
34. Relaxes
36. Attired
39. Saudis, e.g.
40. That woman
43. Baby's bed
45. Pass, as time
46. Former Egyptian leader
47. Bread edges
49. General inclination
50. Shady trees
51. Lunar body
52. Tiresome person
53. Gape
55. Game fish
56. Division word
57. Soupy meat dish
58. Skirt edges
61. Sticky stuff

PUZZLE 572

PUZZLE 573

• MOVIES & TELEVISION •

ACROSS

1. "___ Delicate Condition"
6. "___ Copperfield"
11. Alan Ladd western
16. Actress Verdugo
17. With 39 Down, star of "Fame"
18. "That ___ Girl"
19. "___ Recall"
20. "Frankenstein ___ the Wolf Man"
21. "Staying ___"
22. "Peggy ___ Got Married"
23. Has unpaid bills
25. ___ out (barely made)
27. Irish sea god
28. Plays
30. Formerly, formerly
31. "Hail the Conquering ___"
32. Part of MPH
33. Connie's newsroom partner
34. "I ___ Camera"
36. "___ Street" (Robert Wagner series)
39. "___ Timberlane"
40. Rub out
44. "___ and the Gypsy"
45. Actress Pickford
46. "Field of Dreams" star
48. Erich ___ Stroheim
49. "Bird on a ___"
50. "Who's the ___?"
51. Ziering of "Beverly Hills 90210"
52. "___ Jones and the Last Crusade"
54. "___ and Spars"
55. "___ Fair" (Richard Crenna sitcom)
56. "The ___ Girl" (German film)
57. ___ avis
58. "The ___ Is Silence"
59. Miranda of "Summertime"
61. Marine eagle
62. Fore's partner
64. "___ Appeal" (Lemmon film)
67. Molten rock
69. "Remington ___"
72. "One Day ___ Time"
73. Lane of "The Americano"
74. Natives: suff.
75. Pie ___ mode
77. "Bates ___"
79. Ridiculous
81. "Driving Miss Daisy" star
83. Gillette or Morris
84. Tent caterpillar
85. "The ___ Cantor Story"
86. Ed Sullivan guest Wences
87. British actress Heather ___
88. Claude ___ of "Casablanca"

DOWN

1. "Prime Time ___"
2. Audibly
3. Graves or Falk
4. Alicia of "Falcon Crest"
5. Rita Hayworth film
6. Some coins
7. Greek god
8. Neckline type
9. Michael Callan film, with "The"
10. Schoolroom items
11. Herringlike fish
12. Linden of "Barney Miller"
13. Nimble
14. "___ on Sunday"
15. January: Sp.
24. "___ and Peace"
26. Airport term: abbr.
29. Pinnacle
30. "Earth Girls Are ___"
31. "Entertainment Tonight" host
33. "Truth or ___"
35. "A Fine ___"
36. Linda ___ of "Alice"

37. Actress Massey
38. Repairs
39. See 17 Across
41. Doddering
42. Closes securely
43. Director Lubitsch
45. "____ and Bill"
46. '30s character actress Witherspoon
47. Ladd/Fitzgerald film
49. Methods
50. Hay-storage building
53. "____ No Secret"
54. "Gone With the Wind" home
55. Johnson of "Laugh-In"
57. "____ of the Nerds"
60. Priest's garment
62. Consumed
63. "The Addams Family" uncle
64. "____ Family"
65. Make amends
66. "____ Doll" (Ellington song)
68. "____ Irish Rose"
69. Ham and gang endings
70. '30s actress Elissa ____
71. "Murphy Brown" painter
73. Having wings
74. Unique person
76. Positive votes
78. Eisenhower's command: abbr.
80. Turkish title
82. Hayward/Martin film

PUZZLE 574

ACROSS

1. Narrow opening
5. False name
10. Polish
14. Salary
15. Evade
16. Largest continent
17. Qualified
18. Sag
19. Fish snares
20. Cow's comment
21. Young woman
22. Surrounded by
24. Blasphemous
26. Paid athletes
27. Equip
28. Coastline
32. Silverware item
35. Actor George C. ____
36. Male offspring
37. Suspend
38. Jet, e.g.
39. Clothed
40. Stable morsel
41. Gets word
42. Entryways
43. Belongings
45. Embroider
46. Pilaf ingredient
47. Issue in print
51. Globe
54. Clue
55. The blue above
56. Plunder
57. Presses, as clothes
59. Purple fruit
60. Uncle's wife
61. Worth
62. Nashville's state: abbr.
63. Three, in cards
64. Cairo's country
65. Poses a question

DOWN

1. Boggy area
2. Toil
3. House of snow
4. Golfing peg
5. Doing sums
6. Mr. Moto portrayer Peter ____
7. Graven image
8. In the past
9. Apart
10. Condemn to exile
11. Secondhand
12. Tantrums
13. Abstain from food
21. Increase
23. Largest amount
25. Toad's cousin
26. Unskilled laborers
28. Frightening
29. Norway's capital
30. Lion's yell
31. Finishes
32. Market
33. TV host Jack ____
34. Aware of
35. Bluish-gray stone
38. Become aware of
39. Hooded robe
41. Inheritor
42. Unpaid bill
44. Lovely
45. "____ Boulevard"
47. Poster
48. Small land masses
49. Black and white mammal
50. Church songs
51. Thin board
52. Serve wine
53. Whet
54. Sacred
58. Scrap of cloth
59. School group: abbr.

PUZZLE 575

ACROSS
1. Feline beast
4. _____ as a cucumber
8. Cloth belt
12. Graceful steed
14. Rabbit's kin
15. Site of the 1988 Olympics
16. Horne of song
17. Manipulates
18. Entitled
19. Sail support
20. Error
22. Garment edges
24. Give up a position
28. Wander
30. Milky gem
32. Take to court
33. Jog
34. Heroic poem
35. Dog's pest
36. Baby's bed
37. Stream
38. Endure
39. Comedian Bob _____
40. Ventilates
41. Refuses to
42. Building addition
43. Thought
44. Highways
45. Sheep's coat
47. Red vegetable
48. Dietary necessity
51. List entry
55. Frequently
58. Grade
59. _____ Scotia
60. "Take Me _____"
61. Work gang
62. One who departs
63. Smallest of the litter
64. That woman's
65. Explosive initials

DOWN
1. Sedate
2. Region
3. Prepares leather
4. Friendly
5. Desert spring
6. Raw metals
7. Not as much
8. Daytime TV dramas
9. Upper limb
10. Observe
11. Once possessed
13. Post-shower wear
15. Genuflect
21. Footprint
23. Consume lunch
25. Oahu or Hawaii
26. Visitors
27. Tidy
28. Leisurely walk
29. Three-bag hit
30. Sung drama
31. Apple and mince
34. Great Lake
35. Being buoyed up
36. Head cook
37. Military student
41. Misery
43. Cake frosting
44. Subscribes again
46. Happening
47. One who nips
49. Building curve
50. Stallion's mate
52. Horn sound
53. Level
54. Store
55. Rower's need
56. Winter ailment
57. 2,000 pounds

PUZZLE 576

ACROSS

1. Karate hit
5. Storms
10. Russian, e.g.
14. Bagel
15. French school
16. Bark cloth
17. Tony's cousin
18. Gepetto, e.g.
20. Actress Joanne
22. Milk-producing farm
23. Sea eagle
24. Supplies with fuel
26. Glued
30. Lyon's river
31. "____ Karenina"
32. Generous fellow
33. Three, in Roma
36. Satyrs: 2 wds.
40. ____ and order
41. Sicily's land
42. Word of regret
43. Tall tale
44. Baseball's Mickey
46. Author Du Maurier
48. Hawaiian food
49. Shinto gateway
50. Sorrel tree
55. Ground hogs
58. ____ mater
59. Handle on an urn
60. Century plants
61. Luge
62. Soothsayer
63. English measure
64. ____ Krishna

DOWN

1. Brag
2. Nomad
3. Medley
4. Begged
5. Bounty
6. Chipmunk's snack
7. Acceptable
8. Days of yore
9. Dry, as wine
10. Hull planking
11. C'est ____: 2 wds.
12. Copycats
13. Fluctuate
19. Hebrew God
21. Tiny
24. Annie's pet
25. Student's carryall
26. Pivoted object
27. Sulawesi ox
28. Winter precipitation
29. Little one
30. With gloom
32. Trap
33. Lean to one side
34. Genuine
35. Being, to Cato
37. Made of stone
38. Solar god
39. Use a sunlamp
43. Arachnid
44. Rich dessert
45. Atmosphere
46. Lorna of Exmoor
47. Stood up
48. Gambling game
49. "____ the night before . . ."
50. Edinburgh man
51. Scrub
52. Mexican pot
53. Hebrew measure
54. Miami's county
56. Son of Noah
57. Diminutive ending

PUZZLE 577

SLIDE-O-GRAM

Place the seven words below into the diagram, one word for each across line, so that one of the rows reading down will spell out a 7-letter word that is related to the others.

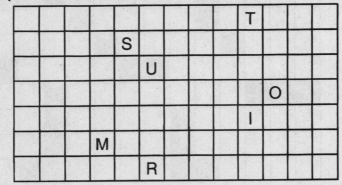

Beetle

Butterfly

Cricket

Grasshopper

Mosquito

Moth

Spider

CODEWORD

Codeword is a special crossword puzzle in which conventional clues are omitted. Instead, answer words in the diagram are represented by numbers. Each number represents a different letter of the alphabet, and all of the letters of the alphabet are used. When you are sure of a letter, put it in the code key chart for easy reference. A group of letters has been inserted to start you off.

1	14 G	2	15
3	16	4	17
5	18	6	19 A
7	20	8	21
9	22	10	23
11	24	12 R	25
13	26		

CODEWORD

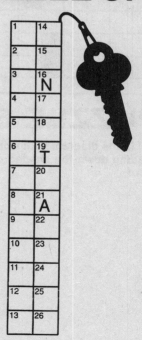

1	14	2	15
3	16 N	4	17
5	18	6	19 T
7	20	8	21 A
9	22	10	23
11	24	12	25
13	26		

PUZZLE 580

ACROSS

1. Sluggish
5. Valuable
10. Leftover fare
14. Volcano output
15. Task
16. Resound
17. Gershwin composition, with "An": 3 wds.
20. Writing utensil
21. Brink
22. Expert
23. Lean
24. Use a lever
25. Modern
28. Greedy
30. Opening
33. Actor Alda
34. "Remember the ___"
35. Reverential fear
36. Song of 1920, with "The": 2 wds.
40. Dined
41. Prevent
42. Emanation
43. That woman's
44. Irish fuel
45. OPEC, e.g.
47. Jailbird
48. French glove
49. Dismay, in Britain
52. Apparent
54. Revolver
57. Sherwood drama: 3 wds.
60. "___ La Douce"
61. Warning flame
62. Conceited
63. Twofold
64. Mary ___ Moore
65. Miss Kett

DOWN

1. Insulting blow
2. Gold cloth
3. Kiln
4. Conflict
5. Emphasis
6. "Jaws" star
7. Melody
8. Great Lake
9. "___ Little Indians"
10. Intoxicating
11. Land measure
12. Vessel
13. Party giver
18. Russian tsar
19. Forgive
23. Miss Horne
24. Kind of cotton
25. Indian ruler
26. Cheer up
27. Prank
28. Warn
29. Huge
30. Entire range
31. Cognizant
32. Regarding punishment
34. On the briny
37. Italian province
38. Smooth
39. Dash
45. George Washington ___
46. One against
47. Waterway
48. Genus
49. Dry
50. Lima's country
51. Cougar
52. Just
53. Small bottle
54. Insect
55. Standard quantity
56. Zola novel
58. Frequently, to a poet
59. Adam's mate

PUZZLE 581

HOCUS POCUS

Fill In the diagram with words formed by unscrambling the letters so that an 8-letter word will be revealed reading down the shaded column. This is a bit tricky as the scrambled letters may form more than one word.

1. A E L P T
2. A E M N S
3. A I N S T
4. A E G L R
5. A E P R S
6. A C E R T
7. E I M S T
8. E I N R S

PUZZLE 582

ACROSS

1. Put away aboard
5. "___ Spee"
9. Nile dam site
14. West African country
15. Rivulet
16. Call
17. Ireland, fondly
18. Play part: 2 wds.
19. Laborers
20. Troy's undoing: 2 wds.
23. Speck
24. ___ hat
25. ___ as she goes
27. Flanked by
31. Tests
34. Masjid or Pasha
35. Halt
38. Beauty shop
39. Skating area
41. Lance
43. Wild plumlike fruit
44. Wooden peg
46. Full
48. Language suffix
49. Markets
51. Top
53. Speaks
56. Hail, to Caesar
57. Graduate degree letters
59. "Gypsy" star: 2 wds.
64. Send payment
66. "The Children's ___"
67. Patron saint of sailors
68. One of the Muses
69. Fairy-tale opener
70. Plod
71. Corn breads
72. Sow
73. Pueblo Indian

DOWN

1. Merganser
2. Poi source
3. Medley
4. Oriel, e.g.
5. Eminent Iberians
6. Affluent
7. Choir members
8. Coquette
9. Seems
10. "___ Done Him Wrong"
11. "Sleeper" star: 2 wds.
12. In the year: Latin
13. Sparrow's abode
21. Kind of energy: abbr.
22. Collection
26. Buenos ___
27. Poets
28. George or T.S.
29. "Wizard of Oz" character: 2 wds.
30. Drowses
32. Free
33. Derisive look
36. Black or Red
37. Chows
40. Actress Deborah
42. Fixed
45. Sheds: hyph.
47. Nose or swan
50. Penn, e.g.
52. Most recent
54. Group character
55. Rhone feeder
57. Certain sch.
58. Public idol
60. Publisher Henry
61. Southwest stewpot
62. Melville book
63. Corgis, e.g.
65. Inhabitant: suffix

KEYWORD   PUZZLE 583

To find the KEYWORD fill in the blanks in words 1 through 10 with the correct missing letters. Transfer those letters to the correspondingly numbered squares in the diagram. Approach with care—this puzzle is not as simple as it first appears.

1. S T _ R T
2. V A L _ E
3. F O R _ Y
4. B _ A S T
5. B L O O _
6. S P _ R T
7. _ A T C H
8. S H _ R K
9. _ O D G E
10. L E A S _

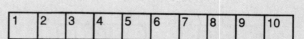

1	2	3	4	5	6	7	8	9	10

493

PUZZLE 584

ACROSS

1. Hoist
6. Munches
11. ___ bleu
12. Cheer
14. Atlanta, Ga.
17. Historical periods
18. Abound
19. Belfry
20. Sothern
21. Containing iron
23. Winter stuff
24. Canning gel
26. Strikebreaker
28. Pentagon VIP
29. Discoloration
30. Intrepid
32. Hiker's path
34. Vicuna's kin
35. Glossy coats
37. Metric measures
40. Lunched
41. Son of Eve
42. Composer Johnny
43. Decorator's advice
45. Hid away
47. Japanese sash
48. Merits
50. Ancient Ireland
51. Double
52. Eskimos
55. Garment part
56. System of self-defense
57. Arabian horse
58. Aspersions

DOWN

1. St. Peter's and Lateran
2. God of war
3. Bachelor's last words
4. Melt
5. Go in
6. Laboratory substances
7. Center
8. Goofs
9. Stoles
10. Nest eggs
11. Band instrument
13. Champions
14. Piles
15. Daughter of Cecrops
16. Seamed and tucked
21. Last exams
22. Actor Reiner
25. Spare, for one
27. Reproached
30. Complimented
31. Asian ruler
33. Cays, to the French
35. Takes without right
36. Daily task
38. Discount
39. Seed coverings
40. Neighborhood
42. Servile
44. Attack
46. Gambles
49. Snow glider
51. Honey
53. Hail, to Caesar
54. Actress Joanne

PUZZLE 585

SHARE-A-LETTER

Fill in each diagram with the words that correspond to each subject. Letters to be filled into the larger areas will be shared by more than one word. Words read across only.

1. ANIMALS

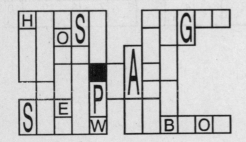

2. COLORS

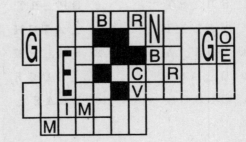

494

ACROSS

1. Actress Kelly
6. Head covers
10. Spool
14. Drives fast
15. Leave out
16. Medicinal plant
17. Special occasion
18. Irritate
19. Baseball team
20. Oater
22. Trickle slowly
24. Before, poetically
25. Floor cleaners
26. Craft
29. Pine tree
31. Defect
33. Turret
35. Beavers' creation
36. Wharf
37. Mexican blanket
38. Makes known
40. Caresses
41. Stringed instruments
42. Made thread
43. Printers' measures
44. Thesis
45. Jump
46. High explosive
47. "___ Loves Me"
48. Great Lake
50. Unlocked, to a bard
52. Impudent child
53. Uneven
57. Confront
60. Roma's language: abbr.
62. Musical drama
63. Level
64. Stitches
65. Conflicting
66. Requirement
67. Sea eagle
68. Rock

DOWN

1. Became larger
2. Rant
3. High cards
4. Middle
5. Organic compound
6. Cereal grain
7. French friend
8. Head rest
9. Precipitous
10. Social class
11. Inventor Whitney
12. Vast age
13. Southern general
21. Makes ready for use again
23. Backward
25. Disfigure
26. Rouse
27. Regret
28. Lock of hair
29. Starve
30. Inflict
32. Guitarist Paul
34. Spanish gold
35. Jackknifes
36. Entreaty
37. Daze
39. Georgia's neighbor: abbr.
40. Resort
42. Visualize
45. Untidiness
46. Kettle
49. Elevate
51. Supports
52. Curve
53. Otherwise
54. Distant: pref.
55. Persia, today
56. Look after
57. Marsh
58. St.
59. Passing grade
61. Grain beard

WHAT AM I?

My first is in father, but never in mother.

My second's in aunt, but never in brother.

My third is in grandma and also in mate.

My fourth is in sister, but never in Kate.

My fifth is in uncle and also in clan.

My sixth is in baby, but never in man.

I've room for many, from sibling to spouse.

If you want to find me, look in most any house.

PUZZLE 588

ACROSS

1. Worn out
5. Trite
10. Cranky one
14. Ornamental fabric
15. Heals
16. Govern
17. Actor Arkin
18. Dwell
19. Eastern continent
20. Abutted
22. Additional
23. By way of
24. Budge
26. Folds
30. Drink
34. Hawk's nest
35. Do gardening work
36. Actor Steiger
37. Hits solidly
38. Heed the alarm
39. Amphibian
40. Actress Bartok
41. Seedy joints
42. Type of writing
43. Presented payment
45. More sluggish
46. Chilled
47. River: Sp.
48. Fiery particle
51. Wound dressings
56. Rub lightly
57. Arm support
59. Big bundle
60. Fish sauce
61. Color
62. Actress Lanchester
63. Assay
64. Put 2 and 2 together
65. Consider

DOWN

1. Chunk
2. Angelic headwear
3. Actor Sharif
4. Baby-sit
5. Frightens
6. Potato, e.g.
7. Like the Gobi
8. Guided
9. Compass dir.
10. Moon feature
11. Big hurry
12. "I cannot tell ___": 2 wds.
13. Bruin
21. Dueling sword
22. More than
24. Allots
25. Baker's need
26. Provide food
27. Depart
28. Church instrument
29. Bro's sib
30. Made cookies
31. Bow missile
32. Silly bird
33. Lawn tool
35. Fluttered
38. Telegram
39. To and ___
41. Pack of cards
42. Trudge
44. Guide
45. Charred
47. Buffalo's home
48. Hit hard
49. Heap
50. Mimics
51. Tie
52. In the sack
53. Storm
54. If not
55. Connecting stitches
57. Depot: abbr.
58. Box top

PUZZLE 589

WORD SPIRAL

Fill in the spiral diagram in a clockwise direction with the 4-letter answer words. The last letter of each word will be the first letter of the next word. When the diagram is completed, a 7-letter word will read down the shaded center column.

1. Musical sign
2. Heating need
3. Extensive
4. U.S. territory
5. Actress Marjorie
6. Waiting-room call
7. Stumble
8. Trail
9. Make a rug
10. Chicken ___
11. Action word
12. Small nail
13. Platform
14. Adventure story
15. Choir member
16. Swear word

PUZZLE 590

ACROSS
1. Damage
4. Insult
8. Land measure
12. Pub drink
13. Ancient weapon
14. Put down
15. Poetic contraction
16. Bakery worker
17. Against
18. Ceramic square
20. Resource
21. Rich cake
23. Scratch
25. Sad expression
26. Says again
30. Garland
31. Paces
32. Topsy's playmate
33. Changes
35. Type of school
36. Raw minerals
37. Singes
38. Revenge
41. Castro's land
42. Own
43. Needy
45. Swindle
48. State
49. Goals
50. Age
51. Military meal
52. Bed support
53. Got off one's feet

DOWN
1. Small rug
2. Muhammed ____
3. Hold back
4. Grin
5. Decorative edging
6. Playing card
7. Each
8. 49th state
9. Containers
10. Ceremony
11. Prepare copy
19. "____ a Miracle"
20. Skills
21. Soft mineral
22. Margarine
23. Defrosts
24. Queries
26. Hard to find
27. Patios
28. Level
29. Weakens
31. Existed
34. Electors
35. Tavern
37. Explode
38. Fake
39. Overlay
40. Currier and ____
41. Cook book
43. Dance step
44. Lubricate
46. Mouths
47. ____ King Cole

PUZZLE 591

ACROSS
1. Red vegetable
5. Beret
8. Surfeit
12. Wild buffalo of India
13. Actress Lupino
14. Conceal
15. Start of quotation: 2 wds.
18. Merchant
19. Goddess of agriculture
20. Teachers' org.: abbr.
21. ____ butter
22. Breakfast option
24. Sleuth Mickey
28. Mineo
29. Forelegs
30. 149, to Caesar
31. Voting into office
33. Western college: abbr.
34. Bee's home
35. Yoko
36. "____ Romance": 2 wds.
38. Texas city
41. End of quotation: 3 wds.
43. Spoken
44. Sea eagle
45. Mine entrance
46. Swamps
47. Billy ____ Williams
48. Hideaways

DOWN
1. Hairless
2. Great Lake
3. Enmesh
4. Names
5. Row
6. Paid notices
7. Corresponding
8. Sung by a choir
9. Admire
10. Poems
11. Affirmative reply
16. Meadow
17. Spools
21. Backbone
22. Compass pt.: abbr.
23. Lass
24. Quaked
25. Praise
26. Nothing
27. Guido's note
29. Ex-Police member
32. Ices
33. Lighten
35. Cereal grain
36. Of flying
37. Banner
38. Copenhagen native
39. Similar
40. Fast jets: abbr.
41. Watch piece
42. Before, to poets

PUZZLE 592

• BATTER UP! •

ACROSS

1. Schoolroom furniture
5. Brit. lawyer
9. Part of QED
13. Jai ____
14. Pen name for Lamb
15. Oak seed
16. Consume with flames
17. Cincinnati Reds, former home
19. Smelting byproduct
20. "____ Maria"
21. Piano piece
22. Palm fruit
24. Pub orders
25. Task
27. Assert
28. Distant
31. Scent
32. Jogged
33. Southern constellation
34. Fly catchers milieu?
39. Hot season, in Sevres
40. Victory sign
41. Companies
42. Afternoon social
43. Zadora and Lindstrom
44. Donkey serenades?
45. King of comedy
46. "____ Russia With Love"
47. Forty-niner, e.g.
49. "Cara ____"
50. Above
54. Home of the Boston Red Sox
56. Pianist Peter ____
57. Zones
58. Toward shelter
59. Mild oath
60. Forest ruminant
61. Hardy heroine
62. Back talk

DOWN

1. Small amounts
2. Hebrew month
3. Poet Teasdale
4. Former home of the Seattle Mariners
5. Chide
6. Animate
7. Rend asunder
8. "Norma ____"
9. Off-whites
10. Cross
11. English composer
12. Explosive letters
15. Following
18. Give in
23. Semite
24. Gardner and Haddad
25. Shipping container
26. Old Testament book
27. Van Gogh home
28. Sprite
29. Cuckoopints, e.g.
30. Male sheep
31. Aid a felon
35. Enclosure for birds
36. Mrs. Sprat's bane
37. Type of hairdo
38. Features of 17 and 54 Across
43. Entreaties
44. Stops the car
45. Egyptian leader Sadat
46. Sacks
47. Simple
48. Arrow poison
49. Man
51. Actress Miles
52. Epochs
53. Decays
54. Craze
55. Benatar or Boone

PUZZLE 593

In the Middle

Fill in the squares to form a word which is the missing link to connect the two given words. For example, if the two given words were CRAB and SAUCE, the missing link would be APPLE (Crab apple, Applesauce).

1.

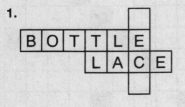

2.

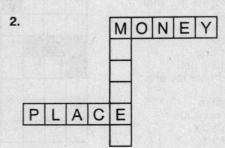

3.

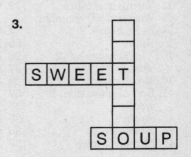

DILEMMA

PUZZLE 594

Except for 1 Across, there are two clues for each number and two identical sides in the diagram. Your Dilemma is to discover which answer goes on the right side and which answer goes on the left. Note: The heavy lines indicate the ends of words as black squares do in regular crosswords.

ACROSS

1. Huge statue honoring Helios
9. Fight
   Actor West
10. ____ Krishna
    Exceptional
11. Celebration
    Ramble
12. French cheese
    Lamb's pen name
13. Paradise
    Spoken
14. Bit of gossip
    Take a nap
15. Never
    Moving
21. Black
    Waste matter
22. Great boxer
    Behold
23. Before, in poetry
    Old French coin
24. Hotel option
    Sandy's owner
26. Ranch rope
    Ventures
27. Ventilate
    Tierra ____ Fuego
28. Taxi
    Remnant
31. Noise
    Itty-bitty
33. Sea bird
    Violinist Bull
34. Two cents worth
    Barter
37. Telegraph developer
    Rotary phone parts
38. "Butterflies ____ Free"
    Toe total
39. Trivial
    Irrigate
41. Belgian resort
    Betel leaf
42. Neighborhood
    Horse's morsels
45. Captain of the Pequod
    Long time periods

46. Mr. Connery
    Margarine
47. Malarial fever
    Ringlet
48. University official
    Classify
49. Major suffix
    Entrepreneur
    Perot

DOWN

1. Indignant
   Merry-go-round
2. Wilma's husband
   Stench
3. Volcanic flow
   Fixed charge
4. Laughing animals
   Breakfast treat
5. Satellites' paths
   Spanish wine
6. Bulls-eye hitter
   Clearance
7. Part of HOMES
   "Trinity" author
8. Throne
   Appear
16. Mrs. Charles
    Killer whale
17. Performs
    ____ de force
18. China's continent
    Magic stick
19. Extraterrestrial
    Admit
20. Suspicious
    Succumb
24. Decides
    Deputy
25. Nary a soul
    Computer operators

28. Range
    Sequoia
29. African succulent
    Diva's solo
30. Small fly
    TV host Parks
32. ____ tree (stumped)
    Ingest
35. Seventh planet
    Leave
36. Allow
    Past and present
40. 1968, e.g.
    Hurry
41. Walt Kelly's possum
    Close
43. Antique auto
    Pub specialty
44. Corn portion
    British brew

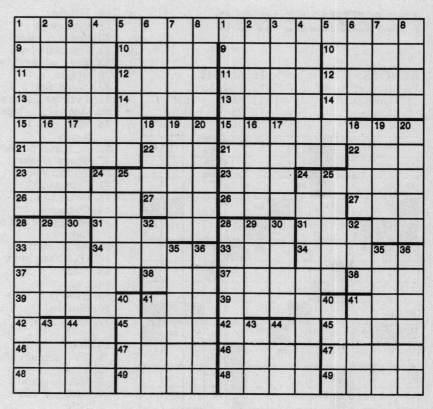

499

PUZZLE 595

ACROSS
1. Ooze
5. Church bench
8. Was contingent (on)
10. Monkeys
12. Chant
13. Divorce city
14. Glide over snow
15. Rains ice
17. Religious denomination
19. Food tin
20. Returned to office
24. Males
25. Large number
27. Twisted out of shape
30. Take advantage of
31. Wicked
32. Worn away
35. Ceramic square
36. Roadside eateries
37. ____ Moines
38. Finest

DOWN
1. Hook, line, and ____
2. Lure
3. Self
4. Ink writer
5. Mom and dad
6. Fencing sword
7. Departed
8. Snake sound
9. Went down
11. Distress signal
16. Varnish ingredient
18. Synagogues
21. Confederate general
22. Evades
23. Sandy wasteland
26. Marries
27. Damp
28. Greedy
29. Annoy
33. Curved bone
34. Single thing

PUZZLE 596

ACROSS
1. Highest cards
5. Requests
9. Unhappy
12. Mislead
13. Fish lure
14. Make a knot
15. Twirl
16. Height
18. Contempt
20. Snow coaster
21. Disencumbers
23. Eyes suggestively
26. Spuds
30. Small cut
31. Lyricist Gershwin
32. Queen ____ lace
34. Suit ____ T: 2 wds.
35. ____ and pepper
37. Opera singers
39. Wide-awake
41. Crimson hues
42. Close by
44. Concerns
47. Money earned on money
50. Actor Alda
52. Gambling cube
53. Sieze
54. Otherwise
55. Elderly
56. Skidded
57. Final

DOWN
1. TV commercials
2. Mugs
3. Heroic poem
4. Spanish wife's title
5. Leaves behind
6. "My Gal ____"
7. Sets of tools
8. Motionless
9. Pupils
10. Help
11. Fourth letter
17. Golf mounds
19. Actress Moreno
22. Husband of 4 Down
24. Mob scene
25. Health resorts
26. Leaning Tower of ____
27. Verbal
28. Skilled
29. Picked out
33. Fizzy drink
36. Woody plant
38. Jewish homeland
40. Small pastries
43. Genuine
45. Songstress Fitzgerald
46. Back talk
47. Wedding promise: 2 wds.
48. Nothing
49. Snow runner
51. Butterfly snare

500

PUZZLE 597

ACROSS

1. Mexican dish
5. Tablets
9. At a distance
13. Inventor Howe
15. Baldwin of films
16. Stretch car
17. Sign on the ___
19. Senior dance
20. English essayist
21. Perform at the Met
23. Piece out
24. Destroyed
26. Chop fine
28. Necklace of flowers
31. Petty dispute
33. Units of gold content
36. Shade trees
38. Enthusiasm
40. Tenth part
41. Rubberneck
42. Summarize
44. Swamp
45. Make amends
47. Snow runners
48. Son of Seth
49. Smaller
51. Thick slice
53. Understand
54. Tennis star Monica ___
56. Untidy person
58. ___ Amin
60. Resorts
62. Marshy ground
66. Bar bills
68. Incapable of emotion
70. "___ Cinders"
71. Midday
72. Claw
73. Encounter
74. Diner sign
75. Require

DOWN

1. Danson and Turner
2. Tons
3. Quote
4. Joyce Carol ___
5. Confidant
6. Baba and MacGraw
7. Jeans material
8. Picturesque
9. European mountain
10. Belligerent
11. Out of control
12. Italian capital
14. Vends
18. More profound
22. Pesky fly
25. Part of the United Kingdom
27. Wrongdoing
28. Judicial
29. Gladden
30. Hopeless
32. Changes heading, nautically
34. Pang
35. "___ thou how faith wrought . . ."
37. Touch or smell
39. Fastens down
43. Book of the Bible
46. Snaky fish
50. Complain
52. Raise
55. Group of islands in the Pacific
57. Actor Keith
58. Component
59. Author Carnegie
61. Location
63. Proficient
64. Kind of gin
65. Dispatch
67. Used a chair
69. Response, briefly

Keyword — PUZZLE 598

To find the Keyword, fill in the blanks in words 1 through 10 with the correct missing letters. Transfer those letters to the correspondingly numbered squares in the diagram. Approach with care—this puzzle is not as simple as it first appears.

1. S _ IFF
2. HO _ SE
3. _ HERE
4. BA _ ON
5. TAR _ Y
6. _ VERT
7. _ OUCH
8. FLAS _
9. TWIN _
10. WO _ DS

501

PUZZLE 599

ACROSS
1. Shovel
6. Temporary lodging
10. Highest point
14. One who errs
15. Seaweed product
16. Hit the ___
17. Doddering
18. Ruthless competition
20. Plague
22. Abundant
23. The Gay Nineties, e.g.
24. Underwater acronym
26. Moroccan port
28. Thickener
31. Tart
32. Parrot
33. Prudent judgment
38. Spiel
40. Ottoman governor
41. Denials
42. String game
46. Johnson or Heflin
47. Thick slice
48. Wail
51. Shining
54. British three-handed card game
55. Inkling
56. Asian wild goat
58. Way out
62. Orange flower
65. Matriculate
66. Verve
67. Pennsylvania port
68. Italian socialist leader
69. Proofreader's mark
70. Govt. bureau
71. Wooded

DOWN
1. Eastern sovereign
2. Andean plateau
3. Arabian prince
4. Gambian coin
5. Menuhin's teacher
6. Rogue
7. Greek marketplace
8. "The Gift of the ___"
9. Introduction
10. Skill
11. Encrypted
12. New Zealand native
13. Mystery writer's award
19. Sponsorship
21. Kindred
25. Tropical tree
27. Arabian Sea gulf
28. Soft mineral
29. Samoan port
30. Confined
31. Safety
34. Auerbach or Adair
35. Variable star
36. Install
37. Serf
39. To be, to Pliny
43. "___ de lune"
44. Talked aimlessly
45. North Sea feeder
49. Pressing
50. Loewe's partner
51. Trod the boards
52. Cunning
53. Lawful
54. Primrose
57. Shamrock land
59. Marine flyer
60. Loudness unit
61. Skidded
63. Cincinnati-to-New York dir.
64. Until now

PUZZLE 600   THROWBACKS

You have to throw your mental gears into reverse to play this game. Reading backward, there are at least three 4-letter words to be found in each of the longer words. You can skip over letters, but don't change the order of the letters. For example, in the word DECLARE you can find the word RACE reading backward by starting with the next-to-last letter and skipping over the L, but you can't find the word READ without changing the order of the letters.

1. RACERS   _____   _____   _____
2. EROTIC   _____   _____   _____
3. SPANKS   _____   _____   _____
4. SEPALS   _____   _____   _____
5. TRAWLS   _____   _____   _____
6. DRABLY   _____   _____   _____
7. GALLEYS   _____   _____   _____
8. BALLOTS   _____   _____   _____

PUZZLE 601

ACROSS
1. Beehive State
5. Pseudonym
10. Animal skin
14. Fury
15. Type of drum
16. Vicinity
17. Rebuff
18. Western show
19. Type of jockey
20. Laboratory gel
21. Some
22. Most dependable
24. Commentator Rooney
26. Stop!
27. Urge to action
30. Callas solo
31. Baseball ref
34. Swamp
35. Mixture
36. Nothing
37. First man
38. Enclose again
39. Sluggish
40. Juniper-flavored liquor
41. Impudence
42. Contest site
43. Before, poetically
44. Rabbit's kin
45. Loved
46. Stringlike
47. Black
48. Upper arm muscles
51. Fireplace shelf
52. Occasionally dry riverbed
56. Wild ox
57. Chubby
59. Test
60. ____ tea
61. Actress Day
62. Governor Grasso
63. Woman
64. Tales
65. Consider

DOWN
1. ____ Major
2. Flavor
3. Water, in Madrid
4. Expression in a Middle Eastern language
5. Rub
6. Daft
7. Type of car racing
8. Birthday number
9. Comforting
10. Italian city
11. Pennsylvania port
12. Smaller
13. Diplomacy
23. Avenue
25. To the ____ degree
26. Inflict
27. Public appearance
28. Low point
29. Construction machine
30. Playwright Edward ____
31. Below
32. Pooh's creator
33. Implore
35. Actor Wallace ____
38. "____ in Blue"
39. Nicholson/ Streep film
41. Cut up
42. Hubbub
45. Convent superior
46. Prepare
47. Red dye
48. Empty water out of
49. Peruvian Indian
50. Female student
51. Mister, in Bonn
53. Wheel shaft
54. Actor Robertson
55. Muslim leader
58. Long scarf

Quotagram

PUZZLE 602

Fill in the answers to the clues. Then transfer the letters to the correspondingly numbered squares in the diagram. The completed diagram will contain a quotation.

1. Profess again
   ── ── ── ── ── ── ── ──
   22 10 25 7 35 15 3 33

2. Life's work
   ── ── ── ── ── ── ── ──
   11 6 36 1 23 18 29 13

3. Wedding participant
   ── ── ── ── ──
   30 38 16 34 5

4. Circumference
   ── ── ── ── ──
   2 27 9 14 24

5. Norwegian, for one
   ── ── ── ── ── ── ── ──
   12 37 31 21 8 39 32 17

6. Strolls
   ── ── ── ── ──
   20 4 28 26 19

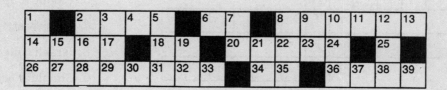

PUZZLE 603

ACROSS
1. City transports
5. Boxing match
9. Stuff
13. Leave out
14. In addition
15. Mortal
17. Grain bin
18. Shed tears
19. Foolish
20. Journey
22. Loss of memory
24. Alexander Hamilton's bill
25. Mist
27. Posed
28. Have obligations
30. Leak
32. Viper
35. Distant
36. Supplement, with out
37. Dot
40. Delicate
43. Dispute
45. Put
46. "___ Day Will Come"
47. First number
48. Spring vegetable
49. Wharf
51. Gear
52. Jolt
55. Percolate
57. Bustle
59. Modifier
62. Arachnid
65. Engine
66. Marine bird
69. Mosaic piece
70. Groom's counterpart
71. Mint
72. Dressed
73. Inquisitive
74. Words
75. Egg layers

DOWN
1. Price
2. Mideast prince
3. Two-sided
4. Cooker
5. Cry
6. Bullring bravo
7. Manipulate
8. November's birthstone
9. Goatee's site
10. Mystical verse
11. Gather
12. Craze
16. Tidy
21. Finale
23. Gauge
25. Recreational trek
26. Mimic
28. Switch position
29. Distort
31. Free
33. Saratoga Springs, e.g.
34. Each
38. Alligator's cousin
39. Card game
41. Space
42. Drink cube
43. Witticism
44. Appendage
46. Unclose, poetically
50. Syncopated talk
52. Doorway post
53. Decorate
54. Proportion
56. Standing
58. Large rut
60. Shells
61. Low card
62. Transmitted
63. Spirit
64. Cincinnati ballplayers
67. Caviar
68. Cancel

PUZZLE 604 — Fore 'n' Aft

Enter the answers to the clues into their correspondingly numbered boxes. The words will begin or end with a letter in WINTERIZE. When finished, the first letters of the words on the left side and the last letters of the words on the right side will spell out a name.

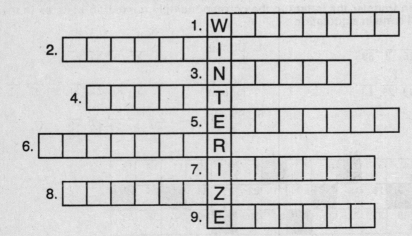

1. "I Was a Teen-age ___"
2. Whirlpool bath
3. Bee attractor
4. Charm
5. Type of coffee
6. Casino employee
7. Narrow strip of land
8. Israeli collective farm
9. Shoulder ornament

504

CIRCULAR CROSSWORD

To complete this Circular puzzle fill in the answers to the Around clues in a clockwise direction. For the Radial clues move from the outside to the inside.

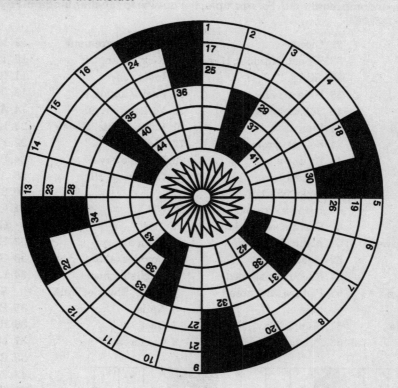

AROUND (Clockwise)

1. Capture
5. Foolish
9. Gambit
13. Fragment
17. Abodes
19. Inventor Howe
21. Paradigm
23. Preferences
25. Needle
26. Fashion
27. Foreboding
28. Realm
29. New York island
31. Type of club
33. Reserved
35. Singer Laine
37. Placid
38. Arab ruler
39. Aspen sites
40. Author Turgenev
41. Indicate
42. Issel and Rather
43. Tantrum
44. Wisdom

RADIAL (Out to In)

1. Sovereignty
2. Milne character
3. Collect
4. Bedevil
5. Shield
6. Solo
7. Evergreen
8. Earmarked
9. Moneygrubbers
10. Exalted composition
11. Peddles
12. Tripods
13. Red wine
14. Charters
15. Alibi ____
16. Cosmetic stick
18. Goggle
20. Alabama city
22. Unsatisfactory item
24. Barrage
30. Reception
32. German article
34. News org.
36. Keen perception

PUZZLE 606

Some of the clues in this crossword are Triple Play clues. They consist of three words separated by commas. The answer to a Triple Play clue is a word that can precede or follow each of the three words to form a common phrase, name, or compound word. For example, the answer to "Shelter, Income, Payer" is TAX (Tax shelter, Income tax, Taxpayer).

ACROSS

1. Cloak
5. Goblet part
9. Nonexploding firework
12. Story, Cut, Hand
13. Peel
14. Composer Thomas ____
15. Body's trunk
16. Land measure
17. Uncouth
18. Deco, Work, Nouveau
19. Tie, Lace, Line
21. Quake
23. Fiscal, Book, End
25. Positively!
26. Charged particle
27. "____ to Joy"
29. Closer
33. Wheat, Number, Hog
36. "King ____"
39. Hole in one
40. Subscribe again
41. Fury
42. Solemn promises
44. Be unwell
45. Once again
46. Make fuddled
47. Using a crowbar
50. Certain evergreen
51. Actor Van Cleef
52. Health resort
54. Racetrack-shaped
58. Picture, Sickness, Less
61. Spinal, Wood, Rip
63. Pub quaff
64. Gumbo ingredient
65. Kick, Cloth, Off
67. Inert gas
69. Praise highly
70. Yorkshire river
71. Robin, Table, House
72. Pigment
73. Father's boys
74. Cap, Deep, High

DOWN

1. Task
2. Main artery
3. Couples: abbr.
4. English school
5. Outer, Shuttle, Walk
6. Nails
7. Goof
8. Conference
9. Major, Snare, Ear
10. Take apart
11. Rein, Hound, Stalker
12. Put, Main, Over
14. Amphitheater
20. Lash, Private, Ball
22. Fish eggs
24. Play, Model, Conflict
28. A.M. condensation
30. Ship deserters
31. Chamber, Location, Gram
32. Home, Easy, Room
33. Gift, Around, Up
34. Loom, Apparent, Ship
35. Exclusively
36. Relatives
37. Mine yield
38. Brand, Born, Comer
42. Japanese sash
43. Flight prefix
45. Committee's schedules
48. Homeric epic
49. ____-Darwinism
50. Away, So, Fetched
52. Contempt
53. Vatican leaders
55. Unclear
56. Leave, Stand, Let
57. Give temporarily
58. Shape
59. All right
60. Love, Blue, Hearted
62. Horse, Ages, Continent
66. ____ Grande
68. Actor/director Howard

MOVIES & TELEVISION

ACROSS

1. "A ____ Is Waiting"
6. "____ Lisa"
10. "There ____ a crooked man . . ."
13. "Easy ____"
14. Kirk Douglas TV film
15. "The ____ on Thelma Jordan"
16. Rub out
17. "Klute" star
19. Horror film director Craven
20. Dan ____ of
    "Cagney and Lacey"
22. Spaces
23. Sun. lecture
24. "____ of Love" (TV film)
25. Roger ____ of
    "Magnum, PI"
29. "____ Match" (TV film)
34. "Happiness ____"
35. "Up in ____"
36. "____: A Dog"
37. Actresses Woods and Grey
38. "The ____" (Jerry Lewis film)
40. Italian resort
41. Food particle
42. "Saturday Night ____"
43. "____ on Sunday"
44. Harry of
    "60 Minutes"
46. "____ Times"
47. "Butterflies ____ Free"
48. Deface
49. Bobby ____
52. "A ____ With a View"
53. Lamb's mom
56. Actor in "Havana"
59. "____ Morning"
61. "Empty ____"
62. "The ____ of Adrian
    Messenger"
63. Simon and Diamond
64. "____ in the Hole"
65. "Peter Pan" pirate
66. "____ Barbara" (TV soap)

DOWN

1. Gang
2. "This Gun for ____"
3. Lupino and Cantor
4. ____ Paul Trio
5. "____ to Kill"
6. "____ Dad"
7. Actor Sharif
8. "____ Stop New York"
9. Peer Gynt's mother
10. "Falcon Crest" product
11. Robert ____ of
    "Rhapsody in Blue"
12. "China ____"
15. Singer Fabian ____
18. "The Three ____
    of Eve"
21. "____ Babu Riba"
24. "This Is the ____"
25. Estate dwelling
26. Chicago airport
27. Actress Berger
28. "The ____ Vegas Story"
29. Spud
30. "48 ____"
31. Oyl of "Popeye"
32. Actor George or Michael
33. Decorate
38. "The Trail of the
    Lonesome ____"
39. Street: abbr.
40. ____ Zeppelin (rock group)
42. Actress Luft
43. Fell and Bates
45. Simon Templar a.k.a The ____
46. ____ Tse-tung
48. "The Count of ____ Cristo"
49. Actress Wynter
50. Guinness or Baldwin
51. Level
52. "____ and Shine"
53. Moran or Gray
54. Basketball's Chamberlain
55. Adamson's lioness
57. "Kidnapped" author's inits.
58. Stanley or Novak
60. Swee' ____ (son of 31 Down)

PUZZLE 608

ACROSS

1. Woodland abode
6. Annoy
9. Martini garnish
10. New York canal
11. Dishes
12. Time-consuming
13. Subways' kin
14. Marionette controllers
16. Game fish
18. Turf
19. I'm all ___!
21. Superlative
24. Knock
26. Like a lawn at dawn
28. Marches in review
32. Golf implement
33. Bakery mainstay
34. Emulates Hans Brinker
36. Show the way
37. Weary
38. "To ___ is human . . ."
39. Pigpens

DOWN

1. Lassie, e.g.
2. 49th state
3. Jot
4. Actor Burl
5. They're for the birds
6. Steel metal
7. Wedding item
8. Beer barrels
10. Omitted phonetically
11. Vim
15. Mr. Reiner
17. Task
20. Melancholy
22. Couch
23. Certain woolens
25. Bothers
27. ___ sirree!
28. Vaulter's need
29. Declare
30. Admiral or echelon
31. Comic routine
35. Mr. Onassis

PUZZLE 609

ACROSS

1. ___ the line (behave)
4. Went by SST
8. Highway approach
12. Samovar
13. Enthusiastic review
14. Cleveland's lake
15. Has faith
17. River deposit
18. Neck of the woods
19. Court events
21. Canine sounds
23. Chief
24. Sets up
25. Attire
29. Summer drink
30. Rural buildings
31. Bard's before
32. Body talk
34. Lowdown sort
35. Goals
36. Archetype
37. Invent
40. It's a ___!
41. Certain paintings
42. Tidy quality
46. Empty
47. Otherwise
48. Small drink
49. Heavy metal
50. Tears
51. Porker's home

DOWN

1. Vat
2. Mined find
3. Blows up
4. Liberates
5. Molten rock
6. Night prior
7. Horse operas
8. Live
9. Opera highlight
10. Flour source
11. Favorites
16. Angers
20. Ewes' mates
21. Boast
22. Military sidekick
23. Jack rabbits
25. Rose tender
26. Unnecessary
27. Maple, e.g.
28. Convince
30. Baseball maneuver
33. Kidded
34. ___ of plenty
36. Little bits
37. Wind
38. Go on horseback
39. Singer Fitzgerald
40. Pant
43. Actor Wallach
44. Pose
45. Secret agent

PUZZLE 610

• TEARJERKERS •

ACROSS

1. U.S. diplomat Whitelaw
5. Lexicon component
9. Actor West
13. Slow, to Bach
18. South American mountains
20. Medicinal plant
21. Small inlet
22. Oscar, for one
23. Rope snare
24. Harvest
25. In the rigging near the deck
26. Hen coop, in Dundee
27. Lillian Roth's story on film
30. Destroys
31. Regrets
32. Tart
33. "St. Elmo's ____"
34. Obscures
37. Dirties
39. Flock
40. Cleopatra's snake
43. Writer James
44. Author Nevil
45. Cup-of-coffee additive
46. Born
47. Sentimental writer
50. Bucket
51. Of a cereal grain
53. Aunt, to Pedro
54. Mimic
55. Canter, as a horse
56. Oblique
57. Practitioner of: suffix
58. U.S. physicist
59. Time unit
60. Female ruff
61. Solar disk
63. Julie London hit song
67. Corn porridge
71. Profound reverence
73. Sea eagles
74. To the sheltered side
76. Golf standard
77. Stock units
80. Those for
81. Perry Mason's challenge
82. Coach Parseghian
83. Multitude
84. Tail shakes
85. Campaign slogan
87. Provide weapons to
88. Tranquillity
90. Carpenter's tool
92. Pump or oxford
93. ". . . merry month of ____"
94. Knot
95. Enticer
96. Subjoin
98. Sharpen
99. School dance
100. Olive genus
101. Assertions
104. Graceful trees
110. Cheerful musical work
111. March flyer
112. Actor Rip
113. Taut
114. More mature
115. Iridescent gem
116. Fencing sword
117. Eagle's nest
118. Out-of-date
119. Depend
120. Bambi, for one
121. Corded fabric

DOWN

1. Princess of India
2. Carbon compound
3. Item of worship
4. Espies
5. Toad features
6. Bread spread
7. Wander
8. Sediment
9. Mite
10. Grief
11. Admit
12. Kitten sound
13. Tearful
14. Mindful
15. Critic's review
16. Grating
17. Pindar's products
19. Immunization agent
28. Affirmative
29. Actor's part
30. The Destroyer, in Hinduism
33. Sense
34. Corsican seaport
35. Selfish one
36. Verbal contest
37. Amber wine
38. Wilder's "____ Town"
39. French cheese
40. Squared column
41. Observed
42. Confined
44. Ox
45. Italian resort island
48. Writer Fleming
49. Ginger and cloves
50. Streams forth
52. Pub drinks
55. Prospective creditors' offerings
56. Apprehend
59. Deli sandwiches
62. Balm of old
64. Join together
65. Unoccupied
66. Make happy
68. "Fort ____, The Bronx"
69. Cookery chestnut
70. Supplicated
72. "____, My Lady"
75. Conger
77. Pretense
78. Israeli dance
79. Military branch
80. Horse's gait
84. Walk in water
85. Unit in music
86. Trellis
89. Time periods
90. Drop heavily
91. Restricted
95. Without restraint
96. The Greatest
97. Greek shield, of yore
98. Conceals
99. Corolla part
100. Proprietor
101. Equestrian's prod
102. "Damn Yankees" temptress
103. No ifs, ____, or buts
104. Dab, as tears
105. Slangy refusal
106. Favor, of yore
107. Fairy-tale monster
108. Cat-o'-nine-tails
109. Put your foot down
111. Hebrew measure

Note to Solvers: This Crossword does not have hints such as "2 wds." and "hyph."

509

PUZZLE 611

ACROSS
1. Fit together
5. Water barrier
8. Goad
12. Scotto highlight
13. Conceit
14. Wander
15. Rivulet
16. Sweet sound
17. Adam's home
18. Bank employee
20. Hinders
22. Be in debt
23. Collection
24. "____ Friends" (1983 Taylor film)
28. Tuneful
32. Exist
33. Tree fluid
35. Actress Merkel
36. Excellent!
39. Dress, e.g.
42. Fuel
44. Foot part
45. Take umbrage at
48. Lose weight
52. River of England
53. GI's address
55. Golf club
56. Penny
57. Managed
58. Matured
59. Work units
60. City railroads
61. Sparks and Beatty

DOWN
1. Store
2. Pennsylvania port
3. Window edge
4. Sanctify
5. Edicts
6. Past
7. States of mind
8. Attractive
9. Took the train
10. Atop
11. Lairs
19. Cote mama
21. Slippery fish
24. Sack
25. Goof
26. Golf mound
27. Pester
29. Regret
30. Small hotel
31. Feline
34. Customers
37. Representatives
38. Beach color
40. Caviar
41. Highway strip
43. Gaze
45. Contest
46. At any time
47. Tune
49. Encourage
50. College girl
51. Ceases
54. Buddy

PUZZLE 612

ACROSS
1. Bullets, for short
5. Shriver of tennis
8. Sprint
12. Lug
13. Adam's ____
14. Hodgepodge
15. Water suppliers: 2 wds.
18. "You ____ Your Life"
19. Join in wedlock
20. Pacino and Waxman
21. Radiate
23. Mork's planet
25. Seer's cards
27. Bored out
31. Troubadour Burl
32. Fan dancer Sally
33. West Point students
36. Mixtures
38. Harden
39. Hollywood's Barrett
40. Billy ____ Williams
43. Of the ear
45. Money man: abbr.
48. Lawyer: hyph.
51. ____ Hari
52. Mao ____-tung
53. Actor Auberjonois
54. Speak sloppily
55. Norm: abbr.
56. Caesar's date with destiny

DOWN
1. Melville captain
2. Stable mate
3. Grumbled quietly
4. Bravo, in Spain
5. Whitewashes
6. Jai ____
7. Teacher
8. "I, Jane ____"
9. ____ breve
10. Window ledge
11. Cartwright son
16. Union or zoot
17. "The Way We ____"
22. Cager Malone
24. Ballerina Kane
25. "____ Tac Dough"
26. Hollywood Gardner
28. Shackled
29. Terminate
30. Tooth man: abbr.
34. Rend
35. Knievel's jobs
36. Heehawed
37. Ms. Falana
40. Weirs
41. And others: abbr.
42. "____, Brute": 2 wds.
44. Pause
46. Window glass
47. Flabbergasts
49. Sculler's tool
50. Three: prefix

MOVIES AND TELEVISION

PUZZLE 613

ACROSS

1. "Planet of the ____"
5. "State ____"
9. "Soap" family name
13. TV host Garroway
14. Avant-____
15. Step ____!
16. Actress MacGraw et al.
17. "Hill Street Blues" actor
19. Comedienne May
21. Join
22. Wilbur Post's horse
23. Actress Sothern
24. "____ to My Heart"
27. Hall of "Coming to America"
31. Forum greeting
32. Annie's dog
34. "____ on Her Fingers"
36. Chip's buddy
38. Lorenzo ____ of "Falcon Crest"
40. Drill
41. Ludden or Funt
43. "Fancy-____"
45. Gp. for Charlie Moore?
46. "The ____ Blade"
48. Certify
50. High school VIPs
51. Ontario Indian
52. Actress LuPone
55. "Nashville" director
58. "Night Court" judge
61. "____ Dirty"
63. "____ Desire"
64. Map within a map
65. "Too ____ the Hero"
66. Chicago district
67. Erwin and Gilliam
68. Sonny Shroyer show

DOWN

1. Susan Hayward film
2. "____ Rider"
3. "____ Under the Sun"
4. Big Bird's street
5. Lost strength
6. "The Long ____"
7. Director May Park
8. Summer TV fare
9. Singer Tennille
10. Subj. for Doogie Howser
11. Wheel covering
12. DDE's command
14. Keaton film, with "The"
18. "____ Sanctum"
20. Cleopatra's maid
23. Nordic
24. Actress Thompson
25. Footballs
26. A Reese
27. Elliot Weston, e.g.
28. Penpoint
29. Hole ____
30. Fairy tale villains
33. Neck parts
35. Usher's find
37. Always, in verse
39. Young actress
42. "____ Habits"
44. Manuscript mark
47. Cary Grant film
49. Shirley ____
51. Walking aids
52. ____ Alto
53. Singer Guthrie
54. "The ____ to Bountiful"
56. King of comedy
57. Defense alliance initials
58. Linden of "Barney Miller"
59. Dynamite letters
60. Columbus sch.
62. "____, Giorgio"

511

PUZZLE 614

• JAZZ IT UP •

ACROSS

1. Bivalve
5. Jewels
9. Hatteras, e.g.
13. Preserve
17. Yorkshire river
18. Actual
19. Wing-shaped
20. Trudge
21. ___ Hari
22. Scat singer
25. Kings' sons
27. Faux pas
28. Panorama
29. Change for publication
30. Advantage
31. Solar disk
33. Confused
35. French holy women: abbr.
36. Tenor sax player
40. Cowardly Lion portrayer
41. Mast support
42. Colleagues
43. Through
44. Wood sorrel
45. Agreement
46. Dark-colored
47. High-school student
48. Rose high
50. Spotless
51. Actor Peter ___
52. Composer and bandleader
56. Tribal symbol
59. Pastries
60. Consumes
64. Arabian gulf
65. Court actions
67. Busy as ___
68. Rubber tree
69. Sawbuck
70. Sources of poi
71. Legal claim
72. At rest
73. Piano great
75. Actress Cheryl ___
76. South American range
77. Tumult
78. Gown
79. Lawyer: abbr.
80. Pertaining to a region
83. Average
84. Mocker
87. Trumpet innovator
91. Provoke
92. Merit
93. Pump, e.g.
94. Fencing blade
95. Enlisted persons: abbr.
96. Greek god of love
97. Swine
98. Lurch
99. Freighter

DOWN

1. Summer vacation spot
2. Fibber
3. Famous clarinetist
4. Stroll about
5. Hail
6. Long fish
7. Bad: pref.
8. Slur
9. "The ___ Mutiny"
10. Choir voice
11. Poet Octavio ___
12. Unit of energy
13. Resilience
14. Word of woe
15. Electrical unit
16. Norse literary work
23. Mists
24. Ties
26. Spy org.
30. And so forth
31. Fits to ___
32. Mountain lake
33. Thanks ___!
34. Mexican dish
35. Digging tool
36. "___ Days in May"
37. At any time
38. Layer
39. Western author Grey
41. Look for
42. Louvre site
45. Cask
46. Reigns
47. Singer Tennille
49. First garden
50. Works at
51. Place for an earring
53. Type of salts
54. Jeered
55. Federal agents
56. See you later!
57. German river
58. Outdoor shelter
61. Drumming great
62. She, in Rouen
63. Looks at
65. Roman statesman
66. Stuck in ___
67. Helper
70. Pursues
71. Worker
72. Hospital employees
74. Retinues
75. Mislaid
76. Supped
78. American Beauties, e.g.
79. Heavenly being
80. To the sheltered side
81. Bellow
82. Continental prefix
83. Urban problem
84. Snicker ___
85. "The Time Machine" people
86. In the order given: abbr.
88. Pulverized lava
89. Greek letter
90. Unlock, in poetry

512

ACROSS

1. Amusing
4. Spoils
8. Caustic remark
12. Style
16. Ever and ____ (occasionally)
18. All: pref.
19. Salmon
20. Currier and ____
21. Craze
22. Levitate
23. Aloud
24. Groupies
25. Brawn
27. Tipsy reef?
30. Skier's tow
32. Cravat
33. Whiskey
34. African range
37. Glacial ridges
39. Galleries
43. Approach
44. Competitors
45. Painter John ____
46. Likely
48. Pattern
50. Walk clumsily
51. ____ Luis
52. Disrespectful
53. Paris river
54. Depleted
56. Heavy weight
57. Playwright Oscar ____
58. Yalie
59. Rendezvous
62. Glass bead
63. Outstanding
67. Baseballer Durocher
68. Campus buildings
69. Feature
70. Raucous cry
71. Oklahoma town
72. Dory
73. Skip
74. Dive
76. Marshal Dillon
77. Low-lying land
78. Catch
79. "Native ____"
80. Expressed admiration
82. Colorful accessory?
86. Shangri-la
90. Witticisms
91. Islamic prince
92. Just
95. African gully
96. Mountain's melody
97. Apollo's mother
98. Reverse
99. Empty, in math
100. Slim
101. Mispronounce
102. City on the Rhone
103. Bandleader Brown

DOWN

1. Till
2. Two-toed sloth
3. Holiday potions
4. Peloponnesus
5. Friend, to Chantal
6. Hosp. employees
7. Naps
8. Teacake
9. Parliament member
10. King of Israel
11. Earth's "hat"
12. Vexed
13. Racetrack
14. Reject
15. Road turn
17. Asphalt ade?
26. Units of wt.
28. Melody
29. Baseball's Nolan ____
31. Haley work
34. Against
35. Pour
36. Tiffany product
38. Cathedral town
39. Isolated
40. Eternal City
41. Comfort
42. Bridge part
44. Mythological figure
45. Playground item
47. Small fry
49. Plunder
50. Prison pads
53. Greek letter
54. Rosebud, e.g.
55. Gossip's pad?
57. Sausage
58. French state
59. What nurses give
60. Gain
61. Caterwaul
62. Trunk
63. Military alliance
64. Bean
65. Blue dye
66. Nerve network
68. Oaf
69. Sultry
71. Govt. agent
72. Pernicious
75. In ____ (together)
76. Me, to Miss Piggy
77. Solidify
79. Razor sharpener
81. Large lake
82. Contest
83. Muslim leader
84. Sacred mountain
85. At ____ end
87. Artist Cezanne
88. Slothful
89. Feels poorly
90. Hairstylist's goo
93. Some
94. Altar words

PUZZLE 616

• PROMINENT PERSONS •

ACROSS

1. Cake portion
5. Asian bigwig
9. ____ Rabbit
13. Scuttles
17. Headdress
18. Type of forest
19. Hoarfrost
20. Statute
22. "Carnal Knowledge" actress
24. "The Barefoot Contessa" actress
26. Wood sorrel
27. Spirit
28. Tips
29. Some
30. Clockmaker Thomas
32. Drubs
35. Texas attraction
37. French tea
38. Nasser's gp.
40. Cookie
41. Memo
42. Faux ____
43. Jack, the joker
46. Comedian Jimmy ____
48. Beat up
51. Football player
53. High notes
54. Ballerina Alicia ____
55. Picnic drink
56. Western Indians
58. Trouble
59. Matted fabric
60. Soak, as flax
61. Impair
62. ____ Peninsula, Alaska
64. Throngs
66. Period
67. Shade
68. "Crime ____ Punishment"
69. Armed conflict
72. Roofing materials
75. John Jacob and family
78. Shade tree
81. Stout
82. Center
83. Ad ____
85. Exchange
86. Open field
87. Exuberant
89. Sculptor Lorado ____
90. Schoolbook
92. Cuddle
93. Actor Peter ____
96. Scornful
97. Reef
98. Ponder
99. Sortie
101. Metallic element
102. Bottom edge
103. Compresses
104. Dummy Mortimer ____
106. Headliner
109. ____ Aviv
110. Whittle
111. Did farm work
113. Sooner than
114. "The Maltese Falcon" actor
118. Oliver Hardy's buddy
121. Ski locale
122. Responsibility
123. Tralee's locale
124. Deviate
125. Clip
126. Captures
127. Joins
128. Author John ____ and family

DOWN

1. Because
2. "Madame X" star
3. Fortify
4. Ovine sounds
5. Disputes
6. "The Wizard of Oz" star
7. Speed
8. Opposite of syn.
9. Bikini part
10. Miss., e.g.
11. Flow out
12. Prevailing system
13. Possessive pronoun
14. Peculiar
15. American songstress
16. Play part
17. New Mexico resort
21. Attempt
23. Actor Morrow
25. Finnish port
31. Abhor
33. Greek letter
34. Preserves, e.g.
35. Chronicles
36. Realtor's land divisions
37. Take to ____ (reprimand)
39. Uncle ____
42. Roles
43. Steamer, e.g.
44. La Scala production
45. Charge
47. Clay, today
48. "I Love Lucy" star
49. Eternally
50. Computer fodder
52. Funnyman Bob ____
54. Actress Audrey ____
57. Fry
59. Church basins
63. Female ruff
65. Possesses
69. Caution
70. Wings
71. Popular comedian
72. Like a krait
73. ____ wolf
74. Wraps
75. Role players
76. Gabs
77. Worn out
78. "Paper Courtship" actress
79. Nasty glance
80. Actress Martin
84. ____-color (risque)
88. News brief
89. Chat
91. Garlands
93. Swiss city
94. Went swiftly
95. Bruce Willis film
98. Strand
100. Nonworking insects
102. "High ____"
103. Crony
105. Neighbor of Md.
107. Zones
108. Depend
109. County parts: abbr.
110. Get ready
112. Track event
115. Pointed roof
116. Depression
117. Road curve
118. Suture
119. Ascot
120. Actress Hagen

PUZZLE 1

```
CALIF TATS  PREP  TAFT
ALONE EIRE  REPO  EMIR
ILONA STORM IBIS  AERY
RESORTS TRAUMA ¢ERS
ONE¢  REB AGNATE UPPER
 SPARE  NITER  MOORE
TONAL ADS ITES  COOLED
ISOBASE EFFS  CORNY
CARRIE ALOI  MOTS  GAB
 ONT PER¢AGES  GOGO
BERATE ANGORAS SCONES
EGAD  FREEBORN  OAT
TOM ROOT  SANE UPTAKE
 PEEVE  HERE  PROOFED
UGANDA SHES TRI TATAS
TANGO ICONS  AZTEC
ASTIN NORRIS TAR ¢AUR
 NEW¢URIONS  REPULSE
CARE HIRO NICER RATED
ABIE EVER  PALO OTARY
NOOR TEDS  ERIS  PERSE
```

PUZZLE 5

```
CLIP ARTE PAVE  FIRM
HERA DOOM EGAL  IDEA
OVAL OMNI TANK  LENT
PINETREESTATE  ELSIE
  TIN   SALE   UNI
COPTS CRAG  CROPPER
OBOE TOUR BLOIS  ILO
TAR PINEYWOODS  SNAP
ENCORES  ALGA  TEENY
 USED MINEO BANC
TOPSY WILD  PANDORA
APIA PINEAPPLES  NIP
BAN BENTS ROAR  DECO
SHEARED  MITT  VISAS
  YAK  DEEM   AIM
MOSEY LODGEPOLEPINE
ALTA HIND VEIL  LOON
PLAY AMOI ARLO  ETON
SAGE MARE LEST  SANS
```

PUZZLE 2

```
SCAM SNOOT ERSE AMMAN
PALO LIVRE VENT LIEGE
ACID ONEAL AREA PSEUD
THEENTERTAINER BETTES
SENSE STEED  ADMIRE
 TEA  OLD  INTREAT
THEODDCOUPLE ASS RACE
HAG DANTE ATES ROTOS
ELAS ANTON PARI ABORT
OFDOOM OPAL SON JENNY
 MAST ILEUM GEAR
CAKES RIA OKAS ASTRAL
ABOLT INNS ANEST SINE
ROTIS BASE SIETE DON
TUCK OUS THEAPARTMENT
ATHEART ISA  YEA
 INDEED REACT RILLS
MANTIS MYSISTEREILEEN
IDAHO MILO KARAT EVOE
SATON ALLA ELECT RENE
TROTS DESK RESTE SEER
```

PUZZLE 6

```
SPARE SCAR RANT BELOW
ALLEE PARE OLEO ELUDE
WOODLDEMCOMMFOREHICEL
STE RAPS EARN LATEST
 PIER ACNE MANE
ADDERS TALC DIET  TVA
CORRESPALMABSCSECDIAM
ROOFS LIES AMES HELLO
INNO DALE SLID LITTER
DEER UNO SALT FINESSE
 MANKREMBEHTAMAR
SENATES DIRT HUB MISS
TAUNTS HULA COCO IRAE
ARECA PUCE SORE INANE
REVERLEGASCCONTFRIDEP
EDE ERST LAPS LONERS
 KINE IRAN LONG
TOWARD FOUR TIES  SON
ABORESOUNSOROTASTOARO
LOREN NEAT ORES ALICE
KEENE ALLY DOME PEDAL
```

PUZZLE 3

```
MEEK SABU ESME SPARK
ALTI URANO SCAM LANAI
GANT MORAL TORO ASTIN
IHATETOBUYNEWCLOTHING
 ITEM  MARL  UREA
NOWOR PEPYS AMBS OFF
IOWAN SOLI SNEE ARAL
FOLKSLOOKATMEANDSMILE
ISEE INNO HADIT CENSE
SET NANA CITES RANGER
 DENY RACER GOLD
GARAGE TICKS ALGA MAI
OZONE PRATE OBOE BANG
BUTEVERYNINEYEARSORSO
EROS LEST MELT TONER
LER SETT SNARL MOTEL
 HOME MIEN SEAS
THEYFINDIMBACKINSTYLE
RIVET DALI TENET RUIN
ALINE ELEA EDINA ALAS
MOLAR DERN ETAL PERE
```

PUZZLE 7

```
FARAD MENU HAHA   CPA
AGILE ALAN OLIVE SRAS
WETBLANKET NIPANDTUCK
NEE INGE IDEES DIODES
 EVILS DERN REVUES
CHINESE OILS  COMET
REVERE PEA ALAI STAR
AMORY CARRYATORCH OTT
TARO MANY ERAT OVULE
ELY DINO BREL PRECIS
 THECENCI ALTHOUGH
OTOOLE ANTS OARS ART
NEWEL URGE ERNE ONER
TRE ABUMPONALOG MIDGE
ORRS ARPS SIB SINGES
 ACRES SIRE CANTORS
 SALARY ATOP RAGES
HALIDE AMINO ADAR BAA
EVENSTEVEN RINGSABELL
MERE TWEET TREE LOYAL
SST ERRS SEER SASSY
```

PUZZLE 4

```
ROAR READE GEESE SLAV
ELBE ELDER ALDER AOLA
CLOSEGLENN ROGERSWILL
AIR RUINS PAPER EERIE
PETRELS PAGE ARDENT
 ENA ATONE PACA
CONNORSMIKE RICHIRENE
AVIEW AIDE HASTE OMOO
MACE GLEE DEBTS SAUNA
ELK COE COMBO NISSEN
 CHAMBERLAINWILT
SAILED ALIEN IDO TIS
ALTER SKIED DELE PAST
IDEA OLEOS CALC WALLA
CARNEYART CALLOWAYCAB
 LEGS LANES ARE
MOHAIR PYRE STRETCH
OLAND ALICE RAISE RHO
WILDERGENE GIBSONHOOT
EVER PEACE ASIAN APSE
DERE MEDES REELS HEEL
```

PUZZLE 8

```
AGENT RECAP  CAKES
BOXER IRADE  AGATE
BUTTE CATASTROPHE
ODE MAES MEAT   PEP
TARPONS WATT  CARS
 MART  MANATEE
CHINS PART  ENDEAR
LENT DRIP  ORIENTE
ALA PROD PIED  TIN
SETTEES WILD  MELD
SNEAKS LASS  HURTS
 BESEECH  DOLT
SPAS EGGS  RELEASE
EAR PROA RELY  ITT
PROPOSITION DINAH
ASSET SENAT  ADELE
LEERS TSARS  YODEL
```

PUZZLE 9

```
HARD  APA  SEAL
EWER  ROB  ERNE
RANUNCULACEAE
DRAMA   NEXT
SEN  COD  EIDER
     CRUSE  OILY
FERRET   BUNGLE
AREA   STOSS
TRICE  ENE  ALP
     KEEN  RADIO
REPERCUSSIONS
OVER  CRI  TREE
WINS  LEN  SEND
```

PUZZLE 10

```
   PLOD   ELMS
   CRAVE  LIONS
  LEGERDEMAIN
YES  NIECE  POW
EATS  VET  MERE
TROOPER  DARED
     FED  PUG
STRAP  SLEIGHT
ERAS  DOE  CLUE
WEB  SEDAN  ALA
  ABRACADABRA
  DIANA  EPEES
   THEY  DEED
```

PUZZLE 11

```
STEP   ERA  ORAL
ARLO DELIS  MEGA
LEAP ERODE  APES
EAT CLAP  ARREST
STEEL  SEW  USA
   LUTE ESE  TAP
LEASER LEND  ELL
EASE EVADE  AREA
ESS  SNIP ARISEN
STE  ADE  SKIN
  RAM DAM  OTTER
BUTLER MINT  ALI
ASIT APPLE  ALIT
REVE PILED  DOTE
NEER  TEE  ONES
```

PUZZLE 12

1. Knock, 2. Plump, 3. Tempt, 4. Dozed,
5. Recur, 6. Cynic, 7. Libel, 8. Outdo, 9.
Eagle, 10. Hitch.

PUZZLE 13

```
STEP FRAT PLAIT
TARE LULU RONDO
IRIS AGAR OUTER
RACEAGAINSTTIME
     TIP  ITE
AHEADOFONESTIME
PAP ALAR  TONES
ANSA EDGAR  MUTT
ROOTS   ALEC REE
TIMEONONESHANDS
     MOP  TEN
INTHENICKOFTIME
CORED NEAR LOOS
OPERA ERNE ENOS
NEEDY DEED RATE
```

PUZZLE 14

BIRDS: Dodo, Eagle, Cormorant, Owl, Robin.

CLOTHING: Dinner jacket, Evening gown, Cloak, Overcoat, Raincoat.

DOGS: Dachshund, English setter, Collie, Otterhound, Rhodesian ridgeback.

ISLANDS: Dominica, Eleuthera, Crete, Okinawa, Ryukyu.

SCIENTISTS: Darwin, Einstein, Curie, Oppenheimer, Roentgen.

PUZZLE 15

```
FACE WRAP ROTE UPON
ELLA HULA ENID NEMO
LAIR ETAS DOES FRAN
LIONHEARTED REDLINE
  EEL MEDEA LII
PERSIST INGE GNATS
ODETS EASTERN ECLAT
DEN TIARA DAN SHARE
SNOB TRILL  ARTISAN
   OPS LEAVE USN
STELLAR SAGAS GARB
KORDA APR LASER MOO
ARIAS PRESENT ITALY
TOAST TOPE INVITES
   BEN PREEN OER
QUARREL INDOMITABLE
URSA PUNS IRIS DOOR
AGES ALIA CITE ERIN
YEAS LULL TATS SANE
```

PUZZLE 16

```
SCRAM COMA SALUTE
STEELE AVER CRANING
HANDEL NEAT ROMANCE
ORTS BRAND GASP MON
AVE SAID DOPE  DIRT
TERSE MACHINE LINER
 PALMS HONE COMEDY
MAINLY FUME  MOLE
ABED STORE PULL SAG
LUCY TRANSPOSE SILO
ETE BEAM TRUST PLEA
  HARP WEIR TRIVET
TIMELY BIAS  SEINE
AREAL SANDMAN VERSE
CELT SERE MORE  SER
OLA HEWN PROBE STAR
MANMADE PAIR BECAME
ANGULAR OLLA ELATED
DEMONS PEEL  LINEN
```

PUZZLE 17

```
DRIFT CHAR GALE  DIS
RODEO RUNE EBON  IRA
OVERT ENID LENT  NEW
PESO OPT UNIT INANE
  CEDE  SCAD SCARED
DOCILE SEEP  DEEM
ALOOF GLAD TOW ECRU
MENU FAIR ROW ISLES
  SWORD DARNED ATE
FAD HOD RUM PIE YES
IDA ELEVEN  MORAL
SATIN NIP ROUE IOWA
TRAM JIM BOOR EMBER
 PROA TOAD AVOIDS
DEFEAT KIND  ESAU
EXALT LIMA PRO SAAR
GEN HOOT NOON FIRMA
ARC ERSE ZANE ONION
STY RATS ARES BEAST
```

PUZZLE 18

```
LAMP RERAN SPATE HALE
ALIA EVADE ARIES ALAS
SIXTHSENSE FIRSTCLASS
EVERYONE DEMIT  HORSE
RESOLUTE PER EASE YON
NAN  BUN  STORE
SOFA DRIER TEA  STOA
AGOG ONESTEP  RATHER
TRUE OSE EAGER SERIF
EER EMIRS BOLE STEEL
  SEVENTH  TWOTIME
ACTOR IOUS SABER SOW
BROOK ATTIC RET PONE
EERIER SECONDS  YMCA
TAEL ORB CUSEC REEK
  EATER HOT  OKA
CPA BASE TAA HOMEMADE
HOUSE PAVOS APPRISES
EIGHTSIDED FIVEANDTEN
ASEA ARENA ACORN ARME
TERM TEDDY DECAY LOSS
```

PUZZLE 19

```
RAMP GOAT LAUD BABE
IDEA INCH ORNE ODIN
BOWLOFCHERRIES NINO
  LUTE SEND PASTEL
ABETS DIVE  MICA
SMOTE FUSS BASTION
LOW REED COPES  RAW
ARLO DUSTBOWL  CAVE
WEEKEND RANEE MANET
  DATA SURFS BORG
SLOPE OPERA SINGERS
RAVI ROSEBOWL  OBOL
APE APART GALS  OLE
PRELATE SPRY PAWED
  PARE BORE MALLS
MARINA GALA  EARL
OVAL BOWLINGGREENKY
TOGO LEEK COOT GAGE
SNAG ERNS EASY EBBS
```

PUZZLE 20

```
CHIC CROC OCTA COLA
LOCO HERO CRAM IBID
ANON IDEA COTE ROAD
PENCILS COUP RACERS
  OLD CHAR CIRL
CLACK CHEF ACCEDED
OAST CLAD COMAS IRE
LIE COOP COVEN CAGE
TRACING CAVIL COLOR
  ATE CORED CAR
COCKY CLUES CANDICE
HALE CHART CART COW
ORO CLINT CURE CEDE
PSYCHIC CURL CASES
  OINK CABS COT
COGNAC CADI CONCERT
AGOG HORN CHIP HAIR
MERE EDEN LATE EVOE
PEER DEWY EYED RETE
```

PUZZLE 21

```
PLOD HARM RAFT CAMP
RUDE OLEO ERIE OLIO
ORES RESPECTED MAST
DESPISE LAS  LISTS
  ACE HILL EPIC
RETIE FUR LADEN ROC
OVER DINER MELT EMU
MEN SORT EVENT TSAR
ERE WEE OVEN STAIRS
  MOA DEPENDS AND
CREATE LARD PIN EGO
RANT SCALE HONK NOW
APT STET STAIN ACRE
MSS HONES OWL FLEES
  RAPT PARK ROT
STEAM AIL REPENTS
AIDS GENTLEMEN RARE
URGE ALOE LANE ERIN
LEES BANS STOW DEPT
```

PUZZLE 22

```
SAL   FARM    FAR
AMOS  ALIEN   DALE
NILE  TITLE   ALAN
DEAN  ACE   PARADE
    ABLE    TIE
 TATE   SATURDAYS
SECOND  FAN   LEA
ONOR  ARTIE  SLAP
LOR   FEE  SEWERS
ERNIEFORD   LENS
   RIO    IAMA
FRIEND  TNT  TARS
EARN  ILENE  EDIE
SLOE  LANES  RATA
SEN   SORT   MAN
```

PUZZLE 26

```
STOW   FAR   PEN
AIDA   AGE  LOOP
SLOT  CONDENSE
SERENE  ERASER
   ROD   WAS
BLAST  DEMERIT
AIR   SOD   ARE
ATTRACT  SPEED
   EVE   APE
UNISON  TARGET
FAREWELL  SAVE
OMIT  RIA  OPEN
ESS   YES  NERD
```

PUZZLE 30

```
RAISE  TOAD  PASS
ANNEX  OGRE  RUNT
PAGET  REID  EDIE
STEREO  ELI  SIDE
    NIP  SCATTER
GRIDDLES   AGO
LACES  TORTE  FAR
IVES  MELEE  ELBE
BED  SERVE  FLEET
PER    ESTIMATE
REPLACE    EAR
OLEO  HAM  BEETLE
ALAW  AGAR  ARRAY
DICE  NERO  RIODE
SEED  TREY  METES
```

PUZZLE 23

```
WARP  BEGAT  BOAT
ALOE  ALINE  URGE
STAN  FORTE  ROOT
HORNOFPLENTY
    OBIE    ITEA
MANON  BULLHORN
POSSE  TINE  ECCE
ANT  STANDIT  EAT
TREE  ARGO  WENDS
HORNPIPE  RAMEE
ENTR     TONI
    HORNSWOGGLED
GURU  HIRES  RITE
ASIS  OCTET  EDAM
GAME  SEATS  SOLO
```

PUZZLE 27

```
GAP    BOA   ODOR
BLOT  QUACK  RAZE
SLUR  UNTIE  ETON
OCELOT  DYE   END
WHEAT      RUDE
   SWAM  FANG
HEN   AJAR  LEAP
ARID  EJECT  YOYO
MAXI  VOTE   NEW
   AVER  TOSS
PALE      VALET
SOL   TIN  BEGONE
CROW  CEDAR  OVAL
ACHE  EXULT  POSE
THAT   TEE    YET
```

1-J, 2-Z, 3-M, 4-X, 5-T, 6-E, 7-A, 8-Q, 9-N, 10-K, 11-I, 12-U, 13-Y, 14-V, 15-G, 16-H, 17-B, 18-S, 19-F, 20-C, 21-P, 22-L, 23-D, 24-R, 25-O, 26-W.

PUZZLE 28

```
JAVELIN  DECIMAL
E  A  U  E  A  O  O  U
ANGER  PAY  NEWER
L  U  K  H  B  Q  E  I
ONETIME  ROUNDED
U  N   WOE   E  L
SHRUG   A   RITZY
   A   AWAKE   A
CRYPTO     BOXER
L   A  OIL  E   E
AFFIXED  ACQUIRE
S  E  I  E  R  U  D  N
HAVOC  NAG  EJECT
E  E  A  L  E  S  A  E
DURABLY  RATTLER
```

1-Y, 2-D, 3-Q, 4-T, 5-S, 6-V, 7-I, 8-C, 9-R, 10-W, 11-M, 12-P, 13-E, 14-F, 15-K, 16-B, 17-L, 18-H, 19-O, 20-G, 21-N, 22-X, 23-U, 24-Z, 25-J, 26-A.

PUZZLE 24

There once was a silly old maid
Who only ate grape marmalade.
At one hundred and ten
She said to the men,
"How nicely preserved I have stayed!"

PUZZLE 31

1. Fisherman: Someone who catches fish by patience, by luck, and sometimes by tale.
2. A good cook is like a sorceress who dispenses happiness.

PUZZLE 32

```
STAB   ALA   DIP
ARGO   BAR  ALOE
DOUBLEDEALERS
DEBITS    RESTS
   LES    ITS
AMIE   ALI   RIB
DOADOUBLETAKE
DAN   RTE   REED
   DIE   PIE
ESTEE   REMAKE
DOUBLEHEADERS
EMEU  GEL  LENT
EST   GAS  EPEE
```

PUZZLE 25

```
SELF  PUN  PRAY
OVAL  ARE  EASE
DEDUCING  PLEA
   FAD  APPEAR
SHAFT   STAY
TINY  THIN  RAP
ART  BRAVE  ICE
BEE  RARE  NOME
   CANE  WATER
SPORTS    SAT
LOVE  FANCIFUL
AREA  EGO  VISE
PERM  ROW  EGAD
```

PUZZLE 29

```
CHATS  SLATE  CRISP
LIMIT  PARER  RETIRE
AROMA  ONCEUPONATIME
REVERENCE  PANEL  VOW
AREA  AGED  TIES  FATE
   NOSE   PINS  VOTER
MIDDLE  COROT  CARESS
ARETE   SATIN   ERST
LEVI  SCRIM  SLITHER
ENID  PEACETIME  ERAT
ELEGANT  TIRED  TOTE
   WIRE  MITER  WIDEN
MEDALS  GAMIN  CAMELS
AVOID   SORE   TARE
RENT  BALI  ACRE  BOSC
IRA  HELEN  MOUNTETNA
ATTHESAMETIME  RITAS
SOARED  RAGES  INERT
RYOTS  SPORT  OGRES
```

PUZZLE 33

```
PAIR   GAR   CHER
AGRA   APE   AONE
LEAVESOFGRASS
SEEM      SEER
   LESS   TRITE
PRESENTS    EAR
LAM  RIATA  SPA
AMI   PRELATES
TASTE   SPAR
   SALE     TIES
CHARLOTTESWEB
EARP  NEO  TETE
ELYS  STY  ASST
```

PUZZLE 34

A

```
TIM   TAR
APACE ALES
GAMES VALET
OLE SHE IRE
ESS ORATED
   KENNY
BESIDE EAT
AVA ISM BOW
RIVET ELATE
LOGE SITED
ROD   ADE
```

B

```
TOM   MUD
ATONE AFAR
CADET TOTAL
ERA EMU EVE
EYE ERASES
   LATER
DECIDE MAT
IDA ORB RIP
MANOR OVINE
MORE WISER
NED   LEE
```

PUZZLE 35

```
MINE   DANA ASP
ALIDA  ALAN ALTO
PETER  LEND LEAK
DANE   ETAT ARTE
   NEST HESTER
LEGAL  EVER
WAVE   SARA IRENE
ANOTHER  SENATOR
REESE  OVEN MORE
   RANA DIANA
ELINOR MESS
LONI   NIPS EWES
MORN   EMIT NAVEE
ASEA   SERE TRIAL
NED    STES ELMS
```

PUZZLE 36

```
SEV ERT ALEDARE
TRAC EHOME RRUN
A ILMAIMEDAIMED
INN ERRE DS OW
SWO RDNE T RIB
REO ROEPRO EASE
PREY SALTNERVE
O GIVEITEMIRE
OVATENEARSLED S
LETRESTDEFTTREE
S HA HOG LEHATE
PEPTINARENANAP
LENTHEELODDSGAS
ANSWERR A SPELI
T OR SAD S EX
```

PUZZLE 37

```
STORESEAFARER
PARENTALEGATE
OPAQUEGGALLON
NATURALATEENA
SLOEEELERSTRUM
OARSWANILEIRE
RIOTINGNEAREST
ETERNALLYEMEN
DOSEDIALEDONA
ALTARSNAPOTAT
REAMILDIASITE
EDGEPEENDIVES
DOERSTRESSESS
```

PUZZLE 38

```
PEAT COMMA PALED FATE
ALMA ALOUD ALINE ATOM
IMPROBINSATIANDNEGOTI
GEL BOOTS ANTES MINER
ERE LOSE LITER NINES
   HIS SOL OIL
MANAGEIMPASSANDDEPEND
ELITE DEAN TRADE IVOR
LACE TINS LAIRS PLATE
TIE SHOD CANER LOOSED
   INIMITANDLAMENT
HORSES COMES TOSS DAS
EROSE SALES PIUS PENT
ALOU SANER IRON PRATE
DETESTATTAINANDPROFIT
PAR   ROY ROD
ORDER APIAN SEAT SAW
SWIRL SCENT MENLO TIA
INVALUPREFERANDINVARI
DEEM NAIVE ARSON AGES
EDNA ADDER STERE TEST
```

PUZZLE 39

```
SCAD ACTA TORN IBID
COLE SLAV AGHA SODA
ADAM SAGO FROBISHER
RARITAN CAFE NURSE
   GAY LACY MACE
ACTOR CADE HAHA MAD
RAID OHIO SERA LASE
ARK AGED SWAB AEGIS
BRIDGES ATOLL UMIAK
AREA BOO ECRU
AMICE PRAWN HOARDED
FENCE EASE CEIL ERA
RIGA EACH PIAF CASH
ONE INKY LEAD YODEL
   BADE AERO TOG
ALARM ISMS THUNDER
PENOBSCOT OKRA ARIA
INTO AUTO NEON TINT
SAID TBAR ANTE EPEE
```

PUZZLE 40

```
SACS FLOW HELP ELAN
ARON IOWA ODOR SAME
SEMI LUNCHTIME PUMA
SAMPLED KALE TERROR
APED WILY EERIE
ANNEX MEET ANNOTATE
TODD TIER BLISS TIN
ONE PEND GLIDE MERV
PERPLEX SOAKS NOSEY
LON LOOSE DOC
ALLOW BEAST LINKAGE
LOAD DRAPE COMO LIL
GAT PEERS DONE BLAB
AMERICAN RING ARENA
CUPID SOME OLAV
ABODES SHAM ABIDING
DAME IMPUDENCE LAIR
ABEL VEIN SONS ETNA
MARY EATS TREE YEAS
```

PUZZLE 41

```
ABAS ELAM ALPS AGER
BOLE NORA SEAT LILY
BLACKJACK SAPODILLA
EDITION ETAS NEE
ANY TSHI LEANSON
TERRA CODE MOAN TSE
AMOY BATONROUGE ISE
SID PERE OISE ACID
STEELER ENURE POKEY
ODIN PLANE LINT
EDDIE BLAND RECEIVE
GORE MOOT ROTE GIS
ARI WANDERLUST SHEP
DIV HIES IONA BETSY
ICELAND FORE TAA
ERS TITI MISLEAD
STAFFTREE CLUBHOUSE
PINT EARL AIRE FREE
ANDY MEAD ETAT FEAR
```

PUZZLE 42

```
ISLES SHOTTHE LANGE
ASPIRE TARRIES ENOUGH
SOONER UNDEALT SEVERE
PLOD GBS EAR ASER
EDNAFERBER ANTOINETTE
RES EVIL OHM ELSA SSS
IRENE BEE SLING
ROTUND NEILS ONCEIN
PENAL HARRIET YEMEN
ADT ERNEST ALWAYS AWA
IDA NUTS LALO MGR
SIR LARUES FEIGNS AAA
ASIDE PREWARN LETTS
HORNOF STANS PEEWEE
GOTUP TIN BRIDE
APT RIGA ELI RING DES
MARIECURIE ERODSEVELT
ARIS ERN AAR ALAI
STOLES OLDHAND AUNTIE
SEDATE TERENCE CLEANS
DEMON STARTER TASSE
```

PUZZLE 43

```
ORBS SOUL APOD CAPE
DUET ORNE CATO ARES
ETTA FLINGUPONESCAP
SHIRLEY IOTA LUSTY
CLAW SERE COLA
IRKED CONE JUBILANT
TILT ERAT LURES VIE
EVE CLIP TODDY NINA
REDRESS AREA EIDER
CLAPONESHANDS
CABAL ROSS MINIMUM
ALEF SCADS DELA ALI
LEA SHANE AONE SKAT
LAUGHING AGED SCENT
LINE ORRS SIAM
ASTIR BRIO EASTERN
THANKONESLUCKY TRIO
TORT UNDO NOES ERGO
UTES TEEN DODO RYAN
```

PUZZLE 44

```
ELM TANS FLAB CAN
SOYS ABIE ROIL DOVE
SOSO WELL UPDO ANEW
ENTRANT LAG ENTRUST
EELY MORAL DOIN
WORSE BAFFLER ENDED
EDIT CALF NOD GRAY
LIE VOLE TIDIED URN
DESPITE PUCE TROMPE
ATE YARER OUR
CELLAR AVID QUIBBLE
ORA LICHEN CURD EAR
BIBB ECO LOIS TWIN
SKYED LOSEOUT BRIDE
REDO SEWUP WAIL
SHIVERY DEN TIRADES
WANE DORA GAIN GELT
ARTS ERAT EIRE ERSE
NTH RETE DRED SEN
```

PUZZLE 45

```
ELBA SPAT ROTA STYE
DARN EACH ORAL THEY
ACID ALTO MELT REAR
MEDEA ARGO CALIBRE
EARTH NOLA ROAR
FRONTIER LACK STIFF
OAF NAIAD TIP EDIE
ORFF ARTIE ASIS END
TERIS TENN STABS
ADLIB TWO MAGOO
NOIRE ELEE ORFEO
ARK PIED DIRKS AFAR
SEER SPY DONAT USA
SYNOD SARI STUNTMEN
SMUG DENT ENNEA
MATADOR AGED ENNIS
OWEN GODS PULP ECRU
LAIC OLEO IDEA THEN
DYNE LEAN DENY SUDS
```

PUZZLE 46

```
GAS LAS CRISP
ADE AFT HOMER
LOP BAY EMPTY
ESTHER ERA
EEL PAINTED
AMY TARS RAY
HUB TRUTH ARE
IRE HUSH ADS
SARDINE ALI
IRK SKATES
PAPAS NOR IRA
EVENT UFO OIL
REPAY TAN NET
```

PUZZLE 47

```
LID BEER ABET
IRE URGE GONE
FIN TROD RODE
ESTATE USE
ROD CHEATS
ALIEN BEE TOE
COLA RID BONE
INK OAT NAMED
DESERT DEN
LET REDEEM
AVID LEAD ARE
DICE EVIL SIN
DEER SANE TED
```

PUZZLE 48

```
MOPS ALEC NOT
AREA LAVA EWE
NEWSPAPER VIA
HAS OMENS
BREED ENLARGE
OARS CREED
APE RARER BOY
AIMED FADE
TRUDGED BINDS
HARSH HUG
EGG TREASURER
SEE LOLL RENO
ESS YELL EDDY
```

PUZZLE 49

```
BOLD PROM SEDAN
ARIA RAVE CRIME
RANT EWER RACES
SNEERS NILE ESS
SASH TEAR
HOP MEET AMICE
APIA DRINK VOLT
LEVI ONE ERIE
EROS ANGEL RATS
ATLAS EDAM LET
EMIT SUIT
TOR PAIL NAILED
OBESE GOLD TALE
MINER EPEE AKIN
STONE REAR NEAT
```

PUZZLE 50

```
POMP RACA PAN
IDEA AROD RIO
SEAL VAGABOND
ASHAMED GEM
CAN MELITA
MONEY HAS SIN
ONES GIN LENT
ACT SAT BASES
BEWRAY WAR
OAR FINGERS
BARNABAS ELAH
ARK HERE SORE
YES SEER TIED
```

PUZZLE 51

```
EKES MILD BALL SEAL
BULL ADORE OLEO ARLO
BRIEFCASES POLOPONIES
STEEL STAIR NEATEST
VAN SHIP BASTE
RENEGED ERICA HEFTS
ALI GARTERSNAKE IRA
FIGS REAL GREW TAU
TAHOE WRIST SETS TIC
TURN SOLID RAT ONE
SPRIT TAMES SCRUB
RAH ONO YENTA KATE
ELI LANG STARK WATER
ALF ILLS MENU HIDE
LIT COATOFPAINT EGO
MESAS AGORA TIRADES
LEAST OARS TUT
ALABAMA IGLOO SLOSH
PAJAMAGAME UNSUITABLE
EVAN TARE TAUNT SEAR
SEXY INIT RBIS TYPO
```

PUZZLE 52

```
YES SHUT ASIA MAST
PARE TAKE CURL ACHE
ALMAMATER TREASURES
TEABAG REEF PLEAT
ERE POND FOES
GOLD CHARD WARN DIP
ADO NOEL SLICED YOU
FOG EARLS EVES SEWN
FROLICS POSED SODAS
UGH GLASS GEM
CATCH CAIRO MINERAL
OBEY MATT NOONS OBI
ALE WIDEST URGE LEE
TEN ACES AGREE VELD
DIET ICES RYE
SHORT IRON SERENE
LIVESTOCK IDENTICAL
AREA ALOE AURA TRIM
PERM MEND LEAP YUL
```

PUZZLE 53

```
ITEM DISC MOW
MOLE AREA ABE
POLARBEAR MET
GAS OKAYS
WOMEN HALE
ODOR CAYENNE
NET LACED OAF
SHRINKS FUSE
ICES MINED
TRADE HEN
HAD NOMINATED
EGO SLUR LAVA
YES EDGE SPED
```

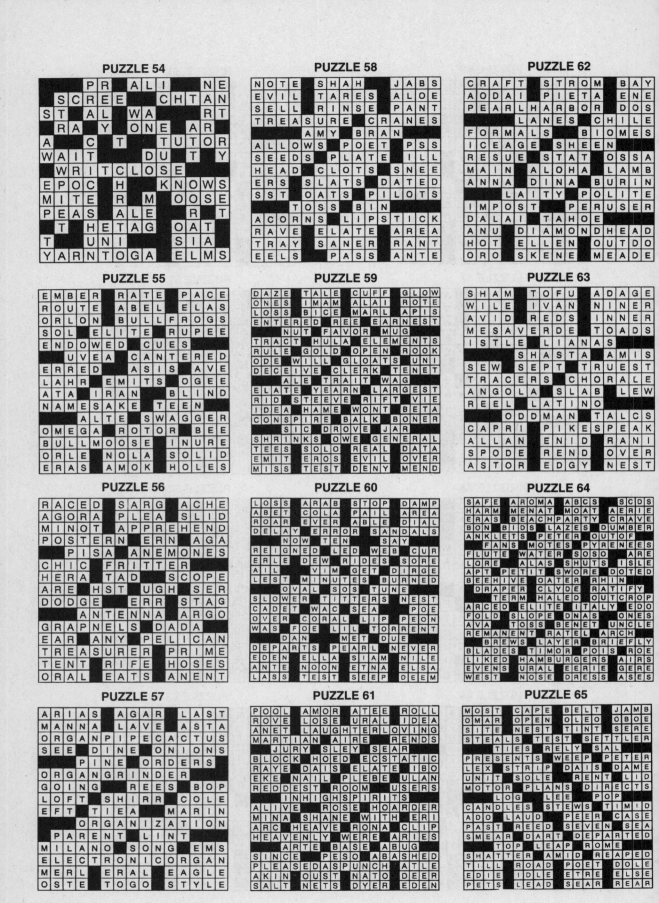

PUZZLE 54   **PUZZLE 58**   **PUZZLE 62**

PUZZLE 55   **PUZZLE 59**   **PUZZLE 63**

PUZZLE 56   **PUZZLE 60**   **PUZZLE 64**

PUZZLE 57   **PUZZLE 61**   **PUZZLE 65**

PUZZLE 66

```
CAP FIR SAP
ADE ARE TWO
NOD RAP EAR
ORATE AVERT
EELS ASIDE
  AUNTS
WORST TEST
TRASH FARCE
AIR ERA ORE
RTE RUT DON
TED SEE EDS
```

PUZZLE 70

```
YAM   COP   WAS
EPIC  ERR  PALE
TENOR LEI BERET
 TROLL   MERRY
  RUE      RIP
  TEST    ANEW
  NOSE    KNOB
  IMP      DRY
  PEON    RITE
  SNAG    MUCH
  DIE      EMU
 LEVEL   STOLE
ALONE ADO RAVES
FACT  ZOO  REAP
TWO   YEN   STY
```

PUZZLE 76

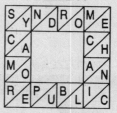

```
LEO     ALP
ERN     MOA
DREAMBOAT
  ROAN TAB    INT
  IAN  OLE    DOE
  DNA NIGHTMARE
      LAS  ERA
      LOO  RAT
 SWEETDREAMS
  LAW  EEL
  ORE  LIS
PIPEDREAM ELM
IRA  FRI  WEE
PEN  TEN TEAR
   DAYDREAMS
   EMP    SEE
   DIE    PTA
```

PUZZLE 71

Be civil to all; sociable to many; familiar with few; friend to one; enemy to none.

1. Bodily, 2. Nominate, 3. Malleable, 4. Waffle iron, 5. Twenty-one, 6. Evocation, 7. Mischief, 8. Riot.

PUZZLE 77

```
S Y N D R O M E
C           C H
M           A N
R E P U B L I C
```

PUZZLE 67

```
PAD     MASH
RIO     SELLER
ODES    PALOMINO
PARADE  WADED
  FOE    NEED
  ENDS
  TYPED
  ADAM
AGOG     ILE
CARAT    CIRCUS
ELEPHANT EASE
LEAVES    SEE
SWAT      ADD
```

PUZZLE 72

```
      SHIP
     SPINES
    CASTLES
   PAPA  OTTO
  RUMANIA SST
LEG ARAT DIP
IRA NET ALEE
PALACE    ASP
STASH    TASTE
 KEY    MANORS
 SERB PIT DON
 TOO SITE ATE
 ARS TALKERS
 RAPS  OISE
 CHALETS
 STATES
 STEN
```

PUZZLE 73

1. Face, Lace, Lice, Life, Lift; 2. Base, Bass, Bans, Buns, Runs; 3. Calm, Call, Cell, Sell, Seal, Seas; 4. Gold, Mold, Mild, Mind, Mink, Link.

PUZZLE 78

```
              ESAU
       SPA   LAMP
       LEAN  SPOIL
       EAST   SNIP
      PAINT   AVER
LOAD          ARENA
HOPTOIT     COMRADES
ACES VOW  RUNS LINE
VARY YEAR FETE ODE
ALA   SNAILS
      TRAIL
     ORNATE      CAW
ALP  PONE MATS TAPE
SEAM GOES DUO OPAL
STROLLER  INAWORD
TREAT      BENT
SEND       SOBER
SIRE       CAPE
NAMED      OVEN
GIVE       PEN
STAN
```

PUZZLE 68

```
NOON        HEMS
AIRED      CAROL
PLATES    ROTATE
SET WAR HUT  SOD
DEN PILOT    PER
SOS DOT      SAD
RAG PECAN
LAD LOW
WAGES PEW
ROD LIT DIP
PEN CANAL TAG
PAL HAY RAH RAT
ARISEN   PIRATE
SEVEN     SIDES
TREE       BEST
```

PUZZLE 74

```
ABLE        SLIP
RAIN        HIRE
MIND        OMIT
SLEEP      PRESS
 DAM        HIT
 YAP        TOT
 PILOT
 PAD
 REGAL
 HIS        YES
 BAG        TIP
STORY      PACES
LOVE        RARE
AREA        ERIE
BEND        SEND
```

PUZZLE 79

```
      ABED
      SILOS
      SCHOOLMAN
LATHES    LASE
AREA      OLIO
PARR      PLAN
STEWS
SOLS      MARE
MILS    SONATINA
AMANANDAWOMAN
NEBULOUS  NARD
 GABS     METS
         SHEBA
      STAR ECON
      HIDE MOST
      ARAM STANCE
      WOMANKIND
       SNEER
       DOPE
```

PUZZLE 69

1. Tracks down, 2. Lifeguards, 3. Brown study.

PUZZLE 75

1. Gelatinous, 2. Weak points, 3. Ravishment.

PUZZLE 80

Haste makes waste.

PUZZLE 81

PUZZLE 82

PUZZLE 83

PUZZLE 84

A. Stratum, B. Himself, C. Seafood, D. Witness, E. Explain, F. Outrage.

PUZZLE 85

PUZZLE 86

1. Fore, Core, Care, Cart, Cast.
2. Post, Port, Part, Park, Mark.
3. Life, Line, Lint, Lent, Bent, Beat, Boat.
4. Draw, Dram, Tram, Team, Beam, Beak, Beck, Back.

PUZZLE 87

PUZZLE 88

PUZZLE 89

PUZZLE 90

Advice is what the wise don't need and the fools won't take.

PUZZLE 91

PUZZLE 92

1. Rent, Rend, Read, Ream, Road, Roam, Room, Roof.
2. Mash, Mast, Malt, Male, Molt, Mole, More, Morn.

PUZZLE 93

PUZZLE 94

One way to stop a runaway horse is to bet on him.

1. Bowie, 2. Harpo, 3. Amos, 4. Toaster, 5. Annoy, 6. Youths, 7. Twine.

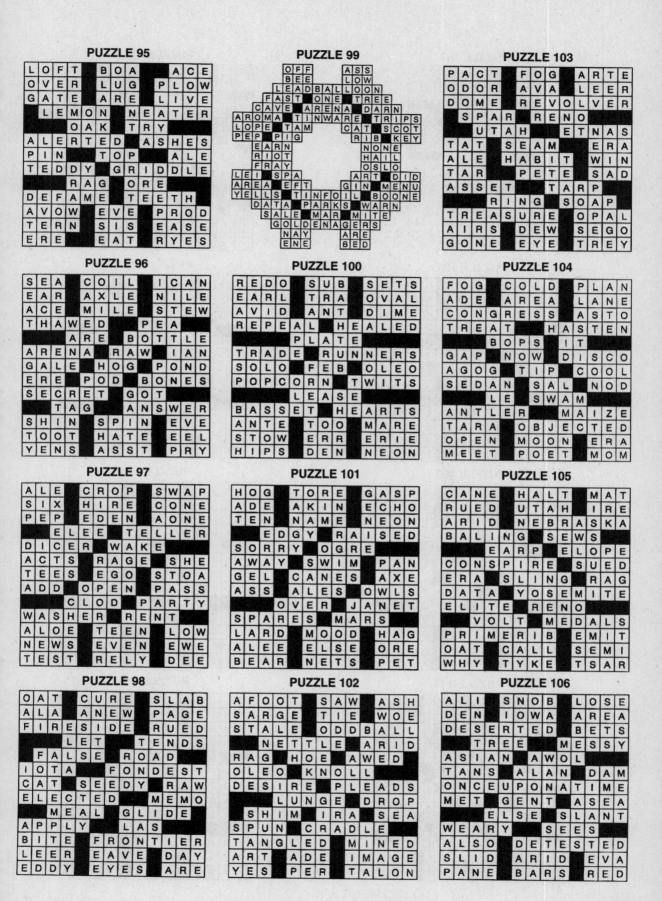

PUZZLE 95

```
LOFT  BOA   ACE
OVER  LUG   PLOW
GATE  ARE   LIVE
 LEMON     NEATER
    OAK   TRY
ALERTED    ASHES
PIN    TOP   ALE
TEDDY   GRIDDLE
    RAG   ORE
DEFAME     TEETH
AVOW  EVE   PROD
TERN  SIS   EASE
ERE   EAT   RYES
```

PUZZLE 96

```
SEA   COIL   ICAN
EAR   AXLE   NILE
ACE   MILE   STEW
THAWED    PEA
    ARE   BOTTLE
ARENA  RAW   IAN
GALE   HOG   POND
ERE    POD   BONES
SECRET     GOT
   TAG    ANSWER
SHIN  SPIN   EVE
TOOT  HATE   EEL
YENS  ASST   PRY
```

PUZZLE 97

```
ALE   CROP   SWAP
SIX   HIRE   CONE
PEP   EDEN   AONE
   ELEE    TELLER
DICER    WAKE
ACTS   RAGE   SHE
TEES   EGO    STOA
ADD    OPEN   PASS
   CLOD    PARTY
WASHER   RENT
ALOE   TEEN   LOW
NEWS   EVEN   EWE
TEST   RELY   DEE
```

PUZZLE 98

```
OAT   CURE   SLAB
ALA   ANEW   PAGE
FIRESIDE     RUED
   LET    TENDS
  FALSE   ROAD
IOTA     FONDEST
CAT   SEEDY   RAW
ELECTED      MEMO
   MEAL   GLIDE
APPLY    LAS
BITE   FRONTIER
LEER   EAVE   DAY
EDDY   EYES   ARE
```

PUZZLE 99

```
      OFF        ASS
      BEE        LOW
     LEADBALLOON
   FAST  ONE  TREE
  CAVE  ARENA  DARN
AROMA  TINWARE  TRIPS
LOPE  TAM   CAT  SCOT
PEP   PIG   RIB  KEY
     EARN      NONE
     RIOT      HAIL
     FRAY      OSLO
LEI  SPA     ART  DID
AREA EFT     GIN  MENU
YELLS TINFOIL   BOONE
DATA   PARKS    WARN
SALE   MAR   MITE
     GOLDENAGERS
      NAY       ARE
      ENE       BED
```

PUZZLE 100

```
REDO   SUB    SETS
EARL   TRA    OVAL
AVID   ANT    DIME
REPEAL     HEALED
       PLATE
TRADE     RUNNERS
SOLO   FEB    OLEO
POPCORN      TWITS
       LEASE
BASSET     HEARTS
ANTE   TOO    MARE
STOW   ERR    ERIE
HIPS   DEN    NEON
```

PUZZLE 101

```
HOG   TORE   GASP
ADE   AKIN   ECHO
TEN   NAME   NEON
   EDGY    RAISED
SORRY    OGRE
AWAY   SWIM   PAN
GEL    CANES  AXE
ASS    ALES   OWLS
   OVER    JANET
SPARES   MARS
LARD   MOOD   HAG
ALEE   ELSE   ORE
BEAR   NETS   PET
```

PUZZLE 102

```
AFOOT    SAW   ASH
SARGE    TIE   WOE
STALE   ODDBALL
   NETTLE    ARID
RAG   HOE   AWED
OLEO   KNOLL
DESIRE     PLEADS
   LUNGE    DROP
SHIM   IRA   SEA
SPUN   CRADLE
TANGLED     MINED
ART   ADE   IMAGE
YES   PER   TALON
```

PUZZLE 103

```
PACT   FOG   ARTE
ODOR   AVA   LEER
DOME   REVOLVER
  SPAR     RENO
   UTAH   ETNAS
TAT    SEAM   ERA
ALE    HABIT  WIN
TAR    PETE   SAD
ASSET      TARP
   RING    SOAP
TREASURE     OPAL
AIRS   DEW   SEGO
GONE   EYE   TREY
```

PUZZLE 104

```
FOG   COLD   PLAN
ADE   AREA   LANE
CONGRESS     ASTO
TREAT     HASTEN
    BOPS    IT
GAP   NOW   DISCO
AGOG   TIP   COOL
SEDAN  SAL   NOD
    LE    SWAM
ANTLER     MAIZE
TARA   OBJECTED
OPEN   MOON   ERA
MEET   POET   MOM
```

PUZZLE 105

```
CANE   HALT   MAT
RUED   UTAH   IRE
ARID   NEBRASKA
BALING     SEWS
   EARP    ELOPE
CONSPIRE     SUED
ERA    SLING   RAG
DATA   YOSEMITE
ELITE      RENO
   VOLT    MEDALS
PRIMERIB     EMIT
OAT    CALL   SEMI
WHY    TYKE   TSAR
```

PUZZLE 106

```
ALI   SNOB   LOSE
DEN   IOWA   AREA
DESERTED     BETS
   TREE    MESSY
ASIAN    AWOL
TANS   ALAN   DAM
ONCEUPONATIME
MET    GENT   ASEA
    ELSE   SLANT
WEARY      SEES
ALSO   DETESTED
SLID   ARID   EVA
PANE   BARS   RED
```

PUZZLE 107

```
CLAW  RAIL  JACK
AIDE  HURRY ALOE
MAZE  ALIKE BITE
PREPARED   HOTEL
    LED   SPAT
MATES QUIZ  TAM
CORE  PURGE AGO
EVENT AIL  LAXER
DEN   ALLEY WINE
ERA   MEET QUEST
    HEAD  FUR
FAVOR  MAINSTAY
EXAM  EJECT LOBE
ELSE  VOTES ANEW
DEER  EYED  BETS
```

1-L, 2-W, 3-M, 4-J, 5-B, 6-H, 7-Q, 8-P, 9-O, 10-C, 11-R, 12-Y, 13-T, 14-V, 15-I, 16-S, 17-Z, 18-K, 19-G, 20-F, 21-N, 22-U, 23-A, 24-D, 25-X, 26-E.

PUZZLE 108

```
PAPA   ASP   USES
ALOE   REE   NERO
SPIRITED     JAIL
    ANY  INURED
ELATE    ACES
PINE   SPUTTERS
IDO  STARS   ROE
CONSPIRE    TATA
    KEPT  NASAL
PARADE   OIL
ABUT   NEGLECTS
SIDE   DAR  SOOT
SEED   STE  ENDS
```

PUZZLE 109

```
PANT   ODE   GROW
ANEW   LAS   ROBE
CORE   ESS   ALOE
KNOLL   HANDLED
   FIN    YOU
SCATTER    TARDY
OUCH   TIE   TIDE
LETGO  PLAINES
   RAH    FRO
ORLATER    KNEAD
WOOD   LEE   DARE
NONE   LAB   ASEA
STIR   ORB   YEAR
```

PUZZLE 110

```
SCAR  DART  CHAD  ALIT
HOPE  ALOE  HUGE  SODA
AMES  LAKEHURON  SALT
MOSELLE  TART  THAMES
   NEY  BELL  SUEY
SLATE  PORT  ERASERS
HALS  VANS  PRIED  RIO
OIL  KERN  CHIN  BIND
OCEANIA  WROTE  COEDS
   GLEN  SAONE  TALC
TAHOE  BOYNE  LAPLATA
ANEW  LONE  BORE  NEW
INN  RHONE  CORN  DALE
LAYSOUT  BRAD  FELLS
   ADDS  FEET  DON
THANES  GLAD  GARONNE
HILT  OHIORIVER  TEAL
ELBE  NILE  TILE  EVIL
NOSE  SEAS  SASS  SALA
```

PUZZLE 111

```
CART  AROMA  TSARS  PET
ALEE  DIVAN  OLLIE  ALAI
TAXEVADERS  REPORTCARD
TAPER  WOODS  FUTILE
ASSERTS  LEANS  ADS  DYS
STORY   ERST   BOOK
SAFE  COMESTOTERMS  PTA
EGAD  LIAR  EATS  SLAM
TER  RELISH  BETA  SPARE
SHOVEL  OWENS  MARION
SCOOTED  OPALS  RELENTS
EAGLES  TRENT  BUTTES
EBOES  BIAS  STILTS  PAM
PLOD  HALT  ESEL  SOLE
SED  EASTERPARADE  TKOS
LIES  ELMS  ARENA
ERG  IRS  GNOME  STRINGS
CORRAL  MATTE  STEEP
OPENSESAME  TEARSAPART
LEAS  SANER  ELIOT  EVOE
EST  SWISS  RASPS  DATE
```

PUZZLE 112

```
CALF   RAJAH   STOP
OPIE   AMIGO   TILE
HENRYCABOTLODGE
ORT   MIRE   ARYAN
      TINA   PAVE
SATIRE  BABI   ALA
OMAN   ARIES   WAG
CASTLESINTHEAIR
HIT   OVINE   TINE
ENE   WIDE   SANTEE
      ABLE   RARA
SPIRO   DAME   PAL
HOLLYWOODPALACE
ORLE   IDEAL   OGRE
TEEN   TERRE   BEER
```

PUZZLE 113

```
TAIL   VET   RENO
IDLE   AGO   AREA
MALT   LAMPPOST
EMU   BED   LISTS
      MEAT   FAD
PRINT   DAY   SPY
REND   FUR   KNEE
ODE   LID   HEART
      OAR   BUNT
SPOTS   SAT   CRY
LIGHTING   SHOE
ALEE   DOE   PEON
PEER   OWL   ARTS
```

PUZZLE 114

```
BOLT   CUT   HALT
IRON   ONE   OLEO
TART   STALLION
ENG   STORED
   NETS   INSULT
FIERY   END   NOR
ARTS   RAG   TIRE
NAT   SOT   MOODS
SNEAKY   NOON
   DIADEM   JAM
TREADLES   RAVE
ROAM   TET   ICES
AIRS   YRS   OKRA
```

PUZZLE 115

```
EBB   SPA    SHAD
LIES  PAD    HARE
STANDARD    ANTE
   EONS    ELDER
 ABET  OGRES
OMAR  INON   TEL
DENSER   REBATE
END  ROSE   ONTO
  SLANT  MADE
PETAL  APER
IRAN    STANDSUP
NINE  EEL   SATE
TEDS  ADE    DEN
```

PUZZLE 119

```
BAR   DELL    POE
USE   ARIA   BRIM
SHOOTINGIRONS
   MEET   NICK
NAMES    ALEE
ICON   REVERSE
LEO  COVET   SIR
 SNOOPER  CERE
  SLUE   DOSED
  STIR  ATOM
SHOOTTHEWORKS
PENS  EONS   YEA
ADE   DYNE   END
```

PUZZLE 123

```
ABBA  LEAK   ODE
SALT  EASE   POE
SHOOTSTHEBULL
  ONES    PESTS
ASPEN    STOA
LEES   STRUMMED
MAR  TAROT   OVA
ASSORTED   ANET
  VEEP   PRONE
AREAS    FACT
CALLSTHESHOTS
ESS   ERIE  ENOS
SEE   SIPS  RENT
```

PUZZLE 116

```
LOST  SEA   REAP
ODOR  LAB   ECRU
GENEROUS    CHAT
   BET   ONIONS
CHILD  BLOT
LACE  BRUNETTE
ATE  CRATE   WIN
DESOLATE    RIND
   PANS   TONES
DEPEND  SOL
OVEN   NAPOLEON
TIRE   EVE  ERNE
SLUR   WED  REED
```

PUZZLE 120

```
GOLF  WEST   MAT
IDOL  ANTE   ICE
FORE  STRESSED
TREES   RASES
   STEEP  VOID
ASP  RAE   DEUCE
LEADER   BURROS
ARROW  PUN   INK
SEAN   TAMED
  KNEAD   SALAD
CREATURE    TILE
AYE   OPEN  ELSE
BET   NESS  STOP
```

PUZZLE 124

```
MOPE   BOW   GROW
AVOW   ALE   RENO
DEPENDED    OVEN
ERE  AGO   AVERT
   RYE   TIER
MIDAS  SAM   ELS
ANEW   CAP   KNIT
NAP  HAY   CATTY
  REED   PAT
ALARM  MAR   SKI
LAVA   MISTREAT
AMES   ANT   DATE
SADE   TEE   STEM
```

PUZZLE 117

```
CONS   OLD   PAVE
UNIT   FAR   ASIA
RELIEFPITCHER
 SELL    PIE
   LIDS   ESSAY
 DISARMED   LIE
JAR   EER    ART
ALA  SWALLOWS
WINCE   REAM
   ARC    MEEK
CENTERFIELDER
ALOE   ARK   EIRE
BARR   MOE   TEND
```

PUZZLE 118

```
ZONE   PAST   RAY
EVEN   SLUR   ORE
REED   ALMANACS
ORDERLY   DUD
   AIM   SENSED
CHARM  FUR   HAY
HOPS   CAN   CORE
ASP   TAN   PAWNS
PEANUT   SAP
   ROB   SCRIPTS
OPERETTA   TOOL
WIN   REEL   ALSO
NET   SAME   LOST
```

PUZZLE 121

```
LADD   BALM   SWAP
ALAI  ALGAE   NILL
SONS  COAST   ESPY
SUCCOTASH    SECS
ODE  GET    OUZO
   FED  SCREENED
ADORE  SPELT   SKI
RACY  DAILY   HIED
ANT  JANET  RONDO
LEOPARDS    MOB
  PACT  EAT   POE
 TURK  MAGNESIUM
BASK  LAIRS   PETE
URSA  AGREE   ATEN
NAYS   GIST  NARD
```

PUZZLE 122

```
BAY   ABOUT   DAB
EGO   LEASE   RUE
DOUBLEFEATURE
  OAT    AGAR
APPLY    BARNS
WEED   DOMESTIC
EAR   WRAPS   ORE
SLITHERS    BRED
  SHOWS   SUEDE
PACE    DUG
ATONESLEISURE
POP   VAULT   PIG
APE   EDGES   SAG
```

PUZZLE 125

```
PAPA   PAR   OMIT
ALES   ARE   RODE
LOSS   SIP   GALE
METERS    ORATED
  NAE    RON
PASTED    TESTER
ADO      IRA
YELLOW    PATENT
  ERA    UTE
DOCTOR    MELTED
ABUT   DIP   LIVE
MORE   ERE   ERIN
PEER   NED   RELY
```

PUZZLE 126

```
ACID RODE LIMA BAIT
PORE ADES ATOM ARTE
TWENTYONE SEVENTEEN
    EERY    MENU
  ATE   CAB    DOC
BLAHS EASES  ENACT
TERR  FIFTEEN ESAU
OGEE ENE NEE  FELT
   EARN    WILL
   OWED    SLOE
   CEDE    MEOW
FALL RYE SHE  ODER
OLEO SIXTEEN VISE
RANCH PIECE TENSE
SKI   TAT    ORE
    DATA    DARN
THREESONS SIXTYFIVE
READ KITT TALE ADAM
ARTS SLAY ALES DANS
```

525

PUZZLE 127

```
JUMP  LEAR  JANE
ERAL SIEGE ALEX
TATA PALED CONE
SLANDERS   DOTES
    ENS DRAB
PRATED FEAT  PAD
LANA PLATE  AGA
ARENA AIL  DETER
ZEN TAINT  RENE
ART TINT  OPERAS
   PART AVE
ALTER  EBENEZER
PEAS LIVER  LANE
SANK SMELT  ANOA
EDGY TALE   NELL
```

PUZZLE 131

```
ACRE  NAPS   AWE
FOES  OPAL   SEA
ALEC  STRICTER
RADAR    ECHO
    PASS  KINGS
PAVEMENT  NILE
ONE PLEAT  SUN
NETS FAMISHED
DWELL  KEEN
   RAIL  DOTES
PEATMOSS  WIRE
URN IDEA  EDIT
GAS TENT  DYES
```

PUZZLE 134

```
SLAB  FAR OCAS IDOL
COMO BIDE CUBA NITA
ANON URAL TROT SSTS
RESIGNS IDO WRAPS
 TINTINABULATION
SHARI NEVER PARLOR
LAO LESS ERSE EVEN
ENVY STER AXES ELS
ATEE ARADA PEA
FORWHOMTHEBELLTOLLS
 ELM SIENA VIEW
WAN PEER DRIP ALVA
ENID ROME INRE TEN
DEGREE SALIC ERASE
 WHOLLBELLTHECAT
TOTAL TAC LISTENS
ATOP PORE HOSS UNIT
LOWE SOUS EDIE NONE
BOLD EDGE SEE ELAN
```

PUZZLE 128
1. Citadel, 2. Exhibit, 3. Concert, 4. Termite, 5. Machine, 6. Cockpit, 7. Dolphin.
MYTHICAL BEAST: Pegasus

PUZZLE 135

```
CARP STEM BOOB BAIZE
ADEEM CASA IGLU OWNER
REATA OMNI NILL RAKEE
 DERROSENKAVALIER
 RIOT  SORE NODDLES
COCOON DIARY POLO ALT
ACES CORI ROSEMARIE
HONEYSUCKLEROSE LATE
INS ELLE BENT BETTER
ETE SEEN BAD ORE
ROSETATTOO ROSEYGRIER
LEV LDS ALIA NNE
EMPIRE AIEA NAST TIS
ROAD SWORDANDTHEROSE
ROSECRANS FREE ORLE
ORC HANS SAFAR FASTED
REHEARD TOUL AIDE
 SWEETROSIEOGRADY
EVASE ERIN CALL MASSE
OATER LUNE TREE SLEEK
STENS SEER SLOT ERNE
```

PUZZLE 132

```
WOMAN    TALCS
ADORED  SAFARI
FILTER  ENAMEL
TOT DUET  REAL
SUED MATE  STY
 SNAG REMOTE
  TOE  RIB
 SHAWLS  TEAS
SKI NOEL  YULE
PATH PEEK  DAM
ATTIRE ENDIVE
REEKED ROUTER
ERRED  BOSSY
```

PUZZLE 129

```
MARE  RIDE  EWER
ARAT SALON  LODE
COTTONWOOD  LOIN
WEEVIL  RECEDED
  IDS   ARNE
SWEDE  PARE  NBA
SHOO  MELEE  SAN
LOON MANED  SHIN
AND BERNE  TORE
PEP ALLY  PREEN
 EMIL   ARA
RECOLOR DAMPER
ASKS WOODYALLEN
ITES ELVES  ALAN
NARY READ   YALE
```

PUZZLE 133

```
NIPA AFRO OLD ACRES
EVER LEAR CEE DROPS
NATCOLEPORTER MONET
ENS PAT EER SHES
 TEN THAT LASSO
AGIO BEER DARE WAR
JAMESDEANMARTIN ARE
ALE AITS NEED BRIE
RET WET TATA MEDAL
 PETEROSEMARIE
PAPER ARKS CON JAB
OMEN BABA SHOE OVA
GET SARAHMILESDAVIS
ONE ARAT IDAS CEDE
RENAL SNIP BAT
ANNS PAS SON REE
REESE JACKBENNYHILL
TARES OAK ERIE EVIL
STONE ERS TATS MASS
```

PUZZLE 136

```
CAN MESA  GAMES
HOME AMER RHODE
APAR SIAM ANODE
HARVESTMOON NAP
SLEEVE  RAGAS
 ESTA  TETCHY
GAMIN ORSE TAOS
ANON RUDER APSE
STOA ATOM GREER
PANNED  RIAL
 RELIT  WEENIE
FLA MOONLANDING
RAKEE WEAR GOTA
AMEER ENID EBON
YARNS REDS  DEW
```

PUZZLE 130
Popular American Golfing Idol
ARNOLD PALMER

PUZZLE 137
If you have knowledge, let others light their candles at it.

1. Tackle, 2. English, 3. Outdoors, 4. Healthier, 5. Flatten, 6. Weighty, 7. Dive.

PUZZLE 138

```
RES  CO  W HAND D   REPAST
SHAM  LARGER   STIR
ISTANBUL  READ  POUTS
    SHARPEN  FULTON
CARAMEL  CIGAR  WANDERED
ROB   FILLING    ROD
TERMINAL  ICER  MARIE
    STEIN    TORN
MAPLE   TEAM   DORMER
GILT   REPLACE   TAIL
CANOE   STEERS   LED
```

PUZZLE 139

A baby is an angel whose wings get smaller as its legs get taller.

PUZZLE 140

```
MAY   DIVE   PUMA
ADE   ONES   ATOM
ROASTERS    RARE
    RASPS  ACHES
CALF    TEACH
ALIEN   SIT   BOB
MONROE   DECADE
PEG   SLY   DOSES
    REFER   MIST
GIVES   LABEL
EDEN   FLIRTING
NEED   ROSE   COO
EARS   OWED   AGO
```

PUZZLE 141

```
FAT   BRAC   GASH
LOU   LALA   LILI
UNBEATEN   ODOR
BEETS   COURAGE
    APT   ELI
BELLHOP   TAMPA
AGE   ENTER   CAR
TOTEM   AVARICE
    REF   ESE
CLEARED   OBESE
ROTS   REMNANTS
ALOE   ALAI   OOP
BAND   LAIC   SAY
```

PUZZLE 142

```
COAT  STEAM  MADAM  WASH
AXLE  KOALA  ADANO  HULA
DEANMARTIN  JOHNNIERAY
INSTATES  ALORS  SCRAM
    YEN  STORE  OTOE
BALLAD  BAERS  DENIZEN
ORION  HIRED  PAIRS  ELI
AGON  BORA  TARNS  OBAN
RUN  EARTHAKITT  SHUTE
DEEPDISH  TETES  THALES
    LOIRE  STEIN  CAIRO
RETOLD  CHINA  TORRENTS
EXILE  LORENZHART  PAP
BUGS  TROPE  EASY  LIMA
ODE  SEATS  ORBIT  BAKER
PERJURY  LIARS  PRYERS
    AGRA  MANTA  FRA
SINAI  SITKA  SOANDSOS
PETERFINCH  BETSYDRAKE
STET  ISERE  LEASE  INRE
TAMS  CLEAR  EGGER  PEAK
```

PUZZLE 143

```
BROW  FIRST  ROPE
EAVE  ETAPE  EBON
ERAL  REGAL  MIND
TALLER  EREMITES
    TAEL  EGIS
ASSORTED  RESIST
BEADS  PAGAN  ROE
ONTO  SERUM  LAWN
USE  HIRES  SITES
TEDIUM  STAMPEDE
    CLUB  STES
REFILLED  TETHER
ERIC  ASIDE  IOTA
PILL  TOKEN  CLOG
SAME  EMEND  KENS
```

PUZZLE 144

```
OPAQUE   OBJECT
F  G PIE X  R
FRO  OWNED  EKE
I  N  T R  N
CHIP   REVOLTED
E Z F  R  O Y
    REQUIREMENT
B   L  U S E Z
OVERLAPS   ECHO
X N N T I K O
ICE   EJECT   TAM
N M S D C I E
GAYEST   SHREWD
```

1-O, 2-M, 3-D, 4-W, 5-Y, 6-Q, 7-U, 8-L,
9-Z, 10-A, 11-R, 12-N, 13-H, 14-I, 15-C,
16-F, 17-P, 18-B, 19-T, 20-V, 21-S, 22-G,
23-X, 24-K, 25-J, 26-E.

PUZZLE 145

```
BRAMBLE   QUAIL
I X E FLUDE  D
DWELL  F  AZURE
O  FLECK  L R
TENOR  T E  TOY
W  O YIELD  V
OKRA  C E  AJAR
I  CENTS  A I
ADZ H O  TOWED
P  O IVORY  G
ARMED  D  LARGE
R BELLE  A N
TRIPS   ENSIGNS
```

1-C, 2-G, 3-E, 4-W, 5-Z, 6-R, 7-Y, 8-F,
9-X, 10-K, 11-Q, 12-D, 13-V, 14-O, 15-S,
16-M, 17-T, 18-H, 19-A, 20-L, 21-P, 22-
N, 23-U, 24-B, 25-J, 26-I.

PUZZLE 146

```
GILT  GASP  HELP  RISK
ODOR  OPAL  OLEO  ARIA
NONE  BELA  RIGS  DONT
GLEAM  SATAN  STRANGE
    TOM  DES  MAR
STEEPER  SIR  LAW  DON
COLD  TUB  SEDAN  PINE
ARK  LAB  CAD  PIECE
NEST  BERATED  HALTED
    EVER  LID  RENO
SHAPED  SLEEPER  TILT
LIMIT  RIO  DIP  TIA
ARID  MONTH  TED  TENT
WED  HOW  SAM  LEGUMES
    VIM  LOS  WAN
RECITED  CEDAR  LEVEL
ALAN  NOVA  EVIL  FADE
MIRE  TRAP  SODA  USES
PATS  SANE  TREY  LENS
```

PUZZLE 147

```
BATH  TOIL  LOW
ASIA  RULE  AGO
RHODEISLANDER
    ROME  EYED
CABINS   RED
ARIA  PET  PRO
PENNSYLVANIAN
SAD  PAY  ANTE
    PAP  SISTER
SKUA   PANT
WISCONSINITES
ATE  REIN  ERNE
BED  BEST  RIDE
```

PUZZLE 148

```
ROBE  ANNS  OWE
ALEX  POOH  PEA
FEATHERDUSTER
    REX  TUSKS
FAKER   PIER
ITEM  EASY  IRA
STREETCLEANER
TAN  VOTE  TREK
    YENS  SHEDS
SHEAR   GEL
CARPETSWEEPER
ALL  SORE  TATA
TOE  TWIN  EDAM
```

PUZZLE 149

```
RATS  CAST  BARD  SLAM
ELAN  ALOU  OHIO  TUBE
BIKE  PAIR  NOGS  ONUS
TEACEREMONY  SPATS
    KID  OWE  YOU
MUSEE  SHINTOTEMPLES
AVER  OPAL  VOLE  AMA
PEA  IVAN  SHELL  SHIV
SAMISEN  SHORE  CARRE
    DIN  TWIST  GAB
BONET  SOARS  SAMURAI
ALOE  LAINE  PELE  ORD
RIA  FOIL  RATE  SUMO
NOHDANCEDRAMA  SATES
    ACE  ION  ART
TWINE  GEISHAGIRLS
RING  SOAP  AURA  AUNT
ONCE  EARP  CLIP  PROA
TEAR  CREE  KALE  SEWN
```

PUZZLE 150

```
MILE  SHUN  AHEM  JILT
ARAB  CORE  TORY  ODOR
DOUBTINGTHOMAS  HERO
END  WOKE  ALE  TENANT
    TIN  NAIL  BEAN
SETON  STIR  CARRYOFF
PRIME  ELM  MANY  OMAR
USED  HEY  GANG  SNIDE
DERIDED  SLID  SETTEE
    CUE  SPINY  HAH
FLAKED  TIDE  CAMELOT
RURAL  CAKE  SOW  SANE
ERIN  HONE  ICE  SPICE
DEADWOOD  CLOD  LOREN
    HALL  CULT  PIT
MALADY  WAR  FORM  LAG
OVER  JOHNBARLEYCORN
LIAR  OLIO  DELE  ASEA
EDDY  EDGE  DEAN  PEAT
```

527

PUZZLE 151

```
ATLE SERED GLEN
SEAR ALATE RODE
HENRYCABOTLODGE
ETC ERN EASIER
SHELLED ACTS
ELD OLT ITS
BOONE SMEE STOA
EDWARDMACDOWELL
DONS EARS LISLE
SRS MRS CES
ADIT BOASTED
SPIRAL EFT ARA
HENRYLONGFELLOW
ASTA ERNIE ELSE
MOOS SCENE EYES
```

PUZZLE 152

Cruet, Truce, Truck, Stuck, Stick, Cling, Thing, Night, Write, Wrote, Tower, Lower.

PUZZLE 153

```
ARIA ATOM OPTS
LENS REVEL FLIP
MATS TRADE TAME
SPOUT SLIMS TEN
RAGE CONTEST
SPHERE NOW
ALE SMILE BIRCH
LEAP STEER TILE
TAPES SOLOS CAR
LED SPEEDS
SISTERS DEAN
TNT PEACE STOLE
AFAR STAND IKON
RELY SENSE TROD
TREE STEW YAPS
```

PUZZLE 154

```
G  GNOMES  OMENS  ONES  M
R  COLLAR  LOCAL  CALL  O
E  ENTERS  RENTS  REST  N
A  KARATE  TAKER  TEAR  K
S  RESIST  RITES  STIR  E
E  YEASTS  STAYS  TASS  Y
```

PUZZLE 155

```
ADD ABT ASTA
MARS PAR STEP
ODIN PHEASANT
REVEAL AGENT
ELLE TEN
BAWLS WESTERN
OVA DAD LEO
PAYDAYS AMEER
EON OLAV
MANNA RELATE
CONTESTS ETON
ARTE TOO SEGO
DEED YEN DOS
```

PUZZLE 156

```
SETS OWED RAP
CLOT CHER EVA
ALOE COLOSSAL
BANANA SOOT
MESS PARED
OMISSION KATE
RIM SOFAR ITA
BLAB NATIONAL
SAGAS SITS
INTO VAMPED
KINGANDI OLGA
EVE STET NEAR
NED HOLY DADE
```

PUZZLE 157

```
CHER SELF ALGA SCAR
BABA ARIL SEAS POSE
CHOCOLATECHIMPCOOKY
ANENT ARES LOTS
CAY AWES FAN
HOCUS SLAW CAIN ESS
AMOR WILY TARNS WOE
NOD MANY BRUIN BELA
SOFTEN SAILS ARSON
ART PUPCAKE RAP
MATES ERROL CANARD
ACHE HAGEN GRUB PEA
IRE MELEE GLIB TEAM
MER ORES SNAP PERMS
ETA STUD EAR
WEST SPUD DINER
DAYSOFSWINEANDROSES
OGRE APAR ALAI UNIT
TEEN TAPE LATE TENS
```

PUZZLE 158

```
POST ELS FEAR SLAM
EVER LIP INLAW TINA
PARADISE NEVERNEVER
SLEDS PANAMA ION
ECU RELY INDOUBT
BASS SWELL DOGE NEE
ETH PEARLYGATES DAN
ALA EFTS OMAR PEST
KINGTUT TIRES SORTS
GIRL CARES SCOW
LARGO WOMEN CHALONS
IRIS WARP BAER ROE
TEL TINPANALLEY LOT
ETA ONES ADULT EDNA
RESOUND AIDE SOT
RTE GRASSO WHOSE
WONDERLAND TWILIGHT
ANNE SATIE EEN CLEO
DOER BEES MDS SEAN
```

PUZZLE 159

```
GRIP ADAGE LIPS
NATES SILAS PARES
UPSETTHEAPPLECART
RYE ONE
APRICOT
LIAR ROMAN GOYA
ALDA COLANUT OVEN
BEDS ADE SAT BAND
SPRAT NATAL
BARA GLEN
RENEW ELLAS
BEAR ABE MEL NOSE
AMIR AVOCADO ARES
DULY ELATE STAT
PRETEND
TAU EVE
STRAWBERRYBLONDES
PRIDE RETIE NOOSE
AIDS ADEPT STEW
```

PUZZLE 160

```
MICE ALATE ASPS
AGAR RABAT BORI
TOTE OPERA ABUT
ORE OMITS SNIDE
GOLAN MUGGED
ELOPES BRAN
TORII SOON ADOS
RAINCATSANDDOGS
ENCE LION ROGET
DORM HERMES
CATNIP HOSEA
ARRAS SPATS TOM
BEER SHAME TITI
ATEE PENAL ESTE
LESS AMENS AMOS
```

PUZZLE 161

OUT: 1. Erupted, 3. Acre, 5. Fin, 6. Ocean, 8. Lucid. 10. Among, 12. Genial.

IN: 14. Lain, 13. Egg, 11. Nomadic, 9. Ulnae, 7. Conifer, 4. Cadet, 2. Pure.

PUZZLE 162

```
MARC SAME MIES BEARS
AGER HIMED UNDO ARIEL
THEAMAZINGMRSHOLLIDAY
SALVAGE SAID STILTED
ANN TARRED YEAR
SPATIATE ERA SEETO
EAT THEANDERSONTAPES
PRO BEATLE STONE OXA
TINGA HIGHS LESS STR
ESCARP CRO TOASTY
THEBRIDGEOFSANLUISREY
EELERS FIT SLEEVE
LAM DOPA CATER ERNES
ALE SEPIA KRONOS ENS
HOWTHEWESTWASWON GEE
RELEE THY DREDGERS
LYME SALARY TOR
CREDENT REDO FINESSE
ALEXANDERSRAGTIMEBAND
HANEY ETUI MEESE ELAN
SWISS DEBS STET SAGA
```

PUZZLE 163

```
EASEL RAW
SCARE REACH
PRUNE ELITE
YEN MESSY
APPROVE
LEAVE
SUSPEND
PRINT RIB
LUNGE CEASE
ULCER AGILE
SEE BONES
```

PUZZLE 164

```
BAT SLAB WACO
ABE TARO ODOR
GEL ATAN ROBE
SLEIGHBELL
DEE ADOBE
TIME ROBS ROD
EROS ENE MAID
AMO IDOL ALLY
MANOR IST
CARPENTERS
SLAT EAVE MAP
HOLE AREA ICE
ABET PERK TED
```

PUZZLE 165

```
SLIM URGES TESTY SPEC
HARI PHONE OAKIE TACO
AMEN READS WRISTWATCH
HANDSOUT SPANS ARSON
 SELDOM TIERS MARC
 EAT BROAD TOMTHUMB
FRISK FAINT POOPS NOR
IONS CURBS PURRS SIRE
DAS OUTRE NURSE GOOSE
ONTIPTOE BINGO TURNED
 REIN BETTE COST
THRONE MINTS FOOTSTEP
RAINS MIDDY MARLO HAS
ADDS VANES BANKS BESS
COG SIREN BARNS SLEET
KNEEPADS JUNKY EMU
 LILI SENDS CRUETS
ASTAR PARKA FINGERED
COATOFARMS GRADE YETI
ELLE ADOBE EAVES EVAN
BOLD NOWAY SMART SILO
```

PUZZLE 166

```
AFT SOS  SHE
LIE LAW  COW
PREPARE  APE
  INSECT
COURT  TOTES
ANNA    PERT
ROUTE  SPRAY
  SERENE
EMU  AVERAGE
LEA SEE  DAY
ILL ERR  ODE
```

PUZZLE 167

```
 PIG      BRAG
SAGA      LACE
CANNY    LAPEL
ALTO     TIMID
MERRY     REED
  YEARLY
   MOIST
   ATTACH
LASS     GRASP
GAMUT     EPEE
ROGUE    TAPER
ONES      ITEM
WERE       PEN
```

PUZZLE 168

```
   OLD    SPA
  PIAF    WIT
  ELMO   MANE
  CRY    IVEY
  BOA     BIG
 BOW  ALE  AHA
CRUX  BYE  LAD
ARID  WOE  BESS
PUN   JAB  RICH
TED   LAX  HOT
   LAC    NUB
   HUSK   FIG
 FLAG   EPIC
 LIT    TONE
 UPS     PER
```

PUZZLE 169

1. Unique, 2. Liquid, 3. Suitor, 4. Narrow, 5. Retina, 6. Kitten, 7. Meteor, 8. Armada, 9. Madrid, 10. Studio, 11. Butter, 12. Rescue.

PUZZLE 170

```
SHOCK      ROT
AERIE   APE SAP
GRATE  VENTURE
BLEND DIN IRIS
    EDEN NEAT
   RELATE
FAVORITE  DEAR
EXILE ARC BURRO
DEAL   MEDITATE
    NINETY
TENT    ANTE
ALOE HUE MARSH
CATALOG  FATED
ONE ASH  AZURE
BET      RENEW
```

PUZZLE 171

DOGS: Greyhound, Rottweiler, Airedale, Newfoundland, Dalmatian.
FAMOUS JOHNS: Garfield, Ritter, Adams, Newcombe, Denver.
UNITED NATIONS: Greece, Rwanda, Albania, Norway, Denmark.
SOUTHERN CITIES: Gulfport, Richmond, Atlanta, New Orleans, Durham.
FLOWERS: Geranium, Rose, Aster, Nasturtium, Daisy.

PUZZLE 172

```
 DIGS       BOG
PECAN      DIVA
ALONE     FINAL
TWINGE   HURDLE
BAR      ROOST
OLIO      COSY
STAR    ABET
SOLE    LEA   SCAN
      LIEN   POPE
      CRAB  ALEE
      AERIE  ODD
ROTUND  MASTER
AVAST    PUPIL
MERE     TRICK
PRO       YANK
```

PUZZLE 173

1. Paris, France; 2. Madrid, Spain; 3. Warsaw, Poland; 4. Rome, Italy; 5. Athens, Greece; 6. Vienna, Austria; 7. Oslo, Norway; 8. Bern, Switzerland.

PUZZLE 174

```
SPAS   ADE   LOY
LARA  PLUS  PAGE
IRED TELESCOPES
TRAINER    ELSE
 SEEN     ALOE
  TORRENT
  REIGN
  FOR
  FETED
  BURSTYN
BURR      EONS
PAPA    ARDUOUS
BINOCULARS RANI
ELAN SECT SKIT
GEL  EAT  ESTE
```

PUZZLE 175

C	CANCEL	CLEAN	LACE	N
H	HUNTER	TUNER	RENT	U
I	GIANTS	GNATS	STAN	G
C	GRACED	GRADE	DEAR	G
K	BAKERS	SABER	BARS	E
E	TITLES	TILTS	LIST	T
N	ENLIST	ISLET	TILE	S

PUZZLE 176

PUZZLE 177
MARINE

PUZZLE 178

```
                CARP
     ABEAM     OBOE
     PONDER    REUP
     ELOISE  NILES
     SALTONSEA
              DOWNED
               PEDRO
MOMS            NEMO
IMAM      SPOT
CARAFE    TIMER GRAM
ENCLOSE  ARMORIAL
LANDORSEAORFOAM
 MEDIATES  ENNEADS
LEAF ALLOT  EDENIC
EARL  SERB    TARA
ORLON         STEN
SPEWED
 SEVENSEAS
TAPIR MAITRE
ELLE  OGLALA
ALAN  SOLON
MATS
```

PUZZLE 179

```
HOBO       STY
AROMA     RARE
TALENT    ELAN
RELENTED   GAP
WOOD     NOMAD
ANY       OMAR
REAR      REND
 LESS     SEEP
 SAME    DRAB
 EVEN     ICE
 BREAD   METE
REV  RETAILED
PURE  DINNER
USED  PETAL
PET    WOKE
```

PUZZLE 180

1. Worked fast, 2. Safe ground, 3. Jealous kid.

PUZZLE 181

```
            MARC
            OBER
            BEDE              NAB
CARD   LIDA              OLE  RTE
AGAR   DONNAS
COCA        TAPE      GASTON
TRIM        MEL       UTAH
IAN    CAMERA         ERNS
   ELEVATE            RIDE
   AMIENS             NASA
   BUENOSAIRES
  SCAR       IGNORE
  HANA       AIRWAYS
  AMID  DAPHNE        POP
  NEMO  IDA           PASO
ANGLER  SARA          ARKS
BAH     CRATER        STAT
EVA          EWER     TARS
SEI          ENID
             LENO
             LEDA
```

PUZZLE 182

```
SOBS         PAT
DETOUR    COMA
OCTANE    ROOM
ERA    SPOILS
SEWS   LAS
   TANGERINE
    EON    SALT
CRETIN     TIE
WHIZ    SEMITE
HIDE    HEAVEN
ONE        DYES
```

PUZZLE 183

```
BEN   WHOM   SAFE
LIE   IOWA   PLAY
ORT   LILYWHITE
BESET       SEE
     WISE   TRUNK
ARDENTLY    ERIE
ROE   GABON  ANY
MONA  GORILLAS
STYLE       WERE
     PRY    VAGUE
LOUISIANA   ART
EARN  PLAN  IGO
ORNE  ELBA  TEN
```

PUZZLE 184

```
MAD   LASS   NEAP
EVE   ESPY   UPTO
TAJMAHAL     TEES
   EASY   LAMENT
UNCLE  VALE
PETE    TOBOGGAN
DEE   GUILE  RIO
ORDNANCE     HANS
   URGE   FATTY
TRAMPS   GURU
IAMB   THESPIAN
ERIE   EIRE   TRA
DEER   NEED   YET
```

PUZZLE 185

```
CLAP  ICED  WIT
LILI  NAME  ALE
OFOZ  FRIGHTEN
   ARID   EERIE
MEZZANINE   LVI
ATOZ  GEE   SOAR
LOO   MEGAPHONE
ENTRY    ORLE
   SOSO   NYLONS
SQUEEGEE    TOOL
OUI   LESS  EZRA
NOT   FESS  REAP
```

PUZZLE 186

```
GREAT  PURL  RAMP  OAF
LEDGE  ASIA  ODOR  RIO
ANGER  SHAM  COLORADO
DOE  MATE  PRO  LOANED
   WIPER   ACT  FIG
RELATED  COCOON  DUNE
EMOTED  BLUE  NOR  TOY
DIVE   CRASS   ROTATE
STERN  HINT  DESTINED
   GIVING   METEOR
CAPUCINE  LOBO  RECAP
OPINES  LORAN  SAME
LIE  RIB  AGAR  ROOMER
DADS  TUNNEL  TORMENT
   POT  TEE  SHADE
CHIMES  ESS  HOME  NOW
REPEALED  PAIR  RHONE
ORE  CURE  ANNA  LIVES
PER  HEED  STYX  YEAST
```

PUZZLE 187

```
MIFF   SLAB   PAT
IDEA   HOLE   ADO
LAZYSUSAN     PEN
   EATS      FANG
GRASPS   EMU
AIR      ERASES
SPINNINGJENNY
ELAINE       TIE
   ILK   PILOTS
DELL      CANE
ADE   TALLSALLY
TEN   ALOE   DEER
ANT   GETS   SETS
```

PUZZLE 188

```
BRAD         ETUI
ARENAS    AKIMBO
CABINETMEMBER
RIAL   RAID   ERA
IST    HERD   GRIN
DEEPENS    MESA
   LAE   PIN
SCOT     CREEDAL
CURT   PAIN   IDO
ORA   AITS   EVOE
OFFICEHOLDERS
SETTER    NOISES
DYES         ATTS
```

PUZZLE 189

```
AHEAD   DICE   EMMA
LORRE  MORAN  KEANU
AMASS  AWARD  ELLIS
NET  THIN  MESS  ATE
ROARED  TIDE  BRAD
   NYE  LON  WEE
PACO  DANE  METAL
OLIN  CARY  PIRATE
LIV  LANA  GAIL  TOW
EDITOR  SALE  MUNI
SALON  SAME  AMES
   RIP  IVE  PST
OPEN  EASE  MATTER
MAD  BENT  TATE  LAS
ARISE  DEVIL  ELLIE
RITES  IRENE  REESE
SHES   ESTA   SIRED
```

PUZZLE 190

```
TOMS  TIARA  TEMP  ECHO
BARAK  ANNAM  IVAR  TOOL
AMATI  SKINOFFONESNOSE
DETONATES  RIFE  SLANTS
EDE  DRED  ROSS  BLISS
SEER  BOUT  COED  KAT
PASTES  OLDS  SHAY  RICO
ONTOP  OTIS  MOAS  BINET
SKIP  SNAP  HALT  PRESTO
HAN  STIR  SOLA  TOOT
GOTYOUUNDERMYSKIN
PEEN  PEAS  ESTE  AEC
PAGANS  HEAD  AMOS  KOLA
OVOLO  POND  ETON  SIMON
LEAS  SARD  ROES  SKEINS
ART  JARS  RENE  RAIL
SPUNK  SOBS  MINN  ENT
ASKING  ACTA  MACEDONIA
SKINOFONESTEETH  IDOLS
TINT  ODIN  ELATE  VOLES
OSSA  RALE  DOLES  ERAS
```

PUZZLE 191

```
BOS  SIT  BEST  CALI
ALI  ERIC  ORATES  AMONG
SIDEREAL  SATURNSRINGS
AVILA  ESAS  RARE  GET
LINK  BRAGS  CAPOTE
TAG  ELITE  MOI  LOAF
ALMUCE  MANN  FRAPPE
SAVOIR  LEON  PIONEER
METEOR  PLANET  EER
ADORN  HAIR  EBONY  PEU
RANT  FASTS  BRAND  ALMS
ENE  TASTE  ERRS  FLAME
AIT  SKYLAB  BAITED
MERCURY  LEAF  ROCKET
ALERTS  CEES  IDEATE
LIDO  ORE  PRINT  PST
CARING  AIMED  CREE
WOO  RANI  NEAT  CAIRN
HALLEYSCOMET  ECLIPSES
ORION  TALARA  ROOT  ONE
SOOT  LENA  BAY  NED
```

PUZZLE 192

```
ABA  SERAPE  CRICS  EWER
PAR  EMILIA  REMAP  RENO
ONE  CENTURYOFPROGRESS
DAMONE  NOWS  ERA  KEA
LAWAND  FREUD  HEARHEAR
INAND  DOUD  EBON  BUNTY
DAYOFDOOM  ADRA  FLED
RIANT  CHORALE  LEM
BAM  DREAM  TOUSLE  HERA
OLORD  ENE  AUG  SAMOANS
TAMALE  DAM  RHS  SOLVES
TREMENS  NAP  ALP  NEESE
LANA  VIRTUE  MARAT  STY
EFT  RECEIVE  LIGHT
ODOR  TMEN  SOMETIMES
MAFIA  LIED  LUMP  OPINE
ARTESIAN  EDAMS  SMUDGE
NER  TNT  MCII  UTOPIA
FOURSCOREANDSEVEN  RRS
OLTU  UNOLD  UNSENT  ODA
RAHS  SANTE  POTASH  NET
```

PUZZLE 193

```
DREAM  G  LLAMA
R  D PANACEA M  B
E  G EYEBROW A  H
SAT  OM  IN  RIO
SIRN  ERN  SERR
IMAGES    KIPPER
N   NO  ILLIE   E
GS  OSEER     TN
LP  IBFRAC    IM
U OR  UTE   TP
MYSELF    SATIRE
BEET  FOP  UVAT
LAD TA  ER  EMU
IN  SOLICIT  GO
N CAPOSTLEL  U
EXALT  M  KNEES
```

530

PUZZLE 194

```
T I S         S E A
S H O O T     S U N D A
S T A N D S   O L D E S T
P A N   I A N   E L F   S T A
B E N   S U R E   N O U N   A S P
S O N   O H M   V E E   R T E   T O E
I O D I N E   E R R   H E L I U M
S T E N O   A R G O N   L E E R S
S R A   B A D   O W E   D R S
      E L L   M A Y   A R E
D R Y   D E I   A R E   A D S
C R E A M   B O R O N   P I E T A
C O P P E R   R A N   C A R B O N
I L E   W I N   A M I   R A T   A R T
L A W   M I N T   O R A L   T S E
L A B   C E E   N O D   E R E
S T I N K S   W I N T E R
T R E E S     S U N N Y
D E L         M E A
```

PUZZLE 195

```
  C O W       P A W
  E W E       O R E
B A L L A D   O N E I D A
E L L   R E E D Y   N O W
D E A R   T A D   F E E L
R A C E R       F A R
      T A R   P A T
      B E T   P E T A L
G O O D   P E A   L O O K
A D O   P I E C E   A L I
S E T T L E   E V A D E D
      E R A       I C E
      D A Y       L E D
```

PUZZLE 196

```
P A T S   H A Y   A B L E
A R E A   O N E   L E A K
L E A F L E T S   M A Z E
        A I D E   C O D E S
S C O R E       P A N
T A X I   D W I N D L E D
O R E   R A I N S   E V E
P E N G U I N S   M A I N
      A D S   S A D L Y
S A B L E   S T U D
O R A L   A N I M A T E S
L A K E   D I N   M A R E
O B E Y   O P T   E P E E
```

PUZZLE 197

```
A W E   C R A B   S W A T
P A L   L O S E   H A L O
E Y E   E A S E   A N E W
      P L A N   H A R D E N
A S H E N   T I M E
C H A T   P A V E   G A P
T O N   A L I E N   O R E
S E T   L E N S   A V E R
      F E A T   T R E A T
B Y P A S S   D O E R
L O A D   U N I T   N A P
E R I E   R I S E   O D E
W E L D   E L K S   R O W
```

PUZZLE 198

```
L A Y   U P O N   B O R E
O D E   N E R O   I D E A
B O A   T E E N   S O N S
  R A I L   S P O R T Y
R A N G E   R E I N
E R I E   F I N E   L E D
S E N D   E S S   L I V E
T A G   T A K E   O P E N
  N O S Y   M O S S Y
S P L I N T   P U N T
W O O F   I R I S   I M P
A U N T   N I L E   C A R
P R E Y   G O L D   K E Y
```

PUZZLE 199

```
R O W     D A D   P U P     F R O
A L A     I R A   A P O     L A S
W E S T E R N E R   D A L E E V A N S
      E R I E       E S T A
L O A N E D   P A P A L   P A R L O R
E L M S     E V A D E     Y O R E
I D A   L O N E R A N G E R   R A T
    N A M E D     A L I E N
    D R I E D     G A B L E
    A N N       B I G
    B I N D S   F L O O R
    L E O N E   R E N T E
A M A   W A N T E D D E A D   E D S
L A K E     A R I E S     A N A T
S T E V E N   M A N E S   E L L E N S
      E T O N       T R O D
R O Y R O G E R S   J O H N W A Y N E
A D E     S I P   I W O     A Y E
E A T     S O Y   M E R     M E L
```

PUZZLE 200

```
B O S S   S H I P   E L A T E
E D I T   C A R E   T U T O R
T O R E   A R E A   C R O N E
  R E W A R D   S C H E M E
      B E E     L E D
M E D A L   R A P I D   P O P
O L I V E S   L I E   W I P E
L O N E   O F T E N   A L I T
A P E R   R U E   T H R O N E
R E D   M E R R Y   E N T E R
      H A S     E R R
  B L A S T S   L A D D E R
F E A S T   L O L L   R E A D
E L I T E   I D O L   A R M Y
E L D E R   D E W Y   T Y P E
```

PUZZLE 201

```
C E D E   A C T E D   A B L E
A M I D   N A I V E   P O O L
R I N G   G R E E N   P A R K
S T E E P L E S   T E A S E S
      L E D   D I A L
A R O M A S   N E S T L E D
W O M E N   O F T   B E D
E D I T   F R Y   N O N E
S E T   C A T   T E N S E
  O S T R I C H   L A W Y E R
      A U N T   G A P
O R A N G E   S E R E N A D E
P A I N   M I N E D   A R E A
T I D E   A R O S E   B I A S
S L E D   S E W E R   S A N E
```

PUZZLE 202

```
S T A B   A F T   G A P S
P A G E   R O E   A R I A
A M E R I C A N   S T E M
R E S E T   L O T   E R E
      T E N   R O A R
P A L   M U D   W R I T E
A R A B   N O W   K E E N
N E V E R   N A P   S A D
      E D E N   G E E
C A N   V O W   A R E N A
R U D E   B E T T E R E D
A R E A   L E E   C I T E
M A R T   E K E   T E S S
```

PUZZLE 203

```
A T E   C O D   S P A D E
W A X   A V A   A L L E N
E X I S T E D   T O T E D
S I T T E R   C I T E
    A R T H U R   R E B
C A S T S   O R E   I R E
A L E E   A P E   S N I T
L O N   L I E   R A G E S
L E O   A N S W E R
    R E S T   A N G E R S
G U I D E   S T E E L I E
A S T E R   P E G   E V A
B E A N S   A R E   E E L
```

PUZZLE 204

```
E V E   S P A       B O N   A N T
L A G   T A L L   F A T E   H O E
F L O W E R B E D   C U L T I V A T E
    R A I S E R   O R I O L E
G Y M S     O H S     S S E
N O R     A N I T A     R A Y
A L E   V E G E T A B L E   O R E
B E E     A D E     E O S   S E T
O N I O N S       S P A D E
      T O E       R A G
      H U R T S   S P I N A L
E M U   A I R     L O A     R O D
R A M   C R A B G R A S S   D I E
R O B     T R E E S     E S S
      I T S     A L A   B R A N
      R E P O T S   R E T A I L
A S P A R A G U S   S E E D L I N G S
S E A   S I L T   R A G E   O A T
P E T   E N E     R E D   D R Y
```

PUZZLE 205

```
N A T   B L A B   E L L A
E L I   L O R E   N E O N
A T E   A T T E N D A N T
P O S E D   T O E
    R E E D   S A L T S
R A T E   M A T E R I A L
A G O   B I T E S   M I A
P R O R A T E S   P A L M
S A T E S   S T A R
    P E A   S O U N D
R E P O S S E S S   S E A
O V E R   P E T E   E R R
W E N T   S L A T   S O N
```

531

PUZZLE 206

```
L A O S   A M P S   S P O O L
O S S A   G O A T   W E A V E
A S I N   E A S E   A S H E N
F E E T O N T H E G R O U N D
S T R A N D   A L U M
        I A N   A S L O P E
A L A M O   A V O N   I D A S
P U T O N E S F O O T D O W N
E C O N   L A W N   H O R N E
D E N T A L   A B E
        B E T S   A R M L E T
F O O T I N O N E S M O U T H
I N K E D   R A T E   I G O R
N O I S E   T I N S   R E N E
D R E S S   S L A T   E R S E
```

PUZZLE 207

```
A U R A   S A G O   T R A D E
A N I L   A M I N   A E R I E
R I C E   T A L E   B E G A N
  T H E W I Z A R D O F O Z
        O N O   W O E
P I A N O   N O M E   D A B S
E N D E D   C O L S   N R A
R U M P E L S T I L T S K I N
E R I   D I K E   R E L E T
S E T S   N I T A   O P E R A
      L E D   S O L
  T H E M A G I C F L U T E
B R E E D   A N E T   P E A K
S O L V E   L I N E   D A R E
A D M E N   A T T N   O R L Y
```

PUZZLE 208

```
B I L K   A S P   C A T O
E R I E   T H A R   M O R O N
G E N T   H E R O   I M A G E
A N D T H E M I D D L E B A R
T E A S E D   S I N
      N A S A   D E S E R T
H A I T I   O N A N   A T A R
I N T H E M I D S T O F T H E
E A S E   O L E S   R E E S E
S T A M P S   S T A D
      A E S   L E A S E D
T O P A S S A F T E R M A N Y
A L A N S   L E E R   A N T E
M A R N E   L A S T   S T E R
S N E E   Y R S   S E R S
```

PUZZLE 209

```
    M A M A       S E T H
    B A S I C     A R I A S
  S E N I L E   L I M B E R
T R A D E   H O G A N   I C I
R A G E   L O P E D   S T E P
A T E   H E M E N   S H A D E
P E R S E V E R E   O A T E N
      P R I M A R I L Y
B A S I N   A T A V I S T I C
I R E N E   K I T E D   E N A
G A V E   N E V E S   W E S T
O R E   B A R E D   M O T E T
T A R G E T   L I V E R Y
  T A I N T     I N E R T
    L A D Y     D E N Y
```

PUZZLE 210

```
C L O D   H A B I T   S L A P
I A G O   O S A K A   T I T I
T H R O W S T H E B O O K A T
E R E M I T E S   B A K E R Y
        G A R   L Y R E
  F A N G S   M A C S   B E T
A R I E L   H O R A   T O L E
T O S S E D A N D T U R N E D
E E L S   O R T S   T E E N S
S S E   A L E E   C O T T A
      B R I M   M A P
A M U L E T   M A R I E T T E
G I V E S T H E H E A V E H O
A T E N   L I A R S   E L A N
R E A D   E S N E S   N E W S
```

PUZZLE 211

```
S M E L T   L E T S   L O A F
C A R E W   A D I T   A I D E
A L I N E   P I E R   P L O W
R E N T E R   T R A   S E R E
      Z I P   S P E E D E R
S C R E E N E D   P A D
C L E A R   T A M E R   R O B
A U N T   H A T E D   T A P E
N E D   P O L E R   S E V E N
      S U M   D I V I D E N D
S C A T T E R   T E N
W A G E   S O B   E N T R A P
E R N E   P U R E   E R O S E
A G E D   U S E S   R O U T E
T O W S   N E W S   S T E A K
```

PUZZLE 212

```
B A S E   S C A L P   A G A R
A T T Y   A R B O R   U R G E
G R E E N H O U S E   S E E D
G E E   E A S T   P O S E R S
Y E L P E R S   G A M I N
      A D A   C O R E   R E O
A N G R Y   G R E E N H O R N
L A R S   R O T   A O N E
G R E E N W I C H   A R M O R
A Y E   O R E S   E R E
      N A D I R   C L I M A T E
S T A T E N   B R A E   R A N
L A W S   G R E E N L I G H T
I R A E   E A R E D   N O O R
M A Y A   R E N D S   K N E E
```

PUZZLE 213

```
T E M P O   M B A   R A R E
A C O R N   A Y R   M E T E R
T H R E E L I T T L E P I G S
E O N S   U N E   A D E L I E
      A W L   S T I N T S
T E N G A L L O N H A T
A R I E L   A W E E   S E A M
T I C   L A D L E R S   T I O
A N K A   V I E R   A S T R O
      S W E E T S I X T E E N
C A P E R S   T E R
A R M I E S   A A A   I N T O
F O U R L E A F C L O V E R S
R U S E S   B A H   N E W E L
O P E S   E R E   O S T E O
```

PUZZLE 214

```
BASS . CHAFF . CRAM
TITHE . OUTRE . LILAC
AGREE . BREAD . OPINE
POI . PERT . MOOT . NIL
STAMINA . WIRY . MEAL
. AND . CANASTA .
WRING . SONG . TARGET
RARE . FORE . PENSIVE
ABE . MODE . FORK . VAN
PANDORA . HISS . REDS
STEALS . SENT . PUREE
. REACHED . DAB .
WANT . LARD . SUNSETS
ADO . PERI . SPOT . LIT
SLOPE . OVATE . HOURI
PINES . MELON . ELDER
BEAT . SLEPT . REED
```

PUZZLE 215

```
MAR . WARP . PLY
ALA . ALAR . RAE
PAINTSTHETOWNRED
SLOE . SOBS . ERA
VAIN . ETA . EMIT
CERTAIN TAXICAB
COAL . SILT . ELIS . ROE
AWN . MALL . STEP . URN
LEVEE . RASES
ART . ASH
POSSE . TEETH
ELS . ROIL . IRAE . DUE
ADE . USED . LOOP . TUBE
SALTIER ENVELOP
NEST . IRA . EDIT
EVE . ALAN . MARE
WITHFLYINGCOLORS
IRE . NONO . LIE
POD . GRUB . LEA
```

PUZZLE 216

```
EVAS . ACME . ARAB . LEFT
BACH . NOIR . RAGE . ERIA
ONTO . GROUNDHOG . OILS
NESTLED . POE . GOATEES
. GAL . STUNT . TBA .
ALOUD . POINTER . ARBOR
COIN . SOLOS . MOA . DOVE
INN . RESIN . SPADE . BAT
DETAINED . WET . DRAWLS
. MINDS . BOW . TRASH .
AVERSE . PAN . DRESSING
FIN . ERROR . MOOSE . TEE
ANTS . SUP . WAITS . REAM
RESTS . RECALLS . PESTS
. RAT . SADLY . LAG .
PANACEA . NEA . CARIBOU
OMEN . SQUIRRELS . OARS
REED . TURN . DRAT . NILE
ENDS . SANE . SAPS . SLED
```

PUZZLE 217

```
PUMA . COTE . CLAD . PAST
IRAN . RAHS . HULA . HIKE
KAYO . UKES . ESAU . ODIN
ALFRED . MARCHINGBAND
. LANES . YAK . TAI .
BOOKS . PEEP . IMITATES
LOWS . PROD . WRENS . EAT
OLE . COIN . THONG . LARA
WARTHOG . FIEND . HILLY
. YUL . GOATS . VAN .
STORM . HOURS . LIMEADE
CODE . BERRA . SEAS . URN
UFO . CURES . PEAL . EGAD
MURMURED . JAWS . SNUBS
. ALL . HAL . TOUTS .
APRILINPARIS . TEETER
GOOD . EELS . NOAH . RIDE
ELSE . SMUT . GAME . ENID
SEEN . TOME . SPAR . DEED
```

PUZZLE 218

```
ALMA . SER . OPS . ARNE
LOOP . SPEE . VEES . SEAL
OLLA . HIES . ERAL . SSTS
ELECTEE . ISR . MELEE
. HELLODOLLYPARTON .
DESERT . DELAY . TITTLE
ARE . RIPE . OPEC . SLIT
DIVA . ERSE . SOSO . EOS
SEEP . ESTER . NUTS .
. ROSEMARIEOSMOND .
DELI . ENERO . ORAL
CAP . ALUM . FIRS . WINE
REED . MARS . OTTS . ENA
ARREST . YOKEL . OPERAS
MYFAIRLADYBEGOOD .
. ERNIE . DEB . OPTICAL
LACE . PATE . INRE . SOLE
ARTS . EVER . NEED . OVEN
GIST . ENS . GAD . NEST
```

PUZZLE 219

```
FLEES . RADAR . STAMP
LARGE . AGATE . LAGER
UNION . CONTAMINATE
ICE . SEE . CADET . NEY
DESSERT . ERIN . OARS
. ODORS . SEATS .
BOSS . SACS . SCRAPED
AHA . DECAMP . EUGENE
SABER . KNARS . TEARS
IRONIC . TROUGH . ROK
SETTERS . TARA . ILLS
. EDITS . SPURS .
SCAR . SETA . AZALEAS
TAM . NEWEL . SEN . SPA
IMPRESARIOS . TOTAL
RELAX . REVUE . EVERT
SLEPT . DOERS . DARTS
```

PUZZLE 220

```
STAB . MARS . OAST . TARP
TAKE . ALEC . SOHO . OBEY
ELIA . CAVECANEM . PEER
MENTION . NIGER . ELKE
. ARN . FETE . BASK .
MOORE . TORE . ECLAIRS
AXLE . AHOY . AUTRY . LOP
TEETERED . COPSE . HIVE
. NORWAY . SARD . BAAED
. EEL . TONTO . SOU .
CLEAR . ULNA . GIANTS
HALT . ANNOY . HOLSTEIN
AMA . FLOES . DEAL . ENVY
DENTIST . VEAL . ADDAX
. OBOE . LEFT . KWH .
RIDS . BOITE . PILOTED
ACES . COMMONEST . URDU
ROLE . DONE . SPIT . SEED
ENID . SKIS . EASY . EYRE
```

PUZZLE 221

```
PETE . APED . RUMP . ROMA
ALAN . ROLE . ERIA . EBON
PANCAKELANDING . SILT
ANGORA . ALOE . DELETES
. DING . SPEW . DAN .
CARESSED . EMIL . STARE
AVE . EATER . SNOB . SNIP
RIDS . SUNUP . GRAB . TOE
EDUCE . PILES . ELEVATE
. NAVE . SEEPS . LAIR .
LADDERS . SPENT . RECTO
USA . RITE . SCARF . STIR
TINE . CAVE . SPARE . INE
ESTER . RELY . SCENICAL
. RUT . NEER . TIES .
REFINED . GLEN . GROPES
ALEE . PARAPSYCHOLOGY
PIES . IRON . TEST . DOGS
SALT . DENT . STAS . ERST
```

PUZZLE 222

```
YAW   SCUD  CLEFT MILE
TOLE  SAUDI RODEO ODES
AGEE  OLLAS EAGER HEAP
JACKOFALLTRADES  RASPY
     EGAD  LAOS   CAW
ARNESS   SUEDEJACKETS
GLIDE VOTE  EDIFY EEL
RIGS  SNIPE PAIGE URSA
ACE   PEEVE FONTS UNITY
YELLOWJACKETS    HIDES
     USED  ONO   MENU
MATED    JACKOLANTERNS
HAZED WHALE MOIRA HAH
ARTS  PRIMA FANNY NENE
DIE   LUIGI GONE  BEANS
JACKINTHEBOX     CHEESY
UPS   IBIS  ROAD
FLOWS    JACKINTHEPULPIT
LARA  LUCRE ERODE ELSA
ANTI  OTTER SARIS SILT
NEST  YESES SPAT  SEE
```

PUZZLE 223

```
TWAIN RAPT  ARES  GATES
LAMIA ELSE  LAGS  ADULT
CLOWN CASA  SNOW  VOLGA
TRICKORTREAT      GOBLIN
     YOU   ORCS  LATEEN
RODE  SPUMONE     SORT
APIS  NOME  WEREWOLF
GHOST AMAS  DAISY RIAL
EIDER LAB   TESTS BASIE
RESOLES ERAS      DEPEND
   JACKOLANTERNS
SCUBAS   RAYS  LOATHES
TALON SPANS OIL   OASES
URNS  AMEND PACE  WITCH
BLACKCAT  TIKI    LETO
ERRS  HOLSTER     ERSE
TARGET   REFS  LAD
GHOULS   HAUNTEDHOUSE
HORDE MAID  EASE  BLIND
ALTER SANE  RUNS  LANKY
TEARS SHED  STET  ANGIE
```

PUZZLE 224

```
CANS  S  PAS HA  REC AST
VAS E STATI C  D  RIER
SE VERS AFFR ONT BRE ED S
R E QUEST  RIB RO AST
   IRRESOLUTE   HE AL
PAR ALL EL NE AT REP ART EE
LOR EN F ASHION ABLE
   MAG EN TA  ES T IMATE
FL OR IST TI RADES E GIS
OUT ER MEM P HIS NE T
S L ATE  PAIR S  S ING
```

PUZZLE 225

Since, Teach, Merit, Stage, Flint.

PUZZLE 226

```
SADA  BABE  SHAG
AGED  ALIAS NOME
PANSYYOKUM  APER
SLY   AONE  ALPINE
   TRUE  DRED
CHAINS   WATERED
RINGS MITE  ALOG
ORNE  WADER GIVE
PEER  ALTS  TOTEM
DELILAH    BONERS
   IDLY  FURS
DAHLIA   ALMS ADE
ALAI  BLUEBONNET
WINE  YOKEL OKLA
NAGS  ASSE  TAIL
```

PUZZLE 227

DISNEY WORLD

PUZZLE 228

```
BOLL  BAT  TEAM
LUAU  AIR  ARTE
TRIG  DDE  YSER
SCORE   NOLTE
   SAG   CRO
SPRING   HARDEN
ASA      IWO
LITTER   PONDER
   ROE   IRE
SOUND   COLOR
CODA  AUK  SNOW
ADEN  USA  OTTO
MAST  BOX  NOSE
```

PUZZLE 229

1. Saturday, 2. Basement, 3. Proposed,
4. Uniquely, 5. Notebook, 6. Cinnamon,
7. Frighten, 8. Coverlet, 9. Animated,
10. Blockade.

PUZZLE 230

```
MISS  DECAL ASPS
ANTI  ELOPE SWAT
MAURITANIA  KANE
ANN   RANGES ZEV
SET   RID   ENSILE
   PAN   TRIAL
AJAR  SASH  CRABS
GABON RUE   KENYA
TRYMA TEND  EDEN
SODAS ETS
HUSSAR   ALA   SRA
ANI   MENTAL TIN
LINE  IVORYCOAST
OTIS  EENIE ALEE
SEAS  SNEAD FEND
```

PUZZLE 231

1. Green (horn, house, tea, card); 2.
Back (kick, out, roll, half); 3. Day
(dream, bed, room, break); 4. Call (cat,
bugle, over, curtain); 5. Boat (sail, row,
life, gravy).
BONUS: Great (divide, guns, ape,
lakes, coat)

PUZZLE 232

```
ANGLE APOD  ROTA  AMAS
LIRAS CARR  UPAS  FLORA
BLACKBERRY  PINKERTONS
SLY   EAST  SEEK  READES
   MORN  ICOME PATRI
ALANS SCORE LOOT  NET
LETT  YELLOWPINE CEDAR
TATA  OREL  AVA   MOTIVE
ONEROUS   AROSE VOYAGES
STRIA AGERS EERO  OSS
   ORANGEFREESTATE
AFB   SLOT  RILLE EXPOS
CAROMED   PASSE INSPECT
ERODES ELM  MONO  LAHR
ROWAN GREENBERET ORRA
BEN   BORA  AINGE IDLED
   STLEO PINTA ANEW
ASTRAL   RAIL NOTA HOO
BLUEDANUBE  REDHERRING
BIDES ALEC  PRIM  UTTER
AMYS  TETE  MAES  GEESE
```

PUZZLE 233

```
CHARDS ARAT IBIS  MAP
LINEAL REPORTING  ALAE
ULTIMO STORIEDSTEROID
TAKEGOOD  MAMET DINGE
   EGAN  JENS  INGER
SLANDER   WONT  POSTE
TETRAD JEST  MADEHASTE
ATEAM CANE  AGED  ITAL
TOS   RIND  CAGES TREND
   PLANE BARI  GAMETE
RETRACETERRACECATERER
AVIATE    MILL  PATEN
BOGIE SPITE GAPE  CRO
IKES  MEAL  MICE  DRAIN
DERELICTS SEAT  SEEDED
   PELTS DEAN  STABILE
HOSEA     BIND  MAIL
OWERS AURAS COMPLAIN
ONESTARSENATOR  PENMAN
DEMI  ELEVATORS LATINO
DEA   SORE  EPEE  EDITOR
```

PUZZLE 234

```
HIS   SAFE  RIMS
ODOR  EVEN  PERIL
WERE  READ  ALONE
LATE  ERRS  CANED
   LINT  SET
SCENE COT   EVER
CLODS ARIA  IRE
RID   EASTERN SAD
ACE   TREE  GUESS
MESS  EAR   TENSE
   TEA   BALL
OPERA ALIAS EACH
DALES PORT  SHOE
ESSAY EDGE  SELL
STEM  DEED  MAP
```

PUZZLE 235

PUZZLE 236

```
SORE  ASTOR LAMB
THIN  SCARE AVER
EASE  TALON MIRE
ERE   HERE  EVADED
DANCER   SEGAR
   OWNS  NARRATE
LAUDS CADDY PAD
ELSE  TEPEE PERE
ATE   MANTA SEDAN
FORSAKE   RACE
   TRESS RARELY
HEARTH PERT LIE
ARIA  OLIVE TUNA
LILY  MANES ODER
TESS  EXERT TERN
```

PUZZLE 237

1. Batter, 2. Aromas, 3. Kneads, 4.
Eclair, 5. Raisin, 6. Spices.
FIRST LETTERS: Bakers.

PUZZLE 238

```
MALL WALE BOMB
ERIE SEPAL ALOE
SEED PREDICTION
HANG RED COHORT
     ERA  FINE
SHA AWE ITS  HIT
AEROPLANE  PAGE
FLINT TIS FABLE
ELSE  EXTORTION
ROE BAR AXE  TOY
    POSY  FEZ
MISLAY EGO  EDGE
INTERLOPER BRAD
SCAB UPEND  RULE
TARE MEET   AMEN
```

PUZZLE 239

Failure is the path of least persistence.
1. Feet, 2. Pertain, 3. Sail, 4. Pose, 5. Cluster, 6. Faith, 7. She.

PUZZLE 240

```
MIME DADOS HEMS
ACED EERIE ERIC
COED SOULS INCA
ENTICING  AEGEAN
    EARS AMAH
STUDIO  ABETTORS
TEN NUBBY  SEPAL
AMPS SLASH NIICE
SPICE ESSAY  NEE
HONEYBEE REVERT
    NEAP HALO
NOMADS  DISLOYAL
EMIR HAIRS  DALE
RANI EMCEE  ORES
ONTO DOERS  ODES
```

PUZZLE 241

```
RAGE ANEW REAMS
AWAY DATA EQUIP
DAZE JINX DUNCE
ARE HULA SUITED
REDRESS  FACT
   OAT  OBEYED
JOKER GORE  WIG
IRE DOLLARS EKE
BEE BODY  HAREM
SNIPER  FOX
   COSY RIVETER
REVISE VANE  ONE
EXACT SIZE  AQUA
VILLA USER  PURL
STEEL EASY  TEEM
```

1-C, 2-O, 3-W, 4-T, 5-N, 6-D, 7-H, 8-K, 9-L, 10-Y, 11-Z, 12-R, 13-I, 14-V, 15-J, 16-M, 17-F, 18-S, 19-E, 20-A, 21-B, 22-U, 23-X, 24-Q, 25-P, 26-G.

PUZZLE 242

1. Feverish, 2. Balloon, 3. Patent, 4. Standing, 5. Learned, 6. Currant, 7. Market, 8. Monitor, 9. Garment, 10. Forage.

PUZZLE 243

```
EGOS SONOF CARE
BALI ABABA HEEL
BRIG LOGAN ARAB
BONNIEANDCLYDE
     IAN AUK
WINNIE PANE  PAM
OMEGA SARG  LILA
DAVIDANDGOLIATH
AGIN NERO  INNER
NON AGEE TAGORE
    PRO ENE
LAURELANDHARDY
ARNO ADORE  IRIS
RIIS NIMUE  NAPE
KATE STEMS  GMEN
```

PUZZLE 244

A.
```
RAPID
ABHOR
PHOTO
IOTAS
DROSS
```

B.
```
BIRTH
INURE
RUPEE
TREAD
HEEDS
```

PUZZLE 245

```
RAMP ULES MART REAL
ALAE NOLO ASIA ELLA
YAKS FULLSTEAMAHEAD
NETTED DATA  SEEDY
  HERD FINE RITA
SCARY HOED DEVOTION
TASS NEAR LADER  CRO
ART SOIL LANDS  WELD
GLEANED MITT  EASES
   GOLIKETHEWIND
STRAW ALES ASSISTS
TIER AIRER IDLE  HIE
ADO THREE CREE FAME
RESTRAIN CHER POKER
   HUBS FOES RARE
ESTES NILE  MORTAL
SWIFTASANARROW ULAN
SALT SUVA EAVE NENE
ETES KEEL DEED EGAD
```

PUZZLE 246

```
APP RO VE  BRE D   FRO M   TRA M
U   A  RS  AD AP TAB LE  ANS WER
QUE ST ION ER  PE L IC AN  CRA IN GE
        AS TE R OID  S CRU B
PLE A S URE S  S PAS  M E A DOW
A   TT ACH TAM PER  T ABLE  M EL
    R ET RI VER  IM MED I ATE
RE ACT  VE NT S  E ND  MA U L
D IVER T  E RA  MEN A GE R IE
       AC ER B  P BAT T LE
CAN T ON  E LA T ION  S EA SHO RE
AR E TE  EP IC URE A N  VER B
D EM UR  S AL  LE AVE  S T ATE
```

PUZZLE 247

```
RAIL PORTO ABBR
EINE ALIEN DRAY
BREAKSDOWN VERA
SEE USES OREADS
    NER STUNK
ABETS  STINTING
CARTA SPACE  NEA
AREA  THERE STAB
LOA SEINE  CAWLS
INKSTAND  RAMOS
   SEAMY SER
SAWERS STLO  PTS
ALIT TAKEABREAK
LATH EVERT  BARI
ASHE RANEE  IRON
```

PUZZLE 248

1.
```
REMOTE
A A R
CIRCUS
K R D
ENOUGH
T W E
```

2.
```
STARCH
O T A
LITANY
A I V
CORRAL
E E S
```

PUZZLE 249

PUZZLE 250

```
SOBER THAW SLAP
ALIVE RIDE TALE
SITES IDOL IDEA
HOE TREE  FALSE
   WOOD HART
ADVERB  ARISEN
LEASE RAVED LOW
SALT ICE  LAVA
ONE LINEN WATER
STRONG  HOMELY
   EATS FIRE
SHADE TUSK  APT
MAID GOES MINER
OGRE ERAS ARENA
PEER RELY NEWSY
```

PUZZLE 251

1. Basset, Basket; 2. Coarse, Hoarse; 3. Accent, Accept; 4. Prance, Prince; 5. Propel, Proper.

535

PUZZLE 252

```
ARC . . . . . LAG . TOY
GAL . . . COLA . . BARE
ENACT . SOUSAPHONES
STREW . SLUR . SEAL .
IDO . . PASSE . TENOR
WANE . SEPTETS . RENO
ARE . APE . NEE . OWED
FIT . LAD . . AWN . .
TASSEL . . . . . CAB .
UTE . . . . . . ODE .
NAG . . . . . REGALE .
ROE . . SEE . . COW
CODA . OUR . ELS . CUE
OVER . TIMPANI . LOTS
SANTA . NAILS . . AIR
IDEA . SNEE . LEDGE
BASSOONISTS . IDIOM
ABET . NICE . . OBI
RAT . SLY . . . NIT
```

PUZZLE 256

```
WED . SILK . EARL
OBI . ERIE . SHOE
OBSOLETE . SODA
. LULL . PRAYED
SKIT . ASSAY . .
INK . GNU . ISSUE
TEE . EDGES . INN
SEDAN . ACE . DID
. PEARL . WETS .
INSIST . AMOS .
TALE . ORIENTAL
EPIC . LORE . EGO
METE . LEST . PET
```

PUZZLE 257

```
HOSTS . . LONER
ADORE . OPERA .
GENIE . TEENY .
. . BRAIN . . .
PATE . POSTER .
AGE . RAN . IVE
LOAFER . BEAD .
. . LATER . . .
SALAD . RODEO .
ALIKE . ATONE .
WIDER . SHEER .
```

PUZZLE 258

```
ODES . ASPS . BAG
POLO . ITAL . ALE
AMAN . LANA . LET
LENIN . NETTLE .
. CORD . EER . .
ALF . TOUR . ROTS
HOUSESPARROWS .
AURA . ACME . MOE
. RLS . OPEN . .
GOTHAM . DOORS
BOW . ARID . IDEA
ONE . VICE . SOAP
BED . EASE . ERRS
```

PUZZLE 259

```
. LES . AMAN . BRA
DIVE . SLADE . OAR
AMEN . TIDAL . PART
NERD . ACE . STATES
. MINE . JOHN . .
FRIEND . ONEAND .
AIR . DELIS . MERE
IVES . ROSIE . AVID
RENE . REEDS . EVE
REASON . WARREN .
. SAFE . NAME . .
ALCOTT . MER . GAVE
BARN . ILIAD . GLEN
ETO . MOLLS . ITSA
LEW . EYES . . EAT
```

PUZZLE 253

```
TOY . ZEST . LEON
ODA . OLLA . AMBO
TIM . DAUB . IBIS
ENSUING . ANA . .
. . FAD . TWERPS
ADHOC . FEE . KIM
VIES . ARE . MENU
OVA . PIA . MIDST
WADDED . HAL . .
. LOT . GONDOLA
PAIL . BARN . LAG
ACNE . APSE . ENE
NEED . DEER . SEE
```

PUZZLE 254

```
NEST . TIFF . WYE
ALTO . AGUE . AUK
BLIP . UNSETTLE .
SARAH . ISSUE . .
. ZESTY . TRAM .
CUP . LIE . NOBLE
ERASED . BAREST
DEVON . SAM . DOE
EYED . CIDER . .
. MOORE . DADDY
STEMWARE . CARA
EON . EZRA . KNEW
COT . SEAR . SEWN
```

PUZZLE 260

```
PURIM . ADDA . FLAY
IRONY . CHOP . AARE
CAMEL . COTILLION
ELIZABETH . ASCOT
. SADE . ODESSA .
BATTLE . GUY . .
SALADS . CORONETS
ASYOU . OAT . FATAL
MESSCALL . OSPREY
. HID . TOHEEL .
COPPER . DOPA . .
ARRAS . NOWSLEEPS
PLAYSSAFE . ORLOP
ROME . AMOR . TILDE
ANSE . PERS . TEASE
```

PUZZLE 255

```
MILL . TIP . SASH
ARIA . ONE . EPEE
CONSERVE . VEER
KNEED . ELSE . .
. RUGS . CRASH .
WAD . CAT . HENCE
ALE . ABIDE . TAR
ROAST . GAD . IRE
MELEE . ABUT . .
. EDIT . LATER .
SPAT . SIDELONG
EACH . LOU . KNOT
ANTE . END . SEWS
```

PUZZLE 261
PLAYWRIGHT

PUZZLE 262

```
HAS . SPAS . RED
ARC . TENT . GARY
RIO . RENO . RILE
MATTER . OPENED
. LEA . SPAT . .
DRANK . TELAVIV
ION . GAD . IRA
MEDICAL . LINEN
VANE . ONE . . .
RECORD . BANGER
ODOR . ARID . ALE
DENY . LATE . RIA
ENS . FEED . YAM
```

PUZZLE 263

```
SOAR . BUM . TAFT
ONCE . ATE . AREA
LECTURED . LILT
. OILS . IDEALS
BARRE . ETON . .
RIDE . CLATTERS
ADE . SLATE . SEA
DEDICATE . SCAT
. NOSE . ETAPE .
MULCTS . FLAP .
ALAI . IRRITATE
UNIT . FOE . EDEN
LACE . YET . DEED
```

PUZZLE 264

```
BAT . BAIL . OBOE
ORE . OGLE . DELE
NEE . LIKE . OVER
DAMSEL . HUE . .
. IRE . BARREL .
DITTO . FIT . ADO
ACRE . GUN . AGES
TEE . PAR . SPENT
ADAGES . EEE . .
. SUN . ANSWER .
GLUE . OATS . ARE
AIRS . FLEE . RID
BEES . TEND . END
```

PUZZLE 265

```
. DOG . CAVE . COD
DOVE . OPEN . AWE
EDEN . PEST . PEW
EGRET . TEST . .
PET . EON . ROUGE
. WAGON . ORAL .
ABLE . RIO . TESS
COED . ESSAY . .
TANGO . EEL . TAB
. DEBT . LARGE .
HOE . OAKS . LARD
ERR . EPEE . TIES
YES . SENT . OLE
```

536

PUZZLE 266

```
PIES   LEA  ALB   DREW
ROTO  POLL COAL  EAVE
ATOM  ROIL COLA  FIAT
MANAGES  OTO  STEIN
LOVELYHULAHANDS
ATTILA ASONE STERES
MOO  FIRM UTES  DORA
ANYA LEIF SPOT  PET
STOP SNAPS  EDIT
SOUTHSEAISLANDMAGIC
SOUR RIOTS  ULNA
ERR  NEVE  ETES  TIFF
BEEF EDIE  ARNE  DEE
BALLET ATTIC OATERS
MOONOFMANAKOORA
COSTA  LAM  APPLAUD
ROAD ETUI BORE  ELSE
ARTE SERA ICER  NOES
NEED DIN  CAD   TURK
```

PUZZLE 267

```
LACE SPIRE PELF   SCAD
ALUM PERON ERIE  PEALE
POTBELLIEDSTOVE  ARSON
FERRIES AIDED   PATHS
TRANCE TILTED   SEPIA
CEE  CARVE   SURER
POPE STEREOSCOPE  OFT
ALAS RAT  ODES  KNEE
LET  BASS MACAW LUSTS
ESCAPADE BARK  MARKET
HAILE HALLS   CACTI
TOWHEE ONTO  BACKSLAP
OBOES MUGGY GENE  LIE
GIRD OOLA  AGE   BEDE
ASK  BLUNDERBUSS ETAL
QUIET RAYON   EEL
BUNNY SHAVER  DEVISE
ERICS SIEGE  ROSETTA
TULLE KEROSENELANTERN
OCTET AVON SINEW LANE
NESS TENS  PLODS ELSE
```

PUZZLE 268

```
SHAFT   TEENSY   HARSH
HONOR   NARRATE  EXILE
OPERA   OPOSSUM  LEVER
PEW  NAMED ADEAL  EWE
SQUARES   ENDOW
IMPOUND  ANNIE   RIDS
HERMIT  CIVET   AESOP
AREEL  TAROT  BONANZA
DEY  CEDAR  GOGETTER
FLAXEN   HEARTH
DIPLOMAT OUTRE   JIM
ENLACES RIGID  CAINE
FRESH  VALET  BALBOA
YEAH ELOPE  SERPENT
YOKEL   RAPIERS
TET  FENCE FANNY  JAW
ALOOF  DANCING  AZURE
PLANE  ENDORSE  LONER
EATER  ROONEY   LOOSE
```

PUZZLE 269

```
MAMA CATO BISCAY FLIT
OLES AWED ASHORE LURE
DENS PANE SAUDIARABIA
ECUADOR DEITY   HUES
SEND PUMAS   ANON
CHASE SARAH  MINTERS
LUCID WOVEN STAND XIII
AMIN BARER  NEWZEALAND
RON  GIDE CURIE  ELSE
ARGENTINA OMIT MATTED
LASS BRIBE   SULU
SANITY ROAN SINGAPORE
ACID MOANS MAGI  FAS
LUXEMBOURG HAPPY OTIS
ATE  EARED FAILS ARENA
DESISTS COYLY  PANSY
SATE DARES   ABET
SLOB POMES  MOROCCO
PHILIPPINES GOBI ROOK
LOAD ESCORT EVES IOWA
YORE TIARAS MARE ONLY
```

PUZZLE 270

```
SCROD MAMA MISC CABAL
OLIVE IBEX ICER ADANO
FIVEMINUTESMORE SERIN
AVER NUTS TENFOOTPOLE
RESTORES CURS   SORT
ILETIONS BOZO   PET
OPERA EDIT BYTE MIDI
FIVEFINGER PORE HAMAN
ILES TOGS TROD BIGAMY
TAR  SHOE RAIN  SILO
FIVEANDTENCENTSTORE
ONCE HATE ORTS  OIL
MARINA AIDA BOAR INDY
UTICA ORNE TENPOUNDER
TOTE TRIG CATS SCORE
IMA  LAID POPE  STER
BABE EINE  EPIDEMIC
FIVEHUNDRED ALIE MINA
ERATO TENCOMMANDMENTS
TONER ALEE HOTE INERT
ANELE LESS ORES STOAE
```

PUZZLE 271

```
ADZE PAAR  SOLE LAMA
PRAM EAVE  ALEX ARAB
SUNBATHED  NIGHTCLUB
EMERGES DIDO  ORIOLE
OAR  CITY  WREN
LAPIS BOSS  CATEGORY
ORAL BACH POSED DEE
BIN  CUBA GRAND SILL
EAGERLY TOAST VINYL
GAB  BRUNT   LET
PSHAW CLARK  RANSACK
LOAD PLAID DINT  PHI
EAR  GRIST POPE  HEAL
APPARENT HOES  PEDRO
BOAT TAMS  AIR
SLALOM CASA  ENLARGE
CUCUMBERS  DIXIELAND
UKES LOOT ERAS  DRAG
MESH ESPY SAME  SATE
```

PUZZLE 272

```
BAND CANS RISE  DOSE
ALOE OPAL ODOR  EVER
SINGAPORE  POLARBEAR
STARRY REBEL  HURTS
CEE  COPES  FAITH
MATE SAWED BARN  EGG
ANI  EAGER MOTTO AIL
INVOLVED HONEY  ERLE
NEEDLES PAVED  LADLE
DID  TAPER  BOG
DOLLS CORPS  BALLADE
AWAY SALTY  HOLLERED
TEN  WILLY TALES RAG
ADD  ARMS PRIED BORE
SPIES PEARS  YEW
LACES PERIL  VEERED
UNALTERED  LIMESTONE
KEPT AURA ENOS  LOTA
EWES REEL DEBT  ETON
```

PUZZLE 273

```
SWAP FAIR STUM  RITE
LINE ECCE PISA  EDIT
ESTA WHIMSICAL  FETE
WHISKEY OILS  IGLOOS
AIR  ADZE  OGRE
STUNT FREE  MONOXIDE
TILT PEEL DOZES NOV
ANT  SENS BATED ASSE
REIGNED REDES  GREET
MAIN BEGOT  BONN
CHAMP MESAS  PARASOL
OUTS AARON SALE  ADO
EMU  ARCED DANE  STER
DEMOCRAT LEFT  STERE
BREW LIFE  VIA
ANGLES AIDA  FARMERS
LENA TENTACLES ITEM
SWAT EVER EASE  NOSE
OSTE RATE SETS  ANTE
```

PUZZLE 274

```
MAST TIFFS RATED CHAD
ASTA INUIT ILONA HATE
CHUCKBERRY STRAWBERRY
SENTRIES LAKES DERMIS
LOAD SISI   PLAY
HELENS HESSE HEEDLESS
ERASE WINTERBERRY RIA
IRIS SHEDS ARKS  FRET
SON  BLISS SOLES TROVE
TRELLIS APRES FOALED
HUCKLEBERRYFINN
CETANE AXLES  ENACTED
ALIST DICED HORAL ESE
NEMA PORE  PEARL BETA
EME  CANOLEBERRY CATER
AIRBASES MANES WASHES
ERSE BITS  AARE
REDSEA CARTA ESTIMATE
ELDERBERRY GOOSEBERRY
FIAT LLANO OWNER NEAR
SAYS EDGES NESTS TAPE
```

PUZZLE 275

```
GAEL CRAMP FIRE APART
ASIA AURAL LOON CACHE
THREADBARE INSTITCHES
EYE  LIE TART TER TEAS
PAZ  MITE  FARAD
MISER BAA TEEN NESTLE
INCA TAILORMADE COHEN
TAI  WALL HAIR AMATIVE
ENSNARE FACT PRAY MEM
RESIDE DART HALT  ABLY
ONE  HORA  PONY  COL
FARE HELM MUTE HONEST
LIT  CAME TIRE GAVEWAY
ASARULE LOSS ROSE LIT
SLIER NEEDLEFISH NEVE
HELPED AIDE ACH  RIDER
DROSS ACRE  BAT
BASE ADE ODOR ALP  RAE
ALLSEWEDUP REDBUTTONS
STATE TUNE PLEBE ATOP
HOTEL SPAN SLEET DENY
```

PUZZLE 276

```
PAIR   SCAT    MOM
OGRE   HUSH    AWE
TEEM   ABSENCES
AUKS     FEEDS
SPARSE   ATE
ALIKE  HIS    NEW
GARS   RED    WADE
ANY    HAM   BRIGS
TAG    EYELET
LOSER    EVES
ANTELOPE  TRAY
ICE   EDEN  LACE
DEW   MEET  EWES
```

PUZZLE 277

```
AJAR   WEB     EEL
DALE   ALE    BADE
DRJEKYLL     EVES
ODE    LAGERS
HAL    PALING
ESS   TWO   TABOO
REOS  EBB   ROOM
BANES EEN    UZI
REDSEA       TET
TAHITI       POI
ALOE   PHYSIQUE
ROSS   POE   LUSH
ATE    YIP   SEES
```

PUZZLE 278

```
BRAT  SPA  ERG  STAN
AURA  OAR  PIE  TONE
IDES  PRECISE  ROTS
TESTS ETA  ESTATES
      EAT  EMS  EON
HAT MUG  PIP  OGLED
AGAR NATURAL  EASY
GENOA RES  RED  GEE
      CHINA  STARK
APR ALI  CON  YEARN
LAIC ESSAYED  GLUE
ALOHA HEN  RUG  BEE
      ARK  ADD  DIP
ELASTIC ORO  GUSTO
DABS CHARADE  READ
ETUI KIN  KEY  SAND
NETS SPY  ERE  ELKS
```

PUZZLE 282

```
PASTE CORRAL  FACT
ALTAR APIECE  OLLA
SLOPE LESSEN  RIAL
SORE MONET  DAMASK
EWER ORE  SCAN  SHY
      STAIRS  AHAB
ARA ATE  PAPA  LASH
BANAL SHAVEN  AGUE
ANGLES ICE  DAMAGE
SEED CAVERS  NEPAL
HERE AMER  CAT  ERS
      RARE  SERBIA
PAR LENT  NEE  SOFA
IRONIC ASSET  HALL
LOBE RUSHIN  TOTAL
OMIT ONSALE  ARENA
TANS WEEDED  PERKY
```

PUZZLE 286

```
ELAN HUMES COOE OWNS
ORALE ERATO ADEN CHAP
NONEWSISGOODNEWS TAMA
ESE STRAIN ENS ORATED
RESUMES ADO PROVIDE
NAP SEASONTICKET
BASIN CHAMP RTES SAC
ENTO SHARP STOOL GALA
STANDARDS COUNSELLOR
TER OKIE SCANT DELES
SAVES OPALS DIANA
SHARE HARTE TERM BOY
CONTRIBUTE DECISIONS
ANDY NORSE TANKS RUDE
RES OTOS CARTS WATER
TALENTSCOUTS WAN
BARTERS PUB ARRIVES
EDITOR ORT TRADER ERA
LOPE UNDISCRIMINATING
ORES PEON PUGET NINES
WEST TART LEANS TESS
```

PUZZLE 279

```
PECAN ASSIST BALSA
ADAGE SLANTED AGATE
IDLES SOONERORLATER
NIL TRET PREED ELI
SETA ASTER ERG TREE
      OPRY EWER SARI
EASE DECAY LETHAL
SCENES SORES SLICE
ETC TRAM MEDIA ETTA
RHOS STAMPEDED STUN
NEUT EERIE ONES HAS
ETNAS DARNS ANTLER
SETTER TESTA LUCY
      EXAM SEAL DOME
DAMS NAP SNIPE PILL
ABA BEREA MINT LEA
TONGUEINCHEEK ILIAD
ERIES ANTENNA RINSE
START ASSETS EDGES
```

PUZZLE 283

```
HAHA BELL KING ABBE
OJOS ERIE AREA BOOT
WASHINGTONPOSTMARCH
EXPOSES NOUNS ULNAS
      RAT MITT ISM
ATSEA EINE ELSE TED
NAP CONCERTBAND UNO
DRUM GEE ABUT OBOE
SONATA FOXED BRASS
      SEMPERFIDELIS
FLUTE LEAFS AZORES
IONS BURN MIV NEVA
FAD COMICOPERAS MAN
EDO HOPE COOK ALONG
      BOB STOW SPA
LEVER UPPER STONILY
UNITEDSTATESMARINES
TOOT NEAR SOUR ERNE
ELLE ASHE TUGS REAR
```

PUZZLE 287

```
HEAD SCAB GLAD CATS
ALMA TULL RENE AVON
SKIN ALOE EATS NILE
PENCILPUSHER SADDLE
      ESE SIT DENY
STERN STEP ERASMUS
AID TREED WALT TORE
SNIT ORE LILT RAGE
STEEPLE SANTA DINER
      NIL LINDA HOP
SHAPE FANCY TUNEFUL
HARE LUCE ERR RILE
OVER SADE POETS RNA
TEACHER TANK OREAD
      EAVE GIL ELA
AVENGE GREASEMONKEY
BART ROLE NERO GATE
ESSE ALEE CLOT ESTA
LEER LAND ELSE RARE
```

PUZZLE 280

```
PLOT SLOB MACE PREP
REAR PAPA EBON LOLA
ONTO OVERSTEPS EWER
THUNDERBIRD ABACK
      POE AERO MAGENTA
NAPES QTR WADE
OLES TUE THUNDEREGG
AAA RUES HORNS AGUE
HIRSUTE PIUS SCONE
      THUNDERSTRUCK
OSIER APSE UNUSUAL
THOR FAULT AMID SPY
THUNDERBAY BET SEER
      URGE HUN PASSE
OREGANO WHEN GUM
CAGED THUNDERBOLT
TMAN DESIGNATE VAIN
AIDE YEAR ANNE ACME
LESS ERRS STAN REED
```

PUZZLE 284

```
BIAS SHE MAR EWES
MERGE WAX OLE RADIO
AGREEMENT ATTENDING
MII PORK EASE TEL
ANTE OVER ERRS POSE
      ARA ERECTED EAR
SATIRE SPEED STRIPE
PRECISE ENS CONTAIN
YES ACCENT GALA LED
      ALIT BALD
SOD SPAN COLLIE ESP
PARAPET BAR SETTLES
AROMAS MAIDS ROOSTS
      MET SONNETS NYE
OPEN STUD REAL SWAB
DAD DARN EVES HUE
ERADICATE TREATMENT
SIREN TEN EER EARTH
SYNE ADA ADS PYES
```

PUZZLE 281

```
  BERATE  AMI  AMID
  EVEREST SON  DORA
ANISETTE SOL  OVAL
MILT HASP  REP  IKE
USE KETTLE  TAME
SOY ERE  AMP  MISDO
ENEMY START  STIR
  ASH TENOR  CAVE
ALOT ARA  AMA  ARAL
NEVA HADAT  PAL
NEED ANILE  BLARE
ERROR GUL  ROB  DEL
  ARID MISERY  ULA
ARC BAG  NOVA  FLAT
BETA NOW  LITERATE
LEEK TOE  OVERATE
EDDA EDE  EDITED
```

PUZZLE 285

```
TATA TIS  RIGA  RAMP
ALOG BONE EVIL ESAU
NORA RISE GALE STET
GENTEEL TRA  ARETE
HAVETHELASTWORD
CREASE RENEW SERIAL
RAN ETTA ODER ESTE
UNDO SECT SETA KEG
MEOW HEARD  POLO
BEWEDDEDTOANOPINION
DEER SILOS  ERIE
ELL LEAH EVES SALE
MOOT NEWT ERAL TED
SPIREA ROBIN LITERS
STUBBORNASAMULE
EMBER DRS  ATTEMPT
HARP LANE URGE TORO
ALEE EGER EONS EROS
TART SETS SEA  REDS
```

PUZZLE 288

```
RARER CATER  BOATS
ABUSE ALONE  ERROL
COMPLIMENTS  SAUNA
EDO END GETAS  BET
DERANGES RENEGADE
      STENCH DIME
HAPPEN REF LENSES
ERA DURABLE RETRO
ARIA EAT AGA TARA
RONDO ECONOMY REP
TWEAKS HAG BEARDS
      GLUM RESLAM
APPEARED SKIRTING
BAR HERON ENL GOA
ORONO INELIGIBLES
VENOM TURIN NOONE
EDEMA STOPS GOODS
```

PUZZLE 289

```
SHOP PEN  EDT  ROSY
LIVE BARE YEAH EPEE
AVER ELIA ELMO TEEN
GERMANE REL  ONAIR
IMARAMBLINGWRECK
SLATER PERON SEETHE
CIL NEAP OWNS STIR
AFAR SLED SPAR ANN
REMI LAIRD  ERAT
FROMGEORGIATECHANDA
SNOW STRAD  MERS
ALP USED THEY EVAN
MYRA DESK IRON EKE
ARISTA AWAIT DEARER
HECKOFANENGINEER
EAGRE LEO  OLDGOLD
ATTN ERAL REVE ETUI
WAAC SIRS OWED NOLA
LUGE HEM  TEL  TELL
```

PUZZLE 290

```
WOOD  PAT   OLE
AIDE  RIOT  PEA
GLEE  ORNAMENT
   DAB   GIANTS
FOSSIL  SLY
ERA  MEN  SOLID
EAVE  MAD  RODE
SLEDS  BAA  RON
   GET  GLADLY
APPEAR   GAB
MOISTURE  BABE
ELL  SLUR  EGOS
SEE   YES   YEAS
```

PUZZLE 291

```
ALTO  BOA   EVER
BOWL  EAT   LAVA
ERIE  ARTISTIC
LET  MUSIC   SLY
   THAT   REV
STEADY   EDIBLE
PURR      SEES
ABSENT  OLIVES
   MAR   KATE
ACT  PAPAS   RAM
CLUMSILY   HALO
HONE  TEE   AGES
EDEN  SAD   TEST
```

PUZZLE 292

```
WARD  CLAMP  SILO
ERIE  OILER  ARAL
EELS  POSTOFFICE
PALOMINO  TEASES
   LEES   GEAR
ALTARS  CUISINES
ROUTE  FLINT  OAK
MOLE  WAILS  MESA
ESS  PONCE  VALET
DEADLOCK  HASSLE
   RELY   GIST
DENIAL  BESTOWED
IDENTIFIES  DALE
MEEK  ERASE  OGLE
ENDS  ROSES  NEAR
```

PUZZLE 293

1. Calendar, 2. Renovate, 3. Estimate, 4. Endeavor, 5. Restrain, 6. Nutrient, 7. Telegram, 8. Merchant, 9. Thousand, 10. Domestic.

PUZZLE 294

```
COME  OMAHA  SHAH
IDEA  DAMES  TUBE
TEAS  OPENS  ELLA
ESTEEM  SCUTTLED
   LYES   ERAS
FALSETTO  EPOCHS
EGO  DEALS  SNOOP
IRAN  RIDER  SCAR
GENES  NINES  ORE
NESTED  ESCAPADE
   WARS   EARL
DEPOSITS  LIABLE
OVER  VITAL  SAIL
SEEK  ELOPE  MINK
ERRS  SEWED  ALES
```

PUZZLE 295

VEGETATION

PUZZLE 296

```
LAST  SABLE  POKE
ETCH  TRUER  EDEN
SOAR  ATTAR  TOED
SPRINGS  GOVERNS
   VIE  PURER
CHEEP  ALE  NESTS
HAWS  GNU  ZODIAC
OLE  KINGDOM  RIO
KOREAN  GOO  HELP
ESSAY  TEE  JESSE
   RATED  AID
ALASKAN  PIGGISH
BACH  CAKES  IDLE
UNTO  KNEEL  NEAR
TEST  STYLE  GAME
```

PUZZLE 297

```
     A T
    A R T
   T E A R
  I R A T E
 R E T A I L
A R T I C L E
C L A R I N E T
```

PUZZLE 298

```
TSAR  FRO   SOFA
AQUA  OAR   OMEN
RUST  RIA   BELT
TAT  JELLY  LIL
ARI  EVE   IRENE
RENEWED  EATER
   PER  ELM
EASEL  TADPOLE
ASTER  AGE  RAN
SPA  YOKED  ACT
TILL  HER  STIR
ERLE  MIL  TONE
REST  STY  URGE
```

PUZZLE 299

```
REACT  COT  LAS
ARGUE  AMI  ELL
HEARA  MEN  VIE
   ISRAEL  DEEP
JUNE  FREQUENT
ASS  STATUE
RETIE    ITALY
   DEPART  GEE
LEMONADE  SIGN
OVAL  RODENT
NOT  WAR  LEAPS
EKE  ODE  LETUP
RES  NED  ARENA
```

PUZZLE 300

```
WARM  BART  STAY
ARIES  IDES  NAME
SONGOFLOVE  ORES
AND  LIL   SWAN
   PONY  RATS
PALS  DOTE  BAH
POLA  DONOR  ANA
ASONGTOREMEMBER
PEN  RENEE  REST
ARE  ALAN   BEST
   ANET  FOLD
SALT   EWE  NIA
CARL  BRIANSSONG
ALEE  OURS  SINGE
BEAN  BEET   SEAS
```

PUZZLE 301

```
LIST  TUGS  MISTS
INTO  ASAP  UNTIE
ALOT  MARL  STALE
RENAME  BATTERED
STYLISH  TEEN
   STAT  ARTIST
ERICS  IRAS  ISEE
TOTO  TRIBE  OLES
OPEN  HYMN  INEPT
NESTLE  SECT
   RAMS  RACECAR
ORNATELY  THRONE
REACH  AIDE  ACNE
CASTE  SPAR  SKID
AMASS  HEMS  EYES
```

PUZZLE 302

1. It's impossible to mend a fence if you're sitting on it.

2. Logic is any line of reasoning that proves you are right.

PUZZLE 303

```
SAP  CANS  AFAR
GAME  AGATE  LAVE
EVEN  ROBIN  ICED
MENDED  SEDATES
   SAIL  SET
TAB  SNAG  DOLED
ADO  TACIT  MALES
LOAM  LEVEE  DALE
ERRED  DEEMS  TAR
EDGED  SNAP  EYE
   BAR  SNIP
ABETTER  ANALOG
AREA  ENACT  LIME
LIAR  REVUE  EMIT
PADS  WEED  DOT
```

PUZZLE 304

1. Sonja Henie, 2. Herman Melville, 3. Fidel Castro, 4. Alfred E. Newman, 5. Horatio Nelson, 6. Harry S. Truman, 7. Annie Oakley, 8. Rudolf Nureyev, 9. Sophie Tucker, 10. Luke Skywalker.

PUZZLE 305

```
CAT   BEAM   RAM
ARID  LADLE  ANEW
LINE  ARISE  VOTE
MATTER  TOT  IDES
   RAG   INERT
GREASES  PAVE
OUNCE  TARDY  JAM
ALIT  PATIO  DUPE
LED  FACED  WIDER
   BANK  EPISODE
SPORT   AFT
OOZE  DIN  REAPED
BLOW  ADOPT  NAVE
SANE  MONEY  TREE
RED   PLEA   END
```

PUZZLE 306

Regale, Alert; Severe, Erect; Muffin, Finish; Tattoo, Tooth; Satin, Tinsel; Scalp, Alpine; Impact, Active; Elbow, Bowler; Father, Herald; Human, Manage.

PUZZLE 307

```
CAT SON     MAP
ABE OUI     SAGE
PEANUTBUTTER
    TRY     NEED
    DEN DIP
            BAR
GAB SUR OLIO USE
EMU PRO MANNER TIN
LIT RIP EYE ROW TAD
TAI     ADORE
EVE       OAR
RESTS     DYE
DAM TIE RAP FAR DAD
ARI MALICE IWO UPI
LIL ANTE DEW PEN
YAK ADD KEG
    TELL    GEE
BUTTERSCOTCH
INTO EAU ERE
TEA DOT DUN
```

PUZZLE 311

```
LAND LEAP SEA
ODOR ARLO ARM
SORE PRETENSE
     AGES ALDEN
POMMEL STS
AVAST  PHOENIX
PEG  GEE  OAR
ARIZONA MANNA
   IOU HERESY
OLAND LATE
SINCLAIR NEAT
LET ERNE ALTO
ONE STEM SLEW
```

PUZZLE 316

```
BAD AURA  GET
ONE PROP AERO
OAF INTO BOIL
STERN  SEEMED
NAG STATE
BEST WELT TIE
EEE SHIES RAW
ALL PINS PINE
  ERASE ARC
ASSIST  LEAST
ROSS LATE LEA
IDLE EVER LAM
DAY RENT YRS
```

PUZZLE 312

```
RUT     PER
INERT  ARID
MINER WAVER
 TOTE    ALE
 ERASE SLED
    ISLET
GOWN  FIRST
OVA     DOTE
BEGET EVENS
NOVA  REPEL
 NET    STY
```

PUZZLE 317

```
PAPA AIMS AWL
ALAN ITEM NEE
REST LANE NET
RETIRE DATE
    CARE REALM
CAR POLO ALOE
ARE SNIPE EVA
NEAR STEP DEN
EASED ERIE
  ODES ACUMEN
BAN CAST LORE
ADE OLEO ELIA
ROD REAR RENT
```

PUZZLE 308

```
WHETS TIMID
REMIT ADORE
ALONE NATAL
POT PAD ETE
 TEA BELLE
   GNOME
 STEER TAM
AMA UTE GOT
PICOT GRADE
ELIDE GIVEN
DETER SMELT
```

PUZZLE 313

```
ROAD CASK ALL
URGE ELAN PIE
BEEP DATE EVE
  EDEN ADDER
ALINED ODE
LADDS RESPECT
ASEA HER LIAR
STABBED HORSE
  LAW TERETE
WIDEN MAMA
ADO NEAP BLOT
ILL ERNE LANE
LET RAYS EPEE
```

PUZZLE 318

```
PASS ALL ROWS
ALIT DOE EVIL
DETONATE GENE
  RAM PARED
SWEEP TSAR
TOAD REINDEER
ERR RANGE ARE
PENTAGON ASIA
USER STEEP
SHARP TAT
TORN GARDENER
ALEE ONE SERE
READ BYE TEND
```

PUZZLE 309

```
EVA DAUB PEON
WAD RISE LEVI
ENDEARED ALAN
 IMPS   AISLE
ARTIE END
MEIR HANDSOME
ADO LEROY MAD
HONEYDEW PICA
 TRY   TOTEM
GRACE SENT
RASH STEADIES
ACHE OWES NAP
DEED DOME GUY
```

PUZZLE 314

```
 TIDE   ODE
 MINOR RANT
PATTER ANTI
ISLE  ULCER
THERMOS ERE
 NEWER
SAG ENDURED
ADULT  MAXI
IDEA NAPKIN
DESK OWLET
RTE WEED
```

PUZZLE 310

```
MALE   PLATE
ALARM EASEL
ZORRO SPINE
ENG TOT DOC
 GENES PERT
   ULCER
WARN ADOPT
ADO TRI EAR
SOBER TRACE
PRIDE SOCKS
SENSE  TEST
```

PUZZLE 315

```
SPAR ABE OTTO
POLO PEN FROM
AUTO PAD TAME
TROTTER SEVEN
  SEA ONE
SOB ARROW LAW
IRA  EAR EVE
PER EDGAR RED
  GAS TUB
SCANS MINUTES
LAID LEO TORE
ANNE INN TALE
MESS BUS EDEN
```

PUZZLE 319

```
ALP ABLE ROSE
WOE DRAW EVER
ESTIMATE FEAR
  DIVE PORTS
DELETE FAR
AREAS TORMENT
TIE FIX  DOE
AEROBIC DUETS
 RAN HORNET
ASIAN PEON
CLOT HELMSMAN
TOTE ISLE OLE
SEAS MOOD WET
```

PUZZLE 320

```
PAPA  MODES  SUPS
OMIT  ELIDE  KNOT
LINT  LINEN  IDLE
EDGE  EVENTS  EKE
     STEER  AURAL
SLATE    OPUS
LAX  RYE  GENERAL
AIL  ROW  LET  IRE
PREPARE  ERE  NEE
    ICES   RADAR
   PLATE  AMASS
RED  SHAPES  SWAB
EGOS  ALERT  EARL
SIRE  STAGE  TRIO
STEW  POKER  SEAT
```

PUZZLE 321

1. Headgear, 2. Church, 3. Dependent, 4. Panhandle, 5. Retire, 6. Seersucker, 7. Indefinite, 8. Cornucopia.

PUZZLE 322

```
SCAT  FLAT  KNOB
SPADE  LAVA  NOVA
ARGON  EVER  OPAL
SEE  EXERT  CELL
HEYDAY    ASK
   EMERGENT  BOA
CHAMP  EON  YEARN
HOBO  CUT  DRAT
OMENS  ADE  AISLE
WET  APPARENT
    OWL  ADSORB
VERB  AFTER  ZOO
ERIE  QUIT  AMOUR
EGGS  UNDO  RANGE
ROSE  EDEN  TREE
```

PUZZLE 323

```
F  SOFTER  STORE  ROTE  S
L  STAPLE  PASTE  STEP  A
Y  YOUTHS  SOUTH  SHOT  U
I  INSECT  CENTS  TENS  C
N  ANSWER  SWEAR  WARS  E
G  GAPERS  SPEAR  APSE  R
```

PUZZLE 324

```
SMOG  CLAW  BAT
PEAL  AIDE  ORE
ANTI  RESTORES
   DUAD  TREAT
LATEST  BET
ERASE  CORSAGE
AIM  LOW  LAW
PLEASED  DRAPE
   LOG  TEASER
ASPEN  LIMB
STREAKED  BOAT
PEA  TINE  INTO
SPY  ANTS  TEEM
```

PUZZLE 325

```
ROOD  ELS  SETS
ENTE  RIO  ASIA
ACIDTEST  ICER
RECUR  POLLARD
  CUP  LOOP
CANTEEN  ORATE
AGO  BROOK  DON
PANEL  DRIVERS
   SNUG  ANI
PRESENT  TERMS
AINU  ARGONAUT
APSE  WEE  NILE
REED  SEE  ADEN
```

PUZZLE 326

```
ART  SPED  CAVE
CAR  PULE  OBOE
THEGOLDENBOWL
SEERS  PAR
   ATE  SPARSE
HENRY  FEE  EON
ARES  FRA  PARD
MIA  HOY  JAMES
SETTER  FOR
   ARE  LISLE
THEBOSTONIANS
EARL  TIRE  TOE
ALEE  SEAR  EWE
```

PUZZLE 327

```
JAWS  BAR  MOLD
ALIENATE  ALOE
BANNERED  GENE
  TAN  BAGGED
START  RANI
TOBY  GIRDERS
AIR  SAVOY  OLE
LIGHTEN  PLAY
   HOER  CREPE
ASLEEP  LEO
LOOT  OPENFACE
MIST  SENTINEL
ALTO  TAD  TIES
```

PUZZLE 328

```
MALE  SCAR  TEAM
ERAS  HALE  DANCE
METS  ERIE  ANVIL
ONE  BET  DOT  YDS
STREETS   REF
   YES  CAB  IRAN
PAPER  DELI  BASE
OLE  VALET  TIE
STOP  ALLS  BREAD
TONE  LEO  SEE
   WEE  SHADOWS
ETC  ASH  PIN  PIE
GRANT  OVER  TERN
OASES  WENT  ORES
SPED  LETS  EASE
```

PUZZLE 329

RAI(N)ICE(M)IT(T)HAT

PUZZLE 330

```
LAST  CLEAR  SITS
ALEE  HORDE  INRE
ITEM  AVAIL  STEN
COMPOSE  TIPTOED
  TIERS  ERE
CAVILS  WAVERING
AGONY  DICEY  ROE
SLUG  RANTS  WORN
TEC  BENDS  MANSE
ETHEREAL  RAISES
   RAN  ELECT
INFANTS  AVERAGE
CARS  ELITE  EVIL
EPEE  RIDER  SOBS
SEER  STORE  SNEE
```

PUZZLE 331

1. Electorate, 2. Diploma, 3. Testator, 4. Concurrent, 5. Pitiless, 6. Erratic, 7. Winsome, 8. Pleasantry.

PUZZLE 332

```
FEAR  INTO  DIP
ERNE  NEED  ARI
RING  BRAD  MIL
NEAR  ROB  APSE
   EYE  ADS
ABATED  GUSHED
MALTA   BEIGE
ASSIST  SAMSON
   NTH  NIB
WHIG  REO  LACE
EON  PURR  ICED
ELK  ISLE  ERDA
KEY  SHED  SEEM
```

PUZZLE 333

```
WANT  READ  EYE
AGAR  ALDA  LOW
SERA  HAIRLINE
PERMS  NONE
  APHIDS  DELI
WET  EDS  OGLED
ERODES  SLEEVE
SIRUP  AID  VIA
TESS  AFRICA
  KARL  EATEN
BABYHOOD  DOME
ERA  ESAU  ERMA
NET  METE  TSAR
```

PUZZLE 334

```
DIME  ABLE  BAA
ODOR  ROAN  OLD
FEAR  GIBE  ROD
FATEFUL  MINES
   DIM  GYM
TWO  TELL  PROW
OARS  NEE  SANE
PREP  TEEN  PET
   ASS  FUR
SPENT  AUTUMNS
WAD  EARL  LOOP
ACE  EVIL  ELSE
MEN  LADY  SEED
```

PUZZLE 335

```
SASS  POT  SAY
PILOT  ADO  HIE
ADORE  PONDERS
DEER  FARGO
  EEL  DRAW
CHILLED  GOOSE
ROC  SWINE  PIE
ABODE  PINHEAD
MONA  NEE
   REESE  ARID
BRITTLE  ALINE
OAR  OLE  LENDS
ATE  NAP  EDGY
```

PUZZLE 336

```
SHIV  ACORN  SLOB
HONE  CANOE  HIVE
ORANGEBOWL  AMEN
PANEL  RESIDENT
SEERESS  DOLES
  ANENT  NESTER
WATT  CARP  ORE
ALOE  TRIAL  ANON
SIP  ETNA  BEST
HABEAS  EDITS
  AMILE  ACROBAT
MONOLITH  AROMA
ETAT  CHERRYBOMB
SINE  EERIE  ETAL
SCAD  DREAD  DYNE
```

PUZZLE 337

```
PAW  CAFE  CACHE
JIBE  AXIS  ALLAY
AQUA  TENT  BLAZE
MUSKET  DEW  IDES
BEE  ALP  RAGE
GREAT  TASTER
DOZEN  VOTED  AVE
ALIT  FEWER  OXEN
SIP  WARNS  THIRD
HOSTED  STEAM
OBEY  SAC  ELF
JOYS  SOP  TORQUE
AROSE  DUKE  OUST
MAKES  EMIR  MATE
SLEDS  LADS  PLY
```

1-R, 2-Q, 3-H, 4-K, 5-V, 6-L, 7-J, 8-B, 9-A, 10-Y, 11-S, 12-P, 13-F, 14-C, 15-U, 16-O, 17-G, 18-T, 19-N, 20-I, 21-M, 22-Z, 23-D, 24-W, 25-X, 26-E.

PUZZLE 338

```
ASH  BAND  LANK  SOD
CLIO  ILIA  OGEE  TOME
AINU  GALVESTON  EDEN
WINSTON  IRES  TEXANS
TOT  TSAR  CULT
MACON  TOES  COCK  ALP
IVAN  MOOS  POLKS  TOA
NER  PARK  HARDY  CLAY
GROWERS  SELF  CLANS
LOOKOUTMOUNTAIN
SCION  SOPS  ORBITED
CONS  MEANS  COOS  APE
OCA  FORGE  CAST  KNEE
WAS  EDGE  PANE  MISER
STES  SIRE  SAC
CARTER  WACO  JACKSON
AGUE  ALABAMIAN  ELKO
PALM  TIDE  EDIT  RUIN
ERE  EVER  DELA  SEE
```

PUZZLE 339

```
IPSO  AMAH  WHAT  CLEF
DEAN  NOPE  HAIR  HOLE
LENT  NOEL  AURA  ASSE
ENGAGED  LOLL  VERSES
REX  HIDE  PEAG
TACIT  HOOD  LESSENED
HERO  LION  DANTE  AWE
ARE  WASP  PARTY  OMEN
TOWARDS  SAIGA  EVERY
LAS  SPIRE  MAE
STRAP  SHINY  SECRETE
LIEN  SLANT  DISH  ERN
ORA  DEEMS  MATS  SLAV
WELCOMES  TILE  WISPY
ALIT  MORE  HAM
HAPPEN  GAMA  SERIOUS
EXIT  OMNI  CRUX  LIME
ALTO  LOAD  LORE  ALBA
TEAR  EATS  EYED  RYOT
```

PUZZLE 340

```
CRUST  CALEB  ROADS
ARISTA  IRATE  ONSETS
SUPERNATURAL  PLANET
HIE  SALEM  OBEY  ORA
ESSE  GAD  RAVED  OMEN
SETTLER  LEVEE  BLISS
WIRY  ABED  PAIN
APSES  SPUR  BYROADS
FACET  SPIT  BORE  TEA
TIAS  DEAN  TRUE  BING
ONT  PIER  FRET  EROSE
NETTLES  FLEW  PINES
EROS  PEAS  SPED
CARED  PRESS  PRELATE
ABBE  FRISK  TIE  ERIS
SER  AEON  ARECA  ALT
ELAINE  CONSIDERABLE
SEIDEL  ERUPT  PEGLER
SNOWS  SENSE  TATER
```

PUZZLE 341

```
SHIP  STAR  COMP  DADO
KOTO  COLA  AMIR  ORAL
ABET  HOTTAMALE  MAUI
TOMATO  OILER  AKIMBO
TOLA  OAR  SCAN
COLORADO  RANCHHOUSE
HUI  ASIAN  SIREN  NOW
ACME  TOTUS  DAR  FINE
RHACHIS  DURUM  GLOSS
BLOC  AGIOS  PEON
SHEAR  SPENT  CREASED
COAT  MYA  GOTHE  THAI
URN  MALIC  ROOST  OCA
MASTERPLAN  TRIUMPHS
UTAH  NAG  EDNA
HORNET  STRUM  EASTER
ILED  HONEYMOON  HALO
SEAR  ODOR  BOLT  IRKS
SORA  NEWS  ODDS  EASE
```

PUZZLE 342

```
RIGID  CADETS  STAGE
ARETE  OREGANO  EIDER
JANES  WINGCOMMANDER
ATE  ICES  TWAIN  USE
HERB  ORIEL  SHE  SPED
ALSO  NAIS  ANAT
GLEE  GREET  SCALES
AIDEDE  SUPRA  TRASH
OTS  DIVA  TIARA  ENTO
REST  SERGEANTS  SCAR
ALIA  CROON  SETH  ETE
TEMPO  SARAH  LAUNCE
EGOISM  RENEW  LEOS
REEF  STAR  PARR
PAWS  RAW  SLICE  OPEC
IDA  ELIOT  TUNA  OLE
QUARTERMASTER  LURID
ULCER  SECTORS  ENATE
ELSIE  NOREST  SOLES
```

PUZZLE 343

```
BASE  ARIZ  STAB  STIR
OMAN  PERU  CARA  URSA
SARA  ALEC  ARIL  BALM
CHICORY  CANTALOUPES
TIT  SHUT  ORR
ANGEL  HEIR  RUTABAGA
NEED  PIANO  EKED  SET
ERR  ARK  IRONED  OPAL
TOMATOES  APE  WARE
INEARTH  SWEETER
RANT  AIR  STANDARD
ALAS  CARTER  ORT  GEE
MAT  PURE  TERNS  CUTE
PREDICTS  USES  LASER
REU  BRIE  SOB
WATERMELONS  RHUBARB
ERIA  BRAN  TOUR  AGIO
SEED  ESNE  EASE  GROW
TARS  REAR  DREW  EATS
```

PUZZLE 344

```
      ATE CRAB
SPADES   HOPE
CAGERS   ELSE
OUR  NEEDLES
USES   SAD
REELS   RADAR
  OAT   ROLE
STAGGER   TON
LIMA  RODENT
IRON  RAISES
MESS   ERG
```

PUZZLE 345

```
 EWE      MAP
AVERT    ACRE
CITRIC   ERIK
ELS ERA  ONE
   SAL VAST
   VISITS
   FEE TEE
   CONDOR
 SLED PET
SHE   TEA ADO
EAVE   TRAVEL
TREY   TREND
ERE      IRE
```

PUZZLE 346

```
          APE
PAPA     RILE
IRAN     SNOW
PEGS ADE DIE
ETA PLACE ASS
REND RERUN ARE
   ACORN GAR
   RAFT PINS
   ERI CANTO
PAD TRADE NOTE
HUR SANDS RIP
ORO GAY IDLE
SPUD     MEDE
ELSE     ARES
EEL
```

PUZZLE 347

1. Timber wolf. 2. Computable. 3. Droplights

PUZZLE 348

```
        HAM
 THAT  ARAB
TRACES TOTAL
TRAVELER WAKE
AIDE PUG DEN
POE BOGUS ORA
JOY MOORS BUS
  JAM   YET
 TABBY
RAM SABER PAW
ERA MUM BENE
STIR GENERATE
TACIT NOVELS
NAPE   WADE
NEE
```

PUZZLE 349

Happiness makes up in height for what it lacks in length. (Robert Frost)

1. Hepplewhite, 2. Knuckles, 3. Shanghai, 4. Paint, 5. Moist, 6. Shaft, 7. Ring.

PUZZLE 350

```
SLOE   LAID
HIVE  ANTED
NOVEL SNIPE
LATER  ASONE
DUD      TORE
ALIAS MRT TIN
BURRO HAIRPIECE
 ENTERTAIN
MENAGERIE ETHER
ERA DOE ROUSE
TOPS      MAD
SKIPS  BAYOU
IRATE LASER
NEVER ELIA
NEWS  DEAR
```

PUZZLE 351

1. Conversions, 2. Quarterback, 3. Official time-out, 4. Line of scrimmage, 5. Goalposts, 6. Third down.

PUZZLE 352

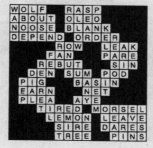

```
WOLF   RASP
ABOUT  OLEO
NOOSE BLANK
DEPEND ORDER
   ROW  LEAK
   FAN  PARE
   REBUT SIN
DEN SUM POD
PIG  BASIN
EARN  NET
PLEA  AYE
TIRED MORSEL
LEMON LEAVE
SIRE  DARES
TREE  PINS
```

PUZZLE 353

Compromise makes a good umbrella, but a poor roof.

1. Amuse, 2. Package, 3. Mirror, 4. Alp, 5. Bloom, 6. Mouse, 7. Foot, 8. Brood.

PUZZLE 354

```
FATAL      BRA
ALKALI    BROW
STARLET  SEOUL
THROE CLAP CHANT
REIN HABIT SIOUX
ANN CIPHER KART
PAGODA POTATION
 MENU   RAPID
 ALINE   ADAM
 NANCY  RISES
  YETI  ANKLE
  UNLIT  GIBE
 DIOGENES NAMELY
FRAU EARWIG LIE
DOOMS SPRAT SETA
CRUMB TABU DUMAS
CRANE  REAGENT
REID    BOTANY
YEN      INERT
```

PUZZLE 355

EXPRESSWAY

PUZZLE 356

```
    YEATS
MUKLUK     FRET
PALETTE  FLESHY
SEE  HOD LACQUER
LES ORACULAR MAY
OPTIC DONATE PRE
PERTH DRIP BRENS
EROSE LETS AIDS
  COSI  BOSC
  KHAN  LEEK
  SANG  ODDS
HAIR ROTC HEEDS
HENNA AMOK ANGRY
EDD BICARB WAGER
AGO OVERTURE HAI
REVENGE SOX ERA
SERIES TUESDAY
RELY  ETCHED
      RESEW
```

PUZZLE 357

As cute as a button

PUZZLE 358

```
RACE     RAP
AWAY     ODE
MERE    FADE
 DREAM  LOW
  ELK   PIE
  IDLE  ADO
  TON  GLEN
WINK PURE ALA
RODE ANIL GAP
CAME PIT CEDE
AGE METE IONS
BEN ORES FLAT
 STOW   ALL
 HAG   EMIT
 ERR   VAN
 TEN FINNS
 OVAL ACID
 NOT  LACE
 EWE  EDEN
```

PUZZLE 359

Waste not, want not.

PUZZLE 360

```
         SLAM
         TITO
        AEONS
SASS  EMOLUMENTS
TUTU NAME YORE
ATOR TOTAL ORAN
TOMFOOLERY RECT RASP
SPERM   EDDY ERAL
RIATA   SALE LANA
STEM ICARUS RATON
FOOLANDHISMONEY
LOMAN STOLEN PROF
ADIT BEDE SALOP
VOLE  AMOS  ERROL
ARES ANOD MAKESMONEY
TINY ALANS NAVE
TODS TITI TIEA
UNAFFECTED ORES
  YOUTH
  OSTE
  LEAD
```

PUZZLE 361

PUZZLE 362

1. Randomizes, 2. Championed, 3. Shockingly.

PUZZLE 363

PUZZLE 364

A: 1. Equip, 2. Ideal, 3. Acorn, 4. Reach, 5. Climb, 6. Moral, 7. Acute, 8. Tweed.
B: 1. Quip, 2. Deal, 3. Corn, 4. Each, 5. Limb, 6. Oral, 7. Cute, 8. Weed.

PUZZLE 365

PUZZLE 366

1.					2.				
P	A	S	T	A	S	W	A	M	P
A	L	E	R	T	D	O	N	O	R
R	I	V	A	L	A	R	G	U	E
E	V	A	D	E	C	R	E	S	S
D	E	L	E	D	S	A	L	E	S

PUZZLE 367

PUZZLE 368

PUZZLE 369

FOOTBALL TERMS: Receiver, Play fake, Completion, Guard.

U.S. ASTRONAUTS: (Scott) Carpenter, (Sally) Ride, (John) Glenn, (Alan) Shepard.

SECTIONS OF A BOOK: Chapter, Preface, Dedication, Foreword.

GOLF GREATS: (Arnold) Palmer, (Curtis) Strange, (Tom) Watson, (Sam) Snead.

GAMES: Red rover, Boccie, Backgammon, Shuffleboard.

PUZZLE 370

PUZZLE 371

PUZZLE 372

1. Burn, Born, Worn, Word, Wood.
2. Boat, Bolt, Bole, Bale, Bake, Lake.
3. Camp, Came, Cane, Cant, Cent, Tent.
4. Hike, Hire, Hare, Pare, Park, Perk, Peak.

PUZZLE 373

PUZZLE 374

PUZZLE 375

PUZZLE 376

```
PESO SLOW FLAG
AGAR PORE RAMAS
COLONIALS AMBLE
ASK ANNO IMPOST
    CIE PANEL
REVOLT INDICTS
ARABS BODE GLUT
BARB SEDER HARE
ITAL TRES ATRIP
NOSEGAY PREENS
    SAILS ARR
MARTIN HERA VAT
SWOON BETSYROSS
SEINE ALTO ELIA
SLED ALAN YEAR
```

PUZZLE 377

From top to bottom: Giant, Enormous, Mammoth, Huge, Gigantic, Colossal, Towering. 7th column down: Immense.

PUZZLE 378

```
SAPS ROMP AMASS
ALOE EVIL DALLY
RUMS SANE ARGON
IMPACT DAMP AWE
    MOOS DATE
THEOREM DERIDE
EWE LEVER DARED
TIRE SETUP SALE
ACORN RENAL TEN
SENIOR STRIDES
EBON SAVE
TOM LEOS DEFACE
AROSE MINI IRON
GALES ALES LEAD
SLEET DOTE EATS
```

PUZZLE 379

```
A B LEST   CONGO   MATCHES
LIAR    NOVA    ESNE
NEMEAN  SERENADE  RISER
    GENEVA   DENTAL
TWIT  ARTISAN  AILING
TRUST   SMEAR   SMITTEN
CHERISH  STITCH   YES
    CINEMAS  HEATING
REDSKIN   SCHEME   RAGOUT
RESERVES  ACETIC   TIRING
SINGS   RESEAL   ESTHS
```

PUZZLE 380

R	PRONE	OPEN	EON	P
U	SALUTE	LEAST	SALT	E
B	BREAST	STARE	REST	A
I	TIRADE	RATED	DATE	R
E	SLATE	LAST	SAT	L
S	SMEARS	REAMS	MARE	S

PUZZLE 381

```
TACT PATE BACON
AGAR OMOO ALAMO
CARILLONS NORIA
OVATION INDEPTH
ETES KNEE ESS
    TREE ADEN
SAC SALTER ATEN
OPAL METRE TELE
WORE RELISH RIB
    TITO ESTE
SPR ADES NAPS
ELITISM BANNOCK
RADON CARNATION
INGOT EDIT ANNE
FEELS EDGE STEW
```

PUZZLE 382

A, Am, Mat, Mast, Meats, Stream, Mastery.

PUZZLE 383

```
CARE SAMBA OUTS
OTIS TROOP SNIP
COST ADOBE IDEA
OPERATORS SEERS
    ACER PURR
RUNTS CARESSES
SONGS PRIES HAT
NUDE GAILY WISE
ATE TALES SHREW
PERFORMS WAITS
SAWS HAGS
LATIN OVERSTATE
ALAN BLOND LIAR
SENT ALICE EDNA
TEDS LADEN RAGS
```

PUZZLE 384

1. Chevy Chase, 2. Alan Alda, 3. Muhammad Ali, 4. Dwight D. Eisenhower, 5. Clarence Darrow, 6. Benny Goodman, 7. Mel Brooks, 8. Charlie Brown, 9. Mary Hartman, 10. Ed Asner.

PUZZLE 385

```
RASPS WOE MELBA
ORARE ADD AREAS
DAVIDANDGOLIATH
ELEMENT INTENSE
    ERK DECA
SPAR AWARE BEER
ORR IRAN SALVE
DAMONANDPYTHIAS
ADORN LEAR DDE
SORT SPEAR MEET
    SEAR REO
SWEETEN SOPRANO
HOLMESANDWATSON
EOSIN MOA CASTE
ADARS ARK TREES
```

PUZZLE 386

My friend, who's a shepherd named Sam,
Stole a costly young pedigreed ram;
  But soon he was caught,
  And charges were brought
For taking a sheep on the lam.

PUZZLE 387

```
GARP FADED BRAY
ALAE IRENE ROVE
LAND EMMET OPEN
ASTERS SMACKERS
    SITE YIPE
SOFTBALL LARDER
HULAS TOTES RAE
ETAL HOARD PATE
EDS CONDO TIMED
POKERS SIDECARS
    SEAS SEAT
PUPTENTS SMUDGE
ERIE NAOMI ROLL
WANE ASHER ERAS
SLAM SHONE SADA
```

PUZZLE 388

Away, Awry, Best, Blob, Blow, Born, Brad, Bran, Bray, Brow, Darn, Dawn, Draw, Dray, Drop, Glob, Glop, Glow, Gory, Gown, Grad, Gray, Grog, Grow, Gryo, Lest, Lobe, Logo, Lord, Lorn, Lory, Mute, Nard, Oboe, Ogle, Oleo, Plop, Plow, Ploy, Poet, Pole, Polo, Robe, Role, Stun, Test, Tube, Tuna, Ward, Warn, Wary, Word, Worn, Yard, Yarn, Yawn, Yoyo.

PUZZLE 389

```
HOPI ACHE ROMA
ADEN DREW SEVER
TOLD DUNE AVERT
REINED RETIRES
    CANES AIL
RUSTED TORRENT
ANTE NORSE ORE
TIED ERA AMID
STE ASIAN RACE
ERASING WARDEN
BIT ELATE
DERIDES ADESTE
ELIDE ELSE TIRO
RIDES TIER EDIE
NESS HERS DEER
```

PUZZLE 390

PUZZLE 391

```
PAD PAPA SHOW
OUR EVENT BLAME
ERA PIANO OILER
MAMA DRAG ATONE
SLANG SLAMS
    YET OTTERS
ARC LANCES EXIT
ROLL MEANT EASE
ALEE PEDDLE MEW
BEFORE YAP
    ARROW TELLS
MAGIC IRIS REAP
EVADE PARES AYE
MOLES STEEL SEA
OWES EDDY ERR
```

PUZZLE 392

Actor, Clerk, Coach, Judge, Model.

PUZZLE 393

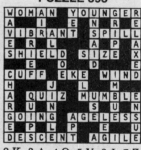

```
WOMAN YOUNGER
A   I   E  N  R  E
VIBRANT SPILL
E   R   L   A P A
SHIELD SIZE X
    E  O   D   E
CUFF EKE WIND
H    J  L   M
A QUIZ MUMBLE
R    U   S  U N
GOING AGELESS
E    P  L P  E U
DESCENT AGILE
```

1-E, 2-K, 3-A, 4-Q, 5-Y, 6-J, 7-Z, 8-C, 9-S, 10-G, 11-W, 12-B, 13-R, 14-F, 15-X, 16-L, 17-D, 18-U, 19-O, 20-H, 21-P, 22-M, 23-I, 24-T, 25-V, 26-N.

PUZZLE 394

```
J R R PROVOKE
AMAZED ERA N
S MAN AVENGED
MAPPED E E
I A G RATTLE
NEGLECTS Y S
EE SHOES WS
    CE ORDINARY
ELIXIR T F S
    I T A BUFFET
SQUALLS AIL E
U NEE STREAM
DENTIST E S S
```

1-K, 2-O, 3-Z, 4-A, 5-L, 6-F, 7-Q, 8-R, 9-I, 10-Y, 11-E, 12-M, 13-B, 14-J, 15-X, 16-D, 17-P, 18-T, 19-C, 20-H, 21-S, 22-N, 23-U, 24-W, 25-G, 26-V.

PUZZLE 395

```
SEPT   BATHS  AFORE
ACROSS ATREE  SLIDES
PRESTO STELE  TETONS
UPSETTHEAPPLECART
  ERSE   STE  LASS
PADS  ART  REAM  ADAM
EVE  SALE   AMY  FIVE
ROBBER SONATA SIRES
INTONE TRET  SPIDERS
 WIT  SAVOR  ORD
SPILLED TINE  SELECT
MARIE IRENES SNEERS
ORAN PLY  IVES  LEA
GANG ALES INA  DYER
   AERO  EOS  SOAR
GOLDENOPPORTUNITY
POLLEN UTILE STERES
TALENT RENDS TIRANA
SLAYS  STEEP  SYST
```

PUZZLE 396

```
LOP  STIR  ACHE  TRIP
EAR  INANE FOOL  AIDE
GREETINGS TREE  SOLE
 SEEP  RIPEN  MASTER
 FILM  RADAR  MERE
BEDS FATED CONCLUDE
ALE MAKES SOUTH NAY
DON ICE  STUNS  FIRE
ENTERED START MUTED
 NET  SPORT  PIN
PRODS ALIVE CONDEMN
RAMS PLANE HUE  SEE
IRE TROTS GRITS SEW
MENTIONS SLEDS LETS
 EDGE  TEASE  TINS
CORNER GIANT BOOT
AVID ATOM COLUMNIST
MATE MARE ERODE ATE
PLED SPED SETS  LYE
```

PUZZLE 397

```
STRODE SPREE SHINER
CREDIT TRILL TIRADE
RACEME RAMIE ELATED
EVE ERGOT AVERT IRE
WEDS NONES ALE HOLY
SLEEPING PETS RANEE
 RATE  TILE  HAH
DRAFTY AIRY DAMAGES
RINSE ANTI SAL SEAT
EFT RESTITUTION STA
ALOE IKE UNAL ASTER
RENDERS FAIT MOPERS
 IDE  TILT  MEMO
PLOTS MARL SADIRONS
LASS WAN YALTA TRUE
ASP FATAL FEELS IAN
ISRAEL GENIE INTEND
NEEDLE EVERT SEANCE
TRYSTS RITES TENTER
```

PUZZLE 398

```
POPS ABA CUPS ALAMB
EMIT TAR ANEW SAREE
RISE OAT STOA STERN
THEONLYTHINGWEHAVE
  PIES  HEE  GORE
CARESS LOW GENT WIG
ALINE CAR CURT RARA
ROD PAY SASS DUNES
ROEDEER SORT  RIB
FRANKLINROOSEVELT
 INE NORM PEASOUP
BOSSA PLOY MEL ITA
ASHY BEET TAW CAREW
TEA BERT RAY TUREEN
  GEES  OER  PIER
TOFEARISFEARITSELF
ALIEN SETS ENT SILT
RINSE TREE STE TRIO
POKED SENS TOR SATE
```

PUZZLE 399

```
DATES  FEVER  DISCO
ARSENO ARISE ACTORS
JOHNTRAVOLTA NEEDLE
ANI STRODE DOCS EON
RENT ERE  WIDE  ERNS
REA ENS  BAND  PASS
  NEVA  SONG  SAR
BOGGLE BEAT SWINGER
HURLS GOER SPIN RAE
ATEE SOUNDROOM PISA
NRA FAST WILT BASED
GETWITH DADO HUSTLE
 ONE  RILE  COST
RARE PEEK POW  ASS
TIME ATOM ARM STEP
OVA USAF SNAILS AVE
WATUSI FUNKYCHICKEN
SLOPED EXILE DRIERS
 SLIDE ROPER SEEDS
```

PUZZLE 400

```
LAPP CAPS PATH NIBS
ASEA OBIT OGEE OTOE
GIRT METE PERMANENT
SATRAP TRIED IGUANA
 IOTAS  EOS  PSIS
CONNECTION DEPLETED
APE ETONS BATHE HAE
VENT SOC MAMIE CASA
ENTER DAMON TRAINED
 NEW  SALAS  ERG
STOOLIE SALEM TAPED
TOUR LATER PAS RAGE
ADS EDGER PINUP NAB
BOTTLERS TRAINLOADS
 AIRE  RIO  ABOUT
SAMSON SEEDY UTTERS
EXISTENCE DEER ALAE
ELLE SEAL EATS GAPE
PEEL SETS DRAT ESTS
```

PUZZLE 401

```
TARP CLAP GRIN STOA
OBOE RIGA ROVE CHAR
ROADTOMANDALAY REST
SUNDOWN NEIL TESTY
 LID  SINN  STEEP
RATEL ACE SHARD ARK
UGHS SCARP AMOS NAE
TIE STEM INSET AIRE
HOOSIER SNIT HANSEL
 RUM BRENNER ETH
STEPPE IRAE OARSMAN
LOGS SUMAC PUNY ANE
APO ETRE EBONY FIGS
BEN READE END BENES
 TWIRL  ROSE  IRS
FIRES POUT KNOTTED
LOAN ROADTOZANZIBAR
ENID LUCE WIRE VARA
EELY SITS SPAR ERST
```

PUZZLE 402

```
BOAS DEW BOSH WALT
ANNE AURA AUTO ALEE
ITER LORDBYRON TOSS
LOWELL SEAL POETESS
 NOON  DRED  REL
RECEIVE DAIL LEONE
ORO NEVER FEES GEL
BILL RIVAL DEPENDED
SNEER NICER RELIED
 RAID  LEVIS  TENN
MISSAL REDAN CENTS
REDEEMED REVEL SARA
ERG PAID SEPAL SEW
DEEDS SPED ABASHES
 AIL  SPUD  LOVE
AUSTRIA OMOO RECEDE
GLUE SWINBURNE TIER
ONER LACE SEED ORAL
GADS EYES ESE RENE
```

PUZZLE 403

```
GAPE   FEE   BEST
EWER   ERA   ALOE
TERRIERS    SAFE
     AND  TAINTS
SPANK   AWLS
HARD  SLAM   HAM
APT  PEERS   ATE
GAY   LARD  PROS
    COLT  TEEMS
DONATE    SIR
APES  VAMPIRES
TEXT  EGO   SOLE
ANTS   LEG  HEFT
```

PUZZLE 404

```
  BETS    SPAR
  MORAL   WIRES
DESIRE   ANTLER
RATE  PEG  EAVE
ADO   STAGE  TED
BENCH   TELLERS
   OAR   ROE
CONTROL    PARES
ARI  PLATE   ASH
LIES   LYE  ANTE
LOCATE   RUGGED
NEVER    STEER
  SETS    EARS
```

PUZZLE 405

```
MET   DRAG   CHAP
APE   RAIL   LACE
MINNELLI    IDEA
ACTUAL   TOM
   TRY  TABLED
FATTY   PER   IVE
OKAY   BAR  KNEW
RIG   EAT   LEERY
ENSIGN    BEN
   ROD  LAYOFF
POLO  ADORABLE
IRAN   GOON   EEL
TEDS   ENDS   YET
```

PUZZLE 406

```
GRANT     VISTA
AURORA   CANNON
BETTER   ORNATE
   AMPLY   PEW
RAVED   ALI
ODOR   DIN   ALA
LOWEST  EGGNOG
ESS   MAP   ONCE
   APE   SOAKS
APT   SPADE
SOOTHE   UNSURE
PLOWED   EDISON
SOLOS    SPEED
```

PUZZLE 407

```
LET   ARAB   ICON
ORE   PONE   NAPE
GENERATE    DRAW
   DOME   TILLS
REIGN    ERA
AIDE   AGENDAS
IRE  BADGE   ICE
LESSONS    FARE
   ART   FILED
SPADE   WEAN
LAND  BARBELLS
ACNE   EVIL   EAT
TEEN   GENE   AMY
```

PUZZLE 408

```
STAY    DEEP
GUIDES   FOLLOW
OPPOSE   REMOTE
APT   WOES   PAD
LEO   WIPE  LETS
RECENT   SOSO
   ORG   RAN
CANE   FEWEST
MASS   PASS   COB
ADS   HERO   AWE
PEELER   ROARED
STREAM   TIGERS
STEP    LESS
```

PUZZLE 409

```
WAR   ACHE   COLT
IRE   BAIL   AREA
RID   OPTS   MEET
EASEL   EWE
   DISH  ERODE
PAD   SHOP  AVID
LIE   HILLS  ARE
ODES   PEAT  LEN
TERMS   SNAG
   ION  ROBIN
PAIL   ORAL  ICE
ACRE   EASE  TOE
LEAD   LEST  END
```

PUZZLE 410

```
ARE      SET
SCALE   HOSES
POCKET  CANCEL
ARK  LACED  ANY
NET  PAL   SPY
TABS   LAKE
LO      IA
HEAL   ARTS
NOS   AIM   EAR
TOO  MIMIC  VIA
ABROAD  DONALD
GLARE   PAGES
EYE      BED
```

PUZZLE 411

```
HOGS   PAT   OGRE
OVEN   LIE   AREA
PANE   ALE   TIES
SLEEPY   TEMPLE
   RAP  HOE
LAD   LET  NAKED
ACID   NOT  LIME
PEDAL   NOW   NUN
   MET   AIR
HAMPER   SNORER
ALOE   ACT  BAKE
LESS   DUE  IRES
TEST   ERR  NEST
```

PUZZLE 412

```
BOAT   GAP   BORE
ARIA   AGO   AWOL
YELL   LEE   REEF
   EYE   TAG
CHASE    SEINE
OAR  SLOOP   SOB
ALE   AND   SIB
SON  EPEES   USE
TSARS    TREED
   EEL   AYE
EDGE   INN  ASIA
LOUD   NOT  LENT
KEYS   EWE  MAKE
```

PUZZLE 413

```
MAT   RAG    ABE
ACE   AGED  CLAW
SHE   TIME  LORE
KENNEL   ALIENS
   ODE   COP
MILD   WON   BAT
ORE  STONE   EYE
BED   AWE  SEEN
   ONE   ARE
BARREN   WEAPON
ARAB  TRAP   APE
LEIS  YORE   GEE
LAD   EEL    END
```

PUZZLE 414

```
WHAM  ARCDE  SCAR
IONA  REHIT  OHIO
SPONGECAKE   REDO
PEANUT  RES  BEET
   SHELS  BES
FAST  ELO  DETECT
ASHES  STAIN  CRO
CHOCOLATEECLAIR
TOR  LOSES  HIKES
SETSIN  ROD  PESO
   BAD  DUPED
CARL  ARS  TOFFEE
ASEA  CASSEROLES
SIAM  EMEER  WELT
ANDI  RASES  LESE
```

547

PUZZLE 415

```
ERAS  LASS  CLOY
LOCHS ALTO  LEAD
MARAT DIAL  EATS
 DEMONSTRATORS
   SERE   SRO
     EWES  PERIL
   DESERT   PICA
OPAL REAPS  ITEM
HUTS    NOTICE
SNEAD   SEEN
    EGO    ECHO
  CALLIGRAPHERS
PAGE  ALOT  ELBOW
ERRS  NEMO  SPIRE
NEAT  TRAM  STET
```

PUZZLE 419

```
QUEST   CHARISMA   MEDEA
ACTOR   STEER      ATOM
KERN  EL    IMMATURITY
      ICON  BASS
HERMITAGE  H    HOBBLE
DUO     ERRATIC   TAUNT
GENTLEMAN  SKINFLINTS
        SIMON  GAP
REACTIONS   PERSISTENT
BURN    TROUT     DEALER
TESTED  OUSTED    SLED
```

PUZZLE 420

1. Speak the truth and shame the devil.
2. Figures won't lie, but liars will figure.

PUZZLE 421

```
  MINORS      DIGEST
ASTEROID  LIVELIEST
HER   LISTENERS  PAM
SLAG  CERES  SERPENT
 CEREMONIAL  LIVERY
   ERRING  PUMICE
  RESTS  CHANGEABLE
MUTED  WASTE   LEAST
TAU  PRETENSE  THEE
TRANSFER     TAPER
STILLER       REARED
```

PUZZLE 422

Distance is a great promoter of admiration. (Denis Diderot)

PUZZLE 423

```
SOW      CON
EPIC   ALOFT
RASH   BEDLAM
FLEE     SURE
    AREA  TON
  INTERPRET
ADO    DATA
NIBS     VAMP
DOLLAR  EVIL
TEENY   LOCO
  DYE     WET
```

PUZZLE 424

```
TIM  PAPA  ARMS
WOE  AGES  BEAK
OUTBREAK  SEMI
 LINK   SEDAN
ADJUST   VAN
GEAR   CASTING
ELM  BOOTH  TEA
DISHRAG   PEAS
    EAR  WARMTH
SWEAT    TRIO
TEAR  WOODSHED
EAST  ANTE  AGO
PREY  SEES  GOT
```

PUZZLE 425

```
MAST  CAL  BASH
ALEE  ARE  ACHE
PEAL  PRO  LION
   LATIN  ADES
HOD    TAVERN
ADO  TIE  ACTED
ROTTEN  SPEEDY
PREEN  FOP  AGE
   ADVICE  RED
ALEC   ELIDE
WASH  ILE  MERE
ETTE  LET  ITEM
DEER  STY  TABU
```

PUZZLE 426

```
LARD  ZAP  CAME
OBOE  ELI  ARIA
ALAS  STEEPLES
MEMENTO  ATONE
    RAY  PRO
WITTY  SUNRISE
ORE   WON   MEL
WADDLES  REPAY
     AID  COT
BRINE  ARCHERS
LANGUAGE  IDOL
URGE  COD  CITE
REAR  EGO  STEW
```

PUZZLE 427

```
PAIR  ISLAM  MODE
OBOE  MEALY  AVID
PETS  PIPER  NEED
STATIONS  THIRTY
   ELSE  FLEA
BANDIT  AREACODE
ADO  EERIE  DAZED
DOME  ROLES  LOCI
GRANT  BERTH  NOT
ENDORSED  EIDERS
   READ  CEDE
WARMED  MOLESTED
OREO  DRIVE  ERGO
LIEU  LINER  RIOT
FADS  EMITS  TOSS
```

PUZZLE 428

1. LEAP / EDGE / AGES / PEST
2. STEM / TAME / EMIT / METE
3. SALE / AVID / LIME / EDEN

PUZZLE 416

```
DIN   FOUR  MATES
EDIT  EASE  INERT
ALEE  STEP  STAGE
RECENT  DEBT  MOW
  RETAIL  NOES
    HIVE  TARNISH
TAT  VENT   ARIA
ABOVE  SAP  APORT
GLEE   POTS  NEE
SEDATES   COIL
   LARK  ORDEAL
PIC  PEAT  REASON
ADORE  TIME  SITE
SOLAR  EDEN  HATS
SLAMS  SENT  NOT
```

PUZZLE 417

```
BAT   EVITA   STY
AGA   GINAS   LEE
DONTROCKTHEBOAT
   KAY     TOO
ALS ENE LOO ALP WEE
WATERS  BARBS  ASTERN
LYRE  TOWBOAT  AIRS
ILL  RAN  EMU  EGG
ILK  IDA   GIG  HIT
RAE  NEW   BAR  ADO
ADS  ELL   ONE  NOT
APR  ERA LEA TIC
FAIR  ROWBOAT  THUS
ABLEST  YEAST  CHOOSE
DES TOE DYE DUO RAW
   END     ARI
ONESSHIPCOMESIN
WAR  ANEAR  TOY
LES  SNARE  SUE
```

PUZZLE 418

```
  MISS  PACE
  AMOK  ELAN
  CANISTERS
    NIA
   CANDLES
DOC  VERY  SATE  COD
ISH  PILE  TART  APE
ELI  ELL   RIO  NAN
DOCILE    CUDDLY
  ARI       COY
MENACE    PASCAL
AVE  ARK  BAN  AHA
MER  NORA  LENS  NOM
ANY  SIGH  SEAT  EYE
   SOUPCAN
     BEE
  BUCCANEER
  ASIA  TREE
  REAP  SELL
```

PUZZLE 429

```
GNAT   NESTS   TRADE
ATLAS     SOARED
THEBELLSARERINGING
   LEE     ILE  ATE
MATE  DUMBBELLS
ALI     SATIRE    BAN
TAN   CRUDEST    EVA
ASKED     ASH  LAY
  ERIN     STILL
  RACES    SADAT
  BLEAT     REDO
ADE  SPA      REWET
GEL   GREATLY    ERR
ELL    EERIER   RIO
   BELLICOSE  USED
EVE  ARE       GOP
BELLBOTTOMTROUSERS
RELIES  ALIEN  RELIT
OPALS   TEXAS  TIDY
```

PUZZLE 430

```
GAM CAST  BLAB
EGO ALTO  RATE
NET UPON  OPEN
EDENS  PEAK
   OER  SPELLS
CROWDED   TRAIL
HID   DIE   COO
IDOLS  PREVENT
PERIOD   EVA
    TWIG  ENVOY
WILT TOWN  APE
EVIL TROT  SAN
BEDE YEWS  ELS
```

PUZZLE 431

```
WAS DADS  PAMS
EMU EPEE  ETUI
PINETREE  LAND
TESTA  PRAIRIE
   HAIL  SIC
ALI NAN  RAPID
LENT  BAY  NAME
STEAL GEM  LPS
   RIO  TERM
LATHERS  REEVE
ALOE LONESTAR
LAME ORES  TIL
ORAL NEWT  ONE
```

PUZZLE 432

```
FEET BOSS  BAT
AVER ARIA  ALE
DELI CARD  TIN
  TITLE  ROBE
SPHERE   UNIT
PEA  ARRIVE
ANT TIARA  VAN
  WEAPON  ICE
SOFA  NEGATE
UPON  RAISE
PER TALC  NEAP
ERA AREA  URGE
RAY PEEL  SNOW
```

PUZZLE 433

```
HELD APSE  OAR
EPEE SOIL  VIA
RING SERENADE
SCARLET  COT
   AIT  STRICT
ABIDE DES  OLE
CONE LEA  GNUS
ELF WAN  BESET
   STOLID SAN
    ROE ATTUNED
COMPLETE  IOTA
AVA DROP  NEAR
PAL SAPS  ELSE
```

PUZZLE 434

```
RAG ATIP  ALAS
AVE RANT  RATA
TAR MCCARTNEY
  SLOT  AIDES
OTHER  ANNS
PAWS AGOG  SOB
ALI BRAVE  URI
LEN ALVA  GLAD
  ALOE  TELLS
AMASS  SEMI
BACHARACH  VIA
LINE OBOE  ACT
EDEN TETE  NEE
```

PUZZLE 435

```
ALP AMPS  ESTE
BOO COAL  NCAA
BROCCOLI  RANT
EERIER  COOL
   TDS  KILLED
PAREE MEL  ILE
SCUD MAR  COLE
ART FED  PANED
TEASED  PER
   BANI AROUND
SCAN CUCUMBER
HUGE ARES  ERA
YEAR LIRE  ROB
```

PUZZLE 436

```
LIMB MILE  BET
AREA OWED  ALE
DENY NONSENSE
  ONO  TENDED
ACQUIRE  LOS
LOU CADS  STOP
AMI EIGHT  ARE
NECK LEER  NAT
   KIN SPINDLE
PASSED   HOE
REASSURE  VEST
ERN TEAR  ERIE
POD SLED  RAND
```

PUZZLE 437

```
SLAB QUIP  ALL
COLE URGE  GOO
AVER ENORMOUS
RECESS  ROE
   TOTE  NAVAL
PEW FIRM  TORE
ATO TONES  LIE
ATOP NILE  TAR
RADAR  EVER
   IAN  IRONED
CHARCOAL  DOLE
RIP EVIL  ERIE
YET RARE  OMAR
```

PUZZLE 438

```
ARCS PLATA  ACTS
TELE ROPES  DUEL
ONUS OGEES  ETNA
POETSCORNER  COP
   EAT  STATORS
STATIONS  SPAR
HAM DROOD  TINTS
ORES SELAH  LEAN
PONCE LOSES  RBI
  CAPS  SHAKESUP
STORING   DIX
AIR CORNERSTONE
RANT RAISE  RHEA
AREA TILTS  AIMS
HARP SLEET  SOOT
```

PUZZLE 439

WORDS: Mysterious, Appended, Canines, Brawl, Earthquake, Threw, Hash.
TRIVIA DESCRIPTION: Shakespearean play with three witches and Banquo's murder.
ANSWER: Macbeth.

PUZZLE 440

```
SMILE  AUNTS
SPINET  SKIRTS
WINNIETHEPOOH
ANNS ROES  ULE
NEE ANON  ABLE
  SPLAT  RELET
AMORAL  SIRENS
SATES  BLOOM
CLAY ARUT  ATE
OAF SLAG  OKRA
TRAINENGINEER
SITTER  ENTRAP
ASSET  ROOST
```

PUZZLE 441

```
SPARK   BLOAT
ARDENT  PLEASE
NODDER  EASTER
   EAVES  SAM
MURAL   ART
IRAS TEE  ADS
MAYHEM  DRIVEL
ELS NOW  RILE
   TOO  REDID
WAS  ERODE
ENCORE  AMORAL
STARED  DILATE
TINED   TEPEE
```

PUZZLE 442

```
TARO JACK  PERE
ALUM ELAND  IDOL
ROBERTELEE  NESS
STELE  LANTANA
   EMIR  DEAF
NAUTILUS  ROVER
EST TINT  STRIVE
ASIN ATONE  ERIS
RELOAD PANT  ETE
STEAM  SHOWBOAT
   HERA  AREA
PASSING  ESTEE
CORA GOLDENHIND
USER IDEAL  ERIN
DESK EERY  SODA
```

PUZZLE 443

1. Daisy, 2. Grand, 3. Rigid, 4. Pansy,
5. Sprig, 6. Aside, 7. Angry, 8. Sneer,
9. Paper, 10. Spray.

PUZZLE 444

```
CLIMB SCAT  BEES
RAREE NERO  IAMA
ARISE ONCE  TROT
WASHCLOTH  JETTY
   HAZE  KOSHER
CART DERAIL
ALOHA  OLDTIMER
PETAL OFF  EVADE
EXERTING  DELED
   AVERSE  SEND
QUARRY  ATEE
ATLAS EVERGLADE
TILT MEIR  RAGED
ALEE ARTE  EMEND
REND YOYO  TESTY
```

PUZZLE 445

If you don't believe in ghosts, you've never been to a family reunion.

PUZZLE 446

H	A	N	K		H	E	A	L		G	M	A	N		R	A	J	A	S
I	C	O	N		A	E	R	I	E		R	A	M	I		E	R	E	C	T
S	H	O	O	T	F	R	O	M	T	H	E	H	I	P		D	I	T	T	O
S	E	N	T	R	I	E	S		C	E	N	E		A	S	P	A	S	I	A
			T	A	R	S		S	H	A	D			W	I	N				
N	O	T	I	M	E		W	E	E	V	E	R		M	I	N	S	T	E	R
A	S	H	E	S		B	A	R	R	E	L	H	O	U	S	E		R	A	E
I	C	E	R		S	A	R	A				E	G	I	S		R	I	S	E
A	A	R		W	I	N	C	H	E	S	T	E	R		P	A	G	E	D	
D	R	I	B	L	E	T	S		A	R	E	T	E		S	I	N	G	L	Y
	F	R	E	D	S		C	O	N	E	S		T	I	N	G	E			
S	A	L	I	N	E		S	O	L	I	D		F	E	T	T	E	R	E	D
A	M	E	N	D		F	I	R	E	E	S	C	A	P	E		F	R	O	
T	A	M	E		D	O	O	N		A	R	E	S		P	I	O	N		
E	R	A		M	A	G	N	U	M	F	O	R	C	E		B	A	S	S	O
D	A	N	C	E	R	S		A	E	R	A	T	E		F	I	S	H	E	R
			A	R	E		G	A	T	E		P	E	R	T					
S	E	A	S	I	D	E		M	A	I	M		P	A	N	T	R	I	E	S
A	C	R	I	D		C	H	A	R	L	E	S	I	N	C	H	A	R	G	E
S	H	I	N	E		R	A	N	I		A	I	N	E	E		M	E	G	A
S	O	L	O	N		U	T	E	S		L	E	S	S			I	D	Y	L

PUZZLE 447

S	L	O	B		A	S	T	E	R		R	A	Z	E
L	A	D	E		S	L	A	V	E		E	B	O	N
A	V	O	W		B	E	R	E	T		L	E	N	D
P	A	R	A	K	E	E	T		E	L	A	T	E	S
			R	I	S	K		F	L	E	X			
A	C	C	E	N	T		M	U	L	T	I	P	L	E
R	A	H		D	O	D	O	S			S	N	A	I	L
O	P	U	S		S	I	X	E	S		G	I	V	E
M	E	T	E	R		T	I	D	E	S		L	E	G
A	D	E	Q	U	A	T	E		C	L	A	S	S	Y
			U	N	D	O		D	R	A	G			
A	L	L	E	G	E		V	I	E	W	A	B	L	E
L	O	A	N		E	J	E	C	T		T	O	O	L
E	P	I	C		M	O	T	E	L		E	L	L	S
S	E	R	E			S	T	O	R	Y		S	O	L	E

1-Z, 2-H, 3-E, 4-U, 5-M, 6-C, 7-V, 8-W, 9-R, 10-Q, 11-S, 12-A, 13-N, 14-G, 15-L, 16-K, 17-P, 18-D, 19-Y, 20-F, 21-X, 22-T, 23-B, 24-J, 25-I, 26-O.

PUZZLE 448

M	A	A	M		H	A	T	E		N	A	R	C	S
E	L	B	A		A	L	O	W		A	T	E	U	P
A	D	A	R		S	O	L	E		S	H	I	R	E
T	A	S	K		H	O	U	S	A	T	O	N	I	C
			T	R	E	F			B	A	S	S	E	S
A	V	O	W	E	R		W	O	O	S				
R	E	L	A	X		C	O	N	D	E	N	S	E	S
C	A	L	I		L	E	V	E	E		E	A	R	L
A	L	A	N	B	A	T	E	S		S	W	I	N	E
			A	D	E	N		B	I	L	L	E	D	
C	H	A	S	T	E		D	A	D	O				
R	A	L	P	H	N	A	D	E	R		N	I	P	S
O	L	L	I	E		S	E	R	E		D	O	R	A
S	L	I	E	R		P	A	M	S		O	T	I	S
S	E	E	D	S		S	L	A	T		N	A	G	S

PUZZLE 449

Q	U	A	R	T		I	S	A	W		L	A	M	P
U	R	I	A	H		N	O	V	A		A	L	A	I
A	G	R	E	E		P	L	A	Y	A	P	A	R	T
Y	E	S		M	O	U	E		F	R	E	N	C	H
			S	A	L	T		J	A	I	L			
P	A	L	A	T	E		B	U	R	L		C	A	N
A	L	I	B	I		S	A	L	E		E	R	N	E
T	A	K	E	C	E	N	T	E	R	S	T	A	G	E
S	T	E	R		L	O	O	P		L	A	Z	E	D
Y	E	N		T	E	R	N		N	A	P	E	R	Y
			L	A	C	E		V	I	N	E			
A	S	P	E	C	T		D	O	N	T		T	I	C
P	E	R	F	O	R	M	E	D		I	N	A	N	E
S	E	A	T		O	I	N	K		N	I	X	O	N
E	M	M	Y		N	O	T	A		G	L	I	N	T

PUZZLE 450

S	P	A	D	E		A	B	A	T	E		D	A	B
P	O	K	E	R		C	R	I	E	R		A	T	E
E	L	I	T	E		R	A	D	A	R		T	O	E
D	O	N	E		I	T	S		A	D	A	P	T	
			S	H	O	D		O	N	E				
H	A	L	T	E	R		R	U	P	T	U	R	E	S
A	L	E		R	E	C	E	N	T		C	O	N	E
S	A	V	E		L	E	T		E	A	S	E		
T	R	E	E		S	A	L	O	N	S		D	U	D
E	M	E	R	A	L	D	S		T	E	A	S	E	S
			I	C	Y		C	H	A	R				
D	E	F	E	R		M	A	R		C	A	R	E	
A	V	E		O	R	A	T	E		L	A	C	E	D
N	E	E		S	O	L	O	S		A	N	T	E	D
E	N	D		S	T	E	M	S		P	E	S	K	Y

PUZZLE 451

S	A	N	S		O	V	A			S	P	E	D	
U	N	I	T		D	I	P		S	W	A	M	I	S
E	T	H	E	R	E	A	L		W	A	R	B	L	E
S	E	I	N	E	S		O	D	I	N		L	A	D
			L	O	T		S	M	U	G		B	E	T	A
D	A	I	S		H	U	B	S		W	O	M	E	N
U	P	S		G	I	N		T	A	R	P			
D	E	T	E	R	S			D	E	S	I	S	T	
			M	I	S	S		T	I	N		N	E	O
S	T	E	I	N		T	A	U	T		S	T	E	P
T	O	U	R		B	U	S	T		F	E	E		
E	R	R		H	U	N	T		M	I	N	G	L	E
A	R	E	N	A	S		R	H	E	T	O	R	I	C
L	I	K	E	L	Y		A	I	L		R	A	S	H
D	A	T	E		Y	E	T		A	L	T	O		

An optimist sees a doughnut; a pessimist sees the hole.

PUZZLE 452

B	R	A	T		H	A	T	E		C	A	S	H		A	L	I	T
L	I	R	E		A	D	E	S		A	W	A	Y		N	I	R	O
A	V	E	R		M	O	N	A		P	E	T	E		A	M	O	R
B	E	A	N	S	P	R	O	U	T	S		E	N	C	H	A	N	T
			P	E	E	R		R	I	P		A	L	E				
A	W	K	W	A	R	D		R	A	Z	E	D		V	I	C	E	S
S	H	A	R	I	S		V	I	C	E	R	O	Y		M	O	V	E
P	A	L	I	N		C	I	T	E	D		C	E	O		L	E	N
S	T	E	T		M	O	D	E	S		S	T	A	N	D	A	R	D
				E	C	O	L	E	S		P	O	O	R	E	R		
A	M	A	R	I	L	L	O		L	E	A	R	N		A	C	E	S
M	O	B		T	A	I		T	E	A	R	S		M	I	A	M	I
I	T	E	M		R	E	V	E	A	L	S		T	A	N	N	I	N
D	O	T	E	D		S	I	N	G	E		P	U	R	S	E	R	S
			T	I	S		P	A	U		H	E	R	D				
A	R	S	E	N	I	C		C	E	L	E	B	R	I	T	I	E	S
N	O	N	O		D	E	L	I		E	L	B	E		O	V	A	L
O	M	A	R		E	D	I	T		D	O	L	T		G	A	V	E
N	A	P	S		D	E	N	Y		A	T	E	S		A	N	E	W

PUZZLE 453

E	P	I	C		C	O	P		T	A	B		S	L	O	G
S	L	I	C	E		A	V	A	R	I	C	E		T	A	L	E	S
P	A	N	E	L		V	A	L	A	N	C	E		O	V	I	N	E
U	T	E		T	I	E		W	E	E		B	R	A	V	E	R
N	E	S	S		N	A	M	E		S	P	R	E	E		E	R	A
			M	A	S	T	E	R	S		T	E	N		S	R	A	
S	E	D	A	T	E		S	E	N	T	I	M	E	N	T		
T	R	I	S	E	C	T	S		A	R	N	O		O	U	S	T	S
A	R	C	H		T	O	Y		R	U	G		I	N	E	R	T
R	A	T		H	S	T		G	E	E		P	E	R		N	O	R
E	T	U	D	E		M	A	D		G	A	D		T	A	P	E
D	A	M	E	S		P	A	R	R		E	M	U	L	A	T	E	S
			A	T	T	R	I	B	U	T	E		C	A	R	E	S	S
P	A	R		I	O	N		M	I	S	L	A	I	D			
S	E	R		S	P	A	T	S		M	E	A	T		Y	A	L	E
C	A	R	O	L	S		A	L	A		T	E	A		R	A	N	
A	L	I	N	E		V	I	A	D	U	C	T		B	L	E	N	D
R	E	V	U	E		I	N	V	E	R	S	E		C	I	T	E	S
D	E	S	K		E	S	E		B	A	R		S	E	E	S	

PUZZLE 454

P	A	G	E		A	S	H	E	R		U	F	O	S
A	L	E	X		F	L	A	R	E		T	A	N	E
N	A	R	A		L	O	I	N	S		U	S	E	R
G	I	M	M	E	A	B	R	E	A	K		T	A	V
			E	M	S			N	I	M	B	L	E	
B	A	B	B	L	E		F	O	D	D	E	R		
A	C	R	E	S		P	A	R	E		S	E	A	S
R	H	E	A		M	A	T	E	D		H	A	L	E
T	E	A	K		A	L	A	S		P	E	K	O	E
		K	E	R	N	E	L		L	A	S	S	E	N
A	L	F	R	E	D			S	A	T				
M	O	A		B	R	E	A	K	T	H	E	I	C	E
B	O	S	N		E	R	N	I	E		S	T	A	Y
E	S	T	E		L	I	N	E	S		T	E	L	E
R	E	S	T		L	E	A	S	T		A	M	I	D

PUZZLE 455

S	L	A	P		A	L	O	H	A		S	K	E	P
P	I	N	E		N	E	V	E	R		T	I	T	O
A	D	I	R	O	N	D	A	C	K		A	L	O	P
			N	A	G		K	A	T	R	I	N	E	
E	T	A		I	L	E			N	O	R	M		
R	E	P	R	O	S		M	A	S	T		A	H	A
A	S	P	E	N		S	A	G	A	S		N	E	T
S	T	A	T		M	O	T	E	S		A	J	A	R
E	E	L		A	C	R	E	S		S	L	A	V	E
S	R	A		I	K	E	S		S	T	A	R	E	S
		C	A	D	I			P	T	A		O	N	T
A	S	H	C	A	N	S		A	R	I				
O	T	I	C		L	A	U	R	E	N	T	I	A	N
N	E	A	R		E	L	S	I	E		A	L	D	A
E	T	N	A		Y	E	A	S	T		P	L	O	T

PUZZLE 456

E	L	A	N		A	C	E	S		P	I	P	E		B	A	N	G
C	A	N	E		D	O	L	L		R	O	O	T		O	L	E	A
H	I	T	T	H	E	N	A	I	L	O	N	T	H	E	H	E	A	D
O	R	E		A	P	E		P	U	N		S	E	L	E	C	T	S
			O	R	T		M	A	L	T	A		R	I	M			
C	A	B	L	E		N	E	W	L	O	O	K		S	I	R	E	N
A	V	I	D		B	A	L	A	S		R	E	A		A	U	R	A
M	E	T		H	A	S	T	Y		S	T	Y	L	E		D	I	G
P	R	E	S	E	N	T	S		S	H	A		A	L	I	E	N	S
			E	D	D	Y		C	O	Y		A	M	I	D			
C	A	N	A	D	A		H	U	N		P	R	O	T	O	C	O	L
A	R	A		A	G	R	E	E		P	R	I	D	E		A	G	E
R	A	M	P		E	O	N		E	R	O	S	E		T	R	E	E
P	L	E	A	D		E	N	C	L	O	S	E		M	E	T	E	R
			S	E	C		A	L	A	T	E		L	E	D			
P	E	S	T	E	R	S		A	T	E		T	O	N		I	M	P
A	C	H	I	P	O	N	O	N	E	S	S	H	O	U	L	D	E	R
T	R	A	M		P	A	R	K		T	O	E	S		E	L	S	E
H	U	G	E		S	P	A	S		S	O	M	E		R	E	A	P

PUZZLE 457

A	L	E	C		S	P	O	T		T	A	L	C		C	A	T	S
V	I	D	A		O	L	E	O		A	R	E	A		A	L	O	W
E	M	I	T		N	O	R	M		B	A	I	T		T	O	G	A
C	A	T	S	P	A	W		C	O	B	B		H	O	N	E	S	T
			E	A	R		M	A	N	Y		D	E	M	I			
F	L	A	Y	S		F	E	T	E		C	A	T	A	P	U	L	T
L	A	D	E		P	R	O	S		L	A	T	E	R		S	E	A
O	V	I		V	I	E	W		P	E	T	E	R		B	E	A	R
C	A	T	L	I	K	E		M	E	A	T	S		F	E	R	N	S
			O	P	E		R	E	A	D	Y		V	I	A			
D	A	R	T	S		S	O	A	R	S		C	A	T	N	A	P	S
I	R	E	S		A	E	O	N	S		M	A	T	S		I	L	E
S	I	N		C	L	A	M	S		C	A	R	S		C	L	A	W
C	A	T	C	A	L	L	S		P	A	T	E		L	A	S	T	S
			A	P	E	S		S	A	T	E		B	I	T			
C	U	R	T	S	Y		O	K	R	A		C	A	T	A	W	B	A
A	R	I	S		C	A	S	E		R	E	A	L		L	A	I	D
L	A	T	U		A	N	T	I		R	A	L	E		O	N	C	E
F	L	A	P		T	E	E	N		H	U	M	S		G	E	E	S

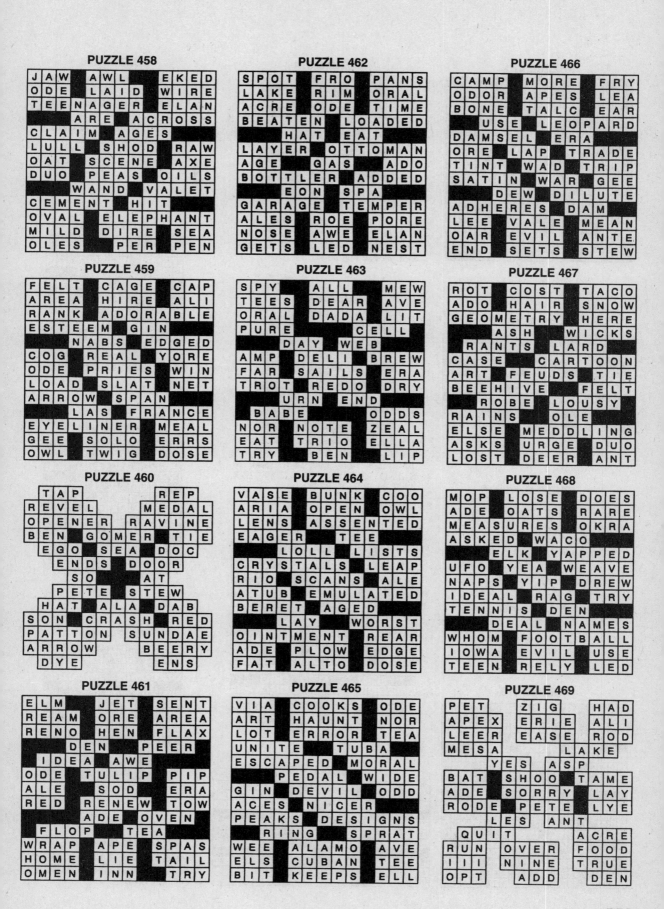

PUZZLE 458

```
J A W   A W L     E K E D
O D E   L A I D   W I R E
T E E N A G E R   E L A N
      A R E   A C R O S S
C L A I M   A G E S
L U L L   S H O D   R A W
O A T   S C E N E   A X E
D U O   P E A S   O I L S
    W A N D   V A L E T
C E M E N T   H I T
O V A L   E L E P H A N T
M I L D   D I R E   S E A
O L E S     P E R   P E N
```

PUZZLE 459

```
F E L T   C A G E   C A P
A R E A   H I R E   A L I
R A N K   A D O R A B L E
E S T E E M   G I N
    N A B S   E D G E D
C O G   R E A L   Y O R E
O D E   P R I E S   W I N
L O A D   S L A T   N E T
A R R O W   S P A N
    L A S   F R A N C E
E Y E L I N E R   M E A L
G E E   S O L O   E R R S
O W L   T W I G   D O S E
```

PUZZLE 460

```
  T A P         R E P
R E V E L     M E D A L
O P E N E R   R A V I N E
B E N   G O M E R   T I E
  E G O   S E A   D O C
  E N D S   D O O R
    S O       A T
  P E T E   S T E W
H A T   A L A   D A B
S O N   C R A S H   R E D
P A T T O N   S U N D A E
A R R O W     B E E R Y
D Y E         E N S
```

PUZZLE 461

```
E L M     J E T   S E N T
R E A M   O R E   A R E A
R E N O   H E N   F L A X
    D E N   P E E R
  I D E A   A W E
O D E   T U L I P   P I P
A L E   S O D   E R A
R E D   R E N E W   T O W
    A D E   O V E N
  F L O P   T E A
W R A P   A P E   S P A S
H O M E   L I E   T A I L
O M E N   I N N   T R Y
```

PUZZLE 462

```
S P O T   F R O   P A N S
L A K E   R I M   O R A L
A C R E   O D E   T I M E
B E A T E N   L O A D E D
    H A T   E A T
L A Y E R   O T T O M A N
A G E   G A S   A D O
B O T T L E R   A D D E D
    E O N   S P A
G A R A G E   T E M P E R
A L E S   R O E   P O R E
N O S E   A W E   E L A N
G E T S   L E D   N E S T
```

PUZZLE 463

```
S P Y     A L L   M E W
T E E S   D E A R   A V E
O R A L   D A D A   L I T
P U R E     C E L L
  D A Y   W E B
A M P   D E L I   B R E W
F A R   S A I L S   E R A
T R O T   R E D O   D R Y
  U R N   E N D
  B A B E     O D D S
N O R   N O T E   Z E A L
E A T   T R I O   E L L A
T R Y   B E N   L I P
```

PUZZLE 464

```
V A S E   B U N K   C O O
A R I A   O P E N   O W L
L E N S   A S S E N T E D
E A G E R   T E E
    L O L L   L I S T S
C R Y S T A L S   L E A P
R I O   S C A N S   A L E
A T U B   E M U L A T E D
B E R E T   A G E D
  L A Y     W O R S T
O I N T M E N T   R E A R
A D E   P L O W   E D G E
F A T   A L T O   D O S E
```

PUZZLE 465

```
V I A   C O O K S   O D E
A R T   H A U N T   N O R
L O T   E R R O R   T E A
U N I T E   T U B A
E S C A P E D   M O R A L
  P E D A L   W I D E
G I N   D E V I L   O D D
A C E S   N I C E R
P E A K S   D E S I G N S
  R I N G   S P R A T
W E E   A L A M O   A V E
E L S   C U B A N   T E E
B I T   K E E P S   E L L
```

PUZZLE 466

```
C A M P   M O R E   F R Y
O D O R   A P E S   L E A
B O N E   T A L C   E A R
    U S E   L E O P A R D
D A M S E L   E R A
O R E   L A P   T R A D E
T I N T   W A D   T R I P
S A T I N   W A R   G E E
    D E W   D I L U T E
A D H E R E S   D A M
L E E   V A L E   M E A N
O A R   E V I L   A N T E
E N D   S E T S   S T E W
```

PUZZLE 467

```
R O T   C O S T   T A C O
A D O   H A I R   S N O W
G E O M E T R Y   H E R E
    A S H   W I C K S
  R A N T S   L A R D
C A S E   C A R T O O N
A R T   F E U D S   T I E
B E E H I V E   F E L T
  R O B E   L O U S Y
R A I N S   O L E
E L S E   M E D D L I N G
A S K S   U R G E   D U O
L O S T   D E E R   A N T
```

PUZZLE 468

```
M O P   L O S E   D O E S
A D E   O A T S   R A R E
M E A S U R E S   O K R A
A S K E D   W A C O
    E L K   Y A P P E D
U F O   Y E A   W E A V E
N A P S   Y I P   D R E W
I D E A L   R A G   T R Y
  D E A L   N A M E S
W H O M   F O O T B A L L
I O W A   E V I L   U S E
T E E N   R E L Y   L E D
```

PUZZLE 469

```
P E T     Z I G     H A D
A P E X   E R I E   A L I
L E E R   E A S E   R O D
M E S A       L A K E
    Y E S   A S P
B A T   S H O O   T A M E
A D E   S O R R Y   L A Y
R O D E   P E T E   L Y E
    L E S   A N T
  Q U I T     A C R E
R U N   O V E R   F O O D
I I I   N I N E   T R U E
O P T   A D D   D E N
```

551

PUZZLE 470

```
  ORAD    SAC     LEIS
ARLENE  SILAS   ARRAS
SAINTPATRICK    SNIDE
ASNOT OARS  HIST   SIN
RUES  TRI   ETE   SHED
AME MDS   DAR   SLAMS
LESTER  EPA   FLEERS
    IRES  SPCA  TETON
SEALANE AERIE   STOA
DER EMERALDISLE   EKG
UNIR  SEATO  STARERS
ANNES   SLOW   SNIT
LAGERS  ASA   DECARE
OMITS SAL PSS     RON
EBBS  OLE   TAR   SCOT
AIR AWOL  CODA  SPANS
SLATE  BLARNEYSTONE
ELGAR  SAGES  ETUDES
  SHOO    SAW    RENE
```

PUZZLE 471

```
BEGAN    AVID   DISPUTE
SIRE   BARES    TORN
DELICATELY  SERGEANT
    NEVER  FERVENT
MORASS  CELL  ISLAND
BILL SHADOWING   CALL
DAYTIME   SHIRK  TREY
    BELLHOP   LOA
DISTRACT  EXPENDABLE
MARLIN  HEARTEN  SMITE
LODE    DAZED    TADS
```

PUZZLE 472

PUZZLE 473

```
GILA  TAMP  UTAH  KANT
ADIT  ASOR  NASA  ATEE
LEAL  PHOENIXARIZONA
LARAMIE  SETI  ROOMER
    NOR  ETAS  LIDO
PLATT  LOOT  RESISTOR
IOWA JINN  HAVOC   AVE
ENE DAMS  MAVIN  ATEN
SEDALIA  RIVEN  LLANO
    LIL  CANES  MUM
MIAMI  AARON  DECATUR
ENGS UNSET  LOSE  ELY
SRO  ANGER  BORA  PANA
SEGOLILY  NAPA  ROMAN
    GIVE  MOSS  SIT
ELAINE  KENT  ANDOVER
DENVERCOLORADO   MENA
INEE  SURE  OHIO  ARIL
TAWS  ERSE  PANT  CADE
```

PUZZLE 474

```
QUALITY    MANIA
U R N   AU   O N
INK  JAMBS   WAX
T       I      I
EFFERVESCENCE
  I  E M     I T
HUE  DEBIT   MAY
E L   E    R B
INDUSTRIALIZE
G       A  P    M
HOW  VAGUE  ASP
T I  A Z R    T
SITED   SKETCHY
```

1-G, 2-D, 3-V, 4-U, 5-B, 6-C, 7-N, 8-K, 9-J, 10-O, 11-Y, 12-R, 13-L, 14-X, 15-H, 16-I, 17-T, 18-Z, 19-E, 20-A, 21-M, 22-P, 23-S, 24-F, 25-Q, 26-W.

PUZZLE 475

```
JAWBONE   JAUNT
E A V P     N A
ACTUALIZATION
N   E   L    O D
SIR  ELOQUENCE
E  X G S      M
ODDITY   WHITES
R   R S E    A
CHARACTER   FAR
H S   R  F    H
APPROXIMATELY
R E   P I T    M
DUNKS   SALVAGE
```

1-T, 2-L, 3-I, 4-G, 5-P, 6-B, 7-U, 8-Z, 9-Y, 10-C, 11-V, 12-Q, 13-J, 14-W, 15-M, 16-S, 17-O, 18-D, 19-A, 20-H, 21-F, 22-X, 23-N, 24-R, 25-K, 26-E.

PUZZLE 476

```
WAND  SLOP  TALC  TEND
ALOE  HOUR  IDEA  OTOE
SASS  AUTO  RASP  RATE
PRESENT  PIE  STARTER
     ERE   ROC   USE
TERRA  LOSES  GRENADE
ALIT  CEDE  TARE  THUD
USS  RHO  DRAPE   ENE
TEEPEE   ALTAR  OMEN
     ALSO  AVE  TASS
BOND  SCALE    NESTLE
ADE   CRISP  AGA  AAA
NOVA  AURA  ROSE  SILT
DRESSER  SHOOK  ATLAS
     SRO   ASP   SIR
REVEALS  IMP  SILENCE
AVER  IOTA  ETAL  TELL
JEST  ALEG  CALL  CRAM
ANTS  NONO  TREY  HOPS
```

PUZZLE 477

```
PERUSE   RENEGE   SCREEN
ABLE   CATO     HONER
LECTURE      GEOLOGY
    NATE    RAPT
DESPITE  MATHEMATIC
VILER   ACHY    DARED
LANGUAGES    RELEASE
    MING     FAT
EXPLORES  UNIVERSITY
AMIABLE  SIDED   ARETE
NEONS   VENTING   RINGS
```

PUZZLE 478

1. Pink, Rink, Risk, Rise, Rose.
2. Last, Lost, Lose, Lore, Lord, Word.
3. Wolf, Woof, Hoof, Hook, Hock, Hack, Pack.
4. Acts, Arts, Arms, Aims, Dims, Dime, Dice, Nice.

PUZZLE 479

```
CRIB   NOM    PALE
LAME   APE    USER
IRAN   VENERATE
PEG   MENTOR
    IRIS   INSIST
PANEL  LOS    MAO
EGAD   RUN    SPIT
ERR   SUM    HALLS
PAYOUT   IOTA
     REGENT   NRA
MOISTENS    ITER
AERO   ROE    SEAM
EDEN   SST    ODDS
```

PUZZLE 480

```
RUSS   ODE    OTIS
UNIT   DIN    URNS
IDEA   IMPOTENT
NOGGIN    LAP
     FED   NATURAL
NORSEMAN    TENO
ANI   MATES   STU
ICED   RADIATED
FEDERAL    ALA
     MAT   UMBRAE
THOUGHTS    ITEM
ROAR   OWE    NERI
YOKE   NOD    ODOR
```

PUZZLE 481

```
SARI   OATS    SPA
IRON   RIATA  DEAF
FELT   ARROW  INCA
TALENTS   PLASTER
ROE        ICE
TAPER  HAREM   NAG
APES   PERILS  CUR
TART   RAILS  FIDO
ARC   REDSEA  ANEW
RTE   ESSES  SIGNS
    PEA      EER
SETTLED   PRELATE
OLIO   DOTER  AMOK
LION   STONE  DIRE
DAN    SEND   YENS
```

PUZZLE 482

1. Scale, 2. Clash, 3. Story, 4. Heart, 5. Rally, 6. Roost, 7. Teach, 8. Relay, 9. Horse, 10. Yeast.

PUZZLE 483

```
ATOP  TED  ARGOT
LIRA  HARP MARIE
ERAS  ERIE OPALS
CENTRALPARK  NET
   RUT  STY STD
LAWYER    EGIS
IRA  ENDS  ALTO
TALLY AYE STOVE
BLUE  PETE  MAR
STAT   STABLE
RTE  EAR  TET
PAR FEDERALHALL
ONEAL EDIT ELLIE
LIEGE NICE NINA
ESTEE DOS  STEP
```

PUZZLE 488

```
LASS  STRIP  TALK
ABET  PEACE  ALOE
TREE  ARSON  LIVE
HARES  RAN  HOTEL
   ROPA  IRON
COS REP CEP  SIR
AROMATIC RETIRE
CANO ANODE  ELAN
ATABAL DEDICATE
OER GEM NOT  SEW
   REDE  ASEA
FREED  DET MODEL
LOAM  LINUS RAVI
ASTI  SCORE TRAM
PEST  TOWER ANNA
```

PUZZLE 494

FISH: Grouper, Ray, Eel, Albacore, Trout.
BIRDS: Grosbeak, Robin, Eagle, Auk, Tern.
LANGUAGES: Greek, Russian, English, Arabic, Tagalog.
DOGS: Greyhound, Rottweiler, Elkhound, Airedale, Tibetan terrier.
AMERICAN CITIES: Gary, Rochester, El Paso, Atlanta, Tampa.

PUZZLE 484

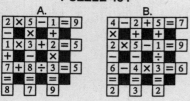

A.

2	×	5	−	1	=	9
−		×		+		
1	×	3	+	2	=	5
+		−		×		
7	+	8	÷	3	=	5
=		=		=		
8		7		9		

B.

4	−	2	+	5	=	7
×		+		+		
2	×	5	−	1	=	9
−		−		÷		
6	−	4	×	3	=	6
=		=		=		
2		3		2		

PUZZLE 489

```
SLAT  RAND   SPAN
HAIR  TERRE  CAGE
ADMIRALFARRAGUT
HES  IRAS   OMENS
   HOOT  SHOP
CHESTERNIMITZ
PAAR   EARS   RIP
ARID  GRAPE  MAGI
WET  ARIL   EDGE
WILLIAMHALSEY
   EATS  ELIA
MADAM  DRUM  LOB
ISOROKUYAMAMOTO
TENN  OVALS  ANTE
TATS  SAND   DIOR
```

PUZZLE 485

```
RIB            ARM
IDEA GAL    REO  IVAN
COLD ARIA TEAL   MAGI
ELLAFITZGERALD  PROP
     ANY  RAE  MERRY
AMASS  DESKS   DUO
COLT  REESE   EVILS
TOT  HAY    ASP  IRAE
OPAL       PRESAGE
ASIDE       ROMAN
DEBATER      ABUT
ALEX  STY   RYE  IFS
BATON  ALAMO    POOL
POD  MILAN   HONEY
SHRED  MAC   OUR
OTTO LOUISARMSTRONG
LEAN TENT  WEAK  IRON
DATE ARI        MESA
     SST   PRY   SEW
```

PUZZLE 490

1. Ginger, Basil, Dill, Sage; 2. Rummy, Poker, Whist, Bridge; 3. Sandal, Boot, Pump, Sneaker; 4. Silk, Chino, Wool, Felt; 5. Cruet, Vial, Beaker, Flask; 6. Onion, Leek, Chives, Shallot.

PUZZLE 491

```
WEST  PLACE  FROM
AVOW  RERUN  LAVA
RIDE  EATER  ICED
PLAN  CRY  AMPERE
   THEN  EGO
STAYED PREACHER
HOG  MEDIA  NAIVE
AWAY  INS   TREE
RETIE VEEPS  END
PREPARED  ROASTS
   CAR  DENT
BRIGHT HIS  OPAL
LODE  TWICE  MANE
OPEN  LADEN  IRON
TEST  EXERT  CENT
```

PUZZLE 495

```
ISNT  ADAGE  SCOW
DOOR  DEBAR  HAVE
LISA  OMEGA  ASEA
ELECTRODES  KERN
   TINS   USE
ACTORS  BARONESS
THERE BOWED  VIA
TONS  TARES  BORN
ARE  SOLES  POKED
RETAILER  LINENS
   IRE   SEED
CARS  REHEARSERS
EVIL  AVERS  MAIL
DOLE  NERVE  ESSE
EWES  TREES  NEED
```

PUZZLE 496

1. Co/m/bi/ne, Ha/ll/w/ay, Di/r/ect/or, S/ta/t/ion.
BONUS: Co/ll/ect/ion
2. Go/g/gl/es, Mo/ld/i/ng, C/on/fin/e, Sc/r/at/ch.
BONUS: Go/ld/fin/ch

PUZZLE 497

```
     MAC          FIN
    BELLE        GENOA
   GALLEY       LINERS
OLD  ARC      BUS  LEA
AND OVER     LETS  ANT
AID DUE EMU  YEP  DEN
DROVER  TAN   TURBAN
DELAY  BERTH   PHASE
DAN  GNU    ADZ  ORE
     EAR      BAA
ICE  EEL    IMP  ACE
SCORN  YACHT  AGAVE
HORNER  SUE  PROPEL
ENS WAD SEW  TAM TRY
SAP MESA     ELAN DAY
ILE COY      DOM  SRI
   RUDDER     SAMPAN
    MAINE      ELIOT
     MET        EAT
```

PUZZLE 486

```
DOTE  EWE   SLED
OVER  SAX   HALE
DALE  TRICYCLE
OLE  LASSO   EAR
GNAT       TOO
PARADE   SNARLS
EXAM       SAIL
REMEDY   GRITTY
SEA       EAST
HAD  SWARM   LAB
ALUMINUM   MILE
RAKE  ERA  ANTE
KNEW  DAN  EGOS
```

PUZZLE 487

```
HEY  ADAM  HOSE
AGO  FILE  APED
MOUNTAIN  SPED
EEL       STONY
PIERS  BEES
BAND  PIANIST
UPS  BAITS  TOW
TAPPING  ZERO
IRAN  TWIST
CARES  URN
OMIT  MANICURE
MINT  ALES  FAR
EDGY  EAST  ONE
```

PUZZLE 492

THE LETTER M

PUZZLE 493

```
FLED  EMBED  ROBS
LIVE  MAUVE  ERIE
ARIA  ANDES  LATE
BALCONY  RIVALED
   OVA  STRIP
BRUNETTE  EASIER
AIR  NEWER  LEDGE
LOGS  DIRER  SORE
STEED  TENET  LED
ASSAIL  SOLOISTS
   SLEDS  ELM
SCHOLAR  PALACES
PAIN  ROBES  GALE
INRE  NOOSE  EPIC
NEED  SPATS  SEAT
```

PUZZLE 498

```
CLOD  SHOE  PEP  SKIT
AIDE  EARN  AYE SPICE
PRESERVED  RELOCATED
PASSAGE  ARC   FURRED
EVE  SNEER   RAT
SHARE  REGALES  PANIC
POST  MATES  DIM  NOVA
APT MAT ROD  PAT  TAN
TEETERED  NIL  DEMONS
RUT  DIG   NAG   SIR
ATONES  PAR  CAPTAINS
LEI RUG BED  TOY  OAT
ENDS MAE LEVEE  DUPE
ESSES  STRIPES  RESET
LAP  CIVET   AIM
SALTED  GEN  ASSUMED
SCREENING  DESPERATE
PAIRS  DEE  ERIE EGOS
ANDS  ODD  DEAN  RINK
```

PUZZLE 499

```
SALAD   WARP
MOLINE DICERS
CORSAGE ELEMENT
ORT REPORTS SAO
MAIM LEVIS LEKS
BLEED REV DINES
ESSES RELENTS
  SCARSDALE
STARLET WEDGE
HOAGY TAV SURGE
ARME TOTES POGO
TRA PARENTS PEN
SELLOUT DRIVERS
LEARNS EATERS
SPET   EPEES
```

PUZZLE 500

Genus, Giant, Globe, Gruel, Guppy.

PUZZLE 501

```
SOSO  TEA  SCADS
SENTA TORME ALLIE
TREAT UNGER LEONE
EVIL BLY NRA ANE
SELLERS OLIVER
ONEAL BRINE
GRANDE OFA CARNE
RAGE NATALIE SAME
ACE STILT DIG
YENS THERESE SELA
STARR RET NEARED
DAISY SALEM
UNSEAT SARACEN
BOO LOW PHI NAPE
BOONS RAREE ATREE
RANGE ENTER SHEER
ATEST TEL PASS
```

PUZZLE 502

```
SCAT REIN  ASST
PALE EMMA PLATE
ANTE PIPS LIMES
TOE LOT THE EMS
ERROR YEAR
ASTER STARES
GASH EDEN STORE
AVE RISES PIE
MONTE TEAM NEED
ENTIRE TRADE
MASH LATER
SST SPA FLY RUM
OHARE RARE ARIA
TIMED EVES POND
SPED MATT ELSE
```

PUZZLE 503

ALLEGIANCE

PUZZLE 504

```
GREATOUTDOORS
VES MRU IW
INJUSTICE TEMPO
SO I TASER
ALIASES SKIDDED
CT UD L
RAILS PERMEABLE
EN EE R
MAGAZINES PIOUS
E II RA
DEADPAN BREADED
IL PSO C CO
ALIBI UPTHEWALL
LEE LCD SL
ENCROACHMENTS
```

PUZZLE 505

```
MATS EACH CLICK
ACHE VILE RADON
DEAD IDEA IGLOO
EDWARD FLAB EST
NOES SUBS
CONSENTS FEEBLE
OBI SCALA DARER
POND ERICA LANE
RETRO SERVE VIC
ASHORE REORIENT
PACE SCOT
OAF CUBA ASANAS
GRILL BEAD LAME
EERIE ERGO IRON
EASES DOES CYST
```

PUZZLE 506

1. Cashew, 2. Ticket, 3. Chorus, 4. Beetle, 5. Poplar, 6. Nugget, 7. Palace, 8. Random.
MOVIE ACTOR: Richard Gere

PUZZLE 507

```
HULA APSES CLAM
ASOF DRAKE HOBO
LEAF MINER ICED
ODDITIES INCITE
ROTS PEEK
FORMAT MASTERED
ORE DECOR SNORE
RACE DRAIN SURE
CLAMP ENSUE SOD
ESPOUSES MASERS
TREK TBSP
DESIRE VENEERED
ECHO SEINE LODE
ERIN ALOES LOGE
RUNS WILTS STEP
```

PUZZLE 508

1.
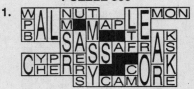

2.

PUZZLE 509

```
BACK BELA SEA
ALOE EGAD ALP
DERRINGDO WIT
SEND ERLE
EAST NADER
GIRL LON DOZE
ADO APE FRA
SLOG VIA AFAR
PETES CRIB
BEEF NAGS
ONE VALENTINE
WOE ERIE EVIL
ERR REEL SETS
```

PUZZLE 510

```
ACT AGAR PILL
DOE BALE AREA
ESTHETES LONG
HATE TRENDS
CHEFS RAID
HURT FORD RAT
AGE SLOTS EGO
RED LOSS CLAW
TOUT BLESS
BREWER IRAN
RILE INDENTED
APSE SEEN EVE
NEED HEAT DAN
```

PUZZLE 511

```
MAD   CODE  STER
DOTES HAIR  HERO
ROOST URGE  ONLY
ARM EARS  ERNES
WESTERN  QUOTE
  ERA BURN SEW
LANAS RAINS STA
OVAL WAITS SETS
LES PINTS SLEEP
ASH APTS  TEA
  VANES CONTEST
ARISE  HATS  ATE
SALS STAR EASES
TILT PORT SLEET
OLES YAMS  ALL
```

PUZZLE 515

```
GRAY  END   LAWS
ROPE  LIE   ACHE
IMPS  OCCASION
PER SPELL  DAD
  OBOE  ADS
AWARD  DRACULA
WACO  TOE  APED
EXHIBIT  ERRED
  LED  MAYO
ACT ABNER  OAT
DAINTIER  ETCH
OKRA  TAR  WERE
SEEP  STY  EDEN
```

PUZZLE 519

```
BALD SCRUB CLAP
OLIO IRANI SINO
MING LUGER COTE
BEEHIVES DRONES
  ONIT  SCUTS
PSEUDO CASTLES
AMASS MARGE AMT
RAGE DEFOE FICO
ISL AWARD FIRER
SHELTER MASSEY
  SULLA  WITH
FENNEL PIGSTIES
OLEG IRISH ACRE
RISE NONET NAME
METS GOERS KNAP
```

PUZZLE 512

```
LIRE STAFF THOR
OTIS TONAL WINE
LEONARDODAVINCI
ARTESIAN MINTED
  SPY  SITE
SPICES ETNA DAM
TAROT SNAG RENO
ALESSANDROVOLTA
KENT GOOS ELLEN
EDE CROW KNEADS
  SHIP  PIE
ATOMIC FASTENER
BENITOMUSSOLINI
REEL LENTE SPOT
INRE ANDES EASE
```

PUZZLE 516

```
SIAM BEST  KOBS
LONI ENLAI RULE
OUTOFDOORS UTES
PSI LEST ODIOUS
  RAW  CLIFF
FLOOR BLOAT MAT
ROUSE RANTS ONO
IOTA GESTE INIT
ESO TITER GRETA
DEF AGORA ROYAL
  ORLON  PIN
SHRILL SLUE EBB
NADA OUTOFFAVOR
AMEN SNIFF SIZE
PERT ARTY PLOW
```

PUZZLE 520

```
KINKS STAR AJAX
INOIL PUPA NONE
STUDY ANTI INON
SON DATE DOMINO
  BONE  HERA
HOMAGE AIRPLANE
AGOG WARNS SHAW
RAW LIT  ODE
EKER BLAST EMIR
MIRACLES EMBERS
  SOON  PLEB
BEACON WHEN OVA
LAVA DORA ABNER
EVIL IRIS CREAM
WEDS ESTE EARLY
```

PUZZLE 513

```
SCOW JARS CUBIC
LONI ELIA ARENA
ARUT EIGHTBELLS
WASHERS LIL LET
  BRET  REBATE
UNREAD  CEASE
POOLS PROD LAMB
TOLL ALINE LIEU
ONES LEES ABNER
OSCAR  SHOUTS
BRONCO  SPAT
AER OVO CASTOFF
BELLWETHER OPAL
ASOUL TANK MARE
RENIS OWES SHOW
```

PUZZLE 517

```
TONG REGAL BART
EMIR EDEMA ODOR
NAPA ASTIN TINA
TRANS UNDERPAY
  NAT  NOISE
MADDENED STEWED
ANTA BEE ASIDE
GNU BARRELS NIL
MACRO TRI ABLE
ASKING HAVEEYES
  PEACE  NRA
UNDERTOW DANCE
ROAN EDIFY TOIL
ADZE AERIE ESNE
LIED USERS DEEM
```

PUZZLE 521

```
HARP RESET WAFT
OLEO ADAGE ARES
STAR VIGOR RITA
PORT ETE MURDER
  URNS  WISE
BARGES PATENTED
IDEAL POSED AVA
NOEL PESTS SCAR
DRS SLATE CHIDE
SNEAKERS HEATED
  DIAL  PINT
STARTS PUN TASS
LOCO ALERT EVIL
ANTI NOOSE ROLE
WEST TUNED SNOW
```

PUZZLE 514

```
PERI ACTS  RACK
OVER LORE PITON
RIDE DRYASABONE
ETA WEE ROC PEW
DASTARD  WEB
  AIRS CREDIBLE
IMBED HAIR DUOS
DOE SERFS  SOT
ODES TREE LEYTE
LETTERED  HORA
  ARE DIVESTS
OVA IWO ONE ART
SICKASADOG EBOE
SARIS TUNE NEVE
ALEN HEED DEEP
```

PUZZLE 518

```
GASP BANGS STUN
RITA ABOLT PAVE
ARES DORIA ABEE
BETTYGRABLE LAD
  SET  LAKE
TASTER FLORIST
ENTER CAAN SPIT
STAN CABLE SOAR
SIBS ARLO LEORA
CLEANSE MORNAY
  ERST  SAT
RAM SEVENGABLES
OMAK RACED AIDA
MITE ENOLA SPIN
ADEN DELLS ESTE
```

PUZZLE 522

```
CAW BRAND  OPAL
OLEG AERIE VERY
PEPPERMILL EPEE
EXTOLLED  EARP
  LEX  GIDE
SASHAY CLAMORED
EDAMS SEATS MER
ELLS LANCE KIRI
TET PARTY HENIE
ORATORIO WINTER
  RING  MIN
ELSE GANGLING
BELL SALTCELLAR
OGLE SLATE MESA
POOR ELDER STY
```

PUZZLE 523

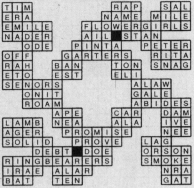

```
TIM      RAP        SAL
ERA EMILE  NAME  MILE
NADER  FLOWERGIRLS
ODE    PINTA    PETER
       AIL STAN
OFF  GARTERS    RITA
RAH  BAN   TON   SNAG
ETO  EST   ELI
SENORS        ALAW
ONIT          GALE
ROAM          ABIDES
APE     CAR       DAM
LAMB NEA  ALA     IVE
AGER   PROMISE    NEE
SOLID  PROVE      LAG
DEBT   DOE    ORSON
RINGBEARERS    SMOKE
IRAE  ALAR        NRA
BAT   TEN          GAT
```

PUZZLE 524

```
    SHE   CAR
   SEAL  OPEN
  NEARS NEVER
PEW KEPT    SIT
AREA   RED  TOO
TORSO  ONE  STY
   SMARTER
ITS IDA    PARES
LET TOT    WAVE
EAR  REAR   VEE
  RADII  BANES
  WARN   EVEN
   MEG   DEW
```

PUZZLE 525

```
HASH   POT  EVAS
ERIE   ANY  MIDI
SIDESTEP    IVAN
  EDIT   EGGARS
ROW     LEADER
ALA ORT    TESTY
NIL  NRA    IRA
TOKEN  ELI  DUN
  RAREAS    EEK
COYOTE  DEAL
HOED   SIDEKICK
INGE  ERI  INRE
NAGS  TEN  MEOW
```

PUZZLE 526

```
SASS  JAW   PINT
ALIT  UTE   IDES
MENU  DELEGATE
EGGNOG  LEE
  TAMP   LOYAL
ESS  TERM  NAME
LEO  SNOOP  LEA
MASH  TUNA  END
STOOD    DART
  BOA    LEADER
SHANGHAI   POPE
AERO  ASS  EVEN
CRIB  BAA  REED
```

PUZZLE 527

```
THOR  RODS   MAT
RARE  INIT   ALA
OVAL  GIGANTIC
DELIGHT    BEE
   EAT   ALERTS
GRAVY  TIE  IRE
LONE   PAD  RAIN
APE  BOX   PILOT
DECREE     EON
  DOT    TRIGGER
FRONTIER   LADE
OAT  EIRE   ELEE
BYE  RIND   TANK
```

PUZZLE 528

```
BRUINS    TABLED
SEEDMEN  ABRADED
ECLIPSE  LEAGUER
EKE  STALKED  CPO
NOAH  SKEET  WASP
ONSET  EAR  OATES
SEARED   SEXTET
  VIP      VET
SCENIC   LAYLOW
SPANS  UTA  EELED
PARS  CRISP  SEER
ORE  GRANOLA  ADO
REFINER  RELATES
EMULATE  DAMPERS
ELATES    ASSESS
```

PUZZLE 529

If it isn't worth fighting for, it isn't worth having.
1. Fright, 2. Thigh, 3. Notion, 4. Wiring, 5. Novi, 6. Twist, 7. Raft, 8. Shift.

PUZZLE 530

```
SAW     TAB      ANT
ARIA  CORER   SLEW
MINT  ALICE   TAXI
DEMAND    ATTEST
  ORT    BLEAR
BASK  ELM    SEAT
MEET  ALA  ATONED
OER  SWIZZLE   INA
SPIRAL  EOS   STEM
SEEN  FRO   BEAT
  STOAS     HAD
SQUAWK   PARADE
FOUL  NINER  TIRE
EMIT  SNORE  EVIL
NET    GNU    EEL
```

PUZZLE 531

1. Tacoma, 2. New Haven, 3. Boise, 4. Tampa, 5. Portland, 6. Denver, 7. Reno, 8. Orlando.

PUZZLE 532

```
RIFLE   ATOM    LAW
ARIEL   ABIDE   ARI
VIRGINQUEEN    DIN
ISMS   OUTS    DYES
   STA     BRAGS
RELATE    MARINO
ALONE   BORED   DAM
PERT  LADEN   RIDE
TED   CARES  SAVES
  NORMAL   BANANA
GENOA     CID
ERLE   ACHE   SSTS
GAS  SIRLANCELOT
IDO  ORION   AROMA
SEN   BEAT   LATER
```

PUZZLE 533

BRIDGE

PUZZLE 534

```
MAZE        TASK
OVENS      JAPAN
REBEL      AMPLE
ERR   EAR    LAW
  TAPER   FED
     OPERA
  MAT   NURSE
HAL   PAL    LAB
ARISE      ELATE
RIVER      RATES
PEEN        PERT
```

PUZZLE 535

```
SIP  ACHE   SHAM
ORE  LAIR   TOGA
NEGATIVE   ROOT
  GENE     HEDGE
ADHERE      BEA
SEES     WEAKENS
EEL  GRANT  POE
ARDUOUS    MEOW
  TEN     PREENS
CHATS      BRAN
HALE    PROCURES
EVER   EASE   ART
FEES   ADES   MAY
```

PUZZLE 536

```
RERAN  SPAT  DANK
IRENE  TONE  EDIE
SLING  ANTE  MINE
KEN  LAND  PETAL
  HERD     GALA
SELECT   TRIANGLE
ALERT  MOODY  HEM
LOVE  SERVE  COVE
APE  SLATE  BLUER
DELICATE  BAILEY
  NAVY     HARP
SIGHT  RANG   ANI
ARIA  LEAN  AILED
RILL  AVID  IDEAL
ISLE  DENY  NACRE
```

PUZZLE 537

```
L  LESSON  NOSES  ONES  S
O  OBLATE  BLEAT  BELT  A
A  ARCANE  CRANE  RACE  N
F  DIFFER  FIRED  RIFE  D
E  LEASES  SEALS  LESS  A
R  PARCEL  PLACE  CAPE  L
```

PUZZLE 538

```
HIRED  SCAR  STEW
ERODE  PLIE  HORA
AMAIN  RENT  OTIS
DARETOEATAPEACH
  ABET    PARLAY
CODDLE     DEN
ALEE  SEMI  IWASA
PEACHESANDCREAM
POLKA  PEGO  ARNO
  LAY     RAPIER
EGGNOG     SAID
VANISHINGCREAMS
IVAN  AGAR  ORLON
TERN  SORE  ILOVE
ALLY  THEE  TEPEE
```

PUZZLE 539

1. Peach, Apple, Mango, Grape; 2. Light, Lamp, Torch, Bulb; 3. Canter, Run, Gallop, Lope; 4. Burn, Char, Sear, Singe; 5. Fold, Pleat, Crease, Bend; 6. March, July, May, June.

PUZZLE 540

```
SWAP  CHAFE   SPA
TAME  AIDES  PLAN
EVES  PRINT  RAIN
WENT  SET  ARABLE
  EATS     STAN
SPARTA    STENCIL
LAW  ENTER  TENOR
ARAB  SONAR  RANI
WISES  MOPES  NEO
SHATTER   ASSERT
  CUES     ASEA
BARONS  FRO  MORE
ERIN  TALON  PRAY
TINS  ERASE  LANE
ADD  DATED   ELKS
```

PUZZLE 541

```
PAID  TRES  MONA  CLAIM
ERGO  SOUSA  ARID  HOTTO
SLOTCLOTPLOTBLOTALLOT
TOR  AILS  OATS  ELAINE
    LIN  AOK  SANE
DRAINGRAINSPRAINTRAIN
EASTS  ISRS  AINT  ALOE
ARTE  SGTS  DAFT  APING
LAIRPAIRHAIRFAIRSTAIR
  NARC  INC  STEW  SAO
    LIKE  PATES  STER
APT  METS  ILO  ALEC
BROILROILSOILFOILCOIL
NITTY  TEEN  DOLL  ASTI
EMEU  AUNT  SAUL  ANTES
RAMPCAMPSAMPTRAMPTAMP
    OTTS  ALS  OPS
BESTIR  LILI  AWOL  LIB
RICENICESPICEDICEVICE
ORATE  ARTS  EDITH  AMEN
WEBER  PASO  ROTH  NORD
```

PUZZLE 542

```
DIBS  ATTAR  LIANA  AWLS
ELLA  NAIVE  OSCAR  SHOO
BLACKSHEEP  WHITETAILS
SEC  LAOS  LIL  DENY  TAO
    KLUTE  DEVIL  SAITE
OPHITE  GRAYFOX  SNOWED
FRIZZ  POUT  EURO  GRAVE
GALA  BEEN  DAMP  ELAN
AIL  ALASKA  GLYNIS  LST
BASHFUL  STRAY  INCISES
    ATE  LIP  KOD
COBWEBS  TAMES  SEWAGES
OUR  ROUSES  SAVOYS  ORA
SION  YIPS  TIRE  SLOT
EDWIN  TATA  FARE  MIDDY
TANNER  REDWING  WILDER
  SAVED  EVENS  COATI
TAT  IDOS  ITA  PALM  GNU
BROWNSWISS  GOLDFINGER
ANNA  EDDIE  LIEGE  BEAN
ROES  AYERS  ELDER  ARTS
```

PUZZLE 543

```
FADS  NERO  GOP  LATHS
ALEC  APER  ERBIL  ORION
LOBO  MICA  AISLE  DANNY
LETTHECATOUTOFTHEBAG
    COD  NOR  LETIN
LIGHT  STREP  ERSE  APSE
ACE  LEIS  GUSTS  RAMROD
RETAINS  LOTTE  LANYARD
ADORNS  SENOR  EARN  IRA
  NAE  SAT  NORDICS  RES
HEL  RABBITPUNCH  GIL
SOS  REFRESH  LAS  SEE
COG  ASEA  LEWES  DARWIN
APOLLOS  MEDES  COMMODE
LEADER  FASOL  TUTU  LEA
ARTS  TEAS  GLARE  REFER
    TEXTS  TRA  SAN
BEARDTHELIONINHISDEN
LORRE  RENAL  OLIO  UELE
ALONE  ARECA  LENA  EELS
POSED  STY  DRAT  SPAT
```

PUZZLE 544

```
SOUVENIR  SABOTS
INNOVATE  IMARET
DEFLATED  LOANER
EPEES  NUTTY  ATE
SITS  DECOY  STEW
LET  WIZEN  EWERS
ICEMAN  DICTA
PERUSER  CHORALE
    STRUT  ANDEAN
TEPEE  RESTS  RUD
ANIS  PANTS  TORO
IRS  VALUE  MISER
LATHES  REGATTAS
EGOIST  EVACUATE
DELETE  SEMESTER
```

PUZZLE 545

```
LASER  ELSA  LLAMA  BEDE
ATONE  SOUL  OASES  IRED
DELTA  TAEL  RISES  EAVE
DAVIDSONDEREK  TURNSIN
STETSON  NOLA  REPELS
  LORI  SLOE  URIAH
MAGENTA  HAMILTONDUMAS
AMID  VOWS  ELEGY  OCT
PEN  SNIPER  HOES  BORA
SNAPPERS  EBONY  GARDEN
  LARK  NOL  SOLE
ARROYO  DUCAT  BOASTERS
TEED  MILE  PSEUDO  LON
ONA  ASIAN  SRAS  DATE
POPPINSMARTIN  ESCENCE
  AMASS  EENS  ATAT
POTTER  ALEC  RELOADS
LAURELS  MADISONMONROE
ATMO  ECLAT  PALE  RADON
NEIN  ROSIE  ALAR  ITEMS
ENDS  STUNS  LENS  CENSE
```

PUZZLE 546

```
AFT  STEP  TEDS  CAPER
AMIE  SHIER  ALIT  ARETE
NEVE  TENLITTLEINDIANS
KEENER  GENIE  TEA  SLAT
ARS  REB  RTE  SPREES
  THREAD  ROAM  PEN
TAU  THREESTRIKES  FAN
BERRY  TORN  TINED  SORA
ALG  ORSONS  OLDE  THUMB
GLENDA  DEUT  SLOWER
SNEER  ERS  NEALS
  ELLENS  AHAS  CEREAL
GIRLS  ATTU  ALLIED  AVA
IDAS  SPOOR  LEAR  SAFES
GEL  OCEANSELEVEN  BCD
  BAR  SEAN  ENAMEL
BEATUP  AMT  EDE  ORO
ALAI  FAS  SCARE  INEVER
MAGNIFICENTSEVEN  RENT
AREEL  LARA  OVINE  IRES
TERSE  STAG  NILE  ESS
```

PUZZLE 547

```
THEN  COTS  CAW  PEER
AURA  RANK  AGO  LAVA
DEANMARTINVANBUREN
STAB  MAE  INNS
ISSUED  DOPY  LONG
NEARS  MIRY  PUNGENT
CAME  CONE  LANCE  AIR
ALP  SHUT  SINGE  STLO
  BAIT  GONG  FATED
RAYCHARLESPERCY
PEALS  MAIN  AMOK
ARID  SPEND  BRIG  RIB
LAS  SCANT  FLIT  PACE
LEOPARD  PEAS  CRIED
DUNE  TART  FOUNDS
ODER  PER  MARS
CHESTERAARTHURASHE
AILS  LIT  ORAL  LIAR
POLA  FOE  TYNE  SAGE
```

PUZZLE 548

```
ERIC  ABATE  SLOSH  MAGS
NOVA  PARRS  AORTA  ALAE
STANLEYCUP  NOBELPRIZE
ENDO  STRAIT  POLITER
  LOSS  HILT  ESSEN
DRENCH  TEAMS  DETER
IRE  SORES  CROCK  SRAS
LOU  TEMPO  YORES  IRV
LOBS  DIRGE  DOYLE  PEP
SLEETS  TALES  WEIR  LDS
  NAILS  TERMS  DEICE
BRA  NUTS  DIETS  REACTS
RAW  ERECT  EARPS  TREE
ADA  PLAID  RIATA  OPT
GIRD  ELLIS  PEELS  WIS
SIDES  PESTO  ATTEND
  TEALS  CASK  DOOR
APPEASE  BANANA  ORES
FIRSTCHAIR  GOLDGLOVES
AMAT  OARED  ELSIE  REMS
RAMS  TRANS  SLOPE  SNIT
```

PUZZLE 549

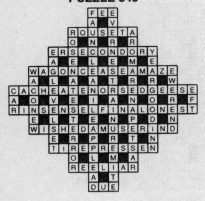

```
        FEE
        A V
      ROUSETA
      O N R R
   ERSECONDORY
   A E L E M E
WAGONCEASEAMAZE
A L A A T R R W
CACHEATENORSEDGEESE
A O V E I A N O R F
RINSENSELFINALONEST
  E L T E N P D N
  WISHEDAMUSERIND
    E R P R T N
    TIREPRESSEN
      O L M A
      REELIAR
        A T
        DUE
```

PUZZLE 550

```
ELSA  SCAN  TRACT
BOON  CLII  OILER
BALI  RANG  FLARE
FOLLOWTHEFLEET
      ELS   LEE
BENGAL WADE  ADE
OTOES  FACE  EDER
SHORESOFTRIPOLI
SINE   TUES  NERVE
ACE    PURR  SCENES
       TAN   BOA
THEHIGHCOUNTRY
RODIN  EARN  ROUT
ARENT  RIND  ALMA
MASKS  ONES  YEAR
```

PUZZLE 551

1. Cleanup, 2. Ashamed, 3. Deflated, 4. Brigade, 5. Shallow, 6. Abused, 7. Brownie, 8. Appease, 9. Shopworn, 10. Aerate.

PUZZLE 552

```
BOWL   DRIP  COY
ERIE   RATE  ONE
GANG   EYES  NAT
SNEAKS MOAN
       LIST  STEAL
ASS    NEAR  ECRU
PAW    DRIES TIN
EVIL   SLAW  SAG
DETER  SCAT
       COAL  TYRANT
ASH    ZERO  IGOR
RUE    OVER  ARTE
END    RIDS  LAST
```

PUZZLE 553

```
POLO   PAT   BELL
OBAN   ORO   INEE
GONETOTHEDOGS
OLE    EDSEL RST
       ALL   ELAM
PADDLE LETOUT
ANOA         EURE
RAGGED BASSET
       PELE  EST
VIA    SERAC PAP
INTHEDOGHOUSE
ECCE   ELL   WRIT
SAHL   DEE   LENS
```

PUZZLE 554

```
REPS  LIBRA  ICED
AREA  INUIT  DODO
TIETHEKNOT  LUGE
ACREAGE  TAPERER
       LED  CIST
CASTES SAKE  SAC
OPTED  HIKED HUR
SHAD   NADIR TIDE
TIL    WIDEN SEPIA
ADE    ACED  RANSOM
       MADE  MAL
ERASING  OVERUSE
WOTS  ELOPEMENTS
EPEE  SEVEN  ATOP
REST  SEARS  DOPY
```

PUZZLE 555

1. Moral, 2. Ether, 3. Viand, 4. Vapor, 5. Taste, 6. Groan, 7. Rider, 8. Layer.
8-LETTER WORD: Rhapsody.

PUZZLE 556

```
RAPT   BET   DAWN
AGUE   RAE   ELIA
SELL   ORDINARY
HELLION  NINES
       BEND  UTA
TSARS  ATELIER
ROC    TONER MOO
AWKWARD  COPSE
       ANT   HONE
BASIC  HOMERUN
LOITERER  DIRE
ANTE   URN   GAIN
BEER   MOE   ELSE
```

PUZZLE 557

```
WISH   LOW   TWO
ACHE   ERA   ORAL
YEARLING  MESA
       PEA EEL AID
APE    BAR   ASKS
DOLE   LYRIC
STYMIE ORACLE
       IDEAL NOEL
HERO   TEN   RAM
LOX    LOT   ERR
ANTI   VIRTUOSO
WORN   ARE   IDEE
RAN    LED   NEAR
```

PUZZLE 558

```
PAMS   CLAP  COSTA
ABEE   AIDE  UNTIL
ALOT   BEAT  COAST
REWAX        MASK
       RAM   LOOSEST
PAPAS        LOCALE
PLAYTIME     ETAL
SEAN   DAY   NINE
HAND   SLEEPING
OCEANS       LOGIC
DESSERT      NON
       LOOP  GRAPE
ACHES  OATS  OVAL
PIANO  TIRE  DORM
EATEN  SLAW  EWES
```

PUZZLE 559

1. Paternal, 2. Fragrant, 3. Stranger, 4. Undulate, 5. Asteroid, 6. Charcoal, 7. Excavate, 8. Forebode.

PUZZLE 560

```
PLACE   RAW
SEESAW  ECHO
HASSLE  PROD
ELSE    LEAD
     TARDY
     SUE
     SPEND
PAST      AJAR
AREA   CINEMA
LIAR   ACCEPT
ART    PEEPS
```

PUZZLE 561

```
LIP   SPAT  GIVE
ADO   POLO  EVER
GAP   ELIMINATE
      OPAL  SINS
COVER  CASE
ANEW  PERU  RAP
PER   FRAME ELI
ESS   LOSS  EDEN
      GAPE  SLEEK
SEAM        SAKE
COMMENTED   MOP
ALIE  IOWA  EWE
NETS  PEST  DEN
```

PUZZLE 562

```
MASH  RAMS  SIVA  CRAB
ALTO  AMAT  OMAN  RODE
TAEL  COLA  DINO  OOZE
TEMPESTINATEAPOT
EPEE  NIPA  SINBAD
SALPA  BOTH  NEEDY
SAD  REEDS  PEEL  REIN
ESEL  TAILS  DROP  RTE
ATLAS  CEILS  MOOS
MILKOFHUMANKINDNESS
ETUI  STINT  SADAT
MAC  SEES  SPEAR  PINE
ARAS  LSTS  SEGOS  TEN
RATED  TOIL  DEBAR
CLARET  PAYS  COSA
WINEWOMENANDSONG
ELBA  NAVE  OLEO  SORT
REAL  EVES  USES  TREE
NESS  TYRE  TORE  SEED
```

PUZZLE 563

```
SOME  BASS  ALAS  TARP
ETAL  ALOU  SALE  IDOL
POLKADOTS  SWINGTIME
TET  FEE  APES  TILTED
BAN  SNIT  ROVE
LAMAR  DANE  COVE  LAB
AGAR  SUGARBLUES  ALA
RUR  BONO  LEER  ESTE
DECLARE  CLEAN  ACTOR
HIRE  HOIST  BLOW
TOKEN  CANES  MALLARD
AMIN  JONG  PIES  LEE
MEN  KINGOFJAZZ  ETNA
ENG  AVES  EAVE  DOZEN
PREY  SAKE  WEN
PRIEST  ATTA  UAR  LAS
LASTTANGO  ROCKNROLL
ARTE  LUNA  TILE  ANDA
NESS  KNIT  ALAN  HEAT
```

PUZZLE 564

```
SCAM  DELI    RAPID
ELSE  ARID    ERASE
MAKE  MODE    AGILE
INSTEAD      ASSURED
        AGE   TOE
CREATE      STANDARD
HELPS  OPAL     SEA
ERIE  GRIPE    HIFI
CUT   OARS    AIDES
KNEEHOLE     ARTERY
       MAD    ARM
OFFENSE      CRYSTAL
WEIRD  DARE    CARE
LARGE  EXES    AMEN
STEED  NEST    READ
```

PUZZLE 568

```
CALM DARE ACHE EMUS
ALOE EDEN LAIN VISA
STAR SODA ARTS ICES
TONICS SCAR SUCCESS
     TOES TIME EAT
PEA GRAB MEAT PEDAL
URN STILL DROP DALE
RITE NEAT LORI  TAG
ENEMY TWIRL KITTENS
     ION ROE MEW
CONTROL SOAPS MILES
ORE ERIE PROP NOVA
MASS MOVE NORTH RIP
ALTER NETS RARE ELS
     COD NEED YEAR
BARONET RAID ARENAS
ICON BRAN SEAT BARE
TROD AURA CAPE EPEE
SETS REEL SLED LEAD
```

PUZZLE 572

```
BONO  GASP    NAMED
OVER  AREA    AGILE
MARE  LOAN    TENSE
BLOSSOM      GRINDER
       TRA    HOT
COOKIE      SPINSTER
ALTER  CHIN    AXE
PITY  ALONE   SKIS
EVE   RANK   CHEST
SERENADE     CRESTS
       LAB    TRI
EMBASSY      RUBBISH
LOOPS  AGES   ANTE
MORSE  WONT   STEM
SNEER  NODS   SOWS
```

PUZZLE 565

```
GRUB  START    DOWN
LURE  HUMOR    AREA
ALAS  ALIBI    VERB
DELI  DID     RISES
       DEEP   TOAD
STEEP  SHRUG    TEE
TONSIL  EAT     HAD
AWE   CARAMEL   EGG
GEM   BAR     RAFFLE
SLY   HOIST   DATES
       TORN   WAYS
SPREE  LID     TIDE
LEAN  STAND    EDEN
IRIS  HEDGE    SEED
DUDE  EASED    TARS
```

PUZZLE 569

```
ALL   ITEM     TORE
DOES  NOPE    ARROW
DONE  TRIM    SUEDE
SNAP       ACCOUNT
     ARCH    BEHIND
STRUT  MOOR    NEE
TRAM  MAMA    SCAN
BRAT  BERET    PORT
LIVE  EARN    CAME
ADE   DENY    LONER
BELIEF      GANG
     DESIRED  LAGS
BASED  COED    EMIT
AREAS  ELSE    DIVE
DIAL  DEER     DEW
```

PUZZLE 573

```
PAPAS DAVID SHANE
ELENA IRENE HAGEN
TOTAL MEETS ALIVE
SUE OWES EKED LER
DRAMAS ERST HERO
   PER DAN AMA
LIME CASS ERASE
ALEX MARY COSTNER
VON WIRE BOSS IAN
INDIANA TARS ALLS
NASTY  RARA  REST
   ISA ERN AFT
MASS LAVA STEELE
ATA ABBE OTES ALA
MOTEL INANE TANDY
ANITA EGGER EDDIE
SENOR SEARS RAINS
```

PUZZLE 566

```
LEAD  RAVES    SPOT
AXLE  ALERT    CAVE
TILE  STARE    OPEN
CLERICAL     ABOARD
HEY   CAR     CLAP
       GEL  EATS RYE
TREAD  BATHE    EEL
AIDS  MERCY    CALM
USE   TEETH   BALLS
TEN   OATH     SOB
     OWLS DEN  MOB
ARTIST      LANDFALL
COAL  IRONS    ALDA
ISLE  MINCE    ITEM
DYED  EDGES    RARE
```

PUZZLE 570

```
SASH  PLUME    SLOE
TRIO  HOTEL    LIRA
ALTO  AWARE    AMES
BOSSES      ECSTASY
     IDEAL    TEE
SHOES  VIA    ADAMS
HOAR  SETTER   LEA
OUR  MON HAS   ILL
USE   ANGLER   MATT
TEDDY  EON    SASSY
     ROT   PSALM
SAFARIS      SYMBOL
WRAP  LEASH    ARTE
ANTE  EMCEE    LION
TOES  RITES    SEED
```

PUZZLE 574

```
SLIT  ALIAS    BUFF
WAGE  DODGE    ASIA
ABLE  DROOP    NETS
MOO   GIRL   AMIDST
PROFANE      PROS
     RIG   SEASHORE
SPOON  SCOTT    SON
HANG  PLANE    CLAD
OAT   HEARS   DOORS
PROPERTY      SEW
     RICE   PUBLISH
SPHERE  HINT    SKY
LOOT  IRONS    PLUM
AUNT  VALUE    TENN
TREY  EGYPT    ASKS
```

PUZZLE 567

```
SACK  LACES    WOLF
AREA  IMAGE    IDOL
GOAT  APRON    TONE
ASSEMBLE     SACRED
NEE   ALE     RICH
     ORE   DEBT  TRI
RELAX  PAILS    EAT
OVER  GORGE    LAKE
BEN   GREEN   HAREM
END   RAMS     LOG
     BITS MOO  TIM
AFLAME      BOOKCASE
RAIL  FORTS    ABLE
ACNE  UNITE    SLAT
BEES  LEMON    HEMS
```

PUZZLE 571

```
RODS  STRAP    SONG
EPIC  CHOIR    AREA
EACH  HELLO    VEAL
FLEE  OIL    FIESTA
     DOOR    PODS
ACTUAL  HAUL    SPA
CHALK  MAINE    HAS
RICE  FOUND    NOUN
ELK   COINS   GOOSE
SIS   HOST   BANKER
     WATT    FUSS
ABSORB  SAG    ELSE
ROAR  ATOLL    NUMB
ARMS  LEASE    SNOB
BEET  LAKES    EGGS
```

PUZZLE 575

```
CAT   COOL     SASH
ARAB  HARE    KOREA
LENA  USES    NAMED
MAST       MISSTEP
     HEMS    RESIGN
STRAY  OPAL     SUE
TROT  EPIC     FLEA
CRIB  CREEK    LAST
HOPE  AIRS     WONT
ELL   IDEA    ROADS
FLEECE      BEET
     VITAMIN   ITEM
OFTEN  RATE    NOVA
ALONG  CREW    GOER
RUNT  HERS     TNT
```

559

PUZZLE 576

```
CHOP RAGES SLAV
ROLL ECOLE TAPA
OBIE WOODCARVER
WOODWARD  DAIRY
    ERN STOKES
PASTED  SAONE
ANNA SANTA TRE
WOODLANDDEITIES
LAW ITALY  ALAS
  STORY MANTLE
 DAPHNE POI
TORII   SOURWOOD
WOODCHUCKS ALMA
ANSE ALOES SLED
SEER METRE HARE
```

PUZZLE 577

From top to bottom: Beetle, Grasshopper, Butterfly, Moth, Spider, Mosquito, Cricket.
7-letter word: TERMITE.

PUZZLE 578

```
FLAT CROAK SCAB
LAVA HELLO ARIA
AMEN ADDER FADS
KERNEL  ADAGES
   ELK LONER
EWERS JAM PIECE
TEN TUXEDO  MAN
HAT GAM LIT ONE
EVE EMBLEM  TOM
RERUN LET TEENY
   PIPED SOL
STEREO  OPAQUE
TIRE RAZOR PURL
ULNA ELOPE SAGA
BEER SLOTS EDEN
```

1-L, 2-J, 3-Q, 4-C, 5-W, 6-D, 7-F, 8-Y, 9-T, 10-U, 11-V, 12-R, 13-I, 14-G, 15-Z, 16-B, 17-E, 18-K, 19-A, 20-S, 21-H, 22-M, 23-X, 24-O, 25-N, 26-P.

PUZZLE 579

```
LOW   SEA   BOA
EPIC SCANT WOOL
GUSH EARTH HAZE
 SHIVER  ADORE
   LED NEWEL
QUIT SOX  LEER
SUN FEDORA JET
HAD SOW DAY EVE
EKE TEACUP  CUE
ERNE GAS  MATE
   ORDER JAB
PHONO   GENIAL
IRIS MAPLE DROP
LAKE ERROR EASE
LYE   MOB   BET
```

1-L, 2-G, 3-D, 4-E, 5-S, 6-H, 7-W, 8-Q, 9-O, 10-M, 11-F, 12-U, 13-Z, 14-R, 15-P, 16-N, 17-B, 18-C, 19-T, 20-Y, 21-A, 22-X, 23-K, 24-I, 25-V, 26-J.

PUZZLE 580

```
SLOW ASSET HASH
LAVA CHORE ECHO
AMERICANINPARIS
PEN VERGE ADEPT
   LANK PRY
RECENT AVID GAP
ALAN ALAMO  AWE
JAPANESESANDMAN
ATE AVERT  AURA
HER PEAT CARTEL
   CON GANT
APPAL OVERT GUN
REUNIONINVIENNA
IRMA FLARE VAIN
DUAL TYLER ETTA
```

PUZZLE 581

1. Plate, 2. Manes, 3. Stain, 4. Regal, 5. Parse, 6. Crate, 7. Times, 8. Resin.
8-LETTER WORD: ANAGRAMS.

PUZZLE 582

```
STOW GRAF ASWAN
MALI RILL PHONE
ERIN ACTI PEONS
WOODENHORSE DOT
  OLD STEADY
BETWEEN  TRIALS
ALI CEASE SALON
RINK SPEAR SLOE
DOWEL SATED ESE
STORES SPINNER
  ORATES AVE
PHD NATALIEWOOD
REMIT HOUR ELMO
ERATO ONCE SLOG
PONES SEED TAOS
```

PUZZLE 583

AUTOMOBILE

PUZZLE 584

```
 RAISE  CHEWS
 CORDON HURRAH
HOMEOFTHEBRAVES
ERAS TEEM SPIRE
ANN FERRIC SNOW
PECTIN SCAB GEN
STAIN FEARLESS
 TRAIL LLAMA
SHELLACS MICRA
ATE SETH MERCER
REDO STORED OBI
EARNS ERIN DUAL
ALASKARESIDENTS
 SLEEVE KARATE
 STEED  SLURS
```

PUZZLE 585

1.

2.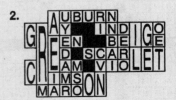

PUZZLE 586

```
GRACE CAPS REEL
RACES OMIT ALOE
EVENT RILE NINE
WESTERN  LEAK
   ERE MOPS ART
FIR FLAW TOWER
DAM PIER SERAPE
IMPARTS STROKES
VIOLAS SPUN ENS
ESSAY LEAP TNT
SHE ERIE  OPE
  BRAT ERRATIC
FACE ITAL OPERA
EVEN SEWS POLAR
NEED ERNE STONE
```

PUZZLE 587

FAMILY

PUZZLE 588

```
SHOT STALE CRAB
LAME CURES RULE
ALAN ABIDE ASIA
BORDERED  OTHER
   PER MOVE
CLOSES BEVERAGE
AERIE WATER ROD
TAGS WAKEN FROG
EVA DIVES PROSE
RENDERED SLOWER
   ICED RIO
SPARK  BANDAGES
WIPE SLING BALE
ALEC TINGE ELSA
TEST ADDED DEEM
```

PUZZLE 589

1. Clef, 2. Fuel, 3. Long, 4. Guam, 5. Main, 6. Next, 7. Trip, 8. Path, 9. Hook, 10. Kiev, 11. Verb, 12. Brad, 13. Dais, 14. Saga, 15. Alto, 16. Oath.
7-LETTER WORD: Foghorn.

PUZZLE 590

```
MAR  SLAP  ACRE
ALE  MACE  LAID
TIS  ICER  ANTI
   TILE ASSET
TORTE MARK
ALAS RESTATES
LEI WALKS  EVA
CONVERTS PREP
  ORES BURNS
SPITE  CUBA
HAVE POOR CON
AVER AIMS ERA
MESS SLAT SAT
```

PUZZLE 591

```
BEET TAM CLOY
ARNI IDA HIDE
LITTLESTROKES
DEALER CERES
  NEA SHEA
EGGS SPILLANE
SAL SHINS CIL
ELECTING UCLA
  HIVE ONO
AFINE DALLAS
FELLGREATOAKS
ORAL ERN ADIT
BOGS DEE DENS
```

PUZZLE 592

```
DESK BARR   ERAT
ALAI ELIA  ACORN
BURN RIVERFRONT
SLAG AVE   ETUDE
     DATE ALES
CHORE  AVER   FAR
AROMA   RAN   ARA
BASEBALLSTADIUM
ETE    VEE  FIRMS
TEA  PIAS  BRAYS
     ALAN FROM
MINER   MIA  OVER
FENWAYPARK   NERO
AREAS  ALEE  DRAT
DEER   TESS  SASS
```

PUZZLE 597

```
TACO   PADS  AFAR
ELIAS  ALEC  LIMO
DOTTEDLINE  PROM
STEELE  SING  EKE
     SLEW MINCE
LEI  SPAT  CARATS
ELMS  ELAN  TITHE
GAPE  RECAP  MIRE
ATONE  SKIS  ENOS
LESSER  SLAB  GET
     SELES SLOB
IDI  SPAS  MORASS
TABS  IMPASSIBLE
ELLA  NOON  TALON
MEET  EATS   NEED
```

PUZZLE 602

A gram of prevention is worth a kilogram of cure.

1. Reaffirm, 2. Vocation, 3. Groom, 4. Girth, 5. European, 6. Walks.

PUZZLE 593

1. Neck, 2. Market, 3. Potato.

PUZZLE 598

NUTCRACKER

PUZZLE 603

```
CABS   BOUT   CRAM
OMIT  ALSO  HUMAN
SILO  WEEP  INANE
TRAVEL   AMNESIA
TEN   HAZE   SAT
OWE  DRIP  ASP
FAR   EKE  SPECK
FRAGILE  QUARREL
PLACE   OUR   ONE
PEA  PIER  COG
JAR   SEEP   ADO
ADAPTER  SPIDER
MOTOR  ERNE  TILE
BRIDE  COIN  CLAD
NOSY   TEXT  HENS
```

PUZZLE 594

```
COLOSSUSOFRHODES
ADAMHAREFRAYRARE
ROVEELIIAFETEBRIE
ORALRESTEDENITEM
UNDERWAYNOTATALL
SOOTYALIDROSSSEE
EREANNIEECUSUITE
LASSODELDARESAIR
CABSOUNDRAGTEENY
OLEINPUTERNTRADE
MORSEAREDIALSTEN
PETTYPANWATERSPA
AREAEONSOATSAHAB
SEANAGUEOLEOCURL
SORTROSSDEANETTE
```

PUZZLE 599

```
SPADE  CAMP  ACME
HUMAN  AGAR  ROAD
ANILE  DOGEATDOG
HARASS  RIFE  ERA
     SCUBA AGADIR
TAPIOCA   ACID
APE   HORSESENSE
LINE   BEY   NOES
CATSCRADLE   VAN
     SLAB ULULATE
AGLEAM   OMBRE
CUE  IBEX  EGRESS
TIGERLILY  ENROL
ELAN  ERIE  NENNI
DELE   DEPT  TREED
```

PUZZLE 604

1. Werewolf, 2. Jacuzzi, 3. Nectar, 4. Amulet, 5. Espresso, 6. Croupier, 7. Isthmus, 8. Kibbutz, 9. Epaulet.
NAME: Jack Frost

PUZZLE 595

```
 SEEP      PEW
HINGED    APES
INTONE    RENO
SKI     SLEETS
SECT  CAN
  REELECTED
    MEN   SLEW
WARPED    USE
EVIL   ERODED
TILE   DINERS
 DES     BEST
```

PUZZLE 600

1. Sear, Scar, Rear; 2. Cite, Core, Tore; 3. Snap, Saps, Naps; 4. Slap, Laps, Apes; 5. Slat, Swat, Wart; 6. Yard, Lard, Bard; 7. Sell, Slag, Yell; 8. Stab, Slab, Toll.

PUZZLE 605

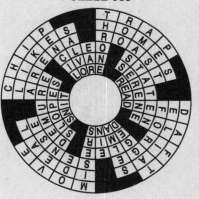

PUZZLE 596

```
ACES  ASKS   SAD
DUPE  BAIT   TIE
SPIN  ALTITUDE
SCORN  SLED
  RIDS   LEERS
POTATOES   SNIP
IRA  ANNES   TOA
SALT  SOLOISTS
ALERT   REDS
   NEAR  CARES
INTEREST   ALAN
DIE  TAKE  ELSE
OLD  SLID   LAST
```

PUZZLE 601

```
UTAH  ALIAS  PELT
RAGE  BONGO  AREA
SNUB  RODEO  DISC
AGAR  ANY  TRUEST
     ANDY  WHOA
INCITE  ARIA  UMP
MARSH  BLEND  NIL
ADAM  REBAG  IDLE
GIN  CHEEK  ARENA
ERE  HARE  ADORED
     ROPY EBON
BICEPS  HOB  WADI
ANOA  OBESE  EXAM
ICED  DORIS  ELLA
LADY  YARNS  DEEM
```

PUZZLE 606

```
CAPE  STEM   DUD
SHORT  PARE  ARNE
TORSO  ACRE  RUDE
ART  NECK  TREMOR
YEAR  YES   ION
   ODE   NEARER
WHOLE  KONG   ACE
RENEW  IRE  OATHS
AIL  ANEW  BESOT
PRYING     FIR
LEE   SPA   OVAL
MOTION  CORD  ALE
OKRA  DROP  ARGON
LAUD  AIRE  ROUND
DYE   SONS  KNEE
```

PUZZLE 607

```
CHILD MONA   WAS
RIDER AMOS  FILE
ERASE JANEFONDA
WES SHOR  AREAS
     SER ACT
MOSLEY THREEONA
AHEAD  ARMS  LAD
NANS PATSY  LIDO
ORT  LIVE  NEVER
REASONER MODERN
     ARE  MAR
DARIN   ROOM EWE
ALANARKIN  APRIL
NEST  LIST NEILS
ACE  SMEE  SANTA
```

PUZZLE 608

```
  CABIN    IRK
  OLIVE   ERIE
PLATES    LONG
ELS   STRINGS
PIKE   SOD
    EARS  BEST
     RAP  DEWY
PARADES    TEE
OVEN   SKATES
LEAD   TIRED
ERR    STIES
```

PUZZLE 609

```
TOE  FLEW  RAMP
URN  RAVE  ERIE
BELIEVES   SILT
   AREA  TRIALS
BARKS   HEAD
RIGS  GARMENTS
ADE  BARNS  ERE
GESTURES   HEEL
    ENDS  MODEL
CREATE    GIRL
OILS  NEATNESS
IDLE  ELSE  SIP
LEAD  RIPS  STY
```

PUZZLE 610

```
REID  WORD  ADAM  LARGO
ANDES ALOE  COVE  AWARD
NOOSE REAP  ALOW  CAVIE
ILLCRYTOMORROW  SHREDS
   RUES  SOUR  FIRE
BEDIMS SOILS BEVY  ASP
AGEE  SHUTE CREAM  NEE
SOBSISTER  PAIL  OATEN
TIA  APER  LOPE ASLANT
IST  NIER  HOUR   REE
ATEN CRYMEARIVER SAMP
 AWE  ERNS  ALEE  PAR
SHARES PROS CASE   ARA
HORDE  WAGS  BATTLECRY
ARM  PEACE  PLANE SHOE
MAY  NODE  FLIRT APPEND
   HONE  PROM  OLEA
CLAIMS WEEPINGWILLOWS
RONDO  KITE  TORN TIGHT
OLDER  OPAL  EPEE AERIE
PASSE  RELY  DEER  REPP
```

PUZZLE 611

```
MESH  DAM  PROD
ARIA  EGO  ROVE
RILL  COO  EDEN
TELLER  DETERS
   OWE  SET
BETWEEN  LYRIC
ARE  SAP  UNA
GREAT  GARMENT
   GAS  TOE
RESENT  REDUCE
AVON  APO  IRON
CENT  RAN  AGED
ERGS  ELS  NEDS
```

PUZZLE 612

```
AMMO  PAM  DASH
HAUL  ALE  OLIO
ARTESIANWELLS
BET  UNITE  ALS
   EMIT  ORK
TAROTS  REAMED
IVES    RAND
CADETS  BLENDS
   SET  RONA
DEE  AURAL  CPA
ATTORNEYATLAW
MATA  TSE  RENE
SLUR  STD  IDES
```

PUZZLE 613

```
APES   FAIR  TATE
DAVE  GARDE  ONIT
ALIS  EDMARINARO
ELAINE    UNITE
   MRED  ANN
SODEAR   ARSENIO
AVE  SANDY  RINGS
DALE  LAMAS  BORE
ALLEN  PANTS  NEA
SARACEN  ATTEST
    SRS  CREE
PATTI    ALTMAN
HARRYSTONE  PLAY
ALLI  INSET  LATE
LOOP  STUS  ENOS
```

PUZZLE 614

```
CLAM  GEMS  CAPE  SAVE
AIRE  REAL  ALAR  PLOD
MATA  ELLAFITZGERALD
PRINCES  NONO   VISTA
EDIT   EDGE   ATEN
ATSEA  STES  STANGETZ
LAHR  SPAR  PEERS  VIA
OCA  DEAL  RAVEN  TEEN
TOWERED  PURE  LORRE
   DUKEELLINGTON
TOTEM   PIES  IMBIBES
ADEN  CASES  ABEE  ULE
TEN  TAROS  LIEN  IDLE
ARTTATUM  LADD  ANDES
   RIOT  ROBE  ATTY
AREAL  SOSO  SNEERER
LOUISARMSTRONG  RILE
EARN  SHOE  EPEE  NCOS
EROS  HOGS  REEL  SHIP
```

PUZZLE 615

```
FUN  MARS  SLAP  MODE
ANON  OMNI  COHO  IVES
RAGE  RISE  ORAL  FANS
MUSCLE   SANDBARFLY
   TBAR  TIE  RYE
ATLAS  OSAR  ARCADES
NEAR  FOES  SLOAN  APT
TEMPLATE  CLOMP  SAO
IMPIOUS  SEINE  SPENT
   TON  WILDE  ELI
TRYST  BUGLE  STELLAR
LEO  DORMS  HEADLINE
CAW  TULSA  BOAT  OMIT
PLUMMET  MATT  SWALE
   NAB  SON  OHED
RAINBOWTIE   UTOPIA
GAGS  EMIR  FAIR  WADI
ECHO  LETO  UNDO  NULL
LEAN  LISP  LYON  LES
```

PUZZLE 616

```
SLAB  AGHA  BRER  HODS
TIARA  RAIN  RIME  EDICT
ANNMARGRET  AVAGARDNER
OCA  SOUL   NIBS  ANY
SETH  BEATS  ALAMO  THE
   UAR  SNAP  NOTE  PAS
CARTER  DURANTE  BASHED
LINEMAN  ELAS  MARKOVA
ADE  UTES  AIL  FELT  RET
MAR  SEWARD  SHOALS  ERA
     HUE   AND
WAR  SLATES  ASTORS  ELM
ALE  CORE  HOC  SWAP  LEA
RADIANT  TAFT  SPELLER
NESTLE  LAWFORD  SNEERY
   KEY  MULL  RAID  TIN
HEM  PACKS  SNERD  STAR
TEL  PARE   HOED  ERE
PETERLORRE  STANLAUREL
SLOPE  ONUS  EIRE  STRAY
SNIP  NETS  WEDS  HAYS
```

DIAGRAMLESS STARTING BOXES

Puzzle 68 starts in box 1
Puzzle 70 starts in box 1
Puzzle 72 starts in box 10
Puzzle 74 starts in box 1
Puzzle 76 starts in box 1
Puzzle 78 starts in box 12
Puzzle 79 starts in box 5
Puzzle 81 starts in box 5
Puzzle 82 starts in box 7
Puzzle 83 starts in box 7
Puzzle 85 starts in box 6
Puzzle 93 starts in box 7
Puzzle 168 starts in box 7
Puzzle 170 starts in box 1
Puzzle 172 starts in box 5
Puzzle 174 starts in box 1
Puzzle 176 starts in box 9
Puzzle 178 starts in box 18
Puzzle 179 starts in box 4
Puzzle 181 starts in box 7
Puzzle 346 starts in box 12
Puzzle 348 starts in box 10
Puzzle 350 starts in box 4
Puzzle 352 starts in box 1
Puzzle 354 starts in box 3
Puzzle 356 starts in box 4
Puzzle 358 starts in box 3
Puzzle 360 starts in box 10
Puzzle 361 starts in box 7
Puzzle 363 starts in box 5
Puzzle 365 starts in box 1
Puzzle 367 starts in box 1
Puzzle 368 starts in box 3
Puzzle 370 starts in box 4
Puzzle 371 starts in box 8